The I.B. Tauris Handbook of Sociology and the Middle East

The I.B. Tauris Handbook of Sociology and the Middle East

Edited by
Fatma Müge Göçek and Gamze Evcimen

I.B. TAURIS
LONDON • NEW YORK • OXFORD • NEW DELHI • SYDNEY

I.B. TAURIS
Bloomsbury Publishing Plc
50 Bedford Square, London, WC1B 3DP, UK
1385 Broadway, New York, NY 10018, USA
29 Earlsfort Terrace, Dublin 2, Ireland

BLOOMSBURY, I.B. TAURIS and the I.B. Tauris logo
are trademarks of Bloomsbury Publishing Plc

First published in Great Britain 2023

Copyright © Fatma Müge Göçek, Gamze Evcimen and contributors, 2023

Fatma Müge Göçek, Gamze Evcimen and contributors have asserted their right under the Copyright, Designs and Patents Act, 1988, to be identified as Editors of this work.

Cover image © The Picture Art Collection/Alamy Stock Photo

All rights reserved. No part of this publication may be reproduced or transmitted in any form or by any means, electronic or mechanical, including photocopying, recording, or any information storage or retrieval system, without prior permission in writing from the publishers.

Bloomsbury Publishing Plc does not have any control over, or responsibility for, any third-party websites referred to or in this book. All internet addresses given in this book were correct at the time of going to press. The author and publisher regret any inconvenience caused if addresses have changed or sites have ceased to exist, but can accept no responsibility for any such changes.

A catalogue record for this book is available from the British Library.

A catalog record for this book is available from the Library of Congress.

ISBN:	HB:	978-0-7556-3942-7
	ePDF:	978-0-7556-3943-4
	eBook:	978-0-7556-3944-1

Typeset by Integra Software Services Pvt. Ltd.
Printed and bound in Great Britain

To find out more about our authors and books visit www.bloomsbury.com and sign up for our newsletters.

Contents

List of Figures	viii
List of Tables	ix
List of Contributors	x
Introduction by Fatma Müge Göçek & Gamze Evcimen	1

Part I. Pivotal Moments

Introduction to Part I by Gamze Evcimen & Fatma Müge Göçek	11
I. Israel and Palestine	15
Segregation and Commingling: Jews and Palestinians in Israel's New Mixed Towns by Gershon Shafir	15
Neoliberal Apartheid in Palestine by Andy Clarno	23
Constructing a Sense of "We" across the Lines of Conflict and Occupation: Joint Peace Movement Organizations in Israel/Palestine by Michelle I. Gawerc	34
II. Iranian Revolution	45
Ideology and Political Action in the Iranian Revolution by Misagh Parsa	45
Gender Politics and the State in Postrevolutionary Iran by Nazanin Shahrokni	57
III. Arab Uprisings and Egypt	67
Front Stage and Back: Assessing "Transition," Citizenship, and Violence in the 2011 Arab Uprisings by Benoit Challand	67
Historicizing Space and Mobilization in Tahrir Square by Atef Said	78
Dual Refusal: How the Labor Movement almost Toppled the Bahraini Monarchy by Amy Austin Holmes	88
Ten Years On: Assessing the Outcomes of the Arab Spring for Bahraini Women by Magdalena Karolak	96
IV. Syrian War and Refugees	105
Extractive Landscapes: The Case of the Jordan Refugee Compact by Julia Morris	105
Schooling in an Environment of Uncertainties: The Case of Syrian Refugee Children in Turkey by Çetin Çelik & Ahmet İçduygu	115

Part II. Public Formal Space: State and Politics

Introduction to Part II by Gamze Evcimen & Fatma Müge Göçek   127

I. Development, Finance, and Neoliberalism   131

    Before the Boom: Oil Wealth, Shariah Scholars, and the Birth of the Islamic Finance Industry by Ryan Calder   131

    The Islamic Ethic and the Spirit of Turkish Capitalism: A Neoliberal History Making by Yıldız Atasoy   140

II. Religion, Politics, and Lifestyles of Islam   149

    Islam as an Experiment in Global Citizenship by Mohammed Bamyeh   149

    When Do Muslims Vote Islamic? by Charles Kurzman and Didem Türkoğlu   163

    Against the "Exception": Rethinking Turkish Secularism through the *Diyanet* by Berna Zengin Arslan and Bryan S. Turner   177

III. Citizenship, Minorities, and Violence   187

    The Kurds and Middle Eastern "State of Violence": The 1980s and 2010s by Hamit Bozarslan   187

    Social Construction of Minority Emotions and Sectarian Boundaries: Christian-Muslim Relations in Post-Arab Uprisings Egypt by Hyun Jeong Ha   196

    Muslimizing Turkish-Origin Migrants and Their Descendants: Diaspora Politics and Integration Politics by Ayhan Kaya   205

Part III. Civic Informal Space: Culture and Society

Introduction to Part III by Gamze Evcimen & Fatma Müge Göçek   233

I. Space and Life Worlds   237

    Israel's Biospatial Politics by Yinon Cohen and Neve Gordon   237

    Post January Revolution Cairo: Urban Wars and the Reshaping of Public Space by Mona Abaza   245

II. Culture and Consumption   265

    Matrimonial Transactions and the Enactment of Class and Gender Difference among Egyptian Youth by Rania Salem   265

    Between Fashion and Tesettür: Marketing and Consuming Women's Islamic Dress by Banu Gökarıksel and Anna Secor   292

    From Aspiration to Self-confidence: What Emotions and Clothing Tastes Tell Us about Class Inequality in Turkey by Irmak Karademir-Hazır   310

III. Gender and Sexuality   319

    Queer Exceptionalism and Exclusion: Cosmopolitanism and Inequalities in "Gay-Friendly" Beirut by Ghassan Moussawi   319

Culture, Class, and Young Women in Turkey by Ayça Alemdaroğlu — 328

Sexuality in Iran Revisited: Queer and Unruly Digital Constellations by Ladan Rahbari — 338

Part IV. Liquified Space: Beyond Borders and Boundaries

Introduction to Part IV by Gamze Evcimen & Fatma Müge Göçek — 349

I. Refugees — 353

Migration, Security, and Insecurity: The Securitization and Hypergovernance of Islam and Muslim Societies and Diasporas by Michael Humphrey — 353

Negotiating Control: Camps, Cities, and Political Life by Silvia Pasquetti — 362

Governing Syrian Refugees through Tech by Elisa Pascucci — 384

II. Diaspora in Europe — 393

Muslims' Civic Participation and Voting in France, Québec, and English-Canada: Do National "Models" Play a Role? by Emily Laxer, Jeffrey G. Reitz, and Patrick Simon — 393

Rethinking Diasporas of the Middle East: Kurdish Diaspora as the Global South in the Global North by Ipek Demir — 403

Jews and Turks in Germany: Immigrant Integration, Political Representation, and Minority Rights by Gökçe Yurdakul — 412

III. Diaspora in United States — 445

The Social Construction of Difference and the Arab American Experience, Revisited by Louise Cainkar — 445

Middle Eastern Muslims and the Ethical Inclusion of America as a New Homeland by Mücahit Bilici — 455

Between Sacred Codes and Secular Consumer Society: The Practice of Headscarf Adoption among American College Girls by Mustafa Gürbüz and Gülsüm Gürbüz-Küçüksarı — 479

Index — 486

Figures

12.1	Islamic banking's share of total banking assets by country, 3Q2019	132
15.1	Seats won by Islamic parties in parliamentary elections, 1970–2020 (individual Islamic parties)	165
15.2	Seats won by Islamic parties in parliamentary elections, 1970–2020 (all Islamic Parties Combined)	166
15.3	Support for selected Islamic themes in Islamic party platforms, 1970–2020	169
15.4	Support for selected democratic themes in Islamic party platforms, 1970–2020	169
21.1	Protest during Morsi's regime	246
21.2	March from Mohandessin quarter to Tahrir Square, commemorating the first year anniversary of the revolution	247
21.3	Islamist officers calling themselves the "bearded officers," protesting and camping opposite the Ministry of Interior, Lazoughly Street	247
21.4	Satellite channel van filming a march from the Mohandessin quarter to Tahrir Square	248
21.5	Ambulant street vendors selling paraphernalia in Tahrir	250
21.6	A protest stand with candles commemorating the Maspero massacre of October 9, 2011, in Talaat Harb Square	250
21.7	Recent graffiti, Mohammed Mahmud Street	252
21.8	The Open-Air Museum of the Revolution in Tahrir	254
21.9	A memorial landmark in Tahrir commemorating the martyrs by displaying photographs and names	255
21.10	Installation of mock tombs in Tahrir Square, commemorating the martyrs	255
23.1	Catalogue image from Sitare, Fall–Winter 2008–9	297
23.2	Catalogue image from SetrMS, Spring–Summer 2008	298
23.3	Catalogue image from Tekbir, Spring–Summer 2007	299
23.4	Catalogue image from Selam, Spring–Summer 2008	301
27.1	Screenshot of a "pansexual" identifying user's post explaining that they look for a "non-sexual" woman or a trans dating partner	342
27.2	Screenshot of a post by a user who identifies as "soft" showing interest in "hairy" bodies and "foot fetish" and looking for [a] "gay" dating partner(s)	343

Tables

8.1	Labor power and revolution	89
9.1	Women in the Bahraini Parliament (re-est. in 2002): Lower House	102
14.1	Historical genres of autonomy and control	154
14.2	Inquisition versus heteroglossia as strategies of faith management	159
15.1	Selected Liberal and Islamic Themes in Major Party Platforms	171
23.1	Basic data on the eleven firms whose catalogues were part of the analysis	295
31.1	Participation in voluntary associations (non-sports), total and co-ethnic, mainstream and minorities by origin and religion: France and Canada (including Québec)	397
31.2	Percent voting in last federal and municipal elections, mainstream and minorities eligible to vote, by origin and religion: France and Canada (including Québec)	398
31.3	Logistic regression on national voting (expressed as relative odds), mainstream and minorities eligible to vote: France and Canada (including Québec)	399

Contributors

Mona Abaza was Professor of sociology in the Department of Sociology, Egyptology, and Anthropology at The American University in Cairo. Abaza's research focused on religious and cultural networks between the Middle East and Southeast Asia, the Hadhrami diaspora in Southeast Asia, and consumer culture and the art market in Egypt. Abaza was the author of several books including *The Cotton Plantation Remembered: An Egyptian Family Story* (2013), *Twentieth Century Egyptian Art: The Private Collection of Sherwet Shafei* (2011), *The Changing Consumer Culture of Modern Egypt: Cairo's Urban Reshaping* (2006), and *Debates on Islam and Knowledge in Malaysia and Egypt: Shifting Worlds* (2002).

Ayça Alemdaroğlu is the Associate Director of the Program on Turkey and Research Scholar at the Center on Democracy, Development and the Rule of Law at Stanford University. Alemdaroğlu is a political sociologist, focusing on social and political inequality and change in Turkey and the Middle East. She is an editor of *Kurds in Dark Times: New Perspectives on Violence and Resistance* (forthcoming), and Middle East Report Issues, Confronting the New Turkey (Fall 2018) and Kurdistan, One and Many (Summer 2020). Alemdaroğlu has also published in several journals including *Turkish Studies, Review of Middle East Studies, Body & Society, Women's Studies International Forum,* and *Social & Cultural Geography.*

Yıldız Atasoy is Professor of sociology, an associate member of the School for International Studies and the Department of Geography, and director of the Center for Sustainable Development at Simon Fraser University. Atasoy grounds her analysis in a theory of social change that links global relations of capital accumulation, political alliances, and the transnational dynamics of social movements with the political and discursive tensions of national politics. Atasoy's published books include *Commodification of Global Agrifood Systems and Agro-Ecology: Convergence, Divergence and Beyond in Turkey* (2017), *Islam's Marriage with Neoliberalism: State Transformation in Turkey* (2009), and *Turkey, Islamists and Democracy: Transition and Globalization in a Muslim State* (2005).

Mohammed Bamyeh is Professor of sociology at the University of Pittsburgh and the Chair of the Board of Trustees of the Arab Council for the Social Sciences. Bamyeh's research interests lie in social movements and revolutions, the nature of conservatism, the sociology of religion, and anarchism and social life organized outside the state. Bamyeh's published books include *Lifeworlds of Islam: The Pragmatics of a Religion* (2019), *Social Sciences in the Arab World: Forms of Presence* (2015: in English, French, Arabic), and *The Social Origins of Islam: Mind, Economy, Discourse* (1999).

Mücahit Bilici is Associate Professor of sociology at John Jay College and CUNY Graduate Center. Bilici's research interests include American Islam, Muslim diasporas including Kurds in the United States, Kurdish identity, and Turkish society. Bilici is the author of *Finding Mecca in America: How Islam Is Becoming an American Religion* (2012).

Hamit Bozarslan is Director of studies at the École des Hautes Études en Sciences Sociales (EHESS) in Paris. Bozarslan's research interests focus on the historical and political sociology of the Middle East. Bozarslan has published extensively on the Kurdish issue, Turkey, and Middle East. His more recent publications include: *Histoire de la Turquie. De l'Empire à nos jours* (2013); *Le luxe et la violence. Domination et contestation chez Ibn Khaldûn* (2014); *Révolutions et état de violence: Moyen-Orient, 2011–15* (2015); *Comprendre le génocide des arméniens. 1915 à nos jours* (with V. Duclert and R.H. Kévorkian, 2015).

Louise Cainkar is Professor of sociology at Marquette University. Cainkar has conducted research on Palestinians in the United States, Arab and Muslim Americans after 9/11, the social experiences of Muslim women in the United States, Islamophobia and hate crimes, citizenship and belonging among transnational Arab American youth living in Yemen, Palestine, and Jordan, the impact of economic sanctions on women and children in Iraq, and the forced migration of Palestinians and Jordanians from Kuwait. Cainkar is the author of *Homeland Insecurity: The Arab American and Muslim American Experience After 9/11* (2009), *Arab American Women: Representation and Refusal* (with Suad Joseph and Michael Suleiman, 2021), and *Sajjilu Arab American: A Reader in SWANA Studies* (with Pauline Homsi Vinson and Amira Jarmakani, 2022).

Ryan Calder is Assistant Professor of sociology at Johns Hopkins University. He is particularly interested in Islamic law, jurisprudence (fiqh), and pious practice under conditions of contemporary capitalism and globalization. Calder has published in various journals including *Sociological Theory, Arab Law Quarterly, European Journal of Sociology,* and *Socio-Economic Review*.

Çetin Çelik is Assistant Professor of sociology at Koç University in Istanbul. Çelik's research interests lie in the field of sociology of migration and education with a particular focus on the links between identity formation and educational achievement of the second-generation migrant youth and broader social policies and institutional regulations. Çelik's articles appeared in several journals such as *Sociology, International Migration, Ethnic and Racial Studies,* and *British Journal of Sociology of Education*.

Benoit Challand is Associate Professor of sociology at The New School for Social Research. Challand's research focuses on political sociology, global critical theory, Arab politics, civil society mobilization, foreign aid, Western European Marxism. Most recently, he was co-editor of *The Struggle for Influence in the Middle East*

The Arab Uprisings and Foreign Assistance (2016) and co-author, with Chiara Bottici, of *Imagining Europe: Myth, Memory and Identity* (2013). His next book is entitled *Violence and Representation in the Arab Uprisings*.

Andy Clarno is Associate Professor of Sociology and Black Studies and coordinator of the Policing in Chicago Research Group at the University of Illinois at Chicago. Clarno's research examines racism, capitalism, colonialism, and empire in the early twenty-first century, with a focus on racialized policing and struggles for social justice in contexts of extreme inequality. Clarno is the author of *Neoliberal Apartheid* (2017) and has published research in various journals such as *Social Problems, Middle East Report, Social Dynamics, Social Psychology Quarterly, Political Power and Social Theory*, and *Antipode*.

Yinon Cohen is the Yosef Hayim Yerushalmi Professor of Israel and Jewish Studies at Columbia University. Cohen's research focuses on international migration, social stratification, and labor markets along with Israeli society on issues of unionization, socioeconomic ethnic and gender gaps, rising inequality, changing immigration and emigration patterns, and the demography of Jewish settlements in the occupied West Bank. Cohen has published in various journals including *Journal of Ethnic and Migration Studies, Sociological Science, Public Culture, Socio-Economic Review, Israeli Sociology, Journal of Palestinian Studies, International Journal of Comparative Sociology*, and *European Sociological Review*.

Ipek Demir is Professor of Diaspora Studies, and the Director of the Centre for Ethnicity and Racism Studies, University of Leeds (UK). Demir's research and publications sit at the intersections of the fields of racism, diaspora studies, ethno-politics, nationalism, decoloniality, indigeneity, global politics as well as epistemology and interdisciplinarity. Her work has been funded by the EU as well as by the UK national funding agencies (ESRC and AHRC). Before joining Leeds, Demir worked at the University of Leicester and also at the University of Cambridge. Her new book is entitled *Diaspora as Translation and Decolonisation* (2022) and introduces a new theoretical framework for understanding diaspora, and examines how diasporas from the Global South decolonize the Global North.

Gamze Evcimen is Visiting Assistant Professor of anthropology and sociology at Kalamazoo College. Evcimen's research addresses global neoliberalism, social inequalities, and contentious politics with a particular focus on twenty-first-century protests and contemporary rise of right-wing politics. Evcimen has published chapters on coalescence of religion and neoliberalism in Global South, fundamentalism and globalization, and political subjectivity of Turkey's anti-capitalist Muslims. In her current book project, Evcimen analyzes the ways in which neoliberal globalization simultaneously enabled and constrained oppositional politics with a particular focus on AKP hegemony and Gezi protests in Turkey.

Michelle I. Gawerc is Associate Professor of sociology and global studies at Loyola University Maryland. She conducts research in the areas of social movements and peace and conflict studies with a primary focus on Israel/Palestine. Gawerc is particularly interested in the ways in which peace activists accomplish working across conflict lines to end injustice and/or advocate for a just peace. She is the author of *Prefiguring Peace: Israeli-Palestinian Peacebuilding Partnerships* (2012). Her research has also been published in numerous journals including *Mobilization; Social Movement Studies; Contention; Research in Social Movements, Conflicts, and Change; Peace and Change; International Journal of Peace Studies; Peace Review;* and *Sociology Compass.*

Fatma Müge Göçek is Professor of sociology at University of Michigan. Göçek's research focuses on the comparative analysis of history, politics, and gender in the first and third worlds. Göçek's most recent sole-authored books include *Denial of Violence: Ottoman Past, Turkish Present and the Collective Violence against Armenians, 1789–2009* (2015) and *The Transformation of Turkey: Redefining State and Society from the Ottoman Empire to the Modern Era* (2011). Göçek has also published several edited volumes including *Contested Spaces in Contemporary Turkey: Environmental, Urban and Secular Politics* (2017) and *Women of the Middle East* (2016). Göçek is currently working on a theory book, constructing social theory from the vantage point of minorities.

Banu Gökarıksel is Professor of geography and The Caroline H. and Thomas S. Royster Distinguished Professor for Graduate Education at The Graduate School at the University of North Carolina, Chapel Hill. Gökarıksel's research examines bodies, intimacy, and everyday spaces as key sites of politics and geopolitics and focuses on religion as manifest in and produced by ordinary people and the ways they make their bodies, traverse spaces of everyday urban life, and encounter others as differently positioned subjects. Gökarıksel has also published in various journals including *Signs, Environment and Planning C, Gender, Place, & Culture, Social & Cultural Geography, Political Geography,* and *Journal of Middle East Women's Studies.*

Neve Gordon is Professor of international law and human rights at Queen Mary University of London. Gordon's research focuses on international humanitarian law, human rights, new warfare technologies, the ethics of violence, and the Israeli-Palestinian conflict. Gordon is author of *Human Shields: A History of People in the Line of Fire* (2020), with Nicola Perugini, *The Human Right to Dominate* (2015), and *Israel's Occupation* (2008).

Mustafa Gürbüz teaches in the Arab World Studies program in the Department of Critical Race, Gender, and Culture Studies at American University in Washington, DC. His research focuses on political violence, social movements, Muslims in the West, and ethnic/sectarian politics in the Middle East. Gürbüz is the author of *Rival Kurdish Movements in Turkey: Transforming Ethnic Conflict* (2016).

Gülsüm Gürbüz-Küçüksarı is an instructor in the history department at University of Northern Iowa. Gürbüz-Küçüksarı's research interests lie in Ottoman history with a particular focus on Kurdish nationalism in the early twentieth century, Kurdish madrasas and their influences on Kurdish consciousness, and the Kurdish media of that time. Gürbüz-Küçüksarı has published in several journals like *Middle Eastern Studies, Turkish Studies, Contemporary Islam,* and *Journal of Muslim Minority Affairs.*

Hyun Jeong Ha is Assistant Professor of sociology at Duke Kunshan University. As a political sociologist and ethnographer, she writes about daily sectarian relations between Christians and Muslims in the post-Arab Uprisings Egypt with a focus on intersectionality. She has published in *Journal of Peace Research, Ethnic and Racial Studies, Research in Social Movements, Conflict and Change,* and *Contexts,* among others.

Amy Austin Holmes is International Affairs Fellow at the Council on Foreign Relations and Public Policy Fellow at Woodrow Wilson International Center for Scholars. Holmes's research addresses US security relations and contentious politics in Europe and the Middle East with a particular focus on governance challenges of the semi-autonomous Kurdish-led region of northern Syria. Holmes is the author of *Coups and Revolutions: Mass Mobilization, the Egyptian Military, and the United States from Mubarak to Sisi* (2019) and *Social Unrest and American Military Bases in Turkey and Germany since 1945* (2014).

Ahmet İçduygu is Professor of sociology and international relations and the Director of the Migration Research Center at Koc (MIREKOC) at Koç University. İçduygu has conducted various research projects for the international organizations such as IOM, UNHCR, EU, OECD, and ILO, and is involved in arranging and participating in a range of projects in order to motivate national and international networks and to strengthen research capacity in the field of migration. İçduygu's most recent books include *Migration and Transformation: Multi-Level Analysis of Migrant Transnationalism,* co-edited with P. Pitkänen and D. Sert (2011), *Countries of Migrants, Cities of Migrants – Italy, Spain, Turkey,* co-edited with M. Balbo and J.P. Serrano (2013), and *Critical Reflections in Migration Research: Views from the South and the East,* co-edited with Ayşem Biriz Karaçay (2014).

Michael Humphrey is a professor at University of Sydney. Humphrey's research addresses large-scale social change and the governability of social life with a particular focus on the impact of globalization on the relationship and connections between societies in the North and South. Humphrey is the author of *The Politics of Atrocity and Reconciliation: From Terror to Trauma* (2002). Humphrey has also published in various journals including *Politics, Religion and Ideology, Journal of Intercultural Studies, Arab Studies Quarterly, International Journal on Multicultural Societies,* and *Bulletin of the Royal Institute for Inter-Faith Studies.*

Magdalena Karolak is Associate Professor of humanities and social sciences at Zayed University, UAE. Karolak's research interests include transformations of societies in the Arabian Gulf and comparative linguistics. Karolak has published more than thirty book chapters and journal articles on the shifting gender relations, social media, culture and identity, and political system transformations in the Gulf Cooperation Council countries in various journals including *Journal of International Women's Studies, Central European University Political Science Journal, Asia Journal of Global Studies, Studia Sociologica,* and the *Journal of North African Studies.*

Irmak Karademir-Hazır is Senior Lecturer in sociology at Oxford Brookes University. Karademir-Hazır's research interests lie in the areas of sociology of consumption, culture, class inequalities and socialization, social mobility, and research methods. Karademir-Hazır is the author of *Enter Culture, Exit Arts? The Transformation of Cultural Hierarchies in European Newspaper Culture Sections, 1960–2010,* co-edited with Semi Purhonen, Riie Heikkilä, Tina Lauronen, Carlos Fernández Rodríguez, and Jukka Gronow (2019). Karademir-Hazır has also published in various journals including *Sociology, International Journal of Fashion Studies, European Journal of Cultural Studies, Turkish Journal of Sociology, Journal of Consumer Culture, Poetics,* and *Sociological Review.*

Ayhan Kaya is Professor of politics and Jean Monnet Chair of European Politics of Interculturalism in the Department of International Relations at Bilgi University in Istanbul. Kaya's research focuses on political theory, ethnicity and the global order, contemporary political ideologies, politics of cultural diversity, international migration, and politics of transnationalism. Kaya is the author of *Turkish Origin Migrants and their Descendants: Hyphenated Identities in Transnational Space* (2018), *Europeanization and Tolerance in Turkey: The Myth of Toleration* (2013), and *Islam, Migration and Securitization* (2012).

Charles Kurzman is Philip Stadter Distinguished Professor of Sociology and co-director of the Center for Middle East and Islamic Studies at University of North Carolina at Chapel Hill. Kurzman's research focuses on Middle East and Islamic studies as well as on political sociology and social movements. Kurzman is author of *The Missing Martyrs* (first edition, 2011; second edition, 2019), *Democracy Denied, 1905–15* (2008), and *The Unthinkable Revolution in Iran* (2004), and editor of the anthologies *Liberal Islam* (1998) and *Modernist Islam, 1840–1940* (2002).

Emily Laxer is Associate Professor of sociology at York University's Glendon Campus in Toronto. Her research spans the fields of political sociology; immigration, race and ethnicity; citizenship and nationalism; and gender. Laxer is the author of *Unveiling the Nation: The Politics of Secularism in France and Québec* (2019). Laxer's recent articles appear in *International Migration Review, Ethnic and Racial Studies,* the *Journal of Ethnic and Migration Studies,* and *Comparative Sociology.*

Contributors

Julia Morris is Assistant Professor of international studies at the University of North Carolina Wilmington. Morris's research focuses on migration and the environment through the framework of resource extraction. Morris's research appears in *American Anthropology, Journal of Refugee Studies, Mobilities* and *The Extractive Industries and Society*, among others. Morris's book on the impacts of the Australian policy of offshoring asylum to the Republic of Nauru is forthcoming with Cornell University Press.

Ghassan Moussawi is Associate Professor of gender and women's studies and sociology at the University of Illinois at Urbana Champaign. Moussawi conducts research in the areas of transnational gender and sexuality, global and transnational sociology, feminist and queer theory, emotions, and social inequalities. Moussawi is the author of the award-winning book *Disruptive Situations: Fractal Orientalism and Queer Strategies in Beirut* (2019). Moussawi has also published in journals including *Departures in Critical Qualitative Research, The Sociological Review, Sociological Forum, Sexualities, Gender, Place and Culture*, including others.

Misagh Parsa is Professor of sociology at Dartmouth College. His research interests lie in dictatorships, social revolutions, political struggle, and Iran. Parsa is the author of *Social Origins of the Iranian Revolution* (1989) and *Democracy in Iran: Why It Failed and How It Might Succeed* (2016). Parsa's research also appears in *Comparative Studies in South Asia, Africa, and the Middle East, Comparative Studies in Society and History, Sociological Forum, Journal of Democracy, Theory and Society, Social Forces,* and the *Middle East Journal*.

Elisa Pascucci is a postdoctoral researcher at Helsinki Institute of Sustainability Science (HELSUS) Centre of Excellence in Law, Identity and the European Narratives. Pascucci's research focuses on two main areas: refugee political agency and political mobilization, and infrastructures and economies of humanitarianism and refuge. Pascucci has published in journals including *Political Geography, International Political Sociology, Refugee, Journal of Contemporary European Research, World Development, Antipode,* and *Migration and Society*.

Silvia Pasquetti is Senior Lecturer in sociology at Newcastle University. Pasquetti's research focuses on the study of forced displacement in comparative and global perspective and in connection to histories and structures of coloniality, race, securitization, militarism, and marginality. Pasquetti is the author of Refugees and Citizens: Control, Emotions, and Politics in a West Bank Camp and an Israeli the co-editor of *Displacement: Global Conversations on Refuge, with Romola Sanyal* (2020). Her research also appears in *Annual Review of Law and Social Science, Law & Society Review, International Journal of Urban and Regional Research, City, Theory and Society, International Sociology, Ethnic & Racial Studies, British Journal of Sociology,* and *Middle East Report*.

Ladan Rahbari is a Political Sociologist and an Assistant Professor at the Department of Sociology, at the University of Amsterdam. She is also a Senior Researcher at the International Migration Institute (IMI). Rahbari was formerly based in Ghent University,

Belgium as the recipient of an FWO (Research Foundation Flanders) post-doctoral fellowship (2019–2022). She is currently a member of Amsterdam Young Academy (2021–2026). Rahbari's research and teaching interests include gender politics and sexuality, migration and race, and (digital) media in the frameworks of feminist and postcolonial theories.

Jeffrey G. Reitz is Professor Emeritus of sociology, and R.F. Harney Professor Emeritus of Ethnic, Immigration and Pluralism Studies, at the University of Toronto at University of Toronto. Reitz has published extensively on immigration and inter-group relations in Canada from comparative perspectives and has frequently contributed to discussions of policies on immigration, multiculturalism, and minority group employment in Canada. Reitz is the co-author of *Multiculturalism and Social Cohesion: Potentials and Challenges of Diversity* (2009); recent articles have appeared in the *International Migration Review, Ethnic and Racial Studies*, the *Journal of Ethnic and Migration Studies*, and *Social Science Research*.

Atef Said is Assistant Professor of sociology at University of Illinois at Chicago. Said's research focuses on spatio-temporalities of revolution, historical analyses of revolutions in relation to knowledge production, and coloniality and de-coloniality. Said's articles have appeared in *Social Problems, Social Research, International Sociology,* and *Contemporary Sociology*. Said is completing a book manuscript on Tahrir Square and the Egyptian revolution entitled *Revolution Squared: The Egyptian Uprising of 2011 Between Historical Possibilities and Counter-Revolutionary Containments*.

Rania Salem is Associate Professor of sociology at University of Toronto. Salem's research interests lie at the intersection of the fields of gender, family, economic sociology, development, and the Middle East. Salem has published sole and co-authored articles in *Population and Development Review, Women's Studies Quarterly, Gender, Work & Organization, Journal of Family Issues,* and *Qualitative Sociology*.

Anna Secor is Professor of human geography at Durham University. Secor's research lies at the intersection of feminist political geography, cultural geography, urban geography, Turkish studies, geographies of religion, and spatial theory and she collaborates with Banu Gökarıksel for research on the role of religion and sectarian difference in public life in Turkey. Secor is among the co-editors of *The Wiley Blackwell Companion to Political Geography* (2015). Her research also appeared in *Gender, Place & Culture, Political Geography, Journal of Middle East Women's Studies, Antipode, Space and Polity,* and *Journal of Women in Culture and Society*.

Gershon Shafir is Distinguished Professor of sociology at University of California San Diego. Shafir's areas of interest are nationalism, ethnicity, citizenship, and human rights and his current research focuses on Israel's settlement policy and international humanitarian law from 1967 to the present. Shafir is the co-author of *Being Israeli: The Dynamics of Multiple Citizenships* (2002) and co-editor of *Struggle and Survival* *in Israel and Palestine* (2012) and of *Lessons and Legacies of the War on Terror: From Moral Panic to Permanent War* (2012). Shafir's articles have appeared in the *American Journal of Sociology,* the *British Journal of Sociology,* the *International Journal of Middle East Studies,* and *Theory and Society.*

Nazanin Shahrokni is Assistant Professor of gender and globalization at London School of Economics. Shahrokni's research interests fall at the intersection of gender politics, feminist geography, and ethnographies of the state in Iran, the Middle East, and beyond with a particular focus on gendered public spaces and spheres, the reconstruction of gender difference in city spaces, and the complex gendered underpinnings of urban governance and political institutions. Shahrokni is the author of *Women in Place: The Politics of Gender Segregation in Iran* (2020). Shahrokni's research have also appeared in Globalizations, *Journal of Contemporary Ethnography,* Current Sociology, *Journal of Middle East Studies, Journal of Middle East Women's Studies* among others.

Patrick Simon is a senior researcher at the French Institute for Demographic Studies. Simon's research interests lie at the intersection of immigration, discrimination, ethnic and racial studies, ethno-racial classification in statistics, social and ethnic division of space. Simon is the co-editor of *Fear, Anxiety and National Identity: Immigration and belonging in North-America and Western Europe* (2015). Simon has also published in journals including *Journal of Ethnic and Migration Studies, Ethnic and Racial Studies, French Politics,* and *Culture & Society.*

Didem Türkoğlu is an assistant professor at Kadir Has University. Türkoğlu's research focuses on political sociology, social movements, and studies of social inequalities. Türkoğlu has published sole and co-authored articles in *Current Sociology, Mobilization, Sociology Compass,* and *Journal of Democracy.* In her current book project, *Political Price of a Public Education,* she conducts a comparative analysis of higher education policies and the protests against tuition hikes over the last two decades in thirty-four OECD countries, with a special focus on England, Germany, Turkey, and the United States.

Bryan S. Turner is Presidential Professor of sociology at Graduate Center, City University of New York. Turner's current research focuses on the role of religion in contemporary Asia, the changing nature of citizenship in a globalizing world, Muslim communities in the United States and Australia with special reference to the Shari'a, and the legal debate about same-sex marriages. Turner has written, co-authored, or edited more than seventy books and more than 200 articles and chapters, including most recently *The Religious and the Political: A Comparative Sociology of Religion* (2013) and *Religion and Modern Society: Citizenship, Secularisation and the State* (2011).

Gökçe Yurdakul is Professor of sociology at Humboldt-Universität zu Berlin. Yurdakul's research focuses on how migratory experiences shape gender and racialized identities in the European context, and she conducts cross-country comparative research in Germany, the Netherlands, the UK, Israel, Canada, and Turkey. Yurdakul is the author of *From Guest workers into Muslims: Turkish Immigrant Associations in Germany* (2009) and co-author of *The Headscarf Debates: Conflict of Belonging in National Narratives* (2014). Yurdakul's research also appears in *Turkish Studies, Journal of Ethnic and Migration Studies, Social Compass, Comparative Sociology, Social Politics, Women's Studies International Forum,* and *Immigrants and Minorities.*

Berna Zengin Arslan is Associate Professor of sociology at Özyeğin University in Istanbul. Zengin Arslan's research areas are studies of secularism and religion, science and religion, gender, science and technology, and Islam and secularism in Turkey and Europe. Zengin Arslan is the author of *Women Engineers in Turkey: Gender, Technology, Education and Professional Life* (2010). Zengin Arslan has also published in journals including *Social Epistemology, Sociological Review, New Perspectives on Turkey,* and *European Journal of Social Theory.*

Introduction

by Fatma Müge Göçek & Gamze Evcimen

There are many challenges to creating a handbook on the Middle East, starting with the most evident one of defining the boundaries of what actually comprises this socially constructed concept. After all, postcolonially put, this region is defined geographically in relation to Western Europe that happened to be hegemonic during the advent of modernity. Even then, what makes up the Middle East has changed over time and across space, often in relation to the interests of involved actors. All scholars agree that the "core" of the Middle East is the Arabian Peninsula geographically, but boundaries get murkier as one moves outward. The late Persian Empire and the contemporary state of Iran, the late Ottoman Empire, and the contemporary state of Turkey have a tense relationship with each other and with the region. While Egypt certainly states that it belongs to the Middle East, the North African region quickly becomes problematic. The same holds true for the al-Andalus province of the Umayyad Caliphate in Damascus that expanded to Spain in Europe during the early years of Islam (622 A.C.E.)—it is unclear how far back in time one ought to go in defining contemporary boundaries. How far south and east one ought to move on the African continent is also challenging, given many states that exist throughout with large Muslim populations. The same holds true for the Balkans in that the region was under Ottoman rule for more than half a millennium. Moving northeast, Central Asian states are also Muslim and Turkish, thereby emerging as potential participants. The same also holds for the southeast; Indonesia, Pakistan, and India contain the largest Muslim populations in the world. In addition, moving to the present, one could also argue, given the increasing number of people from the Middle East moving to the West to form significant Diasporas there, that the boundaries of the Middle East now expand throughout the world, rendering the initial social construction of the East null and void. Such a survey also reveals that religion, specifically Islam, intersects with the region of the Middle East, privileging Islam while obscuring many other characteristics, including the religions of specifically Christianity and Judaism that have been and still are vibrant in the region.

Given these ambiguities in drawing the boundaries of the Middle East across time and space, how does one put together a handbook? Considering this query, we moved our focus from space to social actors, concentrating instead on the intersection of sociologists who have written on the Middle East on the one side and our standpoint as two such sociologists originating in the Middle East on the other. Drawing on our expertise in relation to the region, we decided to privilege what we consider to be the central lands of the Middle East—as well as Islam—historically, namely the Arabian Peninsula, Turkey, Iran, and Egypt. There are many more volumes yet to be written on other parts that we purposefully discussed in the preceding paragraph but do not cover in this one, and we hope many other handbooks will follow from this one. In drawing the list of sociologists who work on the Middle East, we took Charles Kurzman's listserv of sociologists of the Middle East as our starting point: we thank him for generously sharing his list with us and for years gathering us, sociologists of the Middle East annually at two professional meetings, the American Sociological Association, and the Middle East Studies Association. We then researched the sociology departments of universities in the region, Europe and the United States, and Canada. Of course, access to and writing in the English language emerged as another gatekeeper in the process, quickly reducing the number of contributions that could be published here. Once again, we hope that in the future other handbooks would capture the very important contributions of sociologists who write in languages other than English.

Arranging the still vast number of potential contributors still posed a major challenge. Rather than imposing themes around which to structure the contributors, we decided to deduct the themes from what our social actors, namely sociologists working on the Middle East had chosen to write upon. This is how we arrived at the final list of contributors. Searching for patterns among all their valuable contributions, time and space emerged as two significant dimensions, leading us to divide the volume into four parts, Part I. Pivotal Moments, Part II. Public Formal Space, Part III. Civic Informal Space, and Part IV. Liquified Space. The rest of this section discusses in more detail how the Table of Contents came about.

Part I. Pivotal Moments

Given the interest of sociologists on social transformations in general and social conflict in particular, it is not surprising that sociologists have chronically studied study three pivotal events in the region in the aftermath of the two world wars: Israel and Palestine, Iranian Revolution, and Arab Uprisings and Egypt.

Israel and Palestine. The emergence of the state of Israel and the Palestinian forced exile from their ancestral lands in 1948 formulate the first significant conflict in the region to be covered, one that has unfortunately continued to this day. Established through Western support in the aftermath of the horror of the Holocaust, the state and society of Israel has generated many conflicts in the region, especially in relation to the forced exile of Palestinians. The three sociologists included here cover various aspects of this tense coexistence. Gershon Shafir focuses on the historical formation of the conflict, especially in relation to Israel's settlement policy since 1967, narrating the course taken from the vantage point of Jews and Arabs. The works of Andy Clarno and Michelle Gawerc take the analysis from the micro to the macro level. Andy Clarno's work addresses the neoliberal apartheid that exists in Israel since 1994. Intent on concluding on a positive note, we find that Michelle Gawerc's analyses of joint peace organizations as collective actors in Israel and Palestine present a critical if not hopeful insight into the future.

Iranian Revolution. The conflicts generated by the establishment of the state of Israel after the Second World War continued into the Cold War (1947–91) during which period the 1979 Iranian Revolution emerged as the most significant transformation in the region. The Pahlavi dynasty, headed by Reza Shah and supported by the United States was overthrown and replaced by an Islamic Republic under the leadership of Ayatollah Khomeini. A number of sociologists have studied the dramatic change from a Western-style constitutional monarchy to a novel Islamic Republic and prepared the background for the contemporaneous analyses of Misagh Parsa and Nazanin Shahrokni. Misagh Parsa's analyses traversing the Iranian Revolution at past and the democratization movement in contemporary Iran provides a perfect transition into the issues facing Iran today. Nazanin Sharokni bring under lens everyday practices through which the state reproduces its power while being undermined by issues such as poverty, education, and mobility.

Arab Uprisings and Egypt. After the emergence of the Israeli Palestinian conflict in the aftermath of the Second World War and the transformation created by the Iranian Revolution during the Cold War, recent Arab Uprisings (2010–16) constitute the third temporal series of events that sociologists of the Middle East have worked on. Egypt needs special mention here, given the 2011 overthrow of Hosni Mobarak and the holding of democratic elections that led not to democratic rule by the elected leader Mohammad Morsi, but instead military rule that continues to this day. Benoit Challand writes on the larger global context of the Arab Uprisings and emphasizes the role of foreign assistance and subsequent civil society mobilization. Amy Austin Holmes's work on mass mobilization and the military in Egypt—and elsewhere such as Bahrain—provides a nice transition to the case of Egypt that has recently experienced a lot of political turbulence: the re-establishment of autocratic rule in Egypt is also recently turning into a political blueprint followed elsewhere such as Turkey and Syria. Atef Said provides insights into contemporary Egypt as his ethnographic work on Tahrir Square portrays the 2011 Egyptian Revolution.

Syrian War and Refugees. Syrian War (2011–) constitutes the fourth and final temporal series of events that sociologists of the Middle East have worked on. The following group of sociologists specializes on the experiences of Syrian refugees in different societies. Julia Morris studies Syrian refugees in the context of 2016 Jordan Compact; Morris's work highlights how the relationships between the international community and the Jordanian state enable the extraction of Syrian refugees' labor while also constraining their access to relocation in the Global North. Çetin Çelik and Ahmet İçduygu shift the focus to the Syrian refugees in Turkey; Çelik and İçduygu critically evaluate educational opportunities for Syrian children through the accounts of their parents and teachers.

Part II. Public Formal Space: State and Politics

Sociologists working on the Middle East also focus on a spectrum of social spaces, capturing in the process the production and reproduction of meaning and knowledge in these contexts. We cluster their work into three types of space. The first is public, formal space that privileges economic, religious, and political activities. The second comprises the civic, informal space covering the activities of culture, consumption, gender, and sexuality. The final third space we term "liquified" space inspired by Zygmund Bauman's conception of liquified modernity, referring to a set of activities that occur beyond the traditionally defined boundaries. This concept helps us trace and capture the end results of frequent conflict and violence in the Middle East, with many refugees fleeing elsewhere and forming influential diasporas especially in Europe, the United States, and Canada.

The conceptualization of Part II is based on the Western formulation of modernity that prioritizes and privileges the formal public sphere where structurally defined political, economic, and social activities pertaining to the state, market, and religion take place. Sociologists study the negotiation of modernity in the context of the Middle East in three categories: development, finance, and neoliberalism; religion, politics, and lifestyles of Islam; and citizenship, minorities, and violence.

Development, Finance, and Neoliberalism. The emergence and spread of Western modernity predicated on the intersection of the French and industrial revolutions simultaneously advocating democracy and development. This political/economic intersection spread to transform countries throughout the world, including the Middle East. Economically, development became the legitimating aim of the emergent nation-states. Finance was especially significant in actualizing this aim in that it enabled continued development by fueling states and societies with resources in both the short and, more importantly, the long term. Neoliberalism that started to spread throughout the world in the 1970s privileged and legitimated market forces and the profit motive before all else, including human lives. Its hegemony continues to this day. The sociologists in this section work on the impact of neoliberalism in the Middle East. Ryan Calder privileges the negotiation and pull of global neoliberalism on the ground and concentrates on the economic interpretations that Islamic law and Islamic finance, especially the religious ban on usury generate in relation to neoliberal practices in the region. Yıldız Atasoy provides invaluable research on the practices of neoliberalism in Turkey as one of the major economies of the region.

Religion, Politics, and Lifestyles of Islam. In approaching the elements that structure and give meaning to life in the Middle East, the religion of Islam emerges as a major contributing local factor alongside modernity. Many sociologists therefore focus on the role Islam plays in defining, structuring, and mobilizing citizens in the Middle East. Mohammed Bamyeh highlights the cultural and political dimensions of Islam as he focuses on the dynamics of religious tradition, conservatism, and ensuing lifestyles in Islam. Charles Kurzman and Didem Türkoğlu ground these discussions empirically by researching how and why Islam becomes politically transformative in the contemporary world; Kurzman and Türkoğlu not only trace the devolution in the Middle East from democratic revolution to developmental dictatorships, but, in doing so, also highlight the foundation of Islamic extremism. Bryan S. Turner and Berna Zengin Arslan are intent on undergirding the dynamic of the official form of Islam in Turkey as they focus on Diyanet (the Directorate of Religious Affairs) as the state institution that defines the boundaries of ideal religiosity and secularism.

Citizenship, Minorities, and Violence. Continued political instability in the Middle East has led many sociologists to focus on how the state draws the boundaries of belonging and exclusion. Hamit Bozarslan approaches violence, intolerance, and the democratic challenge in the Middle East from a macro perspective, focusing specifically on the practices of state inclusion and exclusion through citizenship. Bozarslan highlights the political dynamics of the Middle East that has recently transformed, as evinced by the Arab Revolutions, from political struggle to self-sacrifice. Continuing this focus on the relationship between structural changes and sectarian relations, Hyun Jeong Ha analyzes the social construction of minority emotions and symbolic boundaries in Egypt through the case of changing daily Christian-Muslim interactions after Mubarak's fall. Ayhan Kaya approaches similar themes through the case of Germany's Muslim youth with Turkish background and addresses the contemporary Muslimization of Euro-Turks in the context of rising nativism and Islamophobia in Europe.

Part III. Civic Informal Space: Culture and Society

This formulation follows upon the insights of critical scholarship that research how power negotiations as well as meaning and knowledge construction and reconstruction extend beyond the formal public into the civic informal space. Everyday practices move to the forefront in the analyses, bringing in a wealth of information on these often-understudied sites. In doing so, they especially capture and demonstrate the vibrancy of non-Western societies that is often missed by structural approaches. The sociologists of the Middle East working on this space specifically focus on space and lifeworlds, culture and consumption, and gender and sexuality.

Space and Lifeworlds. Space, place, and culture arise as a recently growing research area in the sociological literature on the Middle East. The scholars in this section study the interactions of contentious politics, biospatial strategies, and space in the context of different cultural activities and collective practices like protests. Mona Abaza addresses how Egypt's January revolution of 2011 transformed the notion of public space and analyses its continuing reverberations in the case of Cairo's flourishing art scene. Yinon Cohen and Neve Gordon shift our focus to Israel's racial-spatial strategies and analyze how Israel's land-grabbing practices and demographic classifications construct space and people as racialized categories.

Culture and Consumption. Given that embodiment and marriage constitute a significant part of cultural dispositions and identities, it is not surprising that practices of marriage, clothing, and self-representation quickly emerge as prominent topics in studies of culture and consumption in the Middle East. Rania Salem highlights the economies of courtship in Egypt. Banu Gökarıksel and Anna Secor and Irmak Karademir-Hazır provide nuanced empirical analyses of these conceptualizations by concentrating their attention on Turkey. While Gökarıksel and Secor study Islamic culture industry and Islamic dress and fashion, Karademir-Hazır delves into the relationship between taste and inequality, and does so by focusing on the relationship among class, food, and eating in Istanbul and Ankara.

Gender and Sexuality. This topic is probably the most vibrant sociologically, given the need to challenge and counter the Orientalist stereotyping on the publicly inaccessible activities pertaining to women and sex in the Middle East. Ghassan Moussawi delves into the relatively understudied topic of sexualities as he provides insight into the negotiation of the inequalities of gay life in Beirut. Ayça Alemdaroğlu turns our attention to Turkey and studies the relationship between culture, class, and young women. Ladan Rahbari studies the discourses of gender and sexuality in Iranian spaces with a particular focus on a Persian-language LGBTQI+ dating channel on Telegram.

Part IV. Liquified Space: Beyond the Borders and Boundaries

Even though the world has become more accessible through social media, it has also become increasingly mobile and exclusionary. According to the UN Refugee Agency, the current level of displacement is the highest on record: 56.6 million people have been forced to abandon their homes where nearly 22.5 million have become refugees who do not have a chance to return. Breaking the figures down by country, Syria leads with 5.5 million refugees, followed by South Sudan and Afghanistan, all Muslim countries. Such flows out of the Middle East also occurred in the past, but not at this scale. During and after the demise of the Ottoman Empire, many migrants and refugees from the Middle East ultimately settled throughout the Middle East, Europe, and the United States, forming significant diasporas there.

Refugees. The problem of refugees in the modern Middle East can be traced back to the establishment of the state of Israel whereby Palestinians were forcefully displaced into Lebanon, Jordan, Syria, Egypt, and overseas. State violence in Turkey also created Kurdish refugees in the region alongside refugees emanating from regime changes such as those that occurred in Iran and Egypt. The Iraq wars, Arab Revolutions, and Syrian civil war have also generated millions of refugees. Michael Humphrey provides the larger global context within which to situate refugees from the Middle East, specializing on political violence and healing. Silvia Paquetti concentrates on displacement, refugees, and refugee camps in the context of Israel and the West Bank. Elisa Pascucci's analysis focuses on the effects of international humanitarian aid and Jordan's economic policies on the livelihoods of Syrian refugees in Amman.

Diaspora in Europe. Research privileging the religion of Islam often moves to the forefront in this context; it is sometimes accompanied, however, by discussions of ethnic characteristics, such as the migration of Turks and Kurds into Europe that date back to mid twentieth century. This trend has been recently complemented by investigations into the Syrian refugees trying to reach Europe. Emily Laxer, Jeffrey Reitz, and Patrick Simon provide an empirical analysis of the headscarf debate specifically in Paris, France, also expanding their analysis to Quebec, Canada. The next group of sociologists located mainly in Germany and Great Britain underscores the other common element, namely the ethnicity of immigrants from the Middle East. While Ipek Demir researches the Kurdish and Turkish diaspora in London, Great Britain, Gökçe Yurdakul highlights the transformation of guest workers into Muslims in Germany especially in relation to the headscarf debates.

Diaspora in the United States and Canada. In the migration experience to the United States and Canada, many migrants from the Middle East shed their specific ethnic and national identities to be categorized primarily as Muslims. The sociologists analyzing Middle East diasporas here highlight their religious identities as well. Louise Cainkar articulates the past and present experience of the Muslim diaspora in the United States and Canada respectively. Cainkar specifically focuses on the Arab Muslim American experience in the aftermath of 9/11 as well as the experience of transnational Arab youth. Mücahit Bilici's emphasis is instead on the transformation of Islam into an American religion where he culturally highlights the practices of American Islam on the one side and Islamophobia on the other. Mustafa Gürbüz and Gülsüm Gürbüz-Küçüksarı are more interested in the education that Muslim Americans receive in the United States; Gürbüz and Gürbüz-Küçüksarı concentrates on the experiences of head-covered American college girls and Muslim ethnicities.

In summary then, all these selections reveal the immense contributions that sociologists have made to the field. We hope this will be the first of many handbooks on the Middle East to follow.

Part I

Pivotal Moments

Introduction to Part I

by Gamze Evcimen & Fatma Müge Göçek

Given the interest of sociologists on social transformations in general and social conflict in particular, it is not surprising that sociologists have chronically studied four pivotal events in the region in the aftermath of the two world wars: Israel and Palestine, Iranian Revolution, Arab Uprisings and Egypt, and Syrian War and Refugees.

Gershon Shafir addresses the changes and continuities in patterns of social inequality in Israel with a particular focus on the changing practices of upwardly mobile Palestinian citizens and on the continuing practices of discrimination against them. Shafir illustrates that although the new mixed towns have been promoted as places of coexistence for middle-class Jews and Arabs, they perpetuate "technologies of discrimination," such as not selling houses, not providing collective rights or municipal services, and barriers to municipal employment, in contrast to the old mixed towns that provide further rights and political representation for Palestinian citizens. In doing so, Shafir interrogates the dominant views on middle class and upward social mobility as the basis of modernity, progress, and development and illustrates that, in their stead, historical legacies of living together enable coexistence for the Jews and the Arabs.

Shifting our focus to neoliberalism and development, Andy Clarno studies how Israel's apartheid state operates as a political-economic system of racial capitalism that simultaneously excludes economically marginalized Palestinians as disposable while incorporating upwardly mobile Palestinians into Israel's neoliberal apartheid project. Clarno demonstrates that the neoliberal restructuring of Israel's economy caused increasing class divisions among the Palestinians by reducing Israel's reliance on Palestinian workers while also providing employment opportunities either in the construction of Israeli settlements or in the Palestinian Authority (PA) security forces. Clarno highlights how Israel's regime of racial domination and neoliberal capitalism positions Palestinians into different groups of PA security forces, construction workers in Israeli settlements, and business interests while benefitting from these categorizations of exclusion and inclusion.

Intent on concluding on a positive note, Michelle Gawerc's analysis of joint peace organizations as collective actors in Israel and Palestine presents critical insights into the future. Gawerc addresses the ways in which Israelis and Palestinians in the Middle East can work across difference and form collective identities despite their deep-rooted characterizations as enemies. Gawerc's contribution focuses on identifying and analyzing the factors and processes that enabled two bi-national movement organizations, Parents Circle/Families Forum (PCFF), and Combatants for Peace (CFP), to develop a unifying identity against Israel's occupation and for peace. Gawerc emphasizes building trust as the first step, along with standing together in front of an audience and witnessing the commitment of the other side to the shared cause, in creating this collective identity.

Misagh Parsa's study of the Iranian Revolution provides a perfect transition into the issues facing Iran today. Parsa illustrates that although Khomeini and the regime framed the Iranian Revolution as mobilized by the religious groups and for Islamic purposes, leftist students indeed led the revolutionaries, who mobilized also for having better lives. Parsa emphasizes that, rather than Islamic theocracy, a broad coalition of Iranians supported social justice based on Shia egalitarian notions. Parsa also underlines how Khomeini hid his theocratic ideology to forge this coalition while state repression influenced the outcome of revolutionary struggles as those groups that had been oppressed the most by the state lost their struggles to Khomeini and remained oppressed under the Islamic regime as well.

Nazanin Shahrokni analyzes how the shift from the revolutionary to the postrevolutionary state in Iran engendered both continuities and changes in state formation through the case of discourses and policies surrounding women's outdoor exercise. Shahrokni illustrates that Iran's postrevolutionary state changed its coercive and prohibitive policies of women's outdoor exercise to strategies of regulation and control by opening women-only parks and adopting discourses of protection and provision; according to Shahrokni, this shift derives not only from Iran's domestic politics to prevent Western cultural invasion and provide alternative cultural experiences but also from the global opening of Iran's economy with structural adjustment as well as from the global discourses of urban justice and public health regarding nutrition and exercise. Shahrokni also points to the productive aspects of state power and control, underlining that women-only parks both reproduce gender segregation and provide outdoor exercise spaces as services and rights to women; while women internalize and reproduce state's control by exercising separately from men, the state regulates women's bodies by both addressing and exploiting their needs and demands. Departing from the existing works that regard the Iranian state as fixed, repressive, isolated from the global and in constant crises, Shahrokni demonstrates that it indeed reflects conflicts among different actors, productive power, discursive and material links to global processes, and capacity of adaptability and change.

Regarding political transitions as not only short-term institutional changes but also gradual negotiation processes of citizenship, forms of representation and use of violence, Benoit Challand offers a macro-level analysis of the Arab Uprisings. Challand illustrates that, in their call for a new social contract that respects human dignity and advocates a just use of means of coercion, these protests mobilized against both neoliberalism and authoritarian regimes and supported economic reform as well as political change. Challand also underlines that, although counterrevolutionary forces prevented these citizenship agendas by employing violence and threats of chaos, the Arab uprisings offered a new social contract with a shared sense of citizenship and demands for the people's sovereign control over the means of violence.

Focusing on the Egyptian Revolution of 2011, Atef Said's work addresses the ways in which historical meanings and strategies of space that are constituted by previous movements play role in contemporary mobilizations. Said accounts for the relationship between the earlier sit-ins in Taḥrir and the 2011 occupation of the square through three processes: the participants' prior perception of Tahrir Square as a politicized space of protest enabled their mobilization, the previous sit-ins in Tahrir provided the idea of and techniques for occupying the square, and, the meanings of Tahrir, such as protestors liberating themselves and liberating Egypt from dictatorship, inspired the participants for the revolution. Underlining that these three aspects linked the past, present, and future of Egypt's 2011 revolution, Said illustrates how protestors employ the historical and symbolic meanings of space to connect the ideas and tactics of former and new movements for liberation.

Amy Austin Holmes shifts our focus to the reverberations of Arab Spring in Bahrain and investigates the role of labor movement in 2011 mass uprising. Holmes emphasizes the dual forms of disobedience performed by the labor movement in Bahrain; while trade unions and professional associations implemented strikes to stop production and provision of services, they also continued working to provide medical services in support of mass protests. According to Holmes, bringing these two forms of labor activism—work stoppages associated with a militant, masculine tradition and unpaid, volunteer labor associated with feminine care work—strengthened the labor movement and mass protests against the Bahraini ruling family. Holmes also points to the significance of security forces sent by Saudi Arabia, the United Arab Emirates, and Kuwait in maintaining the Bahraini monarchy.

Focusing on the outcomes of the Arab Spring for Bahraini women, Magdalena Karolak studies the puzzle of women's empowerment in the aftermath of Bahrain's 2011 uprising. Karolak demonstrates that although the uprising improved women's chances of representation in electoral politics, Bahraini state also constrained women's issues to particular areas in order to prevent challenges to the establishment and to co-opt women's empowerment agendas. Karolak underlines how the state claimed sole agency for the progress in women's rights based on its policies and projects for women's participation in economic activity and politics from the 2000s onward. Karolak also cautions that although women play important role in protests, they may be invisibilized and the protests may instead result in the increased influence of men in public sphere.

Adopting a perspective of refugee employment as a mode of accumulation with colonial and imperial roots, Julia Morris focuses on the relationships between the immobility of Syrian refugees and the mobility of value in global system of production. Morris investigates how the 2016 Jordan Compact reflects an instance of extractive capitalism that perpetuates global relations of dependency by extracting values from the refugees in the Global South for export to the Global North. Morris underlines how Jordan benefits from hosting (or containing) Syrian refugees that contribute to Jordan's development while also formalizing their precarity by limiting their employment opportunities to lower-paid jobs. Morris also illustrates that the international community creates an illusion of altruism and investment for refugees' well-being while reaping the benefits of rendering the refugees precarious and immobile.

Çetin Çelik and Ahmet İçduygu shift the focus to the experiences of Syrian refugees in Turkey as they critically evaluate educational opportunities for Syrian children through the accounts of their parents and teachers. Çelik and İçduygu emphasize a change in Turkey's approach toward the education of Syrian children from temporary education centers, which provided education in Arabic, by Syrian teachers, and following the Syrian curriculum, toward enrollment in Turkey's public schools. Their analysis demonstrates that although Syrian parents see public education as a way for their children to build a future in Turkey, numerous issues like language difference, stigmatization, and bullying as well as cultural differences in the curriculum and the influences of education over family dynamics create challenges to integration processes.

Further Reading

Barghouti, O. (2011), *BDS: Boycott, Divestment, Sanctions: The Global Struggle for Palestinian Rights*, Chicago: Haymarket Books.

Bayat, A. (2010), *Life as Politics: How Ordinary People Change the Middle East*, Stanford, CA: Stanford University Press.

Bogaert, K. (2013), "Contextualizing the Arab Revolts: The Politics behind Three Decades of Neoliberalism in the Arab World," *Middle East Critique*, 22 (3): 213–34.

Fakhoury, T. (2021), "Refugee Return and Fragmented Governance in the Host State: Displaced Syrians in the Face of Lebanon's Divided Politics," *Third World Quarterly*, 42 (1): 162–80.

Farsakh, L. (2005), *Palestinian Labour Migration to Israel: Labour, Land, and Occupation*, London: Routledge.

Gordon, N. (2008), *Israel's Occupation*, Berkeley: University of California Press.

Hashemi, M. (2019), "Embedded Enclaves: Cultural Mimicry and Urban Social Exclusion in Iran," *International Journal of Urban and Regional Research*, 43 (5): 914–29.

Hasso, F. (2015), "Civil and the Limits of Politics in Revolutionary Egypt," *Comparative Studies of South Asia, Africa and the Middle East*, 35 (3): 605–21.

Holmes, A. A. (2012), "There Are Weeks when Decades Happen: Structure and Strategy in the Egyptian Revolution," *Mobilization*, 17 (4): 391–410.

Lesch, D. W. (2001), *1979: The Year that Shaped the Modern Middle East*, Colorado: Westview Press.

Moss, D. (2020), "Voice after Exit: Explaining Diaspora Mobilization for the Arab Spring," *Social Forces*, 98 (4): 1669–94.

Said, E. (1980), *The Question of Palestine*, New York: Vintage Books.

I ISRAEL AND PALESTINE

Segregation and Commingling: Jews and Palestinians in Israel's New Mixed Towns

by Gershon Shafir

Palestinian Arabs, who currently make up about 20 percent of Israel's citizenry, remain on average poorer, less-educated, and concentrated at the lower rungs of the occupational hierarchy. The government appointed Or Commission's report of August 2003, concluded that "Israel's Arab citizens live in a reality in which they are discriminated against as Arabs."[1] In the past two decades or so, as part of Israel's raising standards of living there is, however, also a growing Arab middle class.

In 2010, the percentage of Arab households in Israel's middle stratum, defined as households headed by salaried workers whose income is 75–125 percent of the median income, was 23.4 percent, as compared with 28.5 percent of Jewish households (Dagan-Buzaglo and Konor-Attias 2013: 3–4). In 2013, 24.3 percent of Israel's Arab population above age fifteen, as compared with 52 percent of its Jews, possessed above high-school education. In just two decades, by 2017, the size of the Palestinian middle class has dramatically swelled from 17 to 27 percent. These numbers place roughly a quarter of Israel's Palestinian citizens in the middle class.[2] The percentage of Palestinian students in Israeli institutions of higher learning has been on rapid rise for two decades and in just seven years, between 2010 and 2017, rose by 58 percent. The share of Palestinian MA students doubled to 13 percent and for the Ph.D. rose from 3.9 percent to 6.3 percent and the overall rate stands at 16.1 percent which is still below their share in the population.[3] A portion of these professionals, academics, and small business owners aspire to improve their living conditions by moving out of their cramped communities that suffer from the absence of detailed zoning plans, discrimination in planning and allocation of land, to enjoy better public services and employment opportunities, and urban anonymity.[4]

About 90 percent of Israel's citizen-Palestinians live in Arab-only towns and villages. Choice of living arrangements comes under the rubric of private decisions par excellence, but for Palestinian citizens of Israel such a choice is thoroughly saturated with political and identity-related considerations (Abreek-Zubeidat and Ben Arie 2014: 221). High rates of residential segregation, I suggest, are rarely voluntary let alone "natural," but reflect policies of exclusion.

Israel's colonial land dynamic and legacy is characterized by three levels of control over territory—presence, ownership, and sovereignty—the former two serving as placeholders until the latter can be asserted. Even after Israel's establishment, the Zionist fear of decolonization—the apprehension that even when territory had come under formal Jewish sovereignty it might effectively revert to Arab hands unless it was buttressed by Jewish ownership and presence—persists (Kimmerling 1983: 27, 134, 139, 146). The fear of the 'return of the native' "is crucial for a fuller understanding of the Israeli attitude to land" (Rabinowitz 1997: 77). This foreboding is particularly evident in regions that have already been colonized and where reversal would be most visible (ibid. 79–81). I argue that the perpetuation of Israel's *landscape of segregation* is best accounted by Israel's continued settler colonial character.

The geographical focus of this study is the Galilee. The UNSC Partition Resolution allocated the central Galilee to the Arab state-to-be because it had a sizeable majority of Palestinians. For this very reason, its conquest by Israel was left to the last stage of the 1948 War and instead of a wholesale repetition of the dynamic of war-flight-expulsion, a sizeable share of the population stayed. The central Galilee is the only region of Israel in which Palestinian citizens—who make up 75 percent of the population—form the majority and, therefore, had been singled out for a policy of Judaization, the construction of Jewish towns in the midst of the Palestinian population. Nazareth Ilit (Upper Nazareth)—which changed its name to Nof Hagalil in 2019 to obscure its association with Nazareth, the largest Arab town in Israel—was constructed in 1954 on 1,200 dunams, half of which were expropriated from Nazareth (Forman 2006: 351) and Karmiel was built in 1962 on 5,123 dunams, expropriated from Deir al-Asad, Bi'ina and Nahf.[5] In each case, small Arab towns were also incorporated into the new city. By 2019, the population of Nazareth Ilit reached 41,734 and Karmiel 46,252. Jewish-Palestinian pull and tug in the Galilee render majority-minority residential dynamics particularly visible.

Mixed Towns

The commonly used terminology for describing an Israeli city with a significant percentage of Palestinian citizens, but majority Jews, is *mixed town*.[6] The term, however, is more wishful than apt since Palestinian citizens, as in other *divided cities*, "deeply mistrust their city-government's willingness and capacity to respond to calls for equal or groups-based treatment." At the same time, unlike *polarized cities* Israeli mixed towns have not turned into the sites of "enduring and consistent inter-ethnic violence laden with political meaning."[7]

Israel has five old mixed cities and towns: Lod, Ramla, and Acre have been Arab cities most of whose inhabitants were expelled and/or fled during the 1948 war, and were repopulated by newly arrived Jewish immigrants, while Jaffa and Haifa were already mixed in Mandatory times.[8] Their percentage of Palestinians citizens in 2019, ranges from 33 percent in Jaffa to 32 percent in Acre, 30.6 percent in Lod, 24 percent in

Ramla to 11.7 percent in Haifa. Altogether, they make up 111,891 individuals.[9] In the old mixed towns, many of the Arab citizens live in rundown historic city centers and the older neighborhoods surrounding them and are among the less desired in the country.

The emergence of new mixed towns is an unexpected by-product of Palestinian inhabitants having outgrown the limits placed by the Israeli land regime on the expansion and development of their villages and towns. It is estimated that between 50,000 and 60,000 Palestinians reside in new mixed towns.[10] These figures, however underestimate the full size of this population since many Arab families that live in Jewish-majority cities "commute for rights," that is they have not changed their official address in order to be able to send their children to Arab-language schools in nearby Arab cities (Blatman-Thomas 2017). These Palestinian citizens live in about fifteen Jewish-majority cities, from Nahariya and Safed in the north, through Hadera and Tel Aviv in the center, to Beer Sheba in the south. By 2019, in Upper Nazareth, the largest new mixed town, Palestinians make up 28.7 percent of the population and in Karmiel 3.6 percent of the population are of Palestinian nationality.[11]

Though the absolute number of Arab citizens who move into Jewish-majority towns is still low, falling between 1 and 4 percent in most new mixed towns, such migration is an ongoing and accelerating process that poses a concrete challenge to the pattern of residential separation of Jews and Arabs in Israel. A report by the Abraham Fund, a joint Jewish-Arab NGO, devoted to "Building a Shared Future for Israel's Jewish and Arab Citizens," finds that it hard to point to "a region or city in Israel that doesn't show mixing in housing, employment or business." The report suggests that "the transformation of the Arab society into an integral part of the public and general space of these cities demonstrates the blurring of their sharp and long-lasting lines of division," and concludes that such mixing is "the future face of Israel."[12]

This new socio-economic dynamic, when combined with the old and new mixed towns' diverging historical trajectories, leads to new expectations, most passionately articulated in regard to Upper Nazareth by journalists Lily Galili and Uri Nir, in 2001:

> This is a mixed town that doesn't have the history of [the War of] 1948, has no memories of battles and expulsion as do Lod and Ramla, does not possess the wretchedness and poverty of Jews and Arabs alike in Acre, and has no religious tensions. From all that is absent, and from the pattern that is formed, a new recipe can be created for a normal life that may be copied to other cities that are potentially mixed towns, like Beer Sheba and Afula.[13]

A further factor that would support this optimistic view is that Palestinian citizens who move into the new mixed towns are usually upwardly mobile. Upper Nazareth and emerging mixed towns attract mostly professional middle-class people seeking to improve their living conditions or to take up attractive job opportunities. The educational level of Palestinians and Jews in Upper Nazareth is about the same and is considerably above that of the rest of the Arab population of Israel.[14] Nevertheless, both old and new mixed towns oppose the arrival of Arab homeowners even though instead of reducing housing prices they contribute to their rise. While claiming to be kept within the legal boundaries of equal protection, novel forms of discrimination have emerged in the new mixed towns and are either thinly veiled or open secrets. I will survey five such practices.

Technologies of Discrimination

To counter the process of mixing cum replacement, some neighborhoods have adopted either an informal "only-Jews" sale policy or operate unofficial Admission Committees. Developers in Ganey Aviv neighborhood of Lod, in the Ajami neighborhood of Jaffa and the planned Kiryat Belz compound in the Har Yona Gimel neighborhood of Upper Nazareth, employ unofficial Admission Committees to let in only Jews or, respectively, only *haredim* (ultra-orthodox Jews).[15] An investigative program of Channel 10, which sent pairs of prospective Arab and Jewish buyers to new developments in the mixed towns of Acre, Ma'alot-Tarshiha, and Jaffa in 2012 and again in 2015, reported that whereas Arab buyers were rejected, Jewish ones were accommodated. A sales person informed the prospective Jewish "buyer" that "I am not allowed to talk about it ... but we don't sell to Arabs ... If they express interest, we just happen to be very busy and just don't have time to meet them."[16]

A second technology of discrimination is the erection of barriers to the sale of homes to potential Palestinian buyers. The former Mayor of Upper Nazareth, Shimon Gafsou, has chosen the preservation of the city's Jewish identity as the main plank of his electoral platform. In a flier distributed before the January 2013 elections, he promised that there would be no more closing of eyes and clinging to laws that allowed every citizen to choose to live wherever he wishes. Instead, he argued that through operations that are best kept under wraps, he successfully arrested Jewish demographic withdrawal (*nesiga*).[17] Although unable to place legal obstacles in the path of Palestinian citizens seeking to move into Karmiel and Upper Nazareth, both cities' municipal leaders publicized the "open secret" that they regularly employ covert methods for the same purpose. In the 2008 elections, a local list ran in Karmiel on the platform of forbidding the sale of homes to Arab buyers.[18] The deputy Mayor of Karmiel, Oren Milstein, called on its Jewish residents to report neighbors whose homes were in the process of being sold to Arab villagers to a restricted email address.[19] When Milstein instructed the local Civil Guard (*mishmar ezrahi*) to keep Arabs out of the city during evening hours, Mayor Eldar, demoted him.[20] In Afula, a nearby town, the mayor and slate of municipal counselors attempted unsuccessfully to close of a municipal park to Arab visitors in 2018 and members of the municipal council participated in a demonstration in front of a house newly purchased by an Arab couple.[21]

Yet another technology of discrimination used by Jewish municipal leadership against their city's rising Arab population blocks the provision of culturally appropriate social services to their Arab residents. Mayor Gafsou put his opposition this way: "Every Arab who comes to Upper Nazareth is happily welcome …. But everyone who arrives … needs to know that it is a Jewish and democratic city, first of all Jewish and only then democratic."[22]

While he is unable to nullify the legal rights that formally allow every individual, Jew and Arab alike, to choose his residence, Mayor Gafsou refuses to recognize the legitimacy of the Arab population's collective needs, such as Arab-language schools, mosques, cemeteries, Christmas displays, and the like, which he views as conduits to the cultural Arabization of the city. In 2012, the parents of the 1,900 Arab students who live in Upper Nazareth demanded that the municipality, jointly with the Ministry of Education, establish an Arab-language elementary school for their children so they will longer have to commute to Nazareth's public and mostly private Christian schools. As long as he serves as mayor, Gafsou warned the parents, there would be no Arab school in Upper Nazareth, a city that was established to Judaize the Galilee.[23]

In contrast to Upper Nazareth, old mixed cities and towns have both Jewish and Arab language elementary, middle, and high schools, though the allocation of resources favor the former over the latter. There also exist five, parent initiated, bi-lingual schools, one each in Jerusalem, Jaffa, and Lod. There is only one in the new mixed city of Beer Sheva, a university city, and another, the Galilee School in the Misgav area Kibbutz Ashbal, near the Arab city of Sakhnin.[24]

A fourth form of discrimination intends to reverse the potential demographic reversal by actively promoting the settlement of new Jewish residents. Mayor Gafsou placed his faith in the recruitment of Hasidic *haredim* into his predominantly secular city.[25] His flagship project, now underway, is the creation of the Kiryat Belz enclave of up to 3,050 haredi families in the Har Yona neighborhood. This urban development project is unusual for several reasons. Unlike new Arab residents, who are likely to be professionals or middle class, *haredim* have above average unemployment rates. Their emphasis on modesty and hostility to Sabbath activities in the public domain frequently lead to conflicts with secular Jewish neighbors, drives the latter out and property values down.[26] Even so, *haredim* offer the advantage of being less likely to leave the city than secular Jewish residents. *Haredim* effectively form closed homogenous communities centered on rabbinic institutions that run their own Admission Committee.[27] There is also less likelihood that individual *haredim* will sell their homes to Palestinians, because by leaving town they would also be leaving their community.

A fifth and significant form of institutional discrimination is in the area of municipal employment. Here the differences between old and new mixed cities and towns are the sharpest. The share of Arab employees in 2010 in Acre was 29 percent, in Ma'alot 19.7 percent, in Haifa 14.2 percent, in Lod 11.2 percent, in Ramla 9.4 percent but in Upper Nazareth it was only 5 percent, and in fact has fallen from 5.8 percent in 2008.

Its Welfare Department and Legal Departments have no Arab employees, and none are in management position.[28]

While a multitude of discriminatory technologies have been applied to prevent Palestinian citizens in the mixed towns from benefitting from and receiving services from their municipalities, there is one arena in which they are making inroads. Palestinian inhabitants in the old mixed towns have been able to translate their growing numbers into political representation. Elected representatives of either all-Arab or joint Arab-Jewish parties have been serving on municipal councils while following the municipal elections of 2018 they were invited to join additional governing coalitions. The longest uninterrupted shared coalition is in the united Jewish-Arab municipalities of Ma'alot-Tarshiha. In Acre, an Arab municipal councilor continues serving as a deputy mayor in charge of the planning and construction department. In Ramla, Arab parties will rejoin the municipal council. In Jaffa, a mixed neighborhood of Tel Aviv, the council will for the first time have Arab councilors. In Lod, probably the most conflicted old mixed town, an Arab municipal council member will serve as deputy mayor and his party will be in charge of the departments of health, environment, Arab education, and new construction is slated in the Arab neighborhoods.

The most far-reaching coalition agreement was reached in Haifa, considered to be the cultural center of Palestinian life in Israel, under the new mayor Einat Kalisch-Rotem. Not only will an Arab counselor serve as Deputy Mayor and Arab parties be represented on all the major municipal committees but the principles of multiculturalism, "shared life," and equality have been affirmed in the coalition agreement. Two committees, one to advance equality, the other to promote coexistence were established to monitor and ensure their implementation. Finally, in Upper Nazareth, the first new mixed town to do so, the corruption trial and departure of the disgraced mayor were followed by the appointment of Dr. Shukri Awad as an unpaid Deputy Mayor in charge of infrastructure and a second Arab counsellor to direct the Commerce and Industry Department. They will also receive representation in the management of community centers and economic development.[29]

Conclusion

Practically all Israeli mixed towns are engaged in institutional discrimination against new Palestinian Arab renters and homeowners, but new mixed towns, especially Upper Nazareth, appear to be the most determined to justify the preservation of their Jewish majority and character. Treating Arab cultural institutions as illegitimate, the city's Arab residents themselves are viewed as interlopers.

The price paid for enshrining Israel's settler colonial formation in Israel's regime and perpetuating it past the country's independence is the persistent fear of the reversal of Zionist colonization. The Israeli settler-colonial framework, and in particular, the Jewish fear of reversal in the Galilee and the Negev, as well as the continued colonization in the West Bank, are an unstable construct. On the one hand, by blocking zoning and new construction of housing, as well as industrial zones, in Arab locales, it leads to the relocation of upwardly mobile Arab citizens into Jewish-majority towns. On the other hand, the replacement of Jewish with Arab citizens and the changing demographic ratios between these two groups in favor of the later feeds the settler colonial fear of reversal. The pressure from some of the Jewish residents of old and, in particular, new mixed towns generates a backlash and institutional, some veiled some open, forms of discriminatory technologies to exclude if not individual Arab residents then to deny their collective presence. The result is Israel's new and veiled landscape of discrimination.

The growing presence of Arab citizens and the transformation of Jewish cities into new mixed towns, however, create a new reality of mixing and comingling which finds its expression in the growing political influence of Arab and mixed Jewish-Arab municipal parties. Their participation in municipal coalition governments, a task easier to accomplish in local than in the national government, puts paid to the denial of mixing, to the reluctant acknowledgement of their needs, and at least in Haifa to the affirmation of the values of multiculturalism and equal access to municipal resources. These tendencies are, however, slow in coming in new mixed towns and it is too early to evaluate the effectiveness of Jewish-Arab political cooperation in both old and new mixed towns.

Notes

1 Or Commission, "National Commission of Inquiry for the Examination of the Confrontations between the Security Forces and Israeli Citizens in October 2000," Jerusalem, August 2003, Par.9, http://uri.mitkadem.co.il/vaadat-or/
2 *Statistical Abstract of Israel 2014*, Table 8.72.
3 *Haaretz*, January 2, 2018; https://www.themarker.com/misc/article-print-page/1.5762853
4 *Haaretz*, December 22, 2014; David B. Green, "The Arabs Next Door," *Tablet,* April 17, 2012.
5 Abraham Fund Initiatives, *The Arab Society in Israel: Information Binder, 2nd ed.*, 2013, Chapter 5, 10N, (Hebrew).
6 Israel doesn't distinguish between towns and cities.
7 See these distinctions in Bollens (2000): 9–10.
8 Khamaisi, Rassem, *The Arab Population in the Mixed Cities in Israel*, Jerusalem: Shatil, Jerusalem, 2008, 15 (Hebrew).
9 https://www.cbs.gov.il/he/settlements/Pages/default.aspx?mode=Yeshuv
10 Beeri-Sulitzeanu, Amnon and UriGopher, *Mixed Cities and Regions: The Future Face of Israel*, Abraham Fund Initiatives, May 2009, 6 (Hebrew).
11 https://www.cbs.gov.il/he/settlements/Pages/default.aspx?mode=Yeshuv
12 Beeri-Sulitzeanu & Gopher, *Mixed Cities*, 5–7.

13 *Haaretz*, December 22, 2014.
14 Hamdan, Hana (2006), "Upper Nazareth as a Mixed Town," in Tovi Fenster and Haim Yacobi (eds.), *Israeli City or City in Israel?*, Jerusalem: van Leer, 118 (Hebrew).
15 http://www.acri.org.il/he/2611; *Ynet*, February 25, 2013.
16 http://www.acri.org.il/he/24770; http://he.kifaya.org.il/mobile/reports/view/274; http://m.nana10.co.il/Article/?ArticleID=1141750&sid=126&sid=120&pid=55&service=news
17 *Haaretz*, April 4, 2013.
18 *Haaretz*, March 3, 2010.
19 *Ynet*, October 21, 2011.
20 *Jerusalem Post*, April 11, 2010.
21 *Haaretz*, 15 June, 2019.
22 http://www.nrg.co.il/online/12/ART2/434/223.html
23 *Haaretz*, January 17, 2013, July 25, 2003; http://www.abrahamfund.org/5931
24 Shwed, Uriet et al., "Integration of Arab Israelis and Jews in School in Israel," in *State of the National Report: Society, Economy and Policy in Israel 2014*, Jerusalem: Taub Center, December 2014, 330–1, 340.
25 *Haaretz*, December 22, 2014.
26 Green, "Arabs Next Door," 4.
27 *Ynet*, February 25, 2013.
28 *Haaretz*, March 7, 2011 and October 21, 2014; http://www.knesset.gov.il/committees/heb/docs/arab_workers17.pdf
29 https://www.mekomit.co.il/ps/67570/

References

Abreek-Zubeidat, F. and R. Ben Arie (2014), "To Be at Home: Spaces of Citizenship in the Community Settlements of the Galilee," in N. Lebovic and R. Ben-Shai (eds.), *The Politics of Nihilism: From the Nineteenth Century to Contemporary Israel*, 205–26, London: Bloomsbury.

Blatman-Thomas, N. (2017), "Commuting for Rights: Circular Mobilities and Regional Identities of Palestinians in a Jewish-Israeli Town," *Geoforum*, 78: 22–32.

Bollens, S. A. (2000), *On Narrow Ground: Urban Policy and Ethnic Conflict in Jerusalem and Belfast*, Albany: SUNY Press.

Dagan-Buzaglo, N. and E. Konor-Attias (2013), *"Israel's Middle Class 1992–2010: Who Are We Talking About?,"* Tel-Aviv: Adva Center. http://adva.org/wp-content/uploads/2015/01/middle-class12.pdf

Forman, G. (2006), "Military Rule, Political Manipulation, and Jewish Settlement: Israeli Mechanisms for Controlling Nazareth in the 1950s," *The Journal of Israeli History*, 25 (2): 335–59.

Kimmerling, B. (1983), *Zionism and Territory*, Berkeley: Institute of International Studies.

Rabinowitz, D. (1997), *Overlooking Nazareth: The Ethnography of Exclusion in Galilee*, Cambridge: Cambridge University Press.

Yacobi, H. (2009), *The Jewish-Arab City: Spatio-politics in a Mixed Community*, London: Routledge.

Neoliberal Apartheid in Palestine

by Andy Clarno

International law defines apartheid as a system of racialized political domination. According to the International Convention on the Suppression and Punishment of the Crime of Apartheid (1973), apartheid involves "inhuman acts committed for the purpose of establishing and maintaining domination by one racial group of persons over any other racial group of persons and systematically oppressing them." The Rome Statute of the International Criminal Court (2002) defines apartheid as a crime involving "an institutionalized regime of systematic oppression and domination by one racial group over any other racial group or groups."

In March 2017, the United Nations Economic and Social Commission for Western Asia (ESCWA) released a report on "Israeli Practices toward the Palestinian People and the Question of Apartheid" (United Nations 2017). Based on a close reading of international law, the report concludes that "Israel has established an apartheid regime that dominates the Palestinian people as a whole" (2017: 1). More specifically, it argues that "the strategic fragmentation of the Palestinian people is the principal method by which Israel imposes an apartheid regime" (2017: 3–4).

As the ESCWA report explains, Israel's apartheid regime fragments the Palestinian population and subjects each fragment to a different form of racial rule. Palestinians in the occupied West Bank and Gaza Strip are *subjects* of Israeli military rule; Palestinians from East Jerusalem have tenuous *residency* rights; Palestinians with formal *citizenship* in Israel face legalized discrimination; and Palestinian *refugees* are systematically prevented from returning to their homes and lands. Yet each group is subject to the same apartheid state.

While highlighting political fragmentation, the ESCWA report overlooks the economic fragmentation of the Palestinian people. Yet class divisions among Palestinians have increased exponentially over the last twenty-five years due to neoliberal restructuring. The ESCWA report misses this fragmentation because international law treats apartheid as a political regime of racial domination. In this chapter, I propose an alternative, sociological understanding of apartheid as a political-economic system of racial capitalism. This allows us to analyze the impacts of neoliberal restructuring on Israeli apartheid. It also facilitates efforts to de-exceptionalize Palestine and build links with other populations facing combinations of racial domination and neoliberal capitalism.

Apartheid

There is a growing recognition among activists, scholars, journalists, and others that Israel is an apartheid state. For many, this recognition is based on similarities in the regimes of racial domination in Palestine/Israel today and South Africa before 1994.[1] But legal scholars point out that the comparisons are not particularly important. What matters more, they argue, are the international legal statutes which prohibit apartheid as a crime against humanity (Jamjoum 2009; MacAllister 2008). Legal analyses, including the 2017 ESCWA report, have repeatedly concluded that Israel violates this prohibition and can be held legally accountable under international law.[2]

Despite the clear value of international law, there are also serious limitations to the legal approach (Erakat et al. 2012; Erakat 2019). Above all, international laws are only effective when acknowledged and enforced by states, and the hierarchical structure of the state system provides a handful of states with veto power. Similarly, international laws often prioritize political rights over broader political-economic conceptions of justice. This can be seen quite clearly in the international legal definition of apartheid. By focusing only on the *political* regime, the definition does not provide a basis for analyzing the *economic* aspects of apartheid.

We can find a more robust sociological understanding of apartheid in the writings of Black radicals from South Africa during the 1970s and 1980s. The critique of apartheid economics was crucial for every segment of the South African liberation movement. The most powerful bloc within the liberation movement—made up of the African National Congress (ANC) and its allies in the South African Communist Party—understood apartheid as "colonialism of a special type." Recognizing that the system of colonial domination was linked to a capitalist system that relied on the exploitation of Black labor, the ANC/SACP bloc argued that liberation would require two stages: first a struggle against the racist/colonial state and then a struggle against capitalism (South African Communist Party 1981). A smaller block within the movement, including the Azanian People's Organization (AZAPO), insisted that racism and capitalism could not be so easily distinguished, and that apartheid was better understood as a system of "racial capitalism." In the Azanian Manifesto, the radical wing argued that racial capitalism "holds the people of Azania (South Africa) in bondage for the benefit of a small minority of white capitalists and their allies, the white workers and the reactionary sections of the black middle class" (Mngxitama et al. 2008: 168). Predicting that the ANC's strategy would simply entrench the inequality generated by apartheid, they called for a one-stage struggle led by Black workers that would confront not just the racial state but the underlying system of racial capitalism.[3]

The ANC framework for understanding apartheid eclipses the international legal definition because of its attention to the significance of capitalism. Yet the intersectional approach developed by the Black radical tradition offers an even more robust sociological framework for analyzing apartheid.

For instance, this framework can help explain the limitations of transformation in South Africa after 1994. When legal apartheid was abolished, Black South Africans gained formal equality under the law—including the right to vote, the right to live anywhere, and the right to move without permits. The democratization of the state was a remarkable achievement that demonstrates the possibility of peaceful coexistence on the basis of legal equality and mutual recognition. This is what makes South Africa so compelling for many Palestinians seeking an alternative to Israeli apartheid.

But just as the Black radicals predicted, the South African transition did not address the structures of racial capitalism. During the negotiations, the ANC made major concessions to win the support of white South Africans and the global capitalist elite. Most importantly, the ANC agreed not to nationalize the land, banks, and mines and instead accepted constitutional protections for the existing distribution of private property—despite the history of colonial dispossession (Bond 2000; Marais 2001). Instead of land redistribution, the ANC adopted a market-based program through which the state helps Black clients purchase white-owned land. This World Bank-approved "willing seller-willing buyer" program has led to the redistribution of just 7.5 percent of South African land (Ntsebeza 2007). In addition, the ANC government adopted a neoliberal economic strategy promoting free trade, export-oriented industry, and the privatization of state-owned businesses and municipal services. Neville Alexander (2002), one of the framers of the Azanian Manifesto, explained that "what we used to call the apartheid-capitalist system has simply given way to the post-apartheid capitalist system." This has given rise to a small Black elite, but the old white elite continues to own the vast majority of land and wealth in the country. In the words of Achille Mbembe (2015), "This is the only country on Earth in which a revolution took place which resulted in not one single former oppressor losing anything." As a result, post-apartheid South Africa is now recognized as one of the most unequal countries in the world.

Israeli Apartheid

Israeli apartheid was a product of Zionism, a settler colonial project to create and expand a Jewish state in Palestine by displacing most Palestinians and dominating those that remain. In 1948, the Zionist movement declared the formation of Israel as a Jewish state, forcibly displaced 750,000 Palestinians from their towns and villages, and took possession of 78 percent of the land in historical Palestine (Masalha 2012; Pappe 2006). For more than seventy years, the Palestinian minority that became citizens of Israel in 1948 has faced formal legal discrimination due to laws and regulations that privilege Jewish nationality.[4] The State of Israel has also systematically prevented the return of the Palestinian refugees displaced from their lands in 1948. These are the foundations of Israeli apartheid. After occupying the West Bank and Gaza Strip in 1967, Israel extended apartheid to the occupied territories. Israel installed a military administration to rule the occupied Palestinian population and began steadily colonizing Palestinian land and building Jewish settlements (Aruri 1983; Gordon 2008; Hajjar 2005). The state also forcibly incorporated the occupied Palestinian population into the Israel economy as low-wage workers and captive markets (Farsakh 2005; Roy 1995). Until the 1980s, Israel managed a racial Fordist economy characterized by state support for industrial and agricultural production, full employment and extensive benefits for Jewish workers, and the superexploitation of low-wage Palestinian and Mizrahi Jewish workers (Shafir and Peled 2000). In 1993, after a six-year uprising in the occupied territories, Israel and the Palestine Liberation Organization (PLO) negotiated a treaty that launched the "Oslo peace process." Rather than creating an independent Palestinian state, the Oslo process has intensified Israel's apartheid project (Gordon 2008; Weizman 2007).

The international legal definition of apartheid has been useful for making sense of the political and geographic fragmentation generated by the Oslo process. Oslo enabled Israel to restructure settler colonial domination in the occupied territories by supplementing direct military rule with aspects of indirect rule. The Oslo agreements established the Palestinian Authority (PA) as a semi-autonomous governing body for Palestinians in the Gaza Strip and parts of the West Bank (excluding East Jerusalem). Fragmenting the occupied territories, Israel effectively separated the West Bank from the Gaza Strip and isolated East Jerusalem from the rest of the West Bank (Weizman 2007). But the fragmentation of Palestine is most evident in the West Bank, which Israel fractured into dozens of separate isolated enclaves by withdrawing its military from the heart of Palestinian cities, surrounding these areas with checkpoints, roadblocks, fences, and walls, imposing a generalized military "closure" of the occupied territories, and introducing a permit regime and a segregated road network to regulate Palestinian movement. The Oslo agreements granted the PA limited autonomy over civil affairs such as education and urban planning inside the enclaves (Areas A and B), which together make up 40 percent of the West Bank, in exchange for working alongside the Israeli military to suppress resistance to the occupation. Meanwhile, Israel retained full jurisdiction over the remaining 60 percent of the West Bank (Area C) and ultimate sovereignty over the entire territory. Despite formally "disengaging" from the Gaza Strip in 2005, Israel has surrounded and besieged the territory for the last fifteen years while repeatedly carrying out deadly military invasions. In the West Bank, Israel's new colonial strategy involves *concentrating* the Palestinian population into the enclaves of Areas A and B and *colonizing* Palestinian land in Area C. During the second *intifada* (2000– 2005), for instance, Israel erected 500 military checkpoints, used roadblocks and trenches to isolate Palestinian communities, detached villages from neighboring cities, and intensified the generalized "closure" with militarily enforced curfews and restrictions on movement between cities (Beinin and Stein 2006; Honig-Parnass and Haddad 2007). For six years, Palestinians rarely left the newly established confines of their micro-enclaves.

East Jerusalem is also a site of particularly aggressive Israeli colonization. Palestinians are currently 40 percent of the population in Jerusalem. Yet the city council's *Jerusalem 2020* master plan outlines a vision of a 70 percent Jewish majority in the city (Jerusalem Municipality 2005). To manufacture this demographic shift, the state is expanding Jewish settlements and displacing Palestinians from the city through regulations and violence. Palestinians in Jerusalem face a severe housing crisis due to planning restrictions and home demolitions. Palestinians who cannot demonstrate that Jerusalem remains their "center of life" risk having their residency permits revoked. And ideologically motivated Jewish settlers use violence to take over Palestinian properties, expel Palestinians from their homes, abuse Palestinians on the streets, and claim control over the Al-Aqsa Mosque and other Islamic holy sites in the Old City.

In short, Oslo has intensified, rather than reversing, Israeli apartheid. The ESCWA report explains all of this in exceptional detail.

Neoliberal Apartheid

While the legal framework of apartheid helps us see this political and geographic fragmentation, it downplays the importance of class fragmentation for contemporary Israeli apartheid. Understanding apartheid as a system of racial capitalism opens the possibility for analyzing Oslo as not merely a political project but a political-economic project that combines the reorganization of settler colonial rule with neoliberal restructuring. Neoliberal restructuring has generated intense class divisions that intersect with the political and geographic divisions described above. At the same time, the neoliberal project incorporates some Palestinians into the system of oppression.

Neoliberalism is a free-market economic philosophy that has led to extreme economic inequality around the world over the last forty years (Harvey 2005). Neoliberal policies like privatization, deregulation, free trade, and cuts to social spending have generated intense crises for poor and working-class people while producing massive corporate profits and concentrating wealth in the hands of a tiny elite. To contain these crises, neoliberal policies are always accompanied by heavy investments in state and private security forces—such as police, prisons, private security, border patrols, immigration enforcement, and the military industrial complex (Clarno 2017).

Since the late 1980s, Israel's economy has been fundamentally reorganized by neoliberal restructuring. State-led production for domestic consumption has been replaced by corporate-driven, high-tech production for the global market (Grinberg and Shafir 2000; Ram 2008; Shalev 2000). Neoliberal restructuring has enabled Israeli corporations to integrate into the global capitalist economy while dismantling the Israeli welfare state, weakening the Israeli labor movement, and increasing inequality in Israel/Palestine. These changes were intimately connected to the Oslo process. In the eyes of Israeli political and business elites, peace with the Palestinians would open the markets of the Arab world to US and Israeli capital (Peres 1993).

In practice, neoliberal restructuring reduced Israeli reliance on Palestinian workers. Israel's transition to a high-tech economy decreased the demand for industrial and agricultural labor while free trade agreements with Jordan and Egypt allowed Israeli manufacturers to shift production from Palestinian subcontractors to export-processing zones in neighboring countries. Moreover, "shock doctrine" neoliberalism in the former Soviet Union and global neoliberal restructuring led to the immigration of more than one million Russian Jews and over 300,000 migrant workers who now compete with Palestinians for the remaining low-wage jobs (Ellman and Laacher 2003; Klein 2007; Lewin-Epstein, Ro'i and Ritterband 2013).

In short, neoliberal restructuring combined with Israel's settler colonial project has transformed the Palestinians into a truly disposable population. This enabled Israel's new colonial strategy of establishing enclosures in the Gaza Strip and the West Bank to concentrate and contain the racialized Palestinian surplus population.

Just like Israel, the Palestinian Authority has embraced a neoliberal economic program based on the vision of an export-oriented, free-market economy for the future state of Palestine (Haddad 2016; Hanieh 2013). The plan involves cuts to public employment, an expansion of private sector investment, and the creation of free-trade industrial zones along the wall. Despite experiments, the industrial zones have failed to attract investors due primarily to Israeli restrictions on imports and exports and the relatively high cost of Palestinian labor compared to neighboring countries.

Although neoliberalism has failed to produce jobs, it has led to the growth of new Palestinian elites who see some benefits from the status quo. Neoliberal restructuring has created opportunities for Palestinian capitalists, yet their businesses all depend on permits from the Israeli military authorities. As a result, most Palestinian capitalists accommodate the occupation while some even profit from Israeli colonization activities (Dana 2014; Hanieh 2013; Nakhleh 2012). Some PA-affiliated business owners in the West Bank, for instance, sell stones and cement to Israeli companies for the construction of settlements and the apartheid wall.

In addition to Palestinian capitalists, Oslo led to the emergence of a Palestinian NGO elite with ties to international donors. After 1994, the flow of donor funding contributed to the demobilization of Palestinian grassroots structures (Hammami 2000). Although many Palestinian NGO officials have backgrounds in community organizing, the salaried elite has become increasingly professionalized, accommodating, and responsive to international agendas (Hanafi and Tabar 2005). Visitors to Ramallah are often surprised to see private mansions, expensive restaurants, five-star hotels, and luxury vehicles. Although mistaken for signs of a thriving economy, these displays are signs of the growing class divide among Palestinians in the West Bank (Taraki 2008).

Most Palestinians in the occupied territories confront intense poverty, permanent unemployment, and constant repression. The only sector of the Israeli economy that has retained a relatively steady demand for Palestinian workers is construction—due largely to the expansion of Israeli settlements and the wall in the West Bank. The Israeli permit regime requires Palestinians from the occupied territories to obtain work permits from the military administration to access jobs in Israel and the settlements. These permits inculcate subservience: individuals with marks on their security record are automatically blacklisted and the state restricts the number of permits whenever there is an uprising in the occupied territories. In a context of widespread unemployment, the permit regime has become an effective disciplinary tool of the occupation (Berda 2017). Israel now directs 50 percent of these work permits to the settlements (Farsakh 2005). According to a 2011 survey, 82 percent of Palestinians employed in the settlements would leave their jobs if they could find a suitable alternative (Democracy and Workers' Rights Center 2011).

The other primary source of employment for West Bank Palestinians is the PA security forces. After the second *intifada*, the PA security forces were rebuilt under the supervision of the United States. More than 80,000 strong, the new PA security forces are trained by the United States in Jordan and deployed in close coordination with the Israeli military to suppress resistance to the occupation (Tartir 2015, 2017). Working together, Israel and the PA target not only Islamists and leftists but all Palestinian critics of Oslo through shared intelligence, coordinated arrests, and weapons confiscations. Security coordination in the occupied West Bank is one of the most sophisticated security assemblages in the world, incorporating both the forces of US empire and the colonized Palestinian population into Israel's colonial security regime. Yet the PA security officers find themselves in an impossible situation— charged, on the one hand, with not doing enough to protect Israel, and, on the other, with being traitors to their people. The psychological costs are amplified by the fact that many people accept work with the PA security forces because there are so few other job opportunities.

In short, two of the only jobs available for West Bank Palestinians are building Israeli settlements on confiscated Palestinian land or working with the PA security forces suppressing Palestinian resistance to Israeli rule. In either case, the jobs conscript Palestinians into Israel's neoliberal apartheid project.

Palestinians from the Gaza Strip do not even have these "opportunities." Gaza is one of the most extreme versions of engineered disposability on earth (Finkelstein 2018; Pappe 2016; Sassen 2014). Since 2006, Israel has almost entirely eliminated work permits for the Gaza Strip. Gaza is surrounded, enclosed, and under siege. And over the last twelve years, Israel has carried out three sustained assaults on Gaza that killed nearly 4,000 Palestinians.

The oppressive conscription of West Bank workers, the deadly exclusion of the Gaza Strip, and the conspicuous consumption of Palestinian elites highlight the growing class divide and the differential incorporation of Palestinians into Israel's neoliberal apartheid project.

Palestine Liberation and Global Social Justice

Finally, understanding apartheid as form of racial capitalism can help shift away from discourses that treat Palestine as an exception. Israel stands out among repressive racial states today for the brutality and extreme violence of its active project of settler colonial displacement. Yet these policies resonate with the racist forms of state violence in the United States, Brazil, and other countries. Indeed, social justice movements are building connections between struggles against racialized state violence in Palestine, South Africa, the United States, and beyond. Yet state violence is not the only thing that Palestinians have in common with Black Americans, Native Americans, Black South Africans, and other racially oppressed populations. In many parts of the world, combinations of racial domination and neoliberal capitalism have led to extreme inequality and racialized poverty along with an expansion of militarized policing to protect the powerful by policing the racialized poor. Understanding these conditions as products of neoliberal racial capitalism can facilitate further connections as movements build radical forms of solidarity in the worldwide struggle against localized apartheid regimes and global neoliberal apartheid.

Notes

1. See, for example: Abunimah (2006); Barghouti (2011); Bishara (2002); Carter (2006); Farsakh (2005); Said (1996, 2001).
2. See also: Human Sciences Research Council (2009); Russell Tribunal on Palestine (2011); Dugard and Reynolds (2013).
3. At the same time, Cedric Robinson (2000) was developing his influential theory of racial capitalism. Pointing out that capitalism emerged in a European context awash in racial logics and hierarchies, Robinson argues that there is no such thing as non-racial capitalism.
4. Moreover, the Israel government recently passed the "Nation State Law," which entrenches the second-class status of its Palestinian citizens by describing Israel as the "nation state of the Jewish people," declaring Jewish settlement a national value, and claiming that Jews have a "unique" right to self-determination in Palestine/Israel.

References

Abunimah, A. (2006), *One Country: A Bold Proposal to End the Israeli-Palestinian Impasse*, New York: Metropolitan Books.

Alexander, N. (2002), *An Ordinary Country: Issues in the Transition from Apartheid to Democracy in South Africa*, Pietermaritzburg: University of Natal Press.

Aruri, N. (1983), *Occupation: Israel Over Palestine*, Belmont, MA: Association of Arab American University Graduates.

Barghouti, O. (2011), *BDS: Boycott, Divestment, Sanctions: The Global Struggle for Palestinian Rights*, Chicago: Haymarket Books.

Beinin, J. and R. L. Stein, eds. (2006), *The Struggle for Sovereignty: Palestine and Israel, 1993–2005*, Stanford: Stanford University Press.

Berda, Y. (2017), *Living Emergency: Israel's Permit Regime in the Occupied West Bank*, Stanford: Stanford University Press.

Bishara, M. (2002), *Palestine/Israel: Peace or Apartheid—Occupation, Terrorism, and the Future*, London: Zed Books.

Bond, P. (2000), *Elite Transition: From Apartheid to Neoliberalism in South Africa*, London: Pluto Press.

Carter, J. (2006), *Palestine: Peace Not Apartheid*, New York: Simon and Shuster.

Clarno, A. (2017), *Neoliberal Apartheid: Palestine/Israel and South Africa after 1994*, Chicago: University of Chicago Press.

Dana, T. (2014), "The Palestinian Capitalists That Have Gone Too Far," *Jadaliyya* (January 23). http://www.jadaliyya.com/pages/index/16075/the-palestinian-capitalists-that-have-gone-too-far

Democracy and Workers' Rights Center (2011), "Executive Summary of a study on 'Palestinian wage workers in Israeli settlements in the West Bank—Characteristics and work circumstances'," *Democracy and Workers' Rights Center*, Ramallah.

Dugard, J. and J. Reynolds (2013), "Apartheid, International Law, and the Occupied Palestinian Territory," *European Journal of International Law*, 24 (3): 867–913.

Ellman, M. and S. Laacher (2003), *Migrant Workers in Israel: A Contemporary Form of Slavery*, Paris: Euro-Mediterranean Human Rights Network and International Federation for Human Rights. https://www.fidh.org/IMG/pdf/il1806a.pdf

Erakat, N. (2019), *Justice for Some: Law and the Question of Palestine*, Stanford: Stanford University Press.

Erakat, N., L. Hajjar, D. Qaddumi, A. Barclay, A. Bali, N. Sultany, and D. Li (2012), "Roundtable on Occupation Law: Part of the Conflict or Part of the Solution?," Jadaliyya (September 11). https://www.jadaliyya.com/Details/27041/Roundtable-on-Occupation-Law-Part-of-the-Conflict-or-Part-of-the-Solution

Farsakh, L. (2005), *Palestinian Labour Migration to Israel: Labour, Land, and Occupation*, London: Routledge.

Finkelstein, N. (2018), *Gaza: An Inquest into Its Martyrdom*, Berkeley: University of California Press.

Gordon, N. (2008), *Israel's Occupation*, Berkeley: University of California Press.

Grinberg, L. L. and G. Shafir (2000), "Economic Liberalization and the Breakup of the Histadrut's Domain," in G. Shafir and Y. Peled (eds.), *The New Israel: Peacemaking and liberalization*, 103–28, Boulder: Westview Press.

Haddad, T. (2016), *Palestine Ltd.: Neoliberalism and Nationalism in the Occupied Territory*, London: I.B. Tauris.

Hajjar, L. (2005), *Courting Conflict: The Israeli Military Court System in the West Bank and Gaza*, Berkeley: University of California Press.

Hammami, R. (2000), "Palestinian NGOs since Oslo: From NGO Politics to Social Movements?," *Middle East Report*, 214: 16–19+27+48.

Hanafi, S. and L. Tabar (2005), *The Emergence of a Palestinian Globalized Elite: Donors, International Organizations, and Local NGOs*, Jerusalem: Institute for Jerusalem Studies.

Hanieh, A. (2013), *Lineages of Revolt: Issues of Contemporary Capitalism in the Middle East*, Chicago: Haymarket Books.
Harvey, D. (2005), *A Brief History of Neoliberalism*. Oxford: Oxford University Press.
Honig-Parnass, T. and T. Haddad, eds. (2007), *Between the Lines: Readings on Israel, the Palestinians, and the U.S. "War on Terror,"* Chicago: Haymarket Books.
Human Sciences Research Council (2009), *Occupation, Colonialism, Apartheid? A Re-Assessment of Israel's Practices in the Occupied Palestinian Territories under International Law*, Cape Town: Human Sciences Research Council.
International Criminal Court (2002), "Rome Statute of the International Criminal Court." https://www.icc-cpi.int/resource-library/documents/rs-eng.pdf (accessed March 8, 2022).
Jamjoum, H. (2009), "Not an Analogy: Israel and the Crime of Apartheid," *The Electronic Intifada* (April 3). https://electronicintifada.net/content/not-analogy-israel-and-crime-apartheid/8164
Jerusalem Municipality (2005), *Jerusalem 2000: Local Outline Plan—Report No. 4: The Proposed Plan and the Main Planning Policies*, Jerusalem: Jerusalem Municipality.
Klein, N. (2007), *The Shock Doctrine: The Rise of Disaster Capitalism*, New York: Metropolitan Books.
Lewin-Epstein, N., Y. Ro'i and P. Ritterband (2013), *Russian Jews on Three Continents: Migration and Resettlement*, London: Routledge.
MacAllister, K. (2008), "Applicability of the Crime of Apartheid to Israel," *Al-Majdal*, 38 (Summer). http://www.badil.org/en/component/k2/item/72-applicability-of-the-crime-of-apartheid-to-israel.html
Marais, H. (2001), *South Africa—Limits to Change: The Political Economy of Transition*, London: Zed Books.
Masalha, N. (2012), *The Palestine Nakba: Decolonising History, Narrating the Subaltern, Reclaiming Memory*, London: Zed Books.
Mbembe, A. (2015), "The State of South African Political Life," *Africa Is a Country* (September). https://africasacountry.com/2015/09/achille-mbembe-on-the-state-of-south-african-politics/
Mngxitama, A., A. Alexander, and N. Gibson, eds. (2008), *Biko Lives! Contesting the Legacies of Steve Biko*, New York: Palgrave Macmillan.
Nakhleh, K. (2012), *Globalized Palestine: The National Sell-Out of a Homeland*, Trenton: Red Sea Press.
Ntsebeza, L. (2007), "Address the Land Question," *Mail & Guardian* (August 17–23): 23.
Pappe, I. (2006), *The Ethnic Cleansing of Palestine*, London: Oneworld Publications.
Pappe, I. (2016), *The Biggest Prison on Earth: A History of the Occupied Territories*, London: Oneworld Publications.
Peres, S. (1993), *The New Middle East*, New York: Henry Holt.
Ram, U. (2008), *The Globalization of Israel: McWorld in Tel Aviv, Jihad in Jerusalem*, New York: Routledge.
Robinson, C. (2000), *Black Marxism: The Making of the Black Radical Tradition*, Chapel Hill: University of North Carolina Press.
Roy, S. (1995), *The Gaza Strip: The Political Economy of De-development*, Washington, DC: Institute for Palestine Studies.

Russell Tribunal on Palestine (2011), "Findings of the South African Session," Bertrand Russell Peace Foundation (November 5–7). http://www.russelltribunalonpalestine.com/en/wp-content/uploads/2011/09/RToP-Cape-Town-full-findings2.pdf

Said, E. (1996), *Peace and Its Discontents: Essays on Palestine in the Middle East Peace Process*, New York: Vintage.

Said, E. (2001), *The End of the Peace Process: Oslo and After*, New York: Vintage.

Sassen, S. (2014), *Expulsions: Brutality and Complexity in the Global Economy*, Cambridge: Harvard University Press.

Shafir, G. and Y. Peled, eds. (2000), *The New Israel: Peacemaking and Liberalization*, Boulder: Westview Press.

Shalev, M. (2000), "Liberalization and the Transformation of the Political Economy," in G. Shafir and Y. Peled (eds.), *The New Israel: Peacemaking and Liberalization*, 129–160, Boulder: Westview Press.

South African Communist Party (1981), "The Road to South African Freedom," in *South African Communists Speak: Documents from the History of the South African Communist Party 1915–1980*, 284–319, London: Inkululeko Publications.

Taraki, L. (2008), "Urban Modernity on the Periphery: A New Middle Class Reinvents the Palestinian City," *Social Text*, 26 (2): 61–81.

Tartir, A. (2015), "The Evolution and Reform of the Palestinian Security Forces 1993–2013," *Stability: International Journal of Security and Development*. http://www.stabilityjournal.org/articles/10.5334/sta.gi/

Tartir, A. (2017), "The Palestinian Authority Security Forces: Whose Security?," *Al-Shabaka: The Palestinian Policy Network*, May 16, 2017. https://al-shabaka.org/briefs/palestinian-authority-security-forces-whose-security/

United Nations (1973), "International Convention on the Suppression and Punishment of the Crime of Apartheid," General Assembly of the United Nations (November 30). https://treaties.un.org/doc/Publication/UNTS/Volume%201015/volume-1015-I-14861-English.pdf

United Nations (2017), *Israeli Practices towards the Palestinian People and the Question of Apartheid*, United Nations: Economic and Social Commission for Western Asia.

Weizman, E. (2007), *Hollow Land: Israel's Architecture of Occupation*, London: Verso.

Constructing a Sense of "We" across the Lines of Conflict and Occupation: Joint Peace Movement Organizations in Israel/Palestine

by Michelle I. Gawerc

The longstanding enmity between Palestinians and Israelis has been so amply documented that it has become something of an unchangeable truth, both in scholarship and in popular political commentary. However, some local activists on the ground in Israel/Palestine perceive this animosity differently; they see it as a created problem to be addressed through joint political action. For collective action to occur and be sustainable, social movements must construct a collective identity (Melucci 1989; Flesher-Fominaya 2010a). This entails reaching a shared understanding of who the collective "we" are, including a mutual understanding of the goals, strategies, and the environment in which the movement operates (Hunt and Benford 2004). While constructing this sense of "we" is a challenge all movements face, it is especially difficult for movements working across difference, since the participants cannot simply define themselves in terms of a common social location (Gamson 2011).

Yet, our understanding of collective identity formation among more diverse groups is limited, and largely based on groups in the United States and Europe who, at most, have some racial, ethnic, gender, and/or class diversity and are not groups with fundamental differences in national identity. Moreover, there is almost *no* literature focused specifically on movement organizations working across conflict lines in situations of protracted conflict. When it comes to constructing a unifying identity, such organizations, arguably, have the greatest challenge given that conflict identities (e.g., Israeli or Palestinian in the Middle East) tend to have an especially strong impact on one's understanding of self (Smithey, Maney, and Satre 2013). Likewise, the cross-cutting ties, which are understood to be beneficial in moderating political conflict (Goodwin and Jasper 2014), tend to pale in significance to the dominant conflict-based division.

Using data collected in the months and days leading up to the 2014 War in Gaza, this research addresses voids in the literature by asking: How is it possible that Israeli and Palestinian activists can develop and sustain a collective identity given the current political environment that casts each side as the enemy of the other?

This research focuses on two movement organizations that define themselves as bi-national organizations: Parents Circle/Families Forum (PCFF) and Combatants for Peace (CFP). PCFF, founded in 1995, consists of Palestinians and Israelis who have lost a first-degree relative in the conflict (e.g., a child, a parent). They "work to end the cycle of bloodshed and towards achieving a diplomatic arrangement agreed upon by both sides" (PCFF website). Founded in 2006, CFP is comprised of former combatants, both Israeli and Palestinian. CFP seeks "to build the social infrastructure necessary for ending the conflict and the occupation: communities of Palestinians and Israelis working together through nonviolent means to promote peace" (CFP website). I conducted forty-six interviews with activists involved in the two organizations between April and June 2014, and observed organizational events and meetings. The interviewees were from different geographical locations in Israel and the occupied West Bank and included thirty men and sixteen women, between the ages of thirty and eighty-five.[1]

The activists of PCFF and CFP have all experienced violence at the hands of "the other" and/or participated in the violence, thus it is far from clear what factors enabled each of these groups to develop a unifying identity. Identifying and analyzing these factors and processes is the main contribution of this chapter.

Collective Identity Formation

Collective identity is a shared definition of "we" (Snow and Corrigal-Brown 2015). Constructed through ongoing interaction and negotiation, it requires the emotional investment of the activists to feel like and act as a collective entity (Melucci 1995).

Taylor and Whittier (1992) highlight three processes involved in building a collective identity: the development of a group consciousness, negotiation including the symbols and actions used to resist, and the drawing of boundaries between oneself and dominant groups. Scholars tend to agree that while "collective identities are talked into existence ... [they] are shaped by collective action" (Hunt and Benford 2004). It is also understood that the environment within which movement organizations operate will inevitably impact the ongoing process of constructing a collective identity and even the likelihood that it will be successful (Melucci 1995).

To construct a sense of "we" across divides, the literature emphasizes the importance of neutral space (Wood 2005), symmetrical relationships (Kay 2007), trust (Smith 2002), and open discussions of activists' claimed identities (Lichterman 1999). The problem, however, in a situation of occupation and asymmetrical conflict, is that there is no neutral space, symmetrical relationships are an impossibility, mistrust is the norm, and the ability of activists to freely discuss their identities is an accomplishment itself. One would then assume that groups working in such a context would be unable to forge a unifying identity. Yet, with clear organizational structures, leadership patterns, and membership requisites, both CFP and PCFF have the indicators of a collective identity (Melucci 1995: 49). The question that emerges is *how* did they manage to construct a unifying identity enabling joint action for peace?

Collective Identity Formation in Cross-Conflict Groups

Combatants for Peace

Building Trust through Storytelling

A group of former Israeli Defense Force officers and previously imprisoned Palestinian fighters from Fatah first met in early 2005. The meeting was initiated by an international activist in contact with both Israeli *refuseniks* and Palestinian ex-prisoners. The meeting took place near Bethlehem and lasted roughly three hours. As the following quotations highlight, the interaction was characterized by tension and fear.

> It was the most difficult meeting in my life. [Imagine,] you are going to meet your "real enemy" ... The same soldiers, the same people who tortured you, arrested you, or damaged your house—who occupied you. We [Palestinians] think that they are maybe from the Israeli Intelligence ... coming to catch us.—Samir[2]

> We had to wait in an olive grove in the dark for cars to pick us up. We were afraid. I remember thinking we were doing something that was just incredibly stupid. We were not at all sure we would come back alive.—Elik
>
> *(Hirschfield 2007)*

During this first meeting, there was no common language, and no sense that the individuals present constituted a "we." As Elik relayed, "It was a very hard meeting ... while talking politics, we were all inflexible, each side barricaded in their most defensive positions" (Elhanan 2011: xiii).

It was also clear to the Palestinians in the meeting that the two sides were far from equal. In the words of Samir, "We were kids who found ourselves as fighters, and they were *real* soldiers." Notwithstanding the tremendous gap and the mistrust, they agreed to meet again to continue to talk.

These early meetings focused largely on story sharing. The Israelis would highlight how and/or why their family came to Palestine/Israel, the beliefs they were socialized into, how they felt entering the army, the turning point for them—often an incident that provoked a "moral shock" and led them to question their involvement in the army—and why they decided to no longer serve in the Palestinian territories. Many Israeli participants found it difficult. In the words of Zohar, "There was much mistrust ... and I was afraid to admit to, what I'd done as a soldier" (CFP website).

The Palestinians shared their stories as well, often emphasizing the impact that the *Nakba* (i.e., 1948 "catastrophe") and the 1967 Israeli military occupation had on their family, their engagement with Fatah and the resistance movement, their time in the Israeli jails, and why they now wanted to pursue nonviolent resistance to the occupation. Given the mistrust—and the reality of military occupation—Palestinians felt the need to withhold aspects of their story. In the words of Ihab, "We were afraid to share what we were involved in, as we were not sure if the Israelis ... were tools of the occupation ... or just wanted to get information from the Palestinians." Over time, he stated, "these doubts became much less ... It took a long time though."

During this formative period, the sharing of their personal stories was the most critical tool they had for building trust. In the words of Elik, "When we started exchanging our personal stories, a wall came down" (Elhanan 2011: xiii). Similarly, Ihab noted, "The personal stories really did help a lot because through the personal stories you understand who the person is ... and what led them to join this organization. So, it really did help in building trust."

From a Palestinian perspective, the stories were also important in that they allowed Palestinians to see how Israeli activists recognized the need for the occupation to end. As Samir noted, "[Realizing and] trusting that we have the same commitment [to ending the occupation] ... we slowly started to see each other as being on the same side."

Largely through this process of sharing, this group of former "combatants" began to build trust. Moreover, the discussions of who they were collectively and what they were committed to, which emerged from the stories, ultimately allowed for the development of a group consciousness.

Constructing Collective Identity through Visible Confirmatory Actions

From its founding, the activists in CFP knew they did not want to be a dialogue group; they wanted to work jointly via demonstrations and presentations to end the occupation. These visible actions, which confirmed the constructed identity, were fundamental for strengthening the group's identity. In Yael's words, "When we work together, when we build something together, and protest together, it's a great tool for strengthening the trust and our identity." Similarly, Rashid argued, "The nonviolent demonstrations against the occupation in Palestine build the trust ... The most important thing is to work on the ground."

In part, what facilitates this strengthening of identity at the demonstrations is the interactions with movement opponents. As Noam argued,

> We are standing [together] ..., in front of the soldiers, in front of the checkpoint, in front of the tear gas, whatever it is. I think that the nature of this symbolic action, and the fact that we are insisting on it, is kind of a contract that allows us to keep on with what we are doing.

Ibrahim would likely agree. Highlighting the solidarity that such actions (and interactions) can build, he explained:

> We [Palestinians] are used to getting arrested and having the soldiers take away our identity cards and take us to interrogation ... It's something different when you have Noam who served in the army ... get arrested because he is protesting the occupation. I really respect that and because of it, I feel close to Noam and want to continue on our journey together.

Parents Circle/Families Forum

Building Trust through Storytelling

Parent Circle/Families Forum (PCFF) was founded in 1995 as an Israeli organization of bereaved parents who advocated for peace. While Palestinians took part, the organization only became a *joint* effort in 2003. Throughout its existence, though, the organization conducted joint lectures in the schools and community centers, and the members came together for different projects.

Prior to joining PCFF, most members attended a meeting which introduced the organization's mission. Many Palestinians, particularly, admitted to fear, anger, and apprehension before attending their first event. Illustrating the fear, Rania shared,

> As a Palestinian, I am asking for peace while living under the occupation. So, it is not easy for me to be involved. I felt a lot of fear in the first meeting ... But I ... wanted to discover who are the Israeli people who believe in making peace ... I wanted to make sure that these people really ... are working for a peace that will give the Palestinian people their rights and will end the occupation.

Anger was also a common emotion. In his first encounter with several Israeli members, who happened to be in his village visiting his brother-in-law, Osama shouted at them calling them "Jewish murderers," exclaiming, "You [Israelis] go around saying that all Palestinians are terrorists ... [but you] killed ... my grandfather, my in-laws, my best friend! ... I was tortured in interrogation!" Osama was stunned though after one of the Israelis acknowledged his pain, and shared that he himself had lost his daughter in a bombing. Persuading Osama to join, the Israeli man said to him, "if the two of us, who lost the people closest to us ... are sitting today and talking, then everyone can" (Ahituv 2014: 4).

Curiosity was another motivating factor. Khaled wanted to know, "Are PCFF members crazy? ... They killed your brother, and [you're] interested in meeting the other side, the perpetrator?" Echoing the experiences of many, though, he noted, "In the story of every one of them, I found my story" (Furman 2013: 127).

Many of the Israelis also expressed apprehension before attending their first meeting. Not wanting to be labeled a bereaved father and used by the group, Mati's decisive moment came after seeing Palestinian bereaved families,

> It was the first time ever in my life, like every good Israeli that I met Palestinians as human beings, not as workers in the streets, not as terrorists, [but] as humans, as people carrying the same burden that I carry, suffering exactly like I suffer ... That instant, I wanted to be part of it.

For some, the apprehension was focused on the fact that they would be meeting Palestinians. For example, Ran, indicated, "I was a bit anxious and I was unfortunately biased ... I thought I was going to see *faladeen* and people who work in the field, and instead, I saw a Palestinian governmental official and a neurologist. It was people like me; it was amazing."

Many mentioned the importance of the stories for building trust. Rania explained, "By listening to their story ... I was able to understand their suffering. And when I shared my story ... [and] saw that they felt very sorry ..., it allowed me to build trust with them."

Trust, however, was clearly reliant on the belief that the two sides shared the same goals. As Aharon noted, "The sharing of personal stories is very important ... But it is not only that—it is also the approach towards the future." Similarly, Nisreen stated, "The storytelling ... makes the first connection between the two sides. But what makes it closer and stronger is the shared belief that the occupation must end."

Constructing Collective Identity through Visible Confirmatory Actions

For many of the interviewees, the act of standing together in front of an audience, where they share their personal stories and call for change, strengthened the sense of "we." As Baruch relayed, "It's a bonding experience to go together in front of an audience."

Several Palestinian interviewees suggested that having an impact helps to keep the identity strong. As Osama commented, "It's affecting other people that makes me identify with the Parents Circle."

It was critical for these visible confirmatory actions to meet each other's expectations, though. For many Palestinian interviewees, this involved the Israelis also being willing to engage in protest activity in Israel. For example, during the 2008–2009 Gaza War, as Suheir recounted,

> [The Israelis] made a demonstration in the middle of Tel Aviv ... [and] they [Israeli police] took Ran to the jail ... It meant a lot to me! ... If I see that my enemy is asking for my rights ... it builds trust.

In the months leading to the 2014 Gaza War, there was some frustration, however, over Israelis not being more active in protests. As Mais argued, "If they can't go against their government, then what's the point?" Several Palestinian interviewees indicated that they were feeling less connected to the organization as a result. While many Israeli interviewees recognized their Palestinian counterparts' desires for more protest activity, most felt conflicted, as they did not want the organization to be deemed "political" and thus lose its ability to conduct joint presentations inside Israeli schools. These lectures were perceived as fundamental for fostering cultural and political change in Israel.

Notwithstanding concerns, during the 2014 Gaza War, which occurred just weeks later, the Israelis in PCFF—and CFP—led the Israeli protests against the war. And in my follow-up interviews after the war, the Palestinian members expressed great pride with what their Israeli counterparts did and indicated such actions both renewed and strengthened their identification with the organization (see Gawerc 2017).

Discussion and Conclusion

It is apparent, from the presented data, that the first step in building a collective identity is building trust. Yet as Goodwin et al. (2004: 419) indicate, there has been little discussion in the social movement literature focused on trust. Many scholars seem to assume trust is a given, and that identity work begins the moment the actors come together. In these two organizations, though, because of the mistrust, a significant amount of work needed to be done *before* the groups could even consider constructing a collective identity. Indeed, this study suggests that for organizations working across conflict lines, trust-building is a distinct stage of identity work, which needs to occur before—as well as alongside—the development of a group consciousness, negotiation over the content of the "we-ness," and the employment of strategic actions. These two cases, therefore, expose what is often taken for granted in the literature: the underlying assumption that trust is a non-issue. In fact, it is a requisite.

As the experiences of these movement organizations reveal, storytelling went a long way toward building this trust and fostering a shared consciousness. Notwithstanding the asymmetrical context, the stories highlighting the personal impact of the occupation and/or conflict facilitated a mutual recognition of similar experiences (e.g., loss, participation in the violence), which Bystydzienski and Schacht (2001: 8–9) deem critical for groups to be able to coalesce.

Such accomplishments, however, are not enough for building a collective identity, as the data make clear. Visible confirmatory actions, focused on meeting their shared goals, were critical. The act of standing together, whether during a protest or a lecture, in front of an external audience, allowed them to present who they were collectively. And witnessing the commitment of the other side to the shared cause was significant—especially for Palestinians, who needed to be assured that their Israeli colleagues were resolute in their opposition to the occupation.

Just as essential though, as the struggles of PCFF show, the actions taken *must* "satisfy both emotional and rational needs in order to generate … collective identification with the group" (Flesher-Fominaya 2010b: 385). The tension experienced by PCFF also epitomizes a significant challenge that cross-conflict groups face. Not only are there different audiences, but the audiences (i.e., various communities) are engaged in conflict and highly polarized. Moreover, strategic actions deemed legitimate in one community (i.e., Palestinians, protests against the occupation) may be deemed "highly political" or illegitimate in the other.

Notwithstanding the tremendous challenges, as this study demonstrates, a collective identity *can* be constructed *even* in situations where the actors had previously understood themselves to be enemies. In such contexts, some sort of internal process, such as storytelling may be utilized to begin the process of building trust, alongside confirmatory actions that meet the varying needs of the collective. While such processes may not always be enough to unite across polarized conflict lines, they are likely to be necessary in the construction of collective identity.

Notes

1   A detailed description of my methods can be found in Gawerc (2016).
2   Names of interviewees have been changed to provide anonymity.

References

Ahituv, N. (2014), "The Saddest—and Most Optimistic—Peace Organization Turns 20," *Haaretz*, October 17, 2014. http://www.haaretz.com/news/features/.premium-1.620808

Bystydzienski, J. M. and S. P. Schacht, eds. (2001), *Forging Radical Alliances across Difference: Coalition Politics for the New Millennium*, Lanham: Rowman and Littlefield Publishing Group.

Combatants for Peace, n.d. "'Who We Are' and 'Personal Stories'." http://cfpeace.org/ (accessed December 2, 2020).

Elhanan, E. (2011), "A Preface in Two Parts: Part One," in D. J. Perry (ed.), *The Israeli— Palestinian Peace Movement: Combatants for Peace*, xi–xiv, New York: Palgrave Macmillan.

Flesher-Fominaya, C. (2010a), "Collective Identity in Social Movements: Central Concepts and Debates," *Sociology Compass*, 4 (6): 393–404. https://doi.org/10.1111/j.1751-9020.2010.00287.x

Flesher-Fominaya, C. (2010b), "Creating Cohesion from Diversity: The Challenge of Collective Identity Formation in the Global Justice Movement," *Sociological Inquiry*, 80 (3): 377–404. https://doi.org/10.1111/j.1475-682X.2010.00339.x

Furman, F. K. (2013), "Bereavement, Storytelling, and Reconciliation: Peacebuilding between Israelis and Palestinians," *Peace and Conflict Studies*, 20 (2): 125–51.

Gamson, W. A. (2011), "From Outsiders to Insiders: The Changing Perception of Emotional Culture and Consciousness among Social Movement Scholars," *Mobilization*, 16 (3): 251–64.

Gawerc, M. I. (2016), "Constructing a Collective Identity across Conflict Lines: Israeli-Palestinian Peace Movement Organizations," *Mobilization*, 21 (2): 193–212.

Gawerc, M. I. (2017), "Solidarity Is in the Heart, Not in the Field: Israeli-Palestinian Peace Movement Organizations during the 2014 Gaza War," *Social Movement Studies*, 16 (5): 520–34.

Goodwin, J. and J. M. Jasper (2014), *The Social Movement Reader: Cases and Concepts*, 3rd edn, Malden: Blackwell Publishing.

Goodwin, J., J. M. Jasper and F. Polletta (2004), "Emotional Dimensions of Social Movements," in D. A. Snow, S. A. Soule, and H. Kriesi (eds.), *The Blackwell Companion to Social Movements*, 413–32, Malden: Blackwell Publishing.

Hirschfield, R. (2007), "Battle Stories Bring Former Enemies Together," *National Catholic Reporter*, February 2, 2007. http://natcath.org/NCR_Online/archives2/2007a/020207/020207i.htm

Hunt, S. A. and R. D. Benford (2004), "Collective Identity, Solidarity, and Commitment," in D. A. Snow, S. A. Soule, and H. Kriesi (eds.), *The Blackwell Companion to Social Movements*, 433–58, Oxford: Blackwell.

Kay, T. (2007), "Labor Transnationalism and Global Governance: The Impact of NAFTA on Transnational Labor Relationships in North America," in D. A. Snow, S. A. Soule, and H. Kriesi (eds.), *The Blackwell Companion to Social Movements*, 87–105. Malden, MA: Blackwell Publishing.

Lichterman, P. (1999), "Talking Identity in the Public Sphere: Broad Visions and Small Spaces in Sexual Identity Politics," *Theory and Society*, 28 (1): 101–41.

Melucci, A. (1989), *Nomads of the Present*, London: Hutchinson Radius.

Melucci, A. (1995), "The Process of Collective Identity," in H. Johnston and B. Klandermans (eds.), *Social Movements and Culture*, 41–63, Minneapolis: University of Minnesota Press.

Parents Circle/Families Forum, n.d., "Our Vision." http://www.theparentscircle.com/ (accessed December 2, 2020).
Smith, J. (2002), "Bridging Global Divides? Strategic Framing and Solidarity in Transnational Social Movement Organizations," *International Sociology*, 17 (4): 505–28.
Smithey, L., G. Maney, and J. Satre (2013), "Explaining Paramilitary Public Symbolic Displays in Northern Ireland: Preliminary Content and Geospatial Analyses," Presented at the 2013 American Sociological Association Conference.
Snow, D. A. and C. Corrigal-Brown (2015), "Collective Identity," in J. D. Wright (ed.), *International Encyclopedia of the Social & Behavioral Sciences*, 174–80. https://www.sciencedirect.com/referencework/9780080970875/international-encyclopedia-of-the-social-and-behavioral-sciences
Taylor, V. and N. E. Whittier (1992), "Collective Identity in Social Movement Communities: Lesbian Feminist Mobilization," in A. D. Morris and C. McClurg Mueller (eds.), *Frontiers in Social Movement Theory*, 104–29, New Haven: Yale University Press.
Wood, L. J. (2005), "Bridging the Chasms: The Case of Peoples' Global Action," in J. Bandy and J. Smith (eds.), *Coalitions across Borders: Transnational Protest and the Neoliberal Order*, 95–120. Lanham, MD: Rowman and Littlefield Publishers.

II IRANIAN REVOLUTION

Ideology and Political Action in the Iranian Revolution

by Misagh Parsa

Scholars of the Iranian revolution have often explained the 1979 overthrow of the Pahlavi regime in terms of the rise of an Islamic movement that inspired Iranians to challenge the shah, confront his powerful army, and embrace martyrdom to bring down the monarchy (Moaddel 1993; Skocpol 1982). Once in power, Ayatollah Ruholla Khomeini, too, presented an ideological explanation for the revolution. Although before the revolution, Khomeini frequently expressed concern about the erosion of Islam in the country and condemned the prevailing political and cultural development, after the removal of the monarchy, he stated, "I cannot and I do not accept that any prudent individual can believe that the purpose of all these sacrifices was to have less expensive melons, that we sacrificed our young men to have less expensive housing .... No one would give his life for better agriculture. Dignity is better than full bellies. Iranian masses have fought only for God not worldly affairs" (Foran 1993: 358). While it is true that segments of Iranian intellectuals and students fought for an Islamic government, the majority of them did not fight for a theocracy, which Khomeini established. Ideologically driven analyses of the Iranian revolution tend toward the tautological and ignore the complexity of revolutionary processes. They cannot account for the various collectivities that entered the revolutionary struggles at different times and presented diverse claims. The majority of individuals who participated in the struggles did not volunteer to give their lives, but instead expected to improve their lives. Their deaths were the result of political repression, not a desire for martyrdom. In fact, people mobilized through the mosque because it was a relatively safe and secure place.

To test ideologically driven explanations of the Iranian revolution, this chapter focuses on the nature of the collective actions of major actors immediately preceding and during the revolution. Specifically, it examines the timing, demands, and claims of major collectivities and challengers that participated in the revolutionary process. It looks at the political conflicts that erupted in Iran beginning in the mid-1970s, the overthrow of the monarchy in 1979, and, finally, the removal of President Abolhassan Bani-Sadr in 1981 and the subsequent establishment of a theocracy.

Students, Intellectuals, and the Revolutionary Struggles

Ideological explanations of the revolution are brought into question by an analysis of the collective actions and ideology of major actors during the revolutionary struggles. When the revolutionary struggles erupted in 1977, leftist students, not religious collectivities, emerged in the forefront. Students initiated some of the most important collective actions that marked the beginning of the insurgencies that eventually culminated in the revolution. In response to a slight reduction of repression and legal reform in 1977, students' usual preoccupation with educative matters dwindled as they converted colleges into centers for political opposition and information. Student protests occurred independently of actions by the clergy.

During the first three and a half months of the 1977–8 academic year, students held at least twenty rallies and demonstrations and twenty-one class boycotts, well before segments of the clergy were mobilized by the Qom massacre in January 1978. Student protests were so intense that by the end of the fall term many colleges and universities were almost completely closed down. In response to student protests the government organized a rally of five thousand on the campus of Tehran University to condemn the students. It is important to note that student mobilization and collective action played an important role to promote mobilization by other groups including the clergy.

An analysis of the ideology espoused by students refutes the claim that rising Islamic ideology was responsible for the revolutionary struggles. Most student activists in the 1970s subscribed to a secular, socialist ideology, which was expressed throughout the country every year in the observance of Shanzdah-e Azar. On that day, students commemorated the slaying of three students by the government in 1953 during the visit of then vice president Richard Nixon. Shanzdah-e Azar became the unofficial student day and was always marked by rallies and protests. In sharp contrast, before the revolutionary struggles, university students never commemorated 5 June, the date of the 1963 rebellion sparked in part by the arrest of Khomeini. Nor did university students ever observe the date Khomeini was exiled from Iran. In contrast, university student support for the Marxist fedayeen was so intense that in 1976 the shah ordered two major universities to close, though he quickly reversed himself for fear of sparking an even greater uproar (Alam 1991: 488). Aware of students' strong support for radical political organizations, the shah once remarked, "The dangerous young communists had made universities their primary bastions" (Kian 1993: 465). The ideological leaning of university students was also demonstrated by the fact that during the revolutionary conflicts they invited leftist intellectuals, not antimonarchy clerics, to speak on their campuses. Khomeini himself regarded students and their universities as unfriendly allies or even enemies. Although his clerical supporters arranged for him to visit Tehran University and make a public statement upon his return to Iran, Khomeini refused and instead visited the cemetery to pay tribute to the martyrs of the revolution.

Grouped into various leftist organizations, students soon clashed with both the liberal and the clerical factions of the Islamic Republic. The student movements supported opposition demands for democratic freedoms, formation of workers' councils, land reform, women's rights, and autonomy for ethnic minorities.

In reaction, government officials complained that the fedayeen and mujahideen were using university resources to attack Islam and the Islamic Republic. According to top clerical officials in the government, the forces of Islam in the universities had been weakened by the activities of these groups.[1] Khomeini, who had earlier lauded university students for their struggle against the monarchy, dictatorship, and imperialism, now sounded like the shah, declaring that "universities were bastions of communists, and they were war rooms for communists."[2] In April 1980 militant clerics, with the support of the liberal faction of the government, unleashed a "cultural revolution" to Islamize the universities. Government forces enlisted club wielders to attack students throughout the country, killing dozens. In an unprecedented move, the government closed all universities and colleges for at least two years, and many remained closed even longer. Thousands of students who were considered leftist or antigovernment were expelled from the universities. Political and religious standards were then applied to all incoming university students, and Khomeini announced that only those without affiliations to either Eastern or Western ideologies would be admitted.[3] As during the revolutionary struggles, students and youth became the principal targets of repression and violence. Between 1981 and 1985 nearly 4,000 students involved in political opposition activities were either executed or killed in armed struggle.[4]

Aside from students, the majority of Iranian intellectuals also adopted some form of socialism or nationalism in the 1970s. A minority of Iranian intellectuals subscribed to some form of Islamic ideology. For example, Jalal Al-e Ahmad abandoned Marxism and encouraged intellectuals to ally themselves with the clergy to resist what he called "Westoxication." Shariati also opposed secular socialism and instead advocated Islamic socialism. He attracted the attention of some intellectuals and young university students who ended up supporting the mujahideen. But the majority of intellectuals remained in the secular or socialist camp in the 1970s. The ideological tendency of Iranian intellectuals was revealed in the fall of 1977 during a series of poetry nights held in Tehran. Of the sixty-four poets and writers who participated, 66 percent were secular socialist, 28 percent were liberal-nationalist, and only 6 percent followed some sort of Islamic ideology.

Ideological divisions between intellectuals and the Islamic regime are also revealed in the relationship between the Writers' Association and the Islamic regime. After the monarchy's ouster, the Writers' Association came into conflict with the ruling clergy. The association attempted to organize a new round of poetry nights in October 1979 to "defend freedom of thought and speech, and oppose absolutely any censorship of writing."[5] However, the poetry nights never materialized because the government could not guarantee the safety and security of the meetings (Parsa 1989: 286). In June 1981, the first secretary of the association, one of its founders, was executed and the association was banned by the Islamic regime.

Bazaaris, Workers, and Popular Struggles

Bazaaris—a term referring to merchants, shopkeepers, and artisans—were very active and significant during Iran's revolutionary conflicts. But their ideology and politics have often been misunderstood and misinterpreted. *Bazaaris* have been viewed as a traditional social class that supposedly was strongly allied with the clergy or willing to follow clerical leadership in political matters (Bashiriyeh 1984: 61; Farhi 1990: 92; Skocpol 1982). A small minority of *bazaaris* did support Khomeini. With the decline of the liberal-nationalist movement in the 1950s and particularly after the conflicts of the early 1960s, some *bazaaris* began supporting Khomeini. During the revolutionary struggles, the hard-core, activist segment of this group consisted of approximately thirty *bazaaris* who worked closely with the clergy during the monarchy's final days.

While it is true that many *bazaaris*, particularly the older generation, were religious and made contributions that were critical for Islamic mosques, functions, and ceremonies, *bazaaris*' religious orientation did not determine their ideology. *Bazaaris*' contributions and participation in mosque activities, including prayers, had declined dramatically in the 1970s.[6]

Most *bazaaris* never pursued religion as a political ideology.[7] Some *bazaari* activists have even claimed that it has always been *bazaaris* who dictated the clergy's politics, rather than vice versa.[8] *Bazaaris*' politics and collective actions can best be explained not by the authority of the clergy but by the politics of liberal-nationalists.

Bazaaris' politics and ideology did not demonstrate any large-scale ideological conversion in the 1970s in favor of an Islamic theocracy. *Bazaaris* did not protest the repression of clerical students in Qom in June 1975, when the students commemorated the uprising of June 1963. *Bazaaris*, like most of the Iranian public, paid no attention to the clerical students' protests and their plight. Despite Khomeini's support for the clerical students, *bazaaris* did not initiate a single shutdown, protest, or mourning ceremony anywhere in the country.

Although economic and political divisions had undermined cohesion among *bazaaris*, government price controls and an "antiprofiteering" campaign in the late 1970s enhanced *bazaari* solidarity. It was not religious activities but *bazaari* activists in support of the National Front and Prime Minister Mosaddeq that led the mobilization against the government. They illegally reestablished the Society of Merchants, Guilds, and Artisans of the Tehran Bazaar (SMGATB) in October 1977. The SMGATB, supported by Azerbaijanis, the single largest group in the Tehran bazaar, played an important role in organizing bazaar shutdowns and strikes throughout the revolutionary struggles.[9] The SMGATB were most resourceful and owned their own printing machines and encouraged religious *bazaaris* to issue public statements and printed their leaflets.[10]

Furthermore, *bazaaris'* mobilization initially was not channeled through the mosque. Instead, *bazaaris* mobilized alongside modern, secular groups that also early on opposed the government. But *bazaaris*, like others, soon found it difficult to mobilize because of state repression. To protect against repression, *bazaaris* needed a space, and mosques were the only safe spaces.

Throughout the revolutionary struggles, *bazaaris'* protests were primarily political in nature and directed against the state, although they also spoke out against various elements of the government's economic policies. As evidence of a high degree of consensus, *bazaaris* in 1978 in major cities issued at least fifteen protest statements, all of them condemning government repression. The despotic nature of the state was condemned by 53 percent of the *bazaaris'* protest statements, and an equal number of statements condemned imperialist influence and the government's dependence on foreign powers. Other issues mentioned in these statements included corruption, governmental and international "pillaging" of national resources, and growing poverty and inequality. Three statements specifically supported the Islamic movement, two backed the clerical community and its struggles, but only a single statement by Esfahan bazaaris explicitly called for the establishment of an Islamic government. Two statements issued late in the year acknowledged Khomeini as the leader of the opposition movement (Parsa 2000: 213).

Significantly, nowhere in their statements did *bazaaris* mention the Islamization of laws or clerical supervision of the government, nor did their statements manifest any interest in establishing a theocratic Islamic state in Iran. Instead, *bazaaris'* backing of Khomeini was derived from his indomitable stance against "despotism" and his political opposition to the regime. A well-known activist *bazaari* who was a devout Muslim and had raised a great deal of money for Khomeini stated that if "bazaaris had known about Khomeini's ideas on theocracy, they would have never supported him."[11]

An analysis of the postrevolutionary conflicts bears out the point that *bazaaris'* support for Islamic leaders was based, not on ideological conversion in favor of theocracy, but on a political coalition. Although in the final stage of their struggle against the monarchy, broad segments of the bazaar shifted to favor the formation of an Islamic government, their postrevolutionary conflicts with the ruling clerics revealed that many opposed a theocratic state as promoted by Khomeini.

As a result of political and ideological conflicts, many *bazaaris* suffered harsh repression by the Islamic government. Prominent *bazaari* activists, such as Lebaschi and Mohammad Shanehchi, were forced to flee the country during the period of intense repression in 1981. In an unprecedented event in modern Iran, Karim Dastmalchi, a leading member of SMGATB, and Ahmad Javaherian, a supporter of the mujahideen in the bazaar, were executed in July of 1981. Mahmoud Manian, a founding member of SMGATB, withdrew from politics and public life, but after three separate attempts on his life, he was eventually killed in a traffic "accident" in front of his own house. Following the removal of Bani-Sadr in 1981, more than one hundred *bazaaris* were killed or executed (Parsa 1989: 282).

Iranian workers did not join the struggles of intellectuals, students, and *bazaaris* until 1977. Although industrial development had expanded the size of the urban labor force, Iranian workers were severely repressed and lacked the solidarity structures to mobilize and initiate collective action. From fall 1977 to fall 1978, when other collectivities protested government repression, workers struck thirty-nine times for merely economic demands in unrelated cases. The absence of labor strikes during mourning ceremonies and political protests indicated that workers' interests, conflicts, and resources differed significantly from those of *bazaaris* and clergy.

In the fall of 1978, a fresh opportunity for mobilization emerged with the appointment of a new prime minister, Sharif-Emami, who promised liberalization and political freedom for all political groups except Communists. The proposed reforms offered nothing to the working classes, however, and as a consequence, workers seized the opportunity and began to mobilize and demand change. Workers who had previously been involved in strikes, arrested, or imprisoned used informal networks in the workplace to form secret cells and committees with trusted coworkers and organize collective actions (Bayat 1998: 91). Soon white-collar employees joined with their own strikes.

Given the context of mounting inflation and a declining standard of living, strikers pressed to relieve their immediate grievances. The initial demands of workers and white-collar employees, unlike those of *bazaaris*, were mainly economic and primarily defensive in orientation. An analysis of strikers' demands during this period reveals that with few exceptions, economic issues were paramount, and job-related problems were a close second. All strikers demanded higher wages, while most also insisted on allowances or loans for housing expenses and medical insurance. Many complained of pay inequities, especially in sectors where foreign workers were employed. Some protested arbitrary promotion rules and secret "rewards" by heads of bureaucracies. Because most strikers worked in state-owned enterprises or were employed in government bureaucracies, they were, of necessity, directly targeting and confronting the state.

As the strikes continued, those segments of the working class that were more concentrated in large-state enterprises and possessed greater skills and greater solidarity structures gradually began issuing political demands as well. Striking oil workers and employees of a steel mill in Esfahan, a mine in the central Elburz mountain range, a railway in Zahedan, and Iran General Motors in Tehran, all demanded the expulsion of various department chiefs. On 2 September, workers in the Tabriz Machine Tool Factory struck and demanded the dissolution of government-sponsored unions and the lifting of martial law. On 4 November, workers in Tabriz Tractor and Tabriz Machine Tool organized a joint strike, condemned government repression, demanded the lifting of martial law, freedom for all political prisoners, and dissolution of government-sponsored unions, and proclaimed support for the political demands of students, teachers, workers, and government employees. Significantly, oil workers in Abadan and Ahvaz demanded freedom for all political prisoners, the dissolution of SAVAK, the lifting of martial law, the dissolution of government-sponsored unions and the formation of independent labor unions, freedom for all political parties, and other political concessions.

The impact of oil workers' strikes during this time was distinct from that of other workers, in part because oil workers controlled the nation's most vital economic asset. They also shared certain characteristics, which increased the likelihood that their actions would become politicized. Oil workers numbered more than 30,000 and were heavily concentrated in specific oil-producing regions, which added to their ability to communicate, mobilize, and act collectively. Moreover, because oil workers were employed by the state, a greater potential existed for them to become politicized during times of conflict. A core of political experience existed among oil workers as a result of their participation in oil strikes in the early 1950s. Aware that they controlled the state's primary source of revenue, oil workers rapidly became more militant in the fall of 1978. Workers with secular leftist ideologies played an important role in their organizations.

An analysis of the timing of popular mobilization and collective action during the revolutionary struggles also fails to support the ideological explanation of the revolution. Significantly, people initiated their struggles in late 1977 and early 1978 as the government reduced, not increased, repression, in response to President Jimmy Carter's human rights campaign. The timing of popular collective action points to a lower, not higher, cost of struggle. In other words, the Iranian people chose the timing of their involvement based on the extent and intensity of political repression. If Iranians were seeking martyrdom, they would have initiated their collective action when repression was high, as it was in June 1975 when clerical students revolted. Because the vast majority of Iranians did not intend to lose their lives, they chose to initiate their dissident activities during a period of declining repression. Thus, the analysis of the timing of popular struggles does not support Khomeini's ideological claim on martyrdom and the causes of the revolution.

Popular slogans during major demonstrations reveal the people's ideological orientation as they struggled to overthrow the monarchy. Bazargan, the first prime minister of the Islamic Republic, and his associates conducted an analysis of revolutionary slogans using the tapes recorded during major religious holidays and protests. The largest category of slogans, about 38 percent, denounced despotism, 31 percent of slogans called for independence, freedom, and the formation of an Islamic republic, 16 percent asserted the leadership of Khomeini, and 15 percent praised other leaders such as Taleqani and Hossein Ali Montazeri and the martyrs of the mujahideen.[12] Once again, the existing data do not support Khomeini's ideological claim.

In the final phase of the Iranian revolution the most widespread slogan of the crowds was "Independence, Freedom, Islamic Republic." Although secular and leftist forces opposed the term "Islamic Republic," viewing it as imposed by pro-Khomeini clerics, many protestors in the final days of the monarchy did not see any contradiction among freedom, civil liberties, political rights, and Islamic Republic. Iranians had fought under the slogans of independence and freedom during the nationalist movement led by Mosaddeq in the early 1950s. In the late 1970s, Iranians added "Islamic Republic" to their slogan because to the majority of Iranians it meant social justice based on Shia egalitarian notions. Given rising inequalities and an increasing concentration of income and wealth in Iran, this interpretation makes the most sense. Significantly, however, prominent features of the postrevolutionary Islamic theocracy—relegation of women to second-class citizenship, stoning of adulterers, execution of homosexuals, bans against classical Persian music, and so on—were never mentioned in prerevolutionary marches, rallies, public pronouncements, or popular slogans.

The Islamic Clergy and Their Political Ideology

An ideological explanation of the revolution fails to illuminate the politics of the Islamic clergy. They were not politically unified, and it is inaccurate to portray them as a cohesive collectivity. While a small minority supported the government, the largest majority remained apolitical and did not intervene in political affairs. Ahmad Khomeini, the son of Ayatollah Khomeini, noted that the clerics who opposed the regime were only a small minority.[13] Because of their limited size and capacity for mobilization, this faction of the clergy failed to take advantage of an opportunity to mobilize against the regime in 1975 during a revolt of pro-Khomeini clerical students.

In ideological terms, they advocated the correct implementation of the constitution to eliminate anti-Islamic laws and practices, rather than the formation of an Islamic government. An examination of fifteen protest statements and declarations by the clerical community (defined as three or more clerics) during major political events or ceremonies in the period from fall 1977 to fall 1978 demonstrated that they never called for the overthrow of the regime and establishment of an Islamic republic. All fifteen statements condemned political violence and repression. Seven statements also denounced despotism, while five deplored imperialist influences in Iran and the lack of national independence. Five statements condemned the absence of civil liberties, and two called for improved economic conditions for workers and peasants. Four statements urged the abolition of anti-Islamic laws, while two demanded clerical supervision of laws passed by the Majlis, which had been a feature of the 1906 constitution. Finally, several issues were mentioned in one statement each: nationalization of pillaged wealth, taxes, poverty, and foreign exploitation. Only one statement called for the formation of an Islamic government.

Ayatollah Khomeini and the Leadership of the Revolution

Khomeini's rise to the position of paramount leader of the Iranian revolution came about primarily for political rather than theological or ideological reasons. He had certain political advantages that helped place him in position of leadership. Although Khomeini's position within the clerical community as one of the preeminent ayatollahs made him relatively immune from government repression, as evidenced by the fact that he was exiled rather than executed in 1964, it was his political stand that distinguished him from others. In addition, Khomeini's exile enabled him to continue the opposition against the shah. As a result, while all other political leaders capitulated to repression, Khomeini was the only religious or political leader who continued for years to call for the overthrow of the regime. While in Iraq, he was able to meet with his followers and, through them, send messages back to Iran. He also received funds from religious contributions, which he used for political purposes, including assisting families of political prisoners.[14] No other political leader enjoyed such advantages. Equally important, unlike moderate political leaders, Khomeini took an uncompromising stand against the shah, which made him popular among segments of the population.

Perhaps because he was very interested in forging a broad coalition, Khomeini never publicly told the Iranian people about his radical, theocratic ideology. In his public statements addressed to the Iranian people in the years before the revolution, he never mentioned doctrinal issues, such as the concept of *velayat-e faqih*, or "jurist's guardianship." Although Khomeini expressed concern over the decline of the status of the clergy and erosion of Islam, he repeatedly claimed to have no aspiration to political position. At the end of 1977, while still in Iraq, Khomeini instructed his clerical supporters to respect and work with students and intellectuals: "Tomorrow we will not become government ministers; our work is different. These are the ones who become ministers and representatives."[15] While in France, he noted that, as in the past, he would be merely a guide to the people.[16]

Most clerics and clerical students who supported Khomeini did not know anything about such concepts and plans. Even some of Khomeini's closest political allies and advisers who had been in Paris with him were completely bewildered after the revolution when they first heard this concept (Abrahamian 1993: 30; Afsahri 1994: 76). Not knowing about the principle of *velayat-e faqih*, some of Khomeini's supporters, after the overthrow of the monarchy, even called for nominating him as the first president of the Islamic Republic. The provisional government, headed by Bazargan, who was appointed by Khomeini, seems to have been unaware of the principle of *velayat-e faqih*. The first draft of the constitution was liberal and democratic and did not mention the *velayat-e faqih*. Interestingly, Khomeini himself endorsed the constitution.

Khomeini's theological ideology was not responsible for his leadership. Rather, Khomeini received the backing of the vast majority of the Iranian population because of his opposition to dictatorship and his defense of freedom and national interests. He borrowed the basic tenets of the liberal-nationalist movement, which were freedom from dictatorship and imperialism and condemnation of the pillaging of the country's national resources. The only concern that Khomeini added to the nationalist demands was the government's violation of Islamic principles. He steadfastly maintained that an Islamic government would guarantee national independence and provide political freedom for all Iranians. In the final weeks of the revolutionary conflicts, Khomeini repeatedly declared that independence and freedom would be the essence of any Islamic republic.[17] While in Paris, he suggested that even Marxists would be free to express themselves under an Islamic republic. Women, too, would be free "to govern their fate and choose their activities." The shah's dictatorial regime, he asserted, reduced women to objects of consumption, while Islam opposed such treatment of women.[18]

As the implicit coalition broke down after the overthrow of the monarchy, Khomeini and his fundamentalist supporters succeeded in maintaining power because of complex factors and processes. To mitigate the intensity of rising domestic conflicts and discredit their opponents, Khomeini promoted or took advantage of external conflicts, first through the hostage crisis and later the war with Iraq. During these conflicts, Khomeini eliminated his former liberal and nationalist allies, banned labor strikes, repressed workers' councils, closed the universities, and repressed leftist dissidents. Khomeini and his allies also isolated and repressed clerics who opposed their rule. His supporters quickly monopolized the mosques and brushed aside their opponents, thereby destroying the autonomy of the mosques and blocking any social group from mobilizing through this venue that had been so crucial during the revolutionary struggles.

More important, rising class conflict, along with the growing strength of the opposition both secular and religious, compelled Khomeini to introduce new ideological elements into the revolution. This time Khomeini was forced to borrow some basic tenets of the radical Left. Khomeini's ideological shift was critical to the survival of the Islamic Republic and the clergy's rise to political supremacy. He met the challenge posed by the Left by shifting his prerevolutionary focus on independence from foreign powers and on freedom from dictatorship to a resolute concentration on social justice. This political shift placed Khomeini farther to the left than any established Iranian politician in the twentieth century, including Mosaddeq. By making such a shift, Khomeini was able to prevail over liberals who lacked plans to restructure the social order or redress social inequality. Khomeini's shift was also designed to reduce the Left's ability to mobilize students, workers, and peasants around the issues of social justice and equality.

Most important, Khomeini and the Islamic Republic relied heavily on the Revolutionary Guards and the informal Hezbollah to effectively demobilize the opposition. Within two years of the revolution most political organizations and parties were outlawed. He also defrocked Shariat-Madari and placed him under house arrest. The regime even executed hundreds of dissident clerics. During the conflicts and the power struggle, the Guards, along with the revolutionary committees, carried out an unprecedented level of repression against the opposition. Between the summers of 1981 and 1985, the Islamic Republic executed or killed approximately twelve thousand people.[19] Khomeini and his regime also killed several thousand supporters of the mujahideen in 1988, bringing the number of deaths to at least 15,000.

In sum, the evidence demonstrates the diverse timing of collective actions and the variation in demands of those who rose up and made political and ideological claims during the Iranian revolution. Significantly, Iranians fought for independence and freedom and saw no contradiction between these slogans and an Islamic republic. They mobilized through the mosque because mosques provided protection and safety from political repression. During the revolutionary process, most people were unaware of the nature of the theocracy that would ultimately be established in Iran. In fact, none of the principal collectivities that took part in the revolutionary struggles called for a theocracy in Iran. Finally, the political conflicts that erupted after the monarchy's overthrow and the torturous establishment of a theocracy underscore that simple, overarching ideological explanations of the revolution do not do justice to the complexity of the causes and processes of the Iranian revolution.

Notes

1. *Jumhuri Eslami*, December 23, 1982.
2. *Christian Science Monitor*, December 19, 1980.
3. *Ettelaat*, August 28, 1982.
4. *Mojahed*, no. 261 (September 6, 1985), app.
5. *Ettelaat*, October 17, 1979.
6. Abolghasem Lebaschi and Mohammad Shanehchi, interviews by the author, Sacramento, CA, 1997, and Paris, 1998, respectively. See also *Kayhan International*, October 2, 1978.
7. Abolghasem Lebaschi, February 28, 1983, Ghassem Ladjevardi, January 29, 1983, interviews by Habib Ladjeverdi, transcript of tape 3, 15, Iranian Oral History Collection, Houghton Library, Harvard University, Cambridge, MA.
8. Author interviews with a number of *bazaaris*. Interviews were conducted between 1979 and 2000.
9. For example, after the massacre of Qom, Azerbaijanis in the Tehran bazaar issued a public statement supporting the SMGATB's mobilization and shutdowns. The Freedom Movement [Abroad], *Dar Bareh-e Ghiam-e Hammaseh Afarinan-e Qom Va Tabriz Va Digar Shahr Haye Iran*, Abroad: About the Epic Uprising of Qom, Tabriz, and Other Cities of Iran, 1978, 136–7.
10. Lebaschi, interview by Ladjevardi, transcript of tape 3, 5, 15.
11. Mohammad Shanehchi, April 1998, personal communication with the author.
12. MehdiBazargan, *Enghelab-e Iran dar du harkat* (*Iran's Revolution in Two Motions*), Tehran: Mazaheri, 1984, 37–8.
13. *Ettelaat*, September 23, 1979.
14. Shanehchi, interview by Ladjevardi, 1983, transcript of tape 3, 15, Iranian Oral History Collection, Houghton Library.
15. Khomeini, *Sahifeh-e nour*, 1:436.

16 *Ayandegan*, January 10, 1979.
17 Khomeini, *Sahifeh-e nour*, 4: 252.
18 *Ayandegan*, January 17, 1979.
19 *Mojahed*, no. 261 (September 6, 1985), app.

References

Abrahamian, E. (1993), *Khomeinism: Essays on the Islamic Republic*, Berkeley: University of California Press.
Afsahri, R. (1994), "A Critique of Dabashi's Reconstruction of Islamic Ideology as a Prerequisite for the Iranian Revolution," *Critique: Journal of Critical Studies of the Middle East*, 3 (5): 67–83.
Alam, A. (1991), *The Shah and I: The Confidential Diary of Iran's Royal Court, 1969–1977*, London: I. B. Tauris.
Bashiriyeh, H. (1984), *The State and Revolution in Iran, 1962–1982*, New York: St. Martin's Press.
Bayat, A. (1998), "Revolution without Movement, Movement without Revolution: Comparing Islamic Activism in Iran and Egypt," *Comparative Studies in Society and History*, 40 (1): 136–69.
Farhi, F. (1990), *States and Urban-based Revolutions: Iran and Nicaragua*, Urbana, IL: University of Illinois Press.
Foran, J. (1993), *Fragile Resistance: Social Transformation in Iran from 1500 to the Revolution*, Boulder, CO: Westview.
Kian, A. (1993), "The Politics of the New Middle Class in Iran and Egypt from the Nineteenth Century until 1979," Unpublished PhD diss., Los Angeles: University of California.
Moaddel, M. (1993), *Class, Politics, and Ideology in the Iranian Revolution*, New York: Columbia University Press.
Parsa, M. (1989), *Social Origins of the Iranian Revolution*, New Brunswick, NJ: Rutgers University Press.
Parsa, M. (2000), *States, Ideologies, and Social Revolutions: A Comparative Analysis of Iran, Nicaragua and the Philippines*, Cambridge: Cambridge University Press.
Skocpol, T. (1982), "Rentier State and Shi'a Islam in the Iranian Revolution," *Theory and Society*, 11 (3): 265–83.

Gender Politics and the State in Postrevolutionary Iran

by Nazanin Shahrokni

Introduction

The establishment of the Islamic Republic of Iran in 1979, following a successful revolution that put an end to the seventy-five years of Pahlavi rein, is one of the pivotal events of the twentieth century that have marked the current shape of the Middle East.[1] It has often been framed as a singular, homogeneous, and overly religious state that set in motion processes that were juxtaposed with what was before. Such was the emphasis on the rupture represented by the revolution that the literature has largely overlooked or underplayed strong elements of continuity with the past, and the "modernity" and dynamism of (post)revolutionary statecraft in Iran (Kadivar 2022). This predominant attitude toward the Iranian postrevolutionary state is particularly evident when discussing women's status, as the gender politics of the Islamic Republic have been seen as monolithic, predominantly aimed at restricting women's public presence, and dogmatic in the sense of drawing on Islamic tradition.

Without underestimating the rupture with the past that the revolution represented, ignoring the elements of continuity in postrevolutionary politics and the extent of flexibility and adaptability in the state that sprung from the revolution reduces our ability to understand the way the postrevolutionary state constitutes a site characterized by conflict and negotiation, one that is not isolated from society and from its international context. This chapter focuses on gender politics by examining the case of women's outdoor exercise and interrogating policy shifts and the discourses underpinning them, as a case study into the elements of continuity and processes of change in state governance.

Surveying the Beaten Paths: Research on the Postrevolutionary State

The literature has focused on the revolution as a "moment" that culminated in a state whose politics remain immutable, fixed in time. Accordingly, change has been seen through the prism of the change of administrations, a simple variation in tone but not the substance of the politics of the state. Accounts of the postrevolutionary state have tended to treat it as more or less monolithic and rigid, guided by Islamic doctrine and powered by the revolutionary zeal of 1979 (Arjomand 1988, 2009; Banuazizi 1994; Chehabi 1991; Moaddel 1986). Such research focuses on the state's negative, prohibitive, and repressive power. Thus, the Islamic republic is seen as an Islamist state thriving on anti-American and anti-West rhetoric (Kraus 2010; Saghafi 2005), a patriarchal state discriminating against women (Moallem 2001, 2005; Tohidi 2007), or an authoritarian state curtailing human rights (Miller 1996; Osanloo 2009). In these studies, the endurance of the Islamic Republic of Iran is attributed to its application of force, coercion, and repression. Finally, the state has invariably been seen as a territorially bounded entity whose political authors are domestic actors oblivious to the international setting in which the Islamic Republic operates.

Approaching the postrevolutionary state in this way tends to deny its complexity, historicity and its situatedness in a regional and global system of governance. It thus fails to acknowledge so much more than the prohibitive, restrictive dimension of governance, the *disabling of undesired effects*, ignoring what social scientists exploring power and the state have identified as the productive capacity of the state, its *enabling of desired effects*. What makes power effective is its ability to produce spaces, ideas, concepts, and categories (Foucault 1995: 194), its productive capacity rather than its ability to bear down on individuals by working only through the mode of censorship, exclusion, blockage, and repression (Foucault 1980: 59). This injection of complexity in the notion of power and the state, some exceptions aside (Harris 2017; Keshavarzian 2005; Najmabadi 2015), is rarely heeded and the Iranian state's productive power rarely discussed. Overstating Iran's repressive power leads to the neglect of the various ways in which the state enables desired effects, rather than (or alongside) disabling undesired effects. Similarly, viewing the state as monolithic and immutable overlooks its internal complexity and dynamics, the conflictual character of decision-making as well as its historical contextualization. Furthermore, focusing on politics as a purely domestic matter, such interpretations extract the state from crucial transnational contexts, discursive in the sense of global discourses and influences, and material, in the shape of the global institutional architecture and politics in which the Iranian state is embedded (Meyer 1999; Steinmetz 1999).

Reflecting the predominance of such approaches, the study of gender politics in Iran has been based on assumptions denying the complexity of the field. Thus, state policies toward women have been seen as springing out of the revolutionary moment, not substantially changing over time and reduced to Islam. Facing this repressive state women and the state have been seen as opposites engaged in a zero-sum game (Moallem 2001, 2005; Tohidi 2007).

Such approaches to the postrevolutionary state provide important insights into the ways the revolution shaped the Islamic Republic and into authoritarian streaks in Iran's politics. Yet, politics and statecraft in Iran have not remained static but have evolved and adapted over time. We need to focus on the political and institutional ecologies that generate policies displaying both elements of coherence and continuity in the state but also to treat the latter as the complex constellation of actors and institutions that make up the Islamic republic. Such a perspective opens up new ways of examining the ways in which the state has been responding to, and managing crises in productive as well as restrictive ways rather than focusing on the state as facing constantly crises and imminent collapse. Focusing on the reflexivity of state institutions (and the actors that inhabit them) one can discern processes of "maturation" of the state as it moves from its revolutionary form to a post-revolutionary one and as actors, priorities, policies change.

In what follows, I make a departure from mainstream scholarship on gender politics and the state in Iran and use the politics surrounding women's outdoor exercise and the state's gender segregation policy in general as a case study bringing nuance and complexity and allowing me to explore the complex interplay of protection, prohibition, and provision in state policy.

Closing and Opening Outdoor Exercise Spaces

During the early 1980s, women found themselves cast as the part of the population that was to virtually "embody" the new revolutionary and religious ethos. The regime's emphasis on women's modesty and its intent of crafting pious mothers, combined with this restrictive attitude, women's leisure and exercise were pushed to the universe of the forbidden, rendered as, not only unnecessary, but also morally decadent.

The 1980s reports of *Zan-e Rooz* magazine, one of the oldest women's weeklies in Iran, suggest that under such circumstances women's exercise in the parks had turned into a stressful activity, carried out under the suspicious gaze of male guards who would monitor them to ensure that no rule was breached and that their moves conformed to Islamic codes and were not provocative.

During this time, women's outdoor exercise was framed as a problem, the solution to which was the prohibition of women to use public green spaces and parks as exercise space. In this context, gender segregation took the form of a moralizing tool. In the decades that followed, women's outdoor exercise came to eventually be reframed, from a problem to a solution to problems caused by the state's earlier policies, namely free market, urbanization, and compulsory veiling.

In the 1990s, with the termination of the eight-year war with Iraq, the reconstruction era began under the Rafsanjani presidency (Karshenas and Pesaran 1995). The incoming Tehran mayor, Gholamhossein Karbaschi, set the city on a path to growth (Adelkhah 2000). The new mayor was well aware of the fact that with the diminishing of revolutionary zeal in the post-war reconstruction era, something other than revolution and war monuments was needed for the citizenry to develop a sense of belonging to the city. While conservative factions in the state continued to advocate prohibitive measures, the municipality, with the backing of Rafsanjani as president, leaned toward the introduction of productive measures by opening up the urban space to different sectors of society. The decoupling of urban space from the glorification of the revolution and the war effort was matched by the introduction of the discussion of leisure, health, and the citizen's needs and expectations. At that time, as urbanization trends continued unabated and the redevelopment of urban space intensified, the dwelling space of urban households, and, together with it, the space available to women, contracted, the discussion on women's outdoor exercise and leisure became part of the new urban planning agenda.

At the same time, the central government, following World Bank-inspired structural adjustment policies, was turning toward a free-market economy, with the aim to integrate Iran into the global economy. Like many other state projects and policies, this structural adjustment produced undesired effects along the lines of what Ayatollah Khamenei, the leader of the Islamic Republic, labeled a western "cultural invasion" in the form of Western (cultural) products (Arjomand 2009). Some state and local officials realized that the state could no longer rely merely on prohibition and banning Western cultural products and advocated that instead, the state should produce alternative (cultural) products and spaces and address (within limits) citizens' needs.

It is in this conjuncture, when women's outdoor exercise shifted from being seen as a problem in itself to a solution to problems posed by the opening up to global markets, urbanization and the lack of healthy spaces for women. In 1993, the Presidential Center for Women's Affairs and Participation, led by Shahla Habibi, pushed Tehran Municipality to convert the seventy-five-acre Taleghani Park into a women-only park so that "women could exercise in open air with their gym clothes and without the veil." The rationale given for providing alternative leisure and exercise spaces was the importance of directing attention away from the infiltrating Western cultural goods and consumption of such goods. Here emerges a discourse that refers to exercise and sports not as a problem but as a solution to problems associated with the "Western cultural invasion." In the same interview, Habibi highlighted the implications of such acts for the mental and physical health of the population and invited women to show their support and visit the park.

But the project suffered from poor advertising and a lack of cooperation from other state organizations. The municipality did not fully convert the park into a women-only park; instead, it implemented the necessary security measures to reserve the park exclusively for women only on select weekdays. The project was a failure not just because other state institutions did not cooperate, but also because, despite Habibi's call, women showed little interest in using the space. Thus, Taleghani Park was deserted on women-only days. Soon the empty space was reclaimed by men, leaving the park as an example of the state's failed attempt to create a women-only park in the early 1990s.

During the same period Habibi had also expressed hope that the parks of all districts in Tehran would allocate a specific space for women's sports and exercise activities, and this call created a chain of activities in district municipalities. As a result, district municipalities became equipped with women's sports offices, which were responsible for organizing and coordinating women's morning and group exercises, now conducted under the supervision of female instructors in public parks, where women, still observing their hijab, could do aerobics and stretching exercises—something unimaginable a decade earlier. Women's morning exercises and competitions in public parks were no longer policed by the state, but rather organized by it.

With the election of Mohammad Khatami, the reformist candidate, in the 1996 presidential elections, the reform era (1996–2004) began. This period was one of political liberalization (see Behdad 2001; Boroujerdi 2004). After two decades of unsuccessful attempts to reinforce bans on Western (cultural) products, different factions within the state acknowledged the need for the provision of alternative spaces, even if in the name of "cultural defence." They unanimously agreed on what the problem was: a lack of conviviality, entertainment, and sports facilities. Within this atmosphere, the idea of women-only parks was revived. In public statements and media interviews, city and government officials alleged that open spaces for women—including women-only parks—constituted responses to concern for women's health problems that arose from lack of fresh air and exercise. For example, a 2000 report, published by "social and cultural experts" at the Education and Training Organization of Tehran, contained information about schoolgirls' poor health conditions, suggesting that their mandatory covering had caused a lack of exposure to sunlight, and, subsequently, hair loss. One of the recommendations listed was the creation of women-only parks.

In this new official discourse, gender segregation and the establishment of women-only parks, were presented, not as an initiative of a moralizing prohibitor state, but as a positive solution to the side effects of the opening of Iran's economy to the world and to globally recognized health problems. In 2002, a bill permitting the municipality to pursue the creation of women-only parks was introduced:

> [To boost women's] mental and physical capabilities, directing their leisure time, and providing them with appropriate opportunities for healthy entertainments in Tehran, the municipality is obliged to provide and allocate proper spaces in the existing parks. Furthermore, it will design and establish exclusive spaces in Tehran to be called "Mothers' Parks".
> *(Tehran City Council 2002)*

In 2003, Mahmoud Ahmadinejad, then the newly appointed conservative mayor of Tehran, demanded that the Tehran Parks and Green Space Organization locate the ideal spots across Tehran and convert them, whether partially or in their entirety, to women-only parks. Four spots were chosen. Nevertheless, Ahmadinejad's attempts to push for the construction of women-only parks failed partly because of the political opposition he received from the Presidential Center for Women's Affairs and Participation, headed by reformist Zahra Shojaee, who allegedly blocked the allocated budget.

After several years of infighting between various factions within the state, the bill was enacted under mayor Mohammad Baqir Qalibaf, another conservative that succeeded Ahmadinejad as mayor of Tehran. With a conservative heading the municipality and a conservative now in the presidential office, there was no political opposition to the project. Thus, in 2007, the Mothers' Paradise, Tehran's first women-only park, was opened in the northeast of Tehran and, in 2008, the Women's Paradise was opened in the southeast of the city.

That the officials made the effort to formulate the construction of women-only parks, not in terms of the requirements of an Islamic morality but, in terms of women's need for exercise is not surprising if we take into account that according to "data from two values surveys conducted by researchers from the University of Tehran, Iran" in 2000 and 2005, "the stress on the Islamic identity of the nation [by the Iranian government]" has begot "oppositional responses from Iranians" (Moaddel 2010: 535). These surveys indicated that among the Iranian population there was a shift toward "social individualism, liberal democracy, [and] gender equality," and also an increasing demand on the state to "take more responsibility for meeting citizens" needs' (ibid. 535, 542).

Women's outdoor exercise in public parks, once characterized as unnecessary and un-Islamic, was now encouraged and promoted by the state. The language used in the officials' interviews and reports on women-only parks highlighted the shift in the state's attitude toward women's leisure-time activities and exercise. Women were recognized as both mothers of the nation (with needs) and citizens (with rights), whose health was in danger and who therefore need be "served" by the state. "As citizens, they have paid their dues during the revolution and the war," wrote 175 Ministers of Parliament in a letter, stating that it was now the state's obligation to serve them. Mokhtari, the head of the Parks and Green Space Organization of Tehran Municipality, in an interview with *Javan* newspaper, also stated, "If, because of our religious and moral beliefs, we impose specific codes of conduct on women, then we have to provide them with a space where they can enjoy the green space peacefully and securely."

Although as early as the late 1980s some state officials had expressed concerns over the lack of exercise space for women and its negative impact on their mental and physical health, the first attempt to establish a women-only park in 1993 failed. The success of this new emphasis on the discourse of "women's health" and its appeal to women can only be understood in the context of the global focus on the mechanisms of achieving a healthy body. Across the globe a focus on cultivating healthy bodies through proper nutrition and sufficient exercise had emerged. In 2005, Tehran Municipality added in its organizational chart health offices, a development backed by WHO. In various events organized by this office to promote urban health and healthy lifestyles, thousands of citizens show up and participate. In 2009 there were thousands of yoga and aerobics classes across the country, including in religious cities like Mashhad, Isfahan, and even Qom (Moaveni 2008, 2009).

Mansoureh, one of the female exercise instructors of Tehran Municipality, stated in her interview with me that the municipality aimed to "provide" women with one women-only park in each district of Tehran. When I shared this news with a group of women in the Mothers' Paradise, they all welcomed the "much-delayed" initiative. Women want more of what the state wants them to want. In the process, the line between "interest at the level of the consciousness of each individual" and "interest considered as the interest of the population" becomes blurry (Foucault 1991: 100). This completes the process through which, in dealing with women's outdoor exercise and activities, the Iranian state shifted from relying on "negative" power and prohibition to deploying "positive" power to provide and produce. Instead of prohibiting outdoor exercise in the name of Islam, it produces new spaces, and it "rationalizes" and "justifies" the need for these segregated spaces by drawing on modern authoritative concepts and discourses such as urban justice and public health. In doing so, the state ultimately enables its desired behaviors and practices, such as women exercising separately from men, not through coercion and prohibition but through protection and provision.

Conclusion

This discussion attempted to chart and analyze the evolving role/character of the Iranian state over time through an examination of the debates and policies with regard to women's outdoor exercise. This charting exercise, while confirming the sea change brought about by the revolution, identified a chain of continuities as the postrevolutionary state has been engaged in and affected by modernization processes whose origins lie in the pre-revolutionary era as the discussion of urbanization and the mitigation of its adverse effects with regard to women indicates. The way the state and its agencies have shifted the modes in which they have framed problems and solutions over time throws light on the ongoing formation of the Islamic Republic and its inner contradictions decades after the revolution. The post-revolutionary state should not be seen as a singular, time-specific event, but rather, as a nonlinear, fractious, and volatile process that is always being constructed, sustained, and reconstructed by a multitude of actors, an affair fraught with inner contradictions but marked by adaptability and change.

What is more, this exploration has shed light to the maturation of the Iranian state as it moved from a revolutionary ideological construct to a postrevolutionary problem-solving machine. While not discounting the influence of Islam and its bureaucratic interpretations on gender politics, it is hard to overlook the impact of this maturation in the form of processes of bureaucratization, professionalization, and specialization and the ways these affected the framing of gender difference and the demands emanating from it. As a result of this maturation, throughout the period examined, the state has shifted from a restrictive and prohibitive role to regulating women's bodies through a productive role, addressing but also exploiting needs and demands: As the state started to (re)shape the public space to facilitate women's presence, it simultaneously increased its grip over previously unregulated spaces of everyday life. With power fragmented due to factionalism, and consumer pressures in response to Iran's opening to the global markets, the state has had to progressively negotiate and orchestrate rather than command. The story of the gradual (re)opening of public space for women, therefore, is the story of the gradual (re)orientation of state power.

Note

1 Parts of this chapter have been published in the Journal of Middle East Women's Studies (Shahrokni, Nazanin [2014], "The Mothers' Paradise: Women-Only Parks and the Dynamics of State Power in the Islamic Republic of Iran," *Journal of Middle East Women's Studies*, 10 (3): 87–107).

References

Adelkhah, F. (2000), *Being Modern in Iran*, New York: Columbia University Press.
Arjomand, S. A. (1988), *The Turban for the Crown: The Islamic Revolution in Iran*, Oxford: Oxford University Press.
Arjomand, S. A. (2009), *After Khomeini: Iran under His Successors*, Oxford: Oxford University Press.
Banuazizi, A. (1994), "Iran's Revolutionary Impasse: Political Factionalism and Social Resistance," *Middle East Report*, 191: 2–8.
Behdad, S. (2001), "Khatami and His "Reformist" Economic (Non-)Agenda," *Middle East Report Online*. May 21. http://www.merip.org/mero/mero052101 (accessed February 25, 2014).
Boroujerdi, M. (2004), "The Reformist Movement in Iran," in D. Heradstveit and H. Hveem (eds.), *Oil in the Gulf: Obstacles to Democracy and Development*, 63–71, London: Ashgate.
Chehabi, H. E. (1991), "Religion and Politics in Iran: How Theocratic Is the Islamic Republic?," *Daedalus*, 120 (3): 69–91.
Foucault, M. (1980), *Power/Knowledge: Selected Interviews and Other Writings: 1972–1977*, New York: Vintage.
Foucault, M. (1991), "Governmentality," in G. Burchell, C. Gordon, and P. Miller (eds.), *The Foucault Effect: Studies in Governmentality with Two Lectures by and an Interview with Michel Foucault*, 87–104, Chicago: University of Chicago Press.
Foucault, M. (1995), *Discipline and Punish: The Birth of the Prison*, New York: Vintage.

Harris, K. (2017), *A Social Revolution: Politics and the Welfare State in Iran*, Oakland: University of California Press.

Kadivar, Mohammad Ali (2022), "Social Development and Revolution in Iran," *Sociology of Development*, 8 (2): 1–25.

Karshenas, M., and H. M. Pesaran (1995), "Economic Reform and the Reconstruction of the Iranian Economy," *Middle East Journal*, 49 (1): 89–111.

Keshavarzian, A. (2005), "Contestation without Democracy: Elite Fragmentation in Iran," in Marsha Pripstein Posusney and Michelle Penner Angrist (eds.), *Authoritarianism in the Middle East: Regimes and Resistance*, 63–90, Boulder: Lynne Rienner Publishers.

Kraus, C. (2010), "The Sources of Anti-Americanism in Iran: A Historical and Psychological Analysis," *Valley Humanities Review* (Spring). http://www.lvc.edu/vhr/2010/Articles/krause.pdf

Meyer, J. (1999), "The Changing Cultural Content of the Nation-State: A World Society Perspective," in G. Steinmetz (ed.), *State/Culture: State-Formation after the Cultural Turn*, 123–43, Ithaca: Cornell University Press.

Miller, K. J. (1996), "Human Rights of Women in Iran: The Universalist Approach and the Relativist Response," *Emory International Law Review*, 10: 779–928.

Moaddel, M. (1986), "The Shi'i Ulama and the State in Iran," *Theory and Society*, 15 (4): 519–56.

Moaddel, M. (2010), "Religious Regimes and Prospects for Liberal Politics: Futures of Iran, Iraq and Saudi Arabia," *Futures*, 42: 532–44.

Moallem, M. (2001), "Transnationalism, Feminism and Fundamentalism," in E. A. Castelli and R. C. Rodman (eds.), *Women, Gender, Religion: A Reader*, 119–45, New York: Palgrave Macmillan.

Moallem, M. (2005), *Between Warrior Brother and Veiled Sister: Islamic Fundamentalism and the Politics of Patriarchy in Iran*, Berkeley: University of California Press.

Moaveni, A. (2008), "Should a Pious Muslim Practice Yoga?," *Time Magazine*. November 30. http://content.time.com/time/world/article/0,8599,1862306,00.html (accessed April 27, 2014).

Moaveni, A. (2009), "How to Work Out While Muslim- and Female," *Time Magazine*. August 16. http://content.time.com/time/magazine/article/0,9171,1924488,00.html (accessed April 27, 2014).

Najmabadi, A. (2015), *Professing Selves: Transsexuality and Same-Sex Desire in Contemporary Iran*, Durham: Duke University Press.

Osanloo, A. (2009), *The Politics of Women's Rights in Iran*, Princeton: Princeton University Press.

Saghafi, M. (2005), "Three Sources of Anti-Americanism in Iran," in T. Judt and D. Lacorne (eds.), *With Us or against Us: Studies in Global Anti-Americanism*, 189–205, New York: Palgrave Macmillan.

Steinmetz, G. (1999), *State/Culture: State-Formation after the Cultural Turn*, Ithaca: Cornell University Press.

Tohidi, N. (2007), ""Islamic Feminism": Negotiating Patriarchy and Modernity in Iran," in I. M. Abu-Rabi (ed.), *The Blackwell Companion to Contemporary Islamic Thought*, 624–43, Oxford: Blackwell Publishing.

III ARAB UPRISINGS AND EGYPT

Front Stage and Back: Assessing "Transition," Citizenship, and Violence in the 2011 Arab Uprisings

by Benoit Challand

Introduction

The 2011 Arab Uprisings took everyone by surprise and generated a moment of euphoria for social scientists: the outbreak of revolutionary movements in Arab countries was a source of global inspiration for activists and theorists. The *indignados* movements in Europe, the Occupy Wall Street type of sit-ins in the United States, protests against corruption in India and Sub-Saharan Africa in 2011 were all inspired by Tahrir Square and the toppling of four long-standing dictators in Tunisia, Egypt, Libya, and Yemen. Synchronously, the "peripheral" paradigm of Middle Eastern studies moved front stage and offered illuminating criticism of the nefarious impacts of neoliberal policies, of the global war on terror, and growing global inequalities. Theory emerged from the Arab democratic laboratory and the Arab uprisings injected a new life in the field of transition studies, away from the Orientalist depictions of Arab Middle Eastern societies as culturally hostile to democracy. A decade later, this generative and creative process of theory-making in the Middle East has receded and tends to be eclipsed by definitive, essentialist statements about "failures" of the revolution, "Arab winters," and of "state collapses" in Yemen, Libya and partly in Syria and Iraq.

This chapter proposes a relational analysis of the issue of political transition. Based on the manifesto of Emirbayer for a relational sociology (1997), I would like to show the transnational impacts of political economy and violence on state-society relations in the Arab worlds. "Arab politics" is thus the sum of "local" Arab forces and power, combined with the influence of external, European in the past, now mostly American, Chinese, or Gulf-based forces that have encroached in novel manners in the region. Relational sociology also allows for combining the larger politics of comparison (beyond the usual units of analysis—and thus adding a transnational or trans-local dimension) and shows the relative meanings of middle class, transition, and democratic participation. Issues of violence and class formations must be assessed in longer-historical process.

Ould Mohamedou and Sisk (2013) have warned us of the widespread tendency to see transitions as "short-term political developments" as limited "periods between the fall of the dictator and a free (or merely) trouble-free election."[1] The focus in this chapter is on informal alliance and the need to consider transnational factors that affected class-formation and distribution of violence within each Arab polity.

The 2011 Arab Uprisings were the best evidence that Arabs, men and women, youth and older people, residents or denizens, all pushed for political reforms that have challenged the thesis of an impossible citizenship among Arab societies (Challand 2017). Many would take the call for dignity, and social justice as evidence that these revolts were a revolt against neo-liberalism and its negative consequences. To be sure, neo-liberalism was a culprit, but the anger against ruthless regimes and past state violence was also a vital source of discontent. Proof of this assertion lies with repeated statements that Arab people had broken the wall of fear built by their own regimes. The 2011 uprisings were synonymous with the call for a renewed social contract respecting human dignity through jobs and equality, but also through a more just use of the means of coercion.

The Arab uprisings need not (only) to be assessed solely against the backdrop of institution changes (elections, writing of a new constitution, the emergence of a party system, etc.). Instead we need to consider the revolts as a set of historical events sharing, beyond the differences that so disparate countries as Tunisia, Yemen, Bahrain, or Egypt can offer, a common aspiration toward a renewed and reactivated sense of citizenship from below, that is from spontaneous forms of civil society, conjugated with innervated trade union movements, and the emergence of new informal coalitions pushing for more participatory politics. Counterrevolutionary forces, from 2013 onward, have managed to undercut these trends by preventing this collective force and the force of presentism in particular through a return to the use of violence to justify autocratic forms of power, such as those witnessed in Egypt with the president Abdel Fatah al-Sisi.

The move to the front stage and then a return to backstage is a continuous process, both for theory-making but also for the actual practices of revolting citizens. In 2019 and 2020, new protests erupted in Algeria, Sudan, Iraq, and Lebanon, generating talks of a "new Arab Spring." The slogans were direct reference to the famous "the people want to bring down the regime" heard ubiquitously in 2011 (Fahmi 2020). The protests in Iraq and Lebanon came later in 2019 and drew influence from the months-long Algerian and Sudanese street protests. This reading about a living legacy of the 2011 uprisings that cannot be associated with class-politics only but that resides in the connecting power of informal coalition might be over-optimistic in the case of Thermidorian regrouping of power in many Arab states. But the 2011 revolutionary moment instilled new life into Arab citizenship, making repeated and converging claims that citizens do not want military rule or an opaque clique of corrupt people protected by a ruthless political police (*mukhabarat*). The middle classes which are said to be the guarantor of democratic processes have had ambiguous attitudes in the years after 2011. Without the important mobilization of historically marginalized and lower-class groups, there would have never been joint demands to make coercion institutions accountable to the demos. I argue that, beyond fight against corruption and the rejection of neoliberal diktats, this was the core of the 2011 demands, a novelty that makes us reconsider the notion of "transitions."

Transition

The legacies of the Arab uprisings can be read on two levels. Deeply, the uprisings have signified a demand for a profound renegotiation of each national social contract, new forms of representation and an increased control by the sovereign power of the people over the means of violence. Transitions are not only about these short-term institutional changes (the second level). They are also about gradual and imperfect processes through which citizenship, forms of representations, and the use of violence have been renegotiated. I believe that any talks of "Arab transitions" must take this qualitative novelty into consideration.

I would like to concentrate on two aspects of political representation. The first one deals with the issue of social classes: Have middle classes, often considered to be "underlying drivers" of political change,[2] played a central role in the unfolding of the Arab transitions? The second dimension of political representation has to do with the place of state coercion and domestication of violence.

Class

Students of revolutions and democratic transitions all face the thorny question of what specific role classes play in the reshaping of political and social systems at critical junctures. Often the middle class is seen as a necessary stepping stone on which new alliances are forged, and thus becomes an essential "ingredient" for political change.

I think it is misleading to ask this question and to posit a role for a given class within the clear realm of national borders for various reasons. First, after two decades of neoliberal policies, the very notion of middle class can be called into question, because of processes of internal fragmentations. Some subgroups have benefited from intense liberalization while others have been marginalized. This process is most visible in Egypt where the emergence of the so-called "business government," led by Ahmad Nazif from 2004 until 2011, generated an internal split inside what became a two-speed middle class, one subpart being faster to reap benefits from liberalization from the other, typically civil servants.[3] Second, it is difficult to identify a clear and identical role for the middle class in complex events such as those of the Arab uprisings.

With regard to the Arab uprisings of 2011, some of these analyses force parallels with European history and try to defend the view that the middle class has been a motor of the Arab uprisings. If by this we mean to assess whether the middle class was a *trigger* and essential component of the wave of protests, it is hard to argue against such view. Revolutions have by and large been bourgeois events—and the original moment of the Arab uprisings fits this pattern, with vast sections of the middle class (though not only) in the early months of 2011 taking to the streets for their first time—from Sanaa to Tunis, and from Cairo to Manama, and joining earlier forms of activism by lower working classes.[4] Indeed, even in the latter case, where revolution is usually described in simplistic terms of a Shiite-Sunni divide, the initial protest in Bahrain included not just the disgruntled local Shiite population, but also segments of the Sunni middle class as well as organized labor (Achcar 2013: 162; Lynch 2012: 136–7). Without the support of (at least) portions of liberal professions and middle class, no revolution is likely to occur—and this has been the case in all Arab countries in 2011. In Tunisia, localized protests after the immolation of Mohammed Bouazizi in Sidi Bouzid became a revolutionary wave when the middle class from the more urbanized coast joined the protests from January 11 onward.

If, however, we are asking whether the middle class has supported a *continuous effort* toward more social justice and a structural change in the pattern of economic and political redistribution, it is obvious that the middle class has not at all been a motor for the Arab uprisings. A look at the role of lower classes in these revolts shows the complex and overlapping composition of political activism. On the other hand, subsequent events—like those in Egypt during the summer of 2013—cast doubt on the automatically positive expectation (in terms of transition and democratization) that is often attached to middle class.

It is obvious that the marginalized and lower classes are the ones willing to exert political pressure to keep the motor of the Arab uprisings going, so to say. Think of Tunisia, where youth and marginalized Tunisians were pivotal in contributing to the second phase of protests, after Ben Ali had departed the country when the second Qasbah protests in February and March 2011 moved into action. These protests and new sit-ins in the old city and near key ministries kept the pressure on the transition government and raised public awareness among the population at large on the need to keep the train of reforms going. It is widely accepted that these February and March 2011 manifestations paved the way for a collective agreement and compromises on how the fall elections would be held (Gana 2013: 18). Think of Yemen, where *akhdam* (lower-caste servants), disenfranchised groups in the northern region of Saada, and excluded portions of the south pushed for realization of a similar national dialogue after the departure of Ali Abdullah Saleh.[5] Similarly, it is youth activists of differing social backgrounds who since March 2011 have called for an end to political divisions in Palestine. At the end of 2011 in Egypt, when it became clear that the police state was still pulling the strings even after the fall of President Mubarak, the November street battles—such as those of Muhammad Mahmoud street—belonged to the lower segments of Egyptian societies, not the *twitterati* that were so central in the January and February 2011 protests.[6] Alliances have surely been formed, but not just between incumbent elites and the middle classes: shared pressures between lower and middle classes also need to be included in our comparative analyses of the Arab uprisings.[7]

The focus of many of the approaches taken in political science and sociology on the subject tends to reinforce a bias toward methodological nationalism—that is, the a priori selection of variables relating uniquely to internal political or sociological processes. For example, if the bourgeoisie (be it the "would-be middle class" of Khosrokhavar (2012: 60–91) or the "middle class poor" (2010: 44) of Asef Bayat) is described as defective, this is due to the nature of the political system (autocracy), or to internal divisions created by political Islam. In other words, all these accounts privilege internalist processes of political change. What these explanations fail to recognize is that the process of class formation is connected as much to external factors as to internal ones. Sandra Halperin (2005) noted long ago that the systematic crushing of left-radical groups during the Cold War led to massive out-migration of the middle class, skewing the balance between different classes and thwarting the emergence of vivid class consciousness (a key ingredient to class participation in political processes).

It is here that an analysis of the middle class needs to engage with regional and international influences. If rent is generally associated with oil, one needs to look not only at the rent provided by international aid (Egypt, Palestine, Jordan have received vast amounts, both from the United States and from the EU), but also at the increasing flow of Gulf capital into countries such as Egypt, Tunisia, and Palestine. Adam Hanieh has powerfully demonstrated that the traditional divisions of state versus society—or a vision of class formation limited to national borders—fail to capture the vivid and massive influence that transnational non-state actors (e.g. global capitalist classes)[8] play in shaping the future of Arab politics.

We have now a transnational bourgeoisie playing a political (conservative) role that is often unaccounted for. Be it in Palestine with president Abbas and some of his network who made their fortune in the Gulf[9], be it in Libya with past interim Prime Minister Mahmoud Jibril whose connections in Kuwait, Lebanon, and Qatar helped him become a key figure of Libyan transition (Prashad 2012: 138–40), or anti-Brotherhood sentiments expressed by the checkbook diplomacy of the Saudi family or from the United Arab Emirates, one can see not only that state rents shape and undermine the prospect of more democratic change in the region, but also that a powerful capitalist class, international in its composition and outlook, is failing the Arab uprisings' genuinely popular aspiration for political change and economic reform in order to preserve its own interests and investments in other countries.

In that sense, questioning the role of an evanescent middle class is misleading. What needs to be assessed is the flow of three different rents: oil rent in its different forms, non-oil rent that is transnational (and mostly intra-Arab) and that has deep capitalist imbrications in the national economies of countries that are part of the "Arab Spring," and the bureaucratic degeneration linked to foreign aid. This last aspect can be connected to a critique of institutionalized or NGO-ized civil society, which might be seen as having a detrimental role in terms of class formation. Indeed, NGOs all too often focus solely on their economic and institutional survival, and reproduce a middle class disconnected, paradoxically, from lower classes and popular aspirations they are supposed to help and represent through social work.

The Arab Middle East is also a region with an enormous degree of external interference, related to the so-called peace architecture around Israel, Egypt, Palestine, and Jordan and many security issues. As a result, military encroachments limit the sovereign exercise of politics, and increase the high political profile presented by non-tax revenues, such as rents or military aid. The difficulty is to disentangle the degree in which external factors hinder or shoulder internal process of social and political change. This difficulty will be illustrated in the following assessment of whether the middle class(es) in Arab countries have played a key role or not. Second, the notion of security is too often reduced to the existence of external interference. Security does play a distorting role in the making of military states in the region,[10] but such essential discussion should not overlook another crucial aspect of the making of democracies: the domestication by internal forces of the legitimate means of coercion. This will form the basis of the second pillar of this chapter.

Violence

Deep underneath the formal aspect of representation and the creation of political institutions and coalitions lies an even more central question, an issue that has always been at the heart of the modern form of politics, namely the challenge to channel violence in a constructive and legitimate way.[11] While the issue of violence has been seen as a problem enshrined in Arab history,[12] the Arab uprisings have tried to question the political economy of violence and offered ways in which the people have attempted to take full control of it—generating a much deeper form of political transition that is often overlooked.

The revolutionary potential of the 2011 uprisings—or rather the truly democratic element of transition (the *demos* taking power)—resides in the possibility of stripping from the incumbent power the capacity to appear as the ultimate justification for violence. This would be a return to the actual definition given by Max Weber of the state, namely as *the human community* that holds the legitimate means of violence.[13] In countries where these equilibriums have been laid bare by the immanent power of the people to resist as a whole, or through the defection of certain armed groups (especially in Tunisia and Yemen), and where representations were organized in a structured way, there has been the possibility to renegotiate the source of legitimate violence and to give to the human community the opportunity to become the actor in charge of violence.

The symbolic foot of the people put in the door of the management of violence, so to say, could not be enacted without the actual defection of certain groups holding security prerogatives. One can even claim that a necessary condition for the revolutionary transition in Arab countries characterized by a high degree of militarism and militarization is a systemic defection from one armed or security group, which in turn, can be seen as a result of a process of questioning the legitimacy of their use of violence.

Indeed, in Tunisia, the Army decided on January 13, 2011, not to use violence against its people leaving President Ben Ali with a limited support of his political police, an effective tool to repress on the long-term dissidence, but unable to quell mass protests as the ones that erupted in mid-January 2011.[14]

The question of legitimate violence becomes thus a political economy in which, starting with the 2011 uprisings, the building and negotiation of a different social contract were a central claim. Where this negotiation is heading is far from clear. But it signified a totally new situation in which the people and its *rather spontaneous representatives* altered the predicament of Arab politicization of violence: Rather than having militarized states in which it has been the structure of state revenues (typically non-tax revenues, such as oil rent, or the rent of military aid, proverbially high in the Middle East) that were pushing toward a state of war preparation (Heydemann 2000), we have seen emerging embryos of different political economies of violence.

There was another significant break during the first months of 2011. People actively pursued a strategy of questioning, at times even visually, how violence had been used against the people. In Egypt, people organized a media campaign called *al-kadhibun* ("the liars" in Arabic)[15] to confront the lies of the regime. Egyptians tagged security vehicles in Cairo, barring the name "shurta" (police) with a new name "silmya" (peaceful) (Shalakany 2014:358). Various Arab uprisings have indeed challenged the long-established political economy of violence precisely because people reclaimed their own participation in it. There are abundant cases of graffiti or slogans calling for the army to stand with the revolutionary demands. In Egypt, we can cite the chants of February 2011: "The People and the Army: One Hand!" (when soldiers moved into Cairo seemingly to depose Mubarak), or the Facebook page "We are all Khaled Sa'id" recalling the regime's terrible acts of violence. In Tunisia, the immolation of Mohamed Tareq Bouazizi in the remote and impoverished town of Sidi Bouzid was a reaction to the arbitrary power of a police agent who confiscated the only means of subsistence of Bouazizi.

The revolutionary potential of the uprisings resided in the very gesture of stripping the ruling power of the capacity to appear as the bearer of the monopoly of the legitimate recourse to violence. It required a new collective imaginary, one through which the people staged their own revolutionary moment through sitting, screening of their actions, and occupation of symbolic spaces, typically in front of governmental offices: the Mugamma in Tahrir Square, Cairo, or the Qasbah Square, seat of the Prime Ministry in Tunis. In these sit-ins, power was not trusted to civil servants, politicians, or deputies, but decisions were taken, it seemed, by the people themselves, sharing the same space.

In Tunisia and Yemen, reforms of the security sector were implemented in 2011 and 2012, with mixed results. Protesters in 2011 and 2012 called for the same rebuffing of military, religious, and tribal powers that had characterized the rule of Yemeni President Salih. "Large youth contingent [...] personified the antithesis of the kind of revolutionary 'civility' [*madaniyya*] they were seeking to promote" (Porter 2017: 269). Yemeni soldiers who defected and collaborated with the revolutionary groups also generated new political alliances between 2011 and 2013 (Porter 2017). Closer to us, in 2019 protests in Sudan and Algeria echoed these demands for civilian rule, with no military inference in the management of governmental affairs. In a few weeks, many millions had forced president Bouteflika to stand down and corrupt businessmen and senior politicians, including former prime ministers, to be arrested (Northey 2021). Campaigns, unions, and associations called for the end of the authoritarian social pact and the instauration of a second republic, through the drafting of a new constitution with the involvement of non-party actors (Boumghar 2019: 35–6). Aware that the protestors were caught between a rock and a hard place, with such an all-powerful army and deeply entrenched economic and political power vested in the name of stability, protestors targeted the clique around Bouteflika and stayed away from too confrontational a stance with the Army. Yet demonstrators "questioned the role of the army in political life, the Army Chief of Staff General Gaid Salah having been the major decision maker within the regime, with signs declaring their demands for a civil and not a military state: '*Dawla madania, machi aaskaria*'" (Northey 2021: 23).

Conclusion

If the wall of fear was broken in 2011 and if effective pluralism was a key ingredient for the success of the citizens' Arab revolts of 2011, it is not surprising to see reverse trends in local countries that have witnessed setbacks or counterrevolutionary movements. Egypt has returned to military rule, after a brief interlude of Mohammed Morsi as the only democratically elected civilian president of Egyptian history. Former Yemeni president Ali Abdallah Saleh who had accepted to step down in 2011, formed an alliance with his former archenemies, the Shiite Houthi rebels in the north of the country, to try to oust the new democratically elected president in the summer of 2014. The Libyan governments, unable to compromise on how to integrate militia men into regular security forces and how to distribute the oil revenue in the three historical parts of the country, eventually collapsed, despite two rounds of parliamentary elections in 2012 and 2014.

Except for Tunisia, where parties have been forced to govern through coalitions or a technocratic administration, the democratic experiments, understood as electoralism, have been short-lived. The revolutionary character of the very open social movements of 2011 was in stark contrast to the secretive and underground activism in most post-independence Arab countries (Meijer 2014: 634). Is there a curse against active Arab citizen participation in more open and pluralistic elections? A culturalist explanation cannot stand the ground, since Arab countries have inspired worldwide and massive social protests calling for more social justice and equality.

The answer to the current "failure" of the Arab revolts is to be found in the reappearance of old recipes, namely of regimes instrumentalizing the threat of wars, chaos, or Islamic jusqu-au-boutism (Da'esh style) to justify a crackdown on civil and political liberties. If citizenship was strong on the 2011 menu, it was rapidly pushed to the margins. The appetite of security forces accrued again because of the failure to substantially reorganize the architecture and institutional nesting of the security forces. Unable to make the security forces and institutions of organized violence truly accountable to democratically elected parliament and civilian control, the 2011 revolts missed a chance to cement the new form of the self-representation *of* and *by* the people that were at the heart of the initial protests. The return to a full military dictatorship in Egypt and the tragedy of the Syrian war are somber reminders that these attempts at renegotiating representation should have been connected to the organization and control of violence.

The most revolutionary dimension of these revolts, in terms of offering an alternative foundation for a new social contract and shared sense of citizenship, has evolved around the attempts to reclaim violence in a just and legitimate manner. Legitimate violence can only exist if it is controlled, at least in part, by the sovereign people (democracy is about the power of the demos, tempered by various institutions accounting for each other's actions and functions). This revolutionary claim on a shared control of violence has raised citizens' expectations very high, a demand that certain regimes managed to deflect into another round of ruthless violence. Syria, Libya, and now Yemen have fallen prey to the blindness of certain leaders who are happy to revert to old patterns of war-making to cling to power. In other instances, such as Tunisia, informal coalitions have managed to harness these destructive forces and introduce substantial reforms in the field of security. The peculiar history of Egypt, where the military as an institution is entrusted with vast economic power[16] and given the connections of Gulf investors with the country (Hanieh 2013), is a reminder that a comparative study of political transition cannot exist without a clear understanding of the economic forces at play and their origins in at least three decades of forced neoliberal policies. Alexander and Bassiouny are right when they state that "military capital as a distinct form of state capital in Egypt is a product of the period of neoliberal reforms" and that the violence expressed by the military has specifically targeted trade unions and other actors, often from lower classes, who denounced these economic privileges. To this assessment of who has paid a high price since the counterrevolution, one must also include groups that have directly questioned the unjust and illegitimate use of violence by Arab regimes.

Notes

1. Mohammad-Mahmoud Ould Mohamedou and Timothy Sisk, *Bringing Back Transitology: Democratisation in the 21st Century*, Working Paper, GCSP Research Series no. 13, Geneva (2013). http://www.gcsp.ch/content/download/14308/171469/download.
2. To take the expression of Ould Mohamedou and Sisk (*op. cit.*, 18): "The advent of the middle class in developing countries has also arguable been an underlying driver of many transitions in the contemporary period."
3. See Samer Soliman, *The Autumn of Dictatorship. Fiscal Crisis and Political Change in Egypt under Mubarak*, Stanford: Stanford University Press, 2011. A similar argument is made by Omar Dahi, "The Political Economy of the Egyptian and Arab Revolts," *IDS Bulletin*, 431 (2012): 51.
4. The countless number of strikes in Egypt in the five years before 2011 is a reminder of the preparatory work done by trade unions. On this, see Joel Beinin, "The Rise of Egypt's Workers," *Carnegie Endowment for International Peace*. June 2012.
5. Tom Finn, "In Revolt: Yemeni 'Untouchables' Hope for Path Out of Misery," *reuters.com*. Reuters, March 7, 2012. Sheila Carapico, "Yemen," in *Dispatches (op. cit.)*, 102–10.
6. See Lucie Ryzova, "The Battle of Cairo's Muhammad Mahmoud Street - Opinion," *Al Jazeera English*, November 29, 2011. On the pressure by lower middle classes and by trade unions who called for substantial reforms in Egypt, see, Anne Alexander and Mostafa Bassiouny, *Bread, Freedom, Social Justice. Workers and the Egyptian Revolution*, London: Zed Books, 2014.
7. For a general discussion on the role of lower classes in keeping revolutions alive, see Vivek Chibber, *Postcolonial Theory and the Specter of Capital*, London: Verso, 2013, esp. chap. 3–4.
8. I prefer using the plural of "global classes" to show the variety within. Hanieh speaks of them in the singular form. See Adam Hanieh, *Lineages of Revolt: Issues of Contemporary Capitalism in the Middle East*, London: Haymarket, 2013.
9. Rabbani, Mouin. "Qatar and the Palestinians." *jadaliyya.com*. Arab Studies Institute, December 1, 2012.
10. Nancy Bermeo, "Democracy Assistance and the Search for Security," in Peter J. Burnell, and Richard Youngs, eds., *New Challenges to Democratization*, London: Routledge, 2010, 73–90.
11. Norbert Elias, *The Civilizing Process. Sociogenetic and Psychogenetic Investigations*, London: Blackwell, 2000, 187–94, and 257–67. See also Gianfranco Poggi, *The State : Its Nature, Development, and Prospects*. Stanford, CA: Stanford University Press, 1990, 1–68.
12. With famous orientalist account imputing the high level of violence to a specific "Arab mind," see Rafael Patai, *The Arab Mind*, New York: Scribner, 1973.
13. My emphasis. This definition is usually truncated of "the human community" and turned into a "structure" or an "organization" that holds the legitimate means of violence.
14. Gana, *op cit*.
15. For an example of this campaign, see Nur Laiq, *Talking to Arab Youth: Revolution and Counterrevolution in Egypt and Tunisia*. New York: IPI Books, 2012.
16. See Yezid Sayigh, "Above the State: The Officers Republic in Egypt," Carnegie Endowment Working Paper, August 2012. For security and transition, see his recent report: "Missed Opportunity: The Politics of Police Reform in Egypt and Tunisia," Carnegie Endowment Working Paper, March 2015.

References

Achcar, G. (2013), *The People Want: A Radical Exploration of the Arab Uprising*, Berkeley: University of California Press.

Bayat, A. (2010), *Life as Politics: How Ordinary People Change the Middle East*, Stanford: Stanford University Press.

Bermeo, N. (2010), "Democracy Assistance and the Search for Security," in P. J. Burnell, and R. Youngs (eds.), *New Challenges to Democratization*, 73–90, London: Routledge.

Boumghar, M. (2019), "Le gant constitutionnel réversible : accessoire de l'uniforme militaire. Regard critique sur la crise constitutionnelle algérienne de 2019," *L'Année du Maghreb*, 21 (2): 35–54.

Challand, B. (2017), "Citizenship and Violence in the Arab Worlds. A Historical Sketch," in B. S. Turner and J. Mackert (eds.), *The Transformation of Citizenship*, Vol. 3: Struggle, Resistance and Violence, 93–112, London: Routledge.

Elias, N. (2000), *The Civilizing Process. Sociogenetic and Psychogenetic Investigations*, London: Blackwell.

Fahmi, G. (2020), "A New Wave of Arab Uprisings," *Rivista Idees,* online, 9 November. https://revistaidees.cat/en/a-new-wave-of-arab-uprisings-what-have-both-arab-protesters-and-european-policymakers-learned-from-the-arab-spring/.

Finn, T. (2012), "In Revolt: Yemeni 'Untouchables' Hope for Path Out of Misery," *reuters.com*. Reuters, March 7, 2012.

Gana, N. (2013), "Tunisia," in P. Amar and V. Prashad (eds.), *Dispatches from the Arab Spring*, 1–21, Minneapolis: University of Minnesota Press.

Halperin, S. (2005), "The Post-Cold War Political Topography of the Middle East: Prospects for Democracy," *Third World Quarterly*, 26 (7): 1135–56.

Hanieh, A. (2013), *Lineages of Revolt: Issues of Contemporary Capitalism in the Middle East*, London: Haymarket.

Heydemann, S., ed. (2000), *War, Institutions, and Social Change in the Middle East*, Berkeley: University of California Press.

Khosrokhavar, F. (2012), *The New Arab Revolutions that Shook the World*, Boulder, London: Paradigm.

Laiq, N. (2012), *Talking to Arab Youth: Revolution and Counterrevolution in Egypt and Tunisia*. New York: IPI Books.

Lynch, M. (2012), *The Arab Spring: The Unfinished Revolutions of the New Middle East*, New York: Public Affairs Books.

Northey, J. (2021). "The Algerian *hirak*. Citizenship, Non-Violence, and the New Movement for Democracy," in J. Mackert et al. (eds.), *The Condition of Democracy*. Vol. 3*: Postcolonial and Settler Colonial*, 17–32, London: Routledge.

Poggi, G. (1990), *The State: Its Nature, Development, and Prospects*, Stanford: Stanford University Press.

Porter, R. (2017), "Freedom, Power and the Crisis of Politics in Revolutionary Yemen," *Middle East Critique,* 26 (3): 265–81.

Prashad, V. (2012), *Arab Spring, Libyan Winter*, Edinburgh: AK Press.

Shalakany, A. A. (2014), "When the Graffiti Died," *London Review of International Law*, 2 (2): 357–78.

Historicizing Space and Mobilization in Tahrir Square

by Atef Said

Introduction

Scholars and observers across the globe have been associating the 2011 uprising in Egypt with iconic images of Tahrir Square filled with protesters. Not only that, in fact, most Egyptian revolutionaries themselves have been doing the same. Admittedly, when I was conducting fieldwork in Egypt during the revolutionary events, I asked Egyptian activists: Why did you go to Tahrir Square? Almost every single person I interviewed told me again and again that they just knew to head there; Tahrir was simply understood as where the revolution would take place, where the protesters knew the action would be. This shared understanding speaks to the existence of something that precedes the mobilization to a revolution, something that challenges dominant frameworks in social movement scholarship that underplay the role and significance of space and time. This begs a question, what is the role that history of places play in revolutionary mobilization? In this chapter, I answer this question through a close examination of the history of mobilization in Tahrir as it relates to the revolution itself. As I demonstrate in this chapter, it is easy to say that "history matters," but it is both more difficult and important to understand how it matters, particularly with regard to space. My goal is to expand our understanding of space historically, to look at how space over time comes to provide a meaningful context and vernacular to a movement. Before proceeding, a quick overview of literature on space and mobilization is needed.

This chapter is a shortened version of this article: Said, A., "We ought to be here: Historicizing space and mobilization in Tahrir Square," *International Sociology*, 30 (4) (2015): 348–66.

Atef Said is an Assistant Professor of Sociology at the University of Illinois at Chicago. He can be reached at atefsaid@uic.edu.

Space in the Scholarship on Mobilization

Space has received increasing attention from social movement scholars, particularly in the last decade. Prominent geographers in a special issue of the journal Mobilization, for example, focused on space in contentious politics and noted: "Research on social movements and contentious politics has generally downplayed the spatial constitution and context of its central concepts such as identity, grievances, political opportunities, and resources. As such, this body of scholarship remains by and large aspatial" (Martin and Miller 2003: 143). In studying space in social movements, we ought to think of space not as "a container of activism, but also constitutive of it" (Martin and Miller 2003: 144).

At the risk of simplification, one can divide this literature into three main trends. The first trend studies contentious politics in general through the lens of space. This literature studies social movements: (1) in terms of their location(s) and how they are affected by the built environment; (2) in terms of their scale; and (3) as networks that reflect and/or embody the movements themselves. For example, David Harvey recently emphasized, among other things, the role of specific urban features in relation to protest:

> It is also clear that certain urban environmental characteristics are more conducive to rebellious protests than others—such as the centrality of squares like Tahrir, Tiananmen, and Syntagma, the more easily barricaded streets of Paris compared to London or Los Angeles, or El Alto's position commanding the main supply routes into La Paz.
>
> *(2012: 117)*

The second trend takes into account issues of contingency and studies movements, their grievances, and actors as intersecting with space in more complex ways. Tilly suggests that we need to look at "the geography of policing, safe spaces, spatial claim making, and control of places as stakes of contention" (2000: 135). Analyses in this trend take the dynamics of movements and their battle over spaces into account.

Finally, the third trend, newly emerging, studies movements in relation to virtual and "cyber" spaces, in which new forms of activism operate alongside or sometimes even in place of that in non-virtual spaces.

Scholarship on the spatiality of contention in general has made important contributions, yet for the most part, this literature continues to examine space and its relation to movements *synchronically*. Notwithstanding Sewell and Tilly, most analyses still tend to approach space as a set of geographical conditions that become relevant only once a specific movement arises, relatively disconnected from history. As such, it cannot explain how protesters "just knew" to head to Tahrir in the first place. Or to put it in sociological terms, this literature does not attend to the historical making and meaning of space in relation to movements.

Here I would like to invoke an important observation from the work of Willian Sewell, Jr. Sewell states: "While insurgent movements make sure of the preexisting meanings of places, they can also—either intentionally or unintentionally—transform the significance of protest locations" (Sewell 2001: 65). In this chapter, I investigate the extent to which this observation applies to Tahrir Square and the Egyptian revolution, with the goal of expanding our understanding of space historically in relation to mobilization.

Tahrir: A Background

Before proceeding, one quick note is needed about the space of Tahrir Square. This important place is located in the heart of downtown Cairo. It is about 11.5 acres of open space, in which one can see layers of architecture representing different eras of Cairo's unique history. It was designed to emulate Charles de Gaulle Square in Paris and was constructed in 1865 under Khedive Ismail (Taher 2012), after whom it was originally named Ismailia Square. Having lived in Paris during the remaking of that city by Baron Haussman, Ismail's vision was to modernize Cairo and create a "Paris on the Nile." Near the heart of the square is Qasr El-Nile Bridge. From 1882 to 1947, British barracks occupied the area near the bridge. Under King Farouk, a huge all-in-one administrative building known as Mogamma in Arabic (or "the complex") was built in 1951.

The name Tahrir Square, meaning "Liberation Square" in Arabic, was first used informally in Egyptian mass protests against British rule in 1919. The name was made official under Nasser when Egypt became independent and changed from a constitutional monarchy into a republic (Farag 1999). The area around Tahrir Square includes other important buildings such as the Egyptian National Museum, the Nile Hotel, the Kasr El Dobara Evangelical Church, the original downtown campus of the American University in Cairo, and buildings housing the headquarters of the Arab League and Mubarak's National Democratic Party (NDP, formed under Sadat), respectively. The NDP headquarters were burned down during the 2011 revolution. Between the Nile Hotel and the Kasr El Dobara Church is the Omar Makram Mosque. Named after one of Egypt's revolutionaries during the French occupation of Egypt (1798–1801), the mosque was used as one of the field hospitals during the violent clashes of 2011. Also, near the square are key government buildings including the Egyptian Parliament, the Shura Council, the headquarters of the Cabinet, as well as the Ministry of Interior.

History of Mobilization in Tahrir and the Revolution

Based on two phases of historical and ethnographic research in Egypt conducted in 2011 and 2012, in the following section, I demonstrate that the historical significance of Tahrir Square took three forms in relation to mobilization for the 2011 revolution. The first is the identification of Tahrir Square as a known target for protest. The second is as source of strategies, specifically providing the revolutionaries with the idea of encampment in Tahrir. The third is the fact that Tahrir was known as a site of meaning and inspirations. In short, given Tahrir's historic and symbolic significance, it provided protestors with inspiration during the revolution. At the same time, protesters appropriated this history and incorporated it into new narratives about the liberation of the square.

Tahrir: Where the Action Is

As noted above, protestors told me that they headed for Tahrir because they knew that Tahrir is already understood as a gathering point for protest. Some remembered that Tahrir was the site of an important anti-war protest in 2003 (against the Anglo-American war on Iraq), while others remembered protests organized by Kefayya (a prodemocracy coalition formed in 2005). In 1972, students gathered in Tahrir to protest the Sadat regime's authoritarianism and the regime's vague plans to liberate Sinai, Egypt's peninsula that was occupied by Israel in the 1967 war.

In fact, the idea of Tahrir as a space of protest stretches back earlier than 1972. The location of British barracks near Tahrir during the colonial period made the square a target of protests since 1919. Leaders of student movements in the 1940s also recalled protests against the British occupation in 1946, led by the National Committee of Workers and Students. On February 21, 1946, the committee called for the evacuation of British troops and a general strike against British occupation. The same day, a massive demonstration of students marched from Giza to the center of Cairo. When they reached Ismailia Square (Tahrir), they were confronted by British troops who opened fire on the protest. Twenty-three demonstrators were killed and some 120 injured (Farag 1999). The day was later chosen to mark the National Students' Day in Egypt.

Contemporary activists recall Tahrir as the space of more recent protests in the last decade—events that have highlighted, in fact, that protesting in Tahrir is not an easy thing. It is always a battle to control the space, especially under an authoritarian regime and heavy police state. Yet, for many of the activists with whom I spoke, Tahrir had become an important, if unattainable (or, perhaps, because unattainable) meeting point for demonstrations. The idea of controlling Tahrir took on special meaning for protesters precisely because the space was rarely under their control. All this is then supplemented by the fact that Tahrir has a number of physical features that make it a convenient and strategic target. These include the massive width of the space, its location in downtown Cairo, its proximity to numerous cafes, where activists and intellectuals can meet and write statements, and the central pedestal, which provides a convenient and symbolic platform for protest leaders. It is Tahrir's central location, then, in both literal and historical space that leads some analysts to say: "Whatever happens in Tahrir immediately becomes a national concern" (Farag 1999).

A History of Sit-Ins

Actual occupation of Tahrir has taken place only three times prior to the 2011 revolution. The first is during the 1972 student protest in Tahrir, where the sit-in lasted for almost one day, on January 24 one day before being evacuated by police force on the dawn of January 25, 1972. The second is on March 21, 2003, during a national protest against the Anglo-American war on Iraq. Again, protestors were able to occupy the square for one night before being forced to leave by violent police force. The third time was on March 16, 2006. The sit-in was organized in solidarity with pro-democracy judges who were prosecuted under Mubarak.

The first time was organized by students, the second time was by different political forces, and the third time was led mainly by bloggers.

For many of the protesters I interviewed, these incidents hold an important place in their memory, even if they only heard about them second-hand. It should be noted that Egyptian activists mostly use the word "sit-in" (in Arabic *ieetsam*), rather than the word "occupation." Though the latter is used internationally to describe this mode of action (due, in part, to the rise of the Occupy movement), in Arabic "occupation" is associated more with the history of colonialism. In this chapter, I use the words "occupation" and "sit-in" interchangeably in order to avoid confusion and because "occupation" is the term most often used by the media and in scholarship about Tahrir.

Each of these incidents has been important in the memories of many activists I talked to. The sit-ins in 1972 and 2003 were especially memorable to most pro-democracy and leftist activists in Egypt. The 1972 protest occupies a special political status in the Egyptian political imaginary. While students have been engaging on protests in different campuses in Egypt, the protest reached a new level when Sadat's regime arrested 1500 students engaged in a campus sit-in on January 24, 1972, at Cairo University. The previous week had seen many sit-ins organized by student unions and groups at various universities. In response to the arrests, about 20,000 students from Cairo and Ain Chams Universities (both in Cairo) rallied in Tahrir. The students occupied the square all day, despite police efforts to dispel them by force. One activist recounted the sit-in experience:

> They [students] started gathering around the campus, and the spontaneous cry was "to Tahrir," this being the closest thing we have to the center of Cairo. The pedestal was probably an obvious choice, being the closest thing to the center of Tahrir. It was also, as I recall, surrounded by a sort of circular garden. It therefore offered an obvious focal point to gather round. It also provided a sort of platform, which was used for speeches, and for Sheikh Imam and Ahmed Fouad Negm to sing their revolutionary songs.[1]
>
> *(Quoted in Farag 1999)*

Throughout the day, more students and other groups soon joined the sit-in, supporting the demands for the release of their colleagues. At midnight on January 25, police came and evacuated the square by force (Abdalla 2009). This occupation became a significant symbol in Egyptian intellectual and cultural history. Amal Donqol penned the famous poem *Oghneyet El-Kaaka El-Hagareya* (The Song of the Brick Cake—in reference to the pedestal in the center of the square), describing the protesters' chants and determination against the tyranny of Sadat. The poem enjoys a powerful place in Egyptian memory and was cited by participants in later events.

In 2011, this history of sit-ins in Tahrir provided protesters with not only the idea of occupying the square, but also concrete strategies for doing so. People gravitated to the square spontaneously, but once there, the massive crowds and space needed to be managed. Experienced activists who had participated in previous sit-ins knew that focusing on issues of survival, such as food, water, and sleeping equipment, would be crucial. Other activists knew that communication would be key and brought large speakers and set up stages throughout the space. Most of these ideas emerged from previous protests. Egyptian bloggers who had led the small 2006 sit-in, in particular, were key players in 2011, drawing on their past experiences and using social media to mobilize protesters. For example, Amr Ezzat, one of the founders of the blogging movement in Egypt in the decade before the revolution, told me, "for many bloggers the experience in the sit-in during the revolution reminded them of their own sit-in in Tahrir in 2006."

Tahrir Means Liberation

Because many of my interviewees also had memories of unsuccessful attempts to occupy the square, their narratives of occupying Tahrir in 2011 during the revolution involved a distinct sense of pride that this was the longest period they had held the square, and that this represented a new form of liberation. One of the most important components in protesters' narratives was the idea that Tahrir should finally live up to its name (liberation). Their hope was that the liberation of Tahrir would lead to the liberation of Egypt from dictatorship. Implicit in activists' narratives was an understanding of Tahrir as not only liberated during the sit-in of 2011 itself, but also as a symbol of liberation both historically and for the future. Ahmed Bahaa Eddin Shaaban, one of the leaders of the student movement in 1972, became the general coordinator of the National Association for Change, a coalition of different political groups that came together to mobilize for democracy under Mubarak. Shaaban himself comes from a leftist background and is about sixty-three years old. He has spent most of his life involved in political activism against both Sadat and Mubarak. When I interviewed him, he told me how the revolution was in many ways a culmination of all the political activism in his life: "I learned from this revolution and I found in it the reward for all of our sacrifices in our political career since the student movement in 1972. In Tahrir we were liberating ourselves."

Previous protests and occupations of Tahrir were an important source of inspiration, and also provided a reference against which to measure contemporary efforts. Nermine Nezar, an independent activist, stated:

> In all my life, I have been reading the poem about the "brick cake," and I have been hearing stories about the students' protest and their occupation of Tahrir. And I have older friends and family members who participated [in] this. I thought that this was the highest point in the political protest history in Egypt. But when the 18 days in Tahrir came, I felt like we are making new and a stronger history. I was proud of my generation. It was like a dream.

And while the history of protests in Tahrir made it the most well-known target for protesters who wanted to join the sit-in spontaneously, other activists explicitly used this history and the image of Tahrir to actively recruit more protesters. The idea of borrowing meanings from the past to encourage more newcomers to join the protests was an important aspect of the first eighteen days of the revolution.

One of the best examples was the use of important political songs from Egypt's history. Protesters sang old national songs, particularly those advocating resistance against occupation and/or liberating lands. One of the most significant songs appropriated and redeployed in Tahrir in 2011 was a song written by poet Ahmed Fou'ad Negm and composed and sung by Sheikh Emam. The song, named "The Valiant is Valiant and the Coward is Coward," was written in 1969 in the context of what is known as the War of Attrition between Egypt and Israel.[2] In that context, the idea of continuing resistance/ war until liberating the occupied Sinai was prominent in the political debates and protests in Egypt. Protesters in the 2011 revolution appropriated the 1969 song to refer to Tahrir. The message was clear: Tahrir is for those who are valiant. The song's words emphasize the significance of resistance and that only brave people will go to the field (square):

> We will raise the strife
> Above all storms
> We will be proceeding all nights
> And bring the morning
> We will defeat defeatism
> If you want to redress all the lost,
> Go to the field
> The valiant is valiant
> And the coward is coward.

Since 2011, the song has also become popular among protesters trying to reoccupy Tahrir. On April 13, 2012, for example, in one of the so-called "million-person rallies" to protect the aspirations of the revolution, tens of thousands of protesters were recorded singing the song at the same time.[3]

Memories of more recent protests were also present in the minds of many protesters. Activists talked particularly about efforts in the early 2000s. Speaking about his experience in 2003, Mohamed Sanad, a young leftist activist, recounted:

> This was my first participation in a demonstration ever. I was in Cairo University, where the students' rally started. I knew that the target was Tahrir. I joined the protesters. In Tahrir, I saw Kamal Khalil leading chants against Mubarak. The atmosphere was impressive for me. I saw young people, men and women, chanting and singing old songs of Sheikh Emam. At night, protesters lighted many candles. For somebody who never experienced or saw any protests outside the university, this was very memorable and impressive experience. I remembered this during the revolution. It was almost the same environment.

Numerous protesters cited similar sentiments when I interviewed them in 2011. Whether recalling songs and narratives passed down through generations, or drawing on their own personal memories, participants in the 2011 revolution consistently framed the meaning of contemporary events in their historical spatial context.

Conclusion

Countering efforts that would frame the Egyptian revolution as an exceptional event disconnected from any previous history of mobilization, this chapter examines how the history of Tahrir as a space of mobilization shaped the 2011 revolution and its meaning for participants. Of course, mobilization and political protests before the revolution are connected to the latter in many ways, not only through the space of Tahrir. But this research shows that the power of the square as a historical idea and inspiration played a constitutive role in the revolution itself. My research shows that previous movements were connected to the new movements—in this case the revolution itself—through space. Also, Tilly (2008, 2010) and Traugott (1995) have advocated the concept of repertoires in contentious politics to highlight how specific modules of action are repeated in similar or different contexts. One can imagine, for example, studying the tactic of occupying Tahrir Square as one such repertoire of contention. Also, one can suggest that instead of studying only one movement in the past or in the present, it is important to study the connections between old movements and new movements, and to investigate the different types and logics of temporal connections between the two.

Recent scholarship has brought more attention to the meaning and effects of spaces in which significant events take place. But as Tahrir and, hopefully, this study reveal, even before or in between moments when events take place, spaces carry meanings that are constructed over time, redeployed and reconfigured in the present, and carried forward as inspiration for the future.

Notes

1 The works of both Negm and Emam are significant in Egyptian political protest history. The two artists were present in 1972, and visited student protesters in the square. They were heroes of resistance movements throughout the 1970s and beyond, including the 2011 revolution. Their songs were banned in Egypt throughout the 1970s and 1980s.
2 The War of Attrition refers to 1969–1970, a period of mutual attacks between Egypt and Israel. This took place between the Six-Day War of 1967 and the 1973 war.
3 This video can be viewed at www.youtube.com/watch?v=T9ULqvTG6qM (accessed June 5, 2013).

References

Abdalla, A. (2009), *The Student Movement and National Politics in Egypt, 1923–1973*, Cairo: American University in Cairo Press.
Farag, F. (1999), "The Center of the Center," *Al-Ahram Weekly*, September 2–8. Available at: weekly.ahram.org.eg/1999/445/feature.htm (accessed May 15, 2013).
Harvey, D. (2012), *Rebel Cities: From the Right to the City to the Urban Revolution*, London: Verso.
Martin, D. G. and B. Miller (2003), "Space and Contentious Politics," *Mobilization: An International Quarterly*, 8 (2): 143–56.
Northey, J. (2021), "The Algerian Hirak. Citizenship, Non-Violence, and the New Movement for Democracy," in J. Mackert et al. (eds.), *The Condition of Democracy. Vol. 3: Postcolonial and Settler Colonial*, London: Routledge, 17–32.

Sewell, W. Jr (2001), "Space in Contentious Politics," in R. Aminzade Aminzade, C. Tilley, D. McAdam, W. H. Sewell, J. Goldstone, S. Tarrow, and E. J. Perry (eds.), *Silence and Voice in the Study of Contentious Politics*, 51–87, Cambridge and New York: Cambridge University Press.

Taher, M. (2012), "Tahrir Square: Where People Make History,". *Al-Ahram Weekly*, January 20. Available at: english.ahram.org.eg/NewsContent/1/114/32175/Egypt/-January-Revolutioncontinues/Tahrir-Square-Where-people-make-history.aspx (accessed April 1, 2013).

Tilly, C. (2000), "Spaces of Contention," *Mobilization: An International Quarterly*, 5 (2): 135–59.

Tilly, C. (2008), *Contentious Performances*. New York: Cambridge University Press.

Tilly, C. (2010), *Regimes and Repertoires*. Chicago: University of Chicago Press.

Traugott, M. (1995), *Repertoires and Cycles of Collective Action*, Durham: Duke University Press.

Dual Refusal: How the Labor Movement almost Toppled the Bahraini Monarchy

by Amy Austin Holmes

The small island kingdom of Bahrain witnessed a mass uprising in 2011 that sent tremors throughout the region. The revolt quickly transformed from one demanding reforms to calls for a Republic, with the potential of toppling the Al Khalifa family, who had ruled for almost two centuries.[1] This was viewed as a threat even by Bahrain's much larger and allegedly more stable neighboring monarchies, in particular Saudi Arabia, the United Arab Emirates, and Kuwait. Bahrain's anti-regime mobilization was due in part to the organizational capacity of trade unions and professional associations, and yet their role in the "near-revolution" (Yom and Gause 2012) has received very little scholarly attention. I contend that the significance of the labor movement in Bahrain was not merely its ability to strike and put an end to production and the provision of services, but also the ability to support the mass protests by continuing to work, in particular through the provision of medical services on a volunteer basis (Table 8.1). Confronted with these two equally vexing forms of disobedience—the refusal to work and the refusal to stop working—the Bahraini ruling family called for help. To keep Al Khalifa on their thrones, the Saudis sent in their national guard, the Emiratis sent police forces, and the Kuwaitis sent their navy to patrol the maritime borders of the island nation.

In Egypt and Tunisia, the official trade union federations played an ambiguous or even hostile role as workers began to organize strikes during the protests against Mubarak and Ben Ali (Langohr 2014; Zemni, Smet and Bogaert 2013). In contrast, the official General Federation of Bahrain Trade Unions (GFBTU) not only supported the protests from the beginning, but called for two general strikes during the first month of the uprising. Indeed, in 2011 the GFBTU was arguably more independent of the regime than any other trade union federation in the Arab world. It is estimated that 60–85 percent of all employees participated in the general strike in February, including both Sunnis and Shias, while the second general strike in March lasted for nine days (BICI Report 2011).

Holmes, A. A. (2016), "Working on the Revolution in Bahrain: From the Mass Strike to Everyday Forms of Medical Provision," *Social Movement Studies*, 15 (1): 105–14.

A long and venerable tradition of scholars have analyzed the various ways in which the voiceless can be given a voice through their ability to organize and engage in collective bargaining. Of all the tactics at their disposal, workers' ability not to work, or to withhold their labor power through strikes and work stoppages has often been seen as key to exercising their collective power. Beverly Silver (2003) demonstrates how the power of the workers' movement derives from its ability to engage in a wide range of labor actions, including general strikes, strikes, riots, unemployed protests, disputes, demonstrations, and lockouts. From a different theoretical tradition, James Scott (1985) defines "weapons of the weak" as including absenteeism, foot dragging, poor workmanship, undeclared slowdowns, pilfering, slander of superiors, and sabotage of the work process. Both Silver and Scott's conceptualizations of labor unrest, as different and broadly defined as they are, still generally refer to the power that arises from a collective decision not to work, or to withhold labor power through various means. I contend that the mass uprising in Bahrain was only possible because some people refused to work and took part in the general strike, while others refused to stop working.

While the economic impact of striking workers may be illustrated, for example, by pointing to the drop in oil production during the uprising in Bahrain, assessing, much less quantifying, the impact of volunteer labor is much more difficult. Historically, work stoppages and the withholding of labor power have often been associated with the militant (and predominantly masculine) tradition of the trade union movement. By contrast, unpaid labor, volunteer labor, and looking after the wounded and dying have often been associated with the (historically feminine) form of care provision, which is more likely to fall within the realm of care work, or what Bayat (2010) called a "social non-movement" than a militant form of labor activism. And yet, I argue that understanding the 2011 wave of mass mobilization in Bahrain and elsewhere requires an encompassing approach to labor that brings together both traditions: one that can conceptualize equally the ability of collectivities to stop working, but also the ability to collectively continue to work, even on an unpaid basis. Finally, judging by the way the

Table 8.1 Labor power and revolution

Activity	Relationship to authorities	Frequency	Labor power	Union	Membership	Regime response
Mass strike	Defiance of regime	Rare	Refusal to work	BTA	60% women	Severe crackdown
Medical provision	Compliance with standards of medical professionalism	Everyday	Refusal to stop working	BNS	90% women	Severe crackdown

Source: A. A. Holmes

regime retaliated against both forms of labor activism, I argue that it was not just the general strike or collective withholding of labor power that threatened the regime, but also the collective offering of labor power, on an unpaid, volunteer basis. I will illustrate the contradictory role of the labor movement with examples from the Bahrain Teachers' Association (BTA) and the Bahrain Nursing Society (BNS). The majority of members of both associations were women.

The 2011 Uprising

Bahrain's revolt began just three days after Mubarak had been toppled in Egypt: on February 14, 2011. Activists had chosen that day because it was the tenth anniversary of the NAC promulgated by King Hamad. Although heralded as a major reform, many felt that little had changed. Precisely for this reason, protests have been a recurrent feature of Bahraini society. During the year 2010, the chief of public security and acting deputy interior minister said the police counted over 1000 protests during that year, or on average 3.4 protests per day (ICG Report 2011: 3). The anti-regime rebellion that ensued on February 14 was a continuation of previous struggles. But 2011 was different. The dynamics of this wave of contention took place against the backdrop of rapidly disintegrating dictatorships: Ben Ali had fled Tunisia, seeking refuge in Saudi Arabia, and Mubarak was airlifted unceremoniously out of Cairo and decamped to one of his villas in the Sinai Peninsula.

These events prompted the Khalifas to dig into their kingdom's coffers. Just hours after Mubarak was ousted in Egypt, King Hamad gave a speech in which he promised to dole out $2650 to each Bahraini family in an attempt to keep them off the streets (Noueihed and Warren 2012: 141). But the people took to the streets anyway. On February 14, 2011, three days after Mubarak had been ousted in Egypt, the Bahraini people rose up, turning the Pearl Roundabout in Manama into a Tahrir-like spectacle. Protesters' demands during the first few days included political and constitutional reform, free elections, a truly representative consultative council, an end to torture and the release of political prisoners, and equal access to socio-economic opportunities. In essence, they wanted the king to make good on the promises he had made ten years earlier.

These demands for reform (islah al-nizam), however, soon became radicalized with youth demanding the removal of the regime (isqat al-nizam). Yet for most of the opposition, including Al-Wefaq, the largest of the various opposition groups, the "removal of the regime" did not mean establishing a republic in Bahrain or toppling the Khalifas. Rather, it meant securing the resignation of the cabinet and the Prime Minister (who had been in office since 1971 and was the longest-serving unelected PM in the world), to be replaced by an elected Prime Minister and a fully empowered parliament (Matthiesen 2013; Ulrichsen 2014).

The First General Strike in February

For the first time since its founding in 2002, the GFBTU issued a statement calling for a general strike. In contrast to the Bahraini government, decisions within the trade union federation are taken democratically. The decision to declare a general strike was voted on within the central committee of the GFBTU, and passed almost unanimously.[2] Employees in both the private and public sector joined the strike, including both Sunnis and Shias. Although professional associations are not members of the GFBTU, they also joined the mass strike. Indeed, the first strikes recorded that day began in schools, starting at 7.30 am, when teachers began protesting in front of the school gates. Lawyers also went on strike, first gathering at the Ministry of Justice and then marching to the Roundabout. By the early afternoon, employees of the Aluminum Company demonstrated on company grounds. In the evening, the Bahrain Engineers' Society staged a march toward the roundabout.

Striking Teachers and Working Nurses

On the following day, the GFBTU announced that it was calling off the general strike, as the crown prince, Sheikh Salman bin Hamad al Khalifa, ordered the security forces to withdraw and called for a "national dialogue." The fact that the GFBTU called off the general strike after a single day was an indication that the unions were willing to both flex their muscles, but also to cooperate with the regime if they made concessions. The BTA, however, decided to continue the strike, with an estimated 80 percent of the schools and 6500 teachers taking part.[3] Women comprised about 60 percent of the BTA members. The BTA set up a tent at the Pearl Roundabout, and collected signatures of teachers who participated in the strike. BTA President Mahdi Abu Deeb explained that they were asking the teachers to sign their attendance so that the Education Ministry could not later deny that they went on strike. After four days, on Thursday, February 24, the BTA announced they were suspending the strike. On February 25, the BTA issued a statement in which it described the strike of the preceding days as "the largest and most daring" in Bahrain's history.

Medical personnel also played a critical role during the protest movement, and yet in a very different way than teachers (Shawkat al-atibba 2013). Like teachers, doctors and nurses are service providers. But while the teachers refused to go to work and withheld their labor power, the nurses continued to work, in some cases even offering their services for free. The Salmaniya Medical Complex (SMC) is located about 2 km from the Pearl Roundabout, and is the only full-service public hospital in the kingdom. It also houses the primary morgue in the country. Already on the second day of protests, a medical tent was set up on the Pearl Roundabout and was run by SMC medical personnel on a volunteer basis.

The BNS issued a statement declaring their support for the protests, but that it was against their ethics to go on strike. According to Rula Al-Safar, the former President of the BNS, they supported the protests not only out of political convictions, but out of their concern for the safety and well-being of the population as medical professionals. Approximately 90 percent of the BNS members were women.[4]

Tuesday, February 22 saw what is believed to have been the largest demonstration since the beginning of the uprising; it is estimated that one out of every four or five Bahrainis took part in the demonstration that day. The percentage of the adult population who participated was even higher.[5] In one of his first concessions, King Hamad agreed to pardon 308 individuals who had been convicted of crimes relating to state security, including several leading opposition figures. On February 26, the Minister of Health was removed and replaced by Dr. Nazer Al Baharna. The government then demanded that Al Wefaq make concessions in return. However, the opposition leaders declined, "citing their inability to control the streets" (Bassiouni 2011: 168).

The GFBTU threw its weight behind the demands for a constitutional monarchy. Sayed Salman Jaffar Al Mahfoodh, the secretary-general of the General Federation of Bahrain Trade Unions, said that opposition demands—including the introduction of a constitutional monarchy—were "genuine and should be looked at carefully."[6] Confident of their increasing strength, the GFBTU threatened another general strike, as reported in the *Financial Times* on February 24: "If the government doesn't fulfill its promise of genuine dialogue then we will call for a general strike." This was still just ten days after the outbreak of protests. For the time being, however, the GFBTU decided to hold back.

The Second General Strike and the Intervention of the Gulf Cooperation Council

By March 8, a "Coalition for a Bahraini Republic" was formed which declared their intention to march on the royal palace in Al-Rifah. They were going to leave the Pearl Roundabout, the Salmaniya hospital, and other protest sites and march on the palace itself. Although the majority of the opposition, including Al Wefaq, did not condone the march, this was nevertheless an indication that sections of the opposition had become further radicalized.

On March 13, the Crown Prince offered the "7 Principles," but by this point the opposition had lost all faith in the willingness of the government to carry out genuine reforms. On the same day the GFBTU issued a statement calling for a second general strike in Bahrain. A precarious unity had been achieved between the political groupings and the labor movement. The GFBTU had called for a second general strike, and the Coalition for a Republic had announced their support for it. One day later, about 5000 troops from Saudi Arabia and the United Arab Emirates staged a military intervention in Bahrain. Kuwait dispatched its naval forces to patrol the waters around the kingdom. The intervention came just one day after a visit by former US Defense Secretary Gates. Although no fatalities were recorded between February 18 and March 14, the ruling family created a narrative that described the events during the first half of March as representing an "escalation" and a "gravely deteriorated state of law and order," hence necessitating the intervention of foreign troops (Bassiouni 2011: 165).

After the intervention by Saudi Arabia and the UAE, the Salmaniya hospital was partly taken under control by the Bahraini military (Bassiouni 2011: 171). The tent on the Pearl Roundabout was again cleared by security forces. Given the influx of foreign troops, the declaration of a state of emergency, and the generalized chaos that ensued, it is difficult to know with certainty how many people participated in the general strike in order to put pressure on the regime, and how many simply stayed home due to fear of being arrested, or the impossibility of passing road blocks. One industry that was affected was BAPCO, a state-owned oil refinery that produces 250,000 barrels of oil per day. It was reported that absenteeism of BAPCO employees on March 16–17 was about 60 percent. On March 21, the *Financial Times* reported that production had slumped as low as 32,000 barrels a day.[7] Standard & Poor's downgraded Bahrain's credit rating from A- to BBB, the lowest investment grade rating. The fact that this happened, despite the $10 billion in aid that Gulf states were offering, indicates how the economy had suffered from the unrest.

On Sunday March 20, in what can only be seen as a remarkable act of defiance—as the country was now occupied by foreign militaries—the trade union federation announced that it would indefinitely extend the general strike. The Secretary General of the union announced, "Workers are scared to go out to work as there are checkpoints everywhere and in some cases they are questioned unnecessarily by authorities" (Bassiouni 2011: 155). Then on Tuesday, March 22, the GFBTU announced the suspension of the strike. A statement issued by the union clarified that it had made the decision on the basis of assurances from senior officials that assaults against workers would cease, and that their harassment in the workplace would not be allowed (Bassiouni 2011: 156).

The Royals Retaliate

Propped up by Saudi, Emirati, and Kuwaiti security forces—and US acquiescence—the regime then proceeded to engage in collective punishment against those who had participated in the uprising. It punished the teachers who took part in the general strike for not working, and it punished the nurses who continued to work and provide medical services. Rula Al Safar, the president of BNS, and Jalila Al Salman, the deputy president of BTA, shared a prison cell for five months in the Isa Town Women's

Detention Center. Both were tortured. Both were tried in military courts. And both were fired from their positions. At the time of writing, neither of them has been rehired.

Understanding the Bahraini Labor Movement's Dual Refusal

The mass strike is a rare moment of collective defiance, an extraordinary occurrence. By contrast, the provision of medical services is an ordinary, everyday practice, usually not considered a form of defiance at all, but simply the compliance with norms of medical professionalism. During a general strike, workers refuse to work. During the provision of medical aid, doctors and nurses refuse to stop working, in order to care for the injured or dying. James Scott (1985) believed that open defiance was more likely to provoke a "ferocious response" from authorities than "everyday forms of resistance." He also bemoaned that scholars were more attracted to the uncommon moments of insurrection than more commonplace types of resistance, which was what happened in-between rebellions. I have argued here that the 2011 repertoire of contention in Bahrain included both. The Bahraini trade union federation led two general strikes during the first month of the anti-regime uprising. The mass strike was called in part out of solidarity with the medical workers who the government had prevented from caring for the injured. In other words, the GFBTU withheld their labor power (in part) in order to allow the medical workers to provide their labor power, who were not taking part in the strike. The "everyday forms of medical provision" did not happen in between rebellions, but were essential during every day of the uprising. Jalila Al-Salman led the teachers who extended their strike even after the GFBTU had called off the general strike. Rula Al-Safar led the nurses in caring for the wounded. The teachers refused to work. The nurses refused to stop working. Jalila and Rula paid a high price: they both lost their jobs, they were both subjected to torture.

The ruling family may never disclose what exactly prompted them to call upon Saudi Arabia, the United Arab Emirates, and Kuwait to send their security forces across the border and protect their palaces. However, the regime's ferocious response—against both forms of labor activism—speaks for itself. As Bahrainis continue to work on the revolution, scholars should be attuned to both forms of labor activism: the teachers and all other employees who refused to work and participated in the general strike, and the nurses and all others who refused to stop working, and contributed to saving lives, caring for the wounded, and sustaining the movement.

Notes

1 After the Khalifa migrated to Bahrain in 1798, their status as rulers of the island was secured by the British in the General Treaty of 1820.

2 Interview with member of the GFBTU central committee, Manama, Bahrain, November 2014.
3 Interview with Jalila al-Salman, Vice President of the Bahrain Teachers' Association in Manama, Bahrain, November 2014.
4 Interview with Rula al-Safar, President of Bahrain Nursing Society in Manama, Bahrain, November 2014.
5 According to the 2010 census, Bahrain has a population of 1,234,571. Of these, 568,399 are Bahraini citizens, or 46 percent of the total.
6 http://www.ft.com/intl/cms/s/0/0a0b7066-4033-11e0-9140-00144feabdc0.html#axzz2yi7OoIXO
7 "Protests take economic toll on Bahrain," *Financial Times*, March 21, 2011.

References

Bassiouni, M. C. (2011), "Report of the Bahrain Independent Commission of Inquiry," Manama, Bahrain. http://www.bici.org.bh/BICIreportEN.pdf

Bayat, A. (2010), *Life as Politics: How Ordinary People Change the Middle East*, Stanford, CA: Stanford University Press.

International Crisis Group (2011), *Popular Protests in North Africa and the Middle East III: The Bahrain Revolt*, Brussels: International Crisis Group.

Langohr, V. (2014), "Labor Movements and Organizations," in M. Lynch (ed.), *The Arab Uprisings Explained: New Contentious Politics in the Middle East*, 180–200, New York, NY: Columbia University Press.

Matthiesen, T. (2013), *Sectarian Gulf: Bahrain, Saudi Arabia, and the Arab Spring that Wasn't*, Stanford, CA: Stanford University Press.

Noueihed, L. and A. Warren (2012), *The Battle for the Arab Spring: Revolution, Counter-revolution and the Making of a New Era*, New Haven: Yale University Press.

Scott, J. C. (1985). *Weapons of the Weak: Everyday Forms of Peasant Resistance*, New Haven, CT: Yale University Press.

Shawkat al-atibbā. (2013). *miḥnat al-kādir al-ṭibbī fī thawrat al-Baḥrayn* [Thorn of doctors: The medics ordeal in the Bahrain revolution]. al-Baḥrayn: Mir'āt al-Baḥrayn.

Silver, B. J. (2003), *Forces of Labor: Workers' Movements and Globalization since 1870*, Cambridge: Cambridge University Press.

Ulrichsen, K. C. (2014), "Bahrain's Uprising: Domestic Implications and Regional and International Perspectives," in F. A. Gerges (ed.), *The New Middle East: Protest and Revolution in the Arab World*, 332–50, New York, NY: Cambridge University Press.

Yom, S. L. and F. G. Gause III (2012), "Resilient Royals: How Arab Monarchies Hang on," *Journal of Democracy*, 23: 74–88. doi:10.1353/jod.2012.0062

Zemni, S., B. D. Smet and K. Bogaert (2013), "Luxemburg on Tahrir Square: Reading the Arab Revolutions with Rosa Luxemburg's 'The Mass Strike'," *Antipode*, 45: 888–907. doi:10.1111/j.1467-8330.2012.01014.x

Ten Years On: Assessing the Outcomes of the Arab Spring for Bahraini Women

by Magdalena Karolak

This chapter assesses the aftermath of the 2011 uprising in the Kingdom of Bahrain looking specifically through the gender lens. The so-called Arab Spring that began in Bahrain with the occupation of the Pearl Roundabout on February 14, 2011, was the culmination of the disenchantment of some segments of the society with the scope of the political liberalization reforms carried out at the beginning of 2000s. Large-scale activism continued till 2017, a year of the final crackdown on the opposition groups that finally cemented the authoritarian status quo. The roles of women in these events and the changes to their status in the aftermath of the uprisings in the Arab world are subject to debate and the perceptions of the progress are certainly nonlinear and must take into account a variety of factors. Women participated alongside men in political movements and were actively involved in shaping the outcomes of these processes, but their political demands were broader than gender rights. Nonetheless, some movements that called for democracy and reforms in the Arab world were staunchly patriarchal and promoted a traditional reading of the gender roles; while, some authoritarian governments engaged for years in state feminism and pushed gender-related reforms, at times, against the public opinion in their respective countries. In addition, women's status is not uniform, but cuts across the social class, wealth, education, religion, and sect. The changes with regard to gender status that occurred in the aftermath of the Arab uprisings are thus multifaceted.

In Bahrain, women from all backgrounds participated in anti-government and pro-government rallies and sit-ins alongside men. The uprising in Bahrain stands out since it was almost unavoidable not to analyze it in sectarian terms. Although the protesters strongly declined against identifying themselves as a Shi'a movement and they were also supported by Sunni pro-reformers, the unfolding events led to a polarization of the society that accentuated sectarian belongings. Nonetheless, with the elimination of the opposition from the political system and the final crackdown on protesters, the de facto return to authoritarianism has created some new venues for women empowerment. The outcomes of the latter are shaped by those who are loyal to the regime and thus, can and are willing to participate in the system, as well as by the state feminism agendas deployed often from above. The following overview presents the extent of the reforms in relation to women before the uprising as well as in its aftermath to analyze why the failure of the revolutionary movement pushed women's rights on the agenda and led to further increase of their participation in the society, especially in politics.

Women and the Political Liberalization Reforms

Liberalization reforms carried out by King Hamad bin Isa Al Khalifa in the early 2000s marked what seemed to be a major shift in the Bahraini politics, and that is especially visible with regard to women's rights. Female empowerment has been always proclaimed an important goal in the agenda of the government. To begin with, women were provided with universal suffrage rights proclaimed in 2002 and that in spite of 60 percent of the Bahraini women opposing this decision (Janardhan 2005). Furthermore, the commitment to women's rights was stressed through the creation of the Supreme Council for Women [SCW] in 2001, a quasi-governmental body advisory to the king, headed by the king's first wife Sheikha Sabika bint Ibrahim Al Khalifa. The council is dedicated to, among others, fostering inclusion of women in the decision-making positions, improving skills of women, creating job opportunities, conducting studies, as well as organizing awareness campaigns aimed at women. Among the many tasks, SCW has been overseeing the implementation of the provisions of the Convention on Elimination of All Forms of Discrimination Against Women (CEDAW) agreement, within the limits of the sharia. The other important initiative is the National Strategy on the Empowerment of Bahraini Women, conducted with the support of United Nations Development Programme (UNDP). It included programs on enhancing economic and political empowerment of women carried out over the years 2009–12. Moreover, SCW carried out a strong campaign to support the unified personal status law and subsequently, implementation of the law for the Sunni branch of Islam. The council promoted female empowerment in three main areas, namely, economic, political, and within the family.

Economic empowerment of women is part of the "Bahrain Economic Vision 2030," a broad initiative of development of the country unveiled in 2008. Oil depletion as well as soaring unemployment rates among Bahraini nationals demanded a shift in policies related to job market strategy. Sustainable development independent from oil resources and competitiveness are a must for future growth of the GCC region overall. Given the fact that women account for 70 percent of all university graduates (BEDB 2009), Bahraini authorities saw women's rising education attainments as a resource for the country's development (SCW, n.d.). Tamkeen, an employment agency developed under the umbrella of the government, promotes greater inclusion of Bahrainis in the economy through multiple initiatives. It provides job training as well as employment programs in cooperation with Bahraini-based companies, scholarships, funding for enterprises, and skill improvement programs. Tamkeen adopted in collaboration with SCW a special approach to increase female employability, including increasing the number of women in male-dominated fields of economy. This comes as an important step given that women constituted the majority of the unemployed. In 2009 and 2010 women made up roughly 80 percent of the unemployed (Al Gharaibeh 2011). Economic advances in Bahrain were strengthened by female business activity. Eased procedures that allowed women to process all paperwork themselves instead of male representatives boosted female entrepreneurship (Ahmed 2010). In 2008 more than one third of Bahraini businesses were owned by women (Gender Gulf 2008).

Women's participation in politics would not have been possible without an active support of the Bahraini authorities. Apart from obtaining suffrage right as well as the right to stand for elections to the lower house of the Bahrain Parliament in 2002, women were appointed in prominent public offices. Cabinets in 2002 and 2006 included women as minister of health, minister of social affairs, and minister of culture and information. Women were also appointed in the Shura Council, the upper chamber of the Parliament. Moreover, women represented Bahrain on an international scene. In 2000, the first Bahraini woman Sheikha Haya Rashed Al Khalifa became a Bahraini ambassador. She was subsequently elected a president of the UN General Assembly. In 2004 women were appointed in the GCC Consultative Corporation. However, these symbolic nominations would not be sufficient to promote participation of women in society overall. Thus, before the 2006 and the 2010 parliamentary elections SCW conducted political empowerment programs providing women with training necessary skills as well as funding to support their political campaign. The goals of such initiatives included altering of social attitudes and stereotypes toward women as well as supporting participation of women in the Parliament and the Municipal Councils (Action Plan for Political Empowerment of Women 2002). Nonetheless, female candidates running in the elections were breaking an established social order, which caused tensions. In 2002 and in 2006 elections many female candidates felt a direct pressure to withdraw put on them by male candidates in electoral districts (Toumi 2006). Moreover, male candidates used traditional division of gender roles to discredit their female opponents and women were unable to secure the support of major political associations that are Islamic in nature. None of the Islamic associations endorsed female candidates. Till 2011, only one female candidate Latifa Al Qaoud was elected to the parliament in general elections in 2006 and again in 2010. Although she was the first woman MP elected in the GCC, she ran both times unchallenged and represented scarcely populated and remote islands of Al Hawar. The example of politics represents an area where there is strong resistance to change. Nonetheless, participation of women in elections had an important effect on the Bahraini society. In 2010 Latifa Salman a candidate in the municipal elections became the first Bahraini woman to win a seat in elections, while directly challenging a male candidate.

With regard to changes in the family sphere, Bahraini activists since the 1980s tried to exert pressure on the government to allow for the creation of a Personal Status Law to replace the traditional application of sharia that in many cases was detrimental to women. Since its establishment, SCW campaigned for a unified written law and took on a task to prepare a draft. Drafting the law created tensions between female activists and conservative clergy. The firm opposition of Shi'a scholars caused the draft committee to abandon the idea of a unified law in favor of a Sunni only version. Consequently, the first written law called Family Provision Act (Law 19/2009) passed in May 2009 applies to the Sunni sect. The law brought important regulations to protect rights of women related to marriage, divorce, and child custody. Within the marriage contract women can stipulate that they do not agree to their husbands marrying additional wives. Both parties can specify in the marriage contract terms and conditions related to family expenditures, housing as well as employment and education. Furthermore, the new law specified cases where women are rightfully entitled to seek divorce such as lengthy imprisonment of the husband, drug addiction, abandonment of the family, and lack of financial support as well as discord and harm between husband and wife. Moreover, judges are allowed to consult psychologists and social workers when ruling custody of children keeping in mind the best interest of child. The law entitles women granted custody of their children to entail housing provided by the father of children as well as to seek alimony. The court may also order DNA tests to establish parenthood. It is important to note however that the Family Provision Act does not establish equality between genders. A woman, for example, still requires the consent of a guardian to get married even though there are amendments to the role of the guardian in the marriage process. Similarly, the law makes a difference between divorces initiated by men and by women, since women have to provide legal grounds to ask for it. The effects of this law are also limited by the fact that it applies to the Sunni sect only. Shi'a sharia courts continue exercising jurisdiction based on the traditional interpretation of the Islamic law.

These reforms were supported by the local media that for most have close links to the government. Newspapers devoted several articles to present female candidates in the national elections and closely follow their campaigns. Similarly, women who break into the traditionally male-dominated jobs, such as female judges or female pilot were highly praised and draw a lot of attention. Despite these important improvements, empowerment of women is hindered by a number of obstacles, which stem mostly from long-standing traditions and gender stereotyping. On the other hand, female activists in the opposition have accused governmental agencies of lack of progress in advancing political empowerment (Hameed 2006). The criticisms include, among others, lack of transparency and standards used in appointment of women to high offices lack of a plan for consistent promotion of female leaders in other areas (The Shadow Report 2008) as well as lack of the above-mentioned personal status law.

The 2011 Uprising and Its Aftermath

Political liberalization experiment in the Kingdom of Bahrain reveals shortcomings in the outcomes of this process. The promising achievement of the reforms, marked by the turn to a constitutional monarchy on February 14, 2002, was undermined by a social upheaval that began on its anniversary in 2011, and ultimately a steady return to authoritarianism cemented in 2017. In the early 2000s, the opposition groups were initially pleased with the announcement of the sweeping political reforms. Nonetheless, the initial euphoria soon turned into disappointment given their limited scope. A parliament was re-established but as a bicameral body, with only the Council of Representatives, the lower house, elected in universal suffrage. In comparison to the Constitution of 1973, the role of the parliament was reduced. The upper house of the parliament, appointed directly by the king, would approve bills proposed by the lower house before they were implemented. Moreover, the king would have the right to veto all bills. The various protest movements that emerged already after the proclamation of the reforms in 2002 culminated in the large-scale movement underpinned by the Arab Spring revolts in the region. Monarchy has been able to gather strong support among the Sunnis in Bahrain, and ultimately, due to the sectarian split, is perceived as a shield against growing Shi'a political ambitions in the region supported by Iran. Although female participation was considerable throughout the period of the uprising, it was marked by a growing sectarian split that divides the Bahraini society until today. While it is clear that "women must themselves advocate for equal rights" (Social Watch 2009), only a minority of female activists petitioned for women's rights during the uprising. Despite the fact that social unrest was contained in March 2011 and the protests that continued in the years 2011–17 were ultimately repressed, some venues for female empowerment emerged through the state-led initiatives.

Despite reforms carried out before 2011, women still have faced multiple impediments with regard to their status. Even though Bahrain adopted progressive legislation that guarantees equality of genders, Bahraini women cannot pass citizenship on their foreign husbands and on their children born from such marriages. Secondly, the Labour Act (Decree No. 23 of 1976) guarantees equality of all employees; however, women tend to be discriminated in the labor market with regard to remuneration as well as promotion opportunities. Nonetheless, labor laws "do not prohibit or provide protections against gender-based discrimination in the workplace" (Al Najjar 2009). On average, a Bahraini woman earned 76 percent of the income of a male worker performing a similar job (The Global Gender Report 2010). Thirdly, violence against women was not prosecuted due to the perception of violence being the traditional right of men to discipline the women. Finally, Islamic sharia law governs inheritance and treats both genders separately. Women may inherit from fathers, mothers, brothers, husbands, and children; however, women's shares are significantly smaller than the men. Some of these limitations were discussed during a series of debates initiated by the king in July 2011 known as the National Dialogue. The aim of the debates was to forge a compromise on the most prominent political, economic, social, and human rights issues among different groups in the Bahraini society in the aftermath of the uprising. The role of the opposition in the dialogue was greatly reduced to 35[1] out of 300 participants, with the major opposition party Al Wefaq ultimately pulling out of the debates. On the other hand, the dialogue included a number of NGOs. Twelve women associations were involved in the talks. The results of the National Dialogue were formed into recommendations to be approved and implemented at a later stage. The participants acknowledged the importance of strengthening women's rights. Firstly, demands were made to guarantee greater protection for women against violence, equal rights in the workplace, and political and economic empowerment. Secondly, a recommendation was made to allow women to pass the Bahraini nationality on their children born from mixed marriages. Finally, a thorough review of salaries of female workers in the private sector was urged. In the last decade, some of these recommendations did take shape. Among the most notable, the anti-violence law, Law No. 17 of 2015 on Protection against Domestic Violence, was adopted in 2015. It provides protection for women against psychological, physical, and sexual violence, but fell short of criminalizing spousal rape. Secondly, Equal Opportunities Units have been set up in governmental organizations and in some large private companies to promote equal work opportunities between men and women. Citizenship and inheritance have proved to be areas with most resistance to change. So far, Bahraini women are allowed to pass the citizenship onto their children only in case when the father was either unknown or paternity was not legally proven. Foreign husband cannot obtain the Bahraini citizenship through marriage with a Bahraini woman. As an ad hoc measure, in 2011, citizenship was conferred on 335 children of Bahraini women married to non-Bahrainis by Royal Order. Further discussions about the extension of citizenship rights have not been conclusive (Toumi 2017), while inheritance laws have not been discussed in a public forum.

Ultimately, the aftermath of the uprising brought changes in the participation of women in electoral politics. The subsequent parliamentary elections testify to major shifts in the female candidates' probability of getting elected as MPs. Since 2002, women have had passive and active suffrage rights, yet their ability to get elected has drastically improved in the aftermath of the uprising as visible in Table 9.1.

In addition to the female success in the parliamentary elections, women also performed with increased confidence in municipal elections. In 2010, one woman was elected to the municipal council, which marks the first win of a woman running against a male opponent. In 2014, the number of female councilors increased to three, and in 2018 to four. Female success in electoral politics in Bahrain is due to a combination of factors with the demise of major political associations, the largest of them being the opposition society Al Wefaq,[2] but also, changes to the perceptions of female involvement in the public sphere as a result of their engagement in the uprising, among others (Karolak 2021). Finally, the strategies of containment in the aftermath of the uprising opened up opportunities for women loyalist to the regime, independently of their sectarian belonging, to participate more broadly in the political system.

Table 9.1 Women in the Bahraini Parliament (re-est. in 2002): Lower House

Year	Women running as candidates	Women in elected seats (out of forty total)
2002	Thirty-one female contestants, two females in runoffs	0 (0%)
2006	Eighteen female contestants	One winning by default (2.5%) running unopposed
2010	Seven female contestants	One winning by default (2.5%) running unopposed
2011 (by-elections)	Four female contestants	One continuing + three elected: two winning by default and one against a male opponent (10%)
2014	Twenty-three female contestants; six made it to runoffs [266 total candidates]	Three winning against male opponents (7.5%)
2018	Forty-one female contestants [293 total candidates]	Six winning; two winning in the first round (15%); first female parliamentary speaker elected by fellow MPs

Source: M. Karolak

All in all, the uprising has had the effect of strengthening the progress of women's rights in areas that do not challenge the establishment. In addition, those loyal to the regime may be co-opted and participate to a higher degree in the initiatives directed from above and in electoral politics.

Conclusion

This chapter aimed at presenting the progress in the area of women's rights in Bahrain taking into account the uprising as a major event in the modern history of the kingdom. While the aftermath of the uprising marks a return to authoritarian policies, it strengthened the state feminism agendas that were already set in place before the social unrest took place. The elimination of the opposition from the political system allowed the regime and its followers to singlehandedly shape the outcomes of the policies regarding women. The lessons of the Arab Spring show, nonetheless, an ambiguity of female empowerment in the Middle East in the aftermath of the uprisings. Women backing the democratic movements may find themselves marginalized after the political changes have taken place. Ultimately, revolutionary movements can result in greater influence of men in the public sphere. Female presence may get severely diminished. Even though women played important roles during the changes, they may be forced back into the shadows. The Egyptian experience is illustrative of this dilemma. The military council annulled the parliamentary quota of compulsory sixty-four women MPs in the Egyptian Parliament. Consequently, the number of female MPs dropped to nine as a result of the 2011–12 elections. It is thus paradoxical that the pro-democracy movements may not be able to secure women's rights but lead to a regression of female empowerment instead. Similarly, in Iraq, the transitional phase to democracy increased, rather than decreased, the prevalence of gender inequality (Social Watch 2009). In Bahrain, the pro-reform groups have also failed to address any female-related issues or to make promises to its female supporters despite a large participation of women during the uprising. Consequently, the state and its supporters can claim the full credit for the progress of women's rights in the kingdom internally and on the international arena.

Notes

1 Opposition sources claim that some of the invited leaders were at that time in prison.
2 Banned and dissolved in 2016.

References

Action Plan for Political Empowerment of Women (2002), http://www.undp.org.bh/Files/APW/46688.pdf (accessed January 6, 2011).
Ahmed, D. A. A. (2010), *Women's Rights in the Middle East and North Africa: Bahrain*, Washington, DC: Freedom House.
Al Gharaibeh, F. (2011), "Women's Empowerment in Bahrain," *Journal of International Women's Studies*, 12 (3): 96–113.
Al Najjar, S. (2009), *Bahrain*, Washington, DC: Freedom House.
Bahrain Economic Development Board (BEDB) (2009), "Bahrain Leads the Way in Building Capabilities of Women." www.bahrainedb.com (accessed January 6, 2010).
The Economist (April 10, 2008), "Gender Gulf.", https://www.economist.com/finance-and-economics/2008/04/10/gender-gulf (accessed January 12, 2011).
The Global Gender Gap 2010 Report (2010). Geneva: World Economic Forum.
Hameed, T. K. (July 9, 2006), "Stop Paying Lip-Service to Rights for Women," *Gulf Daily News*.
Janardhan, N. (June 20, 2005), "In the Gulf Women Are Not Women's Friends," *The Daily Star*.
Karolak, M. (2021), "Authoritarian Upgrading and the 'Pink Wave': Bahraini Women in Electoral Politics," *Contemporary Arab Affairs*, 14 (3), pp. 79–104.
Social Watch (2009), "*Women's Empowerment: A Misunderstood Process.*" http://www.socialwatch.org/node/858 (accessed March 28, 2012).

The Shadow Report on Implementation of the Convention on the Elimination of All Forms of Discrimination Against Women (CEDAW). (2008). http://www2.ohchr.org/english/bodies/cedaw/docs/ngos/Bahrainwomenunion42.pdf (accessed March 1, 2011).

Supreme Council for Women, n.d., *Statistics on Bahraini Women*. www.scw.bh (accessed July 18, 2005).

The Global Gender Gap 2010 Report (2010). Geneva: World Economic Forum.

Toumi, H. (November 27, 2006), "Islamists Hail Huge Election Victory," *Gulf News*.

Toumi, H. (August 11, 2017), "New Hope for Children Born to Foreign Fathers in Bahrain." *Gulf News*. https://gulfnews.com/world/gulf/bahrain/new-hope-for-children-born-to-foreign-fathers-in-bahrain-1.2071264 (accessed December 10, 2020).

IV SYRIAN WAR AND REFUGEES

Extractive Landscapes: The Case of the Jordan Refugee Compact

by Julia Morris

Since the Syrian conflict, over six million people have been displaced (UNHCR 2018). As the crisis has continued into protracted stages, wealthy governments in the Global North have moved away from humanitarian resettlement responses toward funding development projects in regions that neighbor the conflict. By financing less-developed countries, European governments in particular are looking to reduce transit migration from those countries and prevent the arrival of migrants across their borders through foreign investment and trade. Meanwhile, major refugee host states in the Global South have leveraged their proximity to sites of mass displacement in order to negotiate self-serving policies.

Jordan holds the third-largest population of registered Syrian refugees in the region at 671,428 people, but second in demographic ratio of Syrians in the country.[1] Within the wider refugee-development policy trend, the government of Jordan, the European Union (EU), and the World Bank signed the US$1.7 billion Jordan Compact in February 2016, a landmark political declaration. The Compact was designed to transform the challenges of hosting such a significant number of Syrian refugees into a development opportunity for Jordan, while also improving the livelihoods of both Jordanians and the country's Syrian refugee population. The deal combines humanitarian and development funding with pledges of US$700 million in grants to Jordan annually for three years and concessional loans of $1.9 billion. Payment of grants and loans is linked to specific targets. One of these targets is to expand access to the formal labor market for Syrian refugees by issuing 200,000 work permits in specified sectors and support Syrian education through the Accelerating Access to Quality Formal Education plan. The Compact also stipulates that Jordan will institute reforms to improve the business and investment environment and formalize Syrian businesses. In exchange, Jordan would

---

This chapter is reprinted in an abridged format from its original version, Morris, J., "Extractive Landscapes: The Case of the Jordan Refugee Compact," *Refuge: Canada's Journal on Refugees* 37 (2) (2020): 87–96. I thank the *Refuge* editorial team for permitting its use here.

be offered considerable financial support and the opening up of tariff-free trade in the European market to Jordanian goods. Unemployment in Jordan stands at 18.2 percent (around double that for youth) and 14.4 percent in poverty (World Bank 2018). Tying economic incentives directly to work opportunities for refugees attempts to open the job market to Syrians and Jordanians. It is also a means for the Jordanian government to create new economic opportunities by encouraging more international aid to be channeled into the country.

This chapter considers employment programs focused on Syrian refugees in Jordan, on the basis of my empirical findings in the field. Although refugee employment is significantly promoted by organizations like the World Bank and the EU, behind the headlines, the Jordan Compact has been widely considered a failure. In nongovernmental and state reporting, and in migration studies scholarship, a critical body of literature has been produced on the Jordan Compact in recent years (Barbelet et al. 2018; Lenner and Turner 2019). In these studies, the work permit process is found to be complex and time-consuming, with many employers continuing to employ refugees without permits. My findings expand upon this research into the impact of economic policies on migrants' and refugees' subjectivities and Syrian refugee policies focused on employment in particular. I argue that refugee employment efforts are better understood through a framework centered on extractivism: an analytic I have advanced elsewhere to document and critically theorize the expansion of mining sectors into domains of human resources, such as migrants and refugees (Morris 2019a). Extractivism is a mode of accumulation, with deep roots in colonial and imperial endeavors, whereby natural resources are removed at a high intensity for export markets. As a method of colonial appropriation, extractivism has been essential in the industrial development and prosperity of the Global North at the expense of poorer countries, particularly in the Global South (Jacka 2018). The exploitation of raw minerals has also enabled wealthy networks of transnational elites, and the domination of corporations and non-governmental organizations to move into ever-growing resource frontiers globally. Here, capitalist values have encroached into new forms of extractive intrusion that amount to extracting value(s) from humans, whereby countries in the Global South strategically capitalize on the value of refugee hosting and/or containment.

This chapter starts by presenting the particularities of the Jordanian context, placing the country's newest "trade deal" within past national economic development projects and experiences of hosting refugees. I then turn to examine the characteristics of and challenges faced by employment programs in Jordan, detailing how extractive logics have overtaken refugees' well-being. I close by placing the Jordan Compact within a system of globalized production, in which forms of value circulate outside of Jordan at the expense of refugees' immobility. Overall, I find that these policies formalize precariousness, allowing the international community to abdicate global responsibility and reap the benefits of a purported altruism.

Oil Turned Refugee Economies

The Jordan Compact is best understood locally within the Hashemite Kingdom's extractive history and economic dependencies. Jordan has long depended on the support of outside powers such as Great Britain, the United States, and oil-rich Arab states for its economic and political well-being (Piro 1998). Even after independence in 1946, from its establishment as a British protectorate, Jordan's finances remained guided by the British government. But in the 1950s and 1970s, Jordan shot up economically as a result of remittances received from migration to neighboring oil-rich countries. Jordanian workers flocked to Gulf states to work the oil fields as skilled laborers and in professional positions such as engineers, bankers, and teachers (Ryan 1998). The kingdom relied increasingly on these Gulf connections as a source of Jordanian employment, labor remittances, and considerable Arab foreign aid to Jordan. Jordan was viewed as a frontline state in the conflict with Israel, with some 500,000 Palestinians taking refuge in the country following the Arab-Israeli war of 1948, and then subsequent annexation of the West Bank in 1949, which almost trebled the population (Peters and Moore 2009).

In turn, the discovery of phosphate in Jordan in 1908 and later establishment of mining from 1935 through the Trans-Jordan Phosphate Company grew a successful resource extractive industry for the country. The Arab Potash Company was later developed in 1956 to harvest minerals in the Dead Sea, with potassium phosphate and potassic fertilizers remaining the top exports of Jordan to this day. As many Jordanians left to work in the Gulf, increasing numbers of migrant workers moved to Jordan, predominantly from Egypt and Southeast Asia to fill demand for low-wage workers in domestic work, agriculture, construction, and service industries. Thus, low-skilled immigration simultaneously heightened Jordanians' status via a job-ladder effect, and foreign labor became part of the clientelist redistribution of assets to citizens (De Bel-Air 2016). But by the 1980s Jordan's economy began to struggle with low productivity and high unemployment rates. The Iranian Revolution in 1979, the Iran-Iraq War (1980–8), and later Gulf War (1990–1) upset regional oil production rates, resulting in declining labor remittances and Arab bilateral aid to Jordan. This coincided with the establishment of higher government spending by the kingdom's economic planners. Increasing shortfalls in the national budget spurred Jordan onto a greater level of borrowing. With the decline in remittances and aid, Jordan's national debt steadily rose, until by 1988 the country's debt was twice its gross domestic product (GDP).

From this point, Jordan's relationship with the International Monetary Fund (IMF) played a key part in guiding the country's trajectories, with an economic liberalization program in place since 1989 (Harrigan et al. 2006). Then Prime Minister Zayd al-Rifaai turned to the IMF and World Bank for assistance with Jordan's debt payments in a five-year plan for economic adjustment and stabilization, including dramatically cutting government expenditures. However, in Jordan the imposition of neoliberal economic policies since the 1980s has been accompanied by political instability and unrest. Economic adjustment programs removed a key source of welfare for the public, while simultaneously reducing government spending in major sectors (Baylouny 2008). When the government attempted to comply with IMF guidelines, austerity plans produced violent results, with riots spreading across the country in April 1989, August 1996, and June 2018. At times, the Hashemite regime backed down to comply with protestors, at others, they proceeded apace with few concessions.

Within this context of former colonial power relations and economic instability, refugees have played a major part in Jordan's development as forms of human, financial, and symbolic capital. The country has a history as a refugee host state far before it was formalized as state independent from British control in 1946 (Kelberer 2017). Since that time, Jordan has hosted displaced people from Iraq, Yemen, Sudan, Syria, and Palestine, as some of the more significant waves of refugees. According to UNHCR, Jordan ranked as the second-highest host to the largest number of refugees relative to national population in 2017, where one in fourteen people was a refugee under UNHCR's responsibility (UNHCR 2018). When including Palestine refugees under UNRWA's mandate, the figures rise to one in three for Jordan.

The Jordanian government has been astute about its negotiation of international aid through refugee policy. While Syrian refugees currently account for the largest group of refugees registered with UNHCR, Jordan also hosts over two million Palestinian refugees registered with UNRWA. The arrival of Palestinian refugees from 1948, followed by those who fled the Six-Day War in 1967 brought major challenges for the country (Chatelard 2010). Many of the official camps established for Palestinian refugees became enclaves for Palestinian militia and remain severely economically deprived. Yet Palestinian refugees contributed to the country's economic development in significant ways. First, they allowed Jordan to receive large amounts of development assistance from the international community to help resettle and integrate the refugees. Second, the remittances of those Palestinians who went to look for work in Persian Gulf states also helped develop Jordan's public and private sectors. These remittances, together with foreign aid, have contributed to developing sectors of the Jordanian economy by providing start-up money for Jordanian businesses and for large state-sponsored projects.

New opportunities have now emerged for Jordan as a country proximate to the Syrian conflict.[2] The Jordan Compact came about partially through the work of a Jordanian think tank, the West Asia-North Africa Institute (WANA), which submitted a White Paper to the Jordanian government on the potential contribution of Syrian refugees to the Jordanian economy. This was met by the work of Oxford economics and forced migration professors Alexander Betts and Paul Collier (2017), who widely endorsed pathways for Syrians into the Jordanian labor market.[3] At the time, the Jordanian government was already arguing that hosting Syrian refugees has harmed the country's development outcomes. In fact, the World Bank estimated in 2016 that the Jordan government had spent over $2.5 billion a year in direct costs for hosting

Syrian refugees since the onset of the crisis: 6 percent of GDP and 25 percent of the government's annual revenues (World Bank 2016). An increasingly right-wing political climate was also sweeping across Europe, with the EU seeking ways to manage, and halt, the numbers of refugees arriving at European borders. For European states, the Jordan Compact was a way to deter Syrian refugees from migrating to Europe by improving their livelihoods in Jordan. Meanwhile, Jordan was already heavily in debt. For the Jordanian government, the compact presented an opportunity for favorable trade arrangements with the EU (predicted to result in increased investment), in addition to an aid package and concessional loans.

This is what Victoria Kelberer (2017) describes as "refugee rentierism" or "the phenomenon of using host status and refugee policy as primary mechanisms of international rent-seeking." Through the bargaining power of refugees, Jordan was able to extract increased contributions from the international community, in much the same way as the €6bn ($6.8 billion) EU-Turkey deal, in which Turkey agreed to contain refugees within its borders: allegedly as many as three million refugees (Deutsche Welle 2018). However, whereas Turkey agreed to receive deported migrants in exchange for money and visa-free travel to the Schengen zone, the Jordanian government pledged to promote Syrian economic and social integration. Thus, in different ways, the Syrian "refugee boom" yielded new opportunities for Jordan to have access to labor markets and sources of foreign aid.

The next section turns to examine the grounded effects of the Compact in more detail, arguing that extractive logics have overtaken the social concerns of refugees' and migrants' well-being. The contemporary Jordanian strategy for acquiring international aid by hosting Syrian refugees comes at the very expense of the refugees that the project is nominally supposed to support.

Jordan Compact in Practice

I meet with Nadine in her handicraft store several floors up in a tall, nondescript office building, above a bank in a busy street in central Amman. In contrast to the grey exterior, inside the walls are brightly colored shelves heaved with handmade soaps, vials of rosewater, knitted children's toys, shawls, and crocheted table decorations, delicately wrapped in exquisite packaging. Several women wearing headscarves milled around from the end of a shift, all once from far-flung cities and villages across Syria. Nadine is one of the lucky ones as the co-owner of her own business, but not without struggles and perseverance. For Syrians, owning your own business is not an easy prospect. "Work permits, work permits" is a phrase we hear incessantly as Syrians frequently tell us about the complex bureaucratic process of acquiring one. For small business-owners like Nadine, obtaining a work permit is often Kafka-esque, and unsuccessful. There are two routes: either pay 50,000 Jordanian dinars (US$70,462) and partner with a local, or pay 200,000JOD (US$281,850) to be classified as an investor.

Nadine's story is relatively characteristic of others I have heard. She initially partnered with a local businessman to set up her handicraft store in Amman, but he took advantage of her precarious status as a foreign citizen and made off with the majority of her investment and stock—something she found was of little interest to local police, who chalked off the incident as little more than unfortunate. Luckily, before the Syrian conflict, Nadine had a successful business in Damascus. Savings, family connections in Europe, NGO grants, and the partnership of a Syrian cousin enabled her to reignite the small business. Now committed to helping those affected by the war, Nadine has over one hundred Syrian women on flexible contracts (some working from home) to help produce the beautifully packaged goods so intricately placed around her store: a far cry from when she first started in 2013 with five women in a dingy office space. Some of the women are widows, others successful young professionals unable to instrumentalize their skills in Jordan, a number have husbands still fighting in the war or curtailed from working by Jordan's strict immigration rules. "We work on our own terms here," she tells us, describing how the cooperative works to combat the demands of most available employment for Syrian refugees—concerns voiced by the NGO representative in the opening quote to this section. Instead, Nadine now sells products online and on social media, and even advertises through AirBnB Experiences to help guarantee a steady stream of revenue, bulking up her retail with soap-making workshops for tourists, wealthy Ammanites, and NGO workers.

Nadine's experience speaks to just some of the myriad difficulties encountered by Syrian refugees in Jordan. Although wrapped in discourses of innovation, the Jordan Compact has been marred by failures and uneven outcomes. The Compact had two major elements—the development of special economic zones or SEZs (industrial parks for manufacturing goods) and the issuing of work permits to Syrian refugees in specified sectors both in and out of the industrial export zones.[4] Besides development funding, Jordan was promised access to tariff-free trade with the EU, providing it issued at least 200,000 work permits to Syrians. While work permits were made widely available to Syrians from April 2016, by February 2017 only 38,516 permits were issued, the majority in agriculture and construction (Williams 2017). The government sought to meet its quotas by formalizing work in agriculture, construction, and manufacturing. But, according to local NGOs, many of the work permits in the agricultural sector were based on Syrian workers in the country prior to the conflict.

In reality, the Compact has created few if any new jobs, and instead redistributes some positions held by migrant Bangladeshis and Egyptians to Syrian refugees as preferential migrant workers, which helps meet formal targets of donors and implementing agencies. In fact, since January 2019, a Jordanian regulation disallowed UNHCR from certifying anyone except for Syrians as refugees. Meanwhile, although Syrian refugees are allowed to apply for work permits outside of the SEZs, they are barred from applying for some professions, such as engineering, medicine, law, teaching, driving, and hairdressing, for which they have previously been trained, but which are viewed as potentially taking opportunities from Jordanian workers.

Instead, jobs are in backbreaking sectors like garment manufacture, agriculture, and construction that are of little interest to the majority of the population, many just having been through the brutality of conflict and displacement. These jobs are unregulated and are at times rife with overtime physical abuse. The hours are punishingly long (a minimum of ten-hour shifts), wages low, and safety of little concern.

Several NGOs in Jordan have taken an interest in employer-matching programs to ensure more accountability of otherwise occluded business practices. However, these NGOs also hold their own work quotas—one organization I spoke with cited a "20,0000 refugees in employment scheme"—in addition to being understaffed and under-resourced. The drive to reach these sorts of employment targets by contracted NGOs calls into question their ability to act as employer watchdog enforcers. While the Jordanian government has made some changes to ease the work permit process for Syrian refugees, including waiving the work permit fee and prioritizing Syrian refugees over other foreign workers, Syrians continue to face extreme restrictions to employment. Not only do Syrians in Jordan face significant barriers in accessing decent, paid work, but a future Syria is at risk of what was so often described to me by refugees and advocates as "a lost generation," unused to core professions such as medicine, engineering, and education.

For many Syrians, there is little advantage to formalized employment. Instead, the rigid and bureaucratic labor market has resulted in widespread informal work. For some refugees I spoke with there is fear of losing access to UNHCR cash assistance or the chance of resettlement to a third country. "If we do lose our job we could end up without any income at all," Mohammad, a father of three pointed out, voicing the widespread concern that holding a work permit may make one ineligible for cash assistance, and thus unable to cover what a family needs to survive. As a result, refugees must choose between working informally at the risk of arrest and deportation or seeking unskilled work on a one-year working permit. Other refugees suggested that work permits might actually decrease their working conditions because their work permit sponsor exerts extreme controls over their mobility. Being reliant on precarious worker visas places workers in a position where they end up not voicing concerns, perhaps more exploitable and paid lesser wages—or are unaware of the labor standards that should be in place.

Some refugees prefer to remain under the radar rather than risk registering with a government they mistrust. "Sometimes authorities will make it hard for you even if you have papers," Mohammad continued. "They'll make trouble for you just because they feel like it. Nothing—paper or no paper—is really protection." Deportations of Syrians have indeed skyrocketed since 2016, with reports of more than 4,100 Syrians returned to Syria on the grounds that they pose potential security problems, including working without a permit, which is the most prominent reason for deportation in a context where workplace raids have become commonplace (Molnar 2017). It is not uncommon for Syrian refugees to register for work permits as protection from deportation. However, this is clearly counter to the aims of the Compact, which was presented as beneficial for Syrians. Given that refugees in camps have minimal freedom of movement outside, the "opportunity" to work in factories when they have little other option is certainly coercive.

What is clear from these findings is how the concerns of affected populations have been subsumed under the guise of "development." As James C. Scott (1999) famously showed, large-scale authoritarian plans misfire when they fail to integrate local, practical knowledge. In quickstep with this classic critique of development and humanitarian work, the majority of refugees in Jordan were not actively consulted in the Compact programs that affect their lives, nor were experts on the region, NGOs, and research centers in Jordan. Rather, the Compact reveals a high level of donor interest in presenting Jordan as a model of reform and globalization in the MENA region in order to allow for the continued management of refugees outside of Europe. At its core, the Compact aims to reduce the international migration of Syrians, but it should be recognized that migration is an essential part of people's future well-being that is actually an agent of development. Meanwhile, an overwhelming aid industry has grown in Jordan around Syrian refugees as major funding targets of development aid. For many service providers, there is little incentive in directly critiquing the Compact when it runs in opposition to the extraction of revenue.[5] The Compact itself provides little incentive for Jordan to implement the much-needed reforms for overhauling the business development landscape. Instead, the Jordanian government relies largely on the quick cash from the arrangement to kick-start their economy, often at the expense of the people the project is supposed to help.

Conclusion

This chapter has questioned whether employment programs in Jordan offer meaningful work for Syrian refugees or whether they are arrangements for extracting value. What was stark throughout my fieldwork was the many disadvantages for the Compact's perceived beneficiaries. Although presented by the international community through buzzwords like *innovation* and *self-reliance*, and helping refugees *help themselves*, my findings indicated that Syrian refugees (and non-Syrian refugee and migrant worker populations) in Jordan all too often end up in hazardous or precarious informal work in the quest for government and organizational gain. Indeed, the ramping-up of assistance operations has created thousands of jobs within the humanitarian response sector as well as numerous indirect jobs across other sectors. Yet while refugees are immobilized in Jordan, deprived of movement to wealthier countries with established resettlement systems, their immobility makes possible the mobility of value outside of Jordan's borders. Now, the spectacle of border-making generates a multitude of images and discursive formations that fuel anti-immigrant sentiments for European political and organizational profit (De Genova 2013). In the process, a range of actors can extract political, economic, and moral value while refugees' bodies stay in Jordan.

At the same time, the global visibility of arrangements like the Jordan Compact induces new policies to be taken up and embedded in different contexts. Migration studies scholars have identified a trend in asylum outsourcing and development projects as a means for states to shrink spaces of asylum and subvert international refugee law (Bloch and Schuster 2005). Nation states use financially struggling states to warehouse migrants and isolate them from asylum claims processes. Jordan is part of a fashion of geopolitical cooperation between wealthier former colonial states and poorer dependent ones around frontiering projects. In an age of refugee demonization, the Jordan Compact model is now being trialed for other countries as a "solution" for European countries keen to deter migrant and asylum seeker arrivals. Financing refugee-hosting capacities in countries viewed as ones of transit for migrants potentially seeking refuge in Europe have spanned locations such as Ethiopia, Lebanon, Mali, Nigeria, Niger, and Senegal. This tendency signifies a new form of extractive capitalism, which taps into forms of neo-colonial domination and asymmetric relations of dependency.

Notes

1 Turkey, Lebanon, Jordan, Iran, Pakistan, Uganda, Kenya, Ethiopia, Chad, and the Democratic Republic of Congo host the majority of the world's refugees. These statistics are obtainable from UNHCR, "2018 Total Persons of Concern."
2 Jordan has experienced economic benefits from the Syrian conflict; however, the proximity of the conflict has also had negative impacts on the country. See Parker-Magyar (2019).
3 Collier himself was an advisor at the WANA Institute and former director of the Development Research Group of the World Bank.
4 Jordan has a history of zonal development policies, which have offered duty-free and quota-free access to Jordanian companies for international markets. See Azmeh (2019).
5 As international investments have begun to decline, however, discussions have moved to the possibility of initiating formal returns projects for Syrian refugees in Jordan. See Morris (2019b).

References

Azmeh, S. (2019), "Labour in Global Production Networks: Workers in the Qualifying Industrial Zones (QIZs) of Egypt and Jordan," *Global Networks*, 14 (4): 495–513.
Barbelet, V., J. Hagen-Zanker, and D. Mansour-Ille (2018), *The Jordan Compact: Lessons Learnt and Implications for Future Refugee Compacts*, London: ODI.

Baylouny, A. M. (2008), "Militarizing Welfare: Neo-liberalism and Jordanian Policy," *Middle East Journal*, 62 (2): 277–303.

Betts, A. and P. Collier (2017), *Refuge: Rethinking Refugee Policy in a Changing World*, Oxford: Oxford University Press.

Bloch, A. and L. Schuster (2005), "At the Extremes of Exclusion: Deportation, Detention and Dispersal," *Ethnic and Racial Studies*, 28 (3): 491–512.

Chatelard, G. (2010), "Jordan: A Refugee Haven," Migration Policy Institute, August 31. https://www.migrationpolicy.org/article/jordan-refugee-haven.

De Bel-Air, F. (2016), "Migration Profile: Jordan," Migration Policy Centre Policy Brief, European University Institute.

Deutsche Welle (2018), "The EU-Turkey Refugee Agreement: A Review," https://www.dw.com/en/the-eu-turkey-refugee-agreement-a-review/a-43028295

De Genova, N. (2013), "Spectacles of Migrant 'Illegality': The Scene of Exclusion, the Obscene of Inclusion," *Journal of Ethnic and Racial Studies*, 36 (7): 1180–98.

Harrigan, J., H. El-Said, and C. Wang (2006), "The IMF and the World Bank in Jordan: A Case of Over Optimism and Elusive Growth," *Review of International Organizations*, 1: 263–92.

Jacka, J. K. (2018), "Environmental Impacts of Resource Extraction in the Mineral Age," *Annual Review of Anthropology*, 47: 61–77.

Kelberer, V. (2017), "Negotiating Crisis: International Aid and Refugee Policy in Jordan," *Middle East Policy*, 24 (4): 148–65.

Lenner, K. and L. Turner (2019), "Making Refugees Work? The Politics of Integrating Syrian Refugees into the Labor Market in Jordan," *Middle East Critique*, 28: 65–95.

Molnar, P. (2017), "Discretion to Deport: Intersections between Health and Detention of Syrian Refugees in Jordan," *Refuge*, 33 (2): 18–31.

Morris, J. (2019a), "Violence and Extraction of a Human Commodity: From Phosphate to Refugees in the Republic of Nauru," *Extractive Industries and Society*, 6 (4): 1122–33.

Morris, J. (2019b), "The Politics of Return from Jordan to Syria," *Forced Migration Review*, 62: 31–3.

Peters, A. and P. Moore (2009), "Beyond Boom and Bust: Eternal Rents, Durable Authoritarianism, and Institutional Adaptation in the Hashemite Kingdom of Jordan," *Studies in Comparative International Development*, 44: 256–85.

Piro, T. J. (1998), *The Political Economy of Market Reform in Jordan*, Lanham: Rowman & Littlefield.

Ryan, C. D. (1998), "Peace, Bread and Riots: Jordan and the International Monetary Fund," *Middle East Policy Council*, 6 (2): 54–66.

Scott, J. C. (1999), *Seeing Like a State: How Certain Schemes to Improve the Human Condition Have Failed*, New Haven: Yale University Press.

UNHCR, 2018, "Total Persons of Concern," https://data2.unhcr.org/en/situations/syria/location/36

Williams, S. E. (2017), "Jordan Looks to Turn Refugee Crisis into Economic Boon," *IRIN News*, March 21. https://www.irinnews.org/feature/2017/03/21/jordan-looks-turn-refugee-crisis-economic-boon.

World Bank (2016), "The Economic Effects of War and Peace," Middle East and North Africa Quarterly Economic Brief 6.

World Bank (2018), "Jordan's Economic Outlook—April 2018," https://www.worldbank.org/en/country/jordan/publication/economic-outlook-april-2018.

Schooling in an Environment of Uncertainties: The Case of Syrian Refugee Children in Turkey

by Çetin Çelik & Ahmet İçduygu

Introduction

Since the start of Syria's decade-long conflict, millions of refugees have fled to Syria's neighboring countries, more than a half of them sheltered in Turkey. As Turkey hosts over 3.7 million Syrian refugees today, making it the largest host of refugees in the world, their future is a key political, economic, and social concern to involved stakeholders. In the early years of the Syrian conflict, the policies toward Syrians in Turkey foresaw the temporariness of the refugees based on the presumption that the crisis would end, and the refugees would return home: they ensured full protection, upheld the principle of *non-refoulement*, and provided optimal humanitarian assistance in camps (İçduygu 2015; Kirişci 2016).

As the numbers increased over the years, Turkey increasingly adopted a non-encampment policy: today only less than 1 percent of them are in camps, while the remaining ones are spread throughout the country. Consequently, living in and mixing with the local populations in various neighborhoods, Syrian refugees have experienced a spontaneous integration process even though Turkey's ongoing refugee policies have not effusively targeted integration (İçduygu and Şimşek 2016). Over the last ten years, what is mainly observed is that these refugees have lived for the most part in very poor conditions. They had a precarious legal status, a wide range of exploitation in the huge informal employment sector, substandard housing, very limited access to education, and some access difficulties to health services.

While the conflict in Syria continues, local and national authorities in Turkey have already begun to consider some partial integration policies, particularly as neither the possibility of return nor the that of resettlement to third countries is seen as a viable option in the near future. For instance, in this context, Turkey first tended to provide a legal ground for Syrians to be classified as "persons under temporary protection" and then expansively anticipated the likelihood that protracted displacement would turn into long-term settlement. Concordantly, first a work permit system was introduced, and some naturalization opportunities were offered to selected Syrians. However, all these new policy efforts happened in an environment where one thing remains constant—continuing uncertainty (İçduygu and Sert 2019).

This chapter focuses on how the Turkish asylum regime has responded to the issues surrounding Syrian refugee integration by creating several administrative tools in the field of schooling of children over the last few years. The study draws on semi-structured in-depth interviews with eight parents from Syrian background, who came to Turkey between 2013 and 2017 from Syria and have children attending public schools and two Syrian teachers working in these schools. The interviewees were in Arabic and the recorded interview material was translated into English. The translated data were systematically subjected to procedures of summary (reducing the data to smaller parts), explication (formation of categories and coding rules), and structuring (extracting a consistent structure) (Mayring 2007). An earlier study, which utilized the same data, had already given a more detailed account of schooling question of Syrian children in Turkey in 2019 (Çelik and İçduygu 2019). By relying on our data, here we argue that well-established, comprehensive schooling policies are needed to cater to refugee children, not only first to provide for their immediate need for education, but also offer them the best possible education during these challenging times.

Syrians and Schooling in Turkey

The education of Syrian children is essential for their future employment and integration into the host society. Presently, more than 1,200,000 Syrians are in compulsory schooling age, between five and nineteen years old, and slightly over 50 percent of those attend schools (Mülteciler Derneği 2021). The fact that a high number of them do not have access to education yet clearly indicates the necessity of long-term public policies in this field.

The Syrian children mainly had two schooling options if they want to pursue their education in Turkey; they could either attend Temporary Education Centers, which provides education mostly by Syrian teachers in Arabic language and according to the Syrian curriculum (Save the Children 2015) or they could enroll into public schools, which deliver education by Turkish teachers in Turkish language and according to the Turkish curriculum. Currently, Temporary Education Centers have been shutdown. Since 2016, Syrian children and teenagers have been channeled into public schools to create a uniform educational program (MoNE 2016). Temporary Education Centers originated from the policies that addressed the Syrian refugees' situation in Turkey as temporary. Since they were thought to return within a short period of time, the Ministry of Education supported the implementation of the Arabic curriculum in the education of Syrian children, rather than teaching Turkish language and curriculum, particularly between 2012 and 2014 (Nur Emin 2016). While the policy of using Arabic language and curriculum was justified to minimize the problems Syrians may face when they return to Syria, it, as the then-minister of education clearly indicated in one of his speeches, actually intended to prevent Syrians from staying in Turkey for longer time (Dinçer 2012). Presently, for the Syrian children who have temporary education identity card and live outside the camps, public schools have gradually become main option since the curricular in 2014 (MoNE 2014). In the rest of this chapter, we rely on our empirical data to explore schooling of Syrian students in public schools.

Syrian Students in Public School System: Swimming in Unknown Seas

While the interviewees in this study varied in their perceptions and opinions about the quality of education provided in public schools, they all related these schools to their long-term plans of staying in Turkey. Once they embraced the idea of living in Turkey, they consider these schools as a key for their children to learn Turkish and integrate into Turkish educational system. Lamya, a mother of two girls who attend the same school, said that

> We all know how great the universities are here [in Turkey]. People are trying their best to learn the language so they can enrol in university. So that's why I want my kids to learn the Turkish language very well to enrol in these universities in the future.

Despite the theoretical match between attending public school and building a future in Turkey, the data suggested that both parents and students cannot find what they expected in the state school system. As noted earlier, Syrian parents mostly see these schools as the strongest medium of learning Turkish for their children. Yet, once their children start school, they fathom that they cannot monitor their children's educational performance due to the language difference, and that their children are stigmatized, bullied, and exposed to a curriculum, which is not cognizant of Syrian language and culture.

Schools have critical role in facilitating the adaptation of refuge youth into the host society and parent-school interaction is one of the major determinants of school-centered adaptation processes (McBrien 2011). To engage parents with school strongly, school should have ethos of inclusion, celebrate diversity, and promote positive image of refuge students (Taylor and Sidhu 2012). However, Turkish education system lacks these notions; the schools do not employ Syrian teachers nor use translators in Parent Teacher Meetings, which altogether makes Syrian parents' involvement with school nearly impossible. When asked how she was communicating with teachers in school and whether she attended Parent Teacher Meetings, a parent, Salam, who had previously sent her children to public school and then changed to Temporary Education Center remarked;

> Salam: I don't know much, just a few words [of Turkish]. I didn't even attend any parent meetings because I wouldn't understand anything. So, I didn't communicate with them that much. I tried to learn and recently I registered with Mr. Waleed to learn in this course. We took two or three lessons and then we stopped because the center was closed. So, they were calling us but I never went [to school].
> Researcher: Then, how did you follow up with her situation?
> Salam: She [my daughter] went once instead of me. She talked to the instructor there and told her that "I want to attend instead of my mum and dad, because they won't be able to understand anything". So, she went on behalf of us.

We glimpse, through what Salam says, a sense that attending a public school is almost a humbling experience for Syrian children and their parents; one that potentially makes them think their language and culture are devalued and that they are not warmly welcomed. Furthermore, the quote above exemplifies how monocultural school strengths parent-child role reversal among Syrian refugees. Migration is associated with a series of adaptation challenges such as housing, employment, education, and learning that put immense stresses on the family. As children often learn the new language faster than their parents, they are asked to act as translators in facing authorities. Research shows this causes role reversal between parents and children, and may undermine the authority of the parents and generate shame (Weisskirch 2010). Renzaho et al. (2011) for example studied the adaptation process of Arabic speaking migrants in Australia. They argued that the challenges they face cause a parent-child role reversal and state of disharmony in the family. This leads to distrust toward the legal system and the host society, as they perceive that these two entities undermine the core family dynamics and values. Our findings indicate that the exclusive language policy prepares grounds for undermining family values of Syrian refugees by causing role reversal - as exemplified in the quote above. This extremely painful process for parents undermines their authority and potentially leads to mental health problems (Oznobishin and Kurman 2009). It may also cause them to distrust the Turkish authorities, as it was the case for the Arabic-speaking families in Australia.

Salam's sentiments are widely held. They are reflected in another Syrian mother's words in a different way. Speaking of the registration process of her kids to school, she asserted:

> It was hard for us. We were scared to take this step because we didn't even try to integrate into the community and deal with the people here. We were simply just scared and we didn't know the language.

In both women's words, and those of the clear majority of the other parents we interviewed, we are presented with a sort of fear and anxiety as dominant feelings when it comes to contacting the school due to the exclusionary regulations and language policy.

Monocultural school not only undermines the capacity of the parents for monitoring their children's schooling and potentially weakens their authority but also disengages the students from school and depresses them. One parent, Zilal, described that her child felt sad because she could not follow the Turkish course in school; "She could not understand the verbal expressions (in school). They (the teachers) neglected her. She cried and suffered a lot in the classroom." The same parent added that her daughter was the only Syrian in the classroom;

> In that school, there weren't many Syrians. In the whole school, there were only 5 girls. She suffered a lot and she used to say, "I no longer want to go to school". She cried a lot. Even one of the girls with her in the school and lives in the same building with us she pushed her down the stairs to make her fall down ... there are many different types of girls like that, very aggressive especially towards us.

Various studies have focused on interethnic relations in multicultural schools and considered dealing with diversity as a new developmental task for children and adolescents in culturally heterogeneous societies but did not sufficiently focus on the role of schools in these relations (Monks et al. 2008; Strohmeier et al. 2008). Unlike them, our study reveals the ways in which interethnic relations are mediated by schools. What recurrently emerged in the data was that Syrian students feel more rejected and marginalized in schools. They systemically complained about bullying and negative stereotypes in and outside of school by their peers. While some can solve these problems by receiving personal help from teachers, many are depressed, stigmatized, bullied, and alienated to school. Another mother, Manal, spoke about her daughter's feelings of suffocation in classroom and unwillingness to attend school:

> Among all kids, there is always a bit of sensitivity and tension. But the kids in the school were pointing at her (daughter) and told her "go back to your country, why did you come here, we don't want you here with us". So, one day she came home crying and told me, "mum the kids don't want me in that school. They are telling me to go back to Syria".

When asked how her daughter dealt with this process, the mother said:

> It wasn't easy at all. It was so hard because she was hurt. I needed to encourage her so that she can keep attending the school.

Researcher: How could she overcome what happened with her?

Manal: Unfortunately, she didn't. Honestly, in the last period she decided that she doesn't want to go back to school anymore. So, it was a very big problem for us because she couldn't handle it anymore and she didn't want to go and see those kids ... These incidents happened at the end of the year almost at the end, and she had to force herself to go every day and deal with them until the end of the school year. She had no other choice, there were no other solutions so we were forced to accept that situation at the time.

Manal was not unusual in our sample with regard to the fact that she and her daughter did not make a school choice but were compelled to certain options. As it is the case with her daughter, our data systematically reveal that the Syrian students more often feel marginalized and alienated to school particularly when they are few numbers in classroom and school. Combined by lack of communication with teachers and friends, they are regularly subjected to discriminatory behaviors and attitudes. We argue that the exclusionary organization of the school bears role in the emergence of these discriminatory practices toward them.

The parents also voiced their concerns about the monoculture curriculum that focuses exclusively on Turkish culture and history. One parent, Sima, described her daughter's confusion concerning the curriculum;

> They are learning everything about Ataturk and the history of Ataturk and their (Turkish) history. And there's a long poem the kids learn at school, praising Ataturk. So, when she came back home she asked me "what did Ataturk save us from?" .... She wants to know and understand. And she sings the poem all day long at home. While playing, working, she keeps repeating that he saved us and saved our lives. They were praising him like a prophet and me myself didn't know what he did actually!

There is a strong sentiment among parents that their children are only taught Turkish history but all things related to Arabic and Syrian history are deleted. This seems to sadden the parents. Another described how she was disturbed by her children exposure to monoculture curriculum in the school.

> There is a problem with the Turkish school. Our students learn about Turkish history and Turkish culture, and everything about the Turkish country and life. Their curriculum is hard, their history is hard to learn, it is not that easy. Even the phrases they use in teaching mathematics are different from the ones our children knew. This is a negative point. For sure, they will improve in the Turkish language, but I think all the other subjects will recede.

When we shared our findings with the teachers, suggesting that Syrian students are occasionally depressed and that their parents are concerned, they confirmed these findings. They explained that while they try to help the students individually, they do not know what to do. Pakize, who is a primary school teacher, remarked:

> They sit in the classroom and do not speak at all for the first six months, not a single word. They look into my eyes while I am speaking. I use my body language to explain the topics to them. We carry out home visits, try to help, but teachers like me have limited capacity.

While they want to help, we inferred from our interviews that teachers felt disoriented by the increasing number of Syrians students and often panicked, as they lacked institutional support. Another public school teacher, Pervin, whom we met at a workshop on the education of Syrians, made an analogy between Kurdish and Syrian students and complained about the absence of an inclusive approach:

> We are actively participating in panels, conferences to learn how to help Syrian students because our on-the-job training about this topic are not adequate. We lack perspective to think about them, lack material to use in the courses. We experience with the Syrians students what we have experienced with Kurdish students. Perhaps Syrians are luckier because Arabs and Arabic are not perceived "separatists" like Kurds and Kurdish. Anyway, Turkish education has a standard strategy when it cannot cope; "just pretend these students are not there".

Despite the well-intentioned policies of trying to promote the access of Syrian children to public schools, the examples in this study revealed that teachers lack the institutional support to develop intercultural skills; Parent Teacher Meetings are held in Turkish while the Syrian parents do not speak Turkish; there are no welcome, preparation, or orientation classes in schools. The schools also lack efficient counseling services for traumatized Syrian children. These factors together seem to frighten Syrian parents and undermine their trust in state schools.

Concluding Remarks

This study explores how public schools shape educational experiences, learning process, and adaptation of Syrian children to the school context. With the gradual acceptance of Syrians as permanent settlers, the public school, instead of Temporary Education Center, is presented as an inclusive reform to incorporate the Syrian children to the national education system. However, schools are far from being an inclusive institution. The monoculture organization of schools works to exclude students from non-Turkish background. Syrian parents cannot monitor their children and the students feel depressed, alienated, and are often exposed to peer pressure and bullying in schools. While the authorities rightly eliminated Temporary Education Centers and channeled the education system, these schools have yet to facilitate both the parents and students' interactions and contacts with host society in a proper way. Gomolla (2005) contends that schools, not the immigrants and refugees, are to be designed to incorporate different cultures and values in migration society. In a similar vein, we argue that regular public schools should develop an intercultural, inclusive element for the incorporation of students coming from non-Turkish background. We consider the high number of Syrian students as an advantage to develop intercultural schools and suggest policy makers to focus and put energy into developing a multicultural, school-centered integration model for the inclusion of both Syrians and other migrants and refugees in Turkey.

References

Çelik, Ç. and A. İçduygu (2019), "Schools and Refugee Children: The Case of Syrians in Turkey," *International Migration*, 57 (2): 253–67.
Coşkun, İ. and M. N. Emin (2015), "A Road Map for the Education of Syrians in Turkey: Opportunities and Challenges," SETA.
Dinçer, Ö. (2012), "Oyunun Kuralları Değişmeli," *Dünya Bülteni*, 31 July. https://www.dunyabulteni.net/egitim/dincer-oyunun-kurali-degismemeli-h221066.html.
Emin, M. N. (2016), "Türkiye'deki Suriyeli Çoçukların Eğitimi: Temel Eğitim Politikaları," 153, Analiz, SETA.
Gomolla, M. (2005), *Schulentwicklung in der Einwanderungsgesellschaft: Strategien gegen institutionelle Diskriminierung in England, Deutschland und in der Schweiz*, Interkulturelle Bildungsforschung, 14, Münster: Waxmann.
İçduygu, A. (2015), *Syrian Refugees in Turkey: The Long Road Ahead*, Washington, DC: Migration Policy Institute.
İçduygu, A., and D. Şimşek (2016), "Syrian Refugees in Turkey: Towards Integration Policies," *Turkish Policy Quarterly*, 15 (3): 59–69.
İçduygu, A., and D. S. Sert (2019), "Introduction: Syrian Refugees—Facing Challenges, Making Choices," *International Migration*, 57 (2): 121–5.
Kirişci, K. (2016), "Turkey's Role in the Syrian Refugee Crisis: An Interview with Kemal Kirişci," *Georgetown Journal of International Affairs*, 17 (2): 80–5.
Mayring, P. (2007), *Qualitative Inhaltsanalyse: Grundlagen und Techniken*, Weinheim [u.a.]: Beltz.
McBrien, J. L. (2011), "The Importance of Context: Vietnamese, Somali, and Iranian Refugee Mothers Discuss Their Resettled Lives and Involvement in Their Children's Schools," *Compare: A Journal of Comparative and International Education*, 41 (1): 75–90.

MoNE (2014), "Notice of Ministry of Education on Educational Services for Foreigners," ministry of Education. http://mevzuat.meb.gov.tr/html/yabyonegiogr_1/yabyonegiogr_1.html

MoNE (2016), "Demirci: GEM'ler Üç Yıl Içinde Misyonunu Tamamlayacak," MEB. http://meb.gov.tr/demirci-gemler-uc-yil-icinde-misyonunu-tamamlayacak/haber/11850/tr

Monks, C. P., R. Ortega-Ruiz, and A. J. Rodríguez-Hidalgo (2008), "Peer Victimization in Multicultural Schools in Spain and England," *European Journal of Developmental Psychology*, 5 (4): 507–35.

Mülteciler Derneği (2021), "Türkiyedeki Suriyeli Sayısı Şubat 2021," Mülteciler Derneği.

Oznobishin, O. and J. Kurman (2009), "Parent–Child Role Reversal and Psychological Adjustment among Immigrant Youth in Israel," *Journal of Family Psychology*, 23 (3): 405–15.

Parker-Magyar, E. (2019), "Jordanians See More to Worry About in Their Economy than Syrian Refugees,"*Lawfare*, September 15. https://www.lawfareblog.com/jordanians-see-more-worry-about-their-economy-syrian-refugees

Renzaho, A. M. N., M. McCabe, and W. J. Sainsbury (2011), "Parenting, Role Reversals and the Preservation of Cultural Values among Arabic Speaking Migrant Families in Melbourne, Australia," *International Journal of Intercultural Relations*, 35 (4): 416–24.

Save the Children (2015), "Needs Assessment of Hatay's Temporary Education Centers for Syrians under Temporary Protection," Save the Children.

Strohmeier, D., C. Spiel, and P. Gradinger (2008), "Social Relationships in Multicultural Schools: Bullying and Victimization," *European Journal of Developmental Psychology*, 5 (2): 262–85.

Taylor, S. and R. K. Sidhu (2012), "Supporting Refugee Students in Schools: What Constitutes Inclusive Education?," *International Journal of Inclusive Education*, 16 (1): 39–56.

Weisskirch, R. S. (2010), "Child Language Brokers in Immigrant Families: An Overview of Family Dynamics," *Mediazioni*, 10. http://mediazioni.sitlec.unibo.it

Part II

Public Formal Space: State and Politics

Introduction to Part II

by Gamze Evcimen & Fatma Müge Göçek

The conceptualization of public formal space is based on the Western formulation of modernity that prioritizes and privileges the formal public sphere where structurally defined political, economic, and social activities pertaining to the state, market, and religion take place. Like in any other region of the world, development, religion, and violence are inextricably interlinked in the Middle East particularly through the common actor state, state policies, and practices. So, sociologists study the negotiation of modernity in the context of the Middle East in three categories: development, finance, and neoliberalism; religion, politics, and lifestyles of Islam; and citizenship, minorities, and violence.

Ryan Calder analyzes the rise of Islamic finance in the Gulf Arab societies with a particular focus on how shariah boards and interest simulation harmonize contemporary capitalist finance and contemporary fiqh (Islamic jurisprudence). Calder illustrates that the "Gulf model" allows Islamic finance to merge into existing capitalist financial system through shariah scholars' certification of financial products as well as through using transactions like sales and leases to simulate the economic effects of interest, which many Muslims consider unethical. Emphasizing how the oil boom of the 1970s produced newly wealthy businessmen, who connected the Gulf regimes, shariah scholars, and financial markets, Calder also underlines that the historical relationships between the Arab Gulf societies and the capitalist system enabled this marriage of faith and finance as well as the worldwide dominance of Gulf model among other historical possibilities of Islamic finance.

Shifting our focus to Turkey, Yıldız Atasoy offers a snapshot of how Turkey's neoliberal process opened room for an extended state role in economy and society through Islamic ethics as well as for the state's reclamation of public and agricultural lands for commercial use. Atasoy illustrates that Kemalist developmentalism acted as not only an agent of modernity but also an instigator of sociocultural and politico-economic injustices, which enabled Muslim capitalists to mobilize an Islamic ethical orientation in economy and politics for remaking Turkey's neoliberal history. Atasoy highlights that, as it remains heavily dependent on precarious employment conditions, reorganization of land relations, and short-term foreign capital inflows, this neoliberal articulation of liberal democracy and market economy entails uncertain social and ecological challenges for future generations.

Providing the context for religion, politics, and lifestyles of Islam, Mohammed Bamyeh conceptualizes Islam as a universal belief system that incorporates the worldviews of various social groups, expands the options of believers, and establishes a sense of global citizenship. Bamyeh demonstrates how Islam as a mode of global citizenship has historically promoted partial control, or multiple loyalties rather than loyalty to a single political authority, free movement of people, particularly for accumulating wealth through commerce, fulfilling religious obligations through pilgrimage, and creating scholarly circles through global learning networks, and cultural heteroglossia, or an imagined unified narrative for embracing the diversity of Muslim communities and practices across the world. Bamyeh also underlines that the formation of modern states has challenged these characteristics with their emphasis on establishing total control, prohibiting mobility, and imposing orthodoxies. Adopting a sociological perspective on religion as expressing global social realities rather than creating them, Bamyeh's analysis illustrates how Islam as a cultural system has become global through voluntary dynamics and bottom-up processes outside, and at times in spite, of the state.

In a similar vein, Berna Zengin Arslan and Bryan S. Turner regard state's management of religion as a typical practice of the modern, secular nation-state and study the Turkish state's centralized regulation of the religious domain through the institution of Diyanet (the Directorate of Religious Affairs). Emphasizing the productive capacity of secularism as a normative discourse that cultivates ideal (secular and religious) citizens, Arslan and Turner illustrate how the Diyanet has historically produced and represented an official form of Islam that reflects the religion of the majority, Sunni Islam, and upholds nationalism. Arslan and Turner also illustrate the continuities and changes during the AKP (Justice and Development Party) period: while the state still regulates the boundaries of an acceptable form of Islam in a centralized and bureaucratized way, the Diyanet's role and influence have also expanded through the increase in its budget and personnel as well as through the extension of its services into the private sphere, particularly to women's everyday lives, self-expressions, and family dynamics. Echoing Bamyeh's analysis, Arslan and Turner emphasize that although the Diyanet aims to desecularize modern Islam by reintegrating it into the private lives of Turkish citizens, its vision also remains dependent on the state's control and ignores the people's everyday experiences of religion.

Shifting our focus to the changes and continuities in political Islam, Charles Kurzman and Didem Türkoğlu analyze whether and how the "Arab Spring" influenced the electoral victories and platforms of Islamic political parties. Kurzman and Türkoğlu emphasize that Islamic political parties adopted more liberal discourses since the 1990s as their electoral platforms shifted emphasis from Islamic issues like sharia, jihad, and ban on interest to liberal rights like democracy, equality for women, and equality for minorities. While underlining that some Islamic movements support majoritarian democratic processes together with restrictions on minorities' rights, Kurzman and

Türkoğlu also emphasize that the Arab Spring decreased the centrality of political parties in Muslim communities. In sum, Kurzman and Türkoğlu illustrate that the Arab Spring did not bring about a drastic change in the ideologies of Islamic political parties while the elections in its aftermath seem to have reversed the upward trend in the overall seats won by these parties.

Hamit Bozarslan offers a macro-level analysis of the evolution of Kurdish issue since the 2003 occupation of Iraq and the 2011 Syrian crisis. Bozarslan demonstrates that, in contrast to Kurdish actors' victimization by the Middle East conflicts and state of violence during the 1980s, the 2011 Arab uprisings opened a new historical cycle, in which Kurdish organizations gained a position of empowerment in regional conflicts and in countries like Iraq, Syria, and Turkey. Bozarslan also highlights the changing dynamics of Kurdish society in terms of increasing urbanization, growth of middle class, and changing mobilization patterns from political parties to non-partisan forms of struggles. Bozarslan cautions that although this new state of violence offers more chances for Kurdish organizations, it also reflects continuing regional constraints and the pressure of Turkey and Iran on their own Kurdish actors.

Extending this focus on the relationship between structural changes and sectarian relations to the social construction of minority emotions and symbolic boundaries, Hyun Jeong Ha investigates the changes in daily Christian–Muslim interactions in a mixed-income neighborhood of Cairo after Mubarak's fall. Ha illustrates how an increase in Salafi influences in politics and the rise of social discrimination against ethnic and religious minorities during Egypt's regime transition created a hostile environment for this neighborhood's Christian residents, who previously enjoyed integrated lifestyles and peaceful interreligious relationships, and increased their feelings of failed interactions with Muslims. Ha also emphasizes how such interactions and emotions cause Christians to create symbolic boundaries by identifying themselves as a minority rather than as Egyptians and, thus, demonstrates the co-constitutive relationships among broader changes in political dynamics, sectarian boundaries, and emotions of minorities.

Ayhan Kaya studies self-identified Muslim youth with Turkish background in Germany with a particular focus on how young German-Turks mediate between their affiliations with Germany and Turkey. Underlining how the current sociopolitical environment pushes the socially, economically, and politically deprived sectors of European societies to the extremes of either becoming more nativist and Islamophobist or more Muslimized and Islamicized, Kaya illustrates that the growth of right-wing populism in Europe and the Justice and Development Party's Islamization of diaspora politics contribute to the Muslimization of Euro-Turks. Kaya highlights that Euro-Turks construct an Islamic space in which migrants search for recognition beyond the geographical, political, and cultural boundaries of Turkey and the EU and form a transnational, communal solidarity against the West's rejection of Islam.

Further Reading

Adas, E. B. (2006), "The Making of Entrepreneurial Islam and the Islamic Spirit of Capitalism," *Journal for Cultural Research*, 10 (2): 113–37.
Al-anani, K. and M. Malik (2013), "Pious Way to Politics: The Rise of Political Salafism in Post-Mubarak Egypt," *Digest of Middle East Studies*, 22 (1): 57–73.
Ayata, B. (2011), "Kurdish Transnational Politics and Turkey's Changing Kurdish Policy: The Journey of Kurdish Broadcasting from Europe to Turkey," *Journal of Contemporary European Studies*, 19 (4): 523–33.
Bugra, A. (1998), "Class, Culture, and State: An Analysis of Interest Representation by Two Turkish Business Associations," *International Journal of Middle East Studies*, 30 (4): 521–39.
Cınar, A. (2005), *Modernity, Islam and Secularism in Turkey: Bodies, Places and Time*, Minneapolis: University of Minnesota Press.
Demir, O., M. Acar and M. Toprak (2004), "Anatolian Tigers or Islamic Capital: Prospects and Challenges," *Middle Eastern Studies*, 40 (6): 166–88.
Freer, C. (2018), *Rentier Islamism: The Influence of the Muslim Brotherhood in Gulf Monarchies*, Oxford: Oxford University Press.
Gunes, C. and W. Zeydanlıoğlu, eds. (2014), *The Kurdish Question in Turkey: New Perspectives on Violence, Representation and Reconciliation*, London: Routledge.
Hansen, H. L. (2015), *Christian-Muslim Relations in Egypt: Politics, Society and Interfaith Encounters*, London: I.B. Tauris.
Harris, K. (2017), *A Social Revolution: Politics and the Welfare State in Iran*, Berkeley: University of California Press.
Hasan, S. (2003), *Christians versus Muslims in Modern Egypt: The Century-long Struggle for Coptic Equality*, Oxford: Oxford University Press.
Helman, S. (1999), "Negotiating Obligations, Creating Rights: Conscientious Objection and the Redefinition of Citizenship in Israel," *Citizenship Studies*, 3 (1): 45–70.
Kuran, T. (1997), "The Genesis of Islamic Economics: A Chapter in the Politics of Muslim Identity," *Social Research*, 64 (2): 301–38.
Mardin, S. (2006), *Religion, Society, and Modernity in Turkey*, New York: Syracuse University Press.
Navaro-Yashin, Y. (2002), *Faces of the State: Secularism and Public Life in Turkey*, Princeton: Princeton University Press.
Rodinson, M. (1974), *Islam and Capitalism*, London: Allen Jane.

I DEVELOPMENT, FINANCE, AND NEOLIBERALISM

Before the Boom: Oil Wealth, Shariah Scholars, and the Birth of the Islamic Finance Industry

by Ryan Calder

The rise of Islamic finance has transformed the financial landscape of the Middle East. Islamic finance is the practice of banking, securities issuance, and other financial activity conducted according to shariah. Today's Islamic financial institutions avoid interest—which some Muslims believe Islam prohibits—as well as excessive speculation, unclear contractual terms, and the financing of sectors such as pork, alcohol, pornography, and arms. The first for-profit Islamic bank opened in Dubai in 1975. Today, Islamic banking has significant market share in many Muslim-majority countries, especially in the Gulf region. Worldwide, Islamic finance encompasses around $3 trillion in assets as of 2021, accounting for around 1 percent of world financial assets. This makes it larger than Latin America's entire financial sector.

Contemporary Islamic finance presents a paradox for sociologists. Classical social theorists insisted that religious authority cannot govern modern rational capitalism. They pointed to the Catholic church, which in medieval times regulated markets and condemned usurers to hellfire but which today holds no sway over believers' financial and commercial practices (Bentham [1787] 2014; Marx [1953] 1993: 758; Weber [1922] 1978: 581–9). Since Marx and Weber, generations of social theorists have insisted that profit-seeking and economic modernization squeeze religious rules out of the marketplace (Berger [1967] 1990; Bruce 2002). After all, there is no $3 trillion Christian-finance industry, Hindu-finance industry, or Jewish-finance industry. So how has *Islamic* finance managed to thrive in the context of modern rational capitalism, in the Middle East and beyond? Put differently, under what conditions can religious authority govern markets in which firms' activities are highly rationalized toward profit maximization?

I argue that Islamic finance has thrived because an elective affinity exists between contemporary capitalist finance and contemporary *fiqh* (Islamic jurisprudence). Fiqh, as a longstanding edifice of principles and methodologies for scholastic legal reasoning,

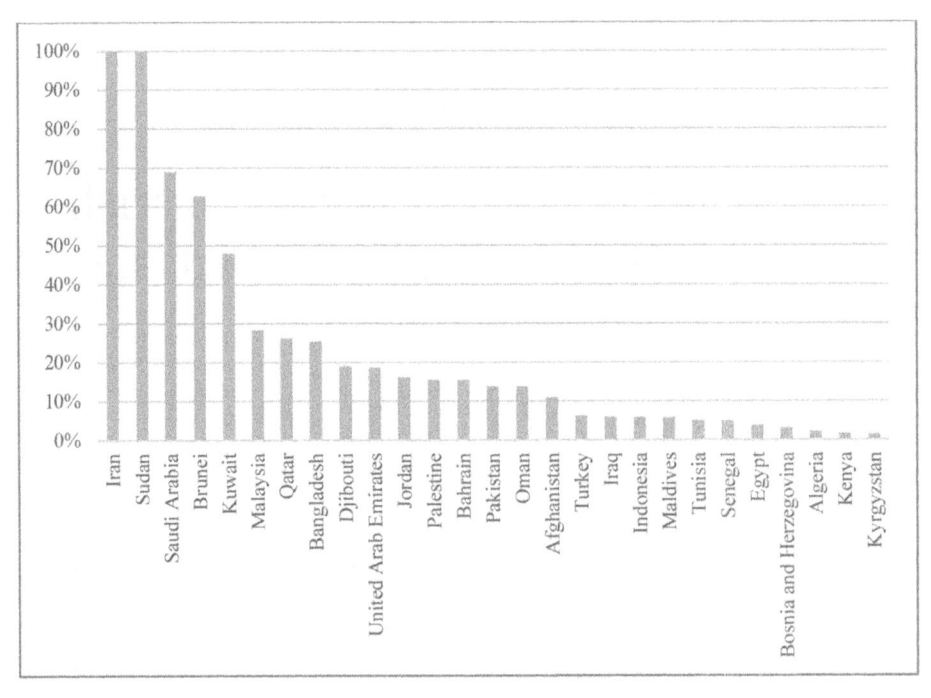

Figure 12.1 Islamic banking's share of total banking assets by country, 3Q2019.

offers widely respected experts in Islamic law who issue fatwas certifying financial products and transactions. These experts, known as shariah scholars (*fuqahā'*), make finance and fiqh compatible. Firms empanel the scholars on shariah supervisory boards that vet their products for shariah-compliance. Thus, fiqh functions as a regime of voluntary ethical regulation layered atop secular state law. Shariah scholars serve as the certification agents, and their fatwas as the certification badges. Their legal interpretations become rules of shariah-compliance that not only restrict financial activity, but give rise to new markets (Schneiberg and Bartley 2008). The scholars also serve an unofficial marketing function, attracting customers and corporate clients who trust them. By certifying financial products as Islamic, the scholars take on the ethical burden of sorting out what pious consumers should and should not buy. Fiqh thus governs financial products much as Fairtrade® standards govern bananas and coffee.

Yet the elective affinity between capitalist finance and fiqh did not result in a $3 trillion industry on its own. It was activated by the historical circumstances of the Arab Gulf societies in the 1970s, which produced newly rich pious entrepreneurs and crucial institutional innovations that merged finance and fiqh into a business-friendly regime of product certification. I call this regime the "Gulf model" of Islamic finance. In addition to certification by scholars, another crucial feature of the Gulf model is that it permits financial transactions that replicate most of the economic effects of interest without technically dealing in it. This acceptance of "interest simulation" has allowed Islamic finance to merge into the existing capitalist financial system instead of clashing with it.

The Gulf model spread worldwide in the 1970s and 1980s and is now virtually the universal way of doing Islamic finance, from Kuala Lumpur to Karachi and London to Lagos. However, it is not the only way that Muslims have sought to practice finance Islamically in the twentieth and twenty-first centuries. This chapter explains the origins of the Gulf model and reflects on what its dominance can tell us about the relationship between religion and capitalism today.

The Gulf Model: One of Many Historical Possibilities

Historically, a significant portion of the world's Muslims have considered interest unethical. From a scriptural perspective, opponents of interest assert that it constitutes usury (*ribā*), which is declared a grievous sin in the Quran (2: 275–9) and the *ḥadīth* literature. From a socioeconomic perspective, Muslim intellectuals and activists have decried interest as a morally corrupting, anti-egalitarian, dishonorable, monopolistic, and non-productive form of profit that keeps Muslims under imperialist subjugation (e.g., al-Kawākibī [1902] 2011: 60). Such critiques echo arguments made against interest throughout world history (Graeber 2011).

In the twentieth century, Muslim intellectuals, activists, and state leaders established a diverse range of financial systems and institutions that sought to avoid interest and comply with Islamic principles. Grassroots developmentalist projects, such as in Egypt and Malaysia in the 1960s, offered interest-free savings accounts to attract rural Muslims and teach them the importance of thrift. Taking a state-led approach, Islamist governments in Pakistan, Iran, and Sudan in the 1980s and 1990s outlawed interest for everyone (Calder 2019; Nomani and Rahnema 1994). Others have reframed or finessed the religious valence of interest. In early-twentieth-century Egypt, for example, Islamic modernists Muhammad Abduh and Rashid Rida disputed the premise that Islam bans all interest (Saeed 1996: 42–3). And in the mid-1970s, Libya's Muammar Gaddafi banned interest between individuals on religious grounds, but allowed banks to deal in it (Mayer 1979).

So what accounts for the present dominance of the Gulf model, in which shariah boards monopolize the authority to declare financial transactions Islamic and interest simulation predominates? More than any other driver, the oil boom of the 1970s set Islamic finance on this fiqh-centric, compliance-oriented path (Henry 1996; Tripp 2006; Warde 2010).

The Arab oil embargo of October 1973, initiated in response to Western support for Israel in the Arab-Israeli war, drove oil prices sky-high. The windfall meant that in the Gulf Arab states, the question of how to structure financial institutions was largely divorced from the developmental problem. Elsewhere, developmental imperatives were paramount: policymakers either subordinated Islamic finance to industrial policy and the economic aims of the state (as in Iran during the Iran-Iraq War and in Malaysia, where the state sought to empower ethnic Malays) or concluded that a truly Islamic financial system would liberate Muslims from the depredations of Western financial hegemony (as in Pakistan and Iran). But in the Gulf, the central question driving financial innovation was not how to create wealth, but how to save and invest it. With banks mushrooming, business opportunities proliferating, incomes rising, and new homes and consumer goods available, millions of ordinary citizens faced the question of whether to deal with interest. Many citizens readily turned to interest-bearing banks, while others, especially in Saudi Arabia, used banks merely as safe-deposit boxes, refusing interest on their savings. The banks loved this, for it lowered their cost of funds. Yet it suggested there was a mass constituency for interest-free capitalist finance.

At the level of haute finance too, Arab Gulf societies became newly implicated in the problem of interest. The Arabian Peninsula had long been an irrelevant backwater for big international banks, but with the oil boom, bankers from Wall Street and the City of London flocked to Jeddah, Riyadh, Abu Dhabi, and Kuwait City. The majority of the Arab Gulf governments' funds were quietly placed in interest-bearing Eurodollar instruments in inconceivable quantities. Yet government dealings in interest remained a sensitive issue at home, particularly for the Saudi, Qatari, and Kuwaiti governments and their ministries of religious affairs and *awqāf* (religious endowments). Privately, some religious scholars rebuked the royal houses for placing oil wealth—a gift from God—in interest-bearing instruments. Some religiously conservative ultra-rich businesspersons eschewed interest too.

Hydrocarbon wealth had produced a stratum of elite capitalist families who dominated sectors such as construction, transport, retail, and oil-related downstream products and enjoyed close personal ties to the ruling houses (Hanieh 2011: 57–84). Together, the royals and these elite families capitalized and launched the first wave of Islamic banks. These appeared between 1975 and 1982, mostly in Arab countries and in offshore hubs such as the Bahamas and Switzerland. (In 1983, Malaysia's plunge into Islamic banking heralded a more global second wave (Rethel 2016; Rudnyckyj 2019.))

The world's first commercial Islamic bank, Dubai Islamic Bank (DIB), was launched in 1975 by Dubai businessman Saeed bin Ahmad Al Lootah. DIB initiated the marriage of modern for-profit commercial banking with fiqh-minded piety. It was explicitly Islamic: it structured its products to comply with shariah, largely by avoiding interest. Yet it was unmistakably a capitalist venture. It competed against existing "conventional" (i.e., non-Islamic) banks and sought to earn a profit. And like its conventional competitors, DIB profited from the spread between the deposits it took and the financing it extended, as well as from familiar trade-finance services such as letters of credit (Saeed bin Ahmad Al Lootah, conversation with author, December 18, 2013). DIB was also capitalized by investors, including prominent Dubai merchants (Wilson 1983: 80). Al Lootah was the first of four businessmen—the other three were Saudi—who launched two-thirds of the Islamic banks founded worldwide between 1975 and 1984. These four had much in common: they were businessmen, the regional oil economy had made them extremely wealthy, and they maintained good relations with Gulf Arab regimes (Seznec and Mosis 2018).

Enter the Scholars

These early Gulf-based entrepreneurs introduced an innovation vital to the future success of Islamic finance: formal product certification by shariah scholars (Kahf 2004). In the second half of the 1970s, scholars began advising the first-wave Islamic banks, often on an ad hoc basis and sometimes for free, as to what financial products and procedures shariah allows. They also publicly legitimated Islamic banking to government officials and the public. Some of these ulama were Gulf-born, such as Abdulaziz ibn Baz, one of the most influential Saudi religious scholars of the late twentieth century (ibn Bāz 1998). Others from outside the Gulf advised Islamic banks—capitalized by Gulf millionaires—in their own countries. These scholars generally hailed from Arab countries that during the 1970s enjoyed warm relations with, and funding from, the Gulf states. Thus, Gulf capital constructed a worldwide network of scholars friendly to Gulf governments, supportive of the Gulf model of Islamic banking, and sympathetic to the belief that shariah can be made compatible with modern finance.

These scholars played a decisive role in the evolution of Islamic finance: they ratified a form of interest-free finance that was consonant with existing capitalist financial practices. To understand why, it helps to understand three ways finance can be practiced without interest.

One way is to offer interest-free loans (*qarḍ ḥasan*), which religious scholars have long lauded as a form of charity. Rentier states use this approach to support homebuyers, but it holds little appeal to for-profit banks.

A second way is to extend capital on a profit-and-loss-sharing ("PLS") basis. Much like private equity or venture capital, PLS financing involves the use of equity or partnership financing instead of loans. A typical PLS instrument is *muḍārabah*, a form of partnership. In muḍārabah, an investor contributes capital while a manager contributes work and know-how. The investor bears all losses, while the manager and the investor split the profits according to a previously agreed ratio. Proponents of Islamic economics and other social-welfare-oriented theoreticians of Islamic banking from the 1940s onward considered PLS to be the most genuinely Islamic and socially just form of finance (Hamidullah [1957] 1997: chap. 10; Siddiqi 1983). They reasoned that lending at interest condemns the borrower to repay even if he suffers unexpected misfortune. Shariah scholars likewise supported PLS because it unquestionably differed from interest-based lending.

The challenge for Islamic banks seeking to implement PLS was that they would have to do business in a fundamentally different way. The first-wave Islamic banks used PLS during the oil boom, especially in large industrial and real-estate projects through which governments injected hydrocarbon rents into the economy. However, most small- and medium-scale financing they extended was not provided on a PLS basis, and from the mid-1980s, "true" PLS—in which the Islamic bank takes liability for a substantial portion of business losses associated with its investment—became increasingly rare in Islamic banking.[1] Islamic banks attempting to implement PLS encountered many difficulties: regulatory restrictions, customer apprehensiveness, information asymmetry, agency problems, high monitoring costs, adverse selection, moral hazard, and asset-liability mismatch (Askari, Iqbal, and Mirakhor 2015). Ultimately, PLS required a fundamentally re-engineering of banking that proved extremely challenging for Islamic banks competing against conventional ones.

Instead, Islamic banks overwhelmingly took the third approach to interest-free finance, which is to use non-interest-bearing transactions, such as sales and leases, to simulate the economic substance of an interest-bearing loan. This interest-simulating approach is illustrated by an arrangement called banking murabaha (*murābaḥah maṣrafīyah*). Banking murabaha has been by far the most common financing mechanism in Islamic finance since the industry's first decade (Asutay 2012). Imagine a customer who wants to buy a $1,000 appliance on credit. The Islamic bank buys the appliance from the store for $1,000, then after some very short time sells it to the customer at a markup—say for $1,070—on a deferred-payment basis. If payment is deferred for one year, for example, this arrangement simulates a 7 percent interest-bearing financing.

From the shariah board's perspective, the bank is trading appliances, not lending money. Defenders of the Islamic finance industry argue that this approach serves as an antidote to financialization, embedding financial operations in the ownership, possession, and movement of real assets—something interest-based lending often fails to do (Pitluck 2012: 439). Critics note that in practice, interest simulation minimizes or transfers to the customer most risks associated with such ownership, possession, and movement of assets.

It was in the 1970s that the interest-simulation approach to Islamic banking was first theorized, applied, and approved by like-minded economists, shariah scholars, and bankers. They repurposed contracts such as murabaha that were used in pre-modern trade and commerce into shariah-compliant analogues of conventional interest-based product offerings. To reach these goals, shariah scholars deployed juridical practices that raised the eyebrows of some of their peers outside the industry, such as liberally selecting minority interpretations from the classical legal corpus and patching together interpretations from different juridical schools (*talfīq*) when it suited their objectives.

A process akin to natural selection aligned capital with those scholars willing to innovate. In the 1970s and 1980s, banks saw no need to work with scholars who rejected techniques such as banking murabaha, and those scholars were quickly sidelined from the industry (Yusuf Talal DeLorenzo, conversation with author, August 10, 2020). The shariah scholars who remained and became the industry's most prominent names were business-minded—often having personal or family backgrounds in business—and saw helping banks engineer shariah-compliant analogues of conventional financial instruments as a way to open the benefits and conveniences of contemporary finance to pious Muslims (Irshad Ahmad Aijaz, conversation with author, October 27, 2016). These scholars felt that if Muslims could now launch businesses, buy homes, and cover medical expenses without falling into the grave sin of interest, this was both a blessing and an economic boon for the *ummah*. Meanwhile, detractors accused them of dealing in interest by another name.

As Islamic banks spread around the globe and offered more and more interest-simulating products, the need for formal legitimation grew. Compounding this need were scandals that usually did not implicate Islamic banks, yet raised public suspicion of newfangled financial institutions. In Kuwait, for example, an unofficial stock market crashed spectacularly in 1982, sending the economy into a tailspin. And in the late 1980s and 1990s, so-called Islamic capital-investment companies (*sharikāt tawẓīf al-amwāl al-islāmīyah*) in Egypt, Pakistan, and Saudi Arabia turned out to be Ponzi schemes, destroying millions of families' savings (Warde 2010).

Beginning in 1976 at Faisal Islamic Bank of Egypt, the entrepreneurs who pioneered Islamic banking introduced a solution for legitimacy problems: the shariah board. Islamic banks needed "the imprimatur of somebody [knowledgeable about] shariah saying 'Yes, [this bank] is really compliant, and not just lying and cheating you,'" recalls Prince Amr bin Mohammed al-Faisal Al Saud, who has helped oversee the international network of Faisal Islamic banks since the 1980s (conversation with author, July 6, 2020). The shariah board is a panel of scholars charged with ensuring that a financial institution's products, services, and operations comply with shariah. Its appearance formalized and systematized the scholars' unofficial advisory relationships with Islamic banks; today, nearly every bank has one. At shariah-board meetings, which typically convene every few months, scholars sit with bank executives and scrutinize the bank's operations, paying special attention to new-product proposals. If all members deem a product halal, they sign a fatwa (Islamic legal decision) certifying this. Shariah-board members are not employees, so they do not receive salaries. However, like members of corporate boards, they receive honoraria. The most prolific shariah scholars in the industry sit on dozens of boards and earn annual incomes ranging into the millions of US dollars for their supervisory and advisory services. They have become expert technicians who bridge the worlds of finance and fiqh.

The Compatibility of Fiqh and Finance

Prevailing Islamic financial practices and ethics changed dramatically in a short period from the 1960s through the 1980s, accelerating their convergence with conventional capitalist finance. This process was facilitated by developments in the Arab Gulf countries: the oil boom, the alliance of capital with shariah scholars, interest simulation, and the institutional innovation of the shariah board. Within a few years, the Gulf model—a pragmatic, fiqh-centric conception of what makes finance Islamic—had squeezed out PLS, a form of finance radically different from conventional interest-based banking. Once made consonant with capitalist finance, Islamic finance was poised to spread worldwide and grow.

So, what can the rise of Islamic finance, grounded in the Gulf model, tell us about the relationship between capitalism and religion in the twenty-first century? It illustrates a set of conditions under which religious authority can, contrary to the expectations of classical sociological theory, govern modern activity. Instead of defining Islamic finance primarily in developmental terms or as resistance against neo-imperialism, pious entrepreneurs from the Gulf region presented it as an interest-free alternative to conventional finance that would succeed based on the competitive advantage offered by scholarly certification. When understood thus, Islamic finance has economically liberal principles built into it. One is the expectation that consumers be free to choose the products they like, certified by whichever religious authorities they trust, instead of being coerced into shariah-compliance by the state. The other is the insistence that producers be free to sell any Islamic products they like, including interest-simulating ones, so long as scholars deem them shariah-compliant. Even as states have played a vital role in the growth of Islamic finance (Apaydin 2018; Pitluck and Adhikari 2018), these basic principles of the Gulf model make it a marriage of faith and finance perfectly suited to a neoliberal age.

Note

1 Many Islamic banks today use PLS contracts such as muḍārabah and mushārakah, but usually in ways that essentially fix in advance the returns that each party will receive on an investment—another form of interest simulation (Farook, Hassan, and Clinch 2012).

References

Apaydin, F. (2018), "Regulating Islamic Banks in Authoritarian Settings: Malaysia and the United Arab Emirates in Comparative Perspective," *Regulation & Governance*, 12 (4): 466–85.

Askari, H., Z. Iqbal, and A. Mirakhor (2015), *Introduction to Islamic Economics*, Singapore: Wiley.

Asutay, M. (2012), "Conceptualising and Locating the Social Failure of Islamic Finance: Aspirations of Islamic Moral Economy vs. the Realities of Islamic Finance," *Asian and African Area Studies*, 11 (2): 93–113.

Bentham, J. (2014), *A Defence of Usury*, Cambridge: Cambridge University Press.

Berger, P. L. (1990), *The Sacred Canopy: Elements of a Sociological Theory of Religion*, New York: Anchor.

Bruce, S. (2002), *God Is Dead: Secularization in the West*, Oxford: Blackwell.

Calder, R. (2019), "How Religio-economic Projects Succeed and Fail: The Field Dynamics of Islamic Finance in the Arab Gulf States and Pakistan, 1975–2018," *Socio-Economic Review*, 17 (1): 167–93.

Farook, S., M. K. Hassan and G. Clinch (2012), "Profit Distribution Management by Islamic Banks: An Empirical Investigation," *The Quarterly Review of Economics and Finance*, 52 (3): 333–47.

Graeber, D. (2011), *Debt: The First 5,000 Years*, Brooklyn: Melville House.

Hamidullah, M. (1997), *Introduction to Islam*, Ankara: Türkiye Diyanet Vakfı.

Hanieh, A. (2011), *Capitalism and Class in the Gulf Arab States*, New York: Palgrave Macmillan.

Henry, C. M. (1996), *The Mediterranean Debt Crescent: Money and Power in Algeria, Egypt, Morocco, Tunisia, and Turkey*, Gainesville: University Press of Florida.

ibn Bāz, ʿAbd al-ʿAzīz bin ʿAbd Allāh (1998), "Ḥukm al-Īdāʿ fī al-Maṣārif]," in al-Saʿdī, ʿAbd al-Raḥmān bin Nāṣr (ed.), *Fatāwá al-Buyūʿ fī al-Islām*, 51, Kuwait: Jamʿīyat Iḥyāʿ al-Turāth al-Islāmī.

Kahf, M. (2004), "Islamic Banks: The Rise of a New Power Alliance of Wealth and Shari'a Scholarship," in C. Henry and R. Wilson (eds.), *The Politics of Islamic Finance*, 17–36, Edinburgh: Edinburgh University Press.

al-Kawākibī, ʿAbd al-Raḥmān (2011), *Ṭabāʾiʿ al-Istibdād wa-Maṣāriʿ al-Istiʿbād*, Cairo: Kalimāt.

Marx, K. (1993), *Grundrisse*, London: Penguin.

Mayer, A. E. (1979), "The Regulation of Interest Charges and Risk Contracts: Some Problems of Recent Libyan Legislation," *The International and Comparative Law Quarterly*, 28 (4): 541–59.

Nomani, F. and A. Rahnema (1994), *Islamic Economic Systems*, London: Zed Books.

Pitluck, A. Z. (2012), "Islamic Banking and Finance: Alternative or Façade?" in K. K. Cetina and A. Preda (eds.), *The Oxford Handbook of the Sociology of Finance*, 431–49, Oxford: Oxford University Press.

Pitluck, A. Z. and S. Adhikari (2018), "Islamic Finance in the Global North: Secular Incubators, Elementary Accommodation and Strategic Negligence," in M. Woodward and R. Lukens-Bull (eds.), *Handbook of Contemporary Islam and Muslim Lives*, 1–28, New York: Springer.

Rethel, L. (2016), "Islamic Finance in Malaysia: Global Ambitions, Local Realities," in J. Elias and L. Rethel (eds.), *The Everyday Political Economy of Southeast Asia*, 116–36, Cambridge: Cambridge University Press.

Rudnyckyj, D. (2019), *Beyond Debt: Islamic Experiments in Global Finance*, Chicago: University of Chicago Press.

Saeed, A. (1996), *Islamic Banking and Interest: A Study of the Prohibition of Riba and Its Contemporary Interpretation*, Leiden: Brill.

Schneiberg, M. and T. Bartley (2008), "Organizations, Regulation, and Economic Behavior: Regulatory Dynamics and Forms from the Nineteenth to Twenty-First Century," *Annual Review of Law and Social Science*, 4: 31–61.

Seznec, J. and S. Mosis (2018), *The Financial Markets of the Arab Gulf: Power, Politics and Money*, Abingdon-on-Thames: Routledge.

Siddiqi, M. N. (1983), *Issues in Islamic Banking*, Lahore: Islamic Foundation.

Tripp, C. (2006), *Islam and the Moral Economy: The Challenge of Capitalism*, Cambridge: Cambridge University Press.

Warde, I. (2010), *Islamic Finance in the Global Economy*, Edinburgh: Edinburgh University Press.

Weber, M. (1978), *Economy and Society: An Outline of Interpretive Sociology*, Berkeley: University of California Press.

Wilson, R. (1983), *Banking and Finance in the Arab Middle East*, London: Macmillan.

The Islamic Ethic and the Spirit of Turkish Capitalism: A Neoliberal History Making

by Yıldız Atasoy

This paper explores "Islam's marriage with neoliberalism" in Turkey since the coming to power of the Justice and Development Party (AKP) in 2002. It focuses on two interrelated processes that connect a market-oriented development model in Turkey to larger changes in global capitalism. They are: (1) the articulation of a *neostatist* perspective of an "Islamic ethic" and (2) the state-reworking of land relations through reclamation of public lands, land titling, and land consolidation schemes for commercial housing, agriculture, and large infrastructural and mining projects. Built in the politics of resentment with Kemalist state domination as implemented in various forms since the 1930s, these processes constitute "a neoliberal history making" in Turkey. It responds to existential inequalities rooted in the previous development pattern while deepening and expanding dispossession-by-accumulation via an enhanced role for the state in the economy and society.

Hüzün

"Neoliberalism" is a historically specific transformation in the system of capital accumulation, commodification, and patterns of domination. Its implementation has not been uniform across the global economy. *The Islamic ethic and the spirit of Turkish capitalism* (Atasoy 2007) exemplifies a geo-historically specific re-formulation of the normative basis of developmentalism and reorganization of its power relations in Turkey which began in the 1980s. This reformulation has opened an opportunity for various social groups to *reposition* themselves in the economy and *rupture* the primacy of civil-military bureaucratic cadres within the Kemalist state.

Kemalism is a constitutionally unchangeable normative referent for state-making. It is rooted in the reform movement of the Ottoman Tanzimat era (1839–76) which upheld an idealized notion of European *civilization* to be emulated on the route to modernity. However, Ottoman reformers were ambivalent about the wholesale replacement of the Ottoman system with a European model versus a synthesis between Ottoman-Islamic culture and European civilization. If a synthesis was deemed to be the best strategy, the means to accomplish it has always been an unsettling question—culturally and emotionally.

Orhan Pamuk captures this unease through the concept of *hüzün* (melancholy) in his autobiographical book *İstanbul*. *Hüzün* results from an ambivalence between the desire to "modernize" along a European path and the long-existing cultural experiences entangled with Muslim beliefs and practices. In his novels *A Mind at Piece* and *The Time Regulation Institute* Ahmet Hamdi Tanpınar describes *hüzün* as cultural derangement. Without a creative synthesis between society's old temporal order and rhythms of life and European ways, the characters in Tanpınar's work suffer eternally. In his poem *Çile* Necip Fazıl Kısakürek describes *hüzün* as deep emotional pain and great suffering. In his *Bu ülke* Cemil Meriç presents *hüzün* as expressing an irreconcilable divide between East and the West which can only be *concealed* temporarily by bureaucratic impositions of westernization.

Turkish literature represents *hüzün* as an outcome of walking the thin line of making developmentalist history. Ottoman reformers advocated the adoption of Western technology but not its culture, as they believed cultural imitation would only generate catastrophe. During the 1930s Kemalist leaders decided that economic development required wholesale adoption of Western ways. For them, modernization was a universal necessity for catching up with the standard of European economic development. Understood as incompatible with European modernity, Islam was kept under state-bureaucratic control through the Directorate of Religious Affairs founded in 1924. It is in the state's reorientation of Islam within Kemalist modernity that an interstitial space of *hüzün* emerged, a space which also opened the possibility for a variety of social groups seeking to remake history.

Concerns over Islam's diminished public role have been an important aspect of politics since the establishment of the multi-party system in 1945. The Democratic Party (1950–61) enlarged the political space for the representation of Muslim religious beliefs and cultural practices in politics. During the 1970s context of world economic crisis, resentment politics was revived within the National Salvation Party, which questioned the presumed universality of a Western model. During the global neoliberal restructuring of the 1980s, the military regime (1980–3) promoted a "Turkish-Islamic synthesis" in reorganizing the power politics of a market-oriented development model. The Motherland Party (1983–95) combined a mixture of market-oriented economic reforms, along with nationalist and Islamic elements. The AKP had initially fused Islamic ethics and engagement with the "globalization" and "democratization" discourses of the European Union (EU). The interstitial relations of resentment have become integral to the complexities of "neoliberal history making" which the AKP has sought through what I describe as *Islam's Marriage with Neoliberalism* (Atasoy 2009).

This historical sketch details the temporality of balances in organizing domination within a developmentalist path which itself expresses the world-historical conditions of capitalism. The AKP's earlier blending of Islam and EU standards represents a *neostatist* approach to a market-oriented development model and to restructuring relations of domination. Muslim grassroots communities are also involved in this restructuring by activating *hüzün* into coalition building under the symbolism of civic engagement in the economy.

The symbolism of civic engagement in the economy has appealed to a variety of social groups affected by class- and region-based inequalities and culture-based grievances against Kemalist state developmentalism. These groups include capitalists from smaller Anatolian cities, highly educated Muslim-salaried professionals from modest families, the urban poor and the marginalized, Muslim women who wear the headscarf, and the Kurdish people. They have been subject, albeit in different ways, to the ebb and flow of a developmentalism that is believed to have created existential inequalities and ontological insecurities. These groups thought of themselves as unequally endowed under Kemalism due to their imputed cultural differences, Muslim orientation, and regional background. An Islamic ethical orientation was thus politically re-signified in tying desires for social inclusion to the developmentalist power structure via a market-economy model.

A "neoliberal synthesis" (van der Pijl 2006: 26) between an attachment to the globalized discourse of liberal democracy and market-oriented development enabled the AKP and other Islamic groups to re-orient developmentalist power relations. The AKP's push for EU membership and the beginning of accession negotiations in 2005 created the context. The AKP's 2002 *Development and Democratization Programme* argued for fundamental rights and freedoms in Turkey to be congruent with "universal standards" as outlined in the EU Copenhagen political criteria for membership. This congruence was described as a precondition for permanent and perpetual growth and for the reordering of the power relations of the Kemalist state.

The Realignment of Turkish Capital

The narrative of *hüzün* has motivated a search for an alternative social base in the realignment of private capital. The divergence of interests between the Turkish Industrialists' and Businessmen's Association (TÜSİAD) and the Independent Industrialists' and Businessmen's Association (MÜSİAD) was central in this narrative. TÜSİAD was founded in 1971, representing secularly oriented big business interests concentrated in the İstanbul region. With strong ties to the Kemalist developmentalist project, it had initially kept its distance from the AKP, although it has always supported a market-economy model. MÜSİAD was founded in 1990 to represent both large and smaller-sized Muslim business interests generally from smaller cities in Anatolia with weak ties to the Kemalist state. MÜSİAD was a key element in the AKP's cross-class coalition. It is important to note that the political articulation of religious, cultural concerns is not synonymous with a class-based shaping of an Islamic orientation. Islamic politics is not overtly aligned with small- and medium-scale, newly emerging Anatolian capitalists; large-scale Muslim capitalists are already among the ranks of big capital located in İstanbul. Rather, it is the differential assessments of Kemalist developmentalism that have had a profound ideological effect on the reproduction of cleavages between large İstanbul-based and small Anatolian-based capitalists. Secularly oriented business groups have been more concerned with the political future of the Kemalist state, seen as an agent of modernity; Muslim groups have a different historical memory. The thin line of a Kemalist path, between an agent of modernity and an instigator of social/cultural injustices, marked an interstitial space for divergent interpretations that shaped Islamic politics.

The articulation of an Islamic ethic was about the placement of a segment of the population having cleavages with Kemalist-state developmentalism on an embourgeoisement trajectory. AKP governments have pursued policies to create an opening for that placement to occur. The bloc-sale style privatization of public companies, which has been the backbone of the Turkish economy since the 1930s, helped to create a political context for state downsizing in this narrative. A new path for *vertically concentrated wealth* among the Muslim bourgeoisie was also opened through state reclamation of common public and agricultural lands for commercial luxury housing, shopping malls, and mega infrastructural, energy, and resource extraction projects (Atasoy 2017). These policies benefited the upward mobility of many companies in their embourgeoisement project, including Ağaoğlu Group, Beytürk İnşaat, Kalyon Holding, IC İçtaş Holding, Kolin Holding, and Cengiz Holding.

TÜSİAD currently has a membership of 4,500 firms and accounts for 50 percent of total value-added in the Turkish economy and 85 percent of Turkish exports.[1] Its founding member firms are family-owned and managed conglomerates with origins in the state-led industrialization project of the 1930s. Indeed, high-level state bureaucrats were involved in the founding of industrial firms, transforming themselves into a private industrial bourgeoisie. Strong historical connections with state bureaucrats and dependence on state backing for growth explain these firms' secularist orientation. TÜSİAD views Turkey's EU membership as part of Turkey's modernization, with roots extending back to the Ottoman Tanzimat. It advocates liberal democratic principles; a secular state of law; a competitive market economy; environmental sustainability; and Turkey-EU integration, along with the modernization of the Customs Union agreement signed in 1995. It is a member of *BusinessEurope* and the *Global Business Coalition*, and has representative offices in Brussels, Washington, DC, Berlin, London, and Paris, and network ties in China, Silicon Valley, and the Gulf Region. TÜSİAD asserts its influence on the AKP government through its involvement within these business structures.

MÜSİAD is central to the coalition politics of the AKP. It rejects the Kemalist cultural hierarchy which has privileged big İstanbul-based bourgeoisie and instead prefers to facilitate the growth of Anatolian businesses. It organizes international fairs and meetings which function as platforms for business groups, bureaucrats, politicians, and the media to support global-Muslim business networks. The International Business Forum, the World Economic Forum for the Muslim World, and annual trade fairs organized within the Organization of Islamic Conference are among these platforms. MÜSİAD has a membership of 60,000 firms, the majority of which are small- and medium-sized, accounting for roughly 20 percent of the Turkish GNP.[2] Its members, 70 percent of which were established after 1980, are typically from modest Muslim-family backgrounds. These firms see their competitive edge in food-processing and retailing, construction, and the new production systems in process technologies and data-driven Industry 4.0 across supply chains.

For MÜSİAD (2019), successful participation in the economy is a civilizational project that requires disciplined work, hence the slogan: "you must work like ants to create monuments like giants." Insofar as it represents the Anatolian bourgeoisie with historically weak connections to the state, it is hardly surprising that MÜSİAD has embraced the World Bank's advocacy of human capital growth. MÜSİAD contends that young and talented human wealth is the most valuable resource available in Turkey. The younger generations must be prepared for success in the economy through education in Islamic beliefs and values, and through nationalist inspiration from history. This preparation must be supplemented by formal education in science and technology. Using the metaphor of a compass, MÜSİAD (2019) argues: "We must station one leg of the compass fixed in our own civilization, while the moveable leg must pivot the world and its developments."

The Naqshbandi and Gülenists

The Naqshbandi order has reimagined a narrative of development since early eighteenth-century Ottoman times. Its narrative is built on the idea of individual self-development to be achieved through silent *dhikr* (recollection of God in the heart), *sohbet* (an intimate spiritual conversation between leader and disciple), and *rabıta* (linking the heart of the follower to the heart of the leader). For Gümüşhanevi, an influential Ottoman-Naqshbandi Sheikh, Muslims must attain knowledge in science and technology through formal education and strengthen their moral standing through the informal processes of Islamic pedagogy (Atasoy 2005: 81–2). Mehmet Zahid Kotku (1897–1980) incorporated the Gümüşhanevi path into a narrative of national industrialization during the 1960s and 1970s. Muslims must thereby escape marginalization and colonization in the world economy—a position that has trapped Turkey since the Ottoman Tanzimat period. Therefore, they must rebuild an independent industrial capacity, competitively engage in the global economy, acquire cultural openness to techno-scientific innovations, strengthen their faith, and adopt Islamic lifestyles (Kotku 1984). The AKP governments have reoriented this narrative within a market-economy model, backed by the Naqshbandi-affiliated İskenderpaşa, Erenköy, Işıkçılar, and İsmailağa communities. While this reorientation marginalized Islamic intellectuals critical of capitalism (e.g., Ali Bulaç, İsmet Özel, and Sezai Karakoç), it created opportunities for many Anatolian entrepreneurs.

The Naqshbandi has a conjunctural perspective of the market economy tied to evaluative judgments on the history of modernity in Turkey. The headscarf ban implemented after the 1997 soft military coup until the AKP's lifting of the ban in 2013 adversely affected the higher education, occupational attainment, and employment prospects of thousands of women who wore the headscarf. The ban has become a symbol of Muslim marginalization, souring relations with state-bureaucratic cadres, fuelling aspirations for *asset building* in human capital for Muslim capitalists, as well as remaking relations of capitalism from below (Atasoy 2018).

The following five words summarize Naqshbandi-affiliated İhlas Holding's business ethics: *integrity*, referring to honesty and trustworthiness; *honour*, to moral righteousness, striving for the country and its values; *loyalty*, to hard work for the strength of society and greater goals; *all-embracing*, to a comprehensive business orientation in local and global markets; and *steadfastness*, to be constant, stable, and continuous in the economy and to maintain strong ties to the past.[3] Other Naqshbandi-affiliated businesses (e.g., Server Holding) adopt similar principles. Formulated in a way that is similar to Rumi's depiction of the "universe as alive," which resonates with James Lovelock's *Gaia*, these principles now constitute an Islamic ethos for sustainable development.

Based on the teachings of Said Nursi (1876–1960) who reinterpreted the Koran to demonstrate that it contains scientific knowledge regarding the laws of order found in nature, Gülenists maintain that an Islamic brand of modernity can emerge. Human capital conceptualized as *homo Islameconomicus* (Atasoy 2018) signifies the making of a "new man and woman" through a continual moral self-renewal within Islamic modernity and formal education in technical fields. The Anatolian populations who were seen to be pushed into backwardness and poverty by the Kemalist state must work to become wealthy and provide *hizmet* (service) to the country. For Gülen (2015), a nation which does not undertake hard work and a search for wealth is bound to be under the domination of another, as "Divine favours [are] granted in return for ... working diligently, night and day." Echoing Adam Smith's view (1759/76) on moral sentiments, Gülen believes that if Muslims do not embody an ethics of conviction to serve their society, they "will wither, and even decay or decompose ... confined in a vicious cycle of fatigue."[4] Moral renewal should inculcate responsiveness within Islamic modernity against an unrestrained pursuit of wealth generation:

> If the inheritors of the earth ... do not pave the way for humanity to reinterpret itself anew by putting forth a new code of morality, a new understanding of economics, a new philosophy of labor, we will experience new catastrophes, ... they will overshadow the destruction of the world wars. (https://fGülen.com/en/recent-articles-en/the-dynamics-of-a-changing-world)

By 2010 when the alliance between the AKP and Gülenists began to dissolve, Gülenists became the dominant group within the AKP, the state bureaucracy, and municipalities. With at least 30,000 affiliated firms organized within TUSKON (the Confederation of Businessmen and Industrialists of Turkey), Gülenists were among the fastest-growing businesses in Turkey. Believing that education constitutes a source of class power, they founded thousands of schools and at least seven universities in Turkey and abroad. After the attempted military coup of 2016 against the AKP government, alleged to have been staged by the Gülenists, thousands of them were detained, arrested, and purged from their public employment positions. Gülenist-affiliated schools and media outlets were banned. TUSKON was closed and its president, general secretary, and high-level administrators from eighty-six TUSKON-member firms were arrested, including Asya Bank, Aydın Holding, Eroğlu Holding, and Metalsac.

Although there is no unified category of Muslim capitalists, they have grown competitively against the old bourgeoisie organized within TÜSİAD. They are heavily concentrated in food processing and retailing, textile and clothing production, and real estate, which tend to be labor intensive. Their phenomenal growth relies on an employment structure delineated by limited trade-union rights, poorly enforced labor laws, the existence of a large pool of unregistered employees, and limited formal employment opportunities for educated young people. While Turkey's official unemployment rate is 13.7 percent in 2020, it is 25.9 percent for young people between fifteen and twenty-four who have a minimum of secondary school education. Informal labor without registration or access to social-security coverage and benefits constitutes 40.2 percent of total employment. The inflow of 3.6 million Syrian refugees further expands the informal employment pool. Women constitute only 30.2 percent of formally employed workers in the economically active age group as compared to 66.2 percent of men.[5] Therefore, a precarious employment structure provides an available, cheap human resource for the transitioning of Muslim capitalists to the ranks of the large bourgeoisie.

These capitalists have integrated the "hidden wealth" of Muslims (i.e., the "idle" gold saved under mattresses as a safety net for future) and remittances from Turkish workers in Europe into their investment capital. The Naqshbandi and Gülenist-affiliated banks (Anadolu Finance House, İhlas Finance, Family Finance, and Asya Bank) and the informal activities of religious communities have provided financial backing for their growth, which also relies on public shareholding. Since the closure of Asya Bank after the attempted military coup, much "idle" gold of Muslims has been channeled into profit-loss sharing accounts by the state-run Vakıf Katılım, Türkiye Finance in partnership with the National Commercial Bank of Saudi Arabia, Bizim Menkul Değerler owned by Erciyes Anadolu Holding, Halk Yatırım in partnership with the state-owned Halk Bank, and Kuveyt Türk. These institutions offer investors financing backed by gold in compliance with Islamic *murabaha* principle (cost + agreed upon marked-up price) while account holders receive revenues on savings without officially being paid interest.[6]

Conclusion

Built upon the politics of resentment with the Kemalist state, an Islamic articulation of a work ethic has offered a chance of upward mobility for Muslim people of modest Anatolian backgrounds in their embourgeoisement project. An Islamic narrative of enhancing individual capacities for *disciplined* and *responsible human capital* supports a personalized cultural orientation to economic rationality which Weber (1915[1946]) seems to have ignored. The effectiveness of this ethic depends on the individual will of believers to correct the historical injustices of the Kemalist state and to provide *hizmet* for society. A *neostatist* path followed by the AKP governments has commenced not-quite-so-open opportunities for the repositioning of Anatolian capitalists in the economy, legitimated by the rapid upward mobility of Muslim entrepreneurs. While privatization has diminished state-bureaucratic power, the state's reworking of land relations for commercial use has generated far-reaching redistributive effects on the social hierarchy. This path was initially promised within a "neoliberal synthesis," between liberal democracy and the market economy; it became heavily reliant on tenuous employment patterns, contraction of agricultural and public lands, and short-term foreign capital inflows that have generated a massive foreign debt[7] in the economy. And all of this—with unknown social and ecological consequences for future generations.

Notes

1 https://tusiad.org/en/tusiad/about
2 https://www.MÜSİAD.org.tr/
3 https://www.ihlas.com.tr/wp-content/uploads/2020/08/IHL_HOL_FRAE_2019_01_uyg6.pdf
4 https://fGülen.com/en/recent-articles-en/to-remain-fresh-and-strive-for-renewal
5 https://data.tuik.gov.tr/Kategori/GetKategori?p=istihdam-issizlik-ve-ucret-108&dil=1
6 https://www.sukuk.com/article/islamic-liquidity-management-murabaha-compliant-liquidity-products-13463/#/?playlistId=0&videoId=4
7 Foreign debt has grown from US$130 billion in 2002 to an all-time high of US$ 467 billion in 2018 and US$ 422 billion in June 2020 (https://tradingeconomics.com/turkey/external-debt).

References

Atasoy, Y. (2005), *Turkey, Islamists and Democracy*, London and New York: I.B. Tauris.
Atasoy, Y. (2007), "The Islamic Ethic and the Spirit of Turkish Capitalism Today," in L. Panitch and C. Leys (eds.), *Socialist Register 2008*, 121–40, London: The Merlin Press.
Atasoy, Y. (2009), *Islam's Marriage with Neoliberalism*, London: Palgrave.

Atasoy, Y. (2017), "Repossession, Re-informalization and Dispossession: The 'Muddy Terrain' of Land Commodification in Turkey," *Journal of Agrarian Change*, 17 (4): 657–79.

Atasoy, Y. (2018), "Neoliberalization and *Homo Islameconomicus*," in A. Almila and D. Inglis (eds.), *The Routledge International Handbook of Veils and Veiling Practices*, 29–43, London: Routledge.

Gülen, F. (2003), "The New Man and Woman," http://fGülen.com/en/fethullah-Gülens-life/1305-Gülens-thoughts/25094-the-new-man-and-woman. (accessed October 3, 2015).

Gülen, F. (2015), "Working Hours of the Devoted Souls," http://fGülen.com/en/fethullah-Gülens-works/thought/endeavor-for-renewal/48623-working-hours-of-the-devoted-souls (accessed September 16, 2015).

Kotku, M. Z. (1984), *Cihad*, Ankara: Seha.

MÜSİAD (2019), *Dönüşen Dünyada Yeni Türkiye*, https://www.musiad.org.tr/icerik/yayin-40/pr-286 (accessed November 29, 2020).

Smith, A. (1976), *The Theory of Moral Sentiments*, New York: Penguin Books.

van der Pijl, K. (2006), "A Lockean Europe?" *New Left Review*, 37: 9–37.

Weber, M. (1946), "Religious Rejections of the World and Their Directions," in H. H. Gerth and C. Wright Mills (eds.), *From Max Weber*, New York: Oxford University Press.

II RELIGION, POLITICS, AND LIFESTYLES OF ISLAM

Islam as an Experiment in Global Citizenship[1]

by Mohammed Bamyeh

From a sociological point of view, the history of monotheism is a series of global experiments in constructing a sense of global citizenship that transcends parochial loyalties. The actual histories show countless fractures, infightings, and exclusions, most of which, however, were justified by the presupposition that a global community ought to reflect the unified nature of its single creator. In the Islamic version of this ongoing, grand historical experiment, we can detect specific sociological support mechanisms that have helped Islam establish itself over the centuries not simply as a "religion," but more importantly for our purposes here as an especially effective way to express a credible mode of global citizenship. Here I would like to focus on three of those mechanisms that have historically lent felt meaning to the otherwise amorphous sense of being a global citizen: partial control, free movement, and cultural heteroglossia. At the most basic level, all three promoted a sense of global citizenship by diversifying the options of believers rather than making them uniform, which is another way of saying that global citizenship is never about creating uniformities, but the exact opposite: it is arrived at by multiplying the options available to the global citizen.

First, partial control meant that for Muslims multiple loyalties tended to be the effective and practical norm, rather than loyalty to a single sovereign or to the state. Second, free movement of people was a natural corollary to the centrality of commerce in Muslim economies, pilgrimage routes, and the global structure of educational networks. Free movement was the fundamental mechanism for wealth accumulation, fulfilment of religious obligations, and creating the scholarly circles at whose hands Islam itself was defined. Third, cultural heteroglossia refers to the ways by which the diversity of Muslim communities around the world appeared unproblematic, so that Muslims could continue to imagine themselves as a single global community, without them being required to act that way, except under exceptional circumstances.

In an earlier book (Bamyeh 2000) I sought to show how global cultural processes have historically served to humanize otherwise pure economic processes—the cold, heartless part of the story about which we seem to fixate entirely today when we discuss what we call "globalization." Yet, the historical tendency has always been for global culture to be inseparable from other global processes. Global culture, in turn, consists not of uniform propositions but of intersecting experiments. These include pronouncements of faith (thereby supplying ready credentials of global citizenship); universalization of ethical and business standards (especially among the trading communities); and loose political arrangements (that made possible the simultaneity of autonomy and communication).

The argument presented here is that the historical Muslim world became established as a predictable world system only to the extent that it adhered to three fundamental principles mentioned above: one political, another social, and a third cultural. These principles persisted remarkably well throughout Islamic history, albeit with occasional interruptions, the latest and most enduring of which occasion the modern colonial epoch and the formation of modern states. The vitality and remarkable career of these principles had little to do with the benevolence or conscious strategies of any particular government or sovereign in Islamic history. In fact, frequently they persisted against the expressed wishes of governments, which until the modern period had simply no means by which to establish total control, prohibit population movements, or impose orthodoxies.

Partial Control

Unlike European states, which especially during the nationalist era presented themselves as ultimate organizing embodiments of society, the Islamic state was historically regarded, by constituents and rulers alike, as only one among several sources of legitimate authority in society. The state itself consisted of multiple centers, especially as the caliph became an increasingly nominal office since the third century. But even at height of its power, the state in Islamic history had to share control with other authorities that were more rooted in the everyday life of society, including religious scholars, tribal networks, merchant and professional guilds, Sufi orders, and local notable families. Thus, a variety of social networks, rather than state agents, governed more or less all aspects of life at the local level—except for imperial taxation, which was usually assessed on a region or a town as a whole, but subdivided according to local rules, and the office of the *muhtasib* or market inspector. Otherwise, it was local elites that meant anything in terms of familiar power structures. The most common form of relation of such local elites to local populations was one of a patron-client, and the various sources of political, financial, and religious authority reinforced each other while also keeping each other from exercising monopoly of social control.

Local elites could benefit from their expressed allegiance to an expansive Islamic state, since such a state gave their authority more reason. The distant state saw them as mediating between it and the local level, and in any case the state could efficiently deal only with a relatively small number of partners in each region. However, local elites also never wanted more state control than was needed to augment their purposes, which were to either have more say over a specific aspect of local life, or protect their constituency as needed, rather than to rule local society as a whole.

The fact that for much of its history the Muslim world was nominally governed by territorially expansive, loose states rather than confined city-states, meant that local civil society, social networks, and collective identities could exist and evolve at some distance from state doctrines. Islam itself was elaborated historically by networks of scholarly communities largely operating out of their own schools rather than through official position in government. The faith was disseminated in society on the basis of their work, and spread geographically through long-distance trade that connected local economies to world systems. States themselves, in spite of their religious claims, usually found it necessary, convenient, or less contentious to leave the task of elaborating Islam to other authorities, namely the scholars of religion and various independent religious orders. Indeed, according to theses spanning a hundred years of arguments (the most notable being an-Na'im (2008) and Abd al-Raziq (1925), the concept of an "Islamic state" is incompatible with Islamic thought theologically and Muslim traditions historically.

In recent literature one encounters an overstated claim regarding how Christianity "essentially" involves a separation of church and state, since Jesus taught that Caesar and god had different requirements. But the historical reality has obviously nothing to do with this standpoint. While the first three centuries of Christianity are characterized by activism from below, with the conversion of Rome to Christianity, religious authority in Europe tended to have an avowed program of political alliances for which the hierarchical structure, particularly of Catholicism, lent instrumental credibility. This would not change in practice until the consolidation of the authority of modern states in the nineteenth century.

In Islam, by contrast, while the ruler was expected to be a Muslim, it was never expected that this should be enough reason for the population to follow his particular creed. Religious authority operated largely in civil society and the ulama were staples of civic life. This was the case even among the shi'a, who had a more hierarchical structure but rarely their own state, apart from the Ismaili Fatimid state (909–1171) in North Africa and the Levant, the Safavid state in Persia as of the sixteenth century, and the Buyid state five centuries earlier. The two centuries of rule over Egypt by the Ismaili Shi'a Fatimid dynasty (969–1171) did not occasion a demographic dominance of their creed, and overall the country lived for six centuries with a Muslim ruler and a non-Muslim majority. None of these states seemed to consider the enforcement of a uniform religious culture to be one of their roles, except in Safavid Persia, where the ultimate outcome from the enforcement of Twelver Shi'ism was the consolidation of the power of the clergy as an independent force that outlasted the Safavid dynasty.

This is clear from the evolution in Sunni Islam of the shari'a, today misunderstood as Islamic "law," even though it had the exact opposite properties of what we understand as "law" today. A proper definition of the shari'a is that it is the sum total of practical ways of being a Muslim in the world. These practical ways far exceed in their scope and purpose legal matters and what we generally understand by "law" today—including such matters as questions of faith, daily manners, rules of hygiene, proper composure, mourning rituals, and thousands of other details concerning how one should lead one's own daily life as a good Muslim. Indeed, more appropriate than the concept of "law" would be to regard the shari'a as an anarchic system of social organization. The anarchic features of the shari'a become evident when we consider its three distinctive historical properties:

1. The shari'a has never been a uniform body of rules. It is elaborated according to the methods of different interpretive schools, both historically and in the present. The four surviving schools in Sunni Islam accept the multiplicity of shari'a as a basic historic and contemporary property of an Islamic way of life.
2. The shari'a may involve contradictory advice that does not require synthesis or resolution. A learned shari'a-based judgment (fatwa) may be contradicted by another. Sociologically speaking, the validity of the judgment depends on the extent to which it is followed, and not on its inner logic or consistency with tradition.
3. The shari'a was elaborated in civil society by scholarly authorities, and not by state legislators. It was not state-oriented in the sense that it did not describe the functions of the state, only how individuals should behave. State matters were addressed in different genre, *siyasa*, which emerged explicitly because the shari'a did not cover its scope.

The shari'a developed over several centuries in historical Muslim civil societies to become a comprehensive but flexible guide for life. The careers of the founders of the main Sunni schools of shari'a, of which only four have survived out of more than twenty schools that flourished at some point or another during the first three centuries of Islam, consistently show a dogged distance from state affairs.

In its general outline, this same story is typical of the clash between the authority of learning, oriented toward elaborating Islam as a basis of an autonomous civic culture, and political authority, which with few exceptions saw Islam largely as a means to its own consolidation. The few exceptions were, as they still are, well-noted by Muslims themselves, precisely because they are exceptions: the first four caliphs, known collectively as Al-Rashidun; the Umayyad caliph Umar Ibn Abd al-Aziz; the Murabitun state founder Yusuf Ibn Tashfin; and a few others. But the general expectation was that the authority of learning and that of the state followed different rather than synergetic requirements.

Modern states in the Muslim world were all well aware of this dynamic, and therefore one of their first acts of "modernization" involved to some degree or other attempts to subdue or co-opt established religious institutions. If there is a problem of authority in modern Islam, therefore, it can be traced to the nature of the modern state rather than to ancient dynamics. All modern states sought to either marginalize Islamic authority in civil society, whose space the modern state wanted to occupy, or co-opt such an authority for state purposes (Abu al-Afjan 1985:325; Carmichael 1997; Fischbach 2001; Khoo Salma 2002; Oberauer 2008; Pianciola and Sartori 2007). Emblematic of this was the transformation of al-Azhar under Jamal Abd al-Nasser into a state institution. Another event that looks very different is in fact similar in its underlying logic: the establishment of a Wahhabi state in Saudi Arabia should also be seen as an example of modern state effort to transform religious life for its own purposes. The Wahhabi state was from the beginning based on a novel proposition that was unfamiliar to most Muslims and that was the proposition that there should be no distance between the men of religious learning and the men of temporal power. And in this form Wahhabism itself was from its beginning in eighteenth-century Arabia unenforceable without a program of political control that was integral to it from inception.

Historically, the civic authority of the learned class was facilitated by the consolidation of charitable endowments (waqf), whose regulation was one of the earlier issues to confront the evolving shari'a. A waqf was typically a private endowment consisting of real estate, although it could also consist of any other property that is able to generate income into perpetuity. It could be used for any charitable purpose, and it was for example used to support hospitals, welfare for the poor, or the upkeep of cemeteries (Arjomand 1999; Assi 2008; Çizakça 2000; Deguilhem 1995; Doumani 1998; Fay 1997, 1998; Hennigan 2004; Hoexter 2002; Layish 2008; Sayyid 1989; Shaham 2000; Shatzmiller 2001).

What has not changed much, however, was the expectation that religious authority in social life must be based on accomplishments and reputation, rather than investiture in a state-office. The institutionalization of religion into state offices in Iran after the Revolution only tarnished the reputation of the clergy, and it appears that toward the end of his life Khomeini himself was becoming aware of that fact (Sadjadpour 2008: 10). Historically as well as today, the validity of any religious opinion, or fatwa, among Muslims rests entirely on how many people believe in it, rather than on its legal enforceability. And the extent to which a fatwa is believed in depends, among other things, on the reputation of the person issuing the fatwa (i.e., on something that requires many years of active participation in civic life). Being dependent on a political power usually diminished such reputation, since reputation could be sustained only by verifiable moral independence.

The fact that the shari'a became not only a code of civic and personal life that had little to do with state politics or the art of administering a state is illustrated by the evolution in North Africa and the Middle East toward the tenth century and after of a different science, *siyasa* or the science of politics, that was explicitly distinguished from the shari'a. Tarif Khalidi (1996: 193–200), who traced that evolution, showed that this science of politics covered three areas, one of which concerned acts of government that were not within the scope of the shari'a. The other two uses of the science of *siyasa*, compiled entirely by advisors to rulers rather than by religious scholars, illustrate what is meant by "acts of government that go beyond the scope of the shari'a." Those concerned effectiveness of state policies, and the management of the state itself (i.e., genres that are equivalent to what Michel Foucault described as "governmentality" in European sciences of state).

On the other hand, the shari'a coexisted as well with another source of regulation of autonomous civic life, namely local customary traditions, often distinguished from shari'a in being called such terms as *taqalid*, *'urf*, *qanun*, *'adat*, all of which referred to local traditions, customs, or mores that were not originated by the shari'a but did not explicitly contradict it either (see Table 3.1). However, those terms connoted a local code that may be traced to tribal customs, highland tradition, or communal identity in a way that was distinct from the shari'a. The degree to which shari'a adapted to or replaced local codes is often difficult to assess, as both shari'a and local customs were marks of a self-organized civic life. But the main distinction between the two was that the shari'a claimed a divine source and thus universal validity, whereas something like a highland qanun tended to be "secular," in the sense that its authority derived from ancient familiarity and local rootedness, rather than universal divine mandates.

Subsequently the shari'a, as a gradual and pragmatic way of elaborating Islam in a variety of social worlds, had to adjust to various localisms, thus the variety of its schools becoming an acknowledged fact from the earliest points of Islamic expansion beyond Arabia. The most inventive were those schools that flourished in new environments like Mesopotamia and Persia, where urban life and local customs required formulating answers to hitherto unforeseen questions. By contrast, the more orthodox and literalist schools, such as that of Ibn Hanbal, held sway largely in relatively isolated territories that saw little social change, such as central Arabia. This multiplicity of the shari'a, which reflected its adjustment to local conditions, required neither streamlining nor

Table 14.1 Historical genres of autonomy and control

Genre	Scope	Attempted earlier mixtures (first three centuries of Islam; continuing)	Attempted later mixtures (beginning circa fourth Hijra century)	Attempted modern mixtures (esp. twentieth century & since)
Shari'a	Universal civics	*Shari'a* & *'Urf*	*Siyasa* & *'Urf*	*Shari'a* & *Siyasa*
Siyasa	State rule			
'Urf (aka *Qanun*, *taqalid*, *'adat*)	Local customs			

Source: M. Bamyeh.

official rules to set the boundaries of orthodoxy. In contrast to Christianity, for example, the doctrines of Islam were never defined in any meeting like the Council of Nicea (or the following twenty councils).

Free Movement

Corollary to the principle of partial control was a principle of free movement of pilgrims, adventurers, merchants, and various communities throughout a Muslim World that remained for centuries at the heart of the world system. Travel eased the concentration of demographic pressures in resource-poor areas, built channels of communication between intellectual communities, provided for a distinct global civil society forged across the great urban centers, and endowed especially the cities with a vibrant multi-ethnic fabric. One Thousand and One Nights may be regarded as one great literary expression of the principle of free movement: The protagonists there are more often on the road from one destination to another than at home. The reality of free movement is evident in the documented histories of scholarly communication within the Muslim world. The main interpretive approaches to Islam established themselves in global learning circuits.

Focusing on the Mediterranean, Goitein (1967–1993, 1: 1–42) mentions that a "journey from Spain to Egypt or from Marseilles to the Levant was a humdrum experience, about which a seasoned traveller would not waste a word. Commuting regularly between Tunisia or Sicily or even Spain and the eastern shores of the Mediterranean was nothing exceptional." He further adds: "Mediterranean man in the Middle Ages was an impassioned and preserving traveler ... the discomfort and insecurity involved in [travel] were insufficient to discourage travel necessary for administrative, business, or social needs" (1967–1993, 1: 273–4).

The centrality of long-distance trade to wealth generation in the Muslim world was one of the defining characteristics of its economy from its earliest point. This is exemplified in one measure by the fact that in addition to illness, travel is the only other ground listed in the Qur'an for exemption from the religious requirement of fasting during the month of Ramadan. And at least one classic source of Islamic economic ethics, al-Hubayshi's fourteenth-century compendium *al-Baraka fi Fadl al-Sa'y wa al-Haraka*, highlights the metaphor of "movement" as the basic character of all economic activity. Geography, as a science of movement, was one of the first sciences established as a distinct genre among the Islamicate learned communities. More than two dozen classic geographic compendia, and countless lesser ones, describing roads, destinations, and manners of distant peoples survive in some form from the early and medieval periods. In more general terms, movement as a basic norm of religious and economic life meant that "borders," which may have meant much to sovereigns, would be given as little attention as possible by everyone else within the Muslim World.

Just as with the principle of partial control, the principle of free movement originated out of dynamics having little to do with the foresight or planning of governments and sovereigns. It emerged rather out of other realities and dynamics: (1) the historical fact that the Muslim world in effect inherited the territorial space of older world systems; (2) a sociological dynamic that lends conversion to Islam the character of being a way to surround connections with global trade partners with a binding ethical cosmos, most notably in central Africa and Southeast Asia; and (3) a connective cosmopolitan urbanity, through which Islam itself appeared as primarily an urban religion appealing most immediately, although of course not exclusively, to the commercial urban classes (Muhammad himself being part of that class before revelation).

Religion therefore expressed rather than simply created global social realities. The clearest examples here may be drawn from early histories of conversion to Islam in Africa (e.g., Robinson 2004), where to become a "Muslim" was an expression of the fact that one belonged to a merchant class defined by its global connections. Of course, the notion that Islam is one expression of global connectedness never meant that Islam meant the same thing to all Muslims, only that it was in the nature of global religions to offer themselves up as ways of expressing a feeling of being part of some global reality.

Apart from the factors mentioned above, the principle of free movement by its nature fostered the further evolution of networks that became over time engraved in the fabric of deep reality. One of these was common educational and mannerist expectations, which allowed for the easy circulation of at least the elites. The *rihla*, or travel narrative, emerged as a distinct genre in Islamic history, including countless great and small collections.

The efforts of historians have helped shed more light on patterns of connection among merchant and scholarly communities in the Islamic world (e.g., Abu-Lughod 1989; Doumani 1995; Fawaz 1983; Goitein 1967–1993). Richard Bulliet has argued that aspiring Muslim rulers who lacked the necessary credentials to be called "caliph" found that they could accumulate significant compensatory prestige by claiming that they were facilitators of pilgrimage and its sites. According to him, Saladin, the first non-caliph to adopt the term *Khadim al-Haramain* ("Servitor of the Two Holy Places"), was also associated with the evolution of the status of Mecca as a magnet for global scholarly communities, a process that ultimately resulted in that "pilgrimage to Mecca replaced the caliphate as the central unifying entity in Islam" (Bulliet 2013: 8).

Historical literature shows the degree of institutionalization of merchant and scholarly networks. The merchant communities used caravans; caravansaries; the practice of using an agent to represent a merchant in distant lands; risk pooling societies (i.e., precursors to the modern "company"); and credit and insurance arrangements. The knowledge communities developed instruments of cultural capital, notably certificates (*ijaza*) that spelled out what a person has learned, from whom, and the branch of knowledge he may be entrusted to teach. The validity of an ijaza depended naturally on the reputation of the scholar issuing it, as well as on his location in a global scholarly network.

Heteroglossia

Islam has frequently been described as a house of harmony or at least well-integrated social order (e.g., Watt 1961). This view, held by many sympathetic observers, is likewise often held by detractors, who wish to highlight the conformity and authoritarianism that for them define the essence of Islam. That Islam was historically and is in the present a very diverse practice is well-known to any serious student of the faith.

I propose to capture this basic property of a sociology of Islam in the term "heteroglossia." The term "heteroglossia" was coined in the 1930s by the Russian literary scholar Mikhail Bakhtin, who used it to analyze the way by which a single literary work housed multiple voices originating in different social standpoints. There are two ways in which this formulation may be expanded to explain the sociology of any discourse that, like a novel, appears as a unified body. The first concerns a distinction between "heteroglossia" and "diversity," the second the social unconscious of religion.

Heteroglossia is not simple "diversity" in the sense that the community of believers does not regard itself as diverse as it is in reality. As Bakhtin outlines it, voices in the novel inhabit the same narrative space, when in effect they originate from a diversity of social locations and interests. "Diversity," the term to which we are more accustomed, describes a condition in which a variety of narratives compete to tell their own story. "Heteroglossia," by contrast, describes a condition in which a single narrative imposes order, but not unity, on the variety of voices within it. Heteroglossia is imagined unity; diversity is proclaimed disunity. The former allows particular voices to express themselves as if they were the voices of all; the latter allows particular voices to express themselves largely to those that are alike.

Each is a different game of social communication, but the basic difference is that while diversity is recognizable at the borderlines of communities, heteroglossia is the unrecognized, and thus unconscious, property of the community. It is due to these properties that heteroglossia, unlike diversity, is better equipped to escape repression or censorship. Likewise, it is also due to these properties that heteroglossia is better equipped to advance toward universalism—its only cause.

Islam is of course not the only belief system with heteroglossic properties. What concerns us here however is how these properties evolved to become indispensable for the social life of the faith. Already at its founding phase, during Muhammad's own lifetime, Islam transformed from being an attempt to create a local, Mecca-centered tradition into a universal belief system into which the interests and viewpoints of various social groups, classes, tribes, and styles of life could be incorporated (Bamyeh 1999). The point of departure could in fact be precisely identified with Muhammad's migration into Medina—in effect abandoning his hometown of Mecca, which had rejected his prophetic claims, for a larger world.

That different social forces and interests saw themselves as addressees of a single divine message meant that the further expansion of Islam worldwide could only do more of the same. Thus, Islam could simultaneously in its long history be used to justify revolutions advocating communist equality—others defending inequalities of wealth. Movements opposed to any political authority not explicitly consented to by the umma—others praising the virtues of despotic rule. Practices oriented toward mystical Sufism—opposing doctrines requiring rational theological sobriety. Propositions defending gender inequality—others advancing the exact opposite point. Economic doctrines oriented toward the interests of the merchant class—others highlighting the needs of the poor. Sayings, all attributed to the prophet, praising austerity and modesty. Others, likewise attributed to the prophet, defending the rights of the wealthy to live ostentatiously.

The basic character of heteroglossia is not simply that for every argument there is a counter-argument and for every position there are many possible opposites within the same tradition. The counter-arguments and the many positions are features of the same system, not of competing systems. Within heteroglossic systems, few talk of "diversity," but all talk about the meaning of the same sentence. And it is the toleration of such a divisive sentence, more so than the toleration of its multiple meanings, that holds together the heteroglossic system.

This common reference possesses by its nature a heteroglossic property, since it allows each person who uses it in her own manner to hypothesize that she is speaking of the essence of the system and not simply of a variation within it. On the other hand, heteroglossia, also by its nature, replaces the propensity toward civil war that is always latent in clashing essentialist standpoints, with a convivial social life characterized by organized anarchy, where authorities remain multiple and the final authority is reserved to god or postponed until his judgment. Until then, heteroglossia governs life on earth.

Heteroglossia versus Inquisition

Just like the two previous principles of historical Islam, namely partial control and free movement, heteroglossia thrives best when existing authorities do not have sufficient power to impose orthodoxies. Global systems tend to give rise to some calls for strong ruling authority or empire, although global systems do not require empire by any necessity, nor even strong authority. The universalist culture of the system, which emerges in stable and voluntary forms only through heteroglossia rather than force, survives best when the system itself includes strong egalitarian claims.

If heteroglossia has been such a central global property of this historical faith, how do we account for what appears to be its recurrent opposite, namely, attempts to impose a single and binding orthodoxy? Here I would like to explore this question by clarifying the distinction between heteroglossia and inquisition as two facets of the social life of any religion.

Both heteroglossia and inquisition are two features of the same phenomenon, namely that religious life is characterized at one and the same time by fragmented

Table 14.2 Inquisition versus heteroglossia as strategies of faith management

	Heteroglossia	Inquisition
Method of organizing fragmented social reality	Organized by voluntary agreements on reference point	Organized by force
Method of observing faith	Observing exteriors	Observing interiors
Cost	Low cost	High cost
Duration	Constant	Recurrent, episodic

Source: M. Bamyeh

reality and organizational impulse. The clash of the two features—reality of fragmentation and impulse to put it into order—should be more frequent the more global and older a religion becomes. That is because longevity and expanse expose religious ideas to the variety of the human experience. It is in fact only in entertaining and resolving a constant clash between heteroglossia and inquisition that a religion may be said to be living, since in so doing it reflects and then absorbs the complexity of humanity itself.

Both heteroglossia and inquisition are strategies of universalism. But while heteroglossia consists of the strategy by which encountered varieties in the human landscape are absorbed into an ever-growing reservoir of religious conceptions, inquisition describes the strategy by which attention is increasingly directed at the real unity of the universal community. At one level, inquisition may be said to be motivated by the fear of the fragmentation that heteroglossia fosters in its natural movement. Inquisition, therefore, is the recurrent rejection of the liberal excess of heteroglossia in religious life. Inquisition consists of the belief that a common social life requires a source of commonality deeper than appearances. Therefore, inquisition requires interrogation or active questioning, and a demand that adherence to an orthodoxy be verified not simply in externally visible rituals, but in such a way that the rituals may allow the observer to see into the interior of the observed. Thus, settings that involve intimate and constant contact, as in the ideal of monastic life, reflect the highest hopes of a strategy of inquisition. The same is essentially true of all forms of religious education that involves lengthy contact between teacher and student, as well as of social movements where members tend to spend much time together, either in fighting camps or when they live together as a matter of principle.

The demands on individual life of the heteroglossic strategy, by contrast, tend to be less intense. It is for this reason that heteroglossia always escapes the claws of inquisition at the last moment. Inquisition requires constant mobilization of precious resources (time, dedicated personnel, organizational resources, coercive capacity, supervision techniques, testing methods, means to overpower resistance, and so on). By contrast, heteroglossia requires little more than hiding away in times of inquisition. At all other times, heteroglossia thrives in the general tenor of pragmatic conservatism, and on the basic intellectual orientations of ordinary life.

Conclusion

In a recent book, Armando Salvatore has proposed the priority of civility over legality in Muslim history (Salvatore 2016: 63–4). In connection to our discussions here, civility would be an aspect of two simultaneous properties of global systems of knowledge: the imperfect knowledge of partners of each other, yet their mutual expectation of some similarity of manners that would allow them to communicate and become predictable to each other. In this sense, civility is the property of uncoerced (since coercion cancels out the need for civility) global systems. This civility, which comes from below and is learned outside of the state (or, as is usually the case in most of the world, in spite of it), is a fundamental building block of global culture. The fact that we learn about civility thus far only with the aid of specific civilizational histories—that of Islam in this case—does not mean that it is a property of any specific culture. Rather, it means that civility is the property of any cultural system that becomes global through voluntary dynamics.

Note

1 This article is a highly condensed version of chapter 3 of Bamyeh, M. A. (2019), *Lifeworlds of Islam* (Oxford: Oxford University Press). Earlier short versions have appeared in Manfred Steger, ed., *Rethinking Globalism* (Rowan & Littlefield, 2004), and Scott Nelson and Nevzat Soguk, eds., *The Ashgate Research Companion to Modern Theory, Modern Power, World Politics* (Farnham, Surrey, England: Ashgate, 2016).

References

Abd al-Raziq, Ali. (1925) 2000. *Al-Islam wa Usul al-Hukm*. Ed. Muhammad Imara. Beirut: Al-Mu'assassah al-'Arabiyyah li al-Dirasat wa al-Nashr.
Abd al-Raziq, A. (2000), *Al-Islam wa Usul al-Hukm*, Ed. Muhammad Imara, Beirut: Al-Mu'assassah al-'Arabiyyah li al-Dirasat wa al-Nashr.
Abu al-Afjan, M. (1985), "al-Waqf 'ala al-Masjid fi al-Maghrib wa al-Andalus," *Dirasat fi al-Iqtisad al-Islami*, 315–42.
Abu-Lughod, J. (1989), *Before European Hegemony*, New York: Oxford University Press.
Arjomand, S. A. 1999. "The Law, Agency, and Policy in Medieval Islamic Society: Development of the Institutions of Learning from the Tenth to the Fifteenth Century," *Comparative Studies in Society & History*, 41 (2): 263–93.
Assi, E. (2008), "Islamic Waqf and Management of Cultural Heritage in Palestine," *International Journal of Heritage Studies*, 14 (4): 380–5.
Bamyeh, M. (1999), *The Social Origins of Islam: Mind, Economy, Discourse*, Minneapolis: University of Minnesota Press.

Bamyeh, M. (2000), *The Ends of Globalization*, Minneapolis: University of Minnesota Press.

Bulliett, R. W. (2013), *"Religion and the State in Islam: From Medieval Caliphate to the Muslim Brotherhood,"* Denver: University of Denver Center for Middle East Studies, occasional paper no. 2.

Carmichael, T. (1997), "British 'Practice' Towards Islam in the East Africa Protectorate: Muslim Officials, Waqf Administration, and Secular Education in Mombasa and Environs, 1895–1920," *Journal of Muslim Minority Affairs*, 17 (2): 293–309.

Çizakça, M. (2000), *A History of Philanthropic Foundations: The Islamic World from the Seventh Century to the Present*, Istanbul: Boğazici University.

Deguilhem, R., ed. (1995), *Le waqf dans l'espace islamique: outil de pouvoir socio-politique*, Damascus: Institut français de Damas.

Doumani, B. (1995), *Rediscovering Palestine: Merchants and Peasants in Jabal Nablus, 1700–1900*, Berkeley: University of California Press.

Doumani, B. (1998), "Endowing Family: Waqf, Property Devolution, and Gender in Greater Syria, 1800 to 1860," *Comparative Studies in Society & History*, 40 (1): 3–41.

Fawaz, L. T. (1983), *Merchants and Migrants in Nineteenth-Century Beirut*, Cambridge: Harvard University Press.

Fay, M. A. (1997), "Women and Waqf: Toward a Reconsideration of Women's Place in the Mamluk Household," *International Journal of Middle East Studies*, 29: 33–51.

Fay, M. A. (1998), "From Concubines to Capitalists: Women, Property, and Power in Eighteenth-Century Cairo," *Journal of Women's History*, 10 (3): 118–40.

Fischbach, M. R. (2001), "Britain and the Ghawr Abi 'Ubayda Waqf Controversy in Transjordan," *International Journal of Middle East Studies*, 33 (4): 525–44.

Goitein, S. D. (1967–93), *A Mediterranean Society: The Jewish Communities of the Arab World as Portrayed in the Documents of the Cairo Geniza*, 6 vols, Berkeley: University of California Press.

Hennigan, P. C. (2004), *The Birth of a Legal Institution: The Formation of the Waqf in Third-century A.H. Hanafi Legal Discourse*, Leiden: Brill.

Hoexter, M. (2002), "The Waqf and the Public Sphere," in M. Hoexter, S. N. Eisenstadt and N. Levtzion (eds.), *The Public Sphere in Muslim Societies*, 119–38, Albany: SUNY Press.

Khalidi, T. (1996), *Arabic Historical Thought in the Classical Period*, Cambridge: Cambridge University Press.

Layish, A. (2008), "Waqfs of Awld al-Nas in Aleppo in the Late Mamluk Period as Reflected in a Family Archive," *Journal of the Economic & Social History of the Orient*, 51 (2): 287–326.

Na'im, Abdullahi an- (2008), *Islam and the Secular State: Negotiating the Future of the Shari'a*, Cambridge: Harvard University Press.

Nasution, K. S. (2002), "Colonial Intervention and Transformation of Muslim Waqf Settlements in Urban Penang: The Role of the Endowments Board," *Journal of Muslim Minority Affairs*, 22 (2): 299–15.

Oberauer, N. (2008), "'Fantastic Charities': The Transformation of Waqf Practice in Colonial Zanzibar," *Islamic Law & Society*, 15 (3): 315–70.

Pianciola, N. and P. Sartori (2007), "Waqf in Turkestan: The Colonial Legacy and the Fate of an Islamic Institution in Early Soviet Central Asia, 1917–1924," *Central Asian Survey*, 26 (4): 475–98.

Robinson, D. (2004), *Muslim Societies in African History*, Cambridge: Cambridge University Press.

Sadjadpour, K. (2008), *Reading Khamenei: The World View of Iran's Most Powerful Leader*, Washington, DC: Carnegie Endowment for International Peace.

Salvatore, A. (2016), *The Sociology of Islam: Knowledge, Power and Civility*, Oxford: Wiley Blackwell.

Shaham, R. (2000), "Masters, Their Freed Slaves, and the Waqf in Egypt (Eighteenth–Twentieth Centuries)," *Journal of the Economic & Social History of the Orient*, 43 (2): 162–88.

Shatzmiller, M. (2001), "Islamic Institutions and Property Rights: The Case of the 'Public Good' Waqf," *Journal of the Economic & Social History of the Orient*, 44 (1): 44–74.

Sayyid, Abd al-Malik (1989), "al-Waqf al-Islami wa al-Dawr alladhi la'ibahu fi numuw al-Ijtima fi al-Islam," in H. al-Amin (ed.), *Idarat wa Tathmir Mumtalakat al-Awqaf*, 225–304, Jeddah: Islamic Research and Training Institute.

Watt, W. M. (1961), *Islam and the Integration of Society*, Evanston: Northwestern University Press.

When Do Muslims Vote Islamic?

by Charles Kurzman and Didem Türkoğlu

A dozen years ago, before the "Arab Spring," Islamic political parties had a poor record in parliamentary elections. Of the 179 Islamic parties that had contested 91 parliamentary elections in 21 countries since 1970, only 14 parties in 8 countries won more than a third of the available seats.[1] More than half of Islamic parties won 6 percent or less of seats, and in more than half the elections, all Islamic parties combined won 15 percent or less of seats.[2] The freer the election, moreover, the worse Islamic parties fared.

At the same time, Islamic parties' electoral platforms had shifted noticeably in a liberal direction: decade by decade, more Islamic parties emphasized democracy and equal rights for women and religious minorities, and fewer of them ran on platforms promising the implementation of *shari'a*, armed *jihad*, or a ban on interest.

In late 2010 and early 2011, uprisings led to the fall of long-ruling autocrats in Tunisia, Egypt, and Libya. The leaders of Jordan, Morocco, and several other Muslim-majority countries inaugurated political reforms for fear of losing power. Elections brought Islamic parties into office across North Africa (except for Algeria), and many Muslim communities witnessed the growth of deeply conservative Salafi movements. The trends that were visible over previous decades seemed to have been reversed.

Or were they? This study updates results from two previous papers, published in *The Journal of Democracy* in 2010 and 2015, that presented systematic evidence on these subjects.[3] Here we present data on Islamic political parties' performance in parliamentary elections through the end of 2020, along with an expanded set of electoral platforms. We find that Islamic parties have not fared much better in elections since the Arab Spring than before. As in earlier years, a handful of Islamic parties have won pluralities of the vote, especially in "breakthrough" elections after long periods of autocratic rule, while most Islamic parties received 2 percent of seats in parliament or less. The Islamic political sector as a whole—that is, the proportion of seats won by *all* Islamic parties in each election—fell slightly to a median of 12 percent since the Arab Spring.

For years, autocrats in Muslim-majority countries sought to justify their rule by warning that free elections would bring radical Islamic parties to power. When the strongmen of Tunisia and Egypt were swept from office by the mass uprisings of early 2011, these warnings were put to a test. Sure enough, Islamic political parties won 41 percent of the seats in the Tunisian constituent assembly in October 2011 and 69 percent of the seats in the Egyptian parliament in December 2011 and January 2012. The latter performance was comparable to the strongest ever by any Islamic political party, the 81 percent vote share that Algeria's Islamic Salvation Front won in late 1991 during the initial round of Algeria's first-ever multiparty parliamentary election. (The Algerian military shut down the voting after that first round, sparking a civil war that killed tens of thousands.)

Tunisia and Egypt proved to be outliers, however. Of the 113 Islamic parties contesting forty-two parliamentary elections in twenty countries during the period from 2011 through 2020, only six won a third or more of seats: the Renaissance Party (Ennahda) in Tunisia, the Freedom and Justice Party (FJP) in Egypt, the Party of God (Hezbollah) in Lebanon, the Justice and Development Party (PJD) in Morocco (just under one-third of seats), the ruling National Congress Party of Sudan, and the incumbent Justice and Development Party (AKP) in Turkey. These countries were the only places where Islamic parties as a whole won a third or more of seats following the Arab Spring. (Islamic parties also won just under one-third of seats in Indonesia and Iraq.)

The most dramatic of these peak performances came in breakthrough elections that offered relatively fair competition after years of repressive secular regimes. This continued a pattern that was visible prior to the Arab Spring as well in Jordan (1989), Algeria (1991), Indonesia (1999), Bahrain (2002), Turkey (2002), Iraq (2005), and Palestine (2006). Islamic parties as a whole won a median of 52 percent of seats in breakthrough elections, as compared with a median of 13 percent in other elections.

In countries where relatively open elections have become routine, support for Islamic parties has tended to decay over time. A prominent example was in Tunisia, where Ennahda and other Islamic parties won a total of 41 percent of seats in 2011 but dropped to the low 30s in 2014 and 2019, moving from government to opposition. In Indonesia, where Islamic parties averaged a combined 38 percent of seats in 1999 and 2004, the total dropped to 30 percent across the 2009, 2014, and 2019 elections. In Turkey, the AKP won more than 60 percent of seats in 2002 and 2007, but has never reached that level in the four elections since then, including two elections in which it dropped below a majority of parliament. In Lebanon, Hezbollah dropped from 52 percent of seats in 2005 to 48 percent in 2009 and 44 percent in 2018.

By contrast, most Islamic parties have been marginal. In the five years after the Arab Spring began, numerous Islamic parties entered the electoral fray, averaging thirteen parties per year as compared with eight per year in the decade before the uprisings and six per year in the last decade of the twentieth century. The bulk of these were fringe parties, however, more than half of which won less than 2 percent of seats in parliament, and only a fifth of which won 10 percent or more. The median percentage of seats won in each election in this period by all Islamic parties, combined, was 14 percent.[4]

In the next half-decade, from 2016 through 2020, fewer Islamic political parties, less than ten per year, participated in parliamentary elections—one of the most prominent Islamic parties, the Muslim Brotherhood's Freedom and Justice Party in Egypt, was labeled a terrorist organization after the coup of 2013 and disbanded, with thousands of its members arrested. For Islamic parties that continued to participate in elections, most won less than 3 percent of seats in parliament. The median percentage of seats won by all Islamic parties dropped slightly to 10 percent.

The overall trend, both for individual Islamic parties and for the Islamic political sector as a whole, has curved downward in recent years. Individual-party performance hit a plateau in the 1990s and began declining gradually in the early 2000s (see the Lowess fitted line in Figure 15.1). The Islamic political sector as a whole garnered an increasing share of electoral sphere until just before the 2011 uprisings (see the Lowess fitted line in Figure 15.2). By these metrics, Islamic parties have been less successful in parliamentary elections after the "Arab Spring" uprisings than before.

Scholars have noted that Islamic parties under semi-authoritarian systems often avoid confrontation with the state by purposefully trying *not* to win elections, usually by restricting the number of candidates they field.[5] We have been able to determine the number of seats contested by almost half the Islamic parties participating in parliamentary elections, including almost all the most successful parties. We found little difference in the average percentage of seats contested before and after the Arab Spring. As anticipated, though, major parties did contest more seats in recent years. Since 2011, almost every election involving Islamic parties has seen at least one of them contest half or more of the available seats in parliament. In Egypt, the political arm of the Muslim Brotherhood ran for more than twice as many seats in 2011 as in earlier elections. In 2011, just over half its candidates won. This was the same share that it managed in

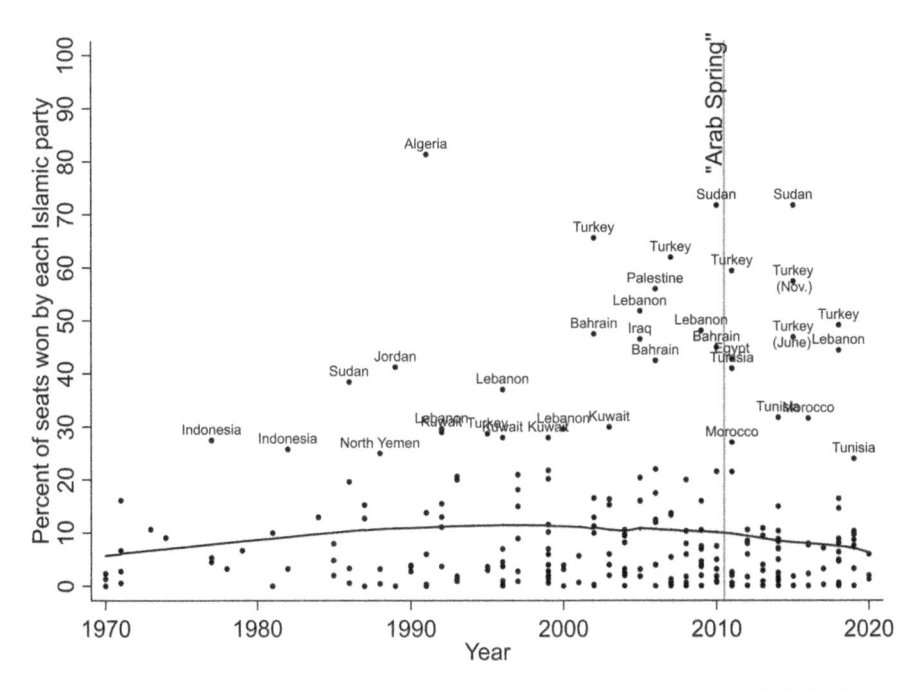

Figure 15.1 Seats won by Islamic parties in parliamentary elections, 1970–2020 (individual Islamic parties).

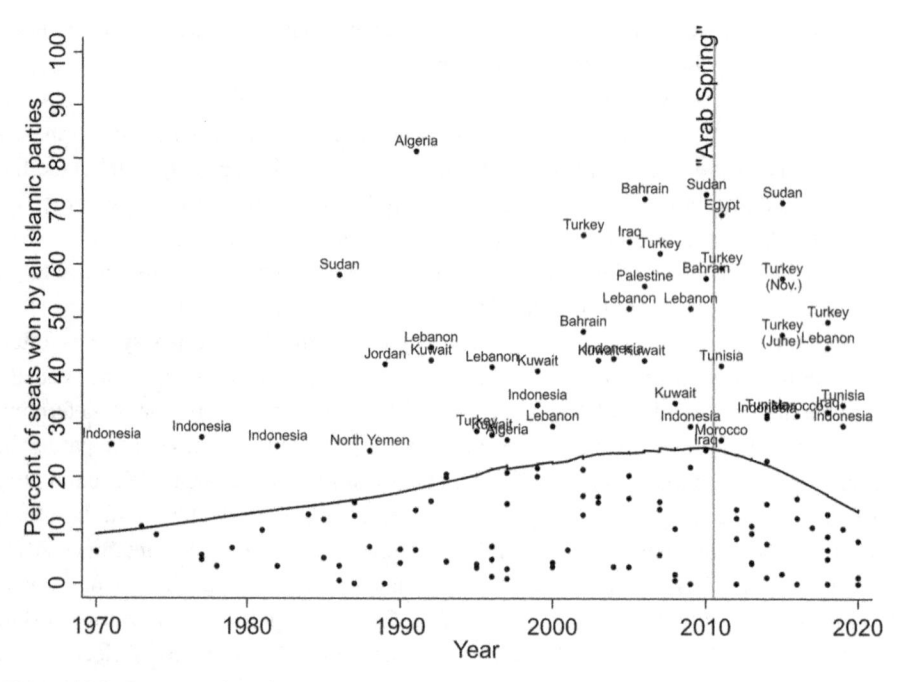

Figure 15.2 Seats won by Islamic parties in parliamentary elections, 1970–2020 (all Islamic parties combined).

2005, its best showing before the Arab Spring. In Morocco, the PJD ran more than three times as many candidates in 2011 as in any previous elections, but with much lower efficiency: in 2007, the party won almost half the ninety-four seats it contested, while in 2011 it won only 27 percent of 393 races.

Complex electoral systems have also played a role in some of these elections. Sources of complexity include the practice of reserving certain seat shares for women and other groups, unevenly populated districts, combinations of proportional representation and single-member districts, electoral thresholds that keep small parties out of parliament, and other factors, some of them intentionally introduced to manipulate electoral outcomes. Overall, however, these complications have had no clear effect on the success of Islamic political parties.

Competition among Islamic Parties

Meanwhile, the existence of multiple political parties claiming an Islamic identity has often led to "inter-Islamist conflicts."[6] The tensions seem to spring in part from ideological differences and in part from political rivalries.

One dramatic example is the rift between Egypt's two leading Islamic parties, the Muslim Brotherhood's FJP and the leading Salafist political organization, the Party of Light (better known in Western media as the Nour Party). In late 2011, as Egypt's landmark parliamentary election loomed, the two formed a coalition along with numerous smaller parties. But Nour soon began complaining that the Brotherhood was dumping Salafist candidates into unpromising spots on the coalition list, and withdrew.[7] Nour's alternative "Islamist Alliance" went on to win 28 percent of the vote and 25 percent of seats, a showing bested only by the FJP's 38 percent of the vote and 43 percent of seats. When the FJP's Mohamed Morsi won the presidency in June 2012, several Nour Party leaders joined his government as junior partners, but left within months. Some Salafist leaders felt from the outset that the Brotherhood was trying to smother the aspirations of other Islamic parties. Yasir al-Borhany, deputy head of Salafist Call (Nour's parent organization), complained that "if they could, the Muslim Brotherhood would eliminate the Salafi movement."[8] By early 2013, Nour had ousted several leaders who had worked most closely with the FJP, and the two parties traded public recriminations.[9] In July 2013, Nour endorsed the military coup that removed the FJP from office, banned the Muslim Brotherhood, assaulted and killed hundreds of its supporters, and imprisoned thousands of its members.[10] Being a fellow Islamic party did not prevent Nour from supporting the destruction of Egypt's largest Islamic movement. The Nour Party continued to participate in the highly restricted elections of 2015 and 2020, winning under 2 percent of seats in parliament.

Outside the electoral arena, hostility among Islamic movements is even more pronounced. Revolutionary Islamic groups have long denounced Islamic parties that take part in the democratic process.[11] One revolutionary captured the tone in 2008: "May those despicable *Ikhwani* [Brotherhood] apostate apes suffer destruction soon and be punished for their crimes."[12] After the Arab Spring, revolutionary leaders railed against the flood of Islamic parties entering the electoral realm. Ayman al-Zawahiri of al-Qaeda, for example, accused Tunisia's Ennahda (and by extension other Islamic parties seeking elected office) of "inventing an 'Islam' that pleases the American Department of State, the European Union and the Gulf scholars. . . . an 'Islam' without jihad, without enforcing the good and prohibiting the malice, without [enforcing] 'loyalty [to believers] and enmity [to disbelievers].'"[13]

In a number of civil-war zones, revolutionaries have physically attacked Islamic leaders who support democratic engagement. At the peak of this violence in 2014, victims included Sheikh Mohammed Idris, chairman of the Council of Imams and Preachers of Kenya, who was shot dead; and Sheikh Abdullah al-Hassan, Muhammad al-Mansuri, and at least twelve other clerics who were executed by the self-declared Islamic State in Mosul, Iraq. Selvedin Beganović, an imam in Trnovi, Bosnia, survived a stabbing. The leaders of the central mosque in Kano, Nigeria, were killed along with dozens of their followers in a suicide bombing during Friday prayers on 28 November 2014. Despite such violence, more Islamic parties have engaged in parliamentary elections in recent years than ever before, averaging 3.3 Islamic parties per election since 2011 as compared to 2.2 in the previous decade and 1.0 in the last three decades of the twentieth century.

The Trend toward Liberalism

Of the 292 parliamentary electoral campaigns by Islamic parties between 1970 and 2020, we have been able to obtain and analyze 106 electoral platforms.[14] We identified how each platform discussed a series of major political issues, including three issues associated with liberal rights and three associated with Islamic movements:

Rights issues:

1. Statement of support for democracy and a secular polity, as opposed to opposition to democracy, no mention of democracy, or statements of support for democracy as defined through Islamic principles such as *shura* (consultation).
2. Statement in support of full legal equality for women, as opposed to no mention of women's rights or statements favoring a distinct women's role in family and society.
3. Statement in support of full legal equality for minorities, as opposed to no mention of minority rights or "separate but equal" style of inclusion with reference to some Islamic criteria.

Islamic issues:

1. Statement in support of implementation of *shari'a*, as opposed to opposition to implementation of *shari'a* or no mention of implementation of *shari'a*.
2. Statement in support of *jihad*, as opposed to opposition to *jihad* or no mention of *jihad*.
3. Statement proposing to ban interest-based banking, as opposed to no mention of interest-based banking or a general statement in support of Islamic banking.

As Figure 15.3 shows, the share of electoral platforms emphasizing these Islamic themes dropped significantly since the last decades of the twentieth century. Twelve out of fifteen platforms from the years 1970–95 proposed to implement *shari'a*, for example; since that time, fewer than half of the platforms (thirty-seven out of ninety-one) adopted this position. A similar pattern is visible in support for a ban on interest-based banking: seven of fifteen platforms during the period 1970–95 proposed to ban interest, as compared with eleven out of ninety-one platforms since then (and none of the ten platforms that we have found for 2016–20). More than half of the platforms in 1970–95 (nine out of fifteen) indicated support for *jihad*; only ten out of ninety-one platforms since then expressed this support. (It should be noted that *jihad*, in these contexts, refers primarily to historical anticolonial movements; in no platform did an Islamic party endorse violent revolution against its own state.)

Support for liberal rights forms an inverse pattern (see Figure 15.4). Support for secular democracy more than doubled from 27 percent of platforms in 1970–95 (four of fifteen) to 63 percent since then (fifty-nine of ninety-one). If we expand the definition

When Do Muslims Vote Islamic?

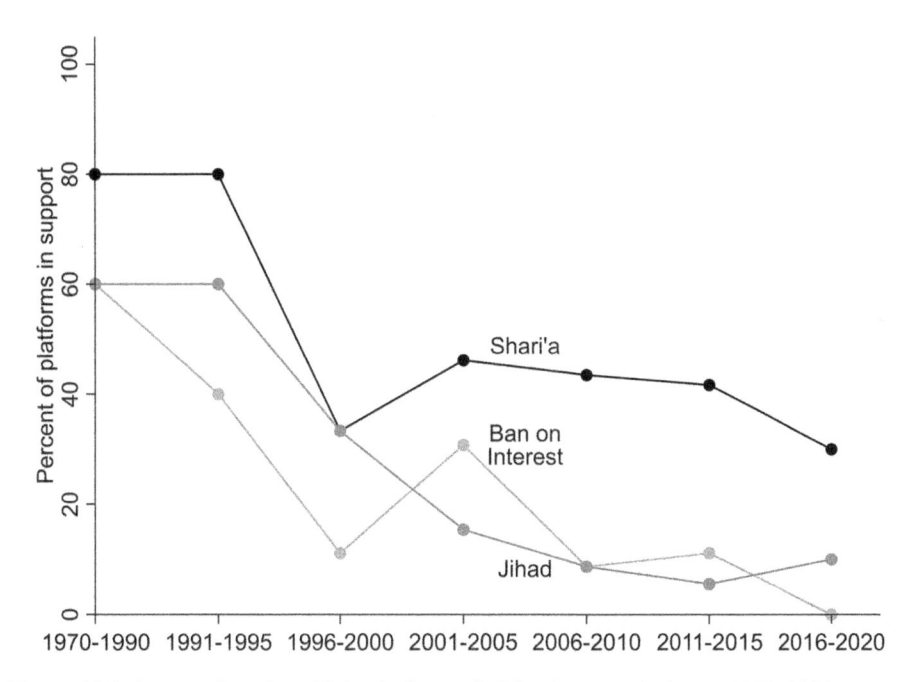

Figure 15.3 Support for selected Islamic themes in Islamic party platforms, 1970–2020.

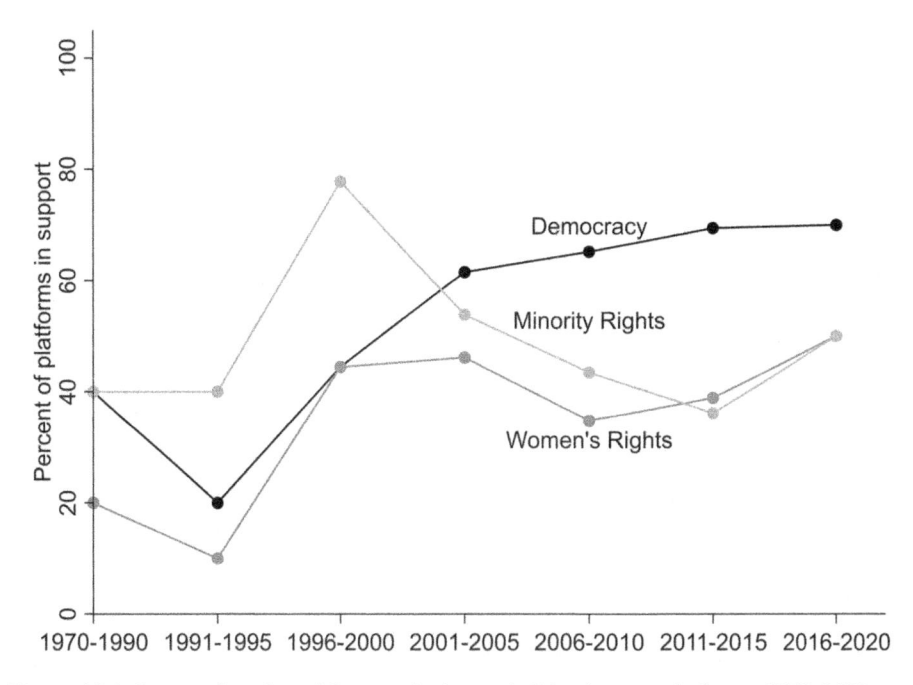

Figure 15.4 Support for selected democratic themes in Islamic party platforms, 1970–2020.

of democracy to include *shura*-style democracy, the rate of support is consistently high. Support for women's rights rose even more sharply, from less than one-seventh of platforms in 1970–95 (two of fifteen) to more than one-third since then (thirty-seven of ninety-one). The rights of minorities rose from 40 percent in 1970–95 (six of fifteen) to more than half in the following decade (fourteen of twenty-two), before dropping back to just over 40 percent since then (twenty-eight of sixty-nine).[15] The Arab Spring does not seem to mark a major turning point in the ideology of Islamic political parties.

Many people assume that democracy and rights naturally go hand-in-hand, but the two concepts are in fact distinct, and even in tension with each other: Democracy involves majority rule, while rights involve protections against the will of the majority.[16] Many Islamic movements—like religious and conservative movements in Christian and other contexts as well—have endorsed democratic processes along with restrictions on rights.

These trend patterns are heavily influenced by the profusion of small Islamic parties, most of which barely figure in the political life of Muslim-majority societies. Let us focus instead on seven of the oldest and most influential Islamic parties: the Muslim Brotherhood and its political arm, the FJP, in Egypt; the Pan-Malaysian Islamic Party (PAS); the PJD in Morocco; the Jamaat-e-Islami in Pakistan; Ennahda in Tunisia; and two parties in Turkey, the AKP and the Welfare (Refah) Party and its successors (summarized in Table 15.1).

A survey of these seven parties' platforms reveals no consistent trends. Ennahda in Tunisia maintained consistently liberal positions over the course of three elections. The AKP's platforms shifted slightly in a liberal direction, emphasizing equal rights for minorities in 2011 ("we have turned our hands toward the unjust treatment of our Alevi, non-Muslim, and Roma citizens, together with the most pressing Kurdish problem")— its platform has maintained this position even as it has jailed numerous elected Kurdish leaders. Morocco's PJD removed references to *shari'a* in its 2007 and later platforms, and added a vague sentence on the rights of minorities ("removing all forms of racial or ethnic discrimination") in 2016. At the same time, the PJD was inconsistent on women's rights: shifting from distinct roles for women to equal rights in 2007, then back to distinct roles in 2011 platform ("taking into account women's family responsibilities"), then dropping all reference to women's rights in 2016. Malaysia's PAS maintained a consistently liberal position on all of the issues coded for this study until conservatives ousted the party's liberal wing in 2015 and re-wrote the party's next electoral platform, introducing references to *shari'a* and *shura*-democracy and removing references to equal rights for women and minorities. The liberals ousted from leadership positions in PAS created a separate party and joined a secular pro-democracy coalition.

Three other major parties wavered on these high-profile issues, shifting back and forth on at least half of the six issues, with the Muslim Brotherhood in Egypt shifting on five of six (it remained consistent only in its vision of implementing *shari'a* through electoral mandate). In 2005, for example, the group's platform proposed an "Islamic method" of democracy, based on the Qur'anic "principle of consultation (*shura*)." In 2010, the

Table 15.1 Selected Liberal and Islamic Themes in Major Party Platforms

Country	Party	Year	Support for Democracy	Women's Rights	Minority Rights	Sharia	Jihad mentioned	Ban on interest
Egypt	MB	1987	Unreserved	No mention	Equal rights	Yes	Yes	No
Egypt	MB	1995	Unreserved	Equal rights	Equal rights	Yes	Yes	No
Egypt	MB	2000	Shura	Distinct roles	Islamic rights	Yes	No	No
Egypt	MB	2005	Shura	Distinct roles	Equal rights	Yes	No	Yes
Egypt	MB	2010	Unreserved	Equal rights	Equal rights	Yes	No	No
Egypt	FJP	2011	Shura	Distinct roles	Islamic rights	Yes	Yes	No
Malaysia	PAS	1999	Unreserved	Equal rights	Equal rights	No	No	No
Malaysia	PAS	2004	Unreserved	Equal rights	Equal rights	No	No	No
Malaysia	PAS	2008	Unreserved	Equal rights	Equal rights	No	No	No
Malaysia	PAS	2013	Unreserved	Equal rights	Equal rights	No	No	No
Malaysia	PAS	2018	Shura	No mention	No mention	Yes	No	No
Morocco	PJD	2002	Unreserved	Distinct roles	No mention	Yes	No	No
Morocco	PJD	2007	Unreserved	Equal rights	No mention	No	No	No
Morocco	PJD	2011	Unreserved	Distinct roles	No mention	No	No	No
Morocco	PJD	2016	Unreserved	No mention	Equal rights	No	No	No
Pakistan	JI	1970	Shura	Distinct roles	Islamic rights	Yes	No	Yes
Pakistan	JI	1988	Shura	Equal rights	Islamic rights	Yes	Yes	No
Pakistan	JI	2013	Shura	Distinct roles	Islamic rights	Yes	No	Yes
Tunisia	Ennahda	2011	Unreserved	Equal rights	No mention	No	No	No
Tunisia	Ennahda	2014	Unreserved	Equal rights	No mention	No	No	No
Tunisia	Ennahda	2019	Unreserved	Equal rights	No mention	No	No	No

Country	Party	Year	Support for Democracy	Women's Rights	Minority Rights	Sharia	Jihad mentioned	Ban on interest
Turkey	AKP	2002	Unreserved	Equal rights	No mention	No	No	No
Turkey	AKP	2007	Unreserved	Equal rights	No mention	No	No	No
Turkey	AKP	2011	Unreserved	Equal rights	Equal rights	No	No	No
Turkey	AKP	2015 (June)	Unreserved	Equal rights	Equal rights	No	No	No
Turkey	AKP	2015 (Nov.)	Unreserved	Equal rights	Equal rights	No	No	No
Turkey	AKP	2018	Unreserved	Equal rights	Equal rights	No	No	No
Turkey	Refah	1973	Unreserved	Distinct roles	No mention	No	No	Yes
Turkey	Refah	1991	Unreserved	Distinct roles	No mention	No	No	No
Turkey	Fazilet	1999	Unreserved	No mention	Equal rights	No	No	No
Turkey	Saadet	2002	Unreserved	Equal rights	No mention	No	No	No
Turkey	Saadet	2007	Unreserved	No mention	No mention	No	No	No
Turkey	Saadet	2011	Unreserved	Distinct roles	No mention	No	No	No
Turkey	Saadet	2015 (June)	Unreserved	Equal rights	No mention	No	No	No
Turkey	Saadet	2015 (Nov.)	Unreserved	Equal rights	No mention	No	No	No
Turkey	Saadet	2018	Unreserved	Equal rights	No mention	No	No	No

group's platform made no mention of *shura* and justified "healthy democracy" and "real pluralism" in terms of the Qur'anic precept that "there is no compulsion in religion." In 2011, *shura* was back in the platform as "the way to achieve the interests of the country so as to keep individuals or groups from becoming tyrannical." (The Brotherhood's rival Nour subordinated democracy even more strongly to Islamic goals: "All the components of the political process should be regulated according to the standards of Islamic *shari'a*, as democracy can only be achieved under Islamic *shari'a*.")

Other successful Islamic parties endorsed democracy in 2011 in civic rather than Islamic terms.

Party of Justice and Development, Morocco: "The empowerment of good governance at the political, economic, social, cultural, and foreign levels, based on true democracy, accountability, fair competition, and integrity emanating from renewed reading of our Islamic sources and pluralist Moroccan identity."

Ennahda, Tunisia: "It is the parliamentary system which guarantees public and private freedoms, independence of the judiciary, freedom of information, and alternation of power through the balanced, dynamic distribution of powers between the various state institutions and through free pluralistic elections."

Justice and Development Party, Turkey: "The AK Party perceives democracy as a process that needs to be constantly developed through the broad participation of the people."

The Muslim Brotherhood's changing positions have drawn much comment in Egypt, especially since 2007, when the movement's internal debates over a draft party platform became public.[17] A number of leading figures in the organization quit to form more liberal Islamic political groups, while others urged the Brotherhood to drop political activity altogether and focus on the Islamization of society.[18] Shifts in the Muslim Brotherhood's platforms may have sharpened questions about what the organization stood for and degraded its ability to convey a credible commitment to an inclusive political system.

The Brotherhood reinforced such concerns with highly public reversals after the 2011–12 parliamentary elections, including running a candidate for president after pledging not to do so. During the Brotherhood's year in power, such inconsistencies—along with the sorts of difficulties that are common to new governments—may have contributed to the withering of the organization's public support between mid-2012 and mid-2013. By contrast, parties with more consistent platforms, such as Morocco's PJD and Turkey's AKP, lost only about 10 percent points in their vote-share. Ennahda in Tunisia, whose platform has been relatively consistent, lost 10 percent of vote-share in 2014 and an additional 10 percent in 2019 when a less liberal Islamic party, I'tilaf al-Karama (the Dignity Coalition), ran to its right.

Of course, electoral platforms are not necessarily a reliable predictor of a party's actions —as voters all over the world know, parties rarely enact everything they promise. What platforms show is the discourse that parties wish to present to constituents. In the case of Islamic parties, that discourse has not changed much since the Arab Spring.

Meanwhile, the political environment in which these parties operate has changed dramatically. In 2011, the uprising in Tunisia triggered massive political mobilizations in many Muslim communities, generating ambitions for democratic empowerment that many Islamic parties scrambled to address. Since then, however, militaries and militias have suppressed democratic openings in Egypt, Libya, and Yemen, while antidemocratic regimes have blunted popular movements in Bahrain and elsewhere. The AKP in Turkey, notwithstanding its pro-democracy discourse—"Our aim of pluralist, egalitarian, and participatory democracy will push Turkey upward in the ranking of the league of democracies," the party's November 2015 platform stated—has degraded electoral and judicial institutions to such an extent that academic experts now characterize the country as an electoral autocracy, not a democracy.[19] Prospects for democracy have been further depressed by civil wars, including particularly violent conflicts in Iraq and Syria, Afghanistan and Pakistan, and Mali and Nigeria.

All political parties—the Islamic kind included—may seem less central to the political life of Muslim communities today than they did in 2011. But as we have learned from the uprisings of that year and their tumultuous aftermath, political environments can change quickly. If and when democratic openings reappear, Islamic parties may again rush in, proclaiming the compatibility of Islam and democracy both through their platforms and through their participation in electoral institutions.

Notes

1. This study identifies parties as Islamic if they defined themselves in Islamic terms, or were identified as "Islamic" in compendia of political parties such as the Interparliamentary Union's "Parline" database. The removal of marginally "Islamic" parties, such as Turkey's AKP—which has defined itself as conservative but not as avowedly "Islamic"—leaves this study's statistical findings substantially unchanged.
2. These election results leave out Islamic parties that boycotted or were banned. The totals do include parties that contested only a limited number of seats.
3. Charles Kurzman and Ijlal Naqvi, "Do Muslims Vote Islamic?" *Journal of Democracy* 21 (April 2010): 50–63; Charles Kurzman and Didem Türkoğlu, "Do Muslims Vote Islamic Now?" *Journal of Democracy* 26 (October 2015): 100–9.
4. Data on percentages of the vote won is not available for as many elections as data on seats won.
5. Shadi Hamid, "Arab Islamist Parties: Losing on Purpose?" *Journal of Democracy* 22 (January 2011): 68–80; Nathan Brown, *When Victory Is Not an Option: Islamist Movements in Arab Politics* (Ithaca: Cornell University Press, 2012).

6   Khalilal-Anani, "Islamist Parties Post-Arab Spring," *Mediterranean Politics* 17 (November 2012): 466–72.
7   Khalilal-Anani and MaszleeMalik, "Pious Way to Politics: The Rise of Political Salafism in Post-Mubarak Egypt," *Digest of Middle East Studies* 22 (Spring 2013): 57–73.
8   "Borhany: Al-Ikhwan Lo Tamkanu sa-Yaqdu 'ala al-Da'wa al-Salafiyya," YouTube, May 21, 2012, www.youtube.com/watch?v=Q2lnstFfAgc; *Sada el-Balad*, May 23, 2012.
9   Khalil al-Anani, "The Salafi-Brotherhood Feud in Egypt," *Al-Monitor*, February 21, 2013; Michael Barak, "The Salafist Al-Nour Party and the Muslim Brotherhood: The End of the Affair?" *Tel Aviv Notes*, April 25, 2013.
10 Jonathan A. C. Brown, "The Rise and Fall of the Salafi al-Nour Party in Egypt," *Al-Jadaliyya*, November 14, 2013; Kristen McTighe, "The Salafi Nour Party In Egypt," *Al-Jazeera Center for Studies*, March 26, 2014.
11 Meir Hatina, "Redeeming Sunni Islam: Al-Qa'ida's Polemic against the Muslim Brethren," *British Journal of Middle Eastern Studies* 39 (April 2012): 101–13.
12 Charles Kurzman, *The Missing Martyrs: Why Are There So Few Muslim Terrorists?*, 2nd edn. (New York: Oxford University Press, 2019), 93.
13 Translation by Flashpoint Partners, "Dr. Ayman al-Zawahiri Calls on Tunisians to Defy Ennahda Party and 'Support Your Sharia' (June 10, 2012)." See also Donald Holbrook, "Al-Qaeda's Response to the Arab Spring," *Perspectives on Terrorism* 6 (December 2012): 6–21.
14 These platforms may be found at http://kurzman.unc.edu/islamic-parties. Additional platforms are included on the website, but are excluded from analysis because they were brief (under six-hundred words) or because they were obtained after the analysis was completed.
15 These trend statistics differ at points from earlier versions of this paper, as additional electoral platforms have become available.
16 Charles Kurzman, "Votes Versus Rights: The Debate That's Shaping the Outcome of the Arab Spring," *Foreign Policy* "Democracy Lab," February 10, 2012.
17 Nathan J. Brown and Amr Hamzawy, "The Draft Party Platform of the Egyptian Muslim Brotherhood: Foray into Political Integration or Retreat into Old Positions?" Carnegie Endowment for International Peace, Carnegie Papers: Middle East Series, No. 89, January 2008.
18 Carrie Rosefsky Wickham, *The Muslim Brotherhood: Evolution of an Islamist Movement* (Princeton: Princeton University Press, 2013); HazemKandil, *Inside the Brotherhood* (London: Polity, 2014); Beverley Milton-Edwards, *The Muslim Brotherhood: The Arab Spring and Its Future Face* (Abingdon, UK: Routledge, 2016); Victor J. Willi, *The Fourth Ordeal: A History of the Muslim Brotherhood in Egypt, 1968–2018* (Cambridge, UK: Cambridge University Press, 2021).
19 Varieties of Democracy (V-Dem), *Democracy Report 2021* (Gothenberg, Sweden: University of Gothenburg, 2021).

References

al-Anani, K. (2012), "Islamist Parties Post-Arab Spring," *Mediterranean Politics*, 17 (3): 466–72.
al-Anani, K. (2013), "The Salafi-Brotherhood Feud in Egypt," *Al-Monitor*, February 21, 2013.
al-Anani, K. and M. Malik (2013), "Pious Way to Politics: The Rise of Political Salafism in Post-Mubarak Egypt," *Digest of Middle East Studies*, 22 (1): 57–73.

Barak, M. (2013), "The Salafist Al-Nour Party and the Muslim Brotherhood: The End of the Affair?" *Tel Aviv Notes*, April 25, 2013.

Brown, N. (2012), *When Victory Is Not an Option: Islamist Movements in Arab Politics*, Ithaca: Cornell University Press.

Brown, N. and A. Hamzawy (2008), "The Draft Party Platform of the Egyptian Muslim Brotherhood: Foray into Political Integration or Retreat into Old Positions?" Carnegie Endowment for International Peace, Carnegie Papers: Middle East Series, No. 89, January 2008.

Hamid, S. (2011), "Arab Islamist Parties: Losing on Purpose?" *Journal of Democracy*, 22 (1): 68–80.

Hatina, M. (2012), "Redeeming Sunni Islam: Al-Qa'ida's Polemic against the Muslim Brethren," *British Journal of Middle Eastern Studies*, 39 (1): 101–13.

Holbrook, D. (2012), "Al-Qaeda's Response to the Arab Spring," *Perspectives on Terrorism*, 6 (6): 6–21.

Kandil, H. (2014), *Inside the Brotherhood*, London: Polity.

Kurzman, C. (2012), "Votes versus Rights: The Debate That's Shaping the Outcome of the Arab Spring," *Foreign Policy* "Democracy Lab," February 10, 2012.

Kurzman, C. (2019), *The Missing Martyrs: Why Are There So Few Muslim Terrorists?*, 2nd edn, New York: Oxford University Press.

Kurzman, C. and D. Türkoğlu (2015), "Do Muslims Vote Islamic Now?" *Journal of Democracy*, 26 (4): 100–109.

Kurzman, C. and I. Naqvi (2010), "Do Muslims Vote Islamic?," *Journal of Democracy*, 21 (2): 50–63.

Milton-Edwards, B. (2016), *The Muslim Brotherhood: The Arab Spring and Its Future Face*, Abingdon: Routledge.

Wickham, C. R. (2013), *The Muslim Brotherhood: Evolution of an Islamist Movement*, Princeton: Princeton University Press.

Willi, V. J. (2021), *The Fourth Ordeal: A History of the Muslim Brotherhood in Egypt, 1968–2018*, Cambridge: Cambridge University Press.

Against the "Exception": Rethinking Turkish Secularism through the *Diyanet*

by Berna Zengin Arslan and Bryan S. Turner

Introduction: Reframing Turkish Secularism

Turkish secularism is often represented as an exceptional case or a deviation from secularism insofar as some state practices violate the principle of the separation of religion and the state. We depart from this view by defining secularism as the state's management of religion (Turner 2007; Turner and Zengin Arslan 2013) and the governing mentality of the nation-state (Asad 2003). Retheorizing Turkish secularism from this perspective, we argue that the Turkish state's interference into the religious domain was not a sign of flawed secularism or a deviation from the norm, but on the contrary a typical practice of the secular nation-state. From this perspective, we analyze the *Diyanet* as the basic institution of the Turkish state that has regulated the religious domain in a centralized way. The AKP period represents a shift in the role of the *Diyanet:* it has expanded significantly and "moved out of the mosques," redefining its boundaries, and integrating the private domain into the state's religious regulative framework. Our approach provides a clear understanding of this transformation as the renewed use of the *Diyanet*, a centralized and powerful organization, for the sake of the state's monopolization of religion in private and public life.

The Turkish Republic, founded in 1923, has largely accepted the French notion of *laïcité* as a key model, adopting its emphasis on the separation of the fields of state and religion and removing all religious symbols from the public sphere. As in France, the Constitution does not allow for an official or established religion. An article added to the Constitution in 1924 recognizing Islam as the state religion was abolished in 1928. Yet secularism in Turkey has its own distinct characteristics. For example, unlike France, the operation of mosques is funded publicly, and the state pays the employees of mosques. Since the early 1950s, the state has trained imams in public Schools of Imams and Preachers (*İmam Hatip*). Islamic theology departments are also state funded at public universities. Similarly, religious instruction based on the Sunni Islamic tradition is mandatory from primary school onward. Most significantly, despite the Constitutional separation of state and religion, the Turkish secular state provides services to the Sunni majority, a provision that has been criticized as a departure from its stated policy of religious neutrality. Founded in 1924, the *Diyanet* has been the major institution of the state to administer and assist with wide-ranging religious services, employing imams (as well as preachers and muftis), funding mosques in Turkey and abroad, and issuing fatwas with no legal power. All these practices have been aspects of secularism in Turkey in which the state has violated the separation principle.

These practices have mostly been interpreted as a compromise between the secularist People's Republican Party and influential religious groups during and after the formation of a secular state in the Early Republican Period (1923–38). The exceptionalism thesis has been dominant in the literature on Turkish secularism. It is frequently framed as incomplete (Parla and Davison 2008), or as a specific form of secularism where the state controls religion (Gözaydın 2009a: 15 and 272, 2008: 224, 2009b; Zücher 1997), or as a deviation from the original model of French *laïcité*. To underline this exceptionalism, Gözaydın (2009b) even differentiates "the term laicists to mean those who prefer the state's control of religion as opposed to secularism which implies the separation of state and religion" and intentionally uses "the term 'laicist' for republican state practice in Turkey" (Gözaydın, 2009b). Thus, Turkish secularism has come to be regarded as an exception to the single model of secularism wherein the state is separated from religion.

Departing from this approach, we argue that the practice of secularism in Turkey, in which the modern state intervenes in the sphere of religion, is not an exception or deviation from the European model, but in fact the rule (Zengin Arslan and Turner 2013).[1] In our theoretical approach, we define secularism as the state's management and regulation of religion rather than the separation of the state and religion. Therefore, the state's management of religion is so common a practice of the modern state as to be a building principle of secularism. Even in the French case—the paradigmatic model of separation—the secular state constantly interferes in the religious domain to regulate it (Fernando 2014; Zengin Arslan and Açımuz 2021). The secular state is nominally accepted as neutral toward religions in order to "secure religious rights and equality" (Mahmood 2015). However, it indeed acts as the authority that governs religious matters and draws the line between the religious and the secular (Agrama 2012; Asad 2003; Mahmood 2015). According to Asad, the secular state actively constructs religion in its secular vision and governs it through laws and norms. Asad's theory emphasizes the productive capacity of secularism as a normative discourse in making proper citizens, both secular and religious; the modern nation-state actively involves itself in building new institutions, conceptual frameworks, and subjectivities. The argument therefore critiques the assumption of the secular nation-state's neutrality toward religion. The example of Turkey also presents a significant case in terms of relations between the religion of the majority and the religions of the minorities, in which the secular state comes to represent the majority religion: in this case, Sunni Islam. The Diyanet does not provide religious services to minorities such as the Alevis, who have a population of almost 12 million.

Since its foundation, the *Diyanet* has been one of the most significant institutions of the Turkish state in managing and governing religion in a centralized way. It has been an important site for the state defining what lies within and outside the borders of acceptable of religion, specifically Sunni Islam. Turkish secularization envisioned creating an "enlightened" version of Islam, a "progressive" and modern interpretation of religion that would be based on reason and science rather than on "superstitions"— like pilgrimages to tombs, following a sheikh, or other "archaic practices." By providing financial support, human capital, and the institutional and bureaucratic foundations, the *Diyanet* created a basis and a discourse for the type of Islam that the Turkish state wanted to promote: a modern and secular notion of "religion" (Hassan, 2011: 455) that is rational, moderate, and national. Claiming to "unify the diversity of religions" in a moderate and peaceful manner, the *Diyanet* has defined the limits and forms that Islam can take in public life. It created and promoted a specific form of modern Islam that affirmed the ideology of the nation-state. In this sense, Republican secularism in Turkey cannot be understood only as a repressive discourse but also as productive of the subjectivities and practices of modern Turkish Islam.

The *Diyanet* and Secularizing Islam

The *Diyanet* was founded on March 3, 1924, the same day that the Shari'a Courts were closed down, the Caliphate and the Office of the *Şeyhülislam* were abolished, the Ottoman dynasty was expelled, and the Unity of Education Law (*Tevhid-i Tedrisat Kanunu*) was enacted. These were the foundational reforms of the Turkish secular state, bringing to a conclusion the old regime's administrative mentality and institutional structure, and creating the basic institutions and grounds of secularism for the new nation-state. The Unity of Education Law brought about the closure of the medreses that had traditionally provided religious education and collected the various educational institutions under a single educational authority: the Ministry of Education, which was founded on premises of modernism and secularism. Also in 1924, the imams and preachers' schools were opened to provide some degree of continuity in religious education, now under the supervision of the state. The abolition of the Caliphate, like other founding reforms of the Republic, was without doubt the most significant step in providing legitimacy for the new state on the basis of a national identity that was seen to be above religion (Berkes 1998; Kadıoğlu 2010: 492). Similarly, by expelling the last remnants of dynastic rule, the new Republic was clearly determined to end the Ottoman regime and disconnect itself from the Islamic past.

However, the new Republican administration had some continuities with the regulation of Islam in the Ottoman period. The foundation of the *Diyanet* as the Directorate of Religious Affairs was a continuation of the legislative process that had abolished the Office of the *Şeyhülislam* and founded the Ministry of Islamic Law and Charitable Foundations (*Şeriye ve Evkaf Vekaleti*) in 1920. The *Şeyhülislam*—the highest ranked mufti in the Ottoman state, the chair of the fatwa institution, and the leader of the ulema—had been responsible for juridical, educational, religious, and administrative affairs. This ministry was replaced by the *Diyanet*, though in fact it had lesser status, being founded as an administrative unit under the office of the prime minister. In this institutional reform process, the Office of the *Şeyhülislam* lost all of its functions, apart from those relating to religion. We can say that the Republican regime adopted the state-run and centralized organization of religious domain from the Ottoman experience, but it secularized and transformed this organization into a modern bureaucratic structure. It also employed medrese-educated imams in its early years, since there were not enough personnel educated in modern religious schools. Over time, the ulema lost their influence over a range of different fields, before being replaced by the new men of religion—that is, by the bureaucrats of the modern state's *Diyanet*. Hassan (2011: 454) notes that the term *diyanet* was carefully chosen in legislative discussions to express "religious affairs" in the sense of "matters of personal piety." Its potential alternative, *diniye*, could have implied the new institution's religious responsibilities in the fields of economy, society, policing, and education, which were instead distributed to other branches of government. Unlike the *Şeyhülislam*, the *Diyanet* did not have any legal function. Thus, the role of Islam in the early Republican era was narrowed to encompass only individual worship and belief.

The foundation of the *Diyanet* not only more narrowly defined "religion" as worship (*ibadet*) and belief (*itikat*), but also provided a ground for early Republic to promote a "true" Islam. Kemalism defined enlightened Islam as the religion of modern Turkish citizens. Thus, it promoted a modernized form of Sunni Islam that would be distanced from the fields of law, education, and science. While outlawing other sites and practices of Islam (such as the tekkes and Sufi lodges), the *Diyanet* regulated mosques as the neutral and acceptable places of worship for all Muslims. Therefore, contrary to the common perception, the early Republican ideology, Kemalism, was not anti-religion or aimed at fully erasing religion from public life. It rather worked toward forming a modern Islam, on the one hand favoring Islamic interpretations believed to be in harmony with modern life (*çağdaş yaşam*) and, on the other hand, repressing other Islamic forms that did not fit this vision. We can say that Kemalist ideology was deeply entangled with the religious domain in its attempt to govern it: it has continually defined and redefined what religion/Islam should be and how it should be practiced. Since the early Republican period, furthermore, Sunni (Hanafi) Islam has been integral to Turkish national identity (Yıldız 2001), and has informed definitions of civic morality (see, e.g., Gürbey 2009). Ironically, it has been a source of symbolic and moral reference for the army that the secular ideology has designated as the major defender of secularism (see, e.g., Türkmen 2009). For Kemalism, the *Diyanet* worked as a site for producing and representing a nationalized, official Islam that is praised by the state for being apolitical, moderate, and neutral.

The *Diyanet* is protected by the constitution: a constitutional change would be required to reform or to close it. The rules and regulations of the *Diyanet* are explained in the legislation prepared by the office of the President (before 2018, the office of the prime minister), which organizes the duties of imams, muftis, and preachers (vaiz); defines the hierarchy among them; determines the content of khutbas (Friday sermons); and regulates dress codes of public offices. Thus, the intention is to create uniformity and homogeneity across mosques in Turkey. The central organization of the activities of the *Diyanet* was consolidated after February 28, 1997, when the office of the prime minister began to determine the content of the Friday sermons as well as the morning prayers of Ramadan and the Feast of the Sacrifice.

The Expansion of the *Diyanet*

In 1965, the scope of the *Diyanet*'s services was extended to include not only worship and belief but also morality. The legislation enacted in June 1965 defines the duties of the *Diyanet* as "conducting affairs of the religion of Islam that are related with the principles of belief, worship and morality; enlightening the society on religious questions with activities such as conferences and preaching; and answering religious questions."[2] The *Diyanet*'s expansion continued with sending religious representatives abroad in 1971 in order to prevent Turkish migrants from employing religious personnel in informal ways and to insulate them from "dangerous political ideas" (Gözaydın 2009: 136). Since 1984 the *Diyanet* has strengthened its position in Europe (Çitak 2013, 2021) through a branch organization, DITIB. DITIB has become an influential institution in Europe, where it operates mosques, and elects delegates to the boards of major organizations representing Muslims. Çitak (2010: 625) argues that the Diyanet has acted as "a foreign-policy instrument of the Turkish government" abroad. Conceived as a "neutral" institution and as representing the Turkish state abroad, *Diyanet* mosques in Europe have become appealing not only to the Turkish immigrants but also to Muslims from other ethnic groups (Çitak, 2010: 625). The result is that the *Diyanet* competes with other Turkish Islamic groups, both in attracting followers to its mosques and for places at the administrative boards of Islamic organizations in Europe. Acting as an umbrella organization for other Turkish immigrant Muslim associations, DITIB is now recognized in Germany as a religious society with the right to provide religious services and teach school courses in some states. The *Diyanet* has a strong presence in Germany: it controls almost a thousand mosques alone, having established a social service network, women's and youth groups, Koran reading courses, and funeral funds.

"Moving out of the Mosques": The *Diyanet* in the AKP Period

Since 2002 when the AKP (Justice and Development Party) came to power, the *Diyanet*'s expansion has continued: its budget has risen drastically, allowing it to expand from a "mosque-based" and worship-oriented remit to one that reaches all sections of society, including women and children, by employing female preachers and founding Family Guidance Bureaus (*Aile Irsat ve Rehberlik Burosu*, AIRB) (Adak 2020; Kocamaner 2019; Maritato 2016; Turner and Zengin Arslan 2013; Tütüncü 2010). It has acquired more economic power, and the number of its employees (imams, preachers, muftis, and teachers of Qur'an courses) has grown dramatically. From 2002 to 2021 the *Diyanet*'s budget increased almost twenty-five times (~13 billion Turkish Lira in 2021); between 2002 and 2009 its personnel almost doubled, from 74,000 to 117,000. Through new projects—such as the foundation of the AIRB at the muftis' offices in various towns and cities and the Religious Services Development Project (*Din Hizmetleri Gelişim Projesi*)—the *Diyanet* has been working on "moving imams out of mosques" and having them engage more actively with the community to provide guidance "under the light of Qur'an and Sunna, based on morality centred knowledge." Thus, the *Diyanet* started working actively on integrating children, women, and the elderly into its religious services in Turkey.[3] As in the case of "I love my mosque" (www.camiyiseviyorum.com) campaign, the *Diyanet* specifically aimed at children, encouraging them to identify with and attend mosques. Identifying mosques as "a symbol representing cultural codes," the then president of the *Diyanet*, Mehmet Görmez, said that they had an important role in the spiritual education of children.[4] In this period, the *Diyanet* also increased its influence in Europe through mosques over which it had gained control (Çitak 2010; Yurdakul and Yükleyen 2009). During the presidency of Bardakoglu, the *Diyanet* started employing many more female officers (Hassan 2011), using new technologies and marketing strategies more effectively for these purposes. In 2012, the *Diyanet* TV channel started broadcasting, targeting children and women in particular. Thus, while aiming to reach a larger and more diverse audience, the *Diyanet* began playing a more active role in assisting state politics and developing activities that would make it, and the religious and moral perspective it represents, more deeply embedded in everyday life.

During the AKP period, the *Diyanet* has had three presidents with different focuses in their policies: Ali Bardakoglu (2003–10), Mehmet Görmez (2010–17), and Ali Erbaş (2017–present). The Bardakoğlu period was characterized by the *Diyanet's* moving "out of the mosque." This new approach radically changed not only the role and the mission of the *Diyanet*, but also the boundaries set around religion by the secular state. In building the *Diyanet*, Kemalism had predominantly confined its vision of religious worship and practice within the boundaries of the mosques and had targeted transforming "religion into a secular form built on abstract and cognitive principles." This form contrasted "starkly with the vision of religion as a living tradition that reveals itself in the diversity of everyday practices and the affectionate bonds between believers" (Zengin Arslan and Açımuz 2021). By moving Islam out of the mosque, the *Diyanet* has moved into a new phase in its history and redefined the boundaries of the *Diyanet* and the state's view on the role of religion.

For example, the AIRBs been providing psychological consultancy services to women and other members of the family on issues, such as divorce, marriage, health, and "family-related" questions. According to the AIRB report, the subjects consulted vary from "problems related to men" (such as "not supporting the family, not letting woman to work," and violence in the family) to "problems related to women" (such as "neglecting care of the house," "causing" sexual problems, and saving money without the permission of husband). In AIRBs, the religious services of the state have expanded into the private sphere and to the domain of privacy that concerns the relationship between couples or a woman's relationship to others in the extended family. Also, this work is not based on a direct teaching of the Quran or preaching in the mosques as it used to be, but rather on discussing family-related problems and offering solutions within an (Turkish) Islamic moral framework. In a similar way to the Kemalist ideology, the *Diyanet* today still defines a "correct" version of Islam and promotes it in a centralized and bureaucratized way. However, through the activities of AIRB, it interferes in the way women make meaning of their everyday lives and express their selves, and it attempts to reconfigure these forms from the perspective of the state's current vision on family and gender. Importantly, it works to regulate the role of Islam in the everyday life of women from the perspective of the current vision of Islam represented by the *Diyanet*. Therefore, it does not recognize the religiosity of the everyday life in Turkey. This is also a response to the fact that the private sphere and privacy in Turkey have increasingly been contested in various aspects of capitalism and popular culture, especially through ideas concerning family, beauty standards, and romantic relations. The Diyanet, today, reclaims the role of religion in shaping those domains.

Following Görmez, Ali Erbaş represented a significant shift to increased focus on monopolizing Islam based on concerns of control and security. Arguing that religious groups were "out of control" and "messy" without the state, he emphasized the need for the state to control the field of religion and identified the *Diyanet* as a mechanism of order and guidance.

Conclusion

The case of the Turkish *Diyanet* is a clear illustration of Talal Asad's argument (Asad 2003) that secularity and religion are mutually constitutive, and that they cannot be separated either conceptually or historically. In our approach, we suggest that the Turkish state's relationship with Sunni Islam has not been merely one of control and oppression, but rather that it has been productive, creating a form of nationalized and modern Islam in the process of its establishment. It is possible to see how this modern nationalized perspective on Islam, disseminated by those who went through the educational system at the Theology Faculties or employment in the *Diyanet*, has been influential in the formation of Islamic movements and communities in Turkey.

Nevertheless, the secular state in Turkey represents and provides funds and services to the majority religion, Sunni Hanafi Islam. It promotes the moral values of a certain interpretation of modern Turkish Islam and opens up more space for its representation.

In this sense, we do not see a significant deviation over the past ninety years from the secular state's practice of integrating itself into the religious field to govern it. However, since 2002, when the AKP came to power, the *Diyanet* has gained more influence through an increase in its budget and personnel. In parallel, it has been focusing on developing services that, on the one hand, integrate Islamic practices into everyday lives, especially those of women, children, and the elderly, and on the other, increasingly reach Europe and other areas outside Turkey. At the same time, since the late 1990s, European states have aimed at "domesticating" and nationalizing Islam through the civic integration of Muslims and their disconnection from outside financial and ideological influences (Laurence 2012). As a part of this process, European States have recently started calling for an end to importing imams from other countries, including Turkey. *Diyanet* imams were asked to leave Austria by 2015 and France by 2020. In 2020, the *Diyanet*'s organization in Germany, DITIB, has started educating imams in German.[5]

Is this the retreat of Turkish secularism or a deepening of its paradox as the *Diyanet* takes an active role in the "deprivatization" of religion? It remains the Turkish state (now governed by a pro-Islamic party) that defines what is religious and what is secular. In fact, the Turkish state has changed its approach from an emphasis on religion as part of the private to the public domain. "Moving out of the mosque," the *Diyanet* gave up the Kemalist vision of a secular Islam, one that was narrowed to religious worship practiced within the boundaries of the mosques and through individualized learning of the principles of Islam. The *Diyanet* works now toward de-secularizing modern Islam by re-integrating it into everyday life and reclaiming Islam as a living tradition. However, the paradox remains that it still relies heavily on the state's apparatuses of control and regulation to instill a vision of Islam that ends up ignoring the everydayness of religion.

Notes

1 An earlier assertion of this argument can be found in Hassan (2011). For a more recent example of a similar approach, see Kocamaner (2019). In an earlier analysis, Berkes (1964: 6) argued that the distinctiveness of Turkish secularism is not a failure but rather a natural result of the union between religion and state in Muslim societies. For Berkes, while the French secularism is based on the separation between state and church, Turkish secularism is more characterized with the clash between the "forces of tradition" and the "forces of change."
2 Diyanet İşleri Başkanlığı kuruluş ve görevleri hakkında kanun (June 22, 1965) İslam Dini'nin inanç, ibadet ve ahlak esasları ile ilgili işleri yürütmek, din konusunda toplumu aydınlatmak ve ibadet yerlerini yönetmek. (https://www.mevzuat.gov.tr/MevzuatMetin/1.5.633.pdf).
3 www.istanbulmuftulugu.gov.tr/aile-irsat-ve-rehberlik-burosu/tanitim.html
4 www.camiyiseviyorum.com/baskanin-mesaji.html
5 https://www.dw.com/tr/ditib-almanyada-imam-yetiştirmeye-başladı/a-51946862

References

Adak, S. (2020), "Expansion of the Diyanet and the Politics of Family in Turkey under AKP Rule," *Turkish Studies*, 22 (2): 200–21.

Agrama, H. A. (2012), *Questioning Secularism: Islam, Sovereignty, and the Rule of Law in Modern Egypt*. Chicago: University of Chicago Press.

Asad, T. (2003), *Formations of the Secular: Christianity, Islam, Modernity*, Stanford: Stanford University Press.

Berkes, N. (1964), *The Development of Secularism in Turkey*. India: McGill University Press.

Berkes, N. (1998), *The Development of Secularism in Turkey*. London: Hurst.

Çıtak, Z. (2010), "Between 'Turkish Islam' and 'French Islam': The Role of the Diyanet in the Conseil Francais du Culte Musulman," *Journal of Ethnic and Migration Studies*, 36 (4): 619–34.

Çıtak, Z. (2013), "The Institutionalization of Islam in Europe and the Diyanet: The Case of Austria," *Ortadoğu Etütleri*, 5 (1): 167–82.

Çıtak, Z. (2021), "Avrupa İslamı, Ulusal İslam(lar) ve Müslüman Konseyleri," *Eğitim Bilim Toplum Dergisi*, 19 (73): 71–91.

Fernando, M. (2014), *The Republic Unsettled. Muslim French and the Contradictions of Secularism*. New York: Duke University Press.

Gözaydın, İ. (2008), "Diyanet and Politics," *Muslim World*, 98 (2/3): 216–27.

Gözaydın, İ. (2009a), *Diyanet: Türkiye Cumhuriyeti'nde Dinin Tanzimi*, İstanbul: İletişim Yayınları.

Gözaydın, İ. (2009b), "The Fethullah Gülen Movement and Politics in Turkey: A Chance for Democratization or a Trojan Horse?," *Democratization*, 16 (6): 1214–36.

Gürbey, S. (2009), "Islam, Nation-State, and the Military: A Discussion of Secularism in Turkey," *Comparative Studies of South Asia, Africa and the Middle East*, 29 (3): 371–380.

Hassan, M. (2011), "Women Preaching for the Secular State: Official Female Preachers (Bayan Vaizler) in Contemporary Turkey," *International Journal of Middle East Studies*, 43: 451–73.

Kadıoğlu, A. (2010), "The Pathologies of Turkish Republican laicism," *Philosophy and Social Criticism*, 36 (3–4): 489–504.

Kocamaner, H. (2019), "Regulating the Family through Religion: Secularism, Islam, and the Politics of the Family in Contemporary Turkey," *American Ethnologist*, 46 (4): 494–508.

Laurence, J. (2012), *The Emancipation of Europe's Muslims: The State's Role in Minority Integration*, Princeton and Oxford: Princeton University Press.

Mahmood, S. (2015), *Religious Difference in a Secular Age: A Minority Report*. Princeton, NJ: Princeton University Press.

Maritato, C. (2016), "Reassessing Women, Religion and the Turkish Secular State in the Light of the Professionalisation of Female Preachers (Vaizeler) in Istanbul," *Religion, State and Society*, 44 (3): 258–75.

Parla, T. and A. Davison (2008), "Secularism and Laicism in Turkey," in A. Davison, J. R. Jacobsen, and A. Pellegrini (eds.), *Secularisms (A Social Text Book)*, 58–75, Durham, NC: Duke University Press.

Türkmen, B. (2009). "A Transformed Kemalist Islam or a New Islamic Civic Morality? A Study of 'Religious Culture and Morality' Textbooks in the Turkish High School Curricula," *Comparative Studies of South Asia, Africa and the Middle East*, 29 (3): 381–97.

Turner, B. S. (2007), "Managing Religions: State Responses to Religious Diversity," *Contemporary Islam*, 1(2): 123–37.

Turner, B. S. and B. Zengin Arslan (2013), "Shari'a and Legal Pluralism in the West," in B. S. Turner, J. K. Tong, A. A. Pereira, and B. Zengin Arslan (eds.), *The Sociology of Islam*, 273–94, Cambridge: Cambridge University Press.

Turner, B. S. and B. Zengin Arslan (2013), "State and Turkish Secularism: The Case of the Diyanet," inB. S. Turner (ed.), *The Religious and the Political A Comparative Sociology of Religion*, 206–24, Cambridge: Cambridge University Press.

Tütüncü, F. (2010), "The Women Preachers of the Secular State: The Politics of Preaching at the Intersection of Gender, Ethnicity and Sovereignty in Turkey," *Middle Eastern Studies*, 46 (4): 595–614.

Yıldız, A. (2001), *Ne Mutlu Türküm Diyebilene Türk Ulusal Kimliğinin Etno-Seküler Sınırları (1919–1938)*. İstanbul: İletişim Yayınları.

Yurdakul, G. and A. Yükleyen (2009), "Islam, Conflict, and Integration: Turkish Religious Associations in Germany," *Turkish Studies*, 10 (2): 217–31.

Zengin Arslan, B. (2015), "Aleviliği Tanımlamak: Türkiye'de Dinin Yönetimi, Sekülerlik ve Diyanet," *Mülkiye Dergisi*, 39 (1): 135–58.

Zengin Arslan, B. and B. Açımuz (2021), "Reforming Laïcité or Reforming Islam? Secularism, Islam, and the Regulation of Religion in France," Journal of Law, Religion and State, 9 (147–177).

Zürcher, E. J. (1997), *Turkey: A Modern History*, New York: I.B. Tauris.

III CITIZENSHIP, MINORITIES, AND VIOLENCE

The Kurds and Middle Eastern "State of Violence": The 1980s and 2010s

by Hamit Bozarslan

The Middle East of the 1980s

The aim of this chapter, which deliberately adopts a macro-level analysis, is to suggest that in order to understand the evolution of the Kurdish issue since the occupation of Iraq in 2003 and the Syrian crisis in 2011, one needs to take into account the dynamics of a middle-term historical period going back to 1979, as well as a broader spatial scale, including other parts of the Middle East.

The choice of the year 1979 is in no one way arbitrary. Through its long-lasting follow-ups and by-products, this date, together with those of 1918/19 and 1948, became the third most important year in the very formation of the Middle East (Bozarslan 2012; Lesch 2001). Following the recognition of Israel by Egypt, the Iranian Revolution and the occupation of Afghanistan by the Red Army, all in this same year, the Middle East broadly speaking entered a new historical cycle determined by the extreme weakening of left-wing movements and an almost hegemonic domination of Islamism. In the following decade, while the heavily authoritarian regimes consolidated their grip in Iraq and Syria, the Iran-Iraq War, the war in Afghanistan and the intensification of the Lebanese Civil War cost the lives of hundreds of thousands of people. Throughout the 1980s, inter-state borders, which Anthony Giddens defines as "power containers" (Giddens 1987: 120), were transformed into intensely violent zones, where frontiers separating state and non-state actors became blurred and a wide-scale military transhumance propelled tens of thousands young men, including the future leaders of al Qaeda such as Bin Laden and al-Zawahari, from the Arab world to Pakistan and Afghanistan. While no external power could play the role of an arbiter or a regulator in the resolution of these conflicts, major regional states and non-state actors found

---

Bozarslan, H. (2014), "The Kurds and Middle Eastern 'State of Violence:' The 1980s and 2010s," *Kurdish Studies* 2 (1): 4–13.

themselves drawn into a "system of transaction" based on violence (Pécaut 1997). This violence, which cannot be understood without taking into account the power relations at the macro-, mezzo-, and micro-levels, thus appeared as a resource allowing the grand and small regional forces to ensure their durability.

Following the French philosopher Frédéric Gros, one can define this long decade as the decade of a "state of violence" (Gros 2006). By this Gros means the "end of discontinuities" between war and peace, periods of mobilization and demobilization, domestic law-keeping and external war-making operations. Beyond this *ad minima* definition, which Gros proposed mainly to understand the evolution of the Western democracies in the 1990s and 2000s, one can also define a "state of violence" as the end of discontinuities between war and ordinary forms of violence, states and non-state agents, state-making and consolidation processes and those of violent contests targeting the states' authorities. In such a configuration, violence does not only affect the peripheries of a given state, but also its very heart, the "center" itself being transformed into a producer of a social, political, and communitarian violence through the systemic use of non-state actors and/or means. Such a "state of violence" challenges, both theoretically and empirically, Eliasian or Weberian sociology, which present the state-building process as the process of pacification of a delineated space and the state itself as an organ monopolizing successfully the instruments of coercion.

The State of Violence of the 2010s

To some extent, the historical cycle which started with the dramatic events of 1979 lasted until the Arab revolutionary contests of 2011. Less than three years after the fall of Ben Ali, Mubarak and al-Ghaddafi, with the beginning of mass-contests in Bahrain, Yemen, and Syria, the Middle East broadly speaking appears, once again, to be gripped by the turmoil of a new state of violence. Notwithstanding the important transformations of the very political landscape of the region, one is in fact struck by the parallels between the situation of today and that of the 1980s. Many parts of the broader Middle East, including Afghanistan and Pakistan, Yemen, Syria (Iraq and Lebanon are also heavily affected by the Syrian conflict), Sinai and Gaza, Libya and the vast neighboring zones in Africa, experience a massive phenomenon of violence. Not only has the internal territorial fragmentation gained a paroxysmal feature in all these spaces, the sectarian dynamics have become much stronger than in the 1980s, re-drawing the entire map of the "narrow" Middle East (Egypt, the "Fertile Crescent," Gulf countries, Iran and Turkey, Pakistan) along sectarian borders. While the frontiers between state and non-state actors are once again blurred and many trans-border or supra-territorial armed militants are active throughout the region, many parts of the so-called national territories are controlled by an increasing number of intra- or supra-state militias. No external power, be it Russia or a Western country, can impose itself as an arbiter or as an "international" Leviathan able to resolve these regional conflicts. As the main world powers have little capacity of intervention or arbitration, the macro-level *status quo* remains unchanged, but as in the 1980s, no state or non-state actor can itself refrain from the use of violence as a survival safeguard.

As in the 1980s, in the 2010s Middle Eastern minorities[1] find themselves, either geographically or politically, in the interstices of these regional conflicts. There is no doubt that they pay a heavy price for these wars, which are, in no way, related to their cause, but they are also obliged to adapt themselves to the constraints of this new situation, or even to try to survive, thanks to the resources and new opportunities that they can engender. In fact, one of the decisive features of the ongoing state of violence (as in the 1980s) is that, the regional powers have deeply contradictory long-term interests and yet, they are condemned to producing almost exclusively day-to-day policies. This uncertainty, which obliges them to favor tactical steps instead of developing coherent long-term strategies, prohibits the formation of a regional system of security, and creates some room for maneuver for non-state actors, among them the trans-border or supra-territorial minorities, including Kurds. The relations that the states establish with non-state actors in the course of this process do not have any transformative effect on the region-wide power equilibrium, nor on the long-term status of the minorities; still, they clearly show the limits of the Westphalian model of state, as it was imposed throughout the twentieth century through forced divisions (Kurdistan, mandatory Arab world of the 1920s), or constraint unifications (Libya, Yemen), to Middle Eastern societies.

The Kurds in the 1980s, the Kurds in the 2010s

The Kurds were among the major victims, but minor actors of state of violence during the 1980s. More than 200,000 Kurds were killed between 1979 and 1991 as a consequence of state coercion in Iran, Iraq and Turkey; thousands of villages have also been destroyed in these two latter countries. Moreover, ethnic cleansing of the Kurds took a dramatic shape in Iraq, with tens of thousands of Kurdish families being expelled from the Kirkuk region (Randal 1997). One should also mention that through the assassination of Abdurrahman Qasimlo, the leader of the Democratic Party of Iranian Kurdistan (*Partiya Demokratîk a Kurdistana Iranê*, PDKI) in 1989 in Vienna, the Iranian government managed to decapitate the Kurdish leadership within Iran.

Conversely, as we shall see later, during this decade Iraqi Kurdish organizations found some shelter in Iran as well as in Syria, while Iraq hosted Iranian Kurdish organizations (van Bruinessen 1988). The Kurdistan Workers' Party (Partiya *Karkerên Kurdistan*, PKK), which gradually became the hegemon Kurdish actor in Turkey, was able to establish an alliance with Syria and to reorganize its combatants in Lebanon during the civil war before launching its long-lasting guerrilla warfare in Turkish Kurdistan in 1984. In sum, *nolens volens* the Kurdish organizations took part, although in a subordinated position, to the regional system of violence as well as to the region-wide military mobility.

As the 2013 fighting between the Party of Democratic Unity (*Partiya Yekîtiya Demokrat*, PYD) and Jabhat al-Nusra (*Front of Victory*, affiliated to al Qaida) in Syria show, Kurdistan is also one of the main theatres of the state of violence of the 2010s. However, compared to that of the 1980s, Kurdish society, politics and politicians present an entirely new shape (Ahmed and Gunter 2013). The dynamism of the Kurdish diaspora, formed in the wake of the arrival of tens of thousands of militants, intellectuals, and young men and women who fled wars and repression in Kurdistan and sought shelter in Europe in the 1980s (Başer 2013; Eliassi 2013), and the vivacity of the Kurdish studies, arts, and literature both in Europe and in the Middle East, suffice to understand the sharp contrasts between the two periods (Scalbert-Yücel 2014). Among the most important differences between the two periods, however, has been the emergence of a Kurdish federal entity in Iraq which, in spite of its domestic problems such as widespread corruption and lack of integration of younger generations, represents one of the most dynamic, politically pluralistic and peaceful spaces in the Middle East. For the first time in the twentieth century, an entire generation has been formed under "Kurdish rule," and, notwithstanding the political clientelism, viable institutions, including parliamentary ones, have been established (Lawrence 2008). The weak post-Saddam Hussein Iraqi state has obviously no means to envision, at least for the foreseeable future, a policy based on a military option against its Kurds as its predecessors did (Ahmed and Gunter 2005).

The second major—and still uncertain—evolution concerns the constitution of a *de facto* autonomous Kurdish region in Syria. After a long decade of repression against any Kurdish civil or political initiative (Tejel 2009), Bashar al-Assad decided to retire his forces from the Kurdish regions in the summer of 2012 in order to consolidate power in his strategic strongholds. Although the formation of this new entity was a result of the al-Assad regime's incapacity to control the entire Syrian territory, as well as its intense conflict with Turkey (which openly armed the Syrian opposition), it has radically changed the very shape of the Kurdish issue in the Middle East.

Finally, in Turkey, where the military has for the moment been politically subordinated, the government of the Justice and Development Party (Adalet ve Kalkınma Partisi, AKP) decided to improve its relations with the Iraqi Kurdish authorities. While Ankara's commercial interests and its will to ease an almost exclusive energy dependency on Iran and Russia push it toward a rapprochement with Iraqi Kurdistan (Idiz 2013),[2] its limited room for maneuver obliges it to accept the existence of a Kurdish entity in Syria (Çandar 2013). The aid it has given to Jabhat-al Nusra in the summer of 2013 and the building of a wall militarizing the intra-Kurdish borders separating Syria and Turkey show however that it has not abandoned its policy of "containment" vis-à-vis the Syrian Kurds.

There is no doubt that Turkey's domestic and region-wide Kurdish policy aim at the transformation of the Kurdish movement into a subordinated actor of AKP's policies inside Turkey; whatever Ankara's short- and long-term aims might be, however, its Kurdish "overture" has largely legitimized the PKK and the legal Peace and Democracy

Party (*Barış ve Demokrasi Partisi*, BDP) and consolidated their social basis (Ekmekçi and Kaya 2013). The formation of a real hegemonic bloc around the PKK-BDP in Kurdistan in Turkey (more than thirty deputies, around hundred municipalities, among them those of seven important large cities) (Watts 2010), should be mentioned not because it is a new phenomenon, but because it has become such a substantial and durable one. The end of the Kurdish taboo in Turkey (Gunes and Zeydanlıoğlu 2014) does not mean that one should exclude the possibility of a return to extremely repressive policies, such as Erdoğan's government followed in 2011–12; but after thirty years of internal war, Ankara seems finally to be aware that "coercion" cannot be its *exclusive* political line. Thus, bar a new military coup or an electoral victory of the Turkish ultra-nationalist parties, a return to a policy of simple denial of the Kurdish issue, which marked the 1980s and 1990s, would be most unlikely.

Given the changes observed in these three countries, it would be possible to say it is only in Iran that the main determinants of the Kurdish question have remained almost untouched over the past decade. However, if it is true that the extremely timid "overtures" of the Muhammed Khatami period (1997–2005) did not survive the repressive presidency of Mahmud Ahmadinejad (Elling 2013), it is also important to underline that, after a decade of heavy fighting between the Party of Free Life of Kurdistan (*Partiya Jiyana Azad a Kurdistanê*, PJAK) and the *pasdaran*s (*Revolutionary Guards*), Tehran, for tactical reasons, agreed to negotiate a cease-fire with PJAK in 2011. Although it would be illusory to expect radical changes in the Iranian domestic and militia-based foreign policy in the short term, the presidency of Hassan Rohani, which started in 2013, may take some steps to reduce the massive Kurdish discontent that marked the 2000s. The intellectual and social vivacity of the Iranian Kurdish society, which has largely boycotted post-Khatami elections, is a clear sign that in the event of a deep political crisis, the Kurdish question will be at the top of the political agenda in this country.

These developments, which would have seemed unbelievable even to the most optimistic observer only two decades ago, naturally do not mark the end of the process of subordination of the Kurds in the Middle East. However, they provide the Kurds with an important capacity of "empowerment" and resistance that no Kurdish movement could have had during the previous periods of military contest (1920s and 1930s, 1946, 1961–75), or between 1979 and 1991. They also go hand-in-hand with profound changes that one observes in Kurdish society, including in the very formulation of "Kurdish politics." During the last decades, Kurdish society in Iraq and Turkey has become a predominantly urban society, where thousands of villages were systematically destroyed during the 1980s and 1990s, and in Iran and Syria, where developments gave way to the emergence of a middle classes, distinct from the former urban notabilities or craftsmen. The emergence of this class metamorphosed the Kurdish urban landscape and gave birth to a new *habitus*, new ways of consuming, living, socializing, thinking, and struggling. An intellectual "class," distinct from the politicized intelligentsia of the 1950s and 1960s, also appeared and became the agent of new forms of socialization, political mobilisations, as well as cultural production. In the 1970s and 1980s, but also in the 1990s, being a "Kurdish militant" primarily meant being a member or sympathizer of a political party; in contrast, the intellectuals of the 2010s develop non-partisan forms of being, behaving, and struggling. Both the middle classes and this intellectual stratum are widely integrated across Kurdistan and entertain close relations with the outside world.

Kurdistan in a Conflicting Regional System

During the last decade, the strategic positions of states in the region-wide power relations, as well as their policies concerning the Kurdish question have, broadly speaking, changed drastically. Despite being one of the most important independent players in the Middle East in the 1980s, Syria has largely become a client state, whose regime depends for its survival on Iranian aid as well as military strategies decided by the pasdarans and Lebanese Hezbollah, in the wake of its internal break-up. Similarly, Iraq, a major independent player and a regional "patron" throughout the 1980s, is today essentially a broken-up client state. While Iraq's fragmentation explains its incapacity to effectively control its own Sunni areas, not to mention the Kurdish ones, Iraq's internal paralysis and clientelization by Iran explain its inability to resist the policies dictated by Teheran.

The absence of Syria and Iraq, two traditional regional players on the regional scene, leaves space for the Gulf countries (which are not under consideration in this article), and two non-Arab countries, Turkey and Iran. Turkey, which in the 1980s was opposed to any Kurdish activism anywhere in the Middle East (but probably hosted non-Kurdish anti-Iranian activities on its soil), is henceforth able to develop complex strategies, seeking an alliance with Iraqi Kurdistan and trying to "co-opt" the Middle-East-wide Kurdish political class. Moreover, Turkey is much more exposed to the domestic impacts of regional conflicts today than in the 1980s, making it even more pressing to seek "regional allies," including those among the non-state actors.

As the ongoing instability along the Turkish-Syrian borders and the Gezi Park protests in the summer of 2013 show, the sectarian orientations of Turkish domestic and regional politics under Erdoğan transformed the Syrian conflict into an intra-Turkish conflict and outraged Turkey's Alawite and Alevi communities. As a paradoxical and largely unpleasant outcome of this evolution, Turkey also feels "obliged" to defend the Sunni communities throughout the region, among them, Iraqi Kurds. It is true that this "generosity" has not been extended to Syrian Kurds, who are almost exclusively Sunni, but after months of hesitation, Ankara recognized the dangers of its policy of supporting Jihadist movements and was obliged to invite the PYD's co-chair Salih Muslim to Turkey in order to establish a link with this pro-PKK organization. Concerning Iran, one should note that it remains a major force in the trans-border Kurdish space, and, by the very "green-light" that it has indirectly given to the pro-PKK PYD in Syria, it exerts a great impact on the Kurdish movement within. Similarly, by holding PJAK, close ally of the PKK, in a position of political hostage through the agreement of a long-lasting cease-fire, Tehran also exerts an undeniable pressure on the PKK itself and encourages it to resume its armed struggle against Turkey.

The Kurdish Movement in the 2010s: Unity or Division?

The trans-border Kurdish movement of the 1980s was, by and large, divided, but strange as it might appear, it could also find some parcels of power in its own divisions, which were dictated by the constrained alliances that it had to negotiate with Iran, Iraq, or Syria. These divisions, which caused a series of internal conflicts, have further aggravated the dark subjectivities of this decade. The alliances of Kurdish movements with the states which had extremely repressive policies vis-à-vis their own Kurds provoked heavy intra-Kurdish tensions and fratricide and created a real malaise among Kurdish public opinion. This was, to some extent, the price that Kurds, but also other Middle Eastern non-state actors, including the Palestinians, had to pay in order to access resources to ensure their physical durability.

Compared to this past situation, the Kurdish "political class" of today seems to be much less vulnerable. It is of course difficult to comment on its future ability to preserve such unity in the context of a major regional conflict, for example, a deeper "cold war" between Iran and Turkey, or a further aggravation of the Syrian state of violence, but one should also admit that it was successful enough to keep peaceful and fluid internal relations throughout the 2000s. To some extent, the Kurdish region-wide political landscape has also become more clear-cut during this decade: after the crisis it went through in the wake of Öcalan's arrest in 1999, the PKK imposed itself almost as the sole reference actor in Turkish Kurdistan. It has also become, at once, the inspirer, organizer, and protector of the PYD in Syria and the PJAK in Iran, two political parties which are directly linked to the Syrian and Iranian Kurdish society's internal dynamics, but which are often regarded as the PKK's local branches.

There is no doubt that Öcalan's party is unchallenged in Turkey itself. In contrast, and in spite of its willingness to establish its total hegemony, the PYD in Syria is obliged to accept a high degree of intra-Kurdish plurality in what is henceforth known as Kurdistan's *Rojava* (*Western Kurdistan*) region. It is obviously difficult to predict the future evolution of Iranian Kurdistan, where any Kurdish political activity remains underground, but in the context of a future political change, the PJAK will probably also be tempted to impose its hegemony and, at the same time, be forced to accept an asymmetric plurality with other Kurdish actors such as the PDKI, Komala, and their dissident branches. One could thus consider the PKK as a major actor with a trans-Kurdish implantation, and therefore, as a structural pillar of the Kurdish political sphere well beyond Turkey.

As far as the Kurdistan Democratic Party (*Partîya Demokrata Kurdistan,* KDP) of Massoud Barzani is concerned, it occupies a dominant (but not a hegemonic) position in the Iraqi Kurdistan, but it imposes itself as a model and protector of the other Kurdish political formations in Iran and Syria, such as the PDKI and the Kurdish National Council (*Encûmena Niştimanî ya Kurdî li Sûriyê*, KNC). It is naturally obliged to accept Iraqi Kurdistan's internal plurality, and the challenge posed by the strong opposition of the Goran (*Change*) movement, now the second major political force in Iraqi Kurdistan, but thanks to important symbolic and material resources at its disposal, it can be considered as the second structuring pillar of the Kurdish political scene.

A Constrained Coexistence

This evolution does not only illustrate a highly fascinating model of construction of a trans-border political space, but also obliges Kurdish organizations, among them the two major players, the PKK and the KDP, to establish a mutual understanding, to fix the rules of coexistence, including those regulating their respective autonomies and interdependence, and to delineate their individual margins of action. It also means that they have to accept that no one can deny the other the possibility of "contracting" tactical alliances with a state, but at the same time, both of them have to agree that these alliances must not threaten a given Kurdish actor and the Kurdish cause broadly speaking as was the case in the 1980s. It is, however, obvious that given regional constraints, as well as policies of blackmail used by Turkey and Iran on their own Kurds, this political system can only evolve on a knife edge.

Notes

1 The term "minority" is understood here not in a demographic sense, but in the sense of the communities that have been reduced to "minorities" as a consequence of relations of domination and subordination of a given political space and through a series of mechanisms of exclusion and denial.
2 See also "New Kurdistan Oil Pipeline Boosts Kurds in Stand-off with Baghdad" (October 17, 2013), *Reuters*.

References

Ahmed, M.M.A. and M. M. Gunter, eds. (2005), *The Kurdish Question and the 2003 Iraq War*, Costa Mesa: Mazda Publishers.
Ahmed, M.M.A. and M. M. Gunter, eds. (2013), *The Kurdish Spring: Geopolitical Changes and the Kurds*, Costa Mesa: Mazda Publishers.

Başer, B. (2013), *Inherited Conflicts: Spaces of Contention between Second-Generation Turkish and Kurdish Diasporas in Sweden and Germany*, unpublished doctoral dissertation, Italy: European University Institute.

Bozarslan, H. (2012), "Revisiting Middle East's 1979," *Economy and Society*, 41 (4): 558–67.

Bozarslan, H. (2014), "The Kurdish Issue in Turkey of 2010s," *Orient*, 1: 6–10.

Çandar, C. (2013, 19 July) "'Süreç' ve 'Rojava Devrimi'," *Radikal*.

Ekmekçi, F. and İ. Kaya (2013), *Çözüm Sürecinin Değerlendirilmesi*, Istanbul: UKAM.

Eliassi, B. (2013), *Contesting Kurdish Identities in Sweden: Quest for Belonging among Middle Eastern Youth*, New York: Palgrave.

Elling, R. C. (2013), *Minorities in Iran: Nationalism and Ethnicity after Khomeini*, New York: Palgrave.

Giddens, A. (1987), *The Nation-state and Violence*, Berkeley and Los Angeles: University of California Press.

Gros, F. (2006), *Etats de violence. Essai sur la fin de la guerre*, Paris: Gallimard.

Idiz, S. (2013, 19 July). "Turkey Adds Fuel to Iraqi Kurds' Fight for Independence," *Al Monitor*. http://www.al-monitor.com/pulse/originals/2013/07/independent-turkish-kurdistan-moves-forward.html (accessed July 19, 2013).

Lawrence, Q. (2008), *Invisible Nation: How the Kurds' Quest for Statehood Is Shaping Iraq and the Middle East*, New York: Walker and Company.

Lesch, D. W. (2001). *1979: The Year that Shaped the Modern Middle East*, Colorado: Westview Press.

Gunes, C. and W. Zeydanlıoğlu, eds. (2014), *The Kurdish Question in Turkey: New Perspectives on Violence, Representation and Reconciliation*, London: Routledge.

Pécaut, D. (1997), "De la banalité de la violence à la terreur: le cas colombien," *Cultures et Conflits*, 24 (25): 159–93.

Randal, J. C. (1997), *After Such Knowledge, What Forgiveness? My Encounters with Kurdistan*, New York: Farrar, Straus and Giroux.

Scalbert-Yücel, C. (2014), *Le champ littéraire kurde en Turquie (1980–2010)*, Paris: Petra.

Tejel, J. (2009), *Syria's Kurds. History, Politics and Society*, London: Routledge.

van Bruinessen, M. (1988), "The Kurds between Iran and Iraq," *MERIP Report*, 141: 14–27.

Watts, N. F. (2010), *Activists in Office. Kurdish Politics and Protest in Turkey*, Seattle: University of Washington Press.

Social Construction of Minority Emotions and Sectarian Boundaries: Christian-Muslim Relations in Post-Arab Uprisings Egypt

by Hyun Jeong Ha

Would belonging to a minority group mean that its members share particular sets of emotions among themselves? If that is the case, how would sociology make sense of the formation of such emotions? This chapter seeks to answer those questions with the case of Egyptian Christians. They represent roughly 10 percent of Egyptians (equivalent to about 10 million) and are the largest Christian population in the Middle East and North Africa (MENA). Thus far, studies on sectarian relations in the MENA region have paid relatively little attention to ordinary ethnic and religious minorities. Studies on sectarianism in Egypt predominantly focus on state-Islamist (mostly, Muslim Brotherhood) or the state-Church relations, leaving ordinary Christian voices largely unheard. Only a few recent studies focus on ordinary Egyptian Christians, including a recent ethnographic study (Heo 2018). In this spirit, we need an addition to help us understand what daily Christian-Muslim interactions look like and how they changed after the fall of the thirty-year regime of Hosni Mubarak. Investigating daily interactions, therefore, will help us understand the social construction of minority emotions.

After the 2011 Arab Uprisings (widely referred to as *thaura* or *yanair khamsa we ishrin* among Egyptians), Egypt underwent regime changes.[1] The transition has led to the rise of social discrimination against ethnic and religious minorities, as recent studies have demonstrated (Akbaba and Fox 2019). The election and subsequent removal of Muhammad Morsi from office in June 2012 and July 2013, respectively, caused a significant spike in attacks on Christians and church buildings in the summer of 2013. While the period after the Arab Uprisings was a fearful time for all Egyptians, Christians as minorities were even more frightened and felt insecure about the future.

This chapter draws data from a published article "Emotions of the weak" (Ha 2017).

Assistant Professor of Sociology, Duke Kunshan University, China. hyunjeong.ha@dukekunshan.edu.cn

This chapter draws on ethnographic data I collected from in-depth interviews and observation in a mixed-income neighborhood of Cairo from January to July 2014. The duration of my research falls in the period between Morsi's removal and the beginning of Abdel-Fattah el-Sisi taking office. During this time, Christians felt most threatened with heightened physical attacks and social discrimination against them. Based on the findings, the chapter builds a theoretical framework that calls for an understanding of interdependence among the three social aspects: power gap in the majority-minority relations, emotions of minorities, and symbolic boundaries. The framework aims to deepen our understanding of the social construction of emotions among minorities as a consequence of the gap in power and status as the key to comprehending sectarian boundaries between Muslims and Christians.

Social Construction of Emotions among Minorities and Sectarian Boundaries

Sociologists have examined social aspects of emotions by discussing how people struggle to meet social expectations during various social events. For example, during parties, weddings, and funerals, people feel embarrassed when their emotional responses are not aligned with "feeling rules" that form "the sense of entitlement or obligation that governs emotional exchanges" (Hochschild 1983: 56).

Face-to-face interactions help us reveal our "social space," a self-realization about where we belong. The realization accompanies a variety of feelings, including "pain, shame, and belittlement, or pride, pleasure and empowerment" (Clark 1990: 308), and such experience reveals the social construction of emotions. Emotions are "an integral part of social interaction," as they are closely related to "social action like identity, role, ideology, and culture" (Smith-Lovin 1990: 238). Emotions are an important sociological resource to study identity, power, and social status, among others.

Repetitive and momentary in-person interactions can succeed or fail, depending on the cultural capital people own, and these interactions carry a certain emotional energy. To be specific, successful interactions would invigorate positive emotional energy, which subsequently enhances group membership, while failed interactions would drain it. These human interactions happen momentarily but repetitively like chains, as Randall Collins (2004) termed it "interaction ritual chains." Emotions elicited from interactions bring people together but also pull people apart.

Theorizing the social construction of emotions offers an understanding of daily majority-minority interactions between Christians and Muslims. When Christians feel that their interactions with Muslim counterparts failed, the negative emotional energy would bring them closer to Christian communities, while self-perceived successful interactions would help them extend their identity as Egyptians, not just minority

Christians. This way, some chains of unsuccessful interactions would create clearer symbolic boundaries among the minority.

What this chapter focuses on is that changes in political dynamics affect sectarian relations, as seen in the rise of Islamist and ultra-conservative Salafi influences in politics during regime transition in Egypt. As the social atmosphere becomes more hostile to Christian minorities, unsuccessful interactions between Christians and Muslims will increase, resulting in more salient boundaries on the minorities' end.

Christians as Egyptians but Not as Minority: Debates on Belonging

Although Christians claim to be "true" Egyptians for existing in Egypt before Islam and Muslims entered the country, they have been historically under-represented in political arenas. Since Egypt's independence from the British in 1922, only a handful of Christians have served as members of Parliament and ministers. The Constitution, as amended in 1973, has allowed only Muslims to be president. The quota system to ensure promotions of Christian police officers was used to keep the minimum number of Christians in the Egyptian police instead of increasing their number, and Christians often had to compete with each other to be promoted.

Despite the under-representation of Christians, the Coptic Orthodox Church, as a representative of Christians, has denied them being referred to as minorities in Egypt. The Church leadership has rather continued to argue that Christians are equal citizens to Muslims. The Church has been consistent with this perspective; in a Parliamentary discussion on minority quota that intends to allow a certain number of seats for women, Christians, younger people, and those with disabilities, the Church refused to receive a fixed number of seats (Al-Arabiya 2010).

The major reason for the Church to deny the minority status may derive from its historical roots. With the first Coptic Orthodox Church being established in the city of Alexandria in AD 42, Egypt was widely Christian by the time Muslims and Islam entered the country in the seventh century. The word Coptic is derived from *Aigyptos* in Greek, meaning Egyptian. However, as the country has gradually Islamized the Christian population has decreased due to people converting to Islam to avoid discrimination and extra taxes. Egyptian Christians' sense of belonging is largely attached to the land. Recent interviews with Christians revealed that ordinary Christians largely subscribe to the belief that they are "true" Egyptians.

Recent studies have examined citizenship discourses regarding Christians among both Muslim and Christian leadership (Pizzo 2015; Scott 2010). Instead of relying on the modern liberal concept of citizenship to make sense of Christian belonging in Egypt, Rachel Scott (2010) calls for a contextualized understanding of Coptic citizenship based on Egyptian social, moral, and political culture. Drawing on discussions by new Islamists, younger and moderate Islamists in Egypt, she shows a discursive shift for Christians from *dhimmis* (mainly refers to Christians and Jews whose religion was recognized by Islam) to citizens. The new Islamists view social systems of *dhimma* and *jizya* (extra taxes imposed on *dhimmis*) under the Ottoman Empire as degrading and burdening non-Muslim minorities. They further argue that Quranic verses that have historically been used to justify the superior status of Muslims require a new interpretation. This new Islamist perspective recognizes the full citizenship of Christians in Egypt, and Scott (2007: 16) further discusses that the Arabic word *muwatana* (meaning "compatriotism") would be more compatible to understand Egyptian Christians' social belonging.

Emotions in Daily Sectarian Interactions: Methods and Analysis

The neighborhood I studied has the strongest reputation in Cairo for peaceful and harmonious relationships between Christians and Muslims. According to my interlocutors, no single conflict between Muslims and Christians took place in the district; rather, its neighbors used to rely on each other for their daily emergency needs, including leaving their children at their neighbors' homes. During the *thaura*, instead of being divisive, the residents cooperated to protect their properties from thieves. Several of my Christian interview participants were proud to say that they spent several nights with their Muslim neighbors outside their apartment buildings. This collective memory seemed to resonate among the residents of the neighborhood until they realized that the removal of Mubarak did not necessarily mean democratic transition.

Christian residents I studied have integrated their lifestyles with the Muslim majority. They live next door to each other in the same apartment buildings, attend the same schools, visit the same doctors, and get groceries from the same vendors. This integrated lifestyle is predominant in the neighborhood, and both Christians and Muslims live up to its reputation for a peaceful interreligious relationship. I conducted in-depth interviews with twenty-seven Christians in total, with the majority of the interviews in Arabic, along with participant observation in two Coptic Orthodox churches. Each interview lasted about an hour.

Heightened Fear and Subdued Behaviors

As they carefully but quickly checked the atmosphere before we began, the Christians I spoke with tried to make sure no one would hear them. Trying to keep a low profile in public space, they spoke in hushed voices, whispered, mouthed their words without making sounds, and replaced sensitive words such as Islam or Muslims with coded words. They did not want to be heard or catch the attention of those nearby and successfully managed to be invisible by doing so. I later realized that these tactics were to ensure that they would not be involved in any trouble, given the widespread impunity culture in Egypt that tends to punish Christians only, or Christians facing more severe punishment than Muslims when both have the same accusations.

As I sat with Bishoy (interview on June 27, 2014) at a sports center's outdoor table, he lowered his voice whenever he had to mention the word "Islam" to answer my interview questions. However, we did not have anyone sitting within earshot. In another incident, during conversation in a coffee shop, Ashraf (physician, also in his late twenties) likewise lowered his voice and used the phrase "other religion" to refer to Islam or "they" in referring to Muslims. Similarly, at a neighborhood restaurant, Esther (private corporation employee in her late twenties) only moved her lips to say the word "Muslim" while completely silencing her voice. These behaviors, which I understood to be based on fear, appeared conscious at times, as well as unconscious—as if they were accustomed to speaking in such ways in public space.

Even though the Christians I interviewed lived in the most harmonious district in Cairo, I still found that they had developed these behavioral patterns as a defense system growing up as minorities. As Demiana (interview on July 4, 2014) explained, Christians try to avoid any potential trouble.

> Because I am not certain what he [Muslim friend] thinks on the other side, I don't want to go in depth with his troubles and thoughts. Rather, I stop at a certain point so as not to encounter any confrontations ... We [Christians] always have heard that somebody can do something wrong to us by making mistakes. If these things cause you a problem, then it can be your problem. Even though that hasn't happened, we should be safe.

As mentioned earlier, the Egypt's widespread impunity culture has made it difficult for Christians to defend themselves in front of authorities. The blasphemy law enacted in 1981 has penalized criticisms against the president, Islam, and its Islamic religious figures. A series of accusations against Christians, including children and schoolteachers, and subsequent punishment with imprisonment, elicited grave fears among Christians. They have learned that they cannot protect themselves. In this circumstance, trying to protect themselves on their own and avoiding every possible misunderstanding from the beginning are a way to ensure safety.

Christians develop such behavioral patterns as they grow up, but a recent incident, the "Maspero massacre," intensified even further their fear after the Arab Uprisings. Early in October 2011, Christians were attempting a sit-in to protest the government's negligence in not protecting the Christian community after an Orthodox church in Aswan was burned by a group of Muslims. The Egyptian army, intending to repress further social unrest after the Arab Uprisings, unleashed a violent attack, leaving over a dozen dead and about a hundred wounded (Tadros 2011). This incident was a "shock to the Copts," as Abanoub (a graduate student in his mid-thirties) recalled it, because they had relied on the government's protection.[2]

Anger

If fear was an overwhelmingly widespread emotion constructed among Christians, anger was another prevalently shared emotion. I could observe and sense the former, however; because Christians do not reveal their anger in front of Muslims, I did not experience this until they discussed it in detail during the interviews. Such anger is elicited from microaggressions in daily interactions.

Sara (interview on May 23, 2014) recalled her recent experience while shopping at a Muslim Brotherhood-run store. The owner ordered her to cover her hair as Muslim women do, but she was embarrassed and responded, "No, I am a Christian," and left. In Egypt, Christian women are not required to cover their hair because it is a practice widely followed by Muslim women. Consequently, Christian women are more visible when they are among Muslim women. This was the case with Sara, who stood out as a Christian in the shop. She said she felt "annoyed" because the shopkeeper told her to cover her hair, even though she was sure he already knew her to be Christian from her crucifix necklace as well as her unveiled hair. She added that she stopped shopping at the store after that. These microaggressions Sara and other Christian women experienced led to drawing even clearer boundaries along religious lines.

Oftentimes, daily greetings stir up irritation or even anger among Christians. The majority of Christians I spoke with expressed feelings of anger, saying they were *az'al'* (angry) or *mitghāz'* (irritated) in these situations. While Egyptians speak Arabic, Muslims and Christians have developed greeting styles specific to their religion and culture. For instance, Muslims usually greet others by saying *salām 'alaikūm* (peace be upon you, responding *alaikūm el-salām*). Christians, however, get used to saying *Ṣabāḥ el-Kheir* (good morning) or *Masā' el-Kheir* (good afternoon), depending on the time of the day. In certain situations, some Christians feel pressured to respond in the Islamic way, and their greetings have been disregarded. For example, there is a Muslim *bawab* (doorman) at Soher's apartment, and when she greets him with "good morning," unconsciously, he responds with *Salām 'alaikūm*. With this, Soher (interview on May 18, 2014) realized that her greeting and kind intention were not acknowledged and accepted, but rather ignored.

Dismissal

Finally, the last discerned emotional reaction among Christians is dismissal through denying their daily frustrations resulting from interactions. Instead of recognizing frustrations and allowing them to sink deep in their emotions, they quickly dismissed the negative emotions verbally and immediately blamed Muslims for creating such situations. They devised their own tactics to control their daily frustrations in order to maintain their self-esteem. The most prevalent way of doing this is by saying "'ādī" during conversations or interviews after discussing examples of microaggressions. This word literally means "ordinary" or "normal," but contextually, it rather means "It's okay" to connote that they do not want to problematize the situations anymore.

This is a sort of a tactic Christians frequently use in their daily verbal discourse. In this context, the term "tactics" refers to implicit ways of daily resistance to state power dominance in modern society (de Certeau 1984). Claiming autonomy and creativity in an already-structured society, various creative ways of living, including taking shortcuts, cooking, and keeping journals, are tactics to utilize in daily lives, according to de Certeau (1984). Understanding the tactics to resist power imposed on ordinary people that largely shape their everyday lives, and to retain autonomy and power, Christians' dismissing their frustrations verbally can be considered a tactic to survive and preserve self-esteem.

An example of how this tactic of denial works is when Irini (interview on April 12, 2014) discusses her experience in a government office that she visited to renew a document.

> I don't feel that it's [living as Christian] a disaster ... but sometimes, you feel that you cannot get what you want. You don't have your rights. So, you see, this time [when it happens] is not nice. But I don't feel shy [or shy away], and *it's okay* ('ādī). I don't think about living by another religion. *It's okay.* If you're not giving me a good grade because I am a Christian? *It's okay.* This happens in everyday life. (emphasis mine)

From this interview, it is clear that Irini was frustrated about the situation, but to diminish or dismiss her irritation, she said, "It's okay" ('ādī) several times. It was a most frequently observed verbal habit among Christians when they discussed experiences like this. As Irini did, many Christians appear to use this discursive pattern frequently and purposefully to dismiss and further deny their feelings of hurt.

Conclusion

This chapter examined emotions shared among Egyptian Christians elicited from daily interactions with the Muslim majority in Egypt's post-Arab Uprisings era. Through an analysis of ethnographic data, I discussed how they as religious minorities tried to keep a low profile in public to avoid any potential (at times false) accusations. Although they kept it at a private level, Christians spoke about anger after experiencing microaggressions by their Muslim counterparts. The analysis of emotions reveals that interreligious emotional cleavages have deepened over time, and they became even more saliently demonstrated after the significant changes, including regime change after the Arab Uprisings. The construction of emotions resonates with social and political situations.

With 2021 marking the ten-year anniversary of the Mubarak regime's fall, the outlook for future sectarian relations in Egypt seems bleak. The country is much more divisive along the lines of religion and faces old but continuing social and economic problems that once motivated Egyptians to topple the thirty-year Mubarak regime. With problems becoming even more challenging due to a rapidly increasing population and much higher unemployment rate, aggravated by the pandemic, Egyptian citizens, regardless of religion, share deeper grievances and anger under the repressive regime. Sisi has made friendly overtures to the Church since 2014 by celebrating Coptic Christmas and Easter, but Christians become the target of hostility for building favorable relationships with the government when grievances against the government grow (Ha 2020).

Notes

1 Egypt was one of four countries, along with Tunisia, Libya, and Yemen, that experienced regime changes after the Arab Uprisings.
2 In recent decades, the Church has formed and maintained favorable relations with the state, particularly between the late former Pope Shenouda III and Hosni Mubarak since 1981. After Mubarak was ousted, however, the clientelist relationship ended, which made Christians feel much less secure. The Maspero massacre particularly increased fears among Christians, making them realize they no longer have state protection.

References

Akbaba, Y. and J. Fox (2019), "Social Rather than Governmental Change: Religious Discrimination in Muslim-majority Countries after the Arab Uprisings," *All Azimuth*, 8 (1): 5–22.

Al-Arabiya (2010), "Egypt Christians Reject Quota Parliament Seats," September 20. https://www.alarabiya.net/articles/2010/11/21/126824.html

Clark, C. (1990), "Emotions and Micropolitics in Everyday Life: Some Patterns and Paradoxes of 'Place'," in T. D. Kemper (ed.), *Research Agendas in the Sociology of Emotions*, 305–34, Albany: State University of New York Press.

Collins, R. (2004), *Interaction Ritual Chains*, Princeton: Princeton University Press.

de Certeau, M. (1984), *The Practice of Everyday Life*, trans. S. Rendall, Berkeley: University of California Press.

Ha, H. J. (2017), "Emotions of the Weak: Violence and Ethnic Boundaries among Coptic Christians in Egypt," *Ethnic and Racial Studies*, 40 (1): 133–51.

Haddad, F. (2017), "'Sectarianism' and Its Discontents in the Study of the Middle East," *The Middle East Journal*, 71 (3): 363–82.

Haddad, F. (2020), "Egyptian Christians under Sisi: Where Do They Go Now?" *Diverse Asia (Seoul National University Asia Center's online quarterly magazine)*, 10. http://diverseasia.snu.ac.kr/?p=4747

Heo, A. (2018), *The Political Lives of Saints: Christian-Muslim Mediation in Egypt*, Berkeley: University of California Press.

Hochschild, A. R. (1983), *The Managed Heart. Commercialization of Human Feeling*, Berkeley: University of California Press.

Pizzo, P. (2015), "The 'Coptic Question' in Post Revolutionary Egypt: Citizenship Democracy Religion," *Ethnic and Racial Studies*, 38 (14): 2598–613.

Scott, R. (2010), *The Challenge of Political Islam: Non-Muslims and the Egyptian State*, Stanford: Stanford University Press.

Scott, Rachel. (2007), "Contextual Citizenship in Modern Islamic Thought," *Islam and Christian-Muslim Relations*, 18 (1): 1–18.

Smith-Lovin, L. (1990), "Emotions as the Confirmation and Disconfirmation of Identity: An Affect Control Model," in T. D. Kemper (ed.), *Research Agendas in the Sociology of Emotions*, 238–70, Albany: State University of New York Press.

Tadros, M. (2011), "Egypt's Bloody Sunday," Middle East Report and Information Project, October 13. http://www.merip.org/mero/mero101311

Muslimizing Turkish-Origin Migrants and Their Descendants: Diaspora Politics and Integration Politics

by Ayhan Kaya

Introduction

This chapter aims to discuss the root causes of radicalization among Turkish-origin youth residing in Europe, especially Germany. The time span that will be covered in the chapter will be mainly the last two decades as ethno-cultural and religious-based radicalization has become prevalent since the September 11, 2001. Based on the desk research as well as the initial findings of an ongoing European Research Council Advanced Grant study held in Germany, France, Belgium, and the Netherlands (Islam-ophob-ism, Grant Agreement No. 785934), this chapter delineates the ways in which self-identified young Muslims of Turkish origin react to the detrimental effects of globalization, modernization, deindustrialization, institutional discrimination, ambiguity, insecurity, and anomy.[1] Hence, the term radicalization will be used in a rather different way from its current usage by different political, academic, and media circles that perceives it with a rather negative connotation.

As will be discussed later, the term radicalization will be used in parallel with the way Craig Calhoun (2011) has earlier used it in new social movements literature. The scope of this chapter will cover the elaboration of the terms of terrorism, populism, and Islamism in the European context in order to explicate the socioeconomic and political context. The second section of the chapter will concentrate on the relevance of the German politics of integration over the last two decades on the Turkish-origin migrants and their descendants. The third section will be about the other side of the coin depicting the role of the Turkish state's diaspora politics on the religio-political

---

I would like to express my gratitude to Bianca Kaiser for her suggestions on the manuscript. This chapter is driven from an ongoing research conducted within the framework of European Research Council Advanced Grant and funded by the European Commission (Islam-ophob-ism, Grant Agreement No. 785934).

radicalization of Turkish-origin youth in Germany. This section will surely cover the period of the Justice and Development Party rule since 2002. The last section will elaborate on the details of Islamist radicalization of Turkish-origin youth in everyday life unravelling the testimonies of youngsters we have interviewed in 2020 and 2021.

Context: Terrorism, Populism, and Islamism

This chapter was written in a context with a very strong visibility of Islamophobia in Europe and elsewhere. The augmentation of Islamophobic discourse in Europe seems to result from three main processes: the growing terrorist threat posed by Islamist groups such as ISIS, al Qaeda, and Boko Haram (CEP 2019); the securitization of Islam in the West (Huysmans 2006; Kaya 2012; Lazaridis and Wadia 2015); and the growing populist and nativist discourse in Europe (Kaya 2019; Kalb 2011; Laclau 2005; Mouffe 2018; Mudde 2004). Islamist terrorism has some specificities that distinguish it from other types of terrorism. The narrative propagated by Islamist terrorists is peculiar in motivating potential recruits and bolstering their membership by focusing on specific elements over others. One essential element in the Islamist terrorists' rhetoric directly taps into victimization, unfairness, and discrimination. The Salafi/Wahhabi-inspired ideology of groups such as ISIS, Al Qaeda, and Boko Haram depicts a struggle opposing Western oppressive military interventions and geopolitical decisions in relation to Muslim countries. Through these ideological lenses, it is not only the European secular states and societies but also secular Muslim states and societies are seen as inherently corrupt and deceitful. Hence, it is not only the European public but also the predominant majority of Muslim-origin people become the targets and victims of such forms of terrorism initiated in the name of Islam.

Islamophobia has been mainstreamed in many European countries over the last two decades since September 11. This is partly because of the rise of terrorist attacks initiated by various organizations in the name of Islam, and partly because of the securitization of Islam by various political actors, mainstream media, and even some academic circles. There is another driver which has become significantly important since the 2008 global financial crisis and the so-called 2015 refugee crisis leading to the escalation of Islamophobic sentiments in Europe: the rise of right-wing populism and nativism. In times of economic crisis, it often happens that exclusionary acts by various political and societal actors become more visible. Racism, xenophobia, Islamophobia, nativism, and nationalism have been common topics of discussion as far as migration, diversity, multiculturalism, interculturalism, living together, and refugees are concerned (Barker 1981; Brubaker 2017; Russon 1995; Rosaldo 1989). Now, *nativism* has become another popular kind of exclusionary discourse promoted by populist parties. Nativism seems to be a powerful tool to be employed by socio-economically and nostalgically deprived individuals to come to terms with the detrimental fear of globalization causing deindustrialization, structural inequalities, unemployment, poverty, heterogeneity, mobility, and diversity (Kaya 2019).

It is in this populist *Zeitgeist* the chapter has been written. In such a context, there is a growing process of culturalization and religionization of socioeconomic and political phenomena. Day by day, a growing number of individuals from both self-identified native groups and self-identified Muslim groups tend to identify themselves with respectively more ethno-cultural and religious identities. While some self-identified natives tend to become more nationalist and Islamophobist, some self-identified Muslims are likely to become more identified with Islamism. Such individuals in both groups who are, on the one hand, socially, economically, and politically deprived and, on the other, are in search of communities to defend themselves against the detrimental effects of globalization, are more likely to be drawn to right-wing populist discourses and Islamist discourses that simplify, binarize, culturalize, civilationalize, and religionize what is social, economic, and political in origin. What is remarkable in the interviews that we have so far conducted in Islamophobism research accords with the observations of Rogers Brubaker (2017: 1208):

> The growing civilizational preoccupation with Islam in European populisms has profoundly transformed the political semantics of self and other: the collective self is increasingly defined in broadly civilizational, not narrowly national terms. The civilizational-level semantics of self and other have internalized liberalism—along with secularism, philosemitism, gender equality, gay rights, and free speech—as an identity marker of the Christian West *vis-à-vis* putatively intrinsically illiberal Islam.

In parallel with the Huntingtonian paradigm of the "clash of civilizations," the term civilization here is reduced to religious differences, and Christianity to a cultural—but not religious—form, to be celebrated by liberals, atheists, agnostics, and others against the rise of radical Islam challenging secular forms of life. Feelings of socioeconomic and political deprivation are not only expressed through resentment against multiculturalism, diversity, migration, and Islam, but also through resentment toward the European Union institutions. The mainstreaming of right-wing populism (Reynié 2016) actually goes beyond current socioeconomic, political, and demographic markers such as the global financial crisis and refugee crisis; it is rather based on the legacy of the civilizational rhetoric, which has its roots in the aftermath of the end of the Cold War leading into the conflict in the Balkans in the 1990s.

The Impact of German Politics of Integration on the Migrant-Origin Individuals and Their Processes of Radicalization

It has become common practice in Europe to label Muslim-origin migrants as persons with a "Muslim identity," the boundaries of which remain unchanged over time (cf. Heitmeyer et al. 1997; Nielsen 2013). This is not only visible in scientific texts, but also in conferences, seminars, media programs, journals, newspapers, and other venues. Prior to the labeling of migrant-origin people mainly as "Muslims," there were other ways to name them in Europe, the genealogy of which may be traced. Migrant workers were simply called "*workers*" in the early days of the migratory process in the 1960s. Then, in the aftermath of the official ban on recruiting migrant labor in 1974, a sharp discursive shift can be observed in their identification by the host societies and states. They became "foreigners," "Turks," "Algerians," "Indians," "Pakistanis," or "Moroccans." In other words, their ethnic labels became the primary reference for host societies. *Ethnicization* of immigrant workers went in tandem with the process of deindustrialization in western European countries, where unemployment started to become a common phenomenon for migrant workers, who were mostly excluded from the processes of integration into spheres of education, politics, housing, and labor market on an equal footing with host society members (Kaya 2001; Lipsitz 1994).

Labeling migrants as "Muslims," or "Muslimizing" them, is an occurrence of the last quarter of a century in Europe as well as in Germany. It actually goes back to the 1990s when some parts of the European public started to associate migrant-origin people with political instabilities emerging in the Middle East and Africa. The 1990s was also critical in the sense that religious and civilizational divides became more outspoken and highlighted in European public space with the birth of the paradigm of "clash of civilizations" and the war in Bosnia. Hence, the changing global context has partly shaped the ways in which migrant-receiving societies and states have begun to frame and identify migrants and their descendants. In other words, labeling migrants as "Muslims" is one consequence of global political and societal changes, and naturally, migrant-origin people and their descendants have responded to these changes and labeling by identifying themselves even more with Islam.

Labeling Turkish-origin migrants and their descendants simply as "Muslims" in Germany has become prevalent since the mid-2000s. Since then, the German debate on integration has revolved around the annual Summit on Integration, and the German Islam Conference founded by Angela Merkel in 2006. The Summit on Integration resulted in the "National Integration Plan" and a "National Action Plan for Integration," focusing on immigrant integration via social and cultural participation. The Expert Council of German Foundations for Integration and Migration identified the drivers of integration as dialogue and recognition of the achievements of the migrants in Germany. On the other hand, the Islam Conference was widely viewed as a positive development in addressing negative discourse on the integration of Turkish-origin migrants and Islam after 9/11 (Wilpert 2013: 119). The German government has established two kinds of consultation procedures: one for issues of immigrant integration and another one for state–Islam dialogue. This initiative anticipated dialogue by giving the state access to immigrants while creating channels through which immigrants and their descendants could get organized (Kaya 2012). The Islam Conference was meant to set up a new form of German-Islam made in Germany, not in Turkey (Humphrey 2009; Kaya 2012). Due to national, ethnic, and doctrinal cleavages dividing Muslim-origin populations, attempts at organizing European Islam were unsuccessful (Kaya 2012: 194). This debate also concerns Germany's accommodation of Islam in which Islam and Muslim identity are defined and perceived in a monolithic manner, reproducing the civilizational discourse (ibid.).

In 2007, a major academic survey called "Muslims in Germany: integration, barriers to integration, religion, and attitudes towards democracy, the rule of law, and politically/religiously motivated violence" was conducted by Katrin Brettfeld and Peter Wetzels, published by the Ministry of the Interior of Germany in 2007. It was presented at the German Islam Conference. The survey explored youth attitudes toward integration, religion, democracy, and violence to identify the "problem group" of those who are at risk of radicalization into Islamist extremism. This survey found that Germany's "Muslims" identified more with their country of origin. It was also revealed that this tendency was highest among school children and it decreased with age. The survey disclosed that identification with the country of origin did not necessarily mean rejection of integration (Brettfeld and Wetzels 2007: 363). However, the design of the survey and its categories of interpretation were criticized for indicating the assumptions of the researchers rather than illustrating the cultural, religious, or political life of "Muslims" in Germany (Dornhof 2009: 75–6). Similarly, Dirk Baier and Christian Pfeiffer (2010) found a correlation between self-reported strong adherence to Islam and the expressed willingness to become violent among fourteen to sixteen-year-old ninth graders. These surveys and systematic studies on "Muslims," risk ethnicizing migrant-origin populations, while asking the participants to validate the well-known stereotypes in the dominant society about their religion or ethnicity (Wilpert 2013: 120). These contribute to stigmatization of Muslim-origin people, which often affects their understanding of opportunities in society, including socioeconomic mobility, labor mobility, and cultural integration prospects. Many characteristics assigned to Muslim-origin people in these studies are the opposite of German citizens, describing them as "potentially" homophobic, anti-Semitic, misogynist, anti-democratic, backward, anti-modernist drawn to violence and criminality (Schiffauer 2013).

Through the 2000s, the debate on German *Leitkultur* (leading culture) was introduced amidst such debates surrounding migration, citizenship, ethnicity, and belonging. Bassam Tibi (1998) first argued that Germany should reposition itself at the democratic heart of this modern and enlightened Europe by acknowledging and accepting

"European *Leitkultur*," which refers to the generation of a set of European core norms and values to be accepted by all individuals in Germany—natives and migrants. Bassam Tibi denounced multiculturalism as an expression of guilt over colonialism and the Holocaust, leading to "disproportionate tolerance" toward immigrants (Pautz 2005: 43). The conception of *Leitkultur* is highly challenging for migrant communities, but it still remains a significant part of the German identity discourse.

The German "self" in the *Leitkultur* discourse relied on constructing the non-German "other," which simply corresponded to the Turkish minority setting up a "parallel society" reinforced by discrimination, xenophobia, limited education, low socioeconomic status, marginalization, and unassimilable cultural and religious life styles (Mueller 2006: 432). *Leitkultur* was an attempt to create a socioeconomic and sociocultural framework for migrants across European countries in the 2000s (Brubaker 2001; Scholten et al. 2017). In parallel with the *Leitkultur* discourse, assimilationist discourse also returned in the 2000s. However, the former became more acceptable in Germany as it was not an analytically debunked and politically disreputable approach in comparison to the latter. This is why, *Leitkultur* discourse was normatively welcome by the majority society (Brubaker 2001: 531).

The debate on *Leitkultur* became prevalent in parallel with the debate on the failure of multiculturalism in early 2010s, which simultaneously recurred in western Europe. The "failure of multiculturalism" has been announced not only by right-wing populist political parties but also by centrist political parties all across the continent.[2] Angela Merkel, for the first time, publicly dismissed the policy of multiculturalism as having "failed, failed utterly" in October 2010, which was swiftly followed by David Cameron's call for a "more active, more muscular liberalism," as well as Nicolas Sarkozy's statement that multiculturalism is a "failed concept" (*Der Spiegel* September 11, 2010). Thilo Sarrazin (2010) has argued that Germany was becoming "naturally more stupid on average" due to immigration from Muslim countries. In his critique of Sarrazin's highly polemical book, Jürgen Habermas has proposed that German *Leitkultur* (leading culture) was then defined not by "German culture" but by religion: "With an arrogant appropriation of Judaism—and an incredible disregard for the fate the Jews suffered in Germany—the apologists of the *Leitkultur* now appeal to the 'Judeo-Christian tradition,' which distinguishes 'us' from foreigners [Muslims]" (Habermas 2010).

Although Sarrazin's arguments were based on a conventional racist rhetoric, he was credited by remarkable segments of the German society for securitizing Germany's citizenship policies (Habermas 2010). His racist reasoning, which was categorically hostile to Turkish and Arabic migrants, was later partly followed by Bavarian Prime Minister Horst Seehofer (Habermas 2010). The German experience also reveals that the European form of secularism is not yet equipped to accommodate Islam, which has recently become very visible in the public space (Kaya 2012; Laitin 2010). Interestingly, the situation in Germany, alongside that in France, Belgium, the Netherlands, Denmark, and the UK, has led to a kind of *holy alliance* of the secular left and the Christian right against Islam (Roy 2007: xii).

Two years after the publication of Sarrazin's book, the expected "Sarrazin party" emerged in opposition to the loans given to Greece as part of the European Stability Mechanism (ESM). This development was preceded by a debate among various business associations. The non-monopolistic capital of these associations of family-run companies protested against the ESM, whereas the monopolistic capital (Federal Association of German Industries—BDI) demanded just such a policy, which was then implemented by the governing coalition parties (Korteweg 2017). In 2013, neoliberal economists and conservatives from the CSU and the Free Democratic Party (FDP) formed *Alternative für Deutschland*. The AfD is also renowned for its suspicion of migration. Initially, AfD was dominated by neoliberal economics professors, who favored tax reductions for the wealthy and cutbacks in the social budget. They did not shy away from demanding that opportunities for the democratic participation of the poor be limited for the benefit of the wealthy.

The flow of political discourses embraced by the mainstream political parties, especially the CDU-CSU, demonstrates that the two tenets of the current right-wing populism were actually rooted in the same conservative mainstream parties: Islamophobia and anti-multiculturalism. While the growing Islamophobia in Germany has made the majority society appeal more to Judeo-Christian tradition since 9/11, it has made many self-identified Muslims identify themselves more with Islam and their country of origin (Kaya 2019). The elevation of civilizational discourse since the 1990s has also been prevalent in Turkey under the Justice and Development Party rule, instrumentalizing Islam in reaching out the Turkish diaspora. In this sense, it was not only the mainstream German politics "Muslimizing" the Turkish-origin migrants and their descendants, but also the Justice and Development Party rule in Turkey.

The Impact of Turkish State's Diaspora Politics under the AKP Rule on the Radicalization of the Turkish-Origin Migrants and Their Descendants

Traditionally, Turkish foreign policy was based on four principles: Westernization, *laicité*, a stable international order, and commitment to international law. Foreign policy was the reflection of the secular elite's conception of state identity (Öztürk and Sözeri 2018). Under the AKP rule, former PM Ahmet Davutoglu conceived Turkey's foreign policy within his doctrine of strategic depth. Davutoglu was the AKP's former minister of foreign affairs and the prime minister between 2014 and 2016, who argued that Turkey could become a global power if it followed a foreign policy that respects the country's Islamic history. Thus, his conception rejected the Westernization of Turkey in favor of an ethno-religiously oriented foreign policy. For Davutoğlu, the strategic depth of Turkey lies in its geopolitical position and its identity that would enable Turkey to unite Islamic countries and create a common front against Western hegemony (Özkan 2014).

Islam and the Ottoman-Islamic identity would enable the country to easily incorporate countries spreading from the Balkans to the Middle East and beyond (Öztürk and Sözeri 2018). It is no surprise that within this conception of foreign policy, *Diyanet* came to play an important role. Before going into a detailed account of the instrumentalization of *Diyanet* in diaspora politics, one should assess some other institutions instrumentalized by the AKP to politically manipulate the Turkish diaspora in Europe.

Turkish migrants and their children in the West were officially defined in Turkey as either "*gurbetçi*" (those away from homeland) or "*Yurtdışındaki vatandaşlarımız*" ("our citizens abroad"). Indeed, it is not only the Turkish state that has perceived emigrants through a paternalistic lens, but also Turkish citizens living in Turkey (Kaya 2018). The latter still stereotypically define Turkish emigrants as either "*Almanyalı*" or "*Almancı*" (German-like), no matter where they come from. Both terms carry rather negative connotations in Turkey (Kaya and Kentel 2008). The Turkish state's framing of these emigrants can be analyzed in three distinctive epochs: (a) 1960s–1980s: as economic agents providing Turkey with remittances; (b) 1980s–2000s: as political agents acting as an extension of the Turkish state in defending its interests against centrifugal groups abroad; and (c) 2000s–present day: utilization of Turkish emigrants as lobbying agents (Kaya 2018).

While Turkish state policies toward management of its emigrants practically started in the 1980s, these policies gained momentum in line with the growing civilizational discourse in the early 2000s. Prior to the 1980s, emigrants were simply perceived and instrumentalized by the Turkish state as economic agents transferring remittances to Turkey. Remittances—the earnings generated and sent back home by migrant workers—have long been an important source of exchange revenue for developing countries, with Turkey being no exception in the trajectory of remittances since the 1960s. In the 1960s especially, remittances were regarded as a major source of external financing that offset trade deficits in particular (Aksel 2019). Subsequently, the period following the 1980 military coup in Turkey, which resulted in the emigration of thousands of asylum seekers such as Kurds, Alevis, radical left-wing individuals, and Assyrians, was mostly juxtaposed with the securitization of the Turkish state's relations with its citizens living abroad, Turkey's insertion into the global economy, and the consolidation of a state-led Kemalist republicanism that incorporated a stricter emphasis on Turkish-Islamist historical and moral values (İçduygu et al. 1999).

In the 1980s, Turkish emigrants were politically instrumentalized by the Turkish state to ensure that centrifugal ethno-cultural and religious elements abroad, such as Armenians, Assyrians, Kurds, Alevis, and Islamists, could be contained by these "decent Turkish citizens living abroad." These citizens were mostly perceived as agents of the state acting on behalf of the Turkish state to control other groups and individuals with oppositional ideological and political opinions challenging the Turkish state's survival (Kaya 2018).

The final epoch, starting in the 2000s, has been marked by the governance of Turkey toward increased market liberalism and European integration in economic, legal, social, and political terms. More importantly, this period has been shaped by the AKP's ascendance to power that has now lasted for five consecutive terms, creating incremental breaches with former governance models and official state ideology in Turkey (Kadıoğlu 2008). In the current phase, the Turkish state tends to perceive emigrants as active lobbying agents who are expected to contribute to the growing hegemony of the Turkish state in European space. This kind of diaspora strategy also tends to see emigrants as electoral constituents to be incorporated into the national electoral body. In this period, the Turkish state has founded new institutions to help emigrants mobilize themselves as active lobbying agents. The Directorate of Turks Abroad and Related Communities (YTB, *Yurtdışı Türkler ve Akraba Topluluklar Başkanlığı* 2010) and Yunus Emre Cultural Centres (YEKM, *Yunus Emre Kültür Merkezleri,* 2007) have been established in this period to mobilize emigrants living abroad (Pusch and Splitt 2013). The YTB aims to establish a strong and successful diaspora with strong ties to Turkey in order to create a political lobby and close economic links with the countries of residence (Pusch and Splitt 2013: 149), while YEKM aims at introducing the world to Turkish language and culture by means of active involvement of Turkish emigrants.[3]

More recently, in the context of mass demonstrations in Belgium and Germany, the Union of European Turkish Democrats (UETD, *Avrupalı Türk Demokratlar Birliği*) has gained some public attention. The UETD was founded in Cologne in 2004 as a lobby group supporting the Turkish government by organizing campaign events such as rallies and live broadcasts (Aksel 2019). The UETD was mobilized by the Turkish government to organize public rallies for the Turkish President in Cologne, Brussels, and Strasbourg, where he gave public speeches in the framework of general elections held in 2015.[4] External voting abroad in 2015 has been enabled by an amendment of May 18, 2014, to the Law on the Fundamental Principles of Elections and Electoral Registries. It has improved the political rights of Turkish emigrants and enables them to vote from abroad in parliamentary elections, presidential elections, and referenda in Turkey (Abadan-Unat et al. 2016). Prior to this change initiated by a constitutional court ruling in 2012, Turkish expatriates had to come to polling stations at the customs section of airports and borders to participate in domestic elections. The new rules were first applied during the direct presidential elections of August 10, 2014. The AKP's close ties with the UETD have always been visible. On May 10, 2015, President Erdoğan addressed Euro-Turks in Karlsruhe in a public event organized by the UETD, where he recommended them to protect their religion and culture:

> You should first preserve your religion, faith and culture strongly and accept that you are a full citizen of the country you reside in. Then, you will make others accept it. If you do not put up this struggle, nobody else will grant a right to you. You will strongly preserve your mother tongue, the Turkish language. Let me say this clearly, one who loses his mother tongue loses everything. Do not forget the language you speak. (PRT 2015)

In the same speech, the president stressed the importance of the Turkish diaspora, even calling them the "most important source of Turkey's regional and global power" (PRT 2015). Then Prime Minister Ahmet Davutoğlu gave a similar public speech in Dortmund on May 3, 2015, in which he underlined Turkey's perspective on integration:

> You should get involved in the social, political and economic life of the country in which you live ... We do not need anyone telling us about integration. We are achieving integration. But as we have always said, we will never accept assimilation ... You should preserve your culture, identity, language and religion. (AKP 2015)

These statements by Turkish politicians appealing to the diaspora reveal that the ruling political elite fosters a religious-cultural closeness to Turkey. This aspect, paired with the recurrent rejection of "assimilation," has become a main aspect of the AKP politicians' speeches. However, there is also anecdotal evidence indicating that official lobbying activities of the Turkish state among the Turkish diaspora are likely to be more destructive than constructive in the way in which they make Euro-Turks compete with each other on ideological grounds (Aksel 2019).

Revitalizing the Ottoman heritage, past, myths, memories, and Islam, the Turkish President, Recep Tayyip Erdoğan, has empowered many Turkish-origin migrants, especially youngsters, to stand against earlier feelings of humiliation created by migrant receiving states and native populations. Turkish-origin migrants and their descendants were also disappointed with the pace of European integration and the obstacles created by the EU member states, primarily by France and Germany. In the second half of the 2000s, following the emphasis on the "open-ended" characteristic of the negotiations and the possibility of "permanent derogations," Turkey's membership prospects became unclear in the eyes of the Turkish migrants residing in Europe (Paçacı and Straubhaar 2012). Growing Islamophobia and Turkophobia within the EU as well as the deterioration of Turkey-EU relations have engendered in many feelings of alienation toward their countries of settlement, and made them feel more affiliated with the homeland.

Within this context, *Diyanet* has grown significantly since it was founded in 1924 by the Kemalist establishment during the early years of the Turkish Republic. Currently, it has an annual budget of 1.6 billion US dollars, and more than 80,000 employees. Its budget is more than that of thirty-seven other state ministries. It subsidizes the construction and maintenance of more than 90,000 mosques in Turkey, decides about the content of the legal sermons, controls the Quran courses in the country, employs all the imams, and organizes annual pilgrimage to Mecca (Öztürk and Sözeri 2018).

Under the AKP rule, *Diyanet* has served to endorse the party's discourse, actions, and policies and grant them religious legitimation.[5] The party has continued the long tradition of state control of Islamic religious activities and using the presidency to determine who has the legitimate religious authority as opposed to the "deviant radicals." Now *Diyanet* has been expanded to see its reach to go beyond the national borders (Lord 2018). It is given a "global vision" and plays an essential role in AKP's foreign policy (Bruce 2019). To that end, within his vision of strategic depth, Davutoglu positioned Turkey as a Muslim country within the global order and structured the role of *Diyanet* around the concept of the "heart hinterland" (*gönül coğrafyası*) in a way that would help Turkey become a "pivotal country" and regain its appeal within the global Muslim community. It should become the "flotation ring" and the reference for Muslims around the world to "deliver the eternal call of Allah and the Prophet to humanity, which is endangered by secularism and nihilism" (Öztürk and Sözeri 2018: 9).

With its sixty-one branches in thirty-six countries, *Diyanet* has become a religious diplomacy actor. The presidency reflects state identity and seems to have substituted secularism with Sunni Islam in foreign policy. Within the Turkish-Islamic Association of Religious Affairs (*Diyanet İşleri Türk İslam Birliği*, DİTİB), *Diyanet* has been active in providing religious services in Europe, the Balkans, and Central Asia, in building mosques, delivering religious teaching, sending *Imams*, and even putting in place educational institutions to train religious personnel (Öztürk and Sözeri 2018). It is also in charge of promoting Turkish Islam abroad with a focus on countries with a high number of Turkish immigrants to prevent the emergence of radical discourses (Öztürk 2016). In order to compete for regional influence with Saudi Arabia and Iran (Lord 2018) and to maintain Turkish Muslims' loyalty to the Turkish state, *Diyanet*, through mosques, religious classes, and dormitories, has started diffusing Sunni Islam with a focus on human rights, ethics, and an explanation of citizen's duties toward their state (Öztürk 2016). *Diyanet* serves to establish and maintain links between the Turkish state and Turkish emigrants in Europe, mainly in Germany, France, Belgium, and the Netherlands. Significantly, European host countries welcomed the presidency because they were afraid that the religious void could lead to a rise in radical Islamic groups and disrupt their societies (Öztürk 2018). *Diyanet* has a vast network of religious institutions in the Turkish diaspora in Europe, influencing the ways in which young Turkish-origin Muslims practice their religiosity. A twenty-four-year-old Turkish-origin woman staying in the dormitory of *Diyanet* in Tegel, Berlin, said the following in the interview held on August 7, 2020, when asked about the role of religion in her everyday life:

> I try to pray five times a day. I try to live in line with the *Sunna* of the prophet as much as I can. I often go to the *Sohbet* (talks organized by Imam). I read about religious topics personally, in particular about Islam. I wear a headscarf. I started to include religion into my everyday life … Thanks to my religion, I also learned to appreciate and respect my parents. The dormitory belongs to DiTiB. They feel responsible for us. We are treated a bit like protégés. We give them our shopping lists and they buy us groceries every second, or third week during the pandemic. I feel extremely comfortable in the dormitory. The support there is immense.

Diyanet has become even more active during the last years in recruiting young self-identified Muslims through such solidarity networks that are also offered by several other competitive religious-based institutions such as the Gülen community, Salafi groups, and others.

Currently, demonstrating loyalty to *Diyanet* is synonymous to loyalty to the Turkish state, and the presidency has become an "international symbol" of the state's religious identity (Öztürk 2018). Thus, the presidency has sought to get a monopoly on who represents "official" and "legitimate" Islam both within the borders of Turkey and abroad (Bruce 2019). Turkish foreign policy has always been an extension of domestic politics, and this has not changed with the rise of the AKP to power in 2002. However, under the AKP *Diyanet*'s responsibilities and activism in foreign policy have been expanded to include providing scholarships (Lord 2018) and building more mosques in Germany and the Netherlands for example. It is now responsible for spreading the AKP's understanding of Islam, secularism, and nationalism, and promoting Islamic moral values both inside and outside Turkey to young generations (Öztürk 2016). *Diyanet* became a major instrument in foreign policy in charge of publishing and distributing the Quran and religious books in different languages to increase the visibility of Sunni Islam (Öztürk 2018). In other words, it has tried to spread the "identity change of the state to society" both domestically and internationally (Öztürk and Sözeri 2018).

The AKP's foreign policy has acquired an ethno-religious identity in charge of "exporting domestic matters" abroad, for instance, the tensions between the AKP and the Gülen movement since 2015 (Öztürk and Sözeri 2018). As a matter of fact, when the AKP ended its partnership with the Gülen movement much earlier than the 2016 failed coup attempt, some *Diyanet* imams were dismissed from their posts in Europe where they were accused of being close to the movement (Bruce 2019). Thus, the AKP has sought to form alliances with the Muslim-origin community abroad as part of its strategy to preserve its control over the religious affairs abroad and what it entails as economic, symbolic, and most importantly political gains. The way the AKP shifts its alliances in Europe is also a reflection of how it shifts its alliances and forms its domestic policies. In addition, the AKP ended the long-lasting state tradition of cooperating only with non-Islamist movements operating in Europe within its diaspora. Thus, the AKP started cooperating with the *Milli Görüş* movement, which runs mosques and provides religious services mainly in Germany (Foreign Policy 2019). Indeed, the boundaries between *Diyanet* and the movement are blurred as *Diyanet* religious officials often attend *iftar* organized by the movement in Europe and accept their requests when they ask for *Diyanet* imams to be appointed at their mosques. This cooperation is seen as an intention to bring together the different Turkish religious communities in Europe (Bruce 2019) in attempt to raise pious young Muslims, seek influence, and convince Turkish citizens in Europe to vote for the party (Foreign Policy 2019).

Islamist Radicalism among Turkish-Origin Youth

As Robert Gurr (1969) pointed out earlier, angry people rebel. Some youngsters become increasingly angry and radicalized as a result of a variety of root causes. No consensus emerged on the root causes of radicalization. Competing narratives coexisted from its inception between socioeconomic and political marginalization and grievances on the one hand and ideological motivations on the other hand. In the aftermath of 9/11, the term radicalization became intertwined with "recruitment" by extremists, who try to persuade these angry individuals to join their war (Coolsaet 2019). Those who recruit these angry individuals may be both Islamist extremists (e.g., ISIS, al Qaeda, Boko Haram) and white-supremacist extremists (e.g., Identitarian movement, Combat-18, and the Soldiers of Odin) (CEP 2019).[6] In the meantime, some other terms, such as "self-radicalization," "flash radicalization," and "instant radicalization," were also added into the vocabulary of radicalization since it appeared that one could also develop into a violent extremist through kinship and friendship networks (Coolsaet 2019). Such a vocabulary can be extended even more. However, one needs to benefit from an interdisciplinary perspective to understand the root causes of radicalization without causing a confusion with regard to the meanings of the terms such as radicalization, extremism, fundamentalism, and terrorism. This confusion can be resolved by analyzing the socioeconomic, political, spatial, and psychological drivers of radicalization. To that effect, some earlier interventions made in the disciplines of Sociology, Politics, Anthropology, Geography, and Psychology could be beneficial in understanding the root causes of radicalization as well as the ways in which radicalizing individuals mobilize themselves.

Due to the lack of space, this chapter will not delve into an extended discussion on the notion of radicalism. However, it will only stress that the term "radicalization" is used in this text in parallel with what Craig Calhoun (2011) has earlier defined it. In doing so, this chapter underlines that the term "radicalization" should be used in a neutral way as it has been used as a descriptive term in social sciences for many decades. Focusing on the early nineteenth-century social movements, Craig Calhoun (2011) makes a threefold classification of radicalism: philosophical radicalism, tactical radicalism, and reactionary radicalism. *Philosophical radicalism of theorists* was concerned with penetrating to the roots of society with rational analyses and programs to understand the structural transformation of the public sphere. *Tactical radicalism of activists* was mainly related to their search for immediate change that required the use of violence and other extreme measures to achieve it. *Reactionary radicalism of those* suffering from the negative effects of modernization was more about their quest for saving what they valued in communities and cultural traditions from eradication by the growth of capitalism. These categories are not mutually exclusive. Following this line of thinking, the leaders of the Reformation were radicals as they claimed to take back what was essential to Christianity from the hierarchical structure of the Catholic

Church. In philosophy, René Descartes was radical in his attempt to analyze knowledge by thinking through its elementary conditions anew. In everyday life, there were also radical individuals who challenged hierarchical order by judging basic matters for herself/himself—guided by her/his divine inner light, senses, and reason (Calhoun 2011). In this sense, some self-identified Muslims can be perceived as radicals since they may generate some reactionary forms of resistance against the perils of globalization, modernization, deindustrialization, and global injustice. One should also be reminded that radicalization does not include violence; it is rather a mental process far from violence. If violence is involved, then it is in a way no longer radicalization; it is rather extremism, or violent extremism, and sometimes even terrorism.

Religion and ethnicity seem to offer attractive "solutions" for people entangled in intertwined problems. It is not surprising that masses with a gloomy view of the future, who cannot benefit from society, and who are cast aside by global capitalism, should resort to honor, religion, ethnicity, language, and tradition, none of which they believe can be pried from their hands, and to define themselves in those terms. However, a detailed analysis must be undertaken to decipher the employment of Islam by self-identified young Muslims of migrant background in frequent acts of violence. If this analysis is not done rigorously, it will merely serve to affirm, and thus reproduce, the existing "clash of civilisations" thesis. Therefore, it is genuinely important to underline that the Islamic identity used by youth who show their resistance to the socioeconomic, cultural, and political regimes of truth in various different ways (music, graffiti, dance, looting, and arson) in France, Germany, Belgium, and the Netherlands is not necessarily essentialist or radical (Kaya 2012a; Roy 2015).

The Islamic reference used in such acts of opposition is mostly expressive of the need to belong to a legitimate counter-hegemonic global discourse, such as that of Islam, and to derive a symbolic power from that. In the absence of a global leftist movement, it may seem that religion is replacing the left. Michel de Certeau (1984: 183) reminds us of the discursive similarities between religion and left: religion offering a *different world* and left offering a *different future*—both offering solidarity. Moreover, it should be remembered that recent acts of violence, such as in Paris (January 7 and November 13, 2015), Nice (July 14, 2016), Istanbul (January 1, 2017), Berlin (February 28, 2017), London (2017), which are rapidly spreading to other cities and countries, are also an indication of solidarity among members of the newly emerging transnational Islam, who, it is claimed, are engaged in religious fundamentalism.

Gilles Kepel (2008, 2017) and Olivier Roy (2007, 2015) are two leading experts working on Jihadist groups in the EU. While Kepel mostly concentrates on France, Roy has recently extended his research to other European countries trying to understand the causes of Islamist radicalism and Jihadism. Kepel addresses the socioeconomic exclusion and colonial memories of Muslim-origin youngsters as well as the promotion of Salafism by the Gulf countries (mainly Saudi Arabia and Qatar) to explain their affiliation with radical Islam and Jihadism. His main assumption is that Islam is becoming radicalized among self-identified young Muslims who are exposed to structural outsiderism in the West. Roy (2015, 2017), on the other hand, argues that the issue is not the radicalization of Islam but rather "the Islamization of radicalism." Roy claims that the Jihadists, mostly second-generation immigrants, have been caught between the tradition-bound world of their parents and the secularism of their French society. Unable to find a place, they adopted a nihilistic rejection of society, expressed through Islam in the absence of a strong Marxist language in the contemporary world (Roy 2015; 2017). What Olivier Roy (2015) indicates with respect to the analysis of such forms of radicalism is very important in a diagnosis of what is happening. In this age of neoliberalism, Roy's Islamization of radicalism corrects the misdiagnosis of radicalization of Islam. Combining the analyses of Roy (2015) and of de Certeau (1984), a better understanding can be reached of what is happening in diasporas: *Islamization of radicalism* among some young Muslims mostly converts and second/third generations of Muslim background, in the absence of a counter-hegemonic global left-wing ideology.

Individuals tend to develop their own *methods of singularization* to come to terms with realities of the external world such as deindustrialization, unemployment, exclusion, racism, and structural outsiderism. Sometimes, constructing counter-cultures, or aligning with global youth cultures such as hip-hop, rock, or grunge, help youngsters come to terms with the difficulties of the present moment. In the absence of such global counter-cultures, constructing communities of faith, ethnicity, and culture may serve the same purpose. For instance, the idea of "going back to basics" among the working-class Turkish diasporic youth is, in fact, a counter-culture of self-defense. Their attempt to reify the Ottoman past in their paintings, rap lyrics, or graffiti arts as the very essence of their Turkishness is, by and large, a fiction or a form of mimicry, which symbolically helps them resist material and psychological hardships of the present day (Kaya 2001).

Islam is perceived by many Westerners as a threat to the European lifestyle. Islamic fundamentalism is often depicted as the source of xenophobic, racist, and violent behavior in the West. However, reverse this thinking, and the rise in religious values may also be interpreted as the result of structural problems such as deindustrialization, poverty, unemployment, racism, xenophobia, isolation, humiliation, constraints in political representation, and the threat of assimilation. In order to cope with these challenges, discourses on culture, identity, religion, ethnicity, traditions, and the past have become the most significant strategies of survival for minorities in general, and immigrants in particular. Reconstituting the past and resorting to culture, ethnicity, religion, past, and myths seem to serve a dual purpose for disenchanted communities: firstly, as a way to be contemporary without criticizing the existing status quo the "glorious" past, authentic culture, ethnicity, and religion are used by diasporic subjects as a strategic instrument to resist exclusion, poverty, and institutional discrimination; and subsequently, as a way to give an individual the feeling of independence from the criteria imposed by the flows of globalization, because the past, traditions, culture, and religion symbolize values and beliefs of the disenchanted subjects cannot, in their eyes, be taken away from them (de Certeau 1984).

The reality in Europe today is that young self-identified Muslims are becoming politically mobilized to support causes that have less to do with faith and more to do with global communal solidarity with their peers in Gaza, Palestine, Syria, Iraq, Afghanistan, or elsewhere, the manifestation of which can be described as an identity based on *vicarious humiliation* (Buruma and Margalit 2004: 10). Some European Muslims develop empathy for Muslim victims elsewhere in the world and convince themselves that their own exclusion and that of their co-religionists have the same root cause: *Western rejection of Islam.* The rejection of Islam has recently become even more alarming due to the rise of populist movements in Europe which often capitalize on the growing institutional visibility of Islam in public space and which are unlikely to observe the individualization and democratization of Islam in everyday life. However, the difficulties of the migration context, to which migrants of Muslim background are being exposed do stem not only from the ways in which they are framed and represented by the political and societal actors of the receiving countries, but also from the state actors of their homeland country.

These examples imply that cultural identities in the diaspora emerge in the process of dialectical and dialogical relations between majorities and minorities. This is a process of vernacularization of Islam in diaspora whereby religion becomes more individualized in line with the changing needs of individuals who are subject to collective impacts due to ongoing structural outsiderism. Thus, an Islamic space becomes a space in which post-migrants, or trans-migrants, search for recognition. Allegiance to Islam by those youths could also be interpreted as a quest for emancipation from the parental culture, which imprisons religion in their authentic culture. However, the allegiance of post-migrant youth into Islam is not limited to their parents' country, but extends to the worldwide Muslim community, especially involving solidarity with, and interest in, struggles such as the Palestinian cause, and conflicts in Bosnia, Chechnya, Afghanistan, Iraq, and Lebanon by means of social media, internet, and TV channels (Roy 2015). For instance, the Paris' *banlieues* identify with Palestinians, Iraqis, and Afghans (Roy 2007). Hence, diasporic youths who are symbolically affiliated with Islam have a rather political stance, which goes beyond separation of religion and politics. The reality in Europe today is that self-identified young Muslims are becoming politically mobilized to support causes that have less to do with faith and more to do with global communal solidarity.

Radicalization of Muslim-origin youngsters is a reaction to the ways in which they perceive to be subordinated by their countries of settlement. Self-identified Muslim youngsters in Germany and elsewhere in Europe are more likely to identify themselves with Islam as a reaction to the growing visibility of Islamophobia, right-wing populism, and white supremacism. This is in a way what Didier Bigo (2019) calls "the maze of radicalisation," because radicalization might provide them with an opportunity to build an imagined home away from the one that has become indifferent and alienating.

Radicalization then becomes a regime of justification and an alternative form of politics generated by some Muslim youth to protect themselves from day-to-day discrimination. They believe that speaking from the margins might be a more efficient strategy to be heard by the ones in the center who have lost the ability to listen to the peripheral ones. As Robert Young (2004: 5) pointed out, it is not that "they" do not know how to speak (politics), "but rather that the dominant would not listen."

Self-identified Muslim youngsters may use different symbols to hold onto while expressing their discontent against various forms of discrimination in everyday life such as anti-Muslim racism, or different manifestations of Islamophobia, or anti-Muslim racism. Headscarf has increasingly become a symbol of resistance that is being employed by some young female Muslims to demonstrate their resistance and reaction against the increasing manifestations of Islamophobia in everyday life. Muslim women are often victims of stereotyping, since their religious beliefs are seen as the only defining element of their identity in those European states where Islam is not the religion of the majority of the population.[7] Unfortunately, the media contribute to this phenomenon by reporting on Muslim women mainly as victims of so-called "tribal matters," "honor crimes," and "blood feuds" and in relation to their clothing.

Muslim women's clothing has continuously been linked with fundamentalism as a radical and undemocratic interpretation of Islam, which has in turn been linked with radicalization and potential terrorism. Political debate and legislative action concerning Muslim women in Europe are mostly concentrated on the issues of the headscarf, and even more the integral veil, instead of focusing on non-discrimination and equal opportunities. The following testimony of a twenty-two-year-old Muslim woman with Turkish origin in Berlin said the following when asked if she is interested in politics in everyday life:

> The discussion [is mostly] about whether the headscarf is being forcefully worn. Well, there are maybe some women who are forced to wear a headscarf. This occurs within a minority, but nobody talks to the majority [of Muslims who wear the headscarf by their own choice]. It is never about what we want. It's only about representing us as a target. If one doesn't talk to us, then one can't know what we want. This is because many Muslims are not interested in politics. Then they talk about integration ... It's simply like this: You can work in day-care with a headscarf but you can't work in a secondary school, because you are not supposed to influence children ... Sometimes I get the impression that wearing a headscarf you are only allowed to take the lower(-skilled) jobs, but not the higher(-skilled) ones. That's a paradox ...
> *(interview conducted in Berlin, June 30, 2020)*

Our interlocutor addresses at the intersectionality of social divisions of class, gender, religion, and ethnicity (Crenshaw 1991) in the case of different professions: headscarf is not a problem if the woman at stake is working as cleaner, or taking care of children in a nursery, but it becomes an impediment in professions which require high skills. Like many other Muslim women, she believes that her individual freedom is restricted under the disguise of individual liberty imposed by the majority society. It is decided for her that she needs to be liberated from the headscarf which keeps her from "doing things." The paradox is that it is not the headscarf that keeps her from doing things, but a dominant regime of representation that is deemed to know better. In such a context, headscarf might become a symbol of resistance for Muslim women to demonstrate their discomfort by appropriating a symbol that is denied and rejected by the members of majority society.

Issues of intersectional discrimination among Muslim women and men have become even more complicated during the height of populism. Supporters of right-wing populist parties in Europe often share the same motivation: to stop foreign infiltration of Europe and resist globalization, which brings with it international mobility, diversity, multiculturalism, trade, and deindustrialization. The perceived infiltrators are mainly those Muslims who are believed to be "stoning their women," "raping European women," "molesting children," and "drug-trafficking." Young Muslim men are also subject to a set of intersectional discrimination in everyday life. For instance, the sexual assaults committed by immigrant men in Cologne on New Year's Eve 2016 have fueled different forms of discrimination that young Muslim men in Europe have been experiencing (Ingulfsen 2016). In addition to multiple forms of discrimination in the labor market, education, politics, and elsewhere, since then young Muslim men are being perceived by many as potential rapists and terrorists. It is a fact that competition between social groups over scarce resources creates tensions that encourage prejudices among individuals, who have a fundamental need to perceive their own in-group as superior to competing out-groups.

Many self-identified Muslim youngsters that we interviewed have stated that the existing societal and political polarization appears to be motivated by a broader authoritarian outlook entailing nostalgia for traditional ways of doing things. These youngsters also perceive that many European citizens see Muslims as signifiers of vast social changes that have disrupted more traditional ways of life since the postwar period. In a similar vein, scientific studies also demonstrate that these changes produce some uncertainty and disquiet in the eyes of many Europeans in ways that threaten the established concepts of nation, identity, culture, and tradition, as well as the constitutive social hierarchies for many individuals (Gest et al. 2017). Resorting to the past and becoming nostalgic, in this sense, is a compensatory and reflective code of conduct to mediate the tension between tradition and change in a globalizing world.

Individuals, or groups, tend to use the languages that they know best in order to raise their daily concerns such as poverty, exclusion, unemployment, and racism. If they are not equipped with the language of deliberative democratic polity, then they are inclined to use the languages they think they know by heart, such as religion, ethnicity, and even violence. In an age of insecurity and uncertainty, to use the term by Franz Fanon (1965), the new "wretched of the earth" becomes more engaged in the protection of their *honor*, which, they believe, is the only thing left. In understanding the growing significance of honor, Akbar S. Ahmed (2003) draws our attention to the collapse of what Mohammad Ibn Khaldun (1969), a fourteenth-century sociologist in North Africa, once called *asabiyya*, an Arabic word which refers to group loyalty, social cohesion, or solidarity. *Asabiyya* binds groups together through a common language, culture, and code of behavior. Ahmed establishes a direct negative correlation between *asabiyya* and the revival of honor. The collapse of *asabiyya* on a global scale prompts Muslims to revitalize *honor*. Ahmed (2003: 81) claims that *asabiyya* is collapsing for the following reasons: massive urbanization, dramatic demographic changes, a population explosion, large-scale migrations to the West, the gap between rich and poor, the widespread corruption and mismanagement of rulers, rampant materialism coupled with the low premium on education, the crisis of identity, and, perhaps, most significantly new and often alien ideas and images, at once seductive and repellent, and instantly communicated from the West, ideas and images which challenge traditional values and customs.

The collapse of *asabiyya* implies for Muslims the breakdown of *adl* (justice) and *ihsan* (compassion and balance). Global disorder characterized by the lack of *asabiyya*, *adl*, and *ihsan* seems to trigger the celebration of honor by many Muslims across the world. Remaking the past or celebrating honor serves at least a dual purpose for the diasporic communities. Firstly, it is a way of coming to terms with the present without being seen to criticize the existing *status quo*. The "glorious" past and the preservation of honor are, here, handled by the diasporic subject as a strategic tool absorbing the destructiveness of the present, which is defined by structural outsiderism. Secondly, it also helps to recuperate a sense of the self not dependent on criteria handed down by others—the past is what the diasporic subjects can claim as their own. In-depth interviews with self-identified Muslim youngsters with Turkish origin have revealed that they all assign Islam a great task guiding them in search of being a better person in the world, which is identified with chaos, insecurity, instability, and polarization. Islam provides them with a set of values that make it possible for them to find meaning and stability.

Islam gives guidance to many Muslim youngsters. This was one of the most recurring tropes that we encountered everywhere when we interviewed Muslims. Islam as a religion restores the Asabiyya, social cohesion, in the eyes of our interlocutors, and it offers each of them a set of values that might help them navigate in the everyday life that is full of intersectional forms of discrimination, racism, inequality, and injustice. Values refer to lasting priorities, aspirations, and wishes, and they inspire attitudes and behavior. Values are useful concepts when we seek to understand consistent patterns of social, political, and cultural preferences (Merino et al. 2021). To that effect, this kind of search for certainty in the age of endemic uncertainties brought about by globalization may prompt some young Muslims to revitalize honor and purity. Essentialization and revival of honor and purity leave no room for the recognition of difference. The search for certainty operates on an individual level irrespective of being in majority, or in minority. Hence, the temptation not to recognize ethno-cultural and religious differences has become a frequent act among individuals of any kind complaining about the destabilizing effects of globalizing uncertainties.

Conclusion

This chapter scrutinized the ways in which some of the Turkish-origin individuals with strong identification with Islam have radicalized in Germany. The focus of the chapter is on the self-identified Muslims who are increasing identifying themselves with Islam. There are of course other forms of radicalization among the Turkish diasporic communities in Germany such as the Grey Wolfes, Alevis, Kurds, and even Kemalists. Due to my ongoing field research activities concentrating on the radicalization of self-identified Muslim youngsters with Turkish and Moroccan origin, I decided to specifically elaborate on the radicalization of self-identified Muslims. Following the line of thinking introduced by Craig Calhoun to define the term "radicalism," the chapter defined current form of radicalization which has become prevalent in Germany as a reactionary response to the negative ramifications of globalization such as deindustrialization, poverty, socioeconomic deprivation, spatial deprivation, and nostalgic deprivation. The chapter also tried to question the dominant regimes of representation that interchangeably use the following terms in the age of neoliberalism such as "radicalism," "extremism," "terrorism," and "fundamentalism."

It was revealed that radicalization of self-identified Muslims with Turkish background, especially youngsters, is, on the one hand, a response to the growing streams of Islamophobia since September 11, 2001, rooted in the civilizational paradigm the polarizing effects of which can be observed over the last three decades. On the other hand, this kind of reactionary radicalization is a response to the German policies of integration, yielding some exclusionary debates such as *Leitkultur*, anti-multiculturalism, anti-Muslim racism, anti-migration, xenophobia, and racism in general. The response among self-identified Muslims to such destabilizing and threatening societal, political, and economic factors such as Islamophobia is more likely to result in increasing identification with Islam and reification of the code of honor to restore destabilized social cohesion, *Asabiyya*.

The chapter also argued that radicalization of self-identified Muslims with Turkish background is partly related to the changing diaspora politics of the Turkish state under the Justice and Development Party rule over the last two decades. It was disclosed that AKP government has increasingly instrumentalized Sunni Islam to reach the members of the Turkish diasporic communities in Germany at the expense of fragmenting, and even polarizing the members of the transnational communities with Turkish background. It was argued that increasing Islamization of the Turkish diaspora seems to be a result of the increasing presence of the *Diyanet* and other liaison institutions such as the UETD/UID instrumentalizing Sunni Islam to reach out Turkish origin people in Germany. An increasing number of self-identified Muslims tend to reciprocate this move of the AKP by aligning themselves with discourses and practices of such institutions offering certain opportunity structures.

Notes

1. For more information on the content and methodology of the European Research Council Advanced Grant Study, see the official wesbite of the Prime Youth Project https://bpy.bilgi.edu.tr/en/
2. Multiculturalism was also criticized by several left-wing scholars with the argument that multiculturalism has become a rather neoliberal and neocolonial form of governmentality, imprisoning ethno-cultural and religious minorities, migrants, and their children in their own ghettoes. For more on this, see Rosaldo (1989); Russon (1995); Koopmans et al. (2005), and Kaya (2001).
3. Due to the scope of this study, the article will only give a detailed account of the Turkish *Diyanet* in relation to the growing visibility and impact of religion on the Turkish diaspora. For further discussion on the Yunus Emre Cultural Centres and the Presidency of Turks Abroad see Kaya and Tecmen (2011).
4. For a detailed account of the UETD see http://www.uetd.org/cms/front_content.php (accessed August 15, 2020). The name of the UETD was changed into the Union of International Democrats in 2018. See https://u-i-d.org/?lang=en (accessed January 20, 2021).
5. While *Diyanet* is influential in organizations in shaping and implementing AKP's diaspora policy, there are also other organizations such as the Presidency of Turks Abroad (Yurtdışı Türkler ve Akraba Topluluklar Başkanlığı), Yunus Emre Cultural Centers, as well as the Union of European Turkish Democrats (UETD, renamed the Union of International Democrats (UID, Uluslararası Demokrat Birliği), which serves as the AKP's liaison in Europe.
6. For further discussion on the Soldiers of Odin see *The Independent* (February 27, 2016), https://www.independent.co.uk/news/world/europe/norwegian-islamists-form-soldiers-of-allah-in-response-to-soldiers-of-odin-patrols-a6899801.html (accessed February 15, 2021).
7. Resolution 1887 of the Council of Europe (2012) on *Multiple discrimination against Muslim women in Europe: for equal opportunities* see https://pace.coe.int/en/files/18921

References

Abadan-Unat, N., Z. Kadirbeyoğlu, V. Çıdam, D. Çınar, M. Erdoğan, S. Kaynak and B. Özay (2016), "*Research Report on the June 1, 2015 General Elections,*" Istanbul: Boğaziçi University and Friedrich Ebert Foundation.

Ahmed, A. S. (2003), *Islam under Siege: Living Dangerously in a Post-Honour World*, Cambridge: Polity Press.

AKP, Adalet ve Kalkınma Partisi (2015), "Preserve Your Culture, Davutoglu Urges Turks in Germany," *Adalet ve Kalkınma Partisi*.

Aksel, D. (2019), *Home States and Homeland Politics: Interactions between the Turkish State and Its Emigrants in France and the United States*, London: Routledge.

Baier, D. and C. Pfeiffer (2010), "Bericht der Kriminologischen Forschungsinsstutes Niedersachsen (KFN)." Hannover: KFN.

Barker, M. (1981), *The New Racism*, London: Junction Books.

Bigo, D. (2019), "The Maze of Radicalization: Justification and Professional Interests," in N. Fadil, M. de Koning, and F. Ragazzi (eds.), *Radicalization in Belgium and the Netherlands: Critical Perspectives on Violence and Security*, 269–80, London: I.B. Tauris.

Brettfeld, K. and P. Wetzels (2007), "Muslime in Deutschland: Integration, Integrationsbarrieren, Religion und Einstellungen zu Demokratie, Rechtsstaat und politisch-religiös motivierter Gewalt; Ergebnisse von Befragungen im Rahmen einer multizentrischen Studie in städtischen Lebensräumen," Bundesministerium des Innern.

Brubaker, R. (2001), "The Return of Assimilation? Changing Perspectives on Immigration and Its Sequels in France, Germany, and the United States," *Ethnic and Racial Studies*, 24 (4): 531–48.

Brubaker, R. (2017), "Between Nationalism and Civilization: The European Populist Moment in Comparative Perspective," *Ethnic and Racial Studies*, 40 (8): 1191–226.

Bruce, B. (2019), *Governing Islam Abroad: Turkish and Moroccan Muslims in Western Europe*, The Sciences Po Series in International Relations and Political Economy. Palgrave Macmillan.

Buruma, I. and A. Margalit (2004), *Occidentalism: The West in the Eyes of Its Enemies*, New York: The Penguin Press.

Calhoun, C. (2011), *The Roots of Radicalism: Tradition, the Public Sphere, and Early 19th Century Social Movements*, Chicago: Chicago University Press.

CEP (2019), Counter Extremism Project, https://www.counterextremism.com/about

Coolsaet, R. (2019), "Radicalization: The Origins and Limits of a Contested Concept," in N. Fadil, M. de Koning and F. Ragazzi (eds.), *Radicalization in Belgium and the Netherlands: Critical Perspectives on Violence and Security*, 29–51, London: I.B. Tauris.

Crenshaw, K. W. (1991), "Mapping the Margins: Intersectionality, Identity Politics, and Violence against Women of Color," *Stanford Law Review*, 43 (6): 1241–99.

Daiute, C. (2014), *Narrative Inquiry: A Dynamic Approach*, New York: Sage Publications.

De Certeau, M. (1984), *The Practice of Everyday Life*, trans. S. Rendall, Berkeley: University of California Press.

Dornhof, S. (2009), "Germany: Constructing a Sociology of Islamist Radicalisation, Commentary, Race and Class," *Institute of Race Relations*, 50 (4): 75–82.

Eisenstadt, S. N. (2000), "Multiple Modernities," *Daedalus*, 129 (1): 1–29.

Fanon, F. (1965), *The Wretched of the Earth*, New York: Grove Weidenfeld, Reprint of Les damnes de la terre. Paris.

Gest, J., T. Reny and J. Mayer (2017), "Roots of the Radical Right: Nostalgic Deprivation in the United States and Britain," *Comparative Political Studies*, 51 (13): 1–26, https://doi.org/10.1177/0010414017720705

Gurr, T. R. (1969), *Why Men Rebel*, Princeton: Princeton University Press.

Ha, Hyun Jeong. 2017. "Emotions of the Weak: Violence and Ethnic Boundaries among Coptic Christians in Egypt." *Ethnic and Racial Studies* 40 (1): 133–51. https://doi.org/10.1080/01419870.2016.1201586.

Habermas, J. (2010), "Leadership and *Leitkultur*," *New York Times* (October 28), available at http://www.nytimes.com/2010/10/29/opinion/29Habermas.html

Heitmeyer, W., J. Müller, H. Schröder eds. (1997), *Verlockender Fundamentalismus*, Frankfurt am Main: Suhrkamp Verlag.

Humphrey, M. (2009), "Securitisation and Domestication of Diaspora Muslims and Islam: Turkish Immigrants in Germany and Australia," *International Journal on Multicultural Societies*, 11 (2): 136–54.

Huysmans, J. (2006), *The Politics of Insecurity: Fear, Migration and Asylum in the EU*, London: Routledge.

Ibn Khaldun, M. (1969), *The Muqaddimah: An Introduction to History*, ed. N. J. Dawood, trans. Franz Rosenthal, Princeton: Princeton University Press.

İçduygu, A., Y. Çolak and N. Soyarik (1999), "What Is the Matter with Citizenship? A Turkish Debate," *Middle Eastern Studies*, 35 (4): 187–208. https://doi.org/10.1080/00263209908701291

Ingulfsen, I. (2016), "Why Aren't European Feminists Arguing against the Anti-immigrant Right?" *Open Democracy* (February 18). https://www.opendemocracy.net/en/5050/why-are-european-feminists-failing-to-strike-back-against-anti-immigrant-right/

Kadıoğlu, A. (2008), *Vatandaşlığın Dönüşümü* (Transformation of Citizenship), Ankara: Metis Yayınları.

Kalb, D. (2011), "Headlines of Nation, Subtexts of Class: Working-class Populism and the Return of the Repressed in Neoliberal Europe," in D. Kalb and G. Halmai (eds.), *Working Class Populism and the Return of the Repressed in Neoliberal Europe*, 1–35, New York and Oxford: Berghahn.

Kaya, A. (2001), *Constructing Diasporas: Turkish Diasporic Youth in Berlin*, Bielefeld: Transcript Verlag.

Kaya, A. (2012), *Islam, Migration and Integration: The Age of Securitization*, London: Palgrave.

Kaya, A. (2018), *Turkish Origin Migrants and Their Descendants: Hyphenated Identities in Transnational Space*, London: Palgrave.

Kaya, A. (2019), *Populism and Heritage in Europe: Lost in Diversity and Unity*, London: Routledge.

Kaya, A. and A. Tecmen (2011), "The Role of Common Cultural Heritage in External Promotion of Modern Turkey: Yunus Emre Cultural Centres," *Working Paper* 4, European Institute, Istanbul Bilgi University, https://eu.bilgi.edu.tr/tr/publications/working-paper-4-the-role-of-common-cultural-herita/

Kaya, A. and F. Kentel (2008), *Belgian-Turks: A Bridge or a Breach between Turkey and the European Union? Qualitative and Quantitative Research to Improve Understanding of the Turkish Communities in Belgium*, Brussels: King Beduouin Foundation.

Kepel, G. (2008), *Beyond Terror and Martyrdom: The Future of the Middle East*, Cambridge: Harvard Belknap Press.

Kepel, G. (2017), *Terror in France: The Rise of Jihad in the West*, Princeton: Princeton University Press.

Koopmans, R., P. Statham, M. Giugni and F. Passy (2005), *Contested Citizenship: Immigration and Cultural Diversity in Europe*, Minneapolis: University of Minnesota Press.

Korteweg, R. (2017), "Unfreezing TTIP: Why a Transatlantic Trade Pact Still Makes Strategic Sense," *Working Paper*, Centre for European Reform, London (May), https://www.cer.eu/sites/default/files/pb_ttip_rk_10.5.17.pdf

Laclau, E. (2005), *On Populist Reason*, London: Verso.

Laitin, D. (2010), "Rational Islamophobia in Europe," *European Journal of Sociology*, 51: 429–47.

Lazaridis, G. and K. Wadia eds. (2015), *The Securitization of Migration in the EU: Debates since 9/11*, London: Palgrave Macmillan.

Lipsitz, G. (1994), "We Know What Time It Is: Race, Class and Youth Culture in the Nineties," in A. Ross and T. Rose (eds.), *Microphone Friends: Youth Music and Youth Culture*, 17–28, New York & London: Routledge.

Lord, C. (2018), *Religious Politics in Turkey: From the Birth of the Republic to the AKP*, Cambridge University Press.

Merino, P. K., T. Capelos and C. Kinnvall (2021), "Getting Inside 'the Head' of the Far Right: Psychological Responses to the Socio-political Context," in G., Macklin, A. Winter, S. Ashe and J. Busher (eds.), *Researching the Far Right: Theory, Method and Practice*, 74–91, London: Routledge.

Mouffe, C. (2018), *For a Left Populism*, London: Verso. Kindle Edition.

Mudde, C. (2004), "The Populist Zeitgeist," *Government and Opposition*, 39 (4): 541–63.

Mueller, C. (2006), "Integrating Turkish Communities: A German Dilemma," *Population Research and Policy Review*, 25 (5–6): 419–41.

Nielsen, J., ed. (2013), *Muslim Political Participation in Europe*, Edinburgh: Edinburgh University Press.

Özkan, B. (2014), "Turkey, Davutoglu and the Idea of Pan-Islamism," *Global Politics and Strategy*, 56 (4): 119–40. DOI: 10.1080/00396338.2014.941570.

Öztürk, A. E. (2016), "Turkey's Diyanet under AKP Rule: From Protector to Imposer of State Ideology?" *Southeast European and Black Sea Studies*, 16 (4): 619–35, https://doi.org/10.1080/14683857.2016.1233663

Öztürk, A. E. (2018), "Transformation of the Turkish Diyanet Both at Home and Abroad: Three Stages," *European Journal of Turkish Studies*, 27 (December 31), https://doi.org/10.4000/ejts.5944

Öztürk, A. E. and S. Sözeri (2018), "Diyanet as a Turkish Foreign Policy Tool: Evidence from the Netherlands and Bulgaria," *Politics and Religion*, 11 (3): 624–48, https://doi.org/10.1017/S175504831700075X

Paçacı Elitok, S. and T. Straubhaar (2012), *Turkey, Migration and the EU: Potentials, Challenges and Opportunities*, Hamburg: Hamburg University Press, https://doi.org/10.15460/HUP.HWWI.5.118

Pautz, H. (2005), *Die deutsche Leitkultur. Eine Identitatsdebatte*, Stuttgart: Ibidem.

PRT, Presidency of The Republic of Turkey (2015), "We Should Build a Brighter Turkey with the Awareness of One Nation, One Flag, One Country and One State," *Presidency of The Republic of Turkey*.

Pusch, B. and J. Splitt (2013), "Binding the Almancı to the 'Homeland'—Notes from Turkey," *Perceptions*, 28 (3): 129–66.

Reynié, D. (2016), "The Spectre Haunting Europe: 'Heritage Populism' and France's National Front," *Journal of Democracy*, 27 (4): 47–57.

Rosaldo, R. (1989), *Culture and Truth: The Remaking of Social Analysis*, London: Routledge.

Roy, O. (2007), *Secularism Confronts Islam*, trans. G. Holoch, New York: Columbia University Press.

Roy, O. (2015), "What Is the Driving Force behind Jihadist Terrorism? A Scientific Perspective on the Causes/Circumstances of Joining the Scene," Paper presented at the BKA Autumn Conference (November 18–19).

Roy, O. (2017), *Jihad and Death: The Global Appeal of Islamic State*, London: Hurst.

Russon, J. (1995), "Heidegger, Hegel, and Ethnicity: The Ritual Basis of Self-Identity," *The Southern Journal of Philosophy*, 33: 509–32.

Sarrazin, T. (2010), *Deutschland schafft sich ab: Wie wir unser Land aufs Spiel setzen (German Does Away with Itself: How We Gambled with Our Country)*, Munich: DVA Verlag.

Schiffauer, W. (2013), "The Logics of Toleration: Outline for a Comparative Approach to the Study of Tolerance," in J. Dobbernack and J. Modood (eds.), *Tolerance, Intolerance and Respect*, 103–26, London: Palgrave Macmillan.

Scholten, P., E. Collett and M. Perovic (2017), "Mainstreaming Migrant Integration? A Critical Analysis of a New Trend in Integration Governance," *International Review of Administrative Sciences*, 83 (2): 283–302.

Tibi, B. (1998), *Europa ohne Identität? Die Krise der multikulturellen Gesellschaft* [Europe without Identity. The Crisis of the Multicultural Society], Munich: Bertelsmann.

Vidino, L. (2019), "Erdogan's Long Arm in Europe," *Foreign Policy* (May 7). https://foreignpolicy.com/2019/05/07/erdogans-long-arm-in-europe-germany-netherlands-milli-gorus-muslim-brotherhood-turkey-akp/

Wilpert, C. (2013), "Identity Issues in the History of the Post-war Migration from Turkey to Germany," *German Politics and Society*, 31 (2): 108–31.

Young, R. J. C. (2004), *White Mythologies*, New York: Routledge.

Part III

Civic Informal Space: Culture and Society

Introduction to Part III

by Gamze Evcimen & Fatma Müge Göçek

This section follows upon the insights of critical scholarship that research how power negotiations as well as meaning and knowledge construction and reconstruction extend beyond the formal public into the civic informal space. Everyday practices move to the forefront in the analyses, bringing in a wealth of information on these often-understudied sites. In doing so, they especially capture and demonstrate the vibrancy of non-Western societies that is often missed by structural approaches. The sociologists of the Middle East working on this space specifically focus on space and life worlds, culture and consumption, and gender and sexuality.

Addressing the ways in which Israel's settler-colonial project creates racialized categorizations of Jews and Palestinians through biopolitical techniques and statistical tools, Yinon Cohen and Neve Gordon analyze how Israel's biospatial politics racialize civilians and the spaces they inhabit while also determining the population's identity. Cohen and Gordon illustrate that, in addition to appropriating space through legal-bureaucratic mechanisms and racializing the appropriated space, Israel's settler-colonial project redefines the categories of "Israeli" and "Arab" to privilege and homogenize the former while marginalizing and fragmenting the latter. Cohen and Gordon highlight how Israel constructs space and people as racialized categories, emphasizing that Israel's biospatial strategies strengthen the connection between the Jews and the land while severing the Palestinians' connection to the same land and also transforming them into criminals.

Mona Abaza investigates Cairo's transformations since the January revolution of 2011 with a particular focus on the effects of urban warfare and artistic forms of expression over the reimagination of public spaces as spaces of contestation, communication, and public interaction. Abaza illustrates how the protesters transformed Tahrir and other urban squares into spaces for confrontation, grieving, and public performance, especially with their occupation of public spaces and collective activities like photography exhibitions, musical and dance performances, installations, exhibitions, and film screenings. Abaza also cautions about the potential co-optation of young artists and revolutionary art into neoliberal urban agendas of gentrification due to the capitalist investors' support for the arts and graffiti artists. Abaza concludes by connecting the contestations over urban public spaces to Egypt's broader socio-political trajectories, emphasizing that the power of the street carries potential to rise against authoritarianism.

Offering a snapshot of the urban Egyptian youth in terms of culture and consumption, Rania Salem focuses on how matrimonial transactions convey important meanings associated with class and gender. Emphasizing how marriage operates as the primary gateway to adulthood processes and practices like residential independence, sexual activity, and childbearing in Egypt, Salem highlights that the engaged couples postpone marriage to build sufficient resources for appropriate matrimonial expenditures. Salem also illustrates how this practice reflects the normative barriers to marriage and how matrimonial transactions perform crucial symbolic work in terms of class status and gender ideals as couples engage in practices of conspicuous consumption for social prestige while they simultaneously enact the normative ideals of manhood and womanhood.

Shifting our focus to Turkey, Banu Gökarıksel and Anna Secor analyze the co-constitutive and conflictual relationship between the marketing of Islamic dress for women (tesettür) and covered women's embodied performances of identity. Gökarıksel and Secor emphasize that companies of fashionable Islamic dress for women represent the new styles as simultaneously tesettür and fashion while marketing a cosmopolitan lifestyle that incorporates covered women within the realms of consumption, style, and beauty. Gökarıksel and Secor also demonstrate how women engage with Islamic fashion by mediating the contradictions between tesettür as modesty and style; such mediations reflect both their sense of self and their redefinitions of fashion, femininity, class, and tesettür. Gökarıksel and Secor highlight that these marketing strategies and clothing practices indicate the redefinition of modern as participation in fashion's economic and cultural cycles.

In a similar vein, Irmak Karademir-Hazır studies how class, rather than religio-political identities, shapes women's clothing practices, interactions as dressed bodies, and emotions of self-presentations in everyday life. Karademir-Hazır illustrates that, regardless of their secular or pious embodiment styles, women holding higher levels of cultural capital devalue the clothing and bodily styles of rural-to-urban migrant women and working-class women. Emphasizing how the culturally cultivated groups of women enact moral judgment, exclusion, and disadvantage for socioeconomically marginalized covered women by associating their looks with categorizations like uneducated and inconsiderate, Karademir-Hazır points to the distinction between a rural/traditional femininity and an urban/modern femininity, which includes the culturally competent and globally oriented sections of secular and pious women.

Interrogating the discourses of Beiruti cosmopolitanism and Lebanese exceptionalism, Ghassan Moussawi focuses on how gender, class, and normativity shape the lives of LGBTQ individuals in Beirut. Moussawi emphasizes that although Lebanon is regarded as exceptional in the Middle East for its diversity, inclusivity, and openness to difference, sexual openness and gay friendliness in Beirut follow normative queerness that reflects the hierarchies of gender, class, and religion. Moussawi demonstrates that modernity's discourses of openness and tolerance exclusively apply to certain gender, class, and religious identities while excluding and marginalizing other identities, especially in terms of unequal access to Beirut's public and "gay-friendly" spaces that require economic, cultural, and social capital. Moussawi also highlights how these excluded LGBTQ persons question Beirut's cosmopolitanism and develop alternative understandings that challenge the dominant notions of modernity and progress.

In a similar vein, Ayça Alemdaroğlu criticizes the dichotomous perspectives that prioritize either the marginalization or the activism of women in the Middle East and, instead, focuses on young women's experiences and formations of femininity across social classes in urban Turkey. Alemdaroğlu analyzes how women's diverging experiences based on unequal access to cultural and economic resources and opportunities influence their strategies of negotiating power as well as their understandings of social change. Alemdaroğlu illustrates that the ways in which these young women perform and negotiate femininity depend on their economic and educational backgrounds as well as on their cultural understandings of womanhood as shaped by their social relations. Alemdaroğlu also emphasizes how these women employ alternative cultural narratives to negotiate self-value and respectability and navigate the contradictions of escaping femininity and maintaining respectability.

Concluding this section on gender and sexuality, Ladan Rahbari studies the discourses of gender and sexuality in Iranian spaces with a particular focus on a Persian-language LGBTQI+ dating channel on Telegram. Rahbari highlights the relationships between Iran's official discourses, which control, stigmatize, and criminalize the genders and sexualities defined as non-normative, and the experiences of LGBTQI+ people, who encounter a constellation of punishment by law, everyday discrimination, and cultural restrictions. Rahbari illustrates how Iran's politics both constrains LGBTQI+ experiences to certain spaces and enables digital practices of open identification and interaction by deeming the LGBTQI+ dating Telegram channel apolitical and unworthy of surveillance. Rahbari also indicates that such digital practices both territorialize the queer digital spaces and deterritorialize the individually embodied sexuality assemblages between bodies in Iran.

Selected Readings

Abaza, M. (2001), "Shopping Malls, Consumer Culture and the Reshaping of Public Space in Egypt," *Theory, Culture & Society*, 18 (5): 97–122.

Deeb, L. (2006), *An Enchanted Modern: Gender and Public Piety in Shi'i Lebanon*, Princeton, NJ: Princeton University Press.

Göle, N. (1996), *The Forbidden Modern: Civilization and Veiling*, Ann Arbor: University of Michigan Press.

Hashemi, M. (2015), "Waithood and Face: Morality and Mobility among Lower Class Youth in Iran," *Qualitative Sociology*, 38: 261–83.

Hasso, F. (2011), *Consuming Desires: Family Crisis and the State in the Middle East*, Stanford: Stanford University Press.

Kandiyoti, D. (1997), "Gendering the Modern: On Missing Dimensions in the Study of Turkish Modernity," in S. Bozdag and R. Kasaba (eds.), *Rethinking Modernity and National Identity in Turkey*, 113–32, Seattle: University of Washington Press.
Khalaf, S. (2012), *Lebanon Adrift: From Battleground to Playground*, London: Saqi Books.
Massad, J. (2007), *Desiring Arabs*, Chicago, IL: University of Chicago Press.
Mikdashi, M. (2013), "Queering Citizenship, Queering Middle East Studies," *International Journal of Middle East Studies*, 45 (2): 350–2.
Savcı, E. (2016), "Who Speaks the Language of Queer Politics? Western Knowledge, Politico-cultural Capital and Belonging Among Urban Queers in Turkey," *Sexualities*, 19 (3): 369–87.
Yacobi, H. (2009), *The Jewish-Arab City: Spatio-politics in a Mixed Community*, London: Routledge.
Yiftachel, O. (2006), *Ethnocracy: Land and Identity Politics in Israel/Palestine*, Philadelphia, PA: University of Pennsylvania Press.

I SPACE AND LIFE WORLDS

Israel's Biospatial Politics

by Yinon Cohen and Neve Gordon

Applying Israel's land-grabbing practices and demographic classifications as a conceptual lens, this chapter makes the following two claims: the first concerns biospatial strategies, including the construction of space as a racialized category; the second is historical and shows the continuity of Israel's expropriation of Palestinian land from 1948 until today.[1] We show that the particular biospatial scaffolding underlying Israel's colonial project has deployed two major strategies—namely, legal-bureaucratic mechanisms of dispossession followed by the movement of Jewish civilians to settle Palestinian land—across the entire territory located between the Jordan Valley and the Mediterranean Sea in order to grab and control as much land as possible (Falah 2003). We go on to draw a connection between these strategies and statistical classifications and techniques of enumeration that Israel has adopted in order to delineate its efforts to racialize the appropriated space. These classifications and forms of enumeration at times not only defy international standards of statistical reporting but are deployed to either cement or sever the connection between people and space. Historically, we identify a boomerang trajectory, beginning with the massive confiscation and Judaization of Palestinian land in the wake of the 1948 war, then extending and duplicating many of the practices originally developed inside Israel to the West Bank in 1967, and finally turning back inward to solidify the racialization of land within Israel. When we consider that settler colonialism, as Patrick Wolfe (2006) has shown, is a structure and not an event, this recoiling movement across space and time is neither surprising nor unexpected.

The Racial—Spatial Logic

Before the 1948 war, there were nearly three hundred Jewish and over six hundred Palestinian villages and towns in the territory that would later become Israel. During and after the war, Palestinian cities were depopulated and about five hundred Palestinian

---

This is a revised, short version of Cohen, Y. and N. Gordon (2018), "Israel's Bio-Spatial Politics: Territory, Demography and Effective Control," *Public Culture* 30 (2): 199–220.

villages were destroyed, while most of their inhabitants either fled or were expelled across international borders, becoming refugees in neighboring countries. In total, about 750,000 Palestinians were displaced and never allowed to return to their homes in what today would be characterized as ethnic cleansing, while thousands more were internally displaced within the nascent Jewish state. By 1951 the Palestinians who had become refugees were "replaced" by a similar number of Jewish immigrants, both Holocaust survivors from Europe and Mizrahi Jews from Arab countries, thus transforming the state's ethnic composition without altering its overall population size (Cohen 2002).

Soon after the war, Israel introduced a series of administrative and legal mechanisms to seize Palestinian land (Zureik 1979). It classified property belonging to Palestinian refugees first as "abandoned" and then as "absentee property" and quickly appropriated it, while also confiscating much of the land owned by the Palestinians residing in the villages that survived the war. The establishment of a military government (1948–66) responsible for governing the Palestinian citizens within the fledgling state facilitated this massive confiscation of land (Sa'di 2013).

A twofold strategy was adopted: Israel confined the estimated 160,000 Palestinians who had remained in the Jewish state to their villages and simultaneously converted Palestinian land into closed military zones and nature reserves, confiscated what it defined as absentee property, and restricted the cultivation of Palestinian agricultural plots, all the while registering their estates as "state land" (Khamaisi 2003). As we will see, the post-1967 strategies implemented in the Occupied West Bank had their origins in these earlier practices. Indeed, as early as 1951, the state effectively owned 92 percent of the land within its territory, up from 13.5 percent in 1948 (Forman and Kedar 2004).

Seizing land alone, however, does not guarantee effective control or the reconstitution of space and its racialization as Jewish. Using the rhetoric of "population dispersal," Israel consequently established new Jewish towns to attract large numbers of immigrants to areas still populated by Palestinians and created agricultural settlements to ensure control over large swaths of Palestinian land. Of the 370 new Jewish settlements established soon after 1948, 350 were built on or in proximity to Palestinian villages that had been destroyed (Kedar and Yiftachel 2006). While Jews of all stripes and classes settled on confiscated Palestinian land, the state sent mostly new Mizrahi immigrants—a poor and racialized group that came from Arab and Muslim countries—to Israel's periphery, especially to the frontiers along its borders (Shohat 1988).

In later years, middle- and upper-middle-class Jews were offered incentives to relocate to the Galilee to live in hilltop communities overlooking Palestinian villages. As Alexander Kedar and Oren Yiftachel (2006) explain, the Palestinian settlement map was "frozen" in 1948 by prohibiting the establishment of new Palestinian villages and towns and arresting the development of those still intact after the war by confiscating most of their land reserves, preventing any construction outside the already-developed area, and surrounding these villages with Jewish settlements. In this way, Israel created a "geography of enclaves" in which the vast majority of Israel's Palestinian citizens have remained to this day—even as their population has increased tenfold. These policies maintained and reproduced extreme residential segregation between Jews and Palestinians.

Residential segregation—characterized by acute disparity in the state's investment in infrastructure and social services—is arguably the most salient feature informing the organization of Israeli space, with the vast majority of localities defined as either Jewish or non-Jewish by the Israeli Central Bureau of Statistics (CBS). To create and maintain such segregation, Israel adopted a variety of biopolitical techniques while harnessing statistical tools to produce and reproduce a series of classifications that create a clear demarcation between Jews and Palestinians; it did so by homogenizing the former and fragmenting the latter. From the outset, the CBS adopted religion as the population's primary classification, while framing the Jews as the norm and contrasting them with all "non-Jews" (or members of other religions) in its statistical reports. To this day the word *Palestinian* does not appear in Israel's statistical abstracts, while only in 1995 did the word *Arab* finally emerge after decades in which Palestinians were referred to as "non-Jews," reminiscent of how they were labeled in the Balfour Declaration and the 1922 British Mandate for Palestine.

Moreover, to determine their "origin," Jews are classified according to their (or their father's) country of birth. Possible "origins" do not include *Mizrahi* or Arab Jews (presumably because these terms are considered divisive) but only continents of birth. If, however, both respondents and their fathers were born in Israel, they are assigned an "Israeli origin." Kenneth Prewitt (2013), a former director of the United States Census Bureau, calls this "Israel's policy of ethnic erasure," explaining that it was "designed to solve any problem of [Jewish] ethnic cleavage."

One of its outcomes was the rapid erasure of the Arab origin of Mizrahim, about half the Jewish population, thus contributing to the "cleansing," in Ella Shohat's (1988) words, of their Arabness, while ensuring that Arab Jews would swiftly become "Israeli." By contrast, Palestinians have never been able to attain the status of "Israeli origin" irrespective of how many generations their ancestors had resided in Israel/Palestine (Cohen 2002). In fact, they have no "origin," only religion. In other words, according to Israel's official statistics, all Jews ultimately become "Israeli" within the span of two generations, and no Palestinian can ever become "Israeli." This produces a bifurcated racial reality where Jewishness trumps all other categories of identification.

The statistical acrobatics carried out following the mass migration from the former Soviet Union in the 1990s underscores the steps the CBS has been willing to take in order to consolidate the strict Jewish/Palestinian divide: adding non-Jews to the Jewish group as long as they are not Palestinians (Lustick 1999). Out of an estimated 1 million immigrants who arrived on Israel's shores, approximately 250,000 had Jewish relatives but were themselves either Christian or had no religious affiliation. The CBS decided to alter the way it classifies the entire population and labeled the new non-Jewish immigrants as "others," uniting them with Jews in a group called "Jews and others." This group is contrasted in the statistical abstracts with the newly created group designated "Arab population," which includes only Muslims, Druze, and Christians. Thus, since the mid-1990s, according to the CBS, there are two kinds of Christians in Israel: "Arab Christians" and "non-Arab Christians." The algorithm developed by the CBS to distinguish between these two groups is based in part on where they live, namely, in a "Jewish locality" or a "non-Jewish" one. This suggests that race and space are mutually constitutive; biotechniques are used to produce a population's racial (and other) identity and in this way to racialize the inhabited space, while space itself helps determine the population's identity.

Territorial Expansion

Following the 1967 war, Israel has used several complementary methods to seize Palestinian land in the newly occupied West Bank, many of which had their basis in the methods first developed within its pre-1967 borders. These include declaring land absentee property; transforming swathes of land into nature reserves; claiming that land has been left uncultivated for many years or, alternatively, simply declaring that a particular area is needed for military or public use (where "public" denotes Jewish). Using these methods, by 1987 Israel managed to restrict Palestinians to living within a territory that comprised less than 60 percent of the West Bank; consequently, and not unlike their co-patriots within the Green Line, many occupied Palestinians have lost all or parts of their land. This de jure land-grab has translated into de facto annexation through the establishment of Jewish settlements, the construction of bypass roads, and, eventually, the erection of the separation barrier. Often the order of this process was actually reversed, whereby the de facto land seizure preceded de jure confiscation, as was the case with many "unauthorized" settlements (Gordon 2008).

Moreover, under the Oslo Accords, the West Bank was divided into Areas A, B, and C, which were drawn according to a biospatial logic and determined the distribution of powers by creating internal boundaries, each one with its own specific laws and regulations. Because Areas A and B—where the Palestinian Authority was given more responsibilities—were densely populated by Palestinians, they were divided into 131 clusters, scattered like an archipelago across the terrain and separated by strategic corridors that facilitated Israeli control, whereas Area C—under complete Israeli control, containing 60 percent of the land and only 4 percent of the Palestinian population—remained contiguous. It is also in the context of such biospatial strategies that one needs to understand the over one hundred Jewish outposts that were erected in the West Bank since the beginning of the new millennium. These outposts were built with government assistance, but labeled "unauthorized" because Israel had promised the US administration not to establish new settlements. They are populated by relatively few—about ten thousand—Jews, many of them second- and third-generation settlers, but they manage to ensure effective control of large swaths of land.

The way Israel enumerates its population bolsters this logic. Since the 1967 war, the state includes in its population count all the people residing within the pre-1967 borders and annexed East Jerusalem, but in the West Bank it includes only those residing in Jewish settlements, leaving out the indigenous population. Statistical virtuosities of this kind—counting Jewish residents while ignoring the existence of millions of Palestinians within the same region—provide a distorted picture of reality. Such misrepresentations are exacerbated given that Israel includes the Palestinian population in East Jerusalem (which was also occupied in 1967 but had been annexed de jure shortly thereafter) in its count. These practices reflect and help reproduce the de facto annexation of this region by engendering a biospatial link between Jews and the land, while severing the Palestinians' connection to it.

The Colonial Leviathan Recoils

Having succeeded in Judaizing large parts of the West Bank, Israel has now turned back inward, and in a boomerang-like trajectory is now completing the project it left unfinished in the Negev. Approximately 695,000 people currently live in the Negev, which contains about 60 percent of the country's land but is home to only 8 percent of its population. Of this population in the Negev, 35 percent are Palestinians, the vast majority of them Bedouin, whose number has grown from about 11,000 in 1949 to about 230,000 today, thanks to their extremely high fertility rate (similar to that of ultra-Orthodox Jews). Nonetheless, only 18 localities out of the 144 in the region are designated for the Bedouin community, while about 65,000 Bedouin citizens continue to reside in 35 villages classified as "unrecognized" by the Israeli government (Rotem and Gordon 2017). This means that these Bedouin are prohibited from connecting their houses to the electricity grid or the water and sewage systems. Construction regulations are strictly enforced, and in 2018 alone 2,326 Bedouin homes and animal pens—usually referred to by the government as "structures"—were demolished (Avrech and Marcus 2019).

No paved roads lead to the villages, and signposts on main roads indicating their location are prohibited. Moreover, the villages do not appear on maps. As a matter of official policy these localities do not exist. Demographically their inhabitants (who are Israeli citizens) are linked to tribes rather than to a locality, thus officially erasing their connection to their land. Indeed, three of the eighteen Bedouin localities that were recently recognized by the state were considered "places" rather than "localities" in the state registry because according to the official records they were deemed empty. Informed by biotechniques that sever this group from their land, Israel's actions indicate that it plans to demolish most of the unrecognized villages and to relocate at least thirty thousand inhabitants into already-established Bedouin towns.

While the confiscation of the Negev's land was accomplished in the state's early years, over the past decade the government has intensified its attempts to strengthen its effective control of this area and to Judaize it fully. The production of the biospatial link, which effectively racializes space, is achieved through the CBS's classification and the by now familiar twofold strategy of dispossessing and settling. On the one hand, the government is restricting Bedouin development within the confined borders of the towns it created and the eleven villages it recently recognized, while transferring many of its military bases to the Negev, deploying a draconic policy of home demolitions in the unrecognized villages, and, until 2007, spraying "illegal" agricultural plots with poison. Since 2007, such plots have simply been plowed over. Simultaneously, the Israeli government has been reinforcing the Jewish presence on the ground, establishing new Jewish settlements and encouraging Jews to move to the region, while planting thousands of "Jewish trees" provided by the Jewish National Fund on large strips of Bedouin land (Rotem and Gordon 2017).

An illustration of how the colonial leviathan is turning back inward is perhaps most obvious in Umm al-Hiran, a village of about 350 Bedouin citizens that was destroyed in 2018 and will be replaced by a Jewish settlement called Hiran. Just a few kilometers away from this Bedouin village, about thirty religious Jewish families have been living in a makeshift gated community, waiting patiently for the government to expel the Bedouin families from their homes. This gated Jewish community is made up of houses scattered around a playground and a new kindergarten. Needless to say, this bucolic setting is both unnerving and surreal, considering its violent undertow. Ironically, the people who are destined to dispossess the residents of Umm al-Hiran are West Bank settlers who made an ideological decision to return to Israel to "redeem Jewish land" from "Bedouin invaders." Because the land itself is constituted as Jewish, the Bedouin who have inhabited it for decades are rendered "invaders," thus revealing not only the classic colonial inversion between the colonist and the colonized, but also how the spatial-racial nexus produces the biocriminal—the person who is deemed a felon due to the racial status ascribed to him or her. In Israel, Foucault's (2003) notion of the biocriminal is further developed since space itself is racialized and the racial mismatch between space and the subject who occupies it is sufficient to transform the latter into a criminal.

Conclusions

By way of conclusion, it may be important to state the obvious. Historically, states have frequently connected the bio with the spatial since at least the eighteenth century, at times with horrific consequences. Contemporary manifestations also abound, ranging from the biospatial strategies Europe has recently adopted to deal with the massive refugee crisis, through US President Donald Trump's Muslim ban and asylum policies, and all the way to Myanmar where Rohingya Muslims are being ethnically cleansed from Rakhine State. Nonetheless, excavating the specificities of each case remains vital. Before Israel's establishment, for instance, the 1937 Peel Commission and the 1947 UN Partition

Plan clearly based their recommendations on a biospatial logic (i.e., the division of territory according to certain population classifications produced by the colonial power). The difference between these partition plans and the Oslo archipelago is instructive, however, since in the latter the biospatial logic was used not to harness and maximize the population's demographic and economic potential or to enable self-determination but rather to guarantee the ongoing subjugation of the colonized Palestinians.

Notwithstanding this difference, both the long history of biotechniques and the different geographical settings in which they are currently being mobilized suggest that Israel is not really an innovator. The novelty of Israeli colonialism is that for decades it has not merely managed to survive but has actually flourished. This is because it receives the unconditional support of almost all liberal democracies, a striking phenomenon in the postcolonial era that is due in part to these countries' perception of Israel as a democracy. The tragic irony is that Israel's biospatial politics have given birth to a reality of a single, Jewish-Palestinian, apartheid state.

Note

1   We derive the term biospatial from Michel Foucault's notions of biopolitics and biopower, where biopolitics focuses on the administration of life and populations, while biopower is the way in which biopolitics is put to work in society (Foucault 2003). Biopower uses statistical devices and scientific methods as well as mechanisms of surveillance to measure and intervene in a set of processes designed to administer, optimize, and multiply the population's productive capacities and at times to repress and subjugate the people. The term biospatial denotes the deployment of such biotechniques to demarcate, control, manage, shape, and ascribe signification to space and helps expose the diverse mechanisms and processes by which space is constituted as racialized or in racialized terms.

References

Avrech, T. and M. Marcus (2019), *Mechanism for Dispossession and Intimidation: Demolition Policy in Arab Bedouin Communities in the Negev/Naqab*. Negev Coexistence Forum for Civil Equality.

Cohen, Y. (2002), "From Haven to Heaven: Changes Patterns of Immigration to Israel," in D. Levy and Y. Weiss (eds.), *Challenging Ethnic Citizenship: German and Israeli Perspectives on Immigration*, 36–56, New York: Berghahn Books.

Falah, G. (2003), "Dynamics and Patterns of the Shrinking of Arab Lands in Palestine," *Political Geography*, 22 (2): 179–209.

Forman, G. and A. Kedar (2004), "From Arab Land to 'Israel Lands': The Legal Dispossession of the Palestinians Displaced by Israel in the Wake of 1948," *Environment and Planning D: Society and Space*, 22 (6): 809–30.

Foucault, M. (2003), *"Society Must Be Defended": Lectures at the Collège de France, 1975–1976*, eds. M. Bertani and A. Fontana, trans. D. Macey, New York: Macmillan.
Gordon, N. (2008), *Israel's Occupation*, Berkeley: University of California Press.
Kedar, A. and O. Yiftachel (2006), "Land Regime and Social Relations in Israel," in H. de Soto and F. Cheneval (eds.), *Realizing Property Rights*, Vol. 1 of *Swiss Human Rights Book*, 129–46, Zurich: Rüffer and Rub.
Khamaisi, R. (2003), "Mechanism of Land Control and Territorial Judaization of Israel," in M. Al-Haj and U. Ben-Eliezer (eds.), *In the Name of Security*, 421–49, Haifa: Haifa University Press.
Lustick, I. (1999), "Israel as a Non-Arab State: The Political Implications for Mass Immigration of Non-Jews," *Middle East Journal*, 53 (3): 417–33.
Prewitt, K. (2013), *What Is Your Race? The Census and Our Flawed Efforts to Classify Americans*, Princeton: Princeton University Press.
Rotem, M. and N. Gordon (2017), "Bedouin Ṣumud and the Struggle for Education," *Journal of Palestine Studies*, 46 (4): 7–27.
Sa'di, A. H. (2013), *Thorough Surveillance: The Genesis of Israeli Policies of Population Management, Surveillance, and Political Control towards the Palestinian Minority*, Manchester: Manchester University Press.
Shohat, E. (1988), "Sephardim in Israel: Zionism from the Standpoint of Its Jewish Victims," *Social Text*, 19/20: 1–35.
Wolfe, P. (2006), "Settler Colonialism and the Elimination of the Native," *Journal of Genocide Research*, 8 (4): 387–409.
Zureik, E. (1979), *The Palestinians in Israel: A Study in Internal Colonialism*, New York: Routledge.

Post January Revolution Cairo: Urban Wars and the Reshaping of Public Space

by Mona Abaza

Introduction

The worth of public space was never so passionately debated on the global scale as it has been since the emergence of the Arab revolutions. The occupation of public spaces as an emerging global configuration of political activism witnessed a novel turn after 2011. We are reminded by Oikonomakis and Roos (2013) that by the second part of 2011, the planet had witnessed protests in more than 1,000 cities across 80 countries. It seems that the chain of occupying successive specific squares, much inspired by the moving images of the Arab Spring, replicated similar tactics of squatting in public spaces. The recent insurrection in Kiev's Midan testifies to the infectious impact of travelling images.[1] "Encampment" together with the "tent," the emblem of nomadism, of the rootless refugee's shelter, became the most circulated and celebrated images in global media (Mitchell 2012; Oikonomakis and Roos 2013). Novel artistic public expressions and highly inventive urban ways of protest and action traveled swiftly, evidently, though with a variety of local divergences. Oikonomakis and Roos, by raising the issues of "diffusion," "transmission," and "adopting," trace numerous similarities between these movements and new inventive urban forms of resistance and action according to the local context. However, the common denominator seems to be the spontaneity of these movements coupled with the fact that these were all leaderless groups lacking an explicit center. Mitchell draws a common denominator among all the "occupation" movements as reproducing an "anti-iconic, non-sovereign image repertoire" (Mitchell 2012: 9). The main argument of this article is that the conjunction of an emerging new public visibility of a unprecedented powerful visual culture (Abaza 2013), associated with a re-constellation of what Mitchell calls "the rhetoric of space"

Abaza, M. (2014), "Post January Revolution Cairo: Urban Wars and the Reshaping of Public Space," *Theory, Culture & Society* 31 (7/8): 163–83.

(Mitchell 2012: 11), teaches us that one of the main material transformations of the city of Cairo since January 2011 has been precisely over the fascinating art and tactics of squatting of public spaces.

The mesmerizing public satire and sense of humor articulated when marching with text messages (Figure 21.1), slogans, songs, or displaying gas masques, the Guy Fawkes V for vendetta masks and the numerous iconic martyrs' face masks (Figure 21.2), perfecting and innovating performance while marching, women dancing publicly in the streets, the urban street wars, the killings and massacres in the city, filming and being filmed, were all unprecedented public performative activities, only witnessed after January 2011. These were ultimately about the competition for public visibility and conquering public space. Identical tactics of occupation were to be observed by both "good" and "evil" or revolutionary/anti-revolutionary actors depending on the situation, for example, the bearded (Islamist) police officers who occupied and squatted the space opposite the Ministry of Interior on Lazoughly Street in March 2013 (Figure 21.3), with the repetition of tents identical to Tahrir's revolutionaries. After ousting President Morsi in July 2013, the occupation of public spaces continued to become the last resort of the defeated Muslim Brothers. However, in summer 2013 the Islamists took alternative squares of the city since they could not occupy Tahrir Square, which was then occupied by the anti-Morsi protesting masses.

While the success of the revolution remains much contested, it is evident that it revolutionized the very notion of what a public space is about. It succeeded in imposing an entirely unprecedented novel choreography for the city in which the "stage" of Tahrir[2]

Figure 21.1 Protest during Morsi's regime. Text messages from right to left: 1. I say it in all languages. Morsi leave silently. 2. I say it time and again. Down with the rule of the Muslim Brothers. 3. All they want is empowerment (or power) and they forget about the problems of the poor (captured May 2013).

Figure 21.2 March from Mohandessin quarter to Tahrir Square, commemorating the first year anniversary of the revolution. The masks portray the late martyr Sheikh Emad Effat, killed in the Mohammed Mahmud street massacres of November–December 2011 (captured January 25, 2012).

Figure 21.3 Islamist officers calling themselves the "bearded officers," protesting and camping opposite the Ministry of Interior, Lazoughly Street. They were advocating that they be allowed to wear beards as officers, thus displaying in public their Islamist sympathies (captured March 2013).

was the exemplary moment that triggered extended and replicated dramaturgical violent public confrontations, public performances and occupations in all the squares of Cairo as well as in other cities of Egypt. The optimists believe that this has led to an unprecedented challenge to the dominant discourses about Third World metropolises, which seemed to be destined to be entrapped in the predicament of both "neoliberalism" and the "war on terror" discourses as insurmountable paradigms that were imposed by US hegemony (Kanna 2012). Not only have these allegedly deterministic visions regarding these two paradigms been challenged by the creativity of the Arab revolutions, but they are equally challenged today by the competing popular discourse of what Lefebvre calls the "right to the city"—a discourse widely circulated today among architects, NGO workers, and political activists.

The Arab revolutions have triggered a stimulating debate about inventing new and real public spaces that merge with a virtual imaginary, public spaces which occur through collective performances and actions. The blending of the virtual world and the instant events of all the square(s) in the Arab world has opened an entirely novel reading of the city in relationship to the velocity of the flow of information through social media and satellite channels and how these have redefined rules, visions, and modes of action in the public sphere (Figure 21.4). These transformations also raise fascinating challenges regarding the overwhelming state of having to deal with "too much information" (Anderson 2012), questioning then the very premises of what expertise and the role of academics in the public sphere should be all about. What is at stake here is the witnessing of the phenomenon of the decomposition of the mechanisms of established powers like academe, pundits, and experts on the Middle East (Anderson 2012: 385). These conditions invite us to think about the impact of the decentering of

Figure 21.4 Satellite channel van filming a march from the Mohandessin quarter to Tahrir Square. Almost all marches for the past three years have been filmed by numerous satellite channels (captured May 17, 2013).

knowledge and power, or rather the effect of the decomposing of traditional forms of authority that go hand in hand with the excess of information. The question is then how to read the city under these novel constellations.

The "Right to the City"

Some architects argue that a novel way of reclaiming the "right to the city" is being observed in Cairo (Nagati and Stryker 2013).[3] Henri Lefebvre argues that under the neoliberal globalized policies of managing cities, the "right to the city" is one way of enhancing democratic empowering through occupying space in novel ways, as a right of participation and its appropriation, to answer the "problems of disenfranchisement" (Purcell 2002: 103). The "right to the city" if then applied to the Cairene context could be read as a turning point. This is either a fascinating and unique historical moment, through which the power of the street has been dictating novel rules of the game and new ways of occupying public spaces that would lead to democratization. Or it is the case that Cairo is entering an escalating violent phase and descending into a circle of hell.

One point is evident: namely, with the growing absence of police forces to regulate everyday life, Cairo has witnessed more than ever the obvious negative effects of the processes of neoliberalism, a point which Asef Bayat analyzed in his article "Politics of the City Inside-Out" (2012) whereby the increasing deregulation due to the retreat of the state in public services is accompanied by a growing privatization of collective consumption and urban spaces. Bayat looks at how the neoliberal city has been affecting the life world and public spaces of the poor who, precisely due to the lack of private space and absence of public services and goods, end up living, interacting, and working in the street. In that scenario, it is the informal sector that becomes a dominant mode of living due to the fragmentation of labor.

The phenomenon of neoliberalizing Cairo actually started three decades ago. I would like to transcend the discussion as to whether or not the neoliberal city as a model contributed in the fostering of the Arab Spring, which is once again an argument much debated among urban social scientists (Bayat 2012: 112). We only need to be reminded that there are today some 180 million Arabs in the Middle East who survive through the informal sector (Bayat 2012: 111). Architect Omar Nagati and Beth Stryker documented recently the practices and tactics of informal street vendors in occupying public spaces—streets, passages, squares, bridges, and highways—to argue that, according to the International Labour Organization, street vendors in Egypt are estimated to vary between 1.5 and 5 million (Nagati and Stryker 2013: 34–5).

What is of interest for us is how precisely after January 2011 an imposing presence of a massive and marginalized segment of the population of Cairo managed to quasi-permanently occupy public spaces. The term quasi-permanently is used here

The Handbook of Sociology and the Middle East

Figure 21.5 Ambulant street vendors selling paraphernalia in Tahrir (captured November 2012).

Figure 21.6 A protest stand with candles commemorating the Maspero massacre of October 9, 2011, in Talaat Harb Square. The clothes on the perch give the impression that they are for sale, typical to Cairene street vendors. In fact, these are the clothes of the martyrs who were crushed by the army tanks in Maspero. The analogy of displaying in the street the clothes of the victims by protesters and victims' families conveyed a very powerful message—the display of cheap clothes that represents how lives can be cheap in Egypt (captured October 13, 2011).

because of the constant street battles and police evictions. Not only did the public visibility of street children, prostitutes, and ambulant vendors reshape the landscape of Downtown, Tahrir Square, and the area around the colossal Mugama administration building, but it equally managed through squatting in the street to slow car traffic, if not render circulation impossible. Street vendors (Figures 21.5 and 21.6) have been in a constant struggle to gain a few meters from the street via movable pillars and boards to display their merchandise. Some display their merchandise on parked cars, as if the streets of the center of town have been turned into a twenty-four-hour living-cum-informal-commercial area.

Camping, Occupying, and Performance in Public Spaces

When confrontation between the pro-Muslim Brotherhood followers and the anti-Morsi protesters escalated during the year of Morsi's government (June 2012–July 2013), Tahrir Square remained the space of opposition to the Muslim Brotherhood. After Morsi had imposed a much-contested constitution that guaranteed him limitless authoritarian powers in November–December 2012, spectacular marches and demonstrations occurred, this time not only in Tahrir Square but all along the large alley of the presidential palace in the quarter of Heliopolis, representing the then symbolic space of power. As the scale of oppositional demonstrations and marches against the Morsi regime continued to multiply, the Islamists, despite holding the government, wanted to flaunt their popularity by also demonstrating and occupying alternative public squares. Nevertheless, they occupied other parts of the city in the western part in the area of Giza around Cairo University and in the eastern part of the city in the quarter of Rabea al-Addawiyya. There, after the ousting of President Morsi, in July 2013, the Islamists—inspired by the eighteen magical days of Tahrir—created an independent walled or barricaded city in yet another square; however, with the difference that the squatters carried Kalashnikovs and weapons. In contrast to the 2011 Tahrir event, there was evidence that the mini-Islamic republic of 2013, with its own police forces, which challenged the government by using women and children as human shields, was partly turning into a torture camp. The six-week site that ended in a bloody massacre was described by Wael Nawara as a "parallel state," a "sprawling town," a "city-state" that kept on growing day after day (Nawara 2013).

At the time of writing, Egyptians are entering the third year of a revolution that is much contested and closely observed on a planetary scale. The ascension to power of the Muslim Brotherhood with Morsi becoming president following a controversial military junta rule has been perceived by many as an obvious "hijack of the revolution." The transition has been clearly problematic due to the blatant violation of human rights, which immediately intensified after the ousting of President Mubarak. Under the reign of the Muslim Brotherhood and, before them, the military, Egypt witnessed two horrifying years marked by systematic killings and intentional harming of protesters. The violation of human rights continued after Morsi was ousted. Incarceration and escalating violence (burning of churches, confrontations in universities between pro-Morsi protesters and the police, assassinations and terrorist attacks on the soldiers, checkpoints and headquarters of the army in Sinai) led to even more confrontations and violence. However, human rights did not improve after Morsi was ousted, with brutal torturing methods considered worse than in Mubarak's time being reported by human rights organizations (Carr and Doss 2014).

The city of Cairo has witnessed during the past three years multiplying numbers of marches, demonstrations, violent clashes between protesters, on the one hand, and police forces and "thugs" paid by the ancient regime, labeled as the "third constituent," on the other hand. Cairo has also seen intensive urban wars, and yet in the midst of these violent incidents, it also witnessed multiple artistic forms blossom when occupying public spaces for various performances. The walls, fences, buildings, bridges, and empty public spaces of the city were transformed into a playground for graffiti, as well as for displaying insults against the regime and for biting, insolent jokes. A new language emerged to visualize the attacks—running and moving back. Al-karr wal farr, meaning attack and retreat, is derived from classical Arabic and has been inserted in the daily lexicon of the media.

Long-lasting Tahrir Effects

The square became *de facto* the space for contestation, for grieving and for public performance, painting and filming (Figure 21.7). In effect, Tahrir triggered a new visual culture. It became the spot to film and to be filmed, as well as being a space to see others and to be seen. This new public culture is formulating a novel understanding of

Figure 21.7 Recent graffiti, Mohammed Mahmud Street. Graffiti artists painted the wall in red, pointing to the bloodshed of the army. The wall was repainted for the hundredth time as an affront to the squatting tanks (captured November 2013).

public spaces as spaces of contestation, of communication, of artistic expression, or public interaction. Tahrir gave birth to numerous instant installations of mock coffins as memorial spaces for victims, of open air museums for the revolution (replicated identically at the presidential palace in Heliopolis), fantastic graffiti, poetry, and insults displayed on walls and, above all, a blooming musical scene. Women's initiatives fostered public performances of dancing of young women in the streets.

Creativity has flourished, be it in the way text messages and jokes are displayed, paraphernalia and gadgets are colorfully arranged, or the way ambulant salesmen occupy the side streets around Tahrir to perform hilarious acrobatics that attract buyers. All these transformations would not have occurred without the alternative poor publics that have found a thousand ways of survival all around Tahrir.

The sense of humor, which Egyptians have been famed for, has more than blossomed, as if the street is experiencing an effervescent carnival, similar to the numerous popular religious saints' anniversaries (the *Mulids*) that take place all over Egypt which are always accompanied with popular markets and all sorts of means for entertainment (Keraitim and Mehrez 2012). The offline world here has been interacting with the world of the online, which has been given a free hand via the growing significance of the YouTube postings of photography and documentary films that are then screened or exhibited in public spaces. This is certainly transforming the visual landscape and people's behavior in public spaces. Yet, this public culture is emerging as part of a new reshaping space of the city.

During 2011 and 2012, Cairo witnessed the most tumultuous and fascinating moments and struggles over the conquest of the center of Tahrir. The "Saniyya," which could be translated as the center, the circle or roundabout of Tahrir Square, continued to epitomize the physical and symbolic seizure of power for all sides, the revolutionaries and the military and the Muslim Brotherhood. Tahrir was then increasingly turning into a contested symbolic space of a still unresolved battle in which different publics keep returning to put pressure on the ruling forces, only to be violently pushed away, time and again.

The Marches

From the very first day of the revolution, the marches were crucial for mobilizing people to reach Tahrir Square. On the first anniversary of the Revolution in 2012, millions poured into Tahrir to convey the message that they were willing to challenge the junta (Figure 21.8). Up to twenty-five different marches came from all the corners of the city and overwhelmed the square.

An example can illustrate how these marches have been organized. To mark the January 25, 2012, march, a map was distributed via Facebook explaining the departure and itinerary of all the marches throughout Cairo and how these would reach Tahrir

Figure 21.8 The open-air museum of the revolution in Tahrir. Open to the public for writing wishes, comments, displaying photographs of victims, or for hanging on the walls information about the missing (captured February 9, 2012).

Square. Al-Ahram Online also provided a map with all the marches, the meeting points, and the itineraries. These marches have increased in number and scope during the past years, in particular after the October Maspero massacre of Coptic protesters. They reveal a sophisticated level of organization and great effectiveness in attracting people by calling upon those standing on the balconies to come down to the street. Many protesters carry striking written messages and symbols. The march of January 25, 2012, departing from Mustafa Mahmud mosque in Mohandessin quarter was even more impressive after several other marches from other neighborhoods merged with it. The march was synchronized with loud speakers, compelling slogans, and large drums. A significant number of the demonstrators had extremely impressive masks of the faces of famous martyrs (Figures 21.9 and 21.10), such as Khaled Said (who was killed by officers in Alexandria and was a symbol that triggered the January revolution), Sheikh Emad (a learned Azharite religious scholar who was killed in the events on Mohamed Mahmud Street in 2011), and Mina Daniel (killed in the Maspero massacre), as well as the Guy Fawkes V for Vendetta mask that was previously attacked by the Muslim Brotherhood newspaper for instigating chaos and anarchy. The Muslim Brotherhood newspaper's campaign against the V for Vendetta mask had misspelled the V as B and called the mask "Bendetta." To the Muslim Brotherhood's misfortune, the revolutionaries did not spare them from a torrent of jokes about their ignorance.

Post January Revolution Cairo

Figure 21.9 A memorial landmark in Tahrir commemorating the martyrs by displaying photographs and names (captured January 27, 2012).

Figure 21.10 Installation of mock tombs in Tahrir Square, commemorating the martyrs (captured June 8, 2012).

Decentering Urban Battle Zones

Since February 2011, Cairo's downtown has witnessed unprecedented and drastic transmutations through experiencing a swift spread of dispersed guerrilla urban battles through confrontations between protesters and police forces. Cairo equally witnessed the multiplication of checkpoints, barbed wire, and tanks all around the area of the Ministry of Interior and at Lazoughly Street and other state institutions as isolated zones after the confrontation that took place in Mohammed Mahmud Street, which is one of the main entrance streets to Tahrir Square (Abaza 2011). It is possible to observe two parallel phenomena. On the one hand, the city center has become segregated through zoning laws. The slicing of the city center (around the area of Kasr al-Aini Street to Lazoughly Square) through walled buffer zones went hand in hand with the phenomenal squatting of large numbers of poor street vendors, street children, and beggars who have equally transformed the urban landscape of the city. On the other hand, it equally witnessed the decentering or the exporting of the battle zones from the area around Tahrir Square to various other quarters of Cairo due to multiple differentiated political events, each pertaining to the unfulfilled demands of the revolutionaries.

Even though the major clashes continued to occur in Tahrir Square and Mohammed Mahmud Street in November 2011, as well as repeated clashes in November 2012, the confrontations during these two years seem to have spread all around the city. Clashes and killings were witnessed in various quarters, such as Abbasiya (296 injured in July 2011) (Ahram Online 2011) and Maspero Street along the Nile Corniche, resulting in the unforgettable massacre of "bloody Sunday" on October 9, 2011, when some twenty-five protesters were killed by the military. It was a protest march organized by the Copts, attacked by army tanks that horrifically crushed the demonstrators (Ibrahim 2012). Clashes around the American Embassy in Garden City and the Simon Bolivar Square in November 2012 resulted in the erection of even more concrete walls. There have been recurrent clashes and protests in front of the High Court of Justice. Attacks on the Israeli Embassy in the quarter of Guizah in September 2011 caused three deaths and more than thousand wounded (Bakr and Aboudi 2011). Then clashes took place in front of the Ministry of Defence, once again in Abbasiya quarter, leaving some ten dead. After that, the supporters of the Salafi leader Hazem Abu Ismail insisted on demonstrating in front of the Ministry after he was disqualified for the candidacy of the presidency (Dale 2012).

These events were followed by spectacular demonstrations that took place in November and December 2012 all around the city, but most importantly the ones that occurred at the presidential palace in Heliopolis when Morsi imposed his hurried and controversial constitution, considered by many to be the worst ever in Egypt's modern history. The incident took place on December 5, when, under the pretext of defending the president, militias spread terror. Because the Muslim Brotherhood sent their armed militias to kill peaceful protesters at the presidential palace and set up torture chambers, a qualitatively different level of dealing with violence and its public display in order to spread terror among the protesters seems to be in the making (Tadros 2012).

Eternally Divided Cairo?

Before discussing the post-revolution transmutations, it is important to shed some light on the major urban plans that were envisioned for creating a more humane Cairo. Prior to January 2011, there was much speculation about the future of the Khedivial *belle époque*, downtown Cairo, known in Arabic as *Wist al-balad*. Since the campus of the American University in Cairo (AUC) moved in September 2008 from the central Tahrir Square to the Quattameyya heights on the outskirts of the desert, an area now designated as "New Cairo," there has been heated media debate among intellectuals and in official circles about what the center should look like.

Similarly, although *Wist al-balad* (Downtown) remains as the symbol of colonial culture, it seems to have been appropriated today as part of the "national heritage." The press sold the idea with slogans like "revamping history," reviving *belle époque* Cairo and colonial culture (Fayed 2009). Nostalgia seems to have been an important component in the process of modernizing the city of Cairo during the nineteenth century that created the split into two parts. Some architects and historians argued that the creation of the cosmopolitan modern Khedivial city took place with a parallel process of "medievalizing" its Islamic part, perceived then as antiquated and problematic. This is the thesis developed in *Making Cairo Medieval* (Al-Sayyad et al. 2005). The 1867 Exposition Universelle in Paris, they argue, was the starting point for "rendering" Cairo medieval. It also triggered an interest in selective restoration and the increase in experts, historians, and travelers who played an important part in "museumizing" the traditional city (2005: 5). Can we apply today the "medievalizing" thesis to the imaginaries of some intellectual elites regarding the "heritage" of downtown?

Architect Mercedes Volait's (2001) research also focuses on the *belle époque* architecture in Cairo and Alexandria and on the history of the profession of Egyptian architecture. The Khedivial city, the modern Haussmannian boulevard center of town with its European-dominated population and modern *grands magasins*, its French cafes and modern apartment architecture, developed, according to Volait, as the counterspace to the Islamic archaic labyrinth city. Urban sociologists such as Janet Abu-Lughod (1971) and later the historian André Raymond (2000) thus spoke at length of the "tale of two cities" with two different if not clashing lifestyles, tastes, sets of garments, and smells. They pointed to the two antagonizing life worlds, one consisting of the modern *khawagat* (the foreigners) European culture that was juxtaposed to the local, Islamic bazaars, and winding narrow roads of the old city. With modernization, the Islamic city then appeared to lag behind even more. Eventually, these two worlds hardly ever met. However, that the *belle époque* belonged mainly to the foreigners is nowadays more than ever questioned.

After January 2011 the center of town, precisely the areas around Tahrir Square, Sheikh Rehan Street up to Lazoughly Square, where the Ministry of Interior is located, and the residential quarter of Garden City, where the American and British embassies are located, were most affected by the street battles and the erection of walls. The space of the quarter of Garden City around the American, Canadian, and British embassies has been turned into a heavily militarized zone sliced into checkpoints with thousands of soldiers, officers, police vans, and civilians that look like the professional thugs (of the Ministry of Interior) who are permanently squatting there to supposedly protect the area. In reality, the quarter has become unliveable.

The business sector in Mohammed Mahmud Street has obviously been ruined after the consecutive clashes of 2011 and 2012. Many shops had to close and several residents experienced looting and theft of their flats during the Mohammed Mahmud incidents. Small shopkeepers, such as newspaper salesmen, suffered from the violent attacks of thugs. Massive lethal teargas rendered the area of downtown a health hazard zone. The entire quarter looks today like a deserted derelict space. The Lycée (architecturally considered as a historical building for its remarkable aesthetic appeal) was entirely destroyed after a fire erupted during the skirmishes between the police and the protesters in November 2012. Most of the people I have spoken to there have complained that life in the quarter has turned hopeless.

Reclaiming Downtown for Art

If the city has strongly been affected by urban warfare, Cairo's transmutations would not be complete without its flourishing art scene. The point of no return is mostly felt in that large numbers of Egyptians, in particular, youth, simply lost fear. Once the taste of rebellion was acquired, it apparently has not faded away. This new state of mind is mostly evident in the multiple artistic spheres. Fantastic photography exhibitions multiplied all over the city. Excellent photo reportage by Egyptians has taken the lead, at the expense often of costing lives and traumatizing experiences. The daily encounters with violent armed "thugs" and with lethal teargas is teaching the reporters, as well as pedestrians, new ways of moving and protecting themselves in the streets (Shaath 2013). Even with escalating urban violence, optimism is felt in the cultural milieu with the blooming alternative art spaces, the public performances, and spontaneous urban street art, as the newly created and well-informed pro-revolution journalists' website Mada Masr has been reporting (Mada Masr 2013).

Various squares were reinvented for simultaneous musical performances, installations, exhibitions, and film screenings. Public dance performances in the street saw light for the first time in the center of town. Noticeable is the fact that graffiti artists earned much attention from the international media and the press. There are countless YouTube postings, excellent bloggers, photographers, and insightful articles in the press, which have been closely following this emergent art. Several publications on graffiti are already out. Some of the graffiti artists have been adopted recently by reputable "chic" galleries, established curators, and reputed foreign cultural and local art centers. These "rising stars" have already been commissioned to reproduce the "street" and entire walls of graffiti for the space of the galleries and garages Downtown. Some of the artists too have already become celebrities on an international scale. The American University in Cairo organized during March 2012 a conference with the group of graffiti artists who painted the walls of Mohammed Mahmud Street (Willows 2012).

There is much discussion today if the *belle époque* center of town ought to be revamped and upgraded through fostering even more art centers and spaces for public installation, a position already circulating well before January 2011. Downtown has a long history of bustling, well-to-do galleries, art and cultural centers. It seems, however, when pertaining to downtown spaces, that little change has occurred regarding the "gatekeepers" and curators of the artistic world, who were anyway well established before the revolution and who continue to dominate the scene. *Plus ça change, plus c'est la même chose*, in the sense that the same galleries and curators who have been controlling the art market for more than a decade continue to do so. The same art "gatekeepers" now invest in revolutionary art. For example, for some time the Ismailia Company for Real Estate Development has been heavily investing in Downtown by purchasing some twenty old buildings. The company has recently sponsored the Contemporary Arts Festival (D-CAF)[4] and also supports the arts by transforming the decrepit flats of the purchased buildings into art spaces for practically no fee. Moreover, it has recently sponsored a major digital street installation by graffiti artist Ganzeer (El-Kamel 2013).

This seems to be going hand-in-hand with an emerging trend among some real-estate capitalist investors in the center of town (*Wist al-balad*) who recently have been sponsoring the arts and graffiti artists as one way of revamping Downtown to perhaps end up with what Sharon Zukin has termed the growing capitalist control of the "symbolic economy" of the city, a trend which started in the 1970s in the United States. Investing in the arts as forums for gentrifying public spaces, as a way of manipulating violence, has become a standard means by which the "culture industry" becomes ever more dependent on financial capitalism (Zukin 1995: 135). The question remains whether this is not a problematic way of co-opting or rather using revolutionary art for neoliberal capitalist agendas with the ultimate aims of gentrifying and upgrading real estate for future speculation and of course, in the process, risking the autonomy and power of revolutionary art.

Meanwhile, those who see hope in change point to the new initiatives launched beyond the well-established Downtown circles, such as the "living newspaper" at Artellewa, located in the popular quarter of Ard el-Lewa, and the Alexandria Contemporary Art Forum. These optimists (Jaquette 2013) argue that numerous independent self-funded and self-organized art spaces initiatives (cinematheques, digital art, theatre, installations, photography) which have been recently founded deserve appraisal. Most noticeably, these young initiatives are almost all located far from the well-established Downtown spaces. The main question that remains unanswered is who will be the winner in the next years? When Morsi was in power, many raised the question whether the Islamist regime would manage to silence the art scene, which is definitively critical, sardonic and rebellious and clearly antagonist to them. After July 2013 many continued to raise the same question but with different players. Simply, all are concerned that the return of the army in the civil sphere will systematically curtail civil society with the continuous violation of human rights and the re-emergence of the unchanged brutal internal security and police system. Will these newer forums gain further ground and continue the struggle against authoritarianism? Will these young artists be quickly infected by the virus of gentrification through real estate companies and "well-intentioned" capitalist sponsors and philanthropists? There are no answers to these questions for the time being except to note that the polarization between a highly conservative ageing ruling class and a very large rebellious young population will continue to escalate.

Conclusion

The optimists believe that since the power of the street managed to oust two dictators in less than three years, it will manage in the longue durée to counteract the army if the military does not deliver the promised goods by solving the catastrophic economic situation and the problems of escalating Islamic terrorism. If General Sissi has gained a pervasive popularity after June 2013, this is because the one-year rule of the Muslim Brothers proved that they were the best doppelgangers of the Mubarak regime. It is ironic that the Morsi regime excelled Mubarak in the greedy monopolization of power, in accumulating wealth, and through enforcing sectarian violent politics against minorities like the Copts and the Shi'as and by perpetrating killings against demonstrators in collaboration with the fierce Ministry of Interior. When the Muslim Brothers sent their militias in December 2012 that killed protesters at the presidential palace, the incident was the prelude that explains why some 22 million Egyptians signed the petition for ousting Morsi, a petition campaign launched by the Tamarud (the Rebel Campaign). The campaign was the trigger that resulted in millions taking to the streets in all cities of Egypt in June 2013, the largest number of demonstrators ever occupying public space in the history of revolutions.

By ousting Morsi, the army re-emerged in civil life with powerful popular support. Many see that the army's popularity is on the rise because it has been trading with the card of stability. The longing for stability is understandable after three highly exhausting and violent years that have created thousands of martyrs and a disastrous economic situation. Having said this, and to the alarm of human rights organizations, the number of incarcerations not only of members of the Muslim Brothers but equally the revolutionaries, street children, and innocent citizens is growing by the day. The concern is whether the army will manage to provide the desired stability, fix the economy, satisfy the pressing needs of the 40 percent living under the poverty line and re-establish the tourist industry, which has been seriously affected by Islamist terrorist attacks. Al-Sissi has recently cultivated the figure of the "strong" man, comparable to anti-colonial, iconic nationalist Nasser. The rhetorical investment in nostalgic nationalist sentiments seems to be going hand-in-hand with mounting chauvinism. Time and again, revolutions are caught in the predicaments of long-term processes, but nonetheless the optimists believe that the army ought to learn from the lesson of the two previous oustings. There is no turning backwards in spite of the nostalgic discursive domains. Therefore, even if much bloodshed is still to come with the return of the army to civil life, if it fails to soon deliver the goods, the next and likely bloodier round of insurrections seems unavoidable.

Notes

1 It is mesmerizing to observe the striking similarities in actions and resistance, such as the creation of ambulant clinics, communal action, the display of text messages, and the art of resistance to violent police forces between Tahrir, Gesi, and the Maidan in Kiev. The fact alone that the word Maidan means literally square in Arabic raises strong emotions for Middle Easterners when observing the unfolding events in Kiev.
2 Regarding Cairo's transformations during the past three years and the political turmoil that is fundamentally redesigning the cityscape, I could not think of a better analogy for Cairo than Lewis Mumford's earlier observations on the city as "a theatre of social action" (Mumford 2002 [1996]: 92) and as a space that "fosters art and is art. The city creates the theater and is the theater" (Mumford 2002: 94).
3 This is the argument of architect Omar Nagati (cited in his Opening Speech at the Conference "Learning from Cairo," April 12–14, 2013, The American University in Cairo).
4 The title is an ironic allusion to SCAF, The Supreme Council of Armed Forces.

References

Abaza, M. (2006), *Changing Consumer Culture: Cairo's Urban Reshaping*, Leiden: Brill/AUC Press.
Abaza, M. (2011), "Downtown Cairo Imagined: Dubaisation or Nostalgia?" *Urban Studies*, 48 (6): 1075–87.
Abaza, M. (2013), "Walls, Segregating Downtown Cairo and the Mohammed Mahmud Graffiti," *Theory, Culture & Society*, 30 (1): 122–39.
Abu-Lughod, J. (1971), *Cairo: 1001 Years of the City Victorious*, Princeton, NJ: Princeton University Press.
AhramOnline (2011), "296 Injured in Abbasiya Clashes," July 24. Available at: http://english.ahram.org.eg/NewsContent/1/64/17154/Egypt/Politics-/-injured-in-Abbasiya-Clashes.aspx (accessed August 18, 2014).
AhramOnline (2013), "Cairo Cathedral Clashes Leave 21 Injured: Egypt Health Ministry," April 7. Available at: http://english.ahram.org.eg/NewsContent/1/64/68692/Egypt/Politics-/Cairo-cathedral-clashes-leave–injured-Egypt-healt.aspx (accessed August 18, 2014).

AhramOnline (2013), "Violent Clashes Erupt in Shubra after Police Officer Kills a Civilian," January 20. Available at: http://english.ahram.org.eg/NewsContentPrint/1/0/62854/Egypt/0/BREAKING-Violent-clashes-eruptin-Shubra-after-pol.aspx (accessed August 18, 2014).

Al-Masry Al-Youm (2013), "Salafi Leader Arrested in Deadly Shubra Family Feud," Egypt Independent, March 19. Available at: http://www.egyptindependent.com/news/public-prosecutor-orders-probe-deadly-shubra-clashes-0 (accessed August 18, 2014).

Al-Sayyad, N., I. A. Bierman and N. Rabbat (2005), "Prologue: The Project of Making Cairo Medieval," in N. Al-Sayyad, I. A. Bierman and N. Rabbat (eds.), *Making Cairo Medieval*, 1–8, Lanham, MD: Lexington Books.

Anderson, L. (2012), "Too Much Information? Political Science, the University, and the Public Sphere," *Perspectives on Politics*, 10 (2): 385–96.

Bakr, A. and S. Aboudi (2011), "Egypt Vows to Try Those Who Targeted Israel Mission," Reuters, September 10. Available at: http://www.reuters.com/article/2011/09/10/us-egypt-protest-idUSTRE7885PH20110910 (accessed August 18, 2014).

Bayat, A. (1997), "Cairo's Poor: Dilemmas of Survival and Solidarity," *Middle East Report*, 202: 2–8.

Bayat, A. (2012), "Politics in the City Inside-out," *City and Society*, 24 (2): 110–28.

Carr, S. and L. Doss (2014), "Too Many to Count," Mada Masr, January 31. Available at: http://madamasr.com/content/too-many-count (accessed August 18, 2014).

Dale, T. (2012), "The Abbaseya Violence and Revolutionary Impasse in Egypt," Open Democracy, May 5. Available at: https://www.opendemocracy.net/tom-dale/abbaseya-violence-and-revolutionary-impasse-in-egypt (accessed August 18, 2014).

Egyptian Initiative for Human Rights (2013), Available at: http://eipr.org/pressrelease/2013/02/19/1635 (accessed August 18, 2014).

El-Kamel, S. (2013), "The Street Is Watching You: Digital Installation Engages Downtown Crowd [video]," AhramOnline, April 25. Available at: http://english.ahram.org.eg/NewsContent/5/25/70075/Arts–Culture/Visual-Art/The-street-is-watching-you-Digital-installation-en.aspx (accessed August 18, 2014).

El-Kouny, N. (2013), "Residents of Ramlet Boulaq District Decry 'Injustices'," AhramOnline, March 18. Available at: http://english.ahram.org.eg/News/67154.aspx (accessed August 18, 2014).

El-Rashidi, S. (2012), "Zabaleen: Egypt's Traditional Garbage Collectors Struggle for Recognition," AhramOnline, October 25. Available at: http://english.ahram.org.eg/NewsContent/1/64/55025/Egypt/Politics-/Zabaleen-Egypts-traditionalgarbage-collectors-str.aspx (accessed August 18, 2014).

El-Sadek, F. S. (2011), *The Streets of Cairo and the Battle for Public Space*, Thesis, IDBE, Cohort 15, University of Cambridge.

Fayed, S. (2009), "Revamping History," Business Monthly Special (Doorknock supplement, June): 49–58.

Ibrahim, E. (2012), "Justice Denied: Egypt's Maspero Massacre One Year on," AhramOnline, October 9. Available at: http://english.ahram.org.eg/NewsContent/1/64/54821/Egypt/Politics-/Justice-denied-Egypts-Masperomassacre-one-year-on.aspx (accessed August 18, 2014).

Jaquette, E. (2013), "Space for Culture," April 30. Atlantic Council, Egypt Source Rafik Hariri Center for the Middle East.

Kanna, A. (2012), "Urban Praxis and the Arab Spring: Beyond the Pathological City?" *City*, 16 (3): 360–8.

Keraitim, S. and S. Mehrez (2012), "Mulid al-Tahrir: Semiotics of a Revolution," in S. Mehrez (ed.), *Translating Egypt's Revolution: The Language of Tahrir*, 25–68, Cairo: The American University in Cairo Press.

Kimmelman, M. (2013), "Who Rules the Street in Cairo? The Residents Who Build It," *The New York Times*, April 27. Available at: http://www.nytimes.com/2013/04/28/arts/design/in-cairo-rethinking-the-city-from-the-bottom-up.html?smid¼fb-share&_r¼2& (accessed August 18, 2014).

Mada Masr (2013), "A Busy Year for Culture Despite Everything," December 31. Available at: http://www.madamasr.com/content/busy-year-culture-egyptdespite-everything (accessed August 18, 2014).

Mehrez, S. (2012), "'Watching' Tahrir," *Global Dialogue*, 2 (3). Available at: http://isa-global-dialogue.net/wp-content/uploads/2013/07/v2i3-english.pdf (accessed August 18, 2014).

Mitchell, W. J. T. (2012), "Image, Space, Revolution: The Arts of Occupation," *Critical Inquiry*, 39 (1): 8–32.

Mumford, L. (2002[1996]), "What Is a City?," in R. T. LeGates and F. Stout (eds.), *The City Reader*, 2nd edn, 92–7, London: Routledge.

Nagati, O. and B. Stryker (2013), *Archiving the City in Flux: Cairo's Shifting Urban Landscape since the January 25th Revolution*, Cairo: CLUSTER.

Nawara, W. (2013), "B'rotherhood's Scorched-earth Strategy Provokes More Bloodshed," August 14. Al-Monitor. Available at: http://www.al-monitor.com/pulse/originals/2013/08/egypt-scorched-earth-strategy-nawara.html (accessed August 18, 2014).

Oikonomakis, L. and J. E. Roos (2013), "'Que no nos representan': The Crisis of Representation and the Resonance of the Real Democracy Movement from the Indignados to Occupy," Paper presented at the "Conference on Street Politics in the Age of Austerity: From the Indignados to Occupy," University of Montreal, February 20–21.

Purcell, M. (2002), "Excavating Lefebvre: The Right to the City and Its Urban Politics of the Inhabitant," *GeoJournal*, 58: 99–108.

Raymond, A. (2000), *Cairo*, Cambridge, MA: Harvard University Press.

Shaath, R. (2013), "Photojournalists in the Land of Sectarian Strife," Egypt Independent, April 11. Available at: http://www.egyptindependent.com/opinion/photojournalists-land-sectarian-strife (accessed August 18, 2014).

Shawkat, N. (2011), "Street Smart: Cairo 2050—Guilty by Design or Association?" AhramOnline, September 10. Available at: http://english.ahram.org.eg/NewsContentPrint/32/0/20828/Folk/0/Street-Smart-Cairo-,-Guilty-bydesign-or-associati.aspx (accessed August 18, 2014).

Sims, D. (2008), *Arab Republic of Egypt: Towards an Urban Sector Strategy*, Washington, DC: The World Bank.

Tadros, M. (2012), "Signs of Islamist Fascism in Egypt?," Open Democracy, December 8. Available at: http://www.opendemocracy.net/5050/mariz-tadros/signs-of-islamist-fascism-in-egypt (accessed February 14, 2013).

Trew, B. (2013), "Egypt's Islamists Turn Violent," Foreign Policy, August 8. Available at: http://www.foreignpolicy.com/articles/2013/08/08/egypt_s_islamists_turn_violent (accessed August 18, 2014).

UN Habitat (2011), *Cairo: A City in Transition* (Cities and Citizens Series, Bridging the Urban Divide), Cairo: The American University in Cairo, UN Human Settlements Programme, UN Habitat for a Better Urban Future.

Volait, M. (2001), *Le Caire: Alexandrie, architectures europe´enes, 1850–1950*, Cairo: Presses de L'IFAO.

Williams, D. (2009), "Swine-flu Slaughter Leaves Cairo without Pigs to Devour Trash," Bloomberg, September 28. Available at: http://www.bloomberg.com/apps/news?pid¼newsarchive&sid¼aMODvyHlOBAE (accessed August 18, 2014).

Willows, P. (2012), "American University in Cairo to Host Graffiti Artists," Bikya, March 28. Available at: http://www.masress.com/en/bikyamasr/64214 (accessed August 18, 2014).

Zukin, S. (1995), "Whose Culture? Whose City?" in R. T. LeGates and F. Stout (eds.), *The City Reader*, 2nd edn, London: Routledge.

II CULTURE AND CONSUMPTION

Matrimonial Transactions and the Enactment of Class and Gender Difference among Egyptian Youth

by Rania Salem

Asmaa and Mustafa met when he was working in a cell phone shop he had opened in partnership with a friend and she was working in a photography studio nearby. At first, they were casual acquaintances, passing the time at work by chatting on the street linking their workplaces, but with time, they grew closer, and they began to consider a long-term commitment. They have now known one another for six years. Since their initial acquaintance, Mustafa has secured a coveted public sector job as a teacher in a local elementary school (his Bachelor's degree is in sports education), but Asmaa is out of work (she holds a vocational secondary school certificate in commerce). Mustafa helps her cover her expenses by giving her a regular allowance, but both Asmaa and Mustafa live with their parents and receive financial help from them.

Mustafa finally came to propose to Asmaa's parents three years ago, and they have been engaged to be married ever since. The length of their engagement is unusual in Egypt,[1] as is Asmaa's advanced age. Nearly thirty-one, Asmaa considers the ideal age for marriage for a young woman to be twenty-three or twenty-four years old, but in her own case, Asmaa confides that circumstances got in the way of a timely marriage.

Interviewer: Would you have liked to marry earlier than this?
Asmaa: Yes, of course.
Interviewer: What caused you not to marry at the time that you wanted?
Asmaa: It was not fated to be (*ma hasalsh naseeb*). It was against my will. Not everything one wishes for can be realized. It was circumstances that made us wait all this time.

Salem, Rania. 2018. "Matrimonial Transactions and the Enactment of Class and Gender Difference Among Egyptian Youth." Qualitative Sociology 41(3): 399–421.

Although Mustafa owns his own apartment, Mustafa's father, she explains, was burdened with the marriage expenses of two engaged daughters when his son proposed to her. Mustafa elaborates:

> Three years ago, I entered [Asmaa's] home and spoke formally [about getting engaged], but circumstances at home prevented me from taking any further steps forward. My sisters were getting married, and of course as a man ... my father is an Upper Egyptian who believes that girls' futures should be secured before boys', so I had to wait my turn.

Now that the two daughters have married,[2] Mustafa's father can turn his attention to helping his son finance his marriage. Asmaa and Mustafa's wedding was scheduled to take place two months after they were interviewed, and they did not anticipate any further delays.

The literature on youth in the Middle East and North Africa (MENA) has identified a host of material constraints that impede young people's successful transitions from adolescence to adulthood. Scholars have argued that these material constraints result in a period of "waithood" in which young people are suspended as they try to attain social adulthood, uncertain when they will be able to complete the transition from school to work and from work to family formation (Assaad and Barsoum 2009; Dhillon, Dyer and Yousef 2009; Hashemi 2015; Singerman 2007).

The stalled transition to marriage depicted in the opening vignette is especially consequential because marriage is the only socially approved gateway to residential independence, sexual activity, and childbearing available to the region's youth (Salem 2016a; Singerman 2007). In Egypt, the MENA region's most populous country, youth are disadvantaged in the labor market relative to other age groups, making it difficult for them to achieve economic self-sufficiency. Young Egyptians face the additional challenge of financing the matrimonial transactions associated with a new marital union (including the costs of housing, furniture, appliances, celebrations, and jewelry) in the context of a tight housing market and few opportunities for obtaining credit (Assaad et al. 2017). In Egypt, young people's postponement of marriage is widely assumed to be involuntary, and in many circles, it is also considered a pressing social problem (Salem 2016a).

In this article, I focus on Egyptian youth who are engaged to be married, a status most (especially most young men) could not achieve without first demonstrating their ability to sustain a new household economically without assistance from their natal families. This allows me to hone in on the challenge represented by matrimonial transactions. Drawing on semi-structured interview data from a sample of sixty-six engaged young people from two urban centers, I corroborate the observation that many young Egyptians wish to marry earlier than they are able to, and that they see marriage costs as a problem to be overcome. But more importantly, my findings show that when couples are faced with a trade-off between marrying at the time of their choice versus marrying with the material trappings of their choice, they almost invariably opt for the latter. The "rational" response to prevailing economic constraints would be to eliminate or reduce matrimonial expenditures, but this instrumental approach ignores the crucial symbolic and relational work that matrimonial transactions perform.

This article offers a corrective to the literature on waithood, with its emphasis on material barriers and the functional importance of matrimonial goods such as furniture and appliances. I argue that existing explanations of youth waithood, focused as they are on material constraints, are incomplete. My findings show that while young people's marriage timing decisions certainly reflect concerns about purchasing goods with functional value before marriage, matrimonial transactions also play an important role as signifiers of class status and gender ideals, a role that is too great for the actors involved to circumvent by forgoing matrimonial outlays. In sum, I look beyond the instrumental role of matrimonial purchases and ask what cultural and symbolic scaffolding props up the institution of matrimonial transactions in spite of the tremendous financial difficulties they impose and the postponement of marriage that results.

Youth Waithood and the High Costs of Marriage

Normative[3] social expectations in the MENA dictate that young people must clear two hurdles before entering a marital union: they must achieve economic self-sufficiency, and they must invest in the matrimonial transactions considered necessary for engagement and the formation of a new household. The literature on youth waithood takes these social expectations as a given, arguing that the structure of opportunities and constraints faced by young people is the prime determinant of their marriage timing behavior. Certainly, timely transitions to marriage for youth are made difficult by unfavorable material conditions in labor, housing, and credit markets (Assaad and Barsoum 2009; Assaad et al. 2017). The Egyptian labor market's high unemployment rates, low wages, and preponderance of precarious jobs disproportionately affect young people (Salem 2016b). These labor market conditions render economic self-sufficiency beyond the reach of many young men before they are in their thirties, and unfavorable labor market experiences can delay Egyptian men's marriage timing (Salem 2016b).[4] The high cost of marriage is complicated by Egypt's insufficient supply of housing units and the dearth of formal lending mechanisms available to young people (Assaad et al. 2017).

The focus of this article is on marriage costs, which, like economic self-sufficiency, are of particular concern to young men. Egyptian grooms and their natal families shouldered approximately 69 percent of the overall costs of marriage in 2006 (Singerman 2007) and 73 percent in 2012. Although there are regional and class variations, the broad categories of transactions included in the overall costs of marriage do not differ dramatically across couples, and custom governs who pays which expense. Grooms are expected to supply an apartment in which the new couple will live, in addition to most items of furniture for the conjugal home. In the case of middle-class Egyptians, this includes master bedroom furniture and living room furniture (including a wood and glass display case, the *niche*). Depending on the agreements they reach with the bride's family, some middle-class grooms buy furniture for a child's bedroom as well as dining room furniture. Grooms are responsible for certain appliances, such as the television, satellite dish and receiver, cassette player, water heater, and fans. On a number of occasions, the groom is required to visit his fiancée and her family to present gifts. This is in addition to the *shabka*, a gift of gold engagement rings or other gold jewelry given by the groom to the bride at the time of the engagement. Finally, grooms bear the cost of various celebrations, with the exception of the engagement party and other minor celebrations, which fall to the bride's side.[5]

Brides and their families have a host of other expenses that they must shoulder. Among middle-class Egyptians, the bride's side usually purchases the kitchen cabinets. Kitchen appliances such as an automatic washing machine, a refrigerator, an oven, and a gas canister are the responsibility of Egyptian brides. They must also provide other minor kitchen appliances, kitchenware, cleaning implements, and linens. Depending on the agreement reached with the groom's side, the bride's side will sometimes supply rugs and curtains for the conjugal home. Together with the furniture, these items are all referred to as the *gihaz*. The bride is also expected to come to the marriage with a whole new wardrobe for everyday use and for special occasions such as visits and weddings. This is called her *kiswa*.

There is a widespread perception in Egypt that marriage is far more costly today than in the past (Hoodfar 1997; Singerman 1995). The cost of marriage has likely been driven up over the course of the last fifty years by the advent of modern amenities such as refrigerators and automatic washers,[6] the attendant expansion in consumption expectations, the retreat from extended-family living arrangements, and the emergence of a housing crisis caused by rapid rural-urban migration in the 1970s (Ali 2002; Bach 1998; Hasso 2011; Hoodfar 1997; Salem 2015; Singerman 1995; Singerman and Ibrahim 2003). However, different metrics yield discrepant results on whether marriage costs have risen (Salem 2015) or declined over time (Salem 2016a; Singerman 2007), based on married survey respondents' retrospective reports on their matrimonial expenditures. Whatever the time trends may be, marriage costs in Egypt are high by international standards.[7] For the average groom, approximately 3.5 years of saved wages are needed to finance marriage (Salem 2016a). The parallel figure for brides is six months (Salem 2016a). Because of the staggering expenses involved, grooms and brides rely heavily on their families to meet the financial demands of marriage, and Egyptian parents save for their children's marriages in much the same way that American parents save for their children's college tuitions (Hoodfar 1997; Singerman 1995).

The Social Meanings of Matrimonial Expenditures

The international literature on marriage payments contains a wide array of accounts regarding the social meanings of such payments. On the most basic level, scholars contend that the exchange of matrimonial goods symbolizes the sealing of a conjugal match, thus legitimizing the union (Comaroff 1980). Most of this literature focuses on the South Asian context, where net resources once flowed from groom to bride (dower), and, since the mid-twentieth century, now flow from bride to groom (dowry). In many instances, dowry payments continue to be made by the bride's family to the groom after marriage, and the groom will sometimes attempt to extract more resources from the bride's family by threatening violence against the bride. Still, parents view dowry as a necessary for securing a husband for their daughters. In Bangladesh, dowry payments are referred to as a "demand" by potential husbands, rather than a voluntary expression of good will on the part of the bride's kin (Amin and Cain 1997; Lindenbaum 1981). South Indians portray dowry payments as necessary because of the scarcity of marriageable husbands, but this has to do with parents' desire to see their daughters marry up, and specifically to marry men with educational credentials and steady urban employment (Caldwell, Reddy, and Caldwell 1983). In Northern India, high-caste youth regard dowry with distaste because of its association with violence against women, but they report that parental pressure would force them to practice it (Billig 1991). Yet other accounts portray dowry in the South Asian context as an attempt to gain status by emulating the customs of high-caste groups, who have long practiced dowry exchange (Amin and Cain 1997; Bhat and Halli 1999).

In the MENA and sub-Saharan Africa, where net transfers from groom to bride (dower) prevail, the meanings of matrimonial transactions have been less comprehensively studied. In Iran, the size of the dower is seen by the community as an indicator of the status and prestige of the bride and her family (Habibi 1997). Other interpretations of the dower cast it more negatively, with some in Turkey and in Palestine viewing the exchange of dower as akin to the purchase of a bride (Moors 1994; Remez 1998). In the sub-Saharan African context, dowers have been similarly condemned as a sign of women's objectification (Wendo 2004). Others have characterized dower as a transfer of inheritance to daughters upon marriage rather than at the death of parents (Goody 1973). Yet others claim that dowers represent compensation to the bride's family for the loss of her labor and reproductive potential, which are relinquished to the groom and his family (Comaroff 1980).

In the contemporary United States, dowries and dowers may not be exchanged, but other material requirements attend marriage. Young people aspire to achieve a set of economic goals before they can marry: acquire certain assets (such as a home), achieve financial stability, settle all debts, and amass the savings necessary to pay for a respectable church wedding (Gibson-Davis et al. 2005; Smock et al. 2005). Several scholars conclude that in the United States, marriage has come to mean that a couple has arrived financially. For instance, Cherlin (2004: 857) has characterized marriage as a "marker of prestige" and Edin and Reed (2015) hold that marriage has become a status symbol in the contemporary United States.

Social Meanings Related to Class, Gender, and Prestige

The fact that American couples announce their attainment of a comfortable and stable middle-class lifestyle with wedding celebrations, the purchase of a home, and other acquisitions (Cherlin 2004) squares with classical accounts of economic behavior and social stratification, which emphasize that the acquisition of goods and the accumulation of wealth are not motivated by the satisfaction of physical needs, but by the quest for reputation and honor (Veblen 1899/1998). Marriage expenditures can be seen as conspicuous displays of consumption and wealth, observed by others in publicly witnessed celebrations. According to Veblen (1899/1998), through these displays, individuals emulate others and compete to live up to (and exceed) the normative material standards that prevail within their social class. Similarly, for Bourdieu (1984), tastes in consumption are patterned according to social class; hence, consumption habits have a symbolic function in signaling class affiliation and class difference.

This insight has not escaped those studying matrimonial expenditures in Egypt. Amin and Al-Bassusi (2004) observe that the purchase and use of matrimonial goods may contribute to status attainment. Singerman (1995) briefly alludes to the symbolic aspect, noting that marriage is a sign of financial achievement for young Egyptian couples as well as their parents. Still, these fleeting observations aside, the Egyptian case has not been adequately examined.

Many scholars point out that consumption and other exchanges of economic resources can be used as a resource for the construction of identities and relations (Bourdieu 1984; DiMaggio 1994; Zelizer 2005). But can this extend beyond class identities and relations? Amin and Al-Bassusi (2004) observe that in Egyptian marriages, gifts and assets are highly gendered, with grooms' and brides' expenditures reflecting the gendered tasks they are expected to perform within marriage. Certainly, ample examples in the literature point to the role material transactions play in constructing gender identities and relations (for the role of married couples' income and housework see Brines 1994; for the role of payments in dating relationships see Lever et al. 2015). But this research has rarely focused on resource exchanges that *precede* marriage and constitute its material foundations. Following Goffman (1976), these expenditure patterns can be interpreted as self-conscious portrayals of what actors would like to convey to others about their gendered natures, natures which are assumed to be based on essential, biological differences between men and women (Ridgeway 2011). As a type of gender display, matrimonial transactions arise from and bolster actors' claim to membership in a sex category (West and Zimmerman 1987). To Goffman's micro-sociological account,

West and Zimmerman (1987) add that the perceived competence and virtue of men and women depend on gender-appropriate performances, causing actors to experience these performances as compulsory. Like social class membership, membership in a given sex category is continually evaluated, and individual actions are strategic insofar as they are designed with attention to how they might be judged by others.

Social class and sex category membership, and by extension, social approval, are thus contingent on the display of appropriate expenditures around the time of marriage. But the stakes associated with suitable matrimonial expenditures may extend beyond mere social approval, and can be theorized to contribute to one's symbolic capital. Bourdieu (1984: 291) defines symbolic capital as "a reputation for competence and an image of respectability and honourability." Briefly stated, symbolic capital refers to an individual's prestige within a social space. The acquisition of symbolic capital is contingent on others' evaluations of the social actor, and these evaluations are informed by existing beliefs about class (Veblen 1899/1998) and gender (Ridgeway 2011). Symbolic capital is associated with gains in others' esteem for the individual, but the literature on symbolic capital points out that other benefits include self-respect and personal dignity for the individual (Hashemi 2015; Sherman 2006). Social actors are implicated in continuous efforts to maintain and augment their social prestige and self-esteem through the display of class- and gender-appropriate performances through their use and consumption of material culture and material goods. The circulation of such goods can contribute to social recognition and symbolic mobility, but at the same time it creates social inequalities, with those who are unable to mobilize material goods to their advantage experiencing exclusion and marginalization (Hannerz 1992; Klaufus 2012). Individuals' efforts to generate symbolic capital can be understood as Goffmanian image management, where successful performances result in greater prestige and honor, and where failed performances result in the loss of "face." Face refers to a social actor's "claimed identity as a competent, intelligent, or moral person" (White 2009: 261), and threats to one's face result in individual embarrassment and social disdain (Scarborough 2012). Like symbolic capital, blocked access to the material goods that are mobilized in individual efforts to save face provides a basis for social exclusion and social inequalities. In the Egyptian context, the presentation of a face that is "correct" for the interaction or situation at hand, as communicated through the deployment of matrimonial goods, can be essential to maintaining one's symbolic capital.

The forgoing discussion suggests that material barriers to marriage, the main impediments to union formation identified by the waithood literature, are not enough to explain on their own why many couples find themselves stalled in a lengthy period of waithood before they may wed. Engaged couples must meet normative expectations that dictate what matrimonial outlays they must make in order to demonstrate their social class and sex category membership. As I go on to show, matrimonial transactions in Egypt have taken on unique symbolic meanings that reinforce their ongoing use.

Methods

I gathered qualitative interview data from youth who were engaged to be married in two Egyptian cities, Cairo and Al-Minya. Customs governing matrimonial exchanges vary geographically, hence the choice of Cairo, a large urban metropolis, and Al-Minya, located in the poorer and more socially conservative region of Upper Egypt. I conducted thirty-three semi-structured interviews with young men and women in Cairo personally. I also trained a female interviewer, who conducted thirty-three interviews with youth in Al-Minya. Snowball sampling techniques were used to identify and recruit respondents. Respondents were selected if they reported being eighteen years old or older, were currently in any stage of the engagement process, and were middle class based on their responses to a short seven-item questionnaire measuring the wealth of their natal households.[8] My selection criteria for inclusion in the study also aimed at a sample that was gender balanced. To the fullest extent possible, both members of each engaged couple were sought out for an interview, although we met with each member separately. I opted not to vary the sample along additional axes of difference (e.g., I did not make urban/rural comparisons or comparisons across social classes) so that I could attribute variations clearly to either gender or location.

Interviews were conducted between January and June 2010. They lasted an average of one hour and took place in a location of the respondent's choosing. Interview schedules were semi-structured and covered three broad themes: the economic prerequisites for marriage, customs and practices related to courtship and matrimonial transactions, and plans for the future. All interviews were digitally audio recorded, and transcribed verbatim in Arabic. The core of the interview data is supplemented by the information contained in field notes taken from conversations with one key informant in each of the two study sites.

Data analysis followed the broad principles of the extended case method (Burawoy 1998). I coded the interview transcripts based on themes identified in the existing literature (e.g., matrimonial transactions as a barrier to timely marriage, or the functional importance of marriage assets), and with an eye to emergent themes not previously reported elsewhere. The coding procedure thus used deductive and inductive approaches. Codes were applied and analysis undertaken using the program MAXQDA. In the analysis, I called up segments of text that had been coded under a specific theme and examined them for internal patterns of variation along the lines of gender and location, and according to values assigned for other codes. I then searched for and coded outliers or deviations from the general pattern that would illuminate my findings. I examined segments of text under each code, and selected and translated into English a quotation that would most succinctly summarize the theme represented by that code.

The final sample was comprised of thirty-three men and thirty-three women across both locations; this included nine couples in Cairo and eleven couples in Al-Minya. Respondents' ages ranged from eighteen to thirty-four. All had at least some secondary school education, but their educational backgrounds ranged from having dropped out of technical vocational secondary school to having completed five-year university degrees. Although all the young men interviewed were currently employed (with two men working and studying simultaneously), six of the female respondents were neither in school nor working. The majority of respondents were Muslim, and the three Christian respondents interviewed were from Al-Minya.[9] Among women from Cairo, the average respondent had completed technical vocational secondary school, was currently working, and was twenty-three years old. The average man from Cairo had completed university, was currently working, and was twenty-seven years old. Average women from Al-Minya and men from Al-Minya had a university degree and were currently working, and their average ages were twenty-four and twenty-seven, respectively. The age differences between engaged men and women in this study reflect customs in the MENA region that dictate husbands should be older than their wives. Between all four groups of respondents, we interviewed salesclerks, taxi drivers, nurses, carpenters, social workers, teachers, accountants, secretaries, painters, customs officials, market researchers, hotel cooks, factory workers, engineers, sales representatives, and small business owners. In spite of this variation, this is a selective sample of young people in the sense that the sample excludes youth who have not found a partner or who are not yet ready for engagement for various reasons.

Delayed Marriage and Strategies for Financing and Concluding a New Union

A refrain repeated by several respondents was the lament "*elshabab mish 'aref yitgawez elyomein dol*" or "youths are unable to marry these days." Respondents perceived marriage costs as a burden causing economic hardship for young people of their generation, and many attributed their own and others' delayed marriages to the high costs involved. When asked whether she was satisfied with the timing of her own marriage, Naglaa from Cairo answered by stating that the gap between one generation and the next was widening: "My mother is 48 and I'm 28—and I also have an older brother." She elaborated by putting a negative spin on this observation:

> Mama is the one who makes me regret my situation. She tells me that once you're married, the best days of your life will be behind you. You'll have children when you're tired and you won't be able to handle them. And then [our parents] also see that the circumstances of our [generation's] jobs are making earlier marriage impossible. So that's what upsets one. It doesn't make a difference to me, but I still wanted to marry in my twenties.

Naglaa regarded the early years of marriage and childbearing as happy years that should be enjoyed in the prime of one's life—in her view, one's twenties—so that one can withstand all the demands that come with this phase of life. Her account implies that the root of the problem of delayed marriage is in contemporary young people's poor earnings. Not only did Naglaa and other respondents report aspiring to marry at younger ages, but when asked what the ideal age for marriage is for a woman/man in the respondent's circumstances, most replied with an age younger than that at which they themselves planned to marry.

Stories of marriage transitions stalled while young couples amassed the goods and savings needed to conclude a match abounded in respondents' narratives. Like Naglaa, above, Asmaa, described in the opening vignette, and many other respondents, twenty-four-year-old Salah from Al-Minya said he would have liked to marry earlier than he plans to. Employed as a scaffolding carpenter for a large construction firm, Salah had been engaged for nine months at the time of interview. Although the initial agreement was that he would marry a year and a half after his engagement, it now seemed that he would need an additional six months to finish furnishing his apartment and finance his wedding. When asked what caused the delay, Salah replied simply by saying: "My finances." A review of his expenses showed the extent of the strain imposed on him. Salah earned about 600 Egyptian pounds (EGP) monthly,[10] and his meagre income was split between his day-to-day expenses, contributions to the expenses of the household in which he lived with his mother and siblings, and expenses related to his marriage. Unlike Mustafa, no one from Salah's family had helped him out financially, and Salah rejected any help on principle. Because he planned to live in a rented apartment upon marriage, he would not be burdened with expenses related to building. But Salah had bought *shabka* gold for his fiancée for approximately 8,000 EGP, and he had finished paying off the entire 4,000 EGP he was charged for living room furniture. In addition, he contributed 2,000 EGP to the cost of the engagement party; he had bought a TV and a water heater (together costing about 1,250 EGP), cotton filling for the mattress and cloth for curtains and the upholstery of the furniture (together costing about 1,200 EGP). Salah had yet to pay off 10,000 EGP for master bedroom furniture, and he still planned to purchase a niche, rugs, fans, and some clothing for himself, in addition to paying for the painting of his rental apartment and the wedding celebrations.

The young people interviewed deployed several strategies to deal with the challenge of financing marriage. As Mustafa's case above illustrates, mobilizing the efforts and resources of family members was one common strategy.[11] Taking on a second job was another response to the crippling costs of marriage, but it was limited in most cases to young men. Nearly one-third of the grooms in my sample were moonlighting or had moonlighted in the recent past. Men also sought out temporary migration opportunities to increase their earnings and help finance a new union. The fiancés of four of the sampled brides were currently employed in one of the oil-rich Arab Gulf countries, and at least six of the grooms sampled had spent time working abroad. Finally, both men and women accessed credit opportunities by making purchases in installments or participating in rotating savings and credit associations with friends, relatives, or neighbors.

In spite of these efforts, many respondents reported having postponed wedding dates because they were not yet prepared to move into a fully furnished home, as illustrated by the case of Salah above. While extending the engagement period was one solution available to young couples struggling to keep up with the expenditures expected of them, doing so came with the risk of being perceived to lack seriousness of purpose and exposing the young couple to higher chances of disagreements arising.[12] To avoid such situations, engaged couples took great care to adhere to agreements reached during negotiations on marriage expenditures conducted by themselves and their families.

Although financial negotiations occur continuously behind the scenes, the most important negotiations take place at two critical junctures. The first occurs prior to the formal engagement. A well-known script governs the behavior of the groom on the occasion of his first visit to the bride's family.[13] The suitor introduces himself and notes the names of his father's and mother's families. He mentions his educational credentials, his neighborhood of residence, and his and his father's occupations and workplaces so that the bride's family can inquire into their reputations and carry out a character investigation. The groom then describes his income and financial means, including whether he has an apartment. It is not unusual for middle-class grooms to detail the marriage costs they are willing to bear and how long an engagement they will need to accumulate these assets, or to ask the bride's family what their material demands are and launch into detailed negotiations. The discussions held in these early meetings are considered binding, and failure to reach an agreement or to later fulfill the commitments can result in a breakup.

Another critical juncture in the negotiation of the costs of marriage comes with the writing of the *ayma*, an informal contract that lists the contributions of bride and groom to the marriage fund. It is written around the time of the signing of the marriage contract, or the *katb el kitab* for Muslims. All items purchased for the marriage (in addition to a *muakhar*,[14] or deferred dower) are written down, assigned a monetary value, and summed up. Because the *ayma* is meant to be used in the future to claim the property of the bride, her family often gives the items listed an exaggerated Egyptian pound value to correct for future inflation. The groom signs the contract, and it is given to the bride's family for safekeeping, to be used to claim the bride's property (or a sum of money in lieu of that property) in case of divorce or ill-treatment.

As noted above, conflict was a very real risk that attended the extension of engagements, and many respondents said it was not unusual for engagements to break up over marriage expenses. They relayed the stories of friends and relatives who had had engagements called off because of conflicts over the costs of marriage. Some said their own engagements had faltered over material conflicts. The experience of thirty-two-year-old Hussam from Cairo is a case in point. He worked as a customs officer and had been engaged for two years to his second cousin Iman. His mother was the one who first brought her to his attention as a bride, and the families began visiting one another.

The first time they spoke about marriage arrangements, Hussam mentioned he had a one-bedroom apartment, which Iman's parents didn't approve of as a place to start out their married life because of its small size. For about six months, the whole matter was stalled because of the issue of the apartment. At the end of this period, Hussam got in touch with Iman's parents and said that he would look for another apartment that conformed to their expectations, and shortly thereafter they held their engagement party.

Many respondents additionally expressed fear that material conflicts would endanger the prospects of successfully transitioning from engagement to marriage. The negotiation of the *ayma* was often cited as a precarious moment. Aya, a twenty-eight-year-old woman from Cairo, said: "To be honest, [the *ayma*] really worries me because the *gihaz* that I've bought is really expensive, and when it's written up in the *ayma* everything will be given today's prices. The fear is not about him, the fear is about his mother—his mother is very difficult." Aya's concerns centered on her mother-in-law, who might object to an expensive *ayma* because that would represent money owed by her son to Aya in the event of divorce. Mona, a twenty-four-year-old from Al-Minya, described her fiancé's strategy for avoiding a breakup over the *ayma*: "Since the wedding is coming up soon, [my fiancé] told my father we should write the *ayma* now because at the time of the wedding everyone's nerves will be frayed and everyone will insist on their own position, and the marriage could be ruined over a petty matter."

It is important for grooms in particular to demonstrate dedication and resourcefulness in handling the burdensome matrimonial outlays to which they agree. For example, Shaimaa, a twenty-three-year-old from Al-Minya, stated that her parents had at one point been antagonized by her fiancee's requests to postpone their wedding. She described how her parents had been appeased: "When he started to buy furniture they were distracted a bit and they quieted down about the delay because they found that he was enthusiastic and he was buying this and buying that." Shaimaa implied that her fiancé was demonstrating his dedication to the marriage and making concerted progress toward it through the purchase of matrimonial goods. Ibrahim, a twenty-four-year-old man from Cairo, said the engagement constitutes a probation period in which you must prove yourself: "If you do something with that time [find an apartment, buy a *shabka*], then the bride's home will be open to you and they will welcome you. But if you waste your time they will say that you are playing around with their daughter." Since "playing around" indicates a lack of respect for the bride and her family, and a lack of seriousness of purpose, Ibrahim implied that failing to make steady progress with matrimonial purchases would endanger the engagement.

Other respondents said that there were other benefits to making timely and appropriate matrimonial outlays. Twenty-five-year-old May from Al-Minya argued that a groom who has spent a lot of money on his marriage preparations can expect better treatment from his in-laws: "They see that he's 'bought' their daughter (*shary bintohom*); that he's paid a lot for her sake ... 'bought' her means that he wants to live with her. It means he'll take good care of her and protect her." Naglaa, the twenty-eight-year-old from Cairo cited above, reiterated this view when asked whether there are any advantages of high matrimonial expenditures: "The bride's family is affected by such things. I mean, if they see that the groom has bought good [quality] things, they are reassured about their daughter's welfare (*biyitamminoh 'ala bintohom*), and they treat him well." In other words, by displaying his esteem for their daughter with material expenditures, a groom can expect to win the approval of his in-laws and ensure cordial dealings with his new family. Matrimonial transactions can thus be understood as a cultural resource for the construction of social relations. By making timely outlays in line with the agreements they initially made, grooms demonstrate that they are committed to ensuring that their engagements result in marriage; this mitigates the risk of breakup inherent in extending the engagement.

The Functional Importance of Marriage Expenditures

Following Amin and Al-Bassusi (2004), I hold that the marriage fund carries functional and symbolic importance. In Egypt, marriage initiates most young people into independent living arrangements for the first time in their lives. They therefore lack possessions that might be used to outfit the conjugal home. The courtship period is one of intense consumption, and expenditures cover everything from irons to dining tables, from can openers to a hairdresser for the bride, and from freshly painted walls to drinks for wedding guests.

Many purchases related to the conjugal home could obviously be spread out over the first years of marriage. Twenty-five-year-old Ahmad from Al-Minya remarked disapprovingly that today's youth insist on having an apartment that is equipped with everything "from the pin to the rocket";[15] he suggested instead that "we could start out small and build ourselves up." A similar sentiment was voiced by Hesham, a twenty-two-year-old from Cairo, who said that materialistic brides should moderate their expectations to match their grooms' financial means:

> Every girl dreams to have the best apartment possible, to ride in a car, to wear the best clothes. But some girls see that this is what's possible. So instead of going out daily, we can go out once a week, fine. Suppose we saw a dining room set for 5,000 pounds, and there's one just like it for 4,000 pounds. Fine. She shouldn't insist that this is the one she likes, this is the colour she wants.

Like Ahmad, Hesham believed brides should accept the fact that grooms can seldom afford to fulfill their desire to have the best of everything before marriage; with time, he said, many grooms' financial situations will improve and they will be able to fulfill their wives' materialistic whims. Although a minority of grooms, like Ahmad and Hesham, criticized what they saw as excessive consumption and argued that purchases could be postponed until after marriage, none of the brides interviewed echoed such views.

Moreover, an examination of the behavior of those grooms who expressed skepticism about all the outlays expected of them during the engagement period revealed that their purchases were just as extensive as other grooms. In other words, they may have protested, but they did not rebel.

Ultimately, rather than postpone expenditures until after marriage, the vast majority of respondents insisted that all marriage-related purchases had to be made during the engagement period for three reasons. First, most young couples anticipated having enough trouble making ends meet once they got married. Middle-class engaged individuals do not have enough discretionary income to be able to set aside cash to spend after marriage. Instead, all their savings are spent on marriage costs during the engagement period in hopes that they will not have to make any major purchases for several years after they wed. Wafaa, a twenty-five-year-old woman from Al-Minya, is a case in point. She said:

> I know I'm a spendthrift, and I want to buy everything expensive. But girls who marry don't buy anything. There's responsibilities [after marriage]—expenses like the rent, raising children, schooling, and children who need to see the doctor. Mama is telling me, finish up and get married and later on you can get all the things you need for your home, but I know that girls who marry don't buy anything.

'Ali, a twenty-eight-year-old from Cairo, presented a similar point of view. When asked why he was purchasing certain matrimonial goods, he said: "So that the apartment is complete and I don't have to think about buying anything for five or six years after marriage."

Second, most respondents reasoned that immediately after marriage they would begin childbearing, which itself comes with a host of new expenses. When I asked why some acquisitions could not be postponed, Samar, a twenty-three-year-old from Cairo, explained:

> Suppose God blessed them with a pregnancy two or three weeks after getting married. Then there's the doctor, the *Pampers*, and I don't know what else. He won't be able to afford the rent, the cost of food, the doctor's fees, the cost of transportation ... So the best thing is to get married without any obligations or debts ahead of you.

Samar anticipated new financial responsibilities after marriage like those mentioned by Wafaa above, most of which have to do with the added expense of having children.

Third, many respondents expected their households to shift toward reliance on a single earner soon after marriage. For instance, Yasmine, a thirty-one-year-old from Al-Minya, remarked that the engagement period represented an opportunity to buy all the things she needed since she was working in the private sector now, and she didn't know if she would be able to work after marriage. While employment in the private sector often yields higher wages, the long hours and demanding conditions are not easily combined with the housework and caregiving duties that engaged women anticipate after marriage. In fact, the majority of the brides interviewed did not expect to continue working after marriage, in part because they hoped to begin childbearing soon thereafter, a point that echoes the findings of Amin and Al-Bassusi (2004).

The Symbolic Importance of Marriage Expenditures: The Construction of Class

Research in Egypt and elsewhere has described how couples ensure that certain economic arrangements (a stable job, savings, or marriage acquisitions) are set in place before a union is formalized so that consumption aspirations for marriage can be met (Edin and Kefalas 2005; Oppenheimer et al. 1997). But these arrangements do more than guarantee a certain standard of living; they also guarantee the social prestige or symbolic capital that comes with it.

Courtship and marriage are very public undertakings among middle-class Egyptians. The celebrations that accompany the different stages of marriage are often held in the streets adjacent to the couple's homes, with relatives, friends, co-workers, and neighbors in attendance. Conspicuous consumption is blatant in these celebrations.[16] During engagement parties, wedding rings or gifts of gold given to the bride (*shabka*) are often circulated to be admired by the guests. Another example is the *tangeed* celebration which accompanies the preparation of the cotton filling and upholstering of the bride's furniture. Typically held in the street below her house, the *tangeed* often involves displaying all of the bride's bedding and furniture on a small stage. When the time comes to move the goods acquired by the bride from her family's home to the conjugal home, a loud procession takes place with hired cars and trucks blaring horns and music.

In addition to these public celebrations, the young men and women in my sample gave great symbolic weight to the visits they expected to receive after marriage. In the days and weeks following their wedding, couples receive guests who come to relay their congratulations. These visits initiate them into reciprocal gift-giving relationships, but they also represent an occasion when their material lifestyle comes under the scrutiny of friends and family.[17] For example, when Mukhtar, a twenty-three-year-old from Cairo, was asked what would happen if his apartment was not fully furnished and decorated by the time of the wedding, he replied: "It just wouldn't fly in our community. Why? Because suppose the bride's aunt came to visit and found that there's no television. What will she say? She'll say the groom was too stingy to buy a television, that's the first thing she'll say." Clearly, Mukhtar recognized that deviating from certain standards of matrimonial consumption signals negative character attributes.

For other respondents, a groom's unwillingness to make class-appropriate outlays justified ending an engagement. Randa, a twenty-nine-year-old from Al-Minya, described her breakup with a former suitor for material reasons:

> His financial circumstances weren't helping him to be with me. I mean, he couldn't buy even a normal *shabka* and a normal *gihaz* that were at his level (*mustawah*) ... He wasn't trying hard enough, because if he was searching [for work] and doing what he needed to do but God was giving him these means (*rizq*) alone, then I would have continued with him. But he wasn't doing what he should do.

Other respondents similarly reported that the transgression of appropriate material behavior for one's class position would necessarily incur either a social sanction or a loss of face. When Ahmad, a twenty-five-year-old from Al-Minya, was asked what would happen if he failed to bring a gift each time he visited his fiancée at her parents' home, he said: "No one would say anything to me, but I myself would be upset. Because our traditions are that if you are obligated to bring something and you don't bring it, it is something terrible and you would feel you have fallen short (*assart*)." By alluding to the shame he would experience if he didn't present a gift in situations that require it, Ahmad suggested this would involve a loss of face.

Returning to the visits that new couples expect to receive after marriage, many of the purchases made by middle-class brides are meant to create an image of plenty and abundance for such visits. The *niche* display case, for instance, is meant to showcase all of the glassware and china acquired by the bride. One respondent, twenty-one-year-old Nuha from Cairo, said that in addition to two sets of plates and several sets of glasses, the *niche* had to be equipped with four kinds of bowls: soup bowls, rice pudding bowls, ice cream bowls, and glass bowls. Another respondent described how she had bought twelve sets of bedsheets for her *gihaz*. While this kind of excess may be unusual, all the brides interviewed bought an entirely new wardrobe for marriage (complete with winter and summer clothing, along with shoes and purses) and planned not to take any of their old clothing with them to their conjugal homes. For Bourdieu (1984), privileging form over function is one of the ways that the dominant classes mark their distinction. Following Bourdieu, household objects with little use-value that are purchased for the new conjugal home may signal high status, and thus may generate symbolic capital for the individuals involved.

Twenty-three-year-old Ghada from Al-Minya described the advantages of an expensive *gihaz* that gave an impression of plenty: "Many people, when they enter your apartment and see your *gihaz*, they say, look at so-and-so daughter of so-and-so, look what she's bought. *Bismillahi masha' Allah* [God bless] her things. She's bought things better than so-and-so's things." Ghada also confided that although her fiancé's family was wealthier and better-educated than her own, she didn't feel badly about this because she had proved that she was at the same "level" (*mustawa*) as her fiancé through her *gihaz*. Put otherwise, her expensive *gihaz* bolstered her worthiness for claiming higher-class membership. Ghada recognized that adherence to the material standards of her social circle communicated positive messages about class and social prestige. For her, it was important to meet the material standards of their community; failure to do so could incur a loss of face or a loss of status in the hierarchy of new couples.

In determining the appropriate level of expenditures on matrimonial goods, grooms and particularly brides made explicit comparisons with friends and relatives. This reinforces Bourdieu's argument that actors use horizontal rather than vertical references in making consumption decisions. In other words, rather than emulating the dominant classes, actors compete with others in their own social class (Bourdieu 1984). Nuha, a twenty-one-year-old woman from Cairo, explained:

> I am an only daughter, and so Ibrahim [her older brother] says that I have to be the best one in the family. He doesn't want me to end up envying my cousins for what they have. Because my cousins have bought more for their *gihaz* than I have [so far]. So of course I told Ibrahim that I want to get the same things. So he said I'll buy whatever you want. I want to buy the same things, and better still. Every girl has to be proud of her home, just like [the others] are proud of their homes.

Brides also recognized that they would be judged according to their parents' means. For example, twenty-one-year-old Manar from Cairo told the story of a relative whose father lived in Saudi Arabia, and was therefore assumed to have a high income. The daughter, however, bought a hand-operated washer and very few things for her *gihaz*; consequently, there was a lot of talk. According to Manar, the neighbors negatively compared the relative to Manar's sister, who is an orphan but still purchased an automatic washer for her marriage. Grooms do not face the same type of judgments according to their parents' means because young men are considered to be personally responsible for bearing the burden of matrimonial outlays and, unlike brides, any help received from their parents is considered an "extra" rather than an obligation. Young brides are acutely aware that members of their social circles will take their material circumstances and those of their parents into account to draw conclusions about the bride's and her parents' personal attributes and socioeconomic standing. Young grooms know that their matrimonial spending will be taken as evidence of their own hard work and personal socioeconomic position.

The fact that some of the interviewed couples resorted to public deception emphasizes the importance of marriage expenditures to the performance of socioeconomic status and class membership. Several grooms described the tactic of buying *shabka* gold just for the purpose of displaying it during the engagement and wedding parties, then selling the gold immediately after getting married to pay off installments on furniture bought for the conjugal home. The case of Dunya, a twenty-seven-year-old from Al-Minya, is particularly interesting. Her father came from the countryside and therefore had material expectations for marriage that differed slightly from her fiancé 'Essam's. Dunya purchased her own bride's wardrobe (*kiswa*) to prevent a dispute between her father and fiancé. Her father had insisted that 'Essam give her a sum of money for this purpose. Dunya told 'Essam to spend the money on their apartment, but did so behind her father's back. Dunya thus kept the peace between her father and fiancé; in the eyes of others, she had heeded her father's wishes and acquired the articles of clothing expected for a bride of her class. This "backstage work" (Goffman 1959) demonstrates the possibilities for resistance to and negotiation of customs of matrimonial exchanges that are open to individuals while publicly adhering to the community's material standards of respectability.

The Symbolic Importance of Marriage Expenditures: The Construction of Gender

As suggested by my description of the material obligations of bride and groom, marriage gifts and assets are highly gendered. Young women are tasked with outfitting the conjugal home with kitchen appliances, kitchenware, rugs, curtains, and linens (*gihaz*), while the apartment and its furnishings are the responsibility of young men. Respondents rationalized these gendered obligations by pointing to the normative duties of men and women. When I asked why she had to purchase kitchen items, Huda, a twenty-six-year-old from Cairo, said the bride is the one who will "stand in the kitchen," making her more qualified than her fiancé to judge what is needed. Ayman from Cairo made a similar argument, but emphasized the complementarity of bride's and groom's purchases (and by extension, their roles in marriage). He listed the matrimonial goods bought by brides and grooms, and said:

> If there are any items of décor like a table lamp or a vase or flowers, the bride is the one who buys it. The groom doesn't buy any of these little things (*rufaya'at*) at all. He buys the big things like the bedroom furniture. And when he brings his things and furnishes the apartment, it looks ugly. But when the bride comes and brings her things, you find that it's different because she puts in the mattress and the linens and towels and rugs and curtains and flowers.

Whereas Huda highlighted women's cooking acumen, Ayman highlighted their skill in decorating and making a house feel like a home. In response to a question about why he had not purchased kitchen appliances, 'Emad, a thirty-one-year-old from Al-Minya, joked: "What would *I* do with an oven?" 'Emad implied that he would be subject to ridicule if he were to show interest in or purchase goods that were the purview of brides alone. Gendered marriage expenditures can be understood as acts that enact gender differences and signal to others that a groom or bride is competent in the skills and knowledge needed to make gender-appropriate purchases (West and Zimmerman 1987).[18] In other words, gendered matrimonial outlays are taken to be signs of feminine or masculine dispositions, and their performance is part of social actors' face-work and maintenance of an image of competence.

The gendered assignment of marriage purchases also embodies important assumptions about and aspirations for future gender roles within marriage: wives should devote themselves primarily to domestic work and childrearing, while husbands should provide for the household's expenses and pay the rent. Grooms are often expected to display their readiness for the assumption of family duties by providing material support to their fiancées throughout the engagement. This takes the form of gifts of cash, food, or clothing presented at religious holidays; in some instances, it could include a regular allowance for the bride, as in the opening vignette.[19] It is no accident that Egyptian grooms have these obligations, but not brides. These expenditures reinforce the message that the groom will successfully adopt the masculine role of provider and breadwinner after marriage. Gendered marriage expenditures thus signal that each party will conform to the ideal roles husbands and wives are expected to play within marriage.

At the same time, to desist from making the appropriate expenditures would be to invite questions about the bride's ability to be an obedient wife and able homemaker, or about the groom's ability to be a good provider and breadwinner. In other words, to do so would reflect badly on the masculinity and femininity of the groom and bride. Recall the reactions of Mukhtar, Randa, and Muhammad to men's hypothetical or actual deviance from appropriate marriage expenditures described above. These respondents indicated that failure to make suitable outlays resulted in accusations of stinginess, a designation reserved for men alone because of the expectation that they should be competent income earners. A related reaction voiced by other respondents was that some grooms were greedy, a weighty accusation given the assumption that men should be providing and not receiving material resources at marriage. For example, Aya relayed the story of a friend whose fiancé had proposed that they move in with his mother upon marriage. This groom had also been reluctant to buy items of furniture that were often assigned to grooms; instead, he tried to negotiate for the friend's father to pay for these items. When asked for her reaction to the situation, Aya said:

Aya: To be honest, I didn't want her to marry him.
Interviewer: Why?
Aya: First of all, he didn't deserve her ... She told me that she loved him, and I said love wasn't a problem. She could find someone else to love, and who would love her, and it was better to live in her own apartment. I just felt that he was motivated by greed (*tama'*), because her father's [socioeconomic] level (*mustawah*) is high.

Aya suggested that grooms who could not match the socioeconomic standards a bride was accustomed to were not worthy of marriage.[20] Respondents never expressed disapproval of brides in terms that related to stinginess or greed, reserving these characterizations for men because masculine ideals emphasize their roles as providers and breadwinners.

By displaying conformity with the normative ideals of manhood and womanhood, Egyptian matrimonial transactions effectively perform gender (West and Zimmerman 1987). Similar to the purchase of matrimonial goods, negotiations over the value and timing of marriage expenditures represent an occasion for the demonstration of adherence to gender ideals. Brides are often excluded from these negotiations, and if they are present, they remain silent, allowing older members of the family to speak on their behalf. One of my respondents, Naglaa, a twenty-eight-year-old from Cairo, reported that when her fiancé 'Amr came to propose to her family, her uncle made her leave the room by tapping her hand discretely. Her mother, brother, and uncles (Naglaa's father is deceased) conducted the negotiations with 'Amr and his parents. By excluding the bride, her family indicated that the groom was answerable to them, while the bride's silence signaled the feminine attribute of obedience to the will of family elders. The highly scripted behavior reported during marriage negotiations suggests a ritualized situation, organized in a way that enacts and celebrates gendered conduct (West and Zimmerman 1987).

While matrimonial transactions define the roles and obligations of each party to the marriage, they also function as a mechanism that establishes a normative power balance between the genders, giving them an important structural dimension in addition to their symbolic one. Because men provide the conjugal home, they are in a position of power vis-à-vis the wife, who must return to her natal household in the event of marital conflict. Women counter this power imbalance in a number of ways, some of which are institutionalized in the customs of matrimonial transactions. El-Kholy (2000) argues that the *ayma* is a form of insurance against vulnerability in marriage because, in theory at least, it ensures that the wife would leave the marriage with some resources in the event of its dissolution. Respondents echoed this faith in the *ayma* as a document that would provide them with a safety net if their marriages were to break down. In fact, many respondents, like twenty-five-year-old Zeinab from Al-Minya, explicitly referred to the *ayma* as "insurance for a girl" in their narratives. Zeinab explained that if she got divorced, she would at least have a sum of money to enable her to live and cover her children's expenses. Marwa, a twenty-two-year-old from Cairo, said it was important to her to have an *ayma*:

> ... so that I can ensure my rights. So that he doesn't turn against me one of these days. Say he took another wife, or did something to me. How would I be able to get what's mine from him? Because he'll be stronger than me, I won't be able to get my rights. If he did something to me ... I won't be able to punish him. That's where the *ayma* comes in. It will ensure my rights. So if he hit me or humiliated me, I'd be able to get what's mine from him.

Another way marriage payments counter male power is symbolic. As Wafaa, a twenty-five-year-old from Al-Minya, explained, *shabka* gold is not really necessary and, in principle, she herself would be willing to marry without it. But in practice, she cannot marry without a *shabka* because "people would say 'her groom hasn't bought 'her any gold and her parents have thrown her away.'" Basma, a twenty-four-year-old from Al-Minya, echoed the sentiment. She stated that a bride's expensive *gihaz* signals to her husband's family members that her parents have not shortchanged her, and she belongs to a family that supports its daughters. The implications of indicating support for one's daughter are especially weighty in Egypt where married daughters rely on their parents to intervene on their behalf when there is marital conflict (Hoodfar 1997). Parental support is also understood to mean that a married daughter has a home where she will always be welcomed, giving her a fallback position in the event of separation. Displays of family support for the bride through material means thus have as their ends the symbolic enhancement of her gendered power in marriage.

Conclusion

The literature on waithood in the MENA emphasizes the material barriers to marriage given the social expectation that couples should pay for marriage costs and achieve economic independence before they wed. At the same time, several researchers point to the symbolic and relational components of marriage costs (Amin and Al-Bassusi 2004; Singerman 1995). Focusing on engaged couples who have already demonstrated their capacity for economic self-sufficiency, I acknowledge the instrumental role of matrimonial purchases. Material impediments to marriage are neither absent nor unimportant in the MENA, but contrary to the MENA waithood literature, I demonstrate that normative barriers are just as important, at least for those urban middle-class Egyptian youth who have successfully transitioned into the engagement stage of marriage. This study shows that cultural and symbolic rewards for conforming to matrimonial customs—and sanctions for violating them—perpetuate the institution of matrimonial transactions in spite of the tremendous financial difficulties they impose and the postponement of marriage that results.

From a practical standpoint, newlywed couples can certainly live comfortably without living room furniture, furniture for the bedroom of future children, rugs, a television, or the bride's new wardrobe, to give a few examples. But the overwhelming majority of my engaged respondents insisted that their homes be equipped with all the material trappings of a middle-class lifestyle *before* they married, even if it meant delaying marriage. Such large expenditures would be difficult to make after marriage, they said, so making them before marriage ensured their future consumption aspirations were met.

But in addition to its functional importance, I argue that the marriage fund has great symbolic importance, with matrimonial transactions constructing class and gender distinctions. For engaged individuals, making matrimonial outlays involves mobilizing resources to reap returns in their class standing, and by extension, their symbolic capital. Public celebrations and visits to newlyweds' homes involve conspicuous display of matrimonial goods that demonstrate adherence to the material standards that prevail in the middle class. Appropriate matrimonial expenditures are also driven by the desire to secure a favorable social ranking, and the desire to avoid loss of face or negative judgments about one's character or, in the case of brides, the character of one's parents. The need to conform is so strong that public displays of suitable matrimonial outlays sometimes involves deception, with couples resorting to front-stage performances that mask their intention to economize on certain purchases which are perceived to be "unnecessary."

Just as matrimonial transactions afford opportunities to "do class," they also offer opportunities to "do gender." I find that brides are expected to accumulate household goods that presume a feminine interest in decoration, cleaning, and cooking. Grooms are obliged by custom to provide a home and its furnishings, in addition to a steady supply of gifts throughout the engagement, in line with men's normative role as breadwinners. Gendered matrimonial expenditures communicate the individual's competence in the skills and knowledge appropriate to her or his sex category membership, offering rewards in terms of social prestige, while at the same time reflecting and reinforcing normative gender roles within marriage. In addition, ritualized situations related to the negotiation of matrimonial expenditures celebrate and perform gender difference. Marriage payments are also an important way in which the bride's family communicates its support for the bride and its willingness to step in on her behalf if there is any marital discord.

In sum, I find that matrimonial transactions relay important meanings related to class and gender and, as such, cannot be forgone openly without incurring some form of social sanction, often in the form of a loss of face or the attribution of negative characteristics to the young person, and in the case of brides, their parents. The potential to acquire symbolic capital provides an added incentive for young couples to abide by matrimonial customs. The resilience of the institution of matrimonial transactions can be attributed to the social and cultural benefits that accrue from adherence to matrimonial norms, even when they carry little functional meaning.

But this study also uncovers a number of symbolic mechanisms through which the institution of marriage produces and reproduces class and gender norms and hierarchies. First, respondents' narratives revealed that matrimonial transactions are an important vehicle for the transmission of social status inter-generationally. Adherence to matrimonial customs prevents young couples from experiencing downward mobility as they form new households. Matrimonial expenditures thus consolidate middle-class couples' existing privilege and their position of relative power in society. Second, matrimonial transactions position brides and grooms to take on a normative gender division of labor within marriage, and they replicate relations of dominance and subordination between husband and wife. Because men provide the conjugal home and their names are on the leases or ownership titles, women are in a position of vulnerability if the marriage turns sour. But matrimonial customs also provide wives with a form of insurance against male power. The *ayma*, or marriage inventory, provides the wife with a means to claim the contents of the conjugal home, the *shabka* gold, and the *muakhar* payment as her property. Third, I also show that adhering to matrimonial customs offers rewards in terms of reputability, honor, and social prestige. In other words, conformity enhances social actors' symbolic capital, which has the potential to be traded in for other types of Bourdieusian capital, such as economic or social capital. Those who cannot adhere to matrimonial customs not only lose out on such opportunities for generating capital, but they stand to sustain losses in terms of their dignity and self-esteem. Together these findings suggest that matrimonial transactions separate people into class and gender groups based on differences in access to matrimonial resources. Matrimonial goods are thus a medium through which advantaged social actors legitimate their existing social position, and through which disadvantaged actors experience exclusion.

Notes

1 The average duration of engagements in Egypt in 2006 was fifteen months, and in 2012 it was fourteen months (Salem 2015).
2 This vignette illustrates how the marriage of daughters is often prioritized over the marriage of sons in Egypt. This has to do with the cultural definition of marriage as the only legitimate venue for the expression of sexuality, a preoccupation with the preservation of unmarried women's chastity, and the stigma of singlehood for women beyond a certain age.
3 I use the terms normative and norms to refer to shared ideals that guide social actors' conduct, rather than typical behaviors actually enacted by social actors.
4 The same study shows that unfavorable labor market experiences (such as unemployment and low wages) have no effect on Egyptian women's marriage timing (Salem 2016b).
5 Although Islamic tradition requires that grooms provide a prompt dower (*mahr*), all my Muslim respondents reported that they circumvented this by recording a symbolic sum of twenty-five piasters in their marriage contracts. Among those who adhere to this tradition, the prompt dower is given by the groom to the bride and used by her to outfit the marital home. The bride's side typically hosts and pays for most expenses associated with the upholstery celebration (described in greater detail in the results section), which marks the transfer of the newlyweds' furniture and other goods to the conjugal home. The larger *henna* celebration is often held the night before the wedding and involves the application of henna to the bride's skin. This celebration can be hosted by the bride's or the groom's family; however, the majority of the costs are borne by the groom. Both the upholstery and *henna* celebrations can be held in the hosts' home, but more commonly take place in the street in front of the hosts' home. The ceremony in which Muslim couples sign the marriage contract, or the *katb el kitab*, is usually a smaller affair than the *henna*. It is usually hosted by the bride's side, but the groom must pay for all expenses, including the fee of the marriage registrar or *ma'zoun*.
6 It is possible that the increased availability of these amenities has meant lower prices for couples marrying today compared to past generations. The extant literature does not

include analyses of time trends in the cost of modern appliances. We do know, however, that real wages have declined over a twenty-year period (Said 2009), suggesting that the affordability of modern amenities has likely decreased or stayed the same.

7   Rao, for instance, notes that in one area of rural India the total cost of marriage is equivalent to the expenditures of a household for an entire year (1993). Zhang and Chang find that in Taiwan, the average dowry constitutes about six months' earnings for men or ten months' earnings for women, while bride-prices constitute approximately three months' earnings for men and six months' earnings for women (1999).

8   The questionnaire consisted of an asset list including the items television, video or DVD player, fan, air-conditioner, water heater, washer, and car. Respondents were selected into the sample if their natal household owned assets corresponding to those owned by the middle third of the wealth distribution, according to the Egypt Labor Market Panel Survey. Measures of household wealth are a commonly used proxy for socioeconomic status in developing countries, and in Egypt, several large-scale surveys, such as the Demographic and Health Survey and the Egypt Labor Market Panel survey, rely on asset lists to determine household wealth.

9   Christians constitute between 8 and 15 percent of Egypt's population, so they are underrepresented in this study. This can be attributed to our reliance on snowball sampling methods.

10 600 EGP was equivalent to approximately $107 USD at the time of the interview.

11 Parents (and for brides, brothers) often bought matrimonial goods for their engaged children. Brides tended to command greater contributions from family members, and family members often started amassing items for the bride's *gihaz* in her teenage years. In addition, brides and (less frequently) grooms sometimes received gifts of matrimonial goods from other relatives during their engagements.

12 Bride's fathers usually hold grooms accountable for commitments made in negotiations. In recognition of the hardship young people experience in financing marriage, respondents reported that some bride's fathers gave the groom leeway by agreeing to extend the engagement. In some instances, brides explained that their fathers would want the same leniency to be applied to their sons, who were destined to marry and face the same challenges someday.

13 This description is derived from both the respondents' narratives and my conversations with key informants.

14 The *muakhar* is a sum of money to which Muslim wives are entitled after divorce or the husband's death.

15 *Min el ibra lilsarookh* or "from the pin to the rocket" was a well-known mantra of the era of President Gamal Abdel Nasser, when the government emphasized self-sufficiency. The state aimed to manufacture all needs domestically, from the simplest items to the most technologically advanced to reduce dependence on the West.

16 Differences between matrimonial customs in Cairo and Al-Minya exist but are minimal. In Cairo, some grooms reported bearing the cost of the refrigerator and the children's bedroom was a point of negotiation, which was rare in Al-Minya. Unlike Al-Minya, in Cairo the cost of upholstery, rugs, and curtains was almost always assigned to the bride. Unlike Al-Minya, where the bride's gold was an important component of marriage costs, in Cairo most couples simply bought three rings for the bride and the *shabka* engagement party was

a small family affair. The upholstery celebration was bigger in Cairo than in Al-Minya, and *henna* and wedding celebrations were more often held in the street in Cairo.

17 My description of celebrations and visits to the homes of newlyweds is derived from the respondents' narratives and conversations with key informants.

18 All the respondents interviewed stated that in the future, the wife would stop working either after marriage or after childbearing. This suggests that once married, respondents planned to follow a gendered division of labor where wives were responsible for domestic work and childcare.

19 Respondents referred to these payments as a *masroof*, literally an "allowance," the same word used for the monthly allowance given by Egyptian husbands to their wives to cover household expenses. This practice, however, was relatively rare among the middle-class couples I interviewed.

20 This resonates with the Islamic principle of *kafa'a*, or equal status between marriage partners, which is usually gauged by drawing comparisons between the wealth or occupation of the groom and the bride's father (Hasso 2011).

References

Ali, K. A. (2002), *Planning the Family in Egypt: New Bodies, New Selves*, Cairo: American University in Cairo Press.

Amin, S. and M. Cain (1997), "The Rise of Dowry in Bangladesh," in G. W. Jones, R. M. Douglas, J. C. Caldwell and R. M. D'Souza (eds.), *The Continuing Demographic Transition*, 290–306, Oxford: Oxford University Press.

Amin, S. and N. Al-Bassusi (2004), "Education, Wage Work, and Marriage: Perspectives of Egyptian Working Women," *Journal of Marriage and Family*, 66 (5): 1287–99.

Assaad, R. and G. Barsoum (2009), "Rising Expectations and Diminishing Opportunities for Egypt's Young," in N. Dhillon and T. Yousef (eds.), *Generation in Waiting: The Unfulfilled Promise of Young People in the Middle East*, 67–94, Washington, DC: The Brookings Institution.

Assaad, R., C. Krafft and D. J. Rolando (2017), "The Role of Housing Markets in the Timing of Marriage in Egypt, Jordan, and Tunisia," *Economic Research Forum Working Paper Series*, 1081.

Bach, K. H. (1998), "The Vision of a Better Life: New Patterns of Consumption and Changed Social Relations," in N. Hopkins and K. Westergaard (eds.), *Directions of Change in Rural Egypt*, 184–200, Cairo: American University in Cairo Press.

Bhat, P. N. M. and S. S. Halli (1999), "Demography of Brideprice and Dowry: Causes and Consequences of the Indian Marriage Squeeze," *Population Studies*, 53 (2): 129–48.

Billig, M. (1991), "The Marriage Squeeze on High-caste Rajasthani Women," *Journal of Asian Studies*, 50 (2): 341–60.

Bourdieu, P. (1984), *Distinction: A Social Critique of the Judgement of Taste*, Cambridge: Harvard University Press.

Brines, J. (1994), "Economic Dependency, Gender, and the Division of Labor at Home," *American Journal of Sociology*, 100 (3): 652–88.

Burawoy, M. (1998), "The Extended Case Method," *Sociological Theory*, 16 (1): 4–33.

Caldwell, J. C., P. H. Reddy, and P. Caldwell (1983), "The Causes of Marriage Change in South India," *Population Studies*, 37 (3): 343–61.
Cherlin, A. J. (2004), "The Deinstitutionalization of American Marriage," *Journal of Marriage and Family*, 66 (4): 848–61.
Comaroff, J. L. (1980), "Introduction," in J. L. Comaroff (ed.), *The Meaning of Marriage Payments*, 1–47, London: Academic Press.
Dhillon, N., P. Dyer, and T. Yousef (2009), "Generation in Waiting: An Overview of School to Work and Family Formation Transitions," in N. Dhillon and T. Yousef (eds.), *Generation in Waiting: The Unfulfilled Promise of Young People in the Middle East*, 11–38, Washington, DC: The Brookings Institution.
DiMaggio, P. (1994), "Culture and the Economy," in N. J. Smelser and R. Swedberg (eds.), *The Handbook of Economic Sociology*, 27–57, New York and Princeton: Russell Sage Foundation and Princeton University Press.
Edin, K. and J. M. Reed (2015), "Why Don't They Just Get Married? Barriers to Marriage among the Disadvantaged," *The Future of Children*, 15 (2): 117–37.
Edin, K. and M. Kefalas (2005), *Promises I Can Keep: Why Poor Women Put Motherhood before Marriage*, Berkeley: University of California Press.
El-Kholy, H. (2000), "A Tale of Two Contracts: Towards a Situated Understanding of Women's Interests in Egypt," in C. Nelson and S. Rouse (eds.), *Situating Globalization: Views from Egypt*, 301–36, New Brunswick: Transaction Publishers.
Gibson-Davis, C. M., K. Edin and S. McLanahan (2005), "High Hopes but Even Higher Expectations: The Retreat from Marriage among Low-income Couples," *Journal of Marriage and Family*, 67 (5): 1301–12.
Goffman, E. (1959), *The Presentation of Self in Everyday Life*, New York: Anchor Press.
Goffman, E. (1976), "Gender Display," *Studies in the Anthropology of Visual Communications*, 3: 69–77.
Goody, J. (1973), "Bridewealth and Dowry in Africa and Eurasia," in J. Goody and S. J. Tambiah (eds.), *Bridewealth and Dowry*, 1–58, Cambridge: Cambridge University Press.
Habibi, N. (1997), "An Economic Analysis of the Prenuptial Agreement in Contemporary Iran," *Economic Development and Cultural Change*, 45 (2): 281–93.
Hannerz, U. (1992), *Cultural Complexity: Studies in the Social Organization of Meaning*, New York: Columbia University Press.
Hashemi, M. (2015), "Waithood and Face: Morality and Mobility among Lower Class Youth in Iran," *Qualitative Sociology*, 38: 261–83.
Hoodfar, H. (1997), *Between Marriage and the Market: Intimate Politics and Survival in Cairo*, Berkeley: University of California Press.
Hasso, F. (2011), *Consuming Desires: Family Crisis and the State in the Middle East*, Stanford: Stanford University Press.
Klaufus, C. (2012), "The Symbolic Dimension of Mobility: Architecture and Social Status in Ecuadorian Informal Settlements," *International Journal of Urban and Regional Research*, 36 (4): 689–705.
Lever, J., D. A. Frederick, and R. Hertz (2015), "Who Pays for Dates? Following Versus Challenging Gender Norms," *SAGE Open*, 5: 1–14.
Lindenbaum, S. (1981), "Implications for Women of Changing Marriage Transactions in Bangladesh," *Studies in Family Planning*, 12 (11): 394–401.

Moors, A. (1994), "Women and Dower Property in Twentieth-century Palestine: The Case of Jabal Nablus," *Islamic Law and Society*, 1 (3): 301–31.
Oppenheimer, V. K., M. Kalmijn and N. Lim (1997), "Men's Career Development and Marriage Timing during a Period of Rising Inequality," *Demography*, 34 (3): 311–30.
Rao, V. (1993), "The Rising Price of Husbands: A Hedonic Analysis of Dowry Increases in Rural India," *The Journal of Political Economy*, 101 (4): 666–77.
Remez, L. (1998), "In Turkey, Women's Fertility is Linked to Education, Employment and Freedom to Choose a Husband," *International Family Planning Perspectives*, 24 (2): 97–8.
Ridgeway, C. (2011), *Framed by Gender: How Gender Inequality Persists in the Modern World*, New York: Oxford University Press.
Said, M. (2009), "The Fall and Rise of Earnings and Inequality in Egypt: New Evidence from the Egypt Labor Market Panel Survey 2006," in R. Assaad (ed.), *The Egyptian Labor Market Revisited*, 53–82, Cairo: American University in Cairo Press.
Salem, R. (2015), "Changes in the Institution of Marriage in Egypt from 1998 to 2012," in R. Assaad and C. Krafft (eds.), *The Egyptian Labor Market in an Era of Revolution*, 162–81, Oxford: Oxford University Press.
Salem, R. (2016a), "Imagined Crises: Assessing Evidence of Delayed Marriage and Never-marriage in Contemporary Egypt," in K. Celello and H. Kholoussy (eds.), *Domestic Tensions, National Anxieties: Global Perspectives on Marriage Crisis*, 231–54, Oxford: Oxford University Press.
Salem, R. (2016b), "Labor Market Experiences' Gendered Effects on Marriage Timing in Egypt," *Demographic Research*, 35: 283–314.
Salem, R. (2018), "Matrimonial Transactions and the Enactment of Class and Gender Difference among Egyptian Youth," *Qualitative Sociology* 41(3): 399-421.
Scarborough, R. C. (2012), "Managing Challenges on the Front Stage: The Face-work Strategies of Musicians," *Poetics*, 40 (6): 542–64.
Sherman, J. (2006), "Coping with Rural Poverty: Economic Survival and Moral Capital in Rural America," *Social Forces*, 85 (2): 891–207.
Singerman, D. (1995), *Avenues of Participation: Family, Politics, and Networks in Urban Quarters of Cairo*, Princeton: Princeton University Press.
Singerman, D. (2007), "The Economic Imperatives of Marriage: Emerging Practices and Identities among Youth in the Middle East," *Middle East Youth Initiative Working Paper* No. 6.
Singerman, D. and B. Ibrahim (2003), "The Cost of Marriage in Egypt: A Hidden Variable in the New Arab Demography," *Cairo Papers in Social Science*, 24: 80–116.
Smock, P. J., W. D. Manning, and M. Porter (2005), "'Everything's There Except Money': How Money Shapes Decisions to Marry among Cohabiters," *Journal of Marriage and Family*, 67 (3): 680–96.
Veblen, T. (1998), *The Theory of the Leisure Class: An Economic Study of Institutions*, Amherst: Prometheus Books.
Wendo, C. (2004), "African Women Denounce Bride Price," *The Lancet*, 363: 716.
West, C. and D. Zimmerman (1987), "Doing Gender," *Gender and Society*, 1 (2): 125–51.
White, B. T. (2009), "Saving Face: The Benefits of Not Saying I'm Sorry," *Law and Contemporary Problems*, 72: 261–9.
Zelizer, V. (2005), *The Purchase of Intimacy*, Princeton: Princeton University Press.
Zhang, J. and W. Chang (1999), "Dowry and Wife's Welfare: A Theoretical and Empirical Analysis," *Journal of Political Economy*, 107 (4): 786–808.

Between Fashion and Tesettür: Marketing and Consuming Women's Islamic Dress

by Banu Gökarıksel and Anna Secor

What is tesettür? The term comes from the Arabic root s-t-r, meaning covering. It is used in Turkish to signify a set of Islamic practices wherein women cover their heads and bodies and avoid contact with unrelated men. But tesettür has proven to be a slippery signifier in Turkish society. Is it a spiritual concept, an ideal of Islamic womanhood that devout Muslim women may strive toward throughout their lives? Or is it a mode of dress, a set of sartorial signifiers that can shift with the seasons? Since the 1980s, fashionable Islamic dress for women, widely associated with the rise of political Islam and a new Muslim bourgeoisie, has become a growing segment of the textile industry in Turkey. The leading companies in this new tesettür industry present themselves as putting fashion in the service of Islam and thereby counter critics' accusations that they are "selling Islam."

Our research takes place within the taut space of tension between fashion and women's Islamic dress, or tesettür. The global growth of "an Islamic consumer sector, which explicitly forges links between religiosity and fashion, encouraging Muslims to be both covered and fashionable, modest and beautiful" has been the focus of a small but growing literature (Moors and Tarlo 2007: 138; see also Abaza 2007; Akou 2007; Balasescu 2003, 2007; Gökarıksel and Secor 2009; Jones 2007; Kılıçbay and Binark 2002; Sandıkcı and Ger 2002, 2005, 2007). This literature has produced a rich analysis of the emergence of Islamic fashion in a variety of contexts, paying special attention to women's engagements with piety and fashion through their everyday practices of dress. Yet few studies have attempted to work *between and across* the marketing and consumption of Islamic fashion. In this paper we aim to fill this gap by analyzing both how companies represent and sell the new styles and how women respond to such representations and consume Islamic fashion, making it one part of their complex embodied performances of identity. We trace out how marketing images seek to suture tesettür and fashion at the same time as consumers negotiate them as competing pulls to which they devise contingent solutions in their everyday practices of dress.

Gökarıksel, B. and A. Secor (2010), "Between Fashion and Tesettür: Marketing and Consuming Women's Islamic Dress," *Journal of Middle East Women's Studies* 6 (3): 118–48.

This chapter draws mostly from our focus group research with consumers in Istanbul and Konya and seeks to provide a snapshot of some of the ways covered (*kapalı*) women in Turkey negotiate the relationship between style and tesettür. In order to throw into relief what our research participants see as the tension between tesettür-as-Islamic-dress and tesettür-as-fashion, we begin with a visual analysis of the recent (2006–8) catalogues of eleven prominent tesettür-producing firms. Using techniques of visual analysis, we show how these images work to represent these clothes as both stylish and appropriate for pious Muslim women.

Next, we turn to our focus group discussions, in which we asked women to respond to various images from company catalogues. Here we find that, for many covered women in Turkey today, much of what companies call tesettür is simply fashion; for them, tesettür continues to denote an ideal of women's modest dress as interpreted from the Qur'an. And yet at the same time as women dismiss these images as "not tesettür," they also accept that there are questions of age, personal preference, and style when making choices about dress. These focus group discussions betray a general understanding that the way women wear tesettür-fashion is influenced by a series of contingencies and therefore that they wear it in different ways. We argue that, when it comes to covered dress in Turkey, what is acceptable, for whom, and under what circumstances is a contingent and shifting determination. Indeed, the styles presented in the catalogues of prominent companies shimmer on the horizon of what is acceptable, of what may be considered tesettür in Turkish society. Finally, our study of these representations and their reception among their target market[1] reveals the fissured and hybrid practices that emerge in the gap between marketing and embodying Muslim women's dress in Turkey.

The Tesettür-Fashion Nexus in Turkey

The tesettür-fashion nexus in Turkey has emerged over the past thirty years from a particular constellation of economic and political developments. In order to understand the current milieu, it is important to keep in mind that, since its founding in 1923, Turkey has been a constitutionally secular state with a majority Muslim population. As part of the broad cultural reforms attempted by the secular state, the wearing of headscarves was discouraged in the first decades of the Turkish Republic (Göle 1996). Yet while many Turkish women, especially in urban areas, entered into public arenas with their heads uncovered, throughout the first decades of the Republic the headscarf maintained its casual presence among large sectors of Turkish society. With increasing migration from the rural areas of Anatolia into Turkey's urban centers in the 1960s and 70s (Erder 2001; Karpat 1976), the headscarf came to be associated with the lower-class status and rural origins of migrants (Gökarıksel 2007; Secor 2002; Öncü 1999; White 2002).

In the 1980s, however, the role of the headscarf and Islamic dress in Turkey entered into a new phase of political and cultural contention. Economic restructuring in Turkey spurred by IMF structural adjustment in the 1980s and Turkey's entrance into a Customs Union with the EU contributed to the rise of a new entrepreneurial class of conservative businessmen with roots outside of Turkey's urban, secularist elite (Adas 2006; Buğra 1998; 2003; Tokatlı 2003; Yavuz 2003). At the same time, the political restructuring of Turkish society following the 1980 coup d'état led to the repression of leftist politics and the ascendance of Islam as an increasingly prominent political and cultural force. Together, these shifting economic and political sands gave rise to what in Turkey has been called a new Islamic bourgeoisie, an aspiring middle class with tastes and distinctions far removed from the secular, Western-oriented lifestyles of the dominant Turkish elite (Göle 1999; Göle and Ammann 2006; Navaro-Yashin 2002; Saktanber 2002; White 1999, 2002). In this context, a new style of women's modest dress began to appear in the 1980s among young women in urban areas. Neither fashionable nor an industry at that time, tesettür consisted mainly of boxy ankle-length overcoats and large patterned scarves drawn tightly around the face and draped over the neck and shoulders. The colors were muted, dark or neutral. Many of the coats were sewn at home or by tailors; yet, a few early companies began to advertise tesettür styles using simple line-drawn illustrations that left women's faces undrawn (Kılıçbay and Binark 2002; Sandıkcı and Ger 2007). Worn by young, urban women with interests in attending university, this new mode of dress became associated with the headscarf protests that erupted on Turkish campuses beginning in the mid-1980s. Indeed, during this period there was increasing enforcement of a headscarf ban that affected public offices such as courts, government offices, Parliament, military facilities, and public universities (Olson 1985; Özdalga 1998). Over the course of the following decades, the headscarf has become a high-profile political issue in Turkish society (Secor 2005).

From this early emergence of a distinctly urban and modern style of covering has evolved a significant, diverse, and profitable tesettür-fashion industry. Our survey of tesettür-producing firms in Turkey shows that the industry has exploded since the late 1990s, with 50 percent of surveyed firms having been established between 1996 and 2008.[2] The proliferation of the tesettür-fashion industry has taken place in tandem with both the rise of Islam-oriented political parties in Turkey since 1994[3] and a broader trend toward the marketing of Islamic products and lifestyles (Fealy and White 2008; Fischer 2008; Henry and Wilson 2004). Today's tesettür producers market colorful, diverse, and constantly changing styles. In the last decade, Tekbir and its competitors (Aydan, SetrMS, Selam, Armine, and others) have become recognizable brand names with glossy catalogues, advertisements, and even fashion shows that send professional models down the runway wearing not only everyday wear, but also the impossible concoctions of haute couture. With hotel weddings, beach vacations, and country club sports becoming desirable elements of a high-class Islamic lifestyle (Bilici 1999), tesettür-producers manufacture and market covered swimwear, bridal gowns, sportswear, suits, and maternity clothes. The styles, colors, and cuts of this apparel vary greatly, from bold and close-fitting to more conservative looks. Whether and to what extent these styles and their marketing are "Islamic" is a topic of ongoing debate (Aktaş 1991; Eygi 2005; Navaro-Yashin 2002; Şişman 2001). Through an analysis of the representation of these styles in company catalogues, and of the ways in which covered women in Turkey view the styles, the goal of this article is to provide insight into how women's fashion and the question of tesettür become negotiable elements of everyday practice.

Analysis of Catalogue Images

Our visual analysis of the recent catalogues of some prominent tesettür-producing firms surveys the field of images and projected lifestyles that confront consumers of Islamic dress in Turkey. We selected these catalogues because they represent the collections of several of the most prominent brands in the industry (see Table 23.1). In addition, based on our broader survey, we find that these companies are generally representative of the sector in terms of location, when they were founded, their overall size, and the percentage of their production that they would call tesettür.

The approach we take to this analysis is what Gillian Rose (2001) has called a "critical visual methodology." Following Rose, our visual analysis of these catalogues takes place through three modalities: technological, or the visual technology of catalogue images; compositional, or the formal strategies of the image; and social, or more broadly, "the

Table 23.1 Basic data on the eleven firms whose catalogues were part of the analysis

Name	Year founded	Location of HQ	Number of branches	Number of employees	Annual prod. In USD millions	Percent of prod. in tesettür
Armine	1982	Istanbul	4	48	3–7	75–90
Aydan	1980	Istanbul	2	37	NA	>90
Dicle	1991	Istanbul	4	109	3–7	51–75
Eliz	2007	Konya	0	25	0.7–1.0	75–90
Hünerli	1992	Konya	0	61	0.7–1.0	51–75
Selam	1993	Istanbul	2	55	NA	10–25
SetrMS	1974	Ankara	9	215	7–10	51–75
Sitare	1995	Ankara	2	90	0.7–1.0	75–90
Şelale	1993	Ankara	0	73	3–7	26–50
Tekbir	1982	Istanbul	33	1,450	>10	>90
Tuğba	1996	Istanbul	7	303	3–7	51–75

range of economic, social and political relations, institutions and practices that surround an image and through which it is seen and used" (17). While our analysis proceeds from and through catalogue images, we are particularly interested in the social production of these visual representations and the multiplicity of their effects. We regard these catalogues not only as demonstrating the visions of the producers (i.e., their ideas about their potential customers' aspirations and desires), but also as working to *teach viewers to see and to desire in particular ways* (Appadurai 1996). In other words, these images are not passive representations of a particular style, but rather active participants in the ongoing struggle over the (re)definition of fashion, femininity, class, and tesettür. In this section, we present an overview of the catalogues with regard to their technological and compositional modalities before turning to the social modalities of the images in the following section.

In terms of their visual technology, many of these images appear in both print and web catalogues. The print catalogues that we collected are of two varieties: the very large, heavy, often oddly shaped ones, and the small, light ones that are clearly designed to be mailed. For the former, metallic print on the cover (SetrMS, Hünerli, and Sitare), extra high gloss paper (Eliz and Sitare), and vibrant colors lend a feeling of opulence to the catalogues themselves. Oversized with non-standard proportions and filled with professional photographs of models, these catalogues seem to announce that no expense was spared in their production. Visually, the images presented are strikingly different from the very simple line drawings of early industry advertisements. On the websites of these companies, catalogues are usually posted under the title "Collections." Catalogue images are displayed one page at a time, often with accompanying (shopping mall-type) music. The images on the website do not differ from those in the catalogues. These are not sites where consumers can order clothes, since internet shopping has yet to become popular in Turkey. Instead, they are sites that profile the company, display the styles, and provide the addresses of retail outlets carrying the brand. Some sites, such as SetrMS and Tuğba, are up to date, very stylish, and visually appealing. Many, however, are somewhat or very much out of date, with the most recent collections posted a year to six years ago.[4] It appears that the print catalogue is still the leading way for these companies to display images of their products—though print and television advertisements, billboards, and store windows are likely to be more important media for reaching a wide market, since these catalogues are more like coffee table books than circulars. The image of a woman in a white dress, a black and white floral headscarf, dramatic gold jewelry, and an evening bag present on Armine billboards in Istanbul in the summer of 2009, for example, also appeared in the company's 2009 summer collection catalogue.

There are many similarities across these images in terms of their compositional modalities. With the exception of Tekbir's and Dicle's, all of the catalogues display a single woman on each page. She is a vertical shape usually centered in the middle of the page. This verticality is emphasized by the styles portrayed, with the long raincoats and narrow lines usually broken only by a handbag (Figure 23.1). The overcoated model

Figure 23.1 Catalogue image from Sitare, Fall–Winter 2008–09. Courtesy of Sitare Giyim.

is like a pillar, a column placed in the foreground of a scene that is often no more than an artificial montage. As in Figure 23.1, the model is often not actually on location but rather part of a Photoshop assemblage. While many of the catalogues do not show any background environment (just an abstract design behind the image of the woman), others pose the models within luxurious interiors, vacation-like scenes, or European-looking urban environments. The SetrMS catalogue goes furthest with this latter motif by placing models in front of collages of foreign skylines and historical sites (see Figure 23.2). The catalogue is laid out like a scrapbook with travel photos and strips of negatives assembled behind images of chic women wearing headscarves, mid-length

Figure 23.2 Catalogue image from SetrMS, Spring–Summer 2008. Courtesy of SetrMS.

coats, and pants. The images underline the idealized mobility of the SetrMS consumer, her ability to travel, to experience the goods of the world, and to fit in as a member of the cosmopolitan elite.

An alternative narrative of cosmopolitanism structures the images in Şelale's catalogue for their label İklim. The catalogue features models posed in outerwear (ankle-length coats, headscarves, and handbags) within an opulent interior decorated in a style meant to evoke an Ottoman heritage.[5] The walls are decorated with historical maps of the Dardanelles, Greece, and Italy, and miniature portraits of Ottoman figures. Prominently displayed on bookshelves behind the models is a collection of travel and history books with English and Turkish titles such as "Vienna," "Renaissance," and "Troia" (Troy). Thus while SetrMS places its models as tourists in Paris, Şelale likewise blurs the boundaries between "Europe" and "Asia," but by positioning them within a narrative of Ottoman cosmopolitanism. More conspicuously, Tekbir has also drawn on Ottoman motifs in its designs, as illustrated by the ornate detailing and especially the turban-like headgear shown in

Figure 23.3 Catalogue image from Tekbir, Spring–Summer 2007. Courtesy of Tekbir Giyim.

Figure 23.3. Note also that the color of this ensemble, a chartreuse tone, was very much in fashion in spring 2007, as was the hint of suggestive tulle, here improbably peeking out beneath the ankle-length skirt.

The models in these catalogues sometimes gaze directly at the camera, but more often they look off to one side or another, perhaps to signal their modesty. Rarely are they seen in any pose other than standing, though some of the women in Aydan's 2008 catalogue sit, lean, and, in one case, almost sprawl. The models wear full makeup, though they never have bright red lips or colored polish on their fingernails. In line with popular standards of beauty in Turkey, they are generally light-skinned and often green- or blue-eyed. The colors of the clothes are often bright, though white and gray are also popular. Many catalogues feature dramatic red overcoats and outfits, the significance of which we discuss when we turn to our focus group analysis. The overall effect of these images is typical for a clothing catalogue. As in other fashion catalogues, what is on

299

display and being marketed is not just an outfit, but a complex set of aspirations about lifestyle, taste, and beauty.

What is particular to this case is how these tropes intersect with another strong component of these images, and that is their portrayal of Islamic dress. While some catalogues show pictures only of women wearing headscarves (Tekbir, Hünerli, SetrMS, Aydan, and Armine), others mix images of women with heads covered and uncovered. The Sitare catalogue shows women in headscarves from page one to twenty-one, but uses a different, uncovered, light-haired model in the last ten pages. These latter pages also portray more "uncovered"-type styles such as a short-sleeved blouse and a waist-length jacket. While Sitare puts these images in the back of the catalogue—almost as though they were the "interior" images, sequestered from the public in the same way as the covered woman's body might be—Dicle intersperses images of women in headscarves with images of a blue-eyed, long-haired blonde woman modeling floor-length overcoats. This is an odd image strategy because it is generally unlikely that uncovered women in Turkey would wear such dramatically long coats; not only does the length transgress the fashion norms of the moment, but the style is closely associated with tesettür. Perhaps Dicle is attempting to appeal to the broadest possible market by displaying this style on an uncovered woman, but more likely these images work by making *covered* women feel that the style is universally appealing, that they are able to participate in "fashion" in a way that includes them within a broad consuming class. Tuğba, which also intersperses images of covered and uncovered women in its catalogues, seems more convincingly to be trying to appeal to both groups of consumers. The styles shown on the uncovered women are shorter, with coats hitting mid-thigh. These juxtapositions seem to say to the covered woman, "You are included within the realm of style and fashion. There is no difference between you and any other woman. You too desire to be beautiful, chic, and individual."

Finally, there are two exceptional catalogues in the group. The Eliz catalogue uses a single dark-haired, dark-eyed model who displays styles on each page with her head uncovered. Interspersed with floor-length coats are shorter coats modeled with bare legs exposed. On the final page, she wears a short jacket that is open over her midriff, revealing a pierced naval. And at the other end of the spectrum, Selam's catalogue reverts to earlier norms of tesettür advertising and refrains from showing any women's faces throughout. Each page has an image of a woman standing serenely in either a floor-length overcoat or a shorter, tunic-like coat worn over pants. In each case, her head is cut off at the top of the page, though the bottom of the headscarf is visible at the opening of the lapels (see Figure 23.4). This strategy of not showing women's faces was common in the early tesettür ads of the 1980s and reflects concerns for women's modesty and the norms of representation in Islam (see Kılıçbay and Binark 2002).

Of these eleven firms, Selam is the one with the least of its production in specifically tesettür-style clothing. In other words, the choice to produce a markedly conservative

Figure 23.4 Catalogue image from Selam, Spring–Summer 2008. Courtesy of Selam Tekstil Ltd. St.

catalogue does not necessarily reflect a more ideological commitment to tesettür, but rather appears to be a marketing strategy. Indeed, even though Selam goes to the extreme in not showing faces, it features short coats over pants, a combination whose acceptability as tesettür is in question (see focus group discussion below). While other catalogues seem to emphasize the lack of difference between covered and uncovered women, Selam's strategy is to create a unique and explicitly Islamic look for its catalogue. In order to further untangle some of the social modalities of these images, we turn to our focus groups with consumers of Islamic fashion in Istanbul and Konya.

Ways of Seeing: Focus Group Responses to Images

In May–June 2009, we conducted six focus group interviews with consumers of tesettür clothing. There were eight women in each group and the interviews lasted from two to two and a half hours. Five of these focus groups were in Istanbul and one was in Konya. The groups in Istanbul were differentiated according to age and socioeconomic status. We organized our interviews with young/middle-aged women (ages twenty-five to thirty-five)[6] into two groups according to their socioeconomic status (AB and CD). Similarly, we interviewed two groups of older women (ages forty-five to sixty) of AB and CD socioeconomic status. One group in Istanbul consisted of the youngest research participants, spanning the age range eighteen to twenty-five. The consumer group in Konya was mixed in terms of age and socioeconomic status. In addition to open-ended questions about their practices of veiling, fashion, and shopping, we asked women to discuss ten images we had selected from the catalogues and fashion shows of prominent tesettür companies, including Tekbir and Armine. We also included a snapshot of a street scene showing different styles of covering and an image clipped from a newspaper article about a fashion show. We passed around color photocopies of these images two at a time, usually toward the middle of the session.

In all of the groups, women responded to the catalogue images by overwhelmingly stating that none could be considered tesettür by their standards. There was general agreement on this point even in the groups with the most disagreement. The discussion of the images then proceeded to evaluate the styles, colors, fabrics, and cuts, as well as their compositional and professional, technical aspects. The participants described in detail and debated which age group, individual style, and lifestyle the particular outfit under discussion could be appropriate and acceptable for. Another layer was added to the discussion when the participants considered whether or not they themselves would wear a particular style. This series of contingencies determined the wearability of these clothes, not strictly as tesettür but as a mediation between the demands of fashion and the demands of covering.

The first image we asked our participants to respond to was a street scene from the Fatih neighborhood of Istanbul photographed in 2004, showing women dressed in different covered styles. In the foreground there is an older woman wearing a long, blue, loose-fitting overcoat and a large headscarf, carrying a plastic bag. This is generally considered tesettür, the kind of clothing that came to be seen in the 1970s and 80s. It is the headscarf-coat combination that tesettür companies developed, altered, and diversified. In the focus groups it was recognized as tesettür by most, but was quickly dismissed as unwearable by many because it was out of fashion, a style they described as "grandma." To the left of this older woman in the photo are two young women wearing sporty outfits in that year's trendy cuts and colors, underneath bold and colorful headscarves. One wears a bright pink and white-patterned headscarf that matches a pink tunic and ankle-length white skirt. The other has an orange, red, and black headscarf, a pink top, a short white jacket, a long black skirt, and white slouchy boots. Their styles showcase the 2004 youth fashion.

> Moderator: Now we have some photographs we'd like to show you. Please take a look at the first one and tell me what you think. We'll see different tesettür outfits now. Tell me if you like them, and what sort of differences you see between them.
> Nuray: This is what everyone calls "modern" these days. And then there's the old style, what our grandmothers [wear].
> Ayşe: This is a much more colourful and joyful outfit. It has the flair of the new summer season; it's more modern. And then this one is more in line with the old style, what our grandmothers used to wear.
> Zeynep: I don't quite understand what you mean by the "old style." Is that what covering is? [Covering] is not a style of dress but a style of belief, and it has its boundaries and rules. If we believe those rules, if we signify that belief, we have to act within those boundaries.
> Ayşe: But everyone considers age-appropriateness.
> Özge: Well, maybe most people, I mean we all covered because of our faith, obviously. That's for sure. But even when I wasn't covered, there were things I would wear and things I wouldn't wear. You see? I would wear skirts but I wouldn't wear a miniskirt, you know?
> Zeynep: Being covered cannot be your style.
> Özge: We're talking about clothes, not the headscarf.
> Moderator: So you're saying that there cannot be different styles of covering.
> Zeynep: When I say there can't be, I mean there could be a style in colours, or maybe in the cut. However, apart from that, farz and Sünnet determine the rules [of Islamic dress].[7] You have to obey those rules if you're covering because of your faith.

The identification of "old" in contrast to "more modern" fashionable styles of covering in this discussion was echoed in all the other focus groups. Here "modern," a loaded concept that is often understood to be implicitly secular in Turkey, is indexed to fashion and its constant demand for being up to date. It signals participation in the ever-shifting economic and cultural cycles of fashion. Yet this discussion proceeds to reveal the tension between tesettür and style. Zeynep's objection to using "style" as a lens to look at and talk about tesettür stands out.

Paired with the street photo discussed above was a Tekbir catalogue picture. Two women are seen in the square of an exclusive gated community, with pointy high-heeled shoes showing beneath long skirts and coats. The colors are bright. One woman wears a white coat over a white blouse and a long coral-red skirt. The other wears a coat in the same coral shade over a coral, pink, and yellow flowered dress. The women sport matching coral, yellow, and white headscarves. It is an urban and sophisticated scene. In different focus groups women challenged both the fashionableness of these outfits and their appropriateness as tesettür. The objection to these outfits from the perspective of covering was their color. The following discussion from the group of mixed age and socioeconomic status in Konya captures some of these reactions:

> Nala: I might not include the second one completely in tesettür. Someone who's completely covered wouldn't wear this red. This is modern covering, tesettür is different. But this is chic.
> Filiz: I agree.
> Elif: There should be less attention-getting things [in tesettür].
> Moderator: What is the difference between covering and tesettür?
> İlknur: Drawing attention.
> Nalan: The extreme, religiously motivated covering would have a muted palette of colors that doesn't draw attention. This woman [in the picture] is saying, "I'm covered but this is my görgü [cultural capital], my habit, I will dress stylishly. I'm covered and I'm chic."

Ideally, a woman who is covered should not draw attention, but the color red clearly attracts the eye. Across the groups, women debated the colors of tesettür and especially the question of wearing red. They argued that in Islam, red is considered *haram* (banned) for women's outerwear. Yet Tekbir, which prides itself on directing women to appropriate tesettür styles, is promoting this color as stylish and distinctive (see also Gökarıksel and Secor 2010).

For some women, the question of wearing red came down to the delicate distinction between shades: one woman said that a darker red would be acceptable, but not a bright red. Whether one dressed in subdued colors or bright ones seemed to be a defining characteristic of personal style, with many young women (and a fair number of older women) often asserting their preference for lively hues. In these discussions, color became a touchstone for the question of personal preferences and how they mediate religious imperatives.

While some women considered the outfits chic but too showy (as the previous discussion shows), other women considered them boxy and shapeless. Younger women often spoke of Tekbir styles as being lady-ish (i.e., unstylish, for older women). As one woman put it, wearing some of these styles would be "like wearing a tablecloth." Regarding a series of Tekbir catalogue photos, women were critical of the cut and the detailing of the clothes:

> Yelda: I don't think these clothes complement one another, they don't fit [the models] properly.
> Moderator: Which one?
> Yelda: All of them. These denim clothes, for example.
> Özlem: The cut is too simple. There's nothing special about the design. The fabric is simply cut and draped over [the models]. I can take this tablecloth and put it

over my head now. That's what these clothes look like. They definitely don't have anything distinctive, anything different [in their design].

Elif: If these clothes had a bit more detailing, I might wear them. But I wouldn't wear all denim like that [jeans under a long denim tunic], I'd wear something different underneath.

In women's criticisms of catalogue photos, the coordination of colors was significant: the combination of scarf, coat, and whatever is worn underneath was an important element of style. Handbags and shoes were also frequently mentioned as items to be carefully coordinated. Women often objected to tables in which the palette was too narrow, with pants and coat in the same hue, as Elif does above. These outfits looked like uniforms or picnic clothes to them and lacked the frisson of fashion.

In addition to discussing the aesthetics of the fashions themselves, women also shared observations regarding the technological modality of the images: the quality of the catalogue, its production value, and the overall impression of professionalism. The question of presentation was important to them; they did not want to see images that were carelessly put together just to display the clothes. They demanded that all the elements of sleek advertisement be present in the catalogue images: professional photography, professional models, tastefully designed scenes, and attention to every detail, such as the pinning of a scarf. The look as a whole and the model's ability to carry it, to pull it off, were all put into question in the focus group discussions. Just as we observed in our analysis of industry catalogues, it was an entire consumer lifestyle that women considered to be at stake in these photos.

Conclusion

Ayşe: Honestly, tesettür has really gone haywire, it's turned into something else.
Moderator: How did it go haywire?
Ayşe: It did, I swear.
Moderator: How was it originally?
Ayşe: It had to do with faith, covering your head, not revealing the shape of your body. I've been covered since the age of 12 and I covered of my own will. But now I feel like even I have to keep up with the changing fashion trends. Because I can't find what I want.
Özge: "Even I have changed," you're saying.
Ayşe: I started to buy a size smaller, and then another size, and finally now my outfit sticks to my body. Fashion designers have caused this.

There is a deep ambivalence in the relationship between tesettür and fashion. For Ayşe, the decision to veil came early and for religious reasons, but even for her the compulsion of fashion has changed how she interprets covered dress. Ayşe is a twenty-seven-year-old woman who introduced herself as having foregone university education because of her decision to wear a headscarf and instead has been taking various classes, including courses in home tailoring. She said she puts this training to use and often makes alterations to personalize purchased clothing items. She came to the focus group dressed in a majestic long gray coat and a striking gray and purple headscarf, an outfit she jokingly introduced to the group as "elegant." She feels that tesettür has gone haywire, and yet she herself continues to fit into the ever more form-fitting clothes promoted by the tesettür-fashion industry. Despite the piety that underwrites her choice to cover, personal style and fashion are important to her. Thus while she insists that tesettür should be a single piece—that is, a long coat rather than a tunic-pants combination—within these self-imposed parameters she finds room for personal style and interpretation. The coat she wore to the focus group was tailored, with precise detailing, and her comments throughout the group discussion revealed her fashion consciousness.

Ayşe's story underlines women's recognition that fashion is transforming the ways in which tesettür is worn. Thus while some tesettür-producing companies (such as Tekbir and Aydan) claim to be putting fashion in the service of an Islamic ideal of covering, in fact the fashion industry is actively shifting the frontiers and diversifying the realm of tesettür. As the catalogue images we have discussed show, tesettür-fashion companies are marketing a cosmopolitan lifestyle that embraces covered women within the pleasures of consumption, personal style, and beauty. They promote tesettür-fashion as seamlessly combining piety and fashion. Yet our focus group participants challenge this fundamental premise of Islamic fashion marketing. In their view the relationship between tesettür and fashion is fraught with tensions. On the one hand, they see a disjuncture between the Islamic ideal of tesettür and the images these companies put forward. On the other hand, they recognize the role of style, fashion, and personal preference in their own sartorial practices. While there may be no easy reconciliation between the demands for modesty that underlie tesettür and the spectacle of ever-changing fashion, women do not simply reject tesettür-fashion. They accept the disjuncture between tesettür and fashion and knowingly engage in a constant mediation between the two. This mediation becomes central to their sense of self and their embodied performances of identity. Their complex engagements with piety and fashion in the context of their personal preferences, social environments, class, and age demonstrate that it cannot be assumed, even for the devout, that Islamic injunctions regarding modesty operate in a transhistorical, decontextualized way to determine Muslim women's dress. While the women in our focus groups held up this ideal, they also talked about accommodating other aesthetic considerations and personal desires in their lived practices of dress. Neither eyes-to-heaven ascetics nor the vacant-eyed, coquettish Lolitas of the catalogues, these women actively stake out a middle ground in a long continuum of choices between fashion and tesettür.

Notes

1. In 2008, we conducted a survey of 174 tesettür-producing companies in Turkey. Participating firms included both retail and wholesale operations. We estimate this to be 80–90 percent of firms with a significant presence in the tesettür market operating in Turkey today. Half of the firms surveyed considered tesettür clothing to comprise over 90 percent of their production; 75 percent of the firms reported over 50 percent of their production to be tesettür clothing. Our survey research shows that women between the ages of nineteen and forty are the prime target market for the tesettür-producing firms, with a substantial 80 percent of firms also considering women between the ages of forty-one and sixty to be an important market. We conducted focus groups with consumers between the ages of eighteen and fifty. These groups of eight women each were organized by age and socioeconomic status. Participants did not previously know each other. The discussions were conducted in Turkish, and the excerpts quoted here were translated by the authors.
2. See Gökarıksel and Secor (2010) for a more detailed analysis of survey results.
3. In the 1994 municipal elections, an explicitly Islamic political party (Refah Partisi or Welfare Party) surprised the pundits by coming to power not only in many rural municipalities but in Turkey's major urban centers of Ankara and Istanbul. Since then, Islam-oriented political parties have taken increasingly large proportions of the vote in both municipal and national elections. Turkey's current ruling Adalet ve Kalkınma Partisi (AKP, Justice and Development Party) emerged from the more moderate branch of the Islamist parties of the 1990s. It does not call itself an Islamist political party but is generally pro-Islam in orientation.
4. One reason for not making current styles available online may be the concern about other companies replicating the designs as much cheaper knock-offs. This worry was mentioned in focus group discussions with sales assistants as well as in interviews with company representatives.
5. We could not obtain the company's permission to print this image.
6. Many of our research participants viewed themselves as "middle-aged" and referred to those in their teens or early twenties and single as "young."
7. *Farz* (*fardh*) are the obligatory duties specified in the Qur'an, while *Sünnet* (Sunna) are based on the Prophet Muhammad's words, actions, and practices.

References

Abaza, M. (2007), "Shifting Landscapes of Fashion in Contemporary Egypt," *Fashion Theory*, 11: 281–98.

Adas, E. B. (2006), "The Making of Entrepreneurial Islam and the Islamic Spirit of Capitalism," *Journal for Cultural Research*, 10 (2): 113–37.

Akou, H. M. (2007), "Building a New 'World Fashion': Islamic Dress in the Twenty-first Century," *Fashion Theory*, 11: 403–22.

Aktaş, C. (1991), *Tanzimattan Günümüze Kılık, Kıyafet ve İktidar* (Politics and clothing since the Ottoman constitutional period), Istanbul: Nehir.

Appadurai, A. (1996), *Modernities At Large*, Minneapolis: University of Minnesota Press.
Balasescu, A. (2003), "Tehran Chic: Islamic Headscarves, Fashion Designers, and New Geographies of Modernity," *Fashion Theory*, 7: 39–56.
Balasescu, A. (2007), "Haute Couture in Tehran: Two Faces of an Emerging Fashion Scene," *Fashion Theory*, 11: 299–318.
Bilici, M. (1999), "İslam'ın Bronzlaşan Yüzü: Caprice Hotel Örnek Olayı (The suntanning face of Islam: The case of Caprice Hotel)," in Nilüfer Göle (ed.) *İslamın Yeni Kamusal Yüzleri*, 216–36, (The new public faces of Islam), Istanbul: Metis.
Buğra, A. (1998), "Class, Culture and State: An Analysis of Interest Representation by Two Turkish Business Associations," *International Journal of Middle East Studies*, 30: 521–39.
Buğra, A. (2003), "The Place of the Economy in Turkish Society," *South Atlantic Quarterly*, 102: 453–70.
Erder, S. (2001), *Ümraniye: İstanbul'a Bir Kentkondu* (Ümraniye: A squatter city in Istanbul), Istanbul: İletişim.
Eygi, M. (2005), "Müslüman Sosyete (Muslim high society)," Milli Gazete, December 9.
Fealy, G. and S. White (2008), *Expressing Islam: Religious Life and Politics in Indonesia*, Singapore: Institute of Southeast Asian Studies.
Fischer, J. (2008), *Proper Islamic Consumption: Shopping among the Malays in Modern Malaysia*, Copenhagen: Nordic Institute of Asian Studies Press.
Gökarıksel, B. (2007), "A Feminist Geography of Veiling: Gender, Class and Religion in the Making of Modern Spaces and Subjects in Istanbul," in K. M. Morin and J. K. Guelke (eds.), *Women, Religion, and Space*, 61–80, Syracuse, NY: Syracuse University Press.
Gökarıksel, B. and A. Secor (2009), "New Transnational Gegraphies of Islamism, Capitalism and Subjectivity: The Veiling-Fashion Industry in Turkey," *Area*, 41: 6–18.
Gökarıksel, B. and A. Secor (2010), "Islamic-ness in the Life of a Commodity: Veiling-Fashion in Turkey," *Transactions of the Institute of British Geographers*, 35 (3): 313–33.
Göle, N. (1996), *The Forbidden Modern: Civilization and Veiling*, Ann Arbor, MI: University of Michigan Press.
Göle, N. (1999), *İslamın Yeni Kamusal Yüzleri* (The new public faces of Islam), Istanbul: Metis.
Göle, N. and L. Ammann, eds. (2006), *Islam in Public: Turkey, Iran, and Europe*, Istanbul: Bilgi University Press.
Henry, C. M. and R. Wilson, eds. (2004), *The Politics of Islamic Finance*, Edinburgh: Edinburgh University Press.
Jones, C. (2007), "Fashion and Faith in Urban Indonesia," *Fashion Theory*, 11: 211–31.
Karpat, K. H. (1976), *The Gecekondu: Rural Migration and Urbanization*, Cambridge, UK: Cambridge University Press.
Kılıçbay, B. and M. Binark (2002), "Consumer Culture, Islam and the Politics of Lifestyle: Fashion for Veiling in Contemporary Turkey," *European Journal of Communication*, 17: 495–511.
Moors, A. and E. Tarlo (2007), "Introduction," *Fashion Theory*, 11: 133–41.
Navaro-Yashin, Y. (2002), *Faces of the State: Secularism and Public Life in Turkey*, Princeton: Princeton University Press.
Olson, E. A. (1985), "Muslim Identity and Secularisms in Contemporary Turkey: 'The Headscarf Dispute'," *Anthropological Quarterly*, 58 (4): 161–71.

Öncü, A. (1999), "Istanbulites and Others: The Cultural Cosmology of Being Middle Class in the Era of Globalism," in Ç. Keyder (ed.), *Istanbul: Between the Global and the Local*, 95–119, Lanham, MD: Rowman and Littlefield.

Özdalga, E. (1998), *The Veiling Issue, Official Secularism and Popular Islam in Modern Turkey*, Richmond, Surrey, UK: Curzon.

Rose, G. (2001), *Visual Methodologies*, London: Sage.

Saktanber, A. (2002), "'We Pray Like You Have Fun': New Islamic Youth in Turkey between Intellectualism and Popular Culture," in D. Kandiyoti and A. Saktanber (eds.), *Fragments of Culture: The Everyday of Modern Turkey*, 254–76, London: I. B. Tauris.

Sandıkcı, Ö. and G. Ger (2002), "In-between Modernities and Postmodernities: Theorizing Turkish Consumptionscape," *Advances in Consumer Research*, 29: 465–70.

Sandıkcı, Ö. and G. Ger (2005), "Aesthetics, Ethics and Politics of the Turkish Headscarf," in S. Küchler and D. Miller (eds.), *Clothing as Material Culture*, 61–82, Oxford, UK: Berg.

Sandıkcı, Ö. and G. Ger (2007), "Constructing and Representing the Islamic Consumer in Turkey," *Fashion Theory*, 11: 189–210.

Secor, A. (2002), "The Veil and Urban Space in Istanbul: Women's Dress, Mobility and Islamic Knowledge," *Gender, Place and Culture*, 9: 5–22.

Secor, A. (2005), "Islamism, Democracy and the Political Production of the Headscarf Issue in Turkey," in G. Falah and C. Nagel (eds.), *Geographies of Muslim Women: Gender, Religion and Space*, 203–25, New York: Guilford Press.

Şişman, N. (2001), *Kamusal Alanda Başörtülüler: Fatma Karabıyık Karaosmanoğlu ile Söyleşi* (Headscarved women in public space: An interview with Fatma Karabıyık Karaosmanoğlu), Istanbul: İz.

Tokatlı, N. (2003), "Globalization and the Changing Clothing Industry in Turkey," *Environment and Planning A*, 35: 1877–94.

White, J. (1999), "Islamic Chic," in Ç. Keyder (ed.), *Istanbul: Between the Global and the Local*, 77–91, Lanham, MD: Rowman and Littlefield.

White, J. (2002), *Islamist Mobilization in Turkey: A Study in Vernacular Politics*, Seattle: University of Washington Press.

Yavuz, H. (2003), *Islamic Political Identity in Turkey*, Oxford, UK: Oxford University Press.

From Aspiration to Self-confidence: What Emotions and Clothing Tastes Tell Us about Class Inequality in Turkey

by Irmak Karademir-Hazır

Introduction

In the last decades, the practices that we engage in to adorn, dress, and care for our bodies have begun to receive significant scholarly attention from sociologists of consumption. Conceptualized as embodiment practices, they have been scrutinized to understand various dimensions, including but not limited to individuals' capacity to resist structural limitations, the patterning of lifestyles, and the operation of the boundaries between "us" and "them." Most of this literature has, in varying ways, engaged with the debate about how far class inequalities are represented and reproduced through dressed bodies. However, in Turkey, as a predominantly Muslim, rapidly modernized, and secularized state, the focus has been more on how such practices have marked identities religio-politically rather than with class terms. Drawing on my fieldwork and with the use of qualitative as well as quantitative methods, I have proposed a shift in this focus. My work so far has demonstrated the ways in which class shapes women's embodiment experiences, cross-cutting the overly emphasized distinctions between pious and secular styles (Karademir-Hazır 2020, 2017, 2014). In this chapter, I will briefly discuss how women in Turkey experience their dressed bodies in social life and imagine sociologically what their emotions can tell us about the accumulated national class-cultural repertoires.

Clothing Tastes and Class Distinction in Turkey

After the foundation of the Turkish Republic in 1923, comprehensive rules were put into place to rapidly Westernize and secularize the human body, imbuing the "symbolic" and "representational" with huge importance. This modernization process, which mainly started as a top-down project led by bureaucrats and the well-educated of the period, led to an understanding in which changing one's outer layers, including one's clothes, was considered a way of creating "modern" citizens with "modern" dispositions. This shift caused what Bilgin (2004) refers to as Turkey's "obsession with appearance," which has been resistant to change. As in many other similar national contexts, this process also created a hierarchy between traditional and Western cultural forms. From the Ottoman modernization onwards, Alaturka/Turkish styles were granted lower value compared to Alafranga/Western cultural forms (Göle 1997; Kandiyoti 1997). Recent work suggests that this distinction still explains the taste dynamics in Turkey, albeit now working in more complex ways. For instance, Rankin et al. (2013) empirically identified a lifestyle group distinctive in terms of its high economic and cultural capital, which they labeled as "engaged cosmopolitans" because this group comprises people who embrace an urban, globalized, and secular culture instead of Alaturka/local tastes. The discursive construction of "white Turk" and "black Turk" distinctions illustrates how such a hierarchy structured embodiment practices quite forcefully. Rather than racial categories, this black/white distinction has drawn on differences in bodily dispositions as the clothing tastes and embodied manners that emerged after the massive flows of rural-to-urban migration in the 1960s made previously invisible fractions of society and their cultural habits visible. The bodily representations of the newcomers (the "black Turks"), such as their mixing of traditional flower-patterned baggy pants with t-shirts with English slogans, were caricaturized in satire magazines and explicitly ridiculed by Westernized upper middle classes for their in-betweenness and polluting banality. This classification enabled middle classes to redefine their boundaries in opposition to the "absolute other" (Öncü 1999) and triggered spatial distancing through suburbanization as city people's bodily tastes were perceived as being marked by pollution, disease, and early aging (Ayata 2002). As recognized by many, the main carriers of the distinctive "white Turk" repertoire were the new generation of the professional-managerial middle class who accumulated capital after economic liberalization, embodied "Western" cultural habits, and were much more "liberal" in their ideas of gender relations and religion.

Class-cultural conflicts became much more diverse after the 1980s with the rise of political Islam and the associated upward mobility of its supporters, as it challenged the long-established associations between piety and class position. Consumption markets responded to the bifurcation of the bourgeois and the middle class by offering services exclusive to pious fractions (Göle 1999; Navaro-Yashin 2002). The embodiment domain was again at the forefront of the transformation; the new fashionable style of veiling generated an aesthetic variety enabling women to mark their identity in consistency with the particulars of refined urban taste (Sandıkçı and Ger 2010) and distinguish themselves from rural, unsophisticated, and traditional "others." Inevitably this led to the devaluation of certain kinds of self-fashioning representations, leading to the exclusion and marginalization of Muslim identities incompatible with the dynamics of the new market, as Gökarıksel and McLarney suggest (2010).

Emotions and Cultural Class Analysis

In national contexts where appearances have not been at the center of national political and symbolic struggles, embodiment practices are theorized more directly in relation to class processes. Especially after the cultural turn, there has been a recognition of how class can circulate through symbolic and cultural forms (i.e., Lawler 2004; Reay 1998; Skeggs 1997) and be re-made through "claims of entitlement (and of non-entitlement), through symbols and representations, and in the emotional and affective dimensions of life" (Lawler 2005: 797). Class then "is not just about life chances and 'equality of opportunity', but about self-worth, suffering and denigration as well" (Atkinson et al. 2012: 1). Analysis of emotional experiences in many fields, such as education (Reay 2005), femininity (Skeggs 1997), and media (McRobbie 2004), has showcased the ways in which class continues to shape lives despite the lack of overt class consciousness.

It is this stream of research that empirically challenged the reflexive individualization thesis, which suggested that individuals can revise their identities via reflexive practices including embodiment (Bauman 1982; Beck 1992). Bourdieusian concepts have been crucial for unpacking the affective and individualized dimensions of class and thus for critically engaging with theories announcing the death of class. For Bourdieu, even very mundane habits and practices are inculcated not by the rationale of the individual but by the "practical sense" that the habitus generates in relation to locations in social space (Bourdieu 1986, 1989). This sense is embodied in the actor through a long process of socialization and makes the body "the most indisputable materialisation of class taste," revealing "the deepest dispositions of the habitus" (Bourdieu 1984: 190). Embodied cultural capital refers to body hexis, appearances, demeanors, and posture and includes the dispositions of mundane clothing. It can be converted to other forms of capital, such as economic or social, and since it is difficult to "imitate" due to long socialization, its relative lack creates exclusions in everyday life. Once the hierarchy of embodied styles is internalized, it starts to work as a symbolic violence, fixing the vulnerable to their positions and helping others maintain their power to legitimize their own tastes.

In my work, I employed this Bourdieusian framework and drew on class-cultural analysis to see how such processes work in the Turkish context. To capture embodiment tastes and practices of women from different social classes, I conducted interviews (n: 44) and administered questionnaires (n: 229) in Ankara. Respondents were heterogeneous in terms of both class position and proximity to Islamic lifestyles. I have previously shown how women's practices are patterned in quantitative terms (Karademir-Hazır 2014) and qualitative terms (Karademir-Hazır 2020). I have also discussed in more detail how women experience these differences in social life by focusing on their emotions (Karademir-Hazır 2017). In this chapter, I will primarily draw on the latter work and reflect on what my constant comparative analysis (Glaser 1965) revealed in relation to nation-specific class processes.

Resentment, Aspiration, Indifference: Emotional Responses of Restricted Habitus

Unsurprisingly, the most common response among interviewees holding low levels of cultural capital was resentment. They felt resentment in contexts where they thought that their physical appearances were categorized as failure by strangers. These experiences mostly took place in settings where they had to demand service from professionals. "Dressing up" seems to be a common strategic choice made after accepting the fact that one's own routine embodiment practices do not elicit respect. For instance, Zerrin suggests that the staff at hospitals "never try to dismiss people who are well dressed. But when they perceive someone as poor, it is a different case. And it hurts, you know." Like Zerrin, many other interviewees attempted to pass as middle class, but as Skeggs shows (1997: 86), "unless symbolic appearances are converted into symbolic capital through being legitimated by those with power, those lacking the necessary resources will never be capable of knowing what getting it right really means."

Another mode of emotional response was aspiration, again common to those with lower levels of cultural capital. However, unlike in the case of resentment, these experiences were narrated with less defensive tones, considered to be less disturbing, and categorizing gazes were not explicitly criticized. For instance, Ceylan, a cleaner in the local nursery, suggested that "women who work generally wear modern clothes, they are physically well-kept. Their shoes and bags always match." She aspires to be like them but believes she cannot "improve" her style because "the source doesn't come from inside." The "working woman" image that Ceylan has in her mind clearly excludes representations of lower-class working women such as herself. Such self-positioning was common to many other interviewees with limited cultural capital. For instance, Fatma, who migrated to Ankara from a small village, had to motivate herself and cope with stress while she trying what she called an "urban style," thin tights, for the first time, telling herself: "Fatma, look, you might not be lacking anything compared to the other women you have seen." Despite her aspiration, Fatma only rarely wore the tights when she was younger and stopped buying them as she aged. As McRobbie's analysis of TV makeover shows demonstrates, these seemingly "naive" feelings of aspiration show how culturally privileged groups manage to legitimize their ways of engaging with their bodies as representative of good taste and the workings of symbolic violence (McRobbie 2004). Although her response to hierarchy is aspiration, Ceylan never questions why her skirt with an elastic waist is of less symbolic value compared to the power suits of white-collar women. This internalization of the hierarchy is a mark of symbolic violence, which ensures that the situation of the dominated is seen from "the social eyes of a dominant" (Bourdieu 1989: 18).

Interestingly, remaining indifferent to potentially distressing moments of self-presentation was also common to the interviewees with low cultural capital. Respondents who remained indifferent often emphasized the fact that their conscious attempts at improvement would remain partial and would not imbue their appearances with long-lasting high symbolic value. For instance, Eda suggested that she "cannot give them the impression that my [life] conditions are very good. I am who I am; there is no need, why should I present myself above what I really am?" Eda has a clear sense of the hierarchical ordering of aesthetic representations as well as her place in this order. Like others who expressed similar views, she is also aware that her taste has no currency and cannot be converted to social capital by granting access to distinguished social networks. Therefore, from the social location where she stands, aspiratory engagement seems not only artificial but also impractical. One distinctive feature of the interviewees who remained indifferent is that they had the lowest income levels. Consistent with the working-class habitus revealed in Bourdieu's (1984) study, those who have limited economic and cultural capital seem to be more concerned with "being" rather than "seeming."

Self-confidence, Superiority, Complacency: Emotional Responses of the Cultivated Habitus

Presenting one's dressed body in unfamiliar or formal settings is not equally stressful for every individual. Unlike those who had unpleasant experiences, a number of the interviewees were clearly satisfied with the physical outcome of their self-fashioning practices, which consequently imbued them with self-confidence. This response, like the others, is generated by constantly comparing one's embodiment forms with others who participate in the interaction. For instance, after suggesting that clothing tastes are linked to upbringing, Sibel, who wears a headscarf, suggested that she has been consulted by her friends to pick the right clothing items for them. Sibel tied this to her social class background and described one friend who needed advice as follows: "She is my high-school friend. Her family is of peasant origin ... Her father is an electrician, her mother is a housewife. Her parents are quite ordinary." Sibel, the daughter of a culturally privileged urban family who abides by the rules of Islamic covering in a modern style, assumes that she is rightfully entitled to be self-assured and that the lack of command of good taste is directly related to one's restricted class habitus. She, like many of the other culturally and economically distinguished interviewees whose accounts could not be presented here, conceives of her bodily practices as naturally yielding the correct, good-quality aesthetics that are approved of even by those who do not have such competences themselves.

Self-assurance imbued some interviewees with feelings of superiority and made them clearly position themselves above the people that they interact with. This response revealed itself in intentional dressing-down strategies and also in harsh categorizing rhetoric of others' tastes and practices, which might be literally considered as "middle-class gaze." As exemplified by Demet, who wears a headscarf, these interviewees also recognized that the embodiment styles in Turkey are value-wise hierarchically ordered; however, unlike interviewees who resent, aspire, or remain indifferent, they locate themselves closer to the higher end of the spectrum. Talking about the tastes of her husband's extended family, who live in the slums, Demet explained: "They all wear the same style ... large skirts, usually with flower patterns, and an ordinary blouse, and also [a rural style of covering the hair] ... They are undeveloped in many senses, you know. They don't have any sense of matching clothes."

Many similar anecdotes suggest that the culturally cultivated fractions of both covered and not covered interviewees explicitly devalue the clothing and corporeal styles of rural-to-urban migrants as well as the working class. More importantly, this devaluation often exceeds the aesthetic realm and accommodates moral judgments, leading to exclusion and disadvantage on the part of the judged ones. For instance, Şehnaz suggested that people with subordinate embodiment style are badly treated because, thanks to their looks, they are "successfully" categorized as "uneducated" and "inconsiderate."

Quite unexpectedly, the responses of some interviewees with high cultural capital were similar to the "indifference" of the lower cultural capital holders; I labeled this as complacency because they were not marked by negative tones. Especially when there happens to be a mismatch between the respondents' style and the others involved in an event, high cultural capital holders enjoy the comfort of their already acknowledged status. For instance, after attending a celebratory brunch in informal clothes, Melda explained: "I wasn't underdressed; I thought they were the ones who were overdressed!" In a similar vein, Hilal avoided uneasiness and successfully managed a potential style failure at a classical music concert, despite the fact that she was the only covered woman in the audience. She explained why she felt complacent presenting herself in a cultural activity that is framed as "secular" by using class terms: "You learn these rules as you climb those steps."

Concluding Discussion

In this chapter, I have shown how class structures ordinary clothing practices and the emotions that derive from presenting one's self in everyday life. In contrast to studies pointing to the emergence of reflexive consumers, my interviewees' accounts demonstrate the explanatory power of Bourdieu's embodied cultural capital. The dressed bodies of higher social classes elicit respect from others and can be converted to other forms of capital, whereas others face emotionally distressing experiences and exclusions.

The ties between these seemingly individual emotional responses and class processes become visible once the accumulated cultural repertoires are taken into consideration. Skirts with an elastic waist or thick tights are devalued and their wearers feel hesitant in their style because they are perceived as representing rural/traditional femininity, which has been historically much less valued in comparison to modern Westernized femininity and to white-Turk corporeal status. The fractions that have embodied historically valued styles, as revealed in the analysis of their emotions, are very well aware of this taste hierarchy. In this sense, these findings confirm previous studies on Turkish class cultures as they show how the body has become prime grounds for performing distinctions for culturally cultivated fractions. However, they also contradict the widely held view that the hierarchy of embodiment styles is solely or primarily structured by the secular/religious distinction. The new pious female embodiment styles appropriated by upwardly mobile women enable them to differentiate themselves from other traditional "ignorant" (in Şehnaz's terms) and "undeveloped" (in Demet's terms) covered women. As their accounts suggest, being Islamically covered is hardly considered the primary criterion to define "one of us." Interestingly, despite the explicit disapproval of pious styles by some radically secular women, most recognize the hierarchy in class terms, demonstrating how it cross-cuts the secular/religious distinction in Turkey. Whether covered or not, clothing styles imbue the culturally competent and globally oriented sections of each fraction with self-confidence and help them convert this capital to other forms in other social fields. My work has revealed that there is an established understanding of the social hierarchy and its expression through embodiment taste and style in Turkey, which deserves as much—if not more—of the attention that religio-politically embodied tensions have received in our scholarship so far.

References

Atkinson, W., S. Roberts. and M. Savage (2012), "Introduction: A Critical Sociology of the Age of Austerity," in W. Atkinson, S. Roberts and M. Savage (eds.), *Class Inequality in Austerity Britain: Power, Difference, Suffering*, 1–12, Hampshire: Palgrave Macmillan.

Ayata, S. (2002), "The New Middle Class and the Joys of Suburbia," in D. Kandiyoti and A. Saktanber (eds.), *Fragments of Culture: The Everyday of Modern Turkey*, 25–42, New York: I.B Tauris.

Bauman, Z. (1982), *Memories of Class: The Pre-history and After-life of Class*, London: Routledge and Kegan Paul.

Beck, U. (1992), *Risk Society: Towards a New Modernity*, London: Sage.

Bilgin, E. (2004), *Analysis of Turkish Modernity through the Discourses of Masculinities*. Doctor of Philosophy, Middle East Technical University, Ankara.

Bourdieu, P. (1984), *Distinction: A Social Critique of the Judgement of Taste*, Cambridge: Harvard University Press.

Bourdieu, P. (1986), "The Forms of Capital," in J. G. Richardson (ed.), *Handbook of a Theory Research for the Sociology of Education*, 241–58, New York: Greenwood.

Bourdieu, P. (1989), "Social Space and Symbolic Power," *Sociological Theory*, 7 (1): 14–25.

Glaser, G. B. (1965), "The Constant Comparative Method of Qualitative Analysis," *Social Problems*, 12 (4): 436–45.

Göle, N. (1997), "The Quest for the Islamic Self within the Context of Modernity," in S. Bozdağ and R. Kasaba (eds.), *Rethinking Modernity and National Identity in Turkey*, 81–94, Seattle: University of Washington Press.

Göle, N. (1999), *İslamin Yeni Kamusal Yuzleri* (The New Public Faces of Islam), İstanbul: Metis.

Karademir-Hazır, I. (2020), "Narratives of 'Getting it Right': Class, Culture and Good Taste in Clothing," *International Journal of Fashion Studies*, 7 (2): 147–65.

Karademir-Hazır, I. (2017), "Wearing Class: A Study on Clothes, Bodies and Emotions in Turkey," *Journal of Consumer Culture*, 17 (2): 413–32.

Karademir-Hazır, I. (2014), "How Bodies are Classed: An Analysis of Clothing and Bodily Tastes in Turkey," *Poetics*, 44: 1–21.

Kandiyoti, D. (1997), "Gendering the Modern: On Missing Dimensions in the Study of Turkish Modernity," in S. Bozdoğan and R. Kasaba (eds.), *Rethinking Modernity and National Identity in Turkey*, 113–32, Seattle: University of Washington Press.

Lawler, S. (2004), "Rules of Engagement: Habitus, Power and Resistance," *The Sociological Review*, 52 (2): 110–28.

Lawler, S. (2005), "Introduction: Class, Culture, Identity," *Sociology*, 39 (5): 797–806.

McRobbie, A. (2004), "Notes on 'What not to Wear' and Post-feminist Symbolic Violence," in L. Adkins and B. Skeggs (eds.), *Feminism after Bourdieu*, 99–109, Oxford: Blackwell Publishing.

Navaro-Yashin, Y. (2002), *Faces of the State: Secularism and Public Life in Turkey*, Princeton: Princeton University Press.

Öncü, A. (1999), "İstanbulites and Others: The Cultural Cosmology of being Middle Class in the Era of Globalism," in Ç. Keyder (ed.), *Istanbul: between the Global and the Local*, 95–121, New York: Rowman & Littlefield.

Rankin, B., M. Ergin and F. Gökşen (2013), "A Cultural Map of Turkey," *Cultural Sociology*, 8 (2): 159–79.

Reay, D. (1998), *Class Work*, London: University College London.

Reay, D. (2005), "Doing the Dirty Work of Social Class? Mothers' Work in Support of their Children's Schooling," *The Sociological Review*, 53 (2): 104–16.

Sandıkçı, Ö. and G. Ger (2010), "Veiling in Style: How Does a Stigmatized Practice become Fashionable?" *Journal of Consumer Research*, 37 (1): 15–36.

Skeggs, B. (1997), *Formations of Class and Gender: Becoming Respectable*, London: Sage.

III GENDER AND SEXUALITY

Queer Exceptionalism and Exclusion: Cosmopolitanism and Inequalities in "Gay-Friendly" Beirut

by Ghassan Moussawi

Dominant Euro-American discourses describe places where LGBTQ persons do not have mainstream public visibility as repressive, "non-modern," and in need of Western intervention (Long 2009). These descriptions are particularly common in representations of nonnormative gender and sexualities in the Arab Middle East and the Muslim world. However, since the year 2005, the contemporary Euro-American press has hailed Beirut, the capital of Lebanon, as a new, gay-friendly tourist destination in the Middle East. For instance, in 2009, the *New York Times* published an article titled "Beirut, the Provincetown of the Middle East."

Lebanon, a sectarian, Muslim-majority country, has often been regarded as exceptional in the Arab World for its seeming diversity and cosmopolitanism, with cosmopolitanism understood to invoke worldliness, diversity, inclusivity, and "openness" to difference. These representations describe gay life in Beirut using a narrative of linear progress, gauging improvements in the rise of "tolerant" attitudes and the growth of Western-style gay identities, gay-friendly spaces, and LGBTQ organizations. These depictions emphasize Beirut's cosmopolitanism and exceptionalism in a region presently marked by war, conflict, and political and religious violence. While the literature on LGBTQ lives in the Arab Middle East has focused on the marginality of queer communities (El-Feki 2013; Whitaker 2006), another growing body of research has taken into account the multiple positions that queer individuals occupy (Makarem 2011; Merabet 2014; Naber and Zaatari 2014). In this chapter, I build on the latter research by examining how gender, class, and normativity shape LGBTQ individuals' everyday lives and engagements with discourses of cosmopolitanism and national exceptionalism in Beirut. Even though scholars have considered formations and exclusions of LGBTQ spaces in "global cities," exclusions within LGBTQ communities in the Arab World have yet to be examined. Drawing on transnational studies of sexualities, states, and nation, I ask how transnational discourses of modernity and exceptionalism get circulated and articulated by LGBTQ persons in Beirut.

Based on ethnographic research and twenty life-history interviews with LGBTQ individuals, I illustrate how LGBTQ persons in Beirut draw on their experiences of the city to create their own definitions of cosmopolitanism. First, I show that LGBTQ Beirutis create relational understandings of modernity and cosmopolitanism by situating Beirut in relation to other Arab cities, rather than just in relation to Euro-American cities. Whereas discussions of cosmopolitanism tend to assume Western urban centers as reference points for understanding the category, my respondents have different reference points. Second, my interlocutors focus on gendered and classed exclusions that they and other people face, particularly regarding unequal access to public and "gay-friendly" spaces and LGBTQ organizations, which contrast with the narratives of Beiruti cosmopolitanism and exceptionalism.

I find that discourses of sexual openness and gay friendliness in Beirut (seen as markers of cosmopolitanism) are laden with a value structure informed by gender, class, and religion. Building on the notion that cities are sites of "possibility and constraint" (Hubbard 2012; Oswin 2015), I argue that "cosmopolitan Beirut" is accessible as a gay-friendly space to gender-normative, cisgender, secular, and middle-to-upper-class LGBTQ people. Furthermore, Beirut's seeming "tolerance" of middle-to-upper-class, gay and lesbian tourists—and not of groups such as Syrian and Palestinian refugees, migrant domestic workers, gender-nonnormative, trans, and working-class people—is considered a sign of modernity and cosmopolitanism. Finally, I find that marginalized queer Beirutis, particularly gender-nonnormative, genderqueer, and working-class individuals, are most likely to question Beirut's cosmopolitanism and to carve out new understandings of queer life that challenge dominant understandings of modernity and progress.

Narratives of Exceptionalism and Cosmopolitanism

Various scholars have debated cosmopolitanism in the Arab World and the Middle East. Some frame cosmopolitanism in terms of progress narratives (Meijer 1999), as anti-nationalist projects (Seidman 2012), or as high-end and "Western" consumption patterns (Schwedler 2010). Historian Roel Meijer (1999) claims that cosmopolitanism and authenticity are at odds in the Arab World, arguing that Middle Eastern societies opt for "authenticity," rather than what he refers to as moving "forward" toward a European model of cosmopolitanism. Urban comparative methods, such as those used by Meijer (1999), attempt to measure "cosmopolitan progress" using linear progress narratives that employ Eurocentric understandings of cosmopolitanism (Binnie 2014). Such approaches homogenize and neglect colonial histories of the Middle East.

Scholarship examining discourses of cosmopolitanism in the Global South tends to depict it as aspirational, using Euro-American cities as reference points, and envisioning cosmopolitanism as a particularly "Western" phenomenon. In addition to reflecting Eurocentric linear progress narratives, imagining that cosmopolitan discourses are only ever aspirational obscures the many ways that these discourses are employed. My interlocutors conceived of Beirut's cosmopolitanism in relation to cities in the Arab World, rather than to Euro-American cities. While some claimed that Beirut was cosmopolitan and exceptional, others disagreed by pointing to its multiple exclusions. Middle-to-upper-class, cisgender women and men were more likely to highlight Beirut's cosmopolitanism, since their more normative gender and class positions allow them to experience Beirut as exceptional. Those who saw Beirut as cosmopolitan and modern emphasized Beirut's exceptionalism in the Arab Middle East by pointing to religious diversity and the possibility for gay visibility not present in other Arab cities.

Some interlocutors, for instance, tried to prove Beirut's exceptionalism by contrasting its religious diversity to more homogeneous Arab cities. For example, Samira, a twenty-one-year-old cisgender woman, stated that Beirut is exceptional due to the diverse sectarian makeup of the city and its multiple feminist and queer initiatives. Samira identifies as lesbian and was born and raised in the Arab Gulf, but moved to Lebanon to study at a private university. Contrasting her experiences of Beirut to the Arab Gulf, she felt Beirut was exceptional in the Arab World. She says:

> We are known as the most liberal. Technically, we are the only Christian country in the Middle East. Second, we have so many different religions, not one dominates. We have different backgrounds. In Beirut, we all come together. It's beautiful to see 18–19 different sects mash up in one city. Yeah, you still have the Shia area, Sunni, Druze, Maronite. Yes, this is Beirut; drop that shit outside, leave your religions in the villages, and come to Beirut and work.

For Samira, being the "only Christian country in the Middle East" functions as the exception that proves the rule: the Christian country whose presence demonstrates the non-modern, non-secular nature of the rest of the "Muslim" Middle East. For her, leaving one's religious sect behind makes Beirut more diverse and cosmopolitan. Thus, Samira considers people to be "more open" to difference (and therefore "more modern" and "cosmopolitan") in Beirut than in Lebanese villages. Samira invokes what Halberstam (2005: 36) calls "metronormativity": the assumed progressiveness of cities and urban spaces in relation to rural areas.

Samira also presents a relational understanding of cosmopolitanism by contrasting Beirut to other Lebanese and Arab cities and villages. She states:

> In terms of gender and sexuality, people have expressed it in so many different ways and different spaces. It's fascinating, for example, how Helem and Meem started up as underground collectives that slowly branched out to society. In terms of organizing, they organized and reached out. This is history. This is not like Jordan or the

> Gulf where they prosecute you; here they didn't prosecute us. They didn't go out to look for gay people. I don't know if it's the nature of the government to just be careless, but we have freedom [here].

Samira finds Beirut to be exceptional in the Arab World (contrasting it to Jordan and the Gulf). She contrasts the "history" in Beirut and Lebanon to the "timelessness" in other places. Using other Arab countries as reference points, Samira produces hierarchies of "good" and "bad" countries in the Arab World.

Many of my cisgender male interlocutors also contrast the "exceptional" gay life in Beirut to other places in the Arab World. Nonetheless, many point to the difficulty of being openly gay and the gay community's exclusion of gender-nonnormative men. One example is Tarek, a twenty-seven-year-old, gay-identified, Muslim medical doctor. Tarek claims that Lebanon is much better than other Arab countries:

> I am always comparing [Lebanon] to "worse" places: Saudi Arabia, Qatar, Dubai. As far as I know, there is no activism there ... I know friends in Qatar; they tell me that gay life is more underground over there, more so than Beirut. Most gay men are married with kids and then resume their lives.

Tarek's description echoes common discourses of Beiruti exceptionalism, which position it as distinct in the Middle East, yet lagging behind its Euro-American counterparts. He says that Beirut is somewhat, but not completely open. He insists that people in Beirut are "not as openminded" as those in Canada, explaining that people in Beirut don't accept gay men and lesbians. He feels that there is no anonymity in Beirut and that everyone knows everyone else, so he prefers Canada because, he said, "he could do whatever he wanted." To explain Beirut's openness and cosmopolitanism, Tarek distances it from both its Canadian and Arab counterparts.

Unlike findings from other research (Masri 2010; Seidman 2012), many of my interlocutors didn't simply reproduce the claim that Beirut is cosmopolitan. Instead, many contested this claim by citing multiple exclusions targeting them and people they know. Souraya, a twenty-three-year-old Muslim queer Lebanese woman who attended the public university, states that Lebanese gay life is "distinct," not necessarily better than other countries in the Arab World:

> I don't see things better than others. I see that the conditions of Beirut as being different than the conditions in Riyadh. I don't necessarily see Beirut as open: in Riyadh, there is nightlife, and it is all underground. In Beirut, I know how to negotiate some areas more than others. That doesn't mean that I feel safer. Maybe I feel more comfortable, but safety is something else.

Souraya claims that safety and comfort have different meanings in negotiating the city. She does not see Beirut as an "exceptional gay haven"; instead, she focuses on the different conditions and possibilities that make gay life possible. Souraya questions the exceptionalism of Beirut, because she is aware of the multiple exclusions that exist. Souraya is attentive to how social and political economies produce developmental narratives of progress in Lebanon, particularly concerning gender and sexuality. She is critical of those who do not consider the role of government policy in shaping these discourses. Souraya argues that narratives of Beirut's exceptionalism and cosmopolitanism are quite dominant because the Lebanese state and people use them to distinguish Lebanon in the Arab World:

> All things have been worked on: in the government, politics and economics that Lebanon is exceptional … Sexually, it is a sexual haven. The Arabs come here … we have things that other Arab countries don't have, and our women are different. They wear swimsuits; other women in the Arab world don't. We have gay people that other places don't tolerate. But for me, this is all very superficial, of course, and we the people who live here know that it is very superficial.

In post-civil-war Lebanon, the Lebanese state's claims that Lebanon is built on the coexistence of Muslims and Christians are enacted in order to mark Lebanon as modern and cosmopolitan. These narratives of coexistence do not apply to migrants and refugees. Tolerance, as Wendy Brown reminds us, is "a political discourse and practice of governmentality that is historically and geographically variable" (2006: 4). Tolerance of specific groups and not others therefore is a characteristic of progress narratives (Brown 2006). The "modern" narrative of tolerance depends on not tolerating certain groups (gender-nonnormative, trans, and working-class people, as well as refugees) who it regards as non-modern (El-Tayeb 2011).

Whose Gay Beirut? Policing Gender and Class

Gender and class determine who can experience Beirut as "cosmopolitan" and "gay-friendly." The gay-friendly spaces of Beirut require certain performances of classed, normative femininities and masculinities, in addition to economic, social, and cultural capital. Some of my interlocutors suggest that queer normativity is highly racialized in Beirut. Souraya, for example, claims that class, gender, and racial codes govern Beirut and that the people who are welcomed are those who can afford to live in Beirut. She asserts that non-Western (particularly nonwhite) foreigners are excluded much more than the Lebanese, pointing to the experiences of migrant workers from Southeast Asia and North and East Africa. However, she states that, as a Lebanese woman, she feels unwelcome in certain areas, because of her nonnormative gender presentation, particularly her short hair. Class privilege is central in shaping her access to and experiences of the city, which also makes her nonnormative haircut "acceptable." She still has access to Beirut, because she can afford to live there and move relatively safely between certain areas of the city. Since class shapes gender performances (Skeggs 1997), Souraya's gendered and classed position enables her to move safely between areas of the city.

One needs economic and social capital (gained mainly through queer networks) to access private semi-LGBTQ-friendly places. For example, Sirine, a twenty-eight-year-old Lebanese genderqueer individual who was born, raised, and lives in Beirut, argues that, even though certain areas of Beirut seem "more open," they are not necessarily so. Sirine, who prefers feminine pronouns, compares her experiences of Beirut to those in France where she lived while pursuing her MA degree. She claims that in Beirut one is welcome despite one's gender presentation, in private establishments, if one can afford access. This, she feels, is not only common to the Lebanese case. Sirine critiques both Orientalist discourses about the "non-modern" status of Arab societies and discourses of Lebanese exceptionalism. For her, the narrative of modernity in both Lebanon and France is based on the "tolerance" of only particular groups. Randa, a genderqueer Lebanese NGO manager in her early thirties, recounts how places become more expensive when they are marketed as "gay-friendly," especially for tourists. She explains that many Beirutis cannot afford the prices of "gay-friendly" places" in Beirut: "If you are poor, you are excluded: you can't pay in certain places."

Class plays a central role in people's access to "gay space." However, these spaces, as many interlocutors recount, require not only economic capital, but also "acceptable" gendered presentations and performances that embody cultural and/or social capital. Like Sirine, several of my interlocutors suggest that access to gay friendliness in Arab or Western cities depends on privilege. One must embody "acceptable" racial, gender, and class positions, and be part of LGBTQ networks. For example, Mays, a feminist and queer activist in her late twenties in Beirut, refuses the binary of thinking about Lebanon as modern in opposition to the "traditional" Arab World. Mays claims: "Clearly, this is an issue: to understand and define Beirut as progressive in comparison to Arab countries. Usually, Lebanon has all these oppressions: for example, the Dekwaneh incident. It is not true that it is better. We are just as bad."

Mays refutes the idea that Beirut is better than other cities in the Arab World by bringing up the multiple exclusions and oppressions that exist within the city. Significantly, she references the 2013 police raid and shut down of the gay club Ghost in the Dekwaneh neighborhood in East Beirut. During that raid, police detained, humiliated, and verbally and physically abused several gay and trans-individuals (Marwan 2013). Narratives of Beirut's gay exceptionalism treat such incidents as anomalies. However, these incidents illustrate how police maintain "Beirut's cosmopolitanism" by policing subjects that are considered "outsiders" to cosmopolitanism. Police forces regularly harass and assault queer individuals who embody marginalized gendered and class positions. Most people detained at Ghost were both working-class and gender-nonnormative and included

Syrian nationals and refugees. This homonormative, classed, and gendered policing constructs some queer formations as acceptable and others as not (what Mays means when she "Lebanon has all these oppressions"). Those deemed as "less appropriate" queer individuals frequent spaces like Ghost, which many of my more privileged informants distanced themselves from and framed as a "nasty" place. Like other global cities, Beirut's gay friendliness is based on policing classed and gendered boundaries, and producing "others" who embody racialized and "inappropriate" sexualities.

Queer Exclusions

Exclusions take the form of limiting access to spaces, including gay-friendly spaces. Some considered normative queerness in Beirut to be very gendered, classed, and raced. For many, the presence of gay and lesbian places is less indicative of growing openness and "tolerance" than of capitalism and the profitability for establishments becoming gay-friendly. Rabab, for example, talked about how gender, class, and religiosity shaped her experiences in queer and non-queer circles. Rabab, who identified as "bigender," yet at the time, preferred the pronouns she/her, was in her mid-twenties. Rabab, like many of my interlocutors, resists dominant understandings that assume a gay and lesbian subject, who is either out or closeted, and who aspires to certain forms of visibility. She recently stopped wearing the hijab, following a double mastectomy she underwent a few months before we met. She had also moved from a predominantly Shia Muslim area to a Christian quarter in Beirut, and describes people's reactions to her taking the hijab off: "Many people congratulated me when I took off the hijab, both in my [new] neighbourhood and within queer circles." Rabab said that people assumed that she was now "liberated," secular, and "more legitimately queer." She became more intelligible to people around her. Identifying as queer while wearing a hijab did not make sense for many in her LGBTQ circles. This is unsurprising given the "global war on terror," where Muslims are commonly constructed as oppressing women and LGBTQ individuals.

Rabab refuses what I call "reconciliation narratives," which are dominant narratives that present LGBTQ Arabs and Muslims as always having to reconcile what are assumed to be mutually exclusive categories (LGBTQ and Muslim). She considers this framing to be informed by simplistic binaries. However, like many of my interlocutors, she explains how contending and intersecting parts of herself shape her life in Beirut. Rabab stopped wearing the hijab because it was a clear gender marker, rather than because she felt it contradicted her queerness: "I only took the hijab off because I did not want to be viewed as a man or a woman. For me, it depends on the context. I have a flat chest, but I have a feminine voice, and I don't have a beard, but most people assume I am a woman." Rabab rejects the idea, held by many in her new neighborhood and queer circles, that the hijab is oppressive and "not queer." She argues that it has saved her many times and as something that she will strategically use when she finds fit, particularly when visiting family. However, she recounts multiple incidents of harassment she has experienced while wearing the hijab. She said the harassment was worst in private establishments and in what she called "posh" places. These included most "gay-friendly places," where, if she forgot she was wearing a hijab, people's stares often reminded her. She felt that she was most discriminated against when she used to wear the hijab pre-surgery: "I found out, at the end, that nothing tops the harassment that I got from the hijab."

Rabab repeatedly expresses that she is different from the "other queers" for not attending private schools or universities, and for having less access to Beirut growing up (she was born and raised in a Lebanese village). She insists that cultural capital like fluency in English and/or French grants people more access to Beiruti LGBTQ communities, circles, and spaces. These requirements are examples of how some queer activists and circles unwittingly reproduce exclusions that they are critical of. Rabab refuses the claim that Beirut is more modern than villages in Lebanon. She recounts how, growing up in a predominately Shia village, she had very different experiences of sex and sexuality than people in Beirut. Rabab disrupts Samira's binary about Beirut versus the village. She feels that her village, which might be considered more conservative, was more open than Beirut, particularly since people there talked about sex more often than in Beirut. Her characterization of her village as open compared to Beirut critiques the metropolitan discourses that construct Beirut as exceptional and open. Rabab asks, "How are we conservative? How are we traditional/uncivilized because we talk or don't talk about sex?" Rabab thus disrupts the binary between urban and rural, but does so by reproducing the idea that openness around sex and sexuality is a marker of progress and modernity.

By demonstrating Beirut's multiple (often violent, classist, and racist) exclusions, hierarchies, and distinctions, my aim is not to reinscribe the idea that the Middle East is inherently homophobic or "intolerant" toward difference. Rather, using ethnographic research and interviews, I contribute to scholarship that examines the politics of omission of celebratory discourses of exceptionalism and the gay friendliness of cities and nations (Bell and Binnie 2004; Oswin 2012). In addition, I build on urban studies that foreground questions of inequalities and LGBTQ life (Haritaworn 2015; Tucker 2009) by paying attention to gendered and classed inequalities in LGBTQ people's experiences of "gay-friendly Beirut."

References

Bell, D. and J. Binnie (2004), "Authenticating Queer Space: Citizenship, Urbanism and Governance," *Urban Studies*, 41 (9): 1807–20.

Binnie, J. (2014), "Relational Comparison, Queer Urbanism and Worlding Cities," *Geography Compass*, 8 (8): 590–99.

Brown, W. (2006), *Regulating Aversion: Tolerance in the Age of Identity and Empire*, Princeton: Princeton University Press.

El-Feki, S. (2013), *Sex and the Citadel*, London: Chatoo & Windus.

El-Tayeb, F. (2011), *European Others: Queering Ethnicity in Postnational Europe*, Minneapolis and London: University of Minnesota Press.

Halberstam, J. (2005), *In a Queer Time and Place: Transgender Bodies, Subcultural Lives*, New York: New York University Press.

Haritaworn, J. (2015), *Queer Lovers and Hateful Others*, Chicago: University of Chicago Press.

Hubbard, P. (2012), *Cities and Sexualities*, Oxford: Routledge.

Long, S. (2009), "Unbearable Witness: How Western Activists (mis)recognize Sexuality in Iran," *Contemporary Politics*, 15 (1): 119–36.

Makarem, G. (2011). The story of Helem. *Journal of Middle East Women's Studies*, 7: 98–112.

Marwan, Y. (2013), "Lebanese Mayor Cracks Down on Homosexuality in His Town." http://english.al-akhbar.com/node/15610 (accessed October 9, 2016).

Masri, G. (2010), "Resurrecting Phoenicia: Tourist Landscapes and National Identity in the Heart of the Lebanese Capital," in Maitland and B. Ritchie (eds.), *City Tourism: National Capital Perspectives*, 225–38, Oxfordshire, UK: R, CAB International.

Meijer, R. (1999), *Cosmopolitanism, Identity, and Authenticity in the Middle East*, London: Routledge.

Merabet, S. (2014), *Queer Beirut*, Austin: University of Texas Press.

Naber, N. and Z. Zaatari (2014), "Reframing the War on Terror: Feminist and Lesbian, Gay, Bisexual, Transgender, and Queer (LGBTQ) Activism in the Context of the 2006 Israeli Invasion of Lebanon," *Cultural Dynamics*, 26 (1): 91–111.

Oswin, N. (2012), "The Queer Time of Creative Urbanism: Family, Futurity, and Global City Singapore," *Environment and Planning A*, 44 (7): 1624–40.

Oswin, N. (2015), "World, City, Queer," *Antipode*, 47 (3): 557–65.

Puri, J. (2016), *Sexual States*, Durham: Duke University Press.

Savci, E. (2016), "Subjects of Rights and Subjects of Cruelty: The Production of an Islamic Backlash against Homosexuality in Turkey," *Political Power and Social Theory*, 30: 159–86.

Schwedler, J. (2010), "Amman Cosmopolitan: Spaces and Practices of Aspiration and Consumption," *Comparative Studies in South Asia, Africa, and the Middle East*, 30 (3): 547–62.

Seidman, S. (2012), "The Politics of Cosmopolitan Beirut: From the Stranger to the Other," *Theory, Culture, and Society*, 29 (2): 3–36.

Skeggs, B. (1997), *Formations of Class & Gender: Becoming Respectable*, London: Sage.

Tucker, A. (2009), "Framing Exclusion in Cape Town's Gay Village: The Discursive and Material Perpetration of Inequitable Queer Subjects," *Area*, 41 (2): 186–97.

Whitaker, B. (2006), *Unspeakable Love: Gay and Lesbian Life in the Middle East*, London: Saqi.

Culture, Class, and Young Women in Turkey

by Ayça Alemdaroğlu

If an opinion poll were to ask Western publics to name the single most disadvantaged group globally, their response might arguably be Muslim women. Alongside this perception, the historical and pervasive discourse of "saving" this demographic served as a pretext for policies ranging from waging wars in far-away places to anti-immigration regulations at home. This discourse is akin to what Gayatri Spivak (1985) cynically described as "white men saving brown women from brown men" in the context of the abolition of Sati practice during British Colonialism in India (Abu-Lughod 2002). Young women are deemed to be particularly vulnerable to the oppression of "brown men." International organizations, news media, and First-World feminists portray their subjugation as a violation of their most basic rights, often by traditionally or religiously oriented fathers and brothers. Ranging from the veil regarded by many as the utmost sign of oppression to the most extreme cases of "honor crimes," various issues related to young women's lives have helped justify the otherness of Muslim societies (Abu-Lughod 2002; Koğacıoğlu 2004; Mishra 2007; Sweis 2012).

The 2010s uprisings in the Middle East, during which young women were at the forefront, have fostered a different imagination about young womanhood. The heroic images of Neda Agha-Soltan during the mass protests against President Ahmedinejad (even though the paramilitary brutally killed her) in Iran, of Asmaa Mahfouz rallying the masses to Tahrir Square in Egypt, and the iconic image of Ceyda Sungur or "the lady in the red dress" tear-gassed by the Turkish riot police contradicted the stereotypes of submissive Muslim women held by many in North America and Europe.[1] These women urged pundits and the wider public to pay attention to more neglected aspects of women's lives in Muslim-majority societies, namely their up-to-date and omnipresent struggles for resources, rights, and mobility.

How do women get by when they are not being abused or murdered or not out protesting on the streets, which seem to be the only conditions under which they garner international public attention? How do they negotiate meanings and power at the intersections of historically produced gender and class hierarchies? What are the differences and similarities in their experiences of gender? And finally, how does social change manifest itself in their experiences? My research on young women in Turkey, which I summarize below, grappled with these questions.

The Research Method and Concepts

Based on my interview-based ethnographic research, I examined the formations of femininity across social classes in urban Turkey. The interviews with young women entailed open-ended questions about their socioeconomic backgrounds, everyday experiences, and views on social issues. I designed the interviews "as lengthy and focused conversations" to get at young women's sense of hierarchies and negotiations of power and the extent to which these negotiations indicated social change. The interviews frequently turned into open conversations in which young women ask me about my experiences. My candid responses prompted them to share further details about their lives. This dialogue helped rework the power hierarchy created by the research encounter between me and my interviewees and reinscribe my researcher role as a fellow young woman with similar experiences of the double standard of sexuality and everyday patriarchy (Dwyer 1999: 6).

In my final analysis of the research findings, I focused on four young women—Zeynep, Sultan, Nuray, and Sibel—between the ages of twenty and thirty, who come from families with unequal access economic resources and different gender notions. (Alemdaroğlu 2011). I analyzed the structural constraints, everyday struggles, and gender negotiations across social classes in Turkey through their biographies and narratives. Despite their commonalities of being young and female and living in Ankara, their lives differ from each other in significant ways: they have diverse socioeconomic backgrounds, varied levels and quality of education, unequal positions in the labor market, and different household arrangements in disparate neighborhoods.

My approach to social class diverged significantly from the conventional Marxist and Weberian approaches, which treat the class as an entity "out-there," preconfigured based on economic criteria or authority. As Wacquant (1991) notes, the "epistemic ambition" of getting at a correct classification of people is destined to fail because it rests on "a fundamentally mistaken conception of the ontological status of classes." Instead, this paper builds on literature that studies class in relational terms. For instance, from this perspective, "middle-class" becomes a meaningful category only in relation to upper and lower classes. Hence, its effect on cultural identity and gender can only be observed in relation to other class positions and in connection with classed and classifying agents' experiences. Pierre Bourdieu (1985) captures the relative and relational nature of the social class with his suggestion to think about classes as social locations that are determined "on the basis of principles of differentiation and distribution" of economic, cultural, and social resources within social space.

Gender is an essential determinant of one's position in social space. In specifying its effect, I drew on Lois McNay's idea of "gender as a lived relation," which conceptualizes gender as an experience in relation to others instead of a merely structural location within materially and discursively generated hierarchies between men and women (McNay 2004). Conceptualized in these terms, the significance of young women's connections with real and imaginary others in everyday life becomes important for examining their understanding, practice, and negotiation of femininity.

The four young women's narratives particularly compelled me because they exhibited how young women are symbolically connected to each other via their differences. In other words, while they did not know each other in real life and their everyday paths rarely intersect in the city, they habitually refer to each other in the abstract as they narrate their experiences. On the one hand, their narrative relationality indicates how gender hierarchies are formed and negotiated not only through differences between men and women but also through differences from other women. On the other, it also points out the role of common narratives by which they negotiate their identity and power at the intersection of class and gender hierarchies. Their "narrative identities" or the stories they tell about themselves take shape in relation to their knowledge and imagination of other women (Somers 1994). Therefore, when referring to "experience," I do not merely use it as an individual category. Instead, I refer to a social and relational category, given that experiences are continuously formed and narrated in relation to others. Overall, young women's differences and similarities have facilitated an in-depth examination of how class, culture, and gender are entangled in Turkey. Therefore, the paper's contribution lies in its effort to examine similarities and differences between young women's experiences across social classes, their strategies of negotiating power, and what social change looks like in their experiences.

Unequal Resources and Relationality

If society, as Bourdieu prompts us to think, is organized based on principles of differentiation, where agents are distributed according to their share of economic, cultural, and social resources, i.e., income, education, and social networks, Zeynep, Sultan, Nuray, and Sibel have quite different locations in society. These locations entail different experiences, levels of autonomy, spaces of mobility, and performances of respectability. Then, if located spatially regarding the inequalities of access to material resources and everyday mobility, there would be Zeynep, a university-educated professional young woman from an upper-middle-class neighborhood in Ankara on one side, and Sultan on the other, a stay-at-home-young woman in a *gecekondu* neighborhood. Somewhere in the middle, then, are Nuray and Sibel, with significant differences in between. By juxtaposing their stories and narratives about (a) family, educational backgrounds, and work; (b) autonomy, constraints, and struggles; (c) their sense of self in relation to others, my writing on the subject mapped out how femininity is constructed at the intersection of hierarchies of class, gender, and age (a more detailed account of their social positions and experiences can be read in Alemdaroğlu 2015).

The differences in family and educational backgrounds fundamentally affect their access to cultural and economic resources, setting the parameters of their thoughts, beliefs, expectations, and practices. Unequal access to valuable resources and opportunities (such as education and jobs) informs young women's horizons of action or the possible ways they perform and negotiate femininity. The cultural and economic resources available to them primarily depend on their families' location in the socioeconomic distribution (such as parents' education, occupational status, income, and neighborhood of residence) and how opportunities are distributed based on gender within the family.

Attending to young women's biographies in detail allows one to examine how socioeconomic differences are formed and operate in everyday life. Doing so also shows how differences constitute subjects in relational terms (Scott 1991). This relational aspect is evident when young women talk about the self, they also talk about each other without knowing each other in real life. Their place in social hierarchies and their experience of gender are always experienced through their relative and relational position to other women in social space. While their narratives reveal cultural hierarchies about different femininities and play an important part in the formation of gendered subjectivities, they also show how young women classify each other. Finally, however, my research also revealed the similar narratives that young women of different socioeconomic backgrounds employ to negotiate femininity strategically.

Escaping Femininity, Claiming Respectability, and Social Change

While unequal access to valuable resources and gender notions within the family shape young women's knowledge of the expected and possible forms of action, it is evident from my interviewees' narratives that they do not accept their immediate horizons of action as a given. They constantly negotiate what is available and possible for them. Their narratives suggest that young women actively construct their femininity by distancing themselves from other women and escaping from certain forms of femininity. They commonly and strategically identify themselves as "less feminine" and "more masculine" than specific others. Other women are alternately identified as "traditional," "backward," "too feminine," "submissive," and "ignorant." The language they employ to identify other women is not that surprising given the ideological inculcation of the modernization ideology that divided Turkish society into "modern" and "traditional." Their performance of "lesser femininity" is practiced in daily life by smoking and wearing a baseball cap and trouser (Sultan), being solemn and distant to men (Nuray), acting like men, tightly putting up her hair, wearing loose clothes, and speaking vulgarly (Sibel); and working outside the home (Sibel and Zeynep). These performances mean to transgress gender boundaries but do not necessarily subvert gender hierarchies. Instead, they mark the limits of young women's escape, crystallized at the moment, for instance, when Sultan replaced her baseball cap, which she had during our conversation with a headscarf when her male relatives paid a visit. Similarly, Sibel's efforts to get her male colleagues' approval in her male-dominated work environment by acting like them led her to get further stigmatized at work, because her male colleagues find her attempts to integrate as "unnatural" and "improper."

However, it is interesting how young women define "traditional femininity" and perform "less femininity" differently. Their differences are linked to their specific economic and educational backgrounds on the one hand and their cultural notions of womanhood that shape by their relationship to their families, friends, and the larger society. The variation among them provides us with a panorama of social locations and the corresponding symbolic differences in the formation of femininity. For example, Sibel and Zeynep identify "traditional femininity" with women who are less educated, non-working, and more "submissive." Working outside, making their own money, and not being submissive to the expectations of "conservative" boyfriends, friends, and neighbors are fundamental to how they distinguish themselves from their conceptualization of traditional women. However, Sultan, who squarely fits the definition of the "traditional" in Sibel or Zeynep's imagination, also escapes from that role which she associates with her female relatives. Sultan performs the "non-traditional" in several other ways, but most significantly through her religious and somatic practices. While what makes women "traditional" for Sibel and Zeynep is their ignorance of the outside world, for Sultan, it is their ignorance of the religious world.

While young women escape certain forms of femininity, they employ alternative cultural narratives—such as independence, moderation, religiosity, and chastity—to negotiate self-value and respectability in society. The performance of claiming respectability is based on what is culturally and economically available. In Sultan's bounded physical space, her heightened religiosity remains an escape. It warrants her claim to respectability. Whereas for Sibel, respectability is tied to her working women status and "knowing the outside world," unlike her female relatives and neighbors.

In addition to efforts to appear as "less-feminine," young women also avoid specific actions and behaviors that they think might undermine their respectability and chastity in their respective environments. Nuray avoids eye contact with unfamiliar men when she is outside and limits her interactions with those men that she knows; Sibel stays away from the balcony when a male neighbor is outside; Zeynep avoids interaction with her male clients outside the office. It is common for them to think that remaining chaste is their responsibility toward their families and future husbands. The standards of chastity are contextual and family-dependent. For some families like Sultan's, where norms are strict, acts like smoking are seen as dishonoring. For Zeynep, chastity is mainly associated with virginity, an obligation she pragmatically complies with in order to have a peaceful relationship with her family and future husband. That said, Zeynep believes that the conception of virginity is contextual—she would view the issue more liberally if she lived abroad. Even though virginity remains a norm for larger sections of society, it does not entail sexual abstinence for many young women. As Gül Özyeğin (2009) observes, educationally advantaged, upwardly mobile young women purposefully develop "ambiguous identities" about their state of virginity, disconnecting "the physical reality of virginity" and "the moral expression of virginity" in the process of negotiating contradictory social expectations about sexuality. Moreover, anecdotal evidence of hymenoplasty operations are not uncommon. They provide women with leeway in navigating sexual norms and restore respectability and self-confidence in the marriage market (Cindoğlu 1997; Mernissi 1982).

Escaping femininity and maintaining respectability can be seen as contradictory aspirations since how young women escape from femininity may hinder their claims to respectability. Similarly, because respectability is often attained by vindicating social values and norms, it potentially undermines young women's capacity to bargain with restrictive gender regimes. However, young women's narratives indicate that these aspirations work in complementary ways by carving out spaces for young women to challenge social expectations without losing face. The experiences of Zeynep, Sultan, Nuray, and Sibel ultimately show the extent to which family and society control young women's bodies, sexuality, and relationships, and how young women pragmatically mediate between these social impositions, individual desires, changing generational practices, and the security of compliance with their families' demands.

The four young women represent the larger group I studied, demonstrating how youth maneuver within their material and social constraints, juggling between maintaining their parents' protection and expanding their horizons of action. Where social control is the strongest, young women look for outlets that require minimal physical mobility. What appear to be acts of transgressions in Sultan's case, such as her insistence on the ethics of wearing trousers or smoking, are her resistance to the family's impositions. However, they are also acts of exploration within her confined physical and social space. For Nuray, Zeynep, and Sibel, their varying degrees of freedom to move about the city and interact with people beyond their immediate social connections provided them with different autonomy levels. Research on young women in other parts of the world shows similar maneuvering and negotiation strategies within a complex web of meanings, constraints, and relationships framed by patriarchy, cultural stereotypes, youthful desires, economic difficulties, and family control (Dwyer 1999; Mahdavi 2008; Mohammad 2013; Özyeğin 2009).

Young women's escape from femininity and their concern with respectability define their cautious effort to improve their everyday freedoms and mobility and remind us of what Asef Bayat (2010) calls "the collective actions of non-collective actors" that change the society. Bayat debunks the widespread notion that political deficiencies and cultural inertia such as Islam and patriarchy make the Middle East immune to democratization. Based on research on Iran and Egypt, Bayat argues that ordinary people's everyday activities inadvertently promote social transformation. Accordingly, subordinate groups such as youth and women consciously or unconsciously resist, defy, negotiate, or even circumvent discrimination not by the deliberate collective protest theorized by social movements theory, but rather by engaging in ordinary daily practices such as working, grooming, walking, and traveling (Bayat 2010: 98). Youth and women's uncoordinated actions, according to Bayat, replace the politics of protest with the politics of presence, which work in subtle ways in changing society.

The experiences of Sultan, Sibel, Zeynep, and Nuray epitomize uncoordinated change that Bayat theorizes. They participate in social change not through collective action but through daily practices by which they distance themselves from "traditional" and "backward" others. In contribution to Bayat's thesis, however, my study shows the subjective experience of social change, particularly how young women theorize their presence and everyday practices in a changing society. For young women, their practices are more than just "presence." Rather, they are active negotiations mediating between social responsibilities and youthful desires to expand their social confines.

Surveys of urban youth in Turkey confirm some of these findings by comparing young women with young men. They indicate that young women have a less "conservative" and more "egalitarian" approach to gender relations than young men (Artan, Deniz and Güler 2005; Şen et al. 2005; Turkish Youth 98 1999). According to a 2005 study of Turkish university students, most young people struggle to find their way between "individualistic" and "patriarchal" values. However, while female students hold more "liberal" values and seek empowerment, male students are more prone to accept the "traditional" family structure and patriarchal relations (Artan et al. 2005). This is particularly evident in attitudes about sexuality. Studies of sexual attitudes among university students suggest that even though boys engage in premarital sex at a younger age and are more sexually active, they disapprove of nonmarital sex for young women at a higher rate than women themselves. More recent research confirms this finding, indicating young women's unwillingness to comply with a gender order that discriminates against them.

Finally, while my interviewees' critique of submissive women and conservative men hints at the feminist underpinnings of their perspective when asked, all four univocally reject feminism. For them, feminism is an "extreme" and "unrealistic" conviction of women's superiority. Young women's tendency to reject feminism is a common phenomenon not only in Turkey, where there is relatively a strong feminist movement, but also in countries with even stronger feminist political traditions. For instance, in the United States, Baumgardner and Richards (2000) argued that young feminist-minded women were often self-absorbed in their struggles and did not link these individual struggles for autonomy and equality to the larger history of the feminist movement. Hence, even among young women more "feminist-minded" than my interviewees, there is a tangible unwillingness to identify with feminist politics. This unwillingness is tied to several factors not limited to the persistent elitism of feminist movements across the board.

Conclusion

Lila Abu-Lughod (1991: 145) identified three main problems in the way that "culture" or cultural groups are studied in anthropological and feminist literature: the first is to undermine "the connections on each side of the cultural divide and the ways in which they define each other"; the second is to neglect "the differences within each category created by class, race, and sexuality"; and the third is to overlook "the ways in which experiences have been constructed historically and have changed over time." Motivated by this critique, in my work, I first explored the differences within a small group of young Muslim women, who, in the Western discourse, would be deemed as a homogeneously repressed population. I focused on their differing experiences informed by social class and showed access to valuable resources such as education and jobs give women important leverage in bargaining with patriarchy or negotiating their place in society. However, despite these differences, I argued that young women across the board carefully moderate their acts to maintain the respect of others and the support of their families. The family proves to be central to young women's experiences as it sets the boundaries of respectable forms of femininity and draws their horizons of action by creating opportunities and/or constraints in education, work, and physical and social mobility. Depending on one's emotional and economic dependency, the family exerts varying degrees of control over the body, sexuality, and everyday practices. Finally, the young women's stories are also testimonies of social change, embodied in their everyday practices and experiences of generational, cultural shifts within their families and communities. Overall, the paper has provided insights into the entwined relations of gender and class in the context of larger cultural and generational change. Lastly, the four women I examined in depth in my work are in no way to embrace all experiences available to young women in Turkey, nor does my study claim to be representative in the positivist sense. Nevertheless, their experiences and narratives complement each other significantly in depicting a social landscape of young womanhood in the country.

Note

1   For Aga-Soltan's case, see: https://www.youtube.com/watch?v=C4-iLG6FwRc (accessed June 11, 2013), Asma Mahfouz's call is here: http://www.youtube.com/watch?v=ng2PhJMn4uc (accessed June 11, 2013). For Ceyda Sungur's significance for the Turkish uprising, see: http://www.telegraph.co.uk/ news/worldnews/europe/turkey/10108014/Lady-in-the-Red-Dress-and-her-dream-of-a-Turkish-rebirth.html (accessed January 24, 2014). Here is an example of the questioning of previous understandings about Muslim women in main stream media: http://www.nytimes.com/2011/12/21/world/middleeast/violence-enters-5th-day-as-egyptian-general-blames-protesters. html?pagewanted=all&_r=0

References

Abu-Lughod, L. (1991), "Writing against Culture," in R. G. Fox (ed.), *Recapturing Anthropology: Working in the Present*, 137–54, Santa Fe: School of American Research Press.
Abu-Lughod, L. (2002), "Do Muslim Women Really Need Saving? Anthropological Reflections on Cultural Relativism and Its Others," *American Anthropologist*, 104 (3): 783–90.
Afary, J. (2009), *Sexual Politics in Modern Iran*, Cambridge: Cambridge University Press.
Ahmed, L. (1992), *Women and Gender in Islam: Historical Roots of a Modern Debate*, New Haven: Yale University Press.
Alemdaroğlu, A. (2015), "Escaping Femininity, Claiming Respectability: Culture, Class and Young Women in Turkey," *Women's Studies International Forum* 53: 53–62.
Arat, Y. (1997), "The Project of Modernity and Women in Turkey," in S. Bozdogan and R. Kasaba (eds.), *Rethinking Modernity and National Identity in Turkey*, 95–112, Seattle: University of Washington Press.
Artan, H. I., M. D. Börü, G. İslamoğlu, E. S. Yurtkoru, B. Durmuş, K. Calışkan, and H. S. Ergun (2005), *Üniversite Gençleri Değerleri: Korkular ve Umutlar*, Istanbul: TESEV.
Alemdaroğlu, A. (2011), *Knowing Your Place: Inequalities, Subjectivities and Youth in Turkey*, University of Cambridge.
Baumgardner, J. and A. Richards (2000), *Manifesta: Young Women, Feminism, and the Future*, New York: Farrar, Straus and Giroux.
Bayat, A. (2010), *Life as Politics. How Ordinary People Change the Middle East*, Stanford: Stanford University Press.
Beck, L. and N. R. Keddie (1978), *Women in the Muslim World*, Cambridge: Harvard University Press.
Bourdieu, P. (1985), "The Social Space and the Genesis of Groups," *Theory and Society*, 14 (6), 723–44.
Çakır, S. (1994), *Osmanlı Kadın Hareketi*, Istanbul: Metis Yayinlari.
Cindoğlu, D. (1997), "Virginity Tests and Artificial Virginity in Modern Turkish Medicine," *Women's Studies International Forum*, 20 (2): 253–61.
Droeber, J. (2005), *Dreaming of Change: Young Middle-class Women and Social Transformation in Jordan*, Leiden: Brill.
Dwyer, C. (1999), "Veiled Meanings: Young British Muslim Women and the Negotiation of Differences," *Gender, Place and Culture*, 6 (1): 5–26.
Göle, N. (1997), *The Forbidden Modern: Civilization and Veiling*, Ann Arbor: University of Michigan Press.
Kandiyoti, D. (1987), "Emancipated but Unliberated," *Feminist Studies*, 13 (2): 317–38.
Kandiyoti, D. (1988), "Bargaining with Patriarchy," *Gender and Society*, 2 (3): 274–90.
Kandiyoti, D. (1991), "End of the Empire: Islam, Nationalism and Women in Turkey," in D. Kandiyoti (ed.), *Women, Islam and the State*, 22–47, Basingstoke: Macmillan.
Koğacıoğlu, D. (2004), "The Tradition Effect: Framing Honor Crimes in Turkey," *Differences: A Journal of Feminist Cultural Studies*, 15 (2): 119–51.
Mahdavi, P. (2008), *Passionate Uprisings: Iran's Sexual Revolution*, Stanford: Stanford University.

McNay, L. (2004), "Agency and Experience: Gender as a Lived Relation," in L. Adkins and B. Skeggs (eds.), *Feminism after Bourdieu*, 173–90, Oxford: Blackwell.
Mernissi, F. (1982), "Virginity and Patriarchy," *Women's International Forum*, 5 (2): 183–91.
Mernissi, F. (1987), *Beyond the Veil: Male–Female Dynamics in Modern Muslim Society*, Indiana: Indiana University Press.
Mishra, S. (2007), "'Saving' Muslim Women and Fighting Muslim Men: Analysis of Representations in *The New York Times*," *Global Media Journal*, 6 (11).
Moghadam, V. (1993), *Modernizing Women: Gender and Social Change in the Middle East*, Boulder & London: Lynne Rienner.
Mohammad, R. (2013), "Making Gender Ma(r)king Place: Youthful British Pakistani Muslim Women's Narratives of Urban Space," *Environment & Planning A*, 45 (8): 1802–22.
Özdalga, E. (1998), The *Veiling Issue, Official Secularism and Popular Islam in Modern Turkey*, Nordic Institute of Asian Studies Report Series, 33. Richmond, Surrey: Curzon Press.
Özyeğin, Gu. (2009), "Virginal Facades: Sexual Freedom and Guilt among Young Turkish Women," *European Journal of Women's Studies*, 16 (2): 103–23.
Sadeghi, F. (2010), "Negotiating with Modernity: Young Women and Sexuality in Iran," in L. Herrera and A. Bayat (eds.), *Being Young and Muslim: New Cultural Politics in the Global South and North*, 273–90, Oxford: Oxford University Press.
Saktanber, A. (2002), *Living Islam: Women, Religion and the Politicization of Culture in Turkey*, London: I. B. Tauris.
Scott, J. (1991), "The Evidence of Experience," *Critical Inquiry*, 17 (4): 773–97.
Şen, M. (2005), *Gençlik, AB ve zıt hisler: Bedenini İsterim Ama Ruhunu Asla*, Ankara: Türk Sosyal Bilimler Derneği.
Somers, M. R. (1994), "The Narrative Constitution of Identity: A Relational and Network Approach," *Theory and Society*, 23 (5): 605–49.
Spivak, G. C. (1985), "Can the Subaltern Speak? Speculations on Widow Sacrifice," *Wedge*, 7–8: 120–30.
Sweis, R. K. (2012), "Saving Egypt's Village Girls: Humanity, Rights, and Gendered Vulnerability in a Global Youth Initiative," *Journal of Middle East Women's Studies*, 8 (2): 26–50.
Turkish Youth 98 (1999). *Silent Majority Highlighted*, Ankara: Istanbul Mülkiyeliler Vakfı, Konrad Adenauer Association.
Wacquant, L. (1991), "Making Class: The Middle Class(es) in Social Theory and Social Structure," in S. G. McNall, R. Levine and R. Fantasia (eds.), *Bringing Class Back In*, 39–64, Boulder: Westview.

Sexuality in Iran Revisited: Queer and Unruly Digital Constellations

by Ladan Rahbari

Introduction

In 2016, I published a short entry in *The Wiley Blackwell Encyclopaedia of Family Studies* titled "Sexuality in Iran" (i.e. Rahbari 2016). This current chapter attempts to revise that entry and present my updated perspectives on sexuality in Iran, as I now believe that piece to be a short-sighted and unrepresentative description of sexuality and gender discourses in Iran. While there was truth to some of the arguments I presented in that entry, overall, it did not do justice to the complexity of sexuality in Iran. This chapter is thus as much an attempt to revise my 2016 entry, as it is a more in-depth and nuanced account of discourses of gender and sexuality in Iran. I began the 2016 entry by emphasizing the restrictive and problematic nature of some cultural and political discourses of sexuality in Iran. Here, I will start with the same premise: sketching the role of state politics and attitudes in hindering, stigmatizing, and criminalizing unruly and other than cis-heteronormative genders and sexualities. My focus will be on legitimized sexualities and gendered performances, as well as sexual socialization and education.

After discussing the cis-heteronormative nature of institutionalized and state-enforced views on gender and sexuality in Iran, I will broadly outline some of the ways Iranians navigate the state's sexual and gender politics before presenting a short outline of my empirical research on a Persian-language digital LGBTQI+ Telegram dating channel. This latter outline is important because while formalized discourses, from education to politics, adopt a cis-heteronormative and often patriarchal approach to gender and sexuality, sexuality in Iran is not and should not be confined to the realm of official and formal politics and discourses. Sexuality is like gender, impacted by the state's attitude and biopolitics, but not solely defined by it. Had the state-enforced discourses of sexuality in Iran been truly dominant, Ahmadinejad's famous saying "in Iran we don't have homosexuals [*sic*] like in your country"[1] would not have been such an inaccurate, outrageous, and absurd statement. Unlike what Ahmadinejad claimed, queerness, gender, and sexual non-binarism, and stepping outside of cis-heteronormative cultural and official gender and sexuality frameworks are neither rare nor uncommon in Iran. They are, however, pushed into specific spaces and sometimes to the realm of seemingly "apolitical performance," to which I will return at the end of this chapter.

This chapter relies broadly on my work on sexuality and gender in Iranian (digital) spaces and my research on a Persian-language LGBTQI+ dating Telegram channel. Before embarking on my discussion and analysis, I would like to caution the readers that talking about a homogeneous Iran is, for me, problematic per se. The country inhabits above 80 million people from diverse ethnic and religious backgrounds, with an estimated 25 percent living in rural areas, leading to differential access to education and the labor market.[2] The vast geography and demographic differences, coupled with dissimilarities in local and provincial economies and religiopolitical attitudes, have impacted understandings and approaches to gender and sexuality across Iranian populations. There is not one single discourse or cultural framing of sexuality in Iran. The usage of "culture" can sometimes be as problematic as the generalizing term "Iranian." Considering Iranian cultural attitudes to sexuality homogeneous would inevitably lead to bias and reductionism. The "cultural" is not a homogeneous set of ideas, norms, and beliefs and is not independent of the effects of structural factors and state politics. The application of culture as a concept to analyze "Iranian" attitudes toward gender and sexuality masks the vast exiting diversities of local attitudes, mores, traditions, as well as religious and political differences that add important nuances to the discourses on sexuality in Iran. While the education system enforces cis-heteropatriarchal socialization, there are fundamental differences based on regions, families' choices, and socio-political factors such as religious inclinations and political affiliations. I thus use the term Iranian to refer to a geographical territory and not a monolithic cultural or political entity.

Gender and Sexual Politics: Legitimized and Official Discourses

Iran is notorious for its officially implemented sexual and gender policing regime. While some official and cultural rules of conduct limit sociality between men and women, different genders can and do interact and work side by side in most public and private sectors and attend certain entertainment, higher education, health, and government administrative facilities together. Spatial gender segregation is implemented in some transportation, sports, entertainment, administrative, health, and other facilities. Whereas gender segregation has existed as part of the culture and tradition in some Muslim contexts, the systematic effort to implement and institutionalize such a divide is a rather recent phenomenon (Arjomand 2016). Binary gender differentiation and segregation is, however, not only limited to spatial-temporal arrangements and starts at the level of the body. Wearing a state-mandated compulsory hijab covering all body parts except face and hands applies to women and girls over the age of eight (Rahbari,

Longman and Coene 2019). While pious dress codes apply to men as well as women, regulations on men's bodywear are looser and less restrictive.

While gender-based socialization takes place rather widely, sexual education is not central to the Iranian official educational system. In fact, pre-university sexual education takes place on a limited scale. It is only in universities that students must take an obligatory course called "family planning." This course engages with the topic of sex and, to a lesser extent, sexuality. As its title indicates, the course is predominantly geared toward equipping young Iranians with information on pregnancy, contraception, and sexual health/hygiene. Additionally, when getting married, all couples must attend a consultation session to receive a marriage permit. This latter session aims to cover both the emotional and sexual marital obligations of the future spouses. Sexual education in Iran also relies on specific interpretations of Shi'a branch of Islam. Based on these interpretations, the official sexuality discourses do not undermine sex and sexuality. Instead, they recognize sex and desire as central to human development (Sadeghi and Eqbali 2020) but sanction it only within marital relationships. Perhaps partly due to the educational and socialization trends, marriage continues to be widely desired in Iran, but it is no longer the only pathway to long-term cohabitation or sexual relationships.[3]

When it comes to dating limitations, the government's approach is partly performative; that is, a political performance of control is presented by putting in place regulations that are widely ignored. The result is that, while nonmarital dating and sexual relationships are officially forbidden and pushed out of the public eye, in reality, premarital dating is quite common. Contact with the opposite sex is not entirely controlled but rather limited to (semi-)private spaces, which means that premarital dating takes place, albeit as a secret part of the lives of Iranian youth (Rahbari 2020b). Dating is riskier for LGBTQI+ people under the country's penal code, which declares all relationships outside of the legitimized heteronormative model as problematic and subject to punishment by law. The penalties range from flogging to harsher forms of punishment depending on the circumstances of the "crime." Iranian authorities, however, do not actively seek out LGBTQI+ people, making the risk of prosecution for "homosexuality" minimal only as long as their identities are kept strictly covert (Rahbari 2020a). Yet, reducing risks of prosecution does not lead to a risk- and fear-free life, as LGBTQI+ people—especially those who are visibly queer—are at risk of everyday hostility, aggression and violence and systematic and widespread discrimination. Seeking partners, public expressions of affection and other activities that would explicitly or implicitly categorize a person's genders and sexualities as "unruly" may put them at risk.

As perceptions of marriage and relationships have been changing, so have the attitudes toward premarital piety, specifically those regarding women. While in some local traditions, nonmarital cross-gender interactions and loss of "virginity"[4] are still considered unacceptable for female marriage candidates (Nikirashidi et al. 2019) and can damage the woman's reputations and family honor, others tend to value independence and employment as desirable characteristics for women. The attitudes have especially shifted within the younger generations. The Persian saying "not having seen sunlight and moonlight"[5] that was once used to refer to an ideal female marriage partner has turned into a running joke by Iranian youth to mock traditional "piety" frameworks. Besides the official politics, gender and sexuality are also regulated by cultural restrictions, prohibitions, and taboos.

Queer and Unruly in Digital Dating

If one only looks through the mainstream channels—from official state media, educational sources, and official discourses of gender, sexuality, health, etc.—queer gender or sexual identity seems to remain invisible to the Iranian public (Rahbari 2020a). For many Iranian queer, urban spaces are too hostile to claim as territory, although territorialization has been documented on a very small scale in large cities. Despite the dangers associated with queer and gay performance and identification, as Jón Ingvar Kjaran's in-depth study in Iran's gay/queer scenes and spaces has shown, the picture of gay life in Iran is often at odds with the one painted in the global north (Kjaran 2019). Kjaran (2019) traces unruly spaces, practices, and performances that survive and thrive, showing that persecution and victimhood are only one part of the narrative of queer Iranians.

Besides these spaces of unruly presence, many Iranians go digital to claim spaces and territories and to express nonnormative identities. Queer Iranians as well as gender nonnormative people or cis-identifying women and men whose embodiment and performance are simply considered "obscene" use social media not only to connect to each other, but also to be able to freely "identify" (see, e.g., Rahbari 2019, 2020a). Besides the general limitations youth face for dating, LGBTQ+ youth might be exposed to further aggression and violence if their identities are revealed. This added risk makes digital spaces more suitable for them to meet.

In my search for dating and queer interaction spaces, I came across a Persian-language Telegram channel used as an "LGBT [sic] dating" platform.[6] Telegram is a popular messaging application widely used in Iran. Since its launch in 2013, Telegram became one of the main sources of uncensored news and information flow in Iran. The app became so popular that it replaced many functions of other internet services such as emails, other messaging apps, discussion forums, blogs, news websites, e-commerce, social networks, and even television (Kargar and McManamen 2018). In 2017 and 2018, Telegram was used by Iranian for organizing widespread anti-government demonstrations across Iran. As a result, the Iranian government blocked the application in May 2018. While banned, Telegram remains popular in Iran as the government blocking is often circumvented by the more tech-savvy and younger internet users.

One function of Telegram application allows us to create channels, which are platforms where admins are authorized to post messages, but users are not. Users may subscribe to the channels to follow their content. Subscribers to a channel can see the channel's history and all future posts but cannot see other subscribers' information. The "LGBT" dating channel that I studied had 6.38 thousand subscribers at the time of research, during 2020 and January 2021. The channel description explained that it was aimed for "lesbian, gay, trans, shemale [sic],[7] and singles." Users were asked by the admin(s) to send their name, age, location, height, and a picture directly to the admin(s). The admins(s) verified the authenticity of the user accounts and then posted their profile on the channel. There was another channel coupled with the dating channel that exposed non-authentic accounts and warned followers against possibly abusive users. The channel predominantly posted profiles of men users. While less frequent, woman- or trans-identifying profiles also existed.

Besides LGBTQI+ looking for different forms of "rels"—the abbreviated form of relationships used on the platform—there were other forms of non-mainstream dating possibilities on the channel, such as cis-men who sought "sugar-mommies." I did not come across any women looking for sugar daddies on this specific channel, but multiple users sought "sugar-mommies." These *rels* varied between "sex-friends," casual sex, long-term relationships, and marital partner categories.

The channel's posting format did not allow for constant modification in one's profile. This made the initial choice of images and texts even more important. The posts on the channel, an example of which is visible in figure 1, often included information regarding gender, sexual orientation, and dating preference of the person. In the example presented in figure 27.1, the user posted their name, age, and location (all three of which have been anonymized). Then they identified as "pansexual." They explained that they were not looking for a "sexual" relationship and would like to connect with women or trans-individuals who were of similar age and geographically close to them. They emphasized that they sought someone who did not care about "looks" and expressed that they were "fat." It was also mentioned that men who contacted them will get blocked. As the small eye-shaped icon at the bottom of the image reveals, the profile was viewed 10 thousand times at the time the research was conducted.

سلام
اسمم
پن سکشوالم از
سالمه
اصلا اهل رابطه ی جنسی نیستم
پسر بیاد ریپورت میشه
دنبال یه دختر یا ترنسم
من تپلم و اگه این هم براش مهمه و بدش میاد ک همچنان نیاد
10K 2:15 PM

Figure 27.1 Screenshot of a "pansexual" identifying user's post explaining that they look for a "non-sexual" woman or a trans dating partner.

سلام دوستان 😊🌸
■■■ هستم ■ سالمه از ■■■
وزنم ■ قدم ■■■
سافت و فوت فتیش هستم 👞👟👢 💪
هیری دوست دارم 🐻🐾
دوستان همجنسگرا لطفا با اصل و عکس بیان 🌸🌿
👁 8699 2:35 PM

Figure 27.2 Screenshot of a post by a user who identifies as "soft" showing interest in "hairy" bodies and "foot fetish" and looking for [a] "gay" dating partner(s).

The images shared by the users often used filters in the form of digital enhancements, color filters, and digital makeup. Some users made active use of emojis to express or illustrate their sexual preferences. As seen in figure 27.2, for instance, the user did not specify their gender preference. Instead, they posted emojis illustrating men's shoes, implying a preference for men. The terminology used on the profiles sometimes derived from the English language. Terms such as "top," "bot," "soft," "fetish," "butch," "rel," etc., were used parallel to terms deriving from Persian language such as *Fa'el* (dom) and *Maf'ul* (sub).

Considering the precarity of LGBTQI+ people in Iran, it was a significant finding that individuals shared their personal information and profile pictures publicly—albeit sometimes modified to the level that identification became impossible or at least very difficult. In another article on queer fashion in Iran, I have argued that the seemingly apolitical attitude and perceived banality of unruly performances and digital activities could lead to higher levels of tolerance by the Iranian hyper-vigilant cyber police (see Rahbari 2020a). The same argument can apply to the case of the LGBTQI+ dating channel on Telegram.

Discussion and Concluding Remarks

To offer a preliminary analysis of the digital activities of LGBTQI+ Iranians on the Telegram dating channel, I use Jen Jack Gieseking's notion of constellations presented in his book *A Queer New York Geographies of Lesbians, Dykes, and Queer* (Gieseking 2020) and "sexuality assemblage" discussed by Fox and Alldred (2013) to discuss queer and unruly presences in Iranian spaces.

In his book, Gieseking offers a critical cartography of a queer New York across generations using the concept of constellations. Constellations, an analytical term used by Gieseking to discuss queer spaces in New York, consists of accumulations and interruptions in queer spatial presences. Instead of tracing queer presences and performances within networks, the notion "constellations" illustrates that queer networks are not constantly ongoing flows but moments of survival within cis-heteronormative and supposedly "post-queer" discourses. This notion of constellation can be used to analyze queer and unruly gender and sexualities in Iranian cyber-spaces.[8] The application of the concept, like any other analytical framework or concept used outside of the context in which it developed, will inevitably be different when used in the case of Iran. The level of risk and precarity involved with visible queerness and exposure of gay/lesbian identities, and the persecution of queer and non-hetero Iranians dramatically affects their vulnerability, and hence, their embodied experience and performance.

Sexuality assemblages are, in the words of Fox and Alldred (2013: 775), assemblages of biological, psychological, cultural, and socioeconomic relations that produce body capacities including comportments, identities, and subjectivities that establish "masculinity" and "femininity." Sexual attraction, sexual preferences, and proclivities are similarly territorializations toward particular objects of desire, consequent upon the particular mix of relations and affects deriving from physical and social contexts, experience, and culture. Sexuality as assemblage enables an understanding of the sexual, which is more than discourse, discrete bodies, and identities and occurs in the spaces between intra-acting human and non-human entanglements (Allen 2015).

The digital sphere is not merely a medium to convey the messages but is itself a part of the interactive network of images, identities, performances, sounds, and affect. The moments of popping in and out of digital spaces not only allow individuals to identify and disidentify, and hence in the words of José Esteban Muñoz, to survive cis-heteropatriarchy (Muñoz 1999), but also to interact with human and non-human entities, from digital effects such as filters and face/body-altering techniques to emojis, text, sounds, etc. Queer constellations are scattered in online and offline rural and urban spaces. These acts of digital performance, open identification, and interaction involve processes of both territorialization and de-territorialization: they create territorialized queer digital spaces, albeit in the form of digital constellations, and they deterritorialize the otherwise individually embodied sexuality assemblages in between bodies.

For queer and unruly Iranians, the risk and fear of persecution are an everyday reality and one defining factor in navigating their lives online and offline. Yet, Iranians and specifically younger generations have challenged and pushed social and behavioral gender and sexual roles and public and private modes of conduct to their limits. I do not intend to imply that social resistance is exclusive to younger people. While present across generations, the new generations' unruliness has found new platforms and is often more publicized and mediatized because of their internet savviness and competitive knowledge and access to social and digital media compared to their predecessors. I aimed most of all to nuance and to complicate the existing discourses of sexuality in Iranian spaces. The short analysis and discussion in this chapter only revealed one star in the constellations of queer spaces. There are many more that I hope studies on gender and sexuality in Iran will investigate.

Notes

1. For context and exchange, see e.g.: http://news.bbc.co.uk/2/hi/7010962.stm
2. For further estimation, see Enayatrad, M., P. Yavari, K. Etemad, S. Khodakarim, and S. Mahdavi (2019), "Determining the Levels of Urbanization in Iran Using Hierarchical Clustering," *Iranian Journal of Public Health*, 48 (6): 1082–90.
3. There is evidence of increase in "white marriage," which refers to "illegal" nonmarital relationships and cohabitations in Iran. See, e.g., http://lat.ms/3odPxB4
4. I have used quotation marks around virginity because as already shown by studies on hymen, the state of the hymen cannot predict chastity or lack of sex. In Iran, virginity is still associated with visible blood during intercourse, but as post-pubertal hymen is elastic and it is possible to maintain an intact hymen after extensive sexual intercourse (Hegazy and Al-Rukban 2012).
5. In Persian, *Aftab-Mahtab-Nadideh*.
6. The channel's name is left out intentionally to protect the participants.
7. This term is widely considered degrading and offensive in many contexts. On the studied Persian LGBT platforms it was commonly used to refer to others, but I did not come across the usage for self-identification.
8. While as Niki Akhavan explains, "Iranian" cyber-space is transnational, I use this term here to refer to those users who use digital media while being geographically located inside Iran (Akhavan 2013).

References

Akhavan, N. (2013), *Electronic Iran—the Cultural Politics of an Online Evolution*, New Brunswick: Rutgers University Press.

Allen, L. (2015), "Sexual Assemblages: Mobile Phones/Young People/School," *Discourse: Studies in the Cultural Politics of Education*, 36 (1): 120–32.

Arjmand, R. (2016), *Public Urban Space, Gender and Segregation: Women-only Urban Parks in Iran*, New York: Routledge.

Fox, N. J. and P. Alldred (2013), "The Sexuality-assemblage: Desire, Affect, Anti-humanism," *The Sociological Review*, 61 (4): 769–89. doi:10.1111/1467-954X.12075

Gieseking, J. J. (2020), *A Queer New York: Geographies of Lesbians, Dykes, and Queers*, New York: New York University Press.

Hegazy, A. A. and M. O. Al-Rukban (2012), "Hymen: Facts and Conceptions," *The Health*, 3 (4): 109–15.

Kargar, S. and K. McManamen (2018), "Censorship and Collateral Damage: Analyzing the Telegram Ban in Iran," *Berkman Klein Center Research Publication* (2018–4): 1–25. https://papers.ssrn.com/sol3/papers.cfm?abstract_id=3244046.

Kjaran, J. I. (2019), *Gay Life Stories*, Cham: Palgrave.

Muñoz, J. E. (1999), *Disidentifications: Queers of Color and the Performance of Politics*, Minneapolis: University of Minnesota Press.

Nikirashidi, F., Z. Ghorashi, S. Esmaeilzadeh, and Z. Asadollahi (2019), "A Study on Association of Premarital Attitude toward Intact Hymen in New Grooms: A Cross-sectional Study," *Journal of Education and Health Promotion*, 8 (March): 52. doi:10.4103/jehp.jehp_161_18

Rahbari, L. (2016), "Sexuality in Iran," in C. L. Shehan (ed.), *Encyclopedia of Family Studies*, 1–5, Chichester: Wiley Blackwell.

Rahbari, L. (2019), "Pushing Gender to Its Limits: Iranian Women Bodybuilders on Instagram." *Journal of Gender Studies*, 28 (5): 591–602.

Rahbari, L. (2020a), "Duffs and Puffs: Queer Fashion in Iranian Cyberspac," *Middle East Critique*, 29 (1): 69–86.

Rahbari, L. (2020b), "Violence in Premarital Relationships in Iran: An Exploratory Qualitative Research," in A. D. Plat and S. D. Silberman (eds.), *Violence: Probing the Boundaries around the World*, 185–202, Leiden: Brill.

Rahbari, L., C. Longman and G. Coene (2019), "The Female Body as the Bearer of National Identity in Iran: A Critical Discourse Analysis of the Representation of Women's Bodies in Official Online Outlets," *Gender, Place & Culture*, 26 (10): 1417–37.

Sadeghi, S. and A. Eqbali (2020), "A Discourse Reading of Sexual Disputes in Iran," *Journal of Women in Culture and Arts*, 12 (1): 51–70.

Part IV

Liquified Space: Beyond Borders and Boundaries

Introduction to Part IV

by Gamze Evcimen & Fatma Müge Göçek

Starting with the fall of the Ottoman empire and gaining more prevalence in recent years with globalization processes and societal conflicts, mobility and displacement constitute important issues in the region. During and after the demise of the Ottoman Empire, many migrants and refugees from the Middle East ultimately settled throughout the Middle East, Europe, and the United States, forming significant diasporas there. Sociologists study the liquified space of the Middle East by focusing on refugees, diaspora in Europe, and diaspora in the United States.

Focusing on the securitization and hypergovernance of Islam and Muslims since the September 11 attacks, Michael Humphrey addresses how the states in the West transformed Muslim immigrant communities from an ethnic-religious minority to a transnational risk category by framing international migration as a security problem after 9/11. Humphrey illustrates that this securitization of migration shifts the onus from structural issues associated with international migration to the migrants themselves by profiling migrants as potential criminals/terrorists that require policing and regulation. Humphrey also underlines that the hypergovernance of migrants allows the West to govern through cultural and racial difference by constructing the "good" and "bad" Muslim and to legitimize the states of exception that turn migrants' bodies into surrogate borders while preventing migrants from crossing borders and avoiding legal responsibilities toward asylum seekers.

Continuing this focus on the construction of refugees as objects of security, Silvia Pasquetti's comparative ethnographic analysis connects the experiences of two populations of poor Palestinians in Israel and the West Bank. Pasquetti studies how the Palestinian urban poor in Lydda and the Palestinian refugees in Jalazun negotiate different configurations of control and how these negotiations influence their political actions against coercion. Pasquetti illustrates that the Palestinian urban poor's encounters with Israel's security-police state in Lydda cause feelings and interactions of suspicion and influence underground forms of action in the city while the Palestinian refugees' relationships with the control of Israeli army, the United Nations Relief and Work Agency and the Palestinian Authority enable the creation and maintenance of community as well as visible and collective forms of action in the camp.

Elisa Pascucci's work focuses on the ways in which international humanitarian aid and Jordan's economic policies promote particular agendas regarding the economic success and livelihoods of Syrian refugees while the refugees in Amman also challenge such agendas of refugee governance. Pascucci demonstrates that international humanitarian assistance reproduces colonial and racial tropes by aiming to prevent Syrian refugees' migration to Europe while Jordan's development policies limit access for qualified jobs to Jordanian citizens. These agendas coalesce in refugee governance that aims to turn refugees into economically viable subjects and to shift the responsibility of survival and recovery onto refugees themselves. Ending on a positive note, Pascucci also emphasizes the agency of refugees in countering precarity by redefining professional and economic success in terms of support, responsibility, and commitment for extended family and communities in both local and transnational terms.

Shifting our focus to the diaspora in Europe, Emily Laxer, Jeffrey G. Reitz, and Patrick Simon address the influence of integration models in France, Canada, and Québec on Muslim minorities' political and civic engagement. Laxer, Reitz, and Simon underline that French republicanism and Québécois interculturalism consider shared values as limits of tolerance for diverse viewpoints and ethnicity as an illegitimate basis for political mobilization while Canadian multiculturalism makes no reference to an official culture and embraces ethnicity as legitimate component of citizenship. Laxer, Reitz, and Simon illustrate that, rather than these integration models, the structure of political institutions and nation-specific cultures of participation affect the patterns of political and civic engagement among the Muslims in these societies.

Ipek Demir changes our lens from the East/West axis to the North-South axis and reconceptualizes the diasporas of the Middle East in Europe as the Global South in the Global North. Demir emphasizes how the struggles of diasporas have brought foreignizations to the Global North, or contributed to the dislodging of coloniality as well as to the expansion of rights and freedoms in Europe. Demir demonstrates the ways in which the agency and mobilization of the Kurds from Turkey foreignize European publics by offering a counter-history to Turkey's nation building project of modernization and nationalism, by exposing the historical and current links between the Kurdish predicament and Europe, and by forming cosmopolitan justice-based solidarities with the social and political transformations in Syrian Kurdistan.

Gökçe Yurdakul studies how the politically engaged Turkish immigrant groups establish connections with the Jewish minority as victims of racial discrimination in Germany. Yurdakul highlights that the focus of Turkish immigrants in Germany changed from the connections between anti-Semitism and racism against Turks to those between anti-Semitism and Islamophobia with the September 11 attacks. Yurdakul illustrates that organized Turkish immigrants draw analogies between anti-Semitism and Islamophobia, emulate Jewish minority's model of organization as a political lobby, and draw from their model of claiming religious rights. Yurdakul also indicates how these two minority groups in Germany perceive religion differently: while the Jewish leaders see religion as a separating ground between them and Turks, Turkish leaders see religious identity as common ground for these two minorities to connect.

Changing our focus to the diaspora in the United States, Louise Cainkar focuses on how the racialized backlash that held Arab and Muslim American communities collectively responsible for the 9/11 attacks reflects an earlier shift in the racialization of Arabs and Muslims as non-white. Cainkar demonstrates how US global interests, particularly its support for Israel, explains the racial constructions of Arab Americans and Islam as culturally inferior and inherently violent while this stigmatization and marginalization serves to not only delegitimize Arab opposition to Israel's occupation but also legitimize exclusionary domestic policies and discriminatory everyday practices against US Arabs and Muslims. Ending on a positive note, Cainkar emphasizes that recent developments, like Trump's presidency and increasing Islamophobia, enabled Arab and Muslim Americans to enact solidarity with/in BIPOC alliances in issues like opposing Trump's 2017 Muslim ban and supporting Palestinians' liberation.

Complementing Cainkar's analysis, Mücahit Bilici's work addresses Muslims' changing perceptions of America. Bilici focuses on how the coalescence of historical processes and changing experiences influenced changes in Muslims' views, which shifted from seeing America as a non-Muslim place for temporary residence to considering America as a homeland for permanent settlement. Bilici illustrates that this cultural shift from avoidance to ethical inclusion of America as a new Muslim homeland enables Muslim immigrants to balance and harmonize their religious identity and American culture in mutually constitutive and reinforcing ways. Bilici ends on a positive note by highlighting how the recent generations of Muslim Americans combine Muslim self-expressions and American style activism.

In a similar vein, Mustafa Gürbüz and Gülsüm Gürbüz-Küçüksarı analyze how headscarf adoption enables the construction of religious, feminine, moral-cultural, and collective identities among hijabi American college students. Gürbüz and Gürbüz-Küçüksarı point to the particularities of the US context; while individualism of American culture can incorporate the veil as a private choice, dominant secular lifestyle and preconceptions about Muslims also cause the stigmatization of headscarf. Emphasizing that headscarf adoption in the United States serves as part of identity construction of a marginalized minority, Gürbüz and Gürbüz-Küçüksarı illustrate that hijabi college students regard hijab as a symbol of liberation that connects their individual and collective religious identities and as a personal choice that bolsters their identity as both Muslims and Americans.

Selected Readings

Abdo, G. (2006), *Mecca and Main Street: Muslim Life in America after 9/11*, Oxford: Oxford University.

Al-Hardan, A. (2017), "Memories for the Return? Remembering the Nakba by the First Generation of Palestinian Refugees in Syria," *Journal of Holy Land and Palestine Studies*, 16 (2): 177–92.

Bakalian, A. and M. Bozorgmehr (2009), *Backlash 9/11: Middle Eastern and Muslim Americans Respond*, Berkeley: University of California.

Cesari, J. (2004), *When Islam and Democracy Meet: Muslims in Europe and in the United States*, New York: Palgrave Macmillan.

Dunn, K. M., N. Klocker and T. Salabay (2007), "Contemporary Racism and Islamophobia in Australia: Racializing Religion," *Ethnicities*, 7 (4): 564–89.

Eccarius-Kelly, V. (2002), "Political Movements and Leverage Points: Kurdish Activism in the European Diaspora," *The Journal of Muslim Minority Affairs*, 22 (1): 91–118.

Göle, N. (2011), "The Public Visibility of Islam and European Politics of Resentment: The Minarets–Mosques Debate," *Philosophy and Social Criticism*, 37 (4): 383–92.

Hanafi, S. and T. Long (2010), "Governance, Governmentalities, and the State of Exception in the Palestinian Refugee Camps of Lebanon," *Journal of Refugee Studies*, 23 (2): 134–59.

Khalili, L. (2007), "Heroic and Tragic Pasts: Mnemonic Narratives in the Palestinian Refugee Camps," *Critical Sociology*, 33 (4): 731–59.

Killian, C. (2003), "The Other Side of the Veil: North African Women in France Respond to the Headscarf Affair," *Gender & Society*, 17 (4): 567–90.

Moghissi, H. (2009), "Sense of (Not) Belonging," in H. Moghissi, S. Rahnema and M. Goodman (eds.), *Diaspora by Design: Muslim Immigrants in Canada and Beyond*, 168–96, Toronto: University of Toronto Press.

Naber, N. (2008), *Race and Arab Americans before 9/11: From Invisible Citizens to Visible Subjects*, Syracuse, NY: Syracuse University Press.

Nimer, M. (2003), "Muslims in America After 9–11," *Journal of Islamic Law and Culture*, 1 (2): 73–101.

Read, J. G. and J. P. Bartkowski (2000), "To Veil or Not to Veil? A Case Study of Identity Negotiation among Muslim Women in Austin, Texas," *Gender & Society*, 14 (3): 395–417.

Schmidt, G. (2004), "Islamic Identity Formation among Young Muslims: The Case of Denmark, Sweden and the United States," *Journal of Muslim Minority Affairs*, 24 (1): 31–45.

I REFUGEES

Migration, Security, and Insecurity: The Securitization and Hypergovernance of Islam and Muslim Societies and Diasporas

by Michael Humphrey

Since the September 11, 2001, international terrorist attacks, international migration has increasingly been framed as a security problem in the West. Borders and entry have become first and foremost an issue of security. At borders, immigration services no longer merely scrutinize the validity of documents and grant permission to enter but provide "border protection" by assessing the risk of passengers as potential criminals, terrorists or visa over-stayers based on their origin, documents, security profiling, biometrics, and big databanks. The security function of the state has expanded beyond national defense through military preparedness to encompass the protection of citizens through monitoring the complex organizational and technological systems that sustain modern post-industrial societies and making the public feel safe. Agencies whose functions were once regarded as marginal to state security (immigration, customs, ambulance) have now become integral to it. Security has become a pervasive discourse of governments to frame and give priority to public policy.

The securitization of migration, the construction of migration as risk, is an expression of the globalization of security to manage the new threats of international crime and terrorism post-September 11. Securitization is "a political technique of framing policy questions in logics of survival with a capacity to mobilize politics of fear in which social relations are structured on the basis of distrust" (Huysmans 2006: xi). It has become emblematic of the anxieties of state sovereignty seeking to manage migration as an expression of globalization—control borders, plan population growth, promote social cohesion, and support (middle class) sustainability. Each of these issues refers to the national capacity to order and regulate the population and, integral to that, to derive legitimacy from being seen to care for, protect, and determine entitlement. Framing migration as a "security" issue gives it political priority and justifies extraordinary legal, policing, and policy measures to manage it. By making migration a security problem, migrants are constituted as the object of policies directed at managing risk. It misrecognizes structural issues such as refugee flows, urban riots, crime, unemployment, and welfare dependency as the attributes of migrants which need policing and regulating. Blaming migrants becomes a strategy of governance to produce social cohesion, mobilize political support, and claim political legitimacy. Moreover, at the margins cultural and racial differences become the basis of defining sovereignty and delineating a state of exception for those seen not to deserve the same protection of the law.

While securitization frames migration as a national issue concerned with determining "who comes here" (controlling borders), enforcing visa requirements (locating overstayers), selecting the "best" migrants, and policing social categories as risk management, in reality migration, the large-scale transnational flow of populations, is an international issue challenging the capacity of individual states to manage the impact of big structural questions: global inequality, transnational social mobility, and displacement of the most vulnerable through economic crisis, environmental degradation and war. The "security turn" in relation to migration signifies the transformation of security from the problem of producing national order to the problem of managing global disorder. Nationally, governance has combined security (policing, surveillance) with the management of citizen insecurity and public perceptions of danger. Transnationally, the state has outsourced security to other states, to security professionals, corporations, international agencies, and NGOs (Bigo 2008) for them to manage unwanted immigrants through containment. This includes interception and detention en route as well as trying to keep people at home through "human security"-oriented development policies. Securitization extends governmentality beyond the state by providing a common language to connect diverse fields and create a shared political project shaping political identities based on fear of the Other.

This paper examines the securitization of migration and migrants as a national and transnational project seeking to manage global disorder by firstly, creating a transnational border in the North from transnationally shared policies and laws to manage international migration as risk, secondly by turning particular kinds of migrants into transnational categories for transnational management—for example, Muslim immigrants and refugees—and thirdly, the hypergovernance of migrants along migration routes or in countries of origin by externalizing borders and outsourcing sovereignty to other states and NGOs to keep (unwanted) migrants at home or intercept them on the way. Hyper-governance refers to the transnational management of populations, the ability of some states to intervene in and shape other states and societies as a neo-imperial project through military action, humanitarian relief, and the activities of religious and secular NGOs to stop conflict, bring development, and support state building (Bhatt 2007).

Securitization and Governance

Securitization is not just a strategy of policing and risk management; it has become a mode of governance which combines dispersed self-disciplining through surveillance (Foucault 1977) and disciplining through citizen-spectatorship and the management of fear (Debord 1977). The securitization of migration brings about a shift in the focus of policing and surveillance from the panopticon, the surveillance of all under the state's gaze, to the ban-opticon, selective surveillance of social categories based on profiling (Bigo 2008). Bigo (2008:23) argues the ban-opticon is characterized by the

> exceptionalism of power (rules of emergency and their tendency to become permanent), by the way it excludes certain specific groups in the name of their future potential behaviour (profiling), and by the way it normalizes the non-excluded through its production of normative imperatives, the most important of which is free movement (the so-called four freedoms of circulation of the EU: concerning goods, capital, information, services and persons).
>
> *(Bigo 2008: 32)*

The ban-optic security lens institutes a form of governmentality based on the state management of unease by providing a "reassuring and protective pastoral power" (Bigo 2008: 33). It moves away from merely providing protection to proactive policies designed to target risk categories, to anticipate future risk scenarios, and to manage the population's feelings of insecurity. The state's aim is not primarily to make people feel safe but to govern by managing their feelings of insecurity in order to unify them against the threat of the Other. The political technique of the ban-opticon displaces political order based on the social contract for "misgiving as a mode of ruling" concentrating fear on a difficult to identify adversary (Bigo 2002: 81). It thereby makes legible risks in the categories it constructs and identifies as the "enemy" (Krasmann 2007). These social categories are produced through laws and policies designed to police certain dangerous/subversive behavior attributed to them and through policing social surfaces in the media witnessed by the citizen-spectator. "This form of policing emerges with the disappearance of enforceable physical national borders and compensates for the loss of tangible borders by creating new boundary systems that are virtual, mediatized such as electronic, bio-metric, and digital surveillance nets" (Feldman 2004: 74).

Securitization involves the expansion of proactive preventive measures and practices beyond the state which draw on a wide range of agencies that manage risk which include insurance companies, private investigators, retail superstores, banks, and public welfare institutions. Internationally security becomes decentralized through the outsourcing of responsibility to other states, international agencies, private companies, and NGOs. New global surveillance technologies facilitate the emergence of transnational bureaucratic networks and databanks generated by the activities of security professionals managing fear and risk (Bigo 2008). Their professional activities and knowledge transnationalize the security field as the categories of their surveillance and policing are themselves transnationalized. The international securitization of migration has increasingly become the securitization of migrants whose bodies are made surrogate borders.

Muslims and Islam in the West?

Before September 11, 2001, Muslims immigrant communities in the West were largely seen as part of the multicultural mosaic produced by increased South-North migration. Muslim communities were connected to the North through colonization (France, the UK, the Netherlands, Spain), by temporary migrant labor schemes (Germany) and others through mass migration programs (Australia, Canada, United States). They represented a relatively small percentage of the national population ranging from around 9 percent (France) and 8 percent (Germany) to 1.1 percent (United States) and Australia (2.6 percent) of the total population. In general, they were criticized as unwilling to culturally integrate and were stigmatized as culturally conservative and socially marginalized. The impact of September 11, 2001, transformed Muslims from an ethnic/religious minority in a multicultural society to a transnational risk category and potential source of religiously inspired extremist violence. In the post-September 11 era, the "war on terror" saw Muslims securitized and policed, nationally and transnationally, as dangerous encultured bodies (Humphrey 2010). Although implemented nationally, securitization is the product of transnational harmonization of policies and laws controlling counter-terrorism, immigration, and integration to manage Muslims and Islam as a transnational risk category across Western states. Counter-terrorism policy has increased the exceptional powers of the state, immigration policy modified to obstruct Muslim migration to the West and integration policies have policed cultural difference by constructing the "good" and "bad" Muslim.

Since September 11, 2001, the number of counter-terrorism laws in the West has grown enormously. In Australia, for example, between 2001 and 2019, 82 anti-terrorism laws were legislated. The political effect of the growth of anti-terrorism laws has been to create a perpetual state of emergency through extraordinary powers of detention on the grounds of suspicion not crimes committed, through more permissive thresholds for coercive interrogation and through administrative laws facilitating the rapid deportation of non-citizen residents considered security risks. The international harmonization of anti-terrorism laws has helped construct a securitized transnational space reinforced by the ban-optic of global media witnessing by Western publics of terrorist events. Local-global mediation of terrorist events, even at a large geographical distance, constantly remind Western spectator-citizens (us) that they (we) are all potential targets.

Two areas of immigration policy that have become increasingly securitized are the assessment of visa applications and granting citizenship. In response to the threat of terrorist attacks at home Muslims have found it more difficult to immigrate to the West and to obtain citizenship. Reduced quotas for migration from predominantly Muslim countries reflect the growing anti-Muslim sentiment and Islamophobia in Australia, the EU, and the United States. Right-wing populist parties in the West, especially Europe, have tapped into Islamophobia and even advocated complete bans on Muslim migration. Citizenship has also been made increasingly conditional on demonstrated integration. In Australia, Muslim migrants have been judged as "bad" migrants, stigmatized as unwilling to work, too bound by tradition, too controlling of their women, too slow to learn English, and most recently, unwilling to demonstrate their allegiance to Australia by integrating and becoming "Australian." However, the moral panic over terrorism has produced such suspicion toward Muslims that any expression of Islamic religious identity is quickly interpreted as a sign of the menace of Islamic radicalization and a national security threat. Throughout Western states Muslim immigrants have come to symbolize the margins of citizenship. The introduction of new "citizenship tests" in the West designed to measure their language skills and their cultural, social, and political knowledge of their new home societies underline the conditionality of their citizenship (Humphrey 2005).

The "homegrown" terrorist attacks in London on 7/7 2005 by British Pakistanis put the integration of Muslim communities at the top of the political management of Muslim communities in the West. The event was a shock to the host society because it shattered the illusion of the grateful indebted migrant. Instead, the experience of social marginalization, disadvantage, and Islamophobia by many of the second generation had left them disenchanted and alienated. Western governments have sought to counter religious radicalization by trying to "domesticate" Islam and their Muslims communities. They have promoted "moderate" Islam by establishing nationally based Islamic institutions—in President Sarkozy's phrase "to be Muslims of France practicing an Islam of France" (Bowen 2004: 43)–and sought to address social exclusion of Muslim immigrants and their children as a root local cause of Islamic radicalization. As a cultural classification coined by Western governments the term "moderate Islam" is primarily a political judgment about loyalty and values (Aly 2010; Modood and Ahmad 2007). The "moderate Muslim," from the West's perspective, is anti-terrorism, against the use of Islam as a militant political rhetoric and holds modern and progressive views on the religious interpretation of the Qur'an and Hadith. The idea of a Euro-Islam, a secularized Islam informed by human rights, is seen as the most progressive position (AlSayyad and Castells 2002). However, for many Muslims, the term "moderate Muslim" is pejorative referring to a Muslim who has been co-opted and represents no-one, or worse, is so secular that the more religious members of the Muslim diaspora would regard them as lapsed "Muslims."

The state has also sought to promote "moderate" Islam by intervening in the organization of Islamic religious life. A key strategy has been to create more centralized and authoritative national Islamic organizations to counteract the historical absence of a church-like structure in Islam and integrate the ethnically fragmented local religious organizations and structures of diaspora Islam in the West. Muslim women are also a major focus of domestication echoing earlier colonial intervention in Muslim societies which targeted Muslim women as vehicles for cultural change (Abu-Lughod 2002; Massell 1974). Policies targeting Muslim women have invariably been justified on the grounds of cultural and social emancipation. The veil has consistently been a target for legal regulation as a symbolic marker of Muslim gender oppression and focus of legislative attention—for example, wearing the veil French schools (Bowen 2004). In Australia, other gendered cultural practices among some Muslim immigrant communities have been criminalized through legislation against female circumcision and arranged marriage.

A critical aspect of the present securitization of Islam and Muslims is the way "culture" is now constructed under globalization. The nation-state seeks to manage Islam as a transnational cultural system within a national imaginary that is re-emphasizing cultural singularity to reassert sovereignty and unity. Securitizing Islam represents a bureaucratic response to manage potential threats to social order. Hence, current racism toward Muslims (coined as Islamophobia in Europe) is not just a legacy of orientalism reawakened by international jihadist violence but has become integral to the processes of governance as risk management. Securitization only reinforces the essentialization of cultural difference as a strategy to make threats politically legible to their anxious citizens. Muslim immigrant resistance to this bureaucratic project of cultural essentialization has provoked a counter essentialization in the defense of religious authenticity producing movements for the re-authorization of tradition including Muslim revivalist and neo-fundamentalist projects of the recovery of "pristine" Islam (Werbner 2004).

Hypergovernance: Managing Transnational Migration Flows

Integral to the national securitization of migration at home has been the risk management of transnational migration flows to prevent the arrival of illegal immigrants, asylum seekers, and unwanted cultural and political influences from diasporas in the West. The thrust of transnational management of unwanted migration has been to prevent migration flows arriving at the borders of the West through interception, deterrence, and intervention in the countries of origin. The idea of "fortress Europe" was premised upon strengthening the common border and externalizing borders to non-EU members to prevent unwanted migrants reaching the border in the first place. First, a common border was created through the harmonization of EU asylum and migration policies. Second, migrants were intercepted at the borders of non-EU states and either detained or repatriated. Third, Western countries militarily intervened in refugee-producing countries in the Middle East and Africa to keep migrants at home by bringing security and supporting development to alleviate poverty as a push factor. By preventing migrants crossing their borders states in Europe, North America, and Australia avoided legal responsibilities toward asylum seekers. Their mass detention in camps outside their territories made them less politically visible in the West and a major humanitarian problem for countries they had tried to transit. Moreover, the containment policy resulted in the criminalized irregular migration as evidence of "people smuggling." Detention and repatriation of migrants/asylum seekers caught in transit were justified as "saving the lives" because it prevented them embarking on perilous journeys organized by ruthless "people smugglers."

Post 9/11 the prosecution of the "war on terror" through military intervention only intensified the hypergovernance of migration and refugees. Intervention in refugee-producing countries aimed at alleviating the push factors of insecurity and poverty to prevent further emigration and, after stabilization, to permit Western countries to repatriate rejected asylum seekers back home (because they no longer faced any danger). Rather than consolidating state sovereignty, the development and security project produced an assemblage of governance through complex forms of global coordination "to regulate the conflict, post-conflict, migratory, economic, health and educational contingencies of life" (Duffield & Waddell 2006: 10). However, the "war on terror" did not bring security and stabilization, despite the initial military success in Afghanistan. Intervention expanded to a drone war in Pakistan, the invasion of Iraq to remove Saddam Hussein, the war against ISIS in Iraq and Syria, and the proxy wars against jihadist forces in Yemen, Libya, Somalia, and West Africa. The failure to bring stability and development resulted in further large-scale displacement and refugee flows who became the target of new interception efforts. The jihadist counter strategy to military intervention was to portray Western militaries as aggressors inflicting large-scale death and suffering on Muslims and to seek support and jihadi recruits from Muslim diaspora communities in the West. This jihadist strategy seeded further "home grown terrorism" in the Muslim diaspora and intensified the securitization of young Muslim males as terrorism risks and made the focus of "anti-radicalization" programs. The securitizing gaze turned all asylum seekers into potential terrorists, especially during the height of the ISIS "caliphate" (2014–19) in Iraq and Syria.

Hypergovernance as a strategy of transnational governance of populations appears to be becoming more complex and never-ending. The original international agenda of intervention in the Middle East for peacekeeping, peacemaking, and nation-building has fallen well short of its goals. Instead, twenty years after the launch of the "war on terror" the states targeted remain fragile and deeply divided. Moreover, the wars have left behind an ongoing humanitarian crisis of millions of displaced populations strewn across the Middle East and trapped at EU border. The Syrian civil war (2011–19) alone produced around 7 million internally displaced and more than 5 million refugees in the neighboring countries of Lebanon, Jordan, Turkey, Iraq, and Egypt. At its peak during 2015–16, the EU refugee crisis saw more than 1 million cross the EU borders seeking asylum overwhelmingly (almost 80 percent) from Syria, Afghanistan, and Iraq. One reason for the surge of refugee migration across the Mediterranean in 2015 was the breakdown in the EU's externalization of its borders in partnership with Turkey and Libya. The EU refugee crisis has only served to deepen securitization of Muslims and Islam in Europe as right-wing populist parties have capitalized on anti-Muslim feeling. Because of the failure of international military forces to stabilize conflicts in the Middle East the EU has had to return to its strategy of interception, detention, and repatriation of displaced and transient populations based on local deals with states of origin or transit ones. At the same time they have militarized their response to border protection and criminalized refugees as being complicit in people smuggling.

As a consequence, the securitization and hypergovernance of migration will become intensified through the interception, detention, and repatriation, a recycling of displaced and transient populations based on local deals with states of origin or transit ones.

Conclusion

Securitization is an expression of hypergovernance, the transnational management of populations beyond state borders to contain threats at a distance. In the case of international migration this has involved minimizing opportunities for refugees to make asylum applications in the North by intercepting these unwanted migrants—"illegals" and asylum seekers—before they arrive at the border and/or keeping them at home. States in the North seek to distance asylum seekers from electorates by de-humanizing them, by denying their rights through exceptional laws (especial denying them access to national jurisdictions), and by criminalizing them by their resort to people smugglers. Rather disingenuously, states in the North now declare they are saving the lives of refugees by combating people smugglers by breaking their "business model" (stopping dangerous journeys of transit by boat). In other words, interception beyond the border makes them politically and legally invisible and allows the state to avoid having to assume their international legal responsibility to hear asylum claims.

The securitization of migration in the twenty-first century is on course to intensify with the growing anxiety in the North about the South. The impetus for hypergovernance in the North will grow as national order is juxtaposed with global disorder and containment through the externalization of borders becomes the norm. Because military intervention has not been able to achieve liberal peace—the formation of liberal democratic states—we are looking at a complex global "assemblage of governance" in which containment of migration forms an integral part.

References

Abu-Lughod, L. (2002), "Do Muslim Women Really Need Saving? Anthropological Reflections on Cultural Relativism and Its Others," *American Anthropologist*, 104 (3): 783–90.

AlSayyad, N. and M. Castells (2002), *Muslim Europe or Euro-Islam: Politics, Culture, and Citizenship in the Age of Globalization*, Lanham: Lexington Books.

Aly, A. and Green, K. (2010), "Fear, Anxiety and the State of Terror," *Studies in Conflict & Terrorism*, 33 (3): 268–81.

Bhatt, C. (2007), "Frontlines and Interstices in the Global War on Terror," *Development and Change* 38 (6):1073–93.

Bigo, D. (2002), "Security and Immigration: Toward a Critique of the Governmentality of Unease," *Alternatives* 27: 63-92.

Bigo, D. (2008), "Globalized-in-security: The Field and the Ban-opticon," in D. Bigo and A. Tsoukala (eds.), *Terror, Insecurity and Liberty: Illiberal Practices of Liberal Regimes*, 11–48, Abingdon: Routledge.

Bowen, J. (2004), "Does French Islam Have Borders? Dilemmas of Domestication in a Global Religion," *American Anthropologist*, 106 (1): 43–55.

Debord, G. (1977), *Society of the Spectacle*, Cambridge, MA: Zone Books.

Feldman, A. (2004), "Deterritorialized Wars of Public Safety," *Social Analysis* 48 (1): 73–80.

Foucault, M. (1977), *Discipline and Punishment*, New York: Random House.

Hintjens, H. (2019), "Failed Securitization Moves during the 2015 Migration Crisis," *International Migration*, 57 (4): 181–96.

Humphrey, M. (2005), "Australian Islam, the new global terrorism and the limits of citizenship," in S. Akbarzadeh and S. Yasmeen, (eds.), *Islam and Political Violence: Reflections from Australia*,132–48, Sydney: UNSW Press.

Humphrey, M. (2010), "Securitisation, Social Inclusion and Muslims in Australia," in S. Yasmeen (ed.), *Muslims in Australia: The Dynamics of Exclusion and Inclusion*, 56–78, Melbourne: Melbourne University Press.

Huysmans, J. (2006), *The Politics of Insecurity: Fear, Migration and Asylum in the EU*, London and New York: Routledge.

Krasmann, S. (2007), "The Enemy on the Border: Critique of a Programme in Favour of a Preventive State," *Punishment and Society* 9(3): 301–18.

Massell, G. (1974), *The Surrogate Proletariat: Moslem Women and Revolutionary Strategies in Soviet Central Asia*, 1919–1929. Princeton, NJ: Princeton University Press.

Modood, T. and Ahmad, F. (2007), "British Muslim Perspectives on Multiculturalism," *Theory, culture and society*, 24 (2): 187–213.

Werbner, P. (2004), "The Predicament of the Diaspora and Millennial Islam: Reflections in the Aftermath of September 11," *Ethnicities*, 4 (4): 451–76.

Negotiating Control: Camps, Cities, and Political Life

by Silvia Pasquetti

Introduction

Displaced, denied national self-determination, pushed into statelessness, or granted degraded forms of citizenship, Palestinians are routinely deemed as "suspect" or "dangerous" everywhere they live and go. In the context of a "national order of things" (Malkki 1995) that is, geographically and historically, expressive of past and ongoing colonial-military projects (Gregory 2004), they experience multiple states of suspicion and control across different regions of the world. The experience of being treated as objects of suspicion and control links their varied predicaments of displacement, division, and immobility. As Rashid Khalidi (1997: 1) puts it, the regular scrutiny of them because of their suspect identity "brings home to them how much they share in common as a people."

However, throughout their modern history, Palestinians have been forced to live in proximity to different agencies of control and these differences in the forms of control they negotiate in their everyday lives matter for how they inhabit moral-political worlds both locally and globally. With a focus on both sides of the Green Line, the "border" separating Israel from the West Bank, this article develops a comparative ethnographic analysis of how two populations of poor Palestinians have unwillingly established "intimate" relationships with different agencies of control, and argues that there is a link between the forms of control they negotiate and the forms of political expression and action they engage in. Specifically, in this article I trace the bifurcated history of displacement and control that connects the Palestinian urban poor living in Lydda, an Israeli city adjacent to the Ben Gurion International Airport, and Palestinian refugees originally from the Lydda area who now live in Jalazun, a West Bank camp near Ramallah and about 20 miles away from Lydda. I compare these two populations' moral-political responses to state suspicion and coercion.[1]

By conceptualizing the Green Line as a border of control within the broader settler-colonial geography imposed on them,[2] and connecting and comparing poor Palestinians across it, this article pursues two interrelated goals: first, it seeks to problematize "the logic of the nation-state," that still effectively "ensnares" the anthropology and sociology of Palestinians (elsewhere, I called for an "entrapped transnationalism" angle on Palestinian lives on both sides of the Green Line); second, it seeks to break the strict analytical dichotomy between refugees and citizens, and between refugee camps and cities that, beyond the Palestinian case, marks both the urban sociology of the poor and the political sociology of the state across different tiers of the global order.

Put differently, this article conceptualizes the Palestinian urban poor in Lydda and the Palestinian camp refugees in Jalazun as two populations of "urban outcasts" (Wacquant 2008a) living in a settler-colonial context that mixes—and, most crucially, distributes—settler-colonial, colonial, liberal, and neoliberal elements.[3] With such context, both populations of "outcasts" struggle for scarce symbolic and material resources, from recognition to housing, to employment. Yet, their struggles take place in different symbolic-material contexts of control. The Palestinian urban poor negotiate their access to resources against a strikingly stable, if ambiguously hidden, security-police state in Lydda. The Palestinian camp refugees, by contrast, have been forced to establish relationships with a fragmented and highly visible configuration of control, including the United Nations Relief and Work Agency (UNRWA), the Israeli army, and more recently, the Palestinian Authority (PA). In this article, I argue that a focus on these two distinct configurations of control—the convergence of police and security agencies in Lydda and the triadic configuration of Israeli army, UNRWA, and PA—is a required step for understanding how and why the populations differ in their politics. Specifically, I show how camp inhabitants routinely use visible and collective forms of action while urban residents are hesitant to become political in the public sphere and therefore pursue more underground forms of action. I argue that these different political propensities are part of a broader history of adjustments that Palestinians in Lydda and Jalazun have made in their respective relationships with the various agencies of control imposed on them.

De-Essentializing Camps, Cities, and Citizenship: Legal-Spatial Distributions of Control

Excluded from what Malkki calls "the national order of things," refugees negotiate specific urban and national forms of control across different scales of the global order (Pasquetti and Sanyal 2020). Similarly, those citizens that the state considers as potential or real "enemies of the nation" live under forms of control that do not apply to other citizens. This is particularly the case in settler colonial context in which citizenship acts more as a form of "domination" (Tatour 2019) than a regime of rights giving legitimate access to resources. This is also the case in postcolonial societies, in which cities are increasingly becoming spaces of displacement where refugees settle among other impoverished groups (Sanyal 2014). Keeping this mind, a comparative approach to refugees and the urban poor raises questions about how these two groups of "the global poor" (Fraser 2010) experience control and negotiate access to resources. While "practical" notions of citizenship emphasize how state citizenship can be "hollowed" from within by systems of domination, for example, along ethnoracial lines, the scholarship on refugees often implicitly compares them to citizens, emphasizing how they lack a fundamental protective layer within contemporary societies: legal citizenship.

Arendt's (1973: 297) understanding of refugees as people that have lost a protective political community and Agamben's ([1995] 1998) view of camps as spaces that extinguish political life constitute the main intellectual anchors for this conceptualization of refugees and refugee camps in negative terms (e.g., Hanafi and Long 2010; Hyndman 2000). Agier's (2002) call for "an urban ethnography" of camps has convincingly connected refugees and urban spaces, but it has left mostly untouched the political contents usually attributed to concepts of citizenship, cities, and camps. Indeed, while opening up a new important line of research on refugees and cities, the debate generated by Agier's urban approach to camps has reproduced the dominant thinking with regard to refugees and refugee camps as "missing" some urban or political parts. In other words, camps are unfinished cities (Agier 2002: 337), spaces that, unlike cities, do not "entail expectations of citizenship" (Malkki 2002: 355), or again camps, unlike cities, are "'total institutions' ... from which there is no escape" (Bauman 2002: 347).

Recent works have problematized this negative approach to camps and conceptualized them as political spaces and their inhabitants as political agents (e.g., Grbac 2013; Ramadan 2012; Redclift 2013; Sigona 2015). These works have extended the same conceptual language and analytic approaches to the camps that had been developed with regard to the city and the state. Thus, for example, Grbac has argued in favor of "a right to the camp" approach, which is parallel to the "right to the city" approach, and Sigona has used the term "campzenship," a clear parallel to "citizenship," to address issues of political agency within camps. While this "political" turn in the study of camps has effectively destabilized the status of passivity and victimhood typically attached to camps, it has not as effectively challenged the privileged position of cities as political sites and citizens as political agents. However, understanding the variety of political practices and meanings that emerge among marginalized populations, whether they live in camps or in cities, requires challenging both poles of the urban and political spectrum. In other words, scholars must problematize the fixed notions attached to camps as well as those attached to state citizenship and to cities (Sanyal 2012, 2014).

In this article, I problematize such fixed assumption. While I do not turn them on its head conceptually suggesting that refugee status instead of citizenship operates as a layer of protection, I do discuss empirically how the inclusion of a humanitarian agency in the configuration of control at work in the camp on the one hand, and the pervasive presence of Israeli policing and security agencies in the city on the other, play a crucial role in differentiating how Palestinian refugees and the Palestinian urban poor maneuver to obtain scarce material and symbolic resources. Put differently, I do draw attention to an important difference between the various forms of control imposed on "unwanted" populations: the presence of humanitarian organizations in the refugee camps of the Global South (e.g., Agier 2011; Fassin 2012), and the prominent role of the coercive agencies of the state in the lives of the urban poor in both the Global South and the Global North (e.g., Fassin 2013; Graham 2010; Wacquant 2008a, 2008b, 2009, 2014). I speak here about a tendency, not a clear-cut dichotomy. Of course, military, security, and policing agencies can and often do intervene in refugee camps, and welfare agencies and non-governmental organizations (NGOs) can and often are present in the lives of the urban poor. Further, in addition to heavily controlled populations, there are also populations that are "abandoned" rather than controlled by the state or other ruling agencies. Yet, refugee populations tend to establish protracted relationships with humanitarian agencies while the urban poor are more likely to negotiate protracted relationships with the law-enforcement and security agencies.

As argued by sociologists of punishment and critical criminologists, far from operating merely as imposed external domination, the control exercised by the state and other ruling agencies deeply shapes the terrain on which marginalized populations maneuver to improve their living conditions and to formulate their social and political claims (e.g., Palidda 2009; Wacquant 2009). The salience of practices of state control for the study of marginalized populations, whether they live in camps or cities, also emerges from both the colonial and the contemporary urban literature (on the distribution of forms of control in the Palestinian case, see also Pasquetti 2012, 2015). For example, in his model of bifurcated legal rule in colonial South Africa, Mamdani (1996) examines how the legal apparatus of the colonial state differentiated between urban Blacks living in the townships and rural blacks living on the reservations. It also regulated rural Black workers moving to the cities via a system of travel permits, obliging them to stay in urban hostels that were separated from the townships. He argues that this bifurcated colonial regime of legal rule effectively created distinct political expressions and practices among urban and rural subjects and produced distinct forms of organizing within the different spatial configurations of urban townships, rural reservations, and urban hostels for rural workers.

While Mamdani's model of bifurcated control centers on the law—the distinction between citizens and subjects—the literature on urban control in the global north has a more developed spatial dimension (but see Western 1996 on the spatial dimension of control in South Africa) and identifies the emergence of illiberal pockets of control within cities of the global north as well as the role of "brutal top-down control measures" in the management of those at the bottom of the urban-social order. As Scheerer and Hess (1997: 130) put it, "the internal polarization" of post-industrial societies has created distinct forms of control for marginalized "out-groups," especially the urban poor (see also Samara 2011; Wacquant 2009).

In addition to these insights on the productivity and differentiation of control, especially along legal and spatial lines, I draw on Fraser's (2010) approach to "social exclusion" as a key reference in my effort to de-essentialize both camps and cities, viewing both of them as socio-spatial configurations that are shaped by continuous processes of negotiation over material and symbolic resources. Fraser identifies three mechanisms of exclusion: a cultural denial of respect and recognition, an economic denial of resources, and a political denial of participation in decision-making. She highlights how these axes might intersect and combine to further entrench social exclusion in a multiplicity of arenas. Along these lines, contestation might also take different shapes and act in different arenas at the same time.

Lydda and Jalazun: A Bifurcated History of Displacement and Control

Lydda and the Jalazun camp are historically connected through multiple legal-spatial divisions. The first and most crucial of such divisions is between those Palestinians who in 1948 managed to remain within the newly established state, obtaining its legal citizenship but also experiencing its military rule (about 160,000) and those Palestinians who became refugees and were dispersed in Lebanon, Jordan, Syria, the West Bank, and the Gaza Strip (about 750,000). The *Nakba* (literally Catastrophe)— how Palestinians call their societal destruction and mass displacement[4]—also took place in Lydda, which, until 1948 was a Palestinian city. In July 1948, the Israeli army occupied the city and expelled about 50,000 Palestinian residents—including 22,000 regular inhabitants and a roughly equal number of rural Palestinians who had found refuge in the city. Expelled Palestinians left Lydda on foot and those who survived the trek became refugees in Jalazun and in other camps in the West Bank and Gaza Strip.

Since this mass displacement that transformed Lydda into the Jewish Israeli city of Lod and pushed almost all of its former Palestinian inhabitants into camps, urban Palestinian minorities in Lod and Palestinian refugees in the Jalazon camp have experienced distinct forms of control. Like the other Palestinians (about 150,000) that managed to remain inside the newly established Israeli state, the roughly 1,000 remaining Palestinians in Lydda were simultaneously given citizenship and put under military rule. For close to a year, they were forced into two fenced-in areas of the city— one in the old city and one in a Western district of the city—and they could only leave with permits (Yacobi 2009: 33–5). While all-Arab towns and villages inside Israel remained under military rule until 1966, the military restrictions in Lydda were eased in May 1949 due to the very low number of Palestinians there and the emptied city's planned absorption of tens of thousands of Jewish migrants. Indeed, in the 1950s and 1960s, newly arrived Jewish migrants who turned into Israeli citizens constituted about 90 percent of the city's population while the number of urban Palestinians remained the same. However, since the early 1970s, other Palestinian citizens of Israel, mostly poor populations from rural and desert areas, settled in Lydda attracted by the low-paid jobs there and in nearby Tel Aviv. Currently, Palestinians make up about 30 percent of Lydda's population of about 76,000 inhabitants.

The recomposition of the Palestinian population in Lydda has been accompanied by state and public discourses about Palestinians in the city as a demographic-cum-security threat to their Jewish Israeli counterparts and by practices of control, which target them as a "suspect population" to be monitored and rendered legible to state scrutiny. These practices have included, and continue to include today, the widespread use of police informers and the police's logistical support of security agencies and the underground activities these agencies use to identify, arrest, and interrogate "political troublemakers."

In his historical account of the formation of the securitized regime of control imposed over Palestinians in Israel from 1948 to 1966, Cohen (2010: 235; see also Sa'di 2016) describes it in this way:

> one of their [the informers'] central mission ... was to report all nationalist sentiments they heard expressed in their villages and cities ... The result was a comprehensive system of reports from informers ... It was a carefully calculated system through which the security agencies tried to "educate" Arab citizens in what they were permitted and what they were forbidden to say.

As I discuss below, the monopoly of control that the Israeli security agencies have exercised over Palestinian citizens of Israel is still very much at work today in the Palestinian districts of Lydda.

While the Israeli state has historically woven a securitized regime of control around its Palestinian citizens based on the recruitment of informers and the convergence between policing and security agencies, since 1948 Palestinian refugees in the West Bank have negotiated their lives in connection with two strikingly different types of institutions: humanitarian organizations—particularly UNRWA—and military powers—first the Jordanian army (1948–67) and then the Israeli army (since 1967). More recently, the establishment of the PA—an authority of semi-autonomous rule in the West Bank's urban centers—has added an additional third layer to the institutions that refugees must routinely navigate. Thus, in the case of Palestinian refugee camps, "control, more than in other contexts, is partial and in [a] continual process of definition. No monopoly of control exists" (Abourahme and Hilal 2009: 10–11).

In particular, the protracted interplay between military and humanitarian agencies has been particularly consequential for how Palestinian camp inhabitants have struggled to obtain material and symbolic resources. From the very beginning, Palestinian refugees have perceived UNRWA as a tool used by mainly Western international donors to reduce the unsolved question of their political rights to a "problem" of poverty and unemployment. Thus, the first generation of refugees compared UNRWA to a "narcotics castle" and its services to the "giving of a shot of morphine" (Rempel 2009: 418) aimed at convincing them to accept "resettlement" (*tawteen*) while most of them clearly preferred to return to their villages and homes.

Yet, over time, refugees have also found UNRWA to be permeable to their demands, especially as UNRWA hired thousands of them to work in its bureaucratic apparatus, its schools, and its social service departments. As Farah (2010: 391) puts it, the Palestinian refugees working for UNRWA "are the glue that binds refugees to the organization and they blur the boundary between benefactor and beneficiary." UNRWA also became more open to refugees' concerns and desires. One example is UNRWA's support of the establishment of "Youth Centers" in all the refugee camps, which became another important arena for collective cultural and political activities inside the camps. Thus, despite refugees' initial mistrust, UNRWA has emerged over the decades as an institutional layer operating as a protective shield for the reorganization of the collective life of camp inhabitants. Embedded in an everyday reality marked by the Israeli army's attacks on camp inhabitants and their built environment and by expanding Israeli settlements, refugees have come to perceive and use the presence of UNRWA as both a buffer institution against military repression and an arena for the articulation of their own claims and projects.

The establishment of the PA has been accompanied with an increased territorial fragmentation of the West Bank (Farsakh 2005; Hanafi 2009; Parsons and Salter 2008; Weizman 2007): checkpoints, roadblocks, trenches, no-go zones, by-pass roads, fences, and walls have accompanied the administrative division of the West Bank to produce dozens of non-contiguous territorial enclaves (Falah 2005). A second interrelated but less studied feature is the class-moral fragmentation that has accompanied this spatial fragmentation of rule. At the political-institutional level, it is the very struggle over political power between the two main Palestinian factions—Fatah and Hamas—that has acquired a new territorial dimension, with a split, since June 2007, between the Fatah-dominated PA in the West Bank and a Hamas-run government in the Gaza Strip. Despite ongoing efforts, such a split remains far from being stitched. At the social-economic level, new class and moral fractures have contributed to "polarize and demobilize" the Palestinian body politic (El Kurd 2019). In this context, camp refugees feel marginalized and stigmatized by the middle-class oriented "neoliberal" PA (Clarno 2017)[5] and further cling on the bonds to UNRWA as an inadequate but at least partially accountable institution from which they can extract symbolic and material resources collectively.

Political Expression and Action in Jalazun and Lydda: A Study in Contrast

Rami[6] and Bilal are two Palestinian men in their early fifties, both poor, the former an Israeli citizen living in Lydda, and the latter a stateless refugee living in Jalazun. Each has unwillingly established "intimate" relationships with powerful agencies of control, ranging from various Israeli law-enforcement agencies to international humanitarian organizations, and each relates to these agencies through distinct emotions and political orientations. A brief biographical note highlights how each has come in close contact with a distinct configuration of control. Like most poor Palestinians in Lydda, Rami is originally from somewhere else, in his case from the Naqab (H. Negev), a desert area in southern Israel. Rami's life has always been precarious: in the Naqab, his extended family has lost much land to state confiscation; in Lydda, he lives in the segregated and underserved Mahata (railway station) District, and his house, already demolished once, is again under the threat of demolition because he built it without a hard-to-obtain building license. While Rami currently works as car mechanic assistant, when he was in his twenties and early thirties, he engaged in various criminal activities; for example, he used to steal cars and sometime smuggle them across the border into the West Bank. During that period, he was repeatedly arrested and interrogated by Israeli police (Ar. *shurta*). State security was central to these interrogations. For example, once while in police custody, he was warned: "Do whatever you want, but don't touch the security of the state." He interpreted this comment as a reference to the trafficking of arms across the border. Rami's continues to be a "suspect" citizen in the eyes of law-enforcement agents even though over twenty years ago he turned to low-paid jobs to make end meet. Thus, days after a demonstration against house demolitions in his district, he was brought to a local police station to have "a chat," and the police cautioned him not to join future protests.

Rami describes law enforcement as an illegitimate power and contests the legitimacy of the law, whose lack of fairness, he argues, justifies unlawful practices as legitimate attempts to secure access to unjustly denied resources. While these resources are surely material ones such as housing and income, resistance to the law also has for Rami a distinct symbolic dimension. For example, he captivatedly watches on his mobile phone TV clips of political unrest around the world and movies on organized crime. If Rami finds a sense of (political) self-empowerment in (real or imagined) acts of subversion against the law, his encounters with law-enforcement agencies are central to another troubling dimension of his experience of the law: distrust toward fellow Palestinians in Lydda. Specifically, he is concerned that the *Shabak*, the main Israeli security agency,[7] is interested in his whereabouts and that his neighbors, who, like him, live in precarious conditions, are under pressure to monitor and collect information on him. His concern emerges from his own experience: the *Shabak* was involved in some of his interrogations at the police station and pressured him to collect information on friends and neighbors. This concern makes him particularly circumspect in his everyday social relations. Participation in openly collective activities, for example in neighborhood meetings on how to obtain building licenses or prevent house demolitions, interests him but mostly triggers his anxiety of being surveilled and eventually punished (see also Pasquetti 2019).

On the other side of the Green Line, Bilal has quite a bit in common with Rami—not only language and culture, but also protracted experiences of displacement, poverty, and precariousness. Like most refugees in the Jalazun camp, he has lived all his life in Jalazun but his parents were displaced from the Lydda region in 1948. Like Rami, Bilal is an object of security. In his case, however, security has brought him into close contact with the Israeli army (Ar. *jaysh*). Like most men of his generation, Bilal was arrested during the First Intifada, the 1987–93 uprising against the military occupation, and he spent eight years in an Israeli military prison. In addition, on several occasions the Israeli army has rounded him up, along with other men from the camp, and detained them in the camp's small square, where they had to sit in the rain or the heat while the military performed various operations.

Bilal likens the camp to a tree: the camp is rich in branches and leaves, but its life runs inside its trunk. For him, the trunk consists of the social relationships that camp inhabitants establish with one another. What happens within the trunk can strengthen the roots, helping the tree withstand the repetitive storms that come its way. Despite struggling to make ends meet for his family of five, Bilal is active in the camp's associational life. At times, he also helps organize camp visits by foreign delegations (e.g., journalists, architects, lawyers, and students). When he is unable to secure work, mainly in construction or the service sector, he typically spends his mornings in the courtyard of the office for the United Nations Relief and Works Agency (UNRWA, known in the camp as *wakala*, "the agency").[8] There he joins other unemployed men as they drink coffee together. These informal gatherings often lead to animated discussions about the dangers that camp inhabitants face and how to deal with them, including the organization of demonstrations against UNRWA's budget cuts and camp initiatives for reducing tensions between the main political factions. At times, Bilal works as a service worker, "making coffees," as he puts it, in one of the many ministries of the Palestinian Authority (PA, or *Sulta*—"authority"—in Arabic)[9] in the nearby city of Ramallah, where he is exposed to the lifestyles of the PA-oriented urban middle class.

Why does Rami feel distrust toward his neighbors and friends? Why is he fearful of the Israeli authorities? In addition, why does he not participate in neighborhood meetings? By contrast, why does Bilal feel a desire for maintaining and nourishing solidarity within the camp? Moreover, why is he oriented toward open political discussion and participation? Lives that powerful agencies of control mark and target as political-security threats are full of tensions and contradictions: negotiating daily proximity to hostile agencies of control is a process fraught with dilemmas about what to say and do. These dilemmas are particularly intense for the poor, for whom the negotiation of imposed state scrutiny is intertwined with daily attempts to eke out a living from precarious, informal, and at times, unlawful practices. One might say that the experience of being reduced to an object of security is so personal that it varies from individual to individual. Alternatively, one might emphasize how, in each locality, axes such as gender and generation inflect experiences of being controlled. While Rami's and Bilal's life stories surely have idiosyncratic features and important gendered and generational dimensions, they nevertheless also reveal distinct collective affective and political experiences of state suspicion and control among the Palestinian urban poor in Lydda and camp refugees in Jalazun.[10] Along these lines, this article highlights the role that agencies of control play in the day-to-day struggle for material and symbolic resources.

On the one hand, camp inhabitants have developed a disposition to deal with issues of scarce material and symbolic resources collectively through the creation of associations and the organization of protests. They routinely turn to the ethos of "community" when they deal with issues such as unemployment or education: "the ethos [of community] lies group by seeing the group as a community that, because it is harmed collectively, is best helped through collective response" (Collins 2010: 16). They mobilize "the language of community" "not as a kneejerk resistance to social change, but rather as a political tool for protecting families and neighbourhoods" (Collins 2010: 15).

While each layer of control plays a mediating and interactive role in the emergence of this disposition toward collective action, here I focus on the historical interplay between UNRWA and the Israeli army. First, camp inhabitants' access to scarce resources via their relationship with UNRWA is a particularly important site for the elaboration of collective claims. Indeed, camp inhabitants have engaged with UNRWA over decades to deepen its accountability toward them. Through their relationship with UNRWA, camp inhabitants act upon all three dimensions of Fraser's definition of "social exclusion": redistribution, recognition, and representation. As Adnan, a camp refugee who over the years (and decades) has regularly participated in demonstrations against cuts to the UNRWA's budget, puts it:

> Of course, they [UNRWA] did not give anything definite [*ma qadamu ay kalam 'amali*]. For example, when we talked to the head of UNRWA's office he said: "We will look at your request, we will consider your request, we will review your request, we will consider your request, we will talk to the responsible person for your request and we will contact you later." The agency [UNRWA] operates under the principles of prevarication and procrastination [*al-wikala tata'amal bi-madbd'a al-mumatala wa-l-taswif*]. Part of their approach is emotional and the other is based on a military approach [they give orders] but they also negotiate. ... Their approach is also linked to that of foreign governments. They have problems because the donor countries reduced their funding.

This quote illustrates the significant role of UNRWA within Palestinian refugee camp communities. Camp refugees mobilize to buttress UNRWA institutional presence within the camps and remain anxiously vigilant about the precarious position of UNRWA within the geopolitics of Palestinian displacement, due mainly to its dependence on voluntary funding on the part of Western donors (see, for example, Fiddian-Qasmiyeh (2019) on the recent US withdrawal from UNRWA funding). For Adnan, UNRWA mixes a militaristic stance in which they give orders to a negotiating stance through which they engage refugee communities. This latter stance refers to the "emotional" dimension of UNRWA's approach he juxtaposes to the military one. While UNRWA's "military" stance might also have an emotional dimension (e.g., it can produce outrage among camp Palestinians), it is the negotiating one that engages camp Palestinians socially and affectively, creating a space within which they mobilize. A key feature of the process of refugee adjustment to the institutional presence of UNRWA and its stances toward them has historically been a disposition toward "togetherness," a desire to maintain a level of fairness in the distribution of resources both with each refugee camp and among the different camps in a certain field. "Togetherness" is also conducive to collective forms of engagement with issues of rights, justice, and resources. Such engagement includes discussions and negotiations at the camp level, demonstrations in front of UNRWA buildings, and organized meetings with UNRWA officials, mainly local Palestinian ones but at times also international staff, often higher ranked, visiting West Bank camps from headquarters in Jerusalem, Jordan, or elsewhere.

The Israeli army's militarism is another layer of control pushing camp refugees toward collective dispositions of "togetherness" in their political life. This is particularly the case when it has fully embraced an openly aggressive style of control that approximates in its key spatial-colonial characteristics what Mbembe (2003: 28–30) calls necropower:

> the besieged villages and towns are sealed off and cut off from the world. Daily life is militarized. Freedom is given to local military commanders to use their discretion as to when and whom to shoot. Movement between the territorial cells requires formal permits. Local civil institutions are systematically destroyed. The besieged population is deprived of their means of income. Invisible killing is added to outright executions.

In the Jalazun camp, refugees often talk about their experiences of the Israeli army's intermittent but relentless military aggression. As Mbembe aptly puts it, their daily lives are militarized: they live with the Israeli army as much as they live with UNRWA.

Thus, for example, during the First Intifada, the Jalazun camp was put under forty-three days of continuous curfew, and many camp inhabitants were killed, wounded, or arrested. During the Second Intifada, Jalazun and other refugee camps in the Ramallah area experienced a high level of military raids and attacks. More generally, the Israeli army's presence around the camp especially on the side of the Bet El settlement as well as its raids within it are both a routine of camp life and a rupture in it. This is particularly true in the case of the schools that are opposite to a military tower overlooking a no-go zone between the schools and the Bet El settlement. Israeli soldiers have shot camp children and teenagers even when they were sitting on rocks or in parked cars just in the proximity of the no-go zones. At times, the Israeli soldiers shot the Palestinian youth who threw stones or set old tires on fire near or within the valley.[11] Each episode of military violence reinforces refugees' investment in their sense of community, eliciting both a collective awareness of ever-present military dangers and a collective defiant attitude toward such dangers.

For example, conscious of their exposure to military violence, camp teenagers were also highly reflexive in how they traced the social process by which camp youth lose fear and acquire a defiant disposition when they are faced with Israeli soldiers. This affective adjustment emerges from their stories about Israeli soldiers, including this one:

> There is also a disabled girl who has problems in her legs. They [Israeli soldiers] shot a sound and gas bomb at the school while we were leaving the school. The girl who was 7 or 8 years old and in the first grade did not have anything to cover her mouth with, so I removed the cover from my mouth and put it over her mouth. I felt pity for her because she was so little. And when I woke up I found myself in the hospital because of the gas that I inhaled.

The experience of helping other, often weaker members of the camp community during a military raid, is a formative one, with collective feelings and practices of solidarity typically prevailing on more individual fears of military aggression. The social-affective experiences of the Israeli army cannot be fully understood when they are considered in isolation from the collective engagements of refugees with UNRWA as a sort of symbolic-material shield against the Israeli army.[12]

On the other side of the Green Line, in Lydda, control follows a different structural and experiential logic. While Palestinian refugees of the Jalazun camp actively and collectively maneuver within and gradually expand the space created by the different layers of control, especially by the interplay between humanitarianism and military aggression, the monopoly of control established by the Israeli state's security apparatus shrinks the space of maneuver available to poor Palestinians in Lod. In their case, the struggle against material deprivation is individualized and stands in tension with, if not at times in opposition to, the struggle for symbolic recognition and political participation, which, instead, are often identified as two key features of urban political configurations. Like the urban poor in other parts of the world, poor Palestinians in Lod engage in informal practices in various realms of life such as housing and employment. About 50 percent of them live in illegal structures. This is due to the "ethnocratic"[13] logic of urban planning in the city, which constructs their presence as a symbolic demographic threat and effectively "illegalizes" their building activities. As their requests for building licenses are regularly refused, many Palestinian families build their houses without licenses. Many of them also run informal businesses like food stands or second-hand clothing stores. Further, criminality and drug dealing are widespread in the segregated districts of the city where most of them live. This proximity to informal and "illegal" ways of living renders them particularly vulnerable to the securitized forms of monitoring that are imposed on them, and perhaps most especially to the recruitment of police informers.

In particular, the Palestinian urban poor in Lydda experience informing not just as a policing practice but also as a mechanism that distributes reward and punishment. They think that those identified by the authorities as "political troublemakers" are more likely to have their informal businesses closed or their makeshift houses demolished. They are also afraid that their friends and neighbors will strike a deal by "selling information" to the Israeli police at the expense of other Palestinians. Indeed, they believe that police informers and their families are rewarded. As an unemployed resident who failed to obtain a license to sell second-hand clothes put it: "If I were to go to the police station right now, they would give me the license. I have to become a spy to obtain a [shop] license." Most Palestinians in Lydda believe this, though the distribution of rewards and punishment by the security apparatus might be more erratic and less intentional than perceived by Palestinian residents. Though the fact remains that the perception of the link between informing and access to scarce material resources is conducive to a climate of distrust and recriminations. It is also conducive to a generalized fear of "speaking politics," of debating collectively about issues of cultural recognition and political participation. In the words of a middle-aged Palestinian sanitation cleaner: "do you know what they [the authorities] want from us? They want us to make good foul, falafel, and hummus, and to keep silent."

The distrust toward other residents and the fear of being singled out as a political activist hinder a collective approach to shared problems such as housing, employment, and safety. Distrust and fear frustrate attempts at collective organizing to improve material conditions. This is the case of Nisreen (a pseudonym), a woman living in a small housing project who had tried to convince other women from the project to join together and hold regular meetings to pressure the local authorities to solve the problem of the sewage waters that fill the project's streets, especially in the winter. Remembering her efforts, she told me that she was frustrated at herself as well as the other women living in the project because they were not determined enough to build on the initial momentum to give regularity to their meetings. She said that one by one, many women withdrew from the meetings, giving a variety of reasons, including their husbands' opposition to their participation, lack of time due to work and domestic responsibilities, and anxiety about becoming visible "public" figures in the project. This latter problem is, according to Nisreen, the most serious and difficult problem to deal with. With regard to this, she said:

> Even if we start to establish a new committee again we will face the same obstacles that we had before. People ... don't like to be on the summit, or in the first level, they want to be on the second level.

Given the mutual distrust among Palestinians living in Lydda, those who obtain visibility via direct involvement in initiatives such as holding meetings and trying to create committees often face the skepticism of other residents who question their motivations. Further, those who actively participate in such initiatives worry that their participation will make them more vulnerable to state scrutiny because the authorities are likely to interpret this participation in collective organizing as a sign of their interest in "politics."

To sum up, unlike Palestinian camp inhabitants, urban Palestinians experience communal frailty and are not disposed toward associational modalities of action. Further, while Palestinian refugees elaborate their claims of recognition and participation through their day-to-day negotiation over scarce material resources, urban Palestinians' efforts to escape material deprivation frustrate rather than facilitate their expressions of political claims while reproducing their extremely uneven power relations with local and state authorities, especially law-enforcement agencies.

Policed Marginalities, Lived Marginalities: Toward a Comparative Global Agenda

The findings discussed in this article complicate assumptions that increased citizenship rights allow for increased political expression and they reverse the typical opposition between citizenship and refugees, and between cities and refugee camps, as legal and spatial categories that have fixed political content. These fixed oppositions continue to undergird dominant conceptualizations of refugees and refugee camps at one pole of the political and urban spectrums with citizens and cities at the other. My findings show that fixed dichotomies of place (city versus camp) and legal status (citizens versus refugees) cannot explain how and why, despite their access to formal citizenship rights and their incorporation in a post-industrial "advanced" society, poor Palestinians in Lydda such as Rami, experience mutual distrust, feel uneasy about open political expression, and engage in scattered acts of subversion against the law. By contrast, despite their statelessness and their protracted immobility in an impoverished refugee camp under military occupation, poor Palestinians in Jalazun such as Bilal, invest considerable energy in organized solidarity, openly claim rights, and are oriented toward collective forms of political expression and action.

This article has drawn attention to the distribution of forms of control on both sides of the Green Line. More accurately, with the paired study of Jalazun and Lydda, it has examined structures and experiences of control at the bottom of the urban-social order across the West Bank and Israel. By adding an urban marginality angle to the political sociology of the state, this article has highlighted how control works through space and law, wrapping around certain populations and places in distinct ways and with deep implications for their affective-political dispositions.

The challenge ahead is thus to understand how and why, in certain places, like the Jalazun camp, the struggle against material deprivation becomes a privileged site for the expression of political rights-claims and the pursuit of collective action while, in other places, like the Palestinian districts of Lydda, it is experienced as a practice that saps political energies and precludes associational action. The answer to these questions cannot be found without crossing borders of control and unsettling rigid dichotomies between refugees and citizens, and camps and cities. This means challenges the logic of the nation-state and citizenship with its often implicit assumptions about political life. This logic obfuscates the historical and contemporary cross-border distributions of Israeli policing, security, and military discourses and practices of control and deters the emergence of a "transnational" approach to cross-border ties and attempts at communication among differently situated Palestinian populations under (and beyond) Israeli rule.

This also means opening up a new global comparative agenda on how groups that are policed as "suspect" or "dangerous" adjust affectively and politically to the forms of control inhering in the places where they live. For example, how can we put this paired ethnography of Jalazun and Lydda into dialogue with the study of the militarization of urban policing in Brazil (Wacquant 2008b) and its "imperial" origins in the United States (Go 2020)? Further, from a spatial perspective, what can we learn by comparing "urban outcasts" in Cape Town (Western 1996) and Lydda? And, from a spatial-legal perspective, how can we meaningfully discuss experiences of citizenship among Native Americans in cities and reservations (Cornell 1988) and Palestinians in urban Israel and West Bank refugee camps? Further, how and why might political life across borders of settler states (Simpson 2014) converge as in the case of the Kahnawà:ke or by contrast display quite intense level of political fragmentation as in the case of Palestinians across the Green Line?

Asking these questions is a way to support old and new attempts to produce decolonial knowledge about Palestinian society. As I mentioned earlier, Palestinian scholars have historically been at the foreground of this struggle to produce decolonial knowledge about their society (e.g., Zureik published his ground-breaking book *Palestinians in Israel: A study in Internal Colonialism* in 1979). These efforts continue today especially through engagements with settler colonial perspectives (e.g., Sabbagh-Khoury 2021; Salamanca et al. 2012). Asking these questions also means to add a focus on distributions of practices and discourses of control to the study of their global circulation (Khalili 2010).

Along these lines, I conclude this article with an example about how a global comparative approach to control, emotions, and politics can help see further these efforts especially by conceptualizing citizenship as control and breaking off the isolation of the Palestinian urban poor in Lydda. Take for example the case of state control and policing in the United States and Israel. In a thoughtful account of Palestinian intellectuals' reflexive reckoning with the African American experience, Maha Nassar (2019: 27–8) includes two essays that the Palestinian poet Mahmud Darwish wrote in 1966 in an imaginary conversation with Black American intellectuals. In these essays, he oscillates between recognizing commonalities with his own predicament as a Palestinian inside Israel and reflecting upon differences, especially in regard to law and policing. On commonalities, he states: "When Black is said in your country, the listener only sees in the word an oppressed person. That symbol has crossed the borders of your country and reached me, whereupon ... I become 'Black' without needing to ... [have] similar features." On differences, he aptly notices that control might be more visible in the United States than inside Israel:

> I will tell you that we can't go everywhere we want to in our own country! And we can't farm our land because it is, as they say, not for us. And the [policymaker] in the current government here is much smarter than [the policymaker in] your government when it comes to the job of oppression. *For he sees but is unseen.* He tries to take the land under our feet without us feeling his smooth hands.

I added emphasis to "he sees but is unseen" because, like the rest of Darwish's insightful observations about discrimination and policing in the two contexts, this point strongly resonates with what many poor Palestinians in Lydda expressed about their ties with the security state: these anxiety-triggering ties that they have been forced to live with are subterranean. This is just an example of the importance of a global comparative agenda on different Palestinian populations (in cities and camps, with and without Israeli citizenship) within broader histories of imperialism, colonialism, and control in its various militaristic and warlike iterations across the world, including at the urban level.

Notes

1   For a full account of my comparative ethnography, see my forthcoming book *Refugees and Citizens: Control, Emotions, and Politics in a West Bank Camp and an Israeli "Mixed" City* (Oxford: Oxford University Press, 2023). In the book, I draw on Pierre Bourdieu and Abdelmalek Sayad's (2020 [1964]) work on habitus and displacement in colonial Algeria to argue that collective emotions mediate between the spatial-coercive control imposed by the Israeli state, and, for the refugees, by the global humanitarian apparatus, and the political practices that the two populations value and pursue. Further, I also develop a cross-border perspective on the feelings and perceptions that the Palestinian urban poor in Israel and the Palestinian camp refugees in the West Bank have of each other.
2   As I will discuss in the next section, there is a renewed interest in the settler colonial paradigm within Palestinian Studies as an important conceptual tool for understanding the entanglements of displacement, land dispossession, and legal categorization of different Palestinian populations (Barakat 2018; Sabbagh-Khoury 2021; Salamanca et al. 2012). In this article (and in my broader work) I put the settler-colonial perspective in dialogue with additional conceptual tools, including some, such as Wacquant's "advanced" urban marginality perspective, that I import from the global north and others, such as Mamdani's legal colonialism that I borrow from other colonial contexts. This eclectic use of conceptual

sources helps dissect the settler-colonial, liberal (and neoliberal), and global humanitarian aspects of the distribution of control over Palestinians on both sides of the Green Line.

3   From the settler-colonial framework, I take the fundamental point that the distribution of techniques of control across and within the West Bank and urban Israel that I study is intertwined with chains of physical displacement and land dispossession. While maintaining a sustained attention to issues of land, I find Nadia Abu El-Haj's (2010: 40) definition of the Israeli state a good departure point for exploring the distribution of forms of control over different segments of Palestinians. As she puts it, the Israeli state "has both liberal and distinctly illiberal dimensions: it is a colonial state and, for its Jewish citizens, a liberal democracy; it is governed by the rule of law and it operates with a sustained suspension of the law, under the rubric of military rule and the guise of security requirements. The Israeli state *is* that complex multifaceted matrix of forms and tactics of rule."

4   For Palestinians, the memories of the *Nakba* as a historical event (Sa'di and Abu-Lughod 2007) are intertwined with more recent and ongoing experiences of destruction, displacement, and control.

5   "The new middle class is composed of a number of sections. First, there are those in the higher echelons of the PA bureaucracy, and in public services. Second are the directors of Palestinian and international NGOs, as well as university teachers and administrators. Thirdly, there are those in management of the new enterprises, banks, and companies" (Hilal 2003: 169).

6   All names are pseudonyms.

7   The General Security Services (GSS) is the main internal security agency of the Israeli state, also known with its Hebrew acronyms: Shabak and Shin Bet.

8   UNRWA was established by the United Nations in 1949 to address the Palestinian refugee crisis following the creation of the state of Israel, and is still operating today in Lebanon, Syria, Jordan, the West Bank, and the Gaza Strip.

9   The Palestinian Authority (PA) was established in 1993 as an authority of self-rule in certain areas of the West Bank, especially the cities, and of the Gaza Strip. The PA has been increasingly conceptualized as an institution driven by a neoliberal project of proto-statehood through economic development and privileging the small urban-based Palestinian middle class in the West Bank (Clarno 2017).

10   I follow Wacquant (1995: 490, 526n14) in his argument that, while there is a tension between focusing on "the invariants" of a certain "viewpoint" and analyzing possible "variations" within it, "an elucidation of" these variations "presupposes a prior understanding of what these experiential paths hold in common."

11   The list of children and teenagers killed in the proximity is long and, given the bonds between the camp youth and the Israeli army described in this section, it is bound to become longer unless something changes in the triadic configuration of control at work in Jalazun, for example in international and UNRWA forms of protection of Jalazun against the Israeli army. At time of writing, this seems highly unlikely. The children and teenagers from Jalazun killed by the Israeli at the outskirt or within the no-zone area (or at other nearby checkpoints) in the last ten years include: Muhammad Hamdan (sixteen years old, April 2009), Muhammad Alayan (sixteen years old, August 31, 2009), Wajih al-Ramahi (fifteen years old, December 2013), Laith Khalidi (fifteen years old, July 2015), Ahmad Sharaka (thirteen years old, October 2015), Faris Ziyad Ata Bayid (fifteen years

old, October 2016), Muhammad al-Hattab (seventeen years old, March 23, 2017), Jassim Nakhla (fifteen years old, March 23, 2017), and Mahmoud Yousif Nakhla (eighteen years old). Many other camp children and teenagers have been wounded, some very seriously, in the same period of time. Further, young adults have been killed by the Israeli army during raids inside the camp. This is, for example, the case of Ahmed Sabarin (twenty-one years old) who was fatally shot in the chest by Israeli soldiers during a house-to-house search with the camp in June 2014.

12 A full explanation of camp refugees' disposition toward open and collective forms of politics would also require an examination of how the establishment of the PA has reinforced such a disposition by stigmatizing the refugees' poverty and misrecognizing their political action, labeling them as "troublemakers" and "thugs" (see Pasquetti 2012 on the class-moral fragmentation produced by the PA in the West Bank).

13 Yiftachel (2006) uses the concept of "ethnocracy" to refer to a political regime that distributes resources and rights according to the ethnic membership of its citizens. "Ethnocratic" urban planning reorganizes the space in ways that privilege certain ethnic collectivities over others. In the case of Israeli cities with a sizeable Palestinian minority, the urban districts inhabited by Palestinians inside Israeli cities constitute "internal frontiers, into which Jewish presence should expand" or which need to be contained with the construction of Jewish Israeli neighborhoods around them (Yiftachel and Yacobi 2003: 679–80).

References

Abourahme, N. and S. Hilal (2009), "The Production of Space, Political Subjectification and the Folding of Polarity: The Case of Deheishe Camp, Palestine." http://www.campusincamps.ps/wp-content/uploads/2012/12/Nasser-Abourahme-and-Sandi-Hilal_Deheishe-Paper.pdf (1–38).

Abu El-Aj, N. (2010), "Racial Palestinianization and the Janus-Faced Nature of the Israeli State," *Patterns of Prejudice*, 44 (1): 27–41.

Agamben, G. ([1995] 1998), *Homo Sacer: Sovereign Power and Bare Life*, Stanford: Stanford University Press.

Agier, M. (2002), "Between War and City: Towards an Urban Anthropology of Refugee Camps," *Ethnography*, 3 (3): 317–41.

Agier, M. (2011), *Managing the Undesirables: Refugee Camps and Humanitarian Government*, Cambridge: Polity.

Arendt, H. (1973), *The Origins of Totalitarianism*, New York: Harcourt Brace Jovanovich.

Barakat, R. (2018), "Writing/Righting Palestine Studies: Settler Colonialism, Indigenous Sovereignty and Resisting the Ghosts of History," *Settler Colonial Studies*, 8 (3): 349–63.

Bauman, Z. (2002), "In the Lowly Nowherevilles of Liquid Modernity," *Ethnography*, 3 (3): 343–49.

Bourdieu, P. and A. Sayad (2004), "Colonial Rule and the Cultural Sabir," *Ethnography*, 5 (4): 445–86.

Bourdieu, P. and S. Abdelmalek (2020), *Uprooting: The Crisis of Traditional Agriculture in Algeria*, Cambridge: Polity Press.

Clarno, A. (2017), *Neoliberal Apartheid: Palestine/Israel and South Africa after 1994*, Chicago: Chicago University Press.

Cohen, H. (2010), *Good Arabs: The Israeli Security Agencies and the Israeli Arabs, 1948–1967*, Berkeley: University of California Press.

Collins, P. H. (2010), "The New Politics of Community," *American Sociological Review*, 75 (1): 7–30.

Cornell, S. (1988), *The Return of the Native: American Indian Political Resurgence*, Oxford: Oxford University Press.

Elena Fiddian-Qasmiyeh. 2019. The Changing Faces of UNRWA From the Global to the Local. *Journal of Humanitarian Affairs* 1 (1). https://www.manchesteropenhive.com/view/journals/jha/1/1/article-p28.xml

El Kurd, D. (2019), *Polarized and Demobilized: Legacies of Authoritarianism in Palestine*, Oxford: Oxford University Press.

Falah, G. (2005). "The Geopolitics of 'Enclavisation' and the Demise of a Two-State Solution to the Israeli-Palestinian Conflict," *Third World Quarterly*, 26 (8): 1341–1372.

Farah, R. (2010), "UNRWA: Through the Eyes of Its Palestinian Employees," *Refugee Survey Quarterly*, 28 (2–3): 389–411.

Fassin, D. (2012), *Humanitarian Reason: A Moral History of the Present Times*, Berkeley: University of California Press.

Fassin, D. (2013), *Enforcing Order: An Ethnography of Urban Policing*, Cambridge: Polity.

Farsakh, L. (2005). *Palestinian Labour Migration to Israel: Labour, Land, and Occupation*. London: Routledge.

Fiddian-Qasmiyeh, E. (2019). "The Changing Faces of UNRWA: From the Global to the Local." *Journal of Humanitarian Affairs*, 1 (1): 28–41

Fraser, N. (2010), "Injustice at Intersecting Scales: On 'Social Exclusion' and the 'Global Poor'," *European Journal of Social Theory*, 13 (3): 363–71.

Furani, K. and D. Rabinowitz (2011), "The Ethnographic Arriving of Palestine," *Annual Review of Anthropology*, 40: 475–91.

Ghazi-Walid Falah (2005)," The Geopolitics of 'Enclavisation' and the Demise of a Two-stateSolution to the Israeli—Palestinian Conflict. *Third World Quarterly*, 26(8): 1341–372.

Go, J. (2013), "Decolonizing Bourdieu: Colonial and Postcolonial Theory in Pierre Bourdieu's Early Work," *Sociological Theory*, 31 (1): 49–74.

Go, J. (2020), "The Imperial Origins of American Policing: Militarization and Imperial Feedback in the Early 20th Century," *American Journal of Sociology*, 125 (5): 1193–254.

Gordon, N. (2008), *Israel's Occupation*, Berkeley: University of California Press

Graham, S. (2010), *Cities under Siege: The New Military Urbanism*, London: Verso.

Grbac, P. (2013), "Civitas, Polis, and Urbs: Reimagining the Refugee Camp as a City," RSC Working Paper Series 96.

Gregory, D. (2004), *The Colonial Present*, Maiden and Oxford: Blackwell Publishing.

Hanafi, S. (2009). "Spacio-cide: Colonial Politics, Invisibility, and Rezoning in Palestinian Territory," *Contemporary Arab Affairs*, 2 (1): 106–121.

Hanafi, S. and T. Long (2010), "Governance, Governmentalities, and the State of Exception in the Palestinian Camps," *Journal of Refugee Studies*, 23 (2): 39–48.

Holston, J. and A. Appadurai (1996), "Cities and Citizenship," *Public Culture*, 8 (2): 187–204.

Hyndman, J. (2000), *Managing Displacement: Refugees and the Politics of Humanitarianism*, Minneapolis: University of Minnesota Press.
Isin, E. (2000), *Democracy, Citizenship and the Global City*, London: Routledge.
Isin, E. (2002), *Being Political: Genealogies of Citizenship*, Minneapolis: University of Minnesota Press.
Junka, L. (2015), *Late Modern Palestine: The Subject and Representation of the Second Intifada*, London: Routledge.
Khalidi, R. (1997), *Palestinian Identity: The Construction of Modern National Consciousness*, New York: Columbia University Press.
Khalili, L. (2010), "The Location of Palestine in Global Counterinsurgencies," *International Journal of Middle East Studies*, 42 (3): 423–33.
Malkki, L. (1995), "Refugees and Exile: From 'Refugee Studies' to the National Order of Things," *Annual Review of Anthropology*, 24: 495–523.
Malkki, L. (2002), "News from Nowhere: Mass Displacement and Globalized 'Problems of Organization'," *Ethnography*, 3 (3): 351–60.
Mamdani, M. (1996), *Citizen and Subject: Contemporary Africa and the Legacy of Late Colonialism*, Princeton: Princeton University Press.
Mbembe, A. (2003), *Necropolitics*. Durham, NC: Duke University Press.
Meari, L. (2014), "*Sumud*: A Palestinian Philosophy of Confrontation in Colonial Prisons," *South Atlantic Quarterly*, 113 (3): 547–78.
Nassar, M. (2019), "Palestinian Engagement with the Black Freedom Movement Prior to 1967," *Journal of Palestine Studies*, 48 (4): 17–32.
Omar Jabary Salamanca, Mezna Qato, Kareem Rabie, and Sobhi Samour (2012)," Past Is Present: Settler Colonialism in Palestine," *Settler Colonial Studies*, 2 (1): 1–8.
Palidda, S. (2009), "The Criminalization and Victimization of Immigrants: A Critical Perspective," in W. F. McDonald (ed.), *Immigration, Crime and Justice*, 313–26. Bingley: Emerald.
Parsons, N., and Salter, M. (2008). "Israeli Biopolitics: Closure, Territorialisation, and Governmentality in the Occupied Palestinian Territories. *Geopolitics*, 13 (4): 701–723.
Pasquetti, S. (2012), "The Reconfiguration of the Palestinian National Question: The Indirect Rule Route and the Civil Society Route," *Political Power and Social Theory*, 23: 103–46.
Pasquetti, S. (2013), "Legal Emotions: An Ethnography of Distrust and Fear in the Arab Districts of an Israeli City," *Law and Society Review*, 47 (3): 461–92.
Pasquetti, S. (2015), "Subordination and Dispositions: Palestinians' Differing Sense of Injustice, Politics, and Morality," *Theory and Society*, 44 (1): 1–31.
Pasquetti, S. (Forthcoming 2023), *Refugees and Citizens: Control, Emotions, and Politics in a West Bank Camp and an Israeli "Mixed" City*, Oxford: Oxford University Press.
Pasquetti, S. (2019). "Experiences of Urban Militarism: Spatial Stigma, Ruins, and Everyday Life," *International Journal of Urban and Regional Research*, 43 (5): 848–869.
Pasquetti, S. and R. Sanyal, eds (2020), *Displacement: Global Conversations on Refuge*, Manchester: Manchester University Press.
Parsons, Nigel and Mark B. Salter (2008), "Israeli Biopolitics: Closure, Territorialisation and Governmentality in the Occupied Palestinian Territories," *Geopolitics*, 13 (4): 701–23.
Ramadan, A. (2012), "Spatialising the Refugee Camp," *Transactions of the Institute of British Geographers*, 38: 65–77.

Samara, R. H. (2011), *Cape Town after Apartheid: Crime and Governance in the Divided City*, Minneapolis: Minnesota: University of Minnesota Press.

Redclift, V. (2013), "Abjects or Agents? Camps, Contests and the Creation of 'Political Space'," *Citizenship Studies*, 17 (3–4): 308–21.

Rempel, T. (2009), "UNRWA and the Palestine Refugees: A Genealogy of 'Participatory' Development," *Refugee Survey Quarterly*, 28 (2–3): 412–37.

Rodgers, S., C. Barnett, and A. Cochrane (2014), "Where Is Urban Politics?," *International Journal of Urban and Regional Research*, 38 (5): 1551–60.

Sabbagh-Khoury, A. (2021), "Tracing Settler Colonialism: A Genealogy of a Paradigm in the Sociology of Knowledge Production in Israel," *Politics & Society*. https://doi.org/10.1177/0032329221999906

Sa'di, A. (2003), "The Incorporation of the Palestinian Minority by the Israeli State, 1948–1970: On the Nature, Transformation, and Constraints of Collaboration," *Social Text*, 21 (2): 75–94.

Sa'di, A. (2016), *Thorough Surveillance: The Genesis of Israeli Policies of Population Management, Surveillance, and Political Control towards the Palestinian Minority*, Manchester: Manchester University Press.

Sa'di, A. and L. Abu-Lughod (2007), *Nakba: Palestine, 1948, and the Claims of Memory*, New York: Columbia University Press.

Salamanca, O., Qato, M., Kareem, R., and Samour, S. 2012. "Past is Present: Settler Colonialism in Palestine," *Settler Colonial Studies*, 2 (1): 1-8.

Sanyal, R. (2011), "Squatting in Camps: Building and Insurgency in Spaces of Refuge," *Urban Studies*, 48 (5): 877–90.

Sanyal, R. (2012), "Refugees and the City: An Urban Discussion," *Geography Compass*, 6 (11): 633–44.

Sanyal, R. (2014), "Urbanizing Refuge: Interrogating Spaces of Displacement," *International Journal of Urban and Regional Research*, 38 (2): 558–72.

Scheerer, S. and H. Hess (1997), "Social Control: A Defence and Reformulation," in Bergalli and C. Sumner (eds.), *Social Control and Political Order*, 96–130. Newbury Park: Sage.

Shalhoub-Kevorkian, N. (2015), *Security Theology, Surveillance, and the Politics of Fear*, Cambridge: Cambridge University Press.

Sigona, N. (2015), "Campzenship: Reimagining the Camp as a Social and Political Space," *Citizenship Studies*, 19 (1): 1–15.

Simpson, A. (2014), *Mohawk Interruptus: Political Life across the Borders of Settler States*, Durham: Duke University Press.

Tatour, L. (2019), "Citizenship as Domination: Settler Colonialism and the Making of Palestinian Citizenship in Israel," *Arab Studies Journal*, 27 (2): 8–39.

Wacquant, L. (2008a), *Urban Outcasts: A Comparative Sociology of Advanced Marginality*, Cambridge: Polity Press.

Wacquant, L. (2008b), "The Militarization of Urban Marginality: Lessons from the Brazilian Metropolis," *International Political Sociology*, 2 (1): 56–74.

Wacquant, L. (2009), *Punishing the Poor: The Neoliberal Government of Social Insecurity*, Durham: Duke University Press.

Wacquant, L. (2014), "Marginality, Ethnicity and Penality in the Neo-Liberal City: An Analytic Cartography," *Ethnic and Racial Studies*, 37 (10): 1687–711.

Weber, M. (1966), *The City*. New York: Free Press.
Western, J. (1996). *Outcast Cape Town*. Berkeley, CA: University of California Press.
Weizman E. (2007). *Hollow Land: Israel's Architecture Of Occupation*. New York: Verso Press.
Yacobi, H. (2009), *The Jewish-Arab City: Spatio-politics in a Mixed Community*, London: Routledge.
Yiftachel, O. (2006), *Ethnocracy: Land and Identity Politics in Israel/Palestine*, Philadelphia: University of Pennsylvania Press.
Yiftachel, O. and H. Yacobi (2003), "Urban Ethnocracy: Ethnicization and the Production of Space in an Israeli 'Mixed City'," *Environment & Planning D*, 21 (6): 673–93.
Zureik. E. (1979), *The Palestinians in Israel: A Study in International Colonialism*, London: Routledge.
Zureik, E., D. Lyon, and Y. Abu-Laban (2011), *Surveillance and Control in Israel/Palestine: Population, Territory, and Power*, New York: Routledge.

Governing Syrian Refugees through Tech

by Elisa Pascucci

This chapter offers a critical approach to the question of refugee work and entrepreneurship in the context of restrictive asylum policies and shrinking humanitarian assistance for Syrians in the Middle East. Focusing on ICT training programs targeting refugees in Jordan, it explores how Syrian youths approach a humanitarian regime in which, in the absence of full legal and social rights for refugees, the question of their material and financial subsistence is addressed through the paradigms of self-reliance, creativity, technological innovation, and entrepreneurship. It argues that policies targeting refugees as individualized economic subjects are countered by the intimately entangled family and community relations that characterize the experience of refugeeness, both at a local and at a transnational level (Kallio 2018; Mountz and Hyndman 2006). The findings expand upon recent scholarship that has explored the complex intersections of neoliberal governmentality and subjectivity and the migrant and refugee condition (Ehrkamp 2017). They also offer a critical snapshot of humanitarian innovation "from below," highlighting the racialized tropes and colonial continuities that characterize this major policy trend (Turner 2020).

The entry proceeds in three parts. The first section describes the international aid and development policies that have targeted Syrian refugees in Jordan. In particular, it discusses the rise of resilience, entrepreneurship, and IT training programs targeting youths in the context of global shifts toward economic self-reliance in refugee governance. The following section analyses ethnographic and interview material collected through fieldwork in Jordan, in 2017. In the conclusions, I offer some reflections on the implications of the study for both refugee governance and future social sciences research on the Middle East.

The chapter draws on participant observation was conducted for a total 2 months at events organized as part of coding training programs targeting young refugees in the capital, Amman. In addition to that, eleven in-depth unstructured interviews with refugee trainees and training staff and four, shorter follow-up interviews with refugees were analyzed. As a Southern-European who has lived and worked in the Middle East for

---

This chapter is part of an Accepted Manuscript of an article published by Taylor & Francis in *Geographical Review* on November 12, 2019, available online: https://doi.org/10.1111/gere.12315

several years, I shared some of the life trajectories of the young research participants—particularly experiences of graduate unemployment and struggles to fund postgraduate studies and maintain transnational family relations. These did not mitigate the racialized inequalities between my condition of European expatriate and theirs as Syrian refugees in Jordan. However, the focus on shared work experiences helped to bridge the gap between our positionalities, facilitating the research encounter (see also Pascucci 2018).

Refugee Economies and the Syrian Crisis in Jordan

The yellowish, majestic buildings and well-kept gardens of King Hussein Business Park (KHBP) occupy a large area on the western outskirts of central Amman. Built initially as a military facility, the park is at the heart of Jordan's ICT ecosystem, which, in 2016, was one of the biggest in the Middle East with over 700 companies, with a total revenue of $682,204,679 (ICT Association in Jordan—INTAJ 2016). The park's trajectory from a military site to a Special Economic Zone (SEZ) devoted to hi-tech industries reflects the Hashemite Kingdom's neoliberal development policies under King Abdullah, in which urban development has been mostly based on Public Private Partnership (PPP; Baghaeen 2006). However, it is also emblematic of a trend that has invested the wider Middle East since the early 2010s. KHBP is often described as one of the most important sites of the Arab "startup spring" (Ahmari 2015). This is how fanciful developmental narratives qualified some of the economic changes that occurred across the region in the aftermaths of the 2011 uprisings, as the revolts were receding and stability was being restored, in some cases by military juntas.

Syria, however, remained a significant exception in this alleged landscape of technology, entrepreneurship, and manu militari–secured stability. As the country plunged further into war, by the end of 2016 the so-called Middle Eastern "startup spring" had intersected with what, according to the United Nations High Commissioner for Refugees (UNHCR), was the biggest refugee crisis in the world, with over 5.4 million people having left Syria since 2011 (UNHCR 2017). Jordan, a country with no formal domestic asylum legislation, whose refugee policies are regulated only by a Memorandum of Understanding (MOU) with the UNHCR, was hosting over 600,000 displaced Syrians, as well as the largest refugee camp in the Middle East, Zaatari. A rapidly urbanizing conglomerate of prefabricated temporary housing and tents in the middle of the desert, about an hour from Amman, in 2017 Zaatari was home to around 78,500 people. Approximately another 36,600 refugees were in the Azraq camp, in the Zarqa governorate, while a few thousand more were lodged in small camps like Murijep al Fhoud, funded by the United Arab Emirates. The vast majority of Syrians in Jordan, however, had settled autonomously in the major urban areas, including Amman. Since 2014, as the internationally praised open-door policy of Jordan had taken an increasingly restrictive turn, leading to the borders with Syria being shut in 2015, most had found themselves "stuck" in the Hashemite Kingdom, getting by through precarious work, savings, and transnational networks of social and financial support.

Securing the livelihoods of refugees in Jordan beyond the reliance on humanitarian assistance and preventing their irregular movement soon became of paramount importance for international donors. In turn, the Jordanian government saw in the global concern about Syrian refugees a potential chance for economic development. Through the Jordan Compact, approved during the London conference on Syria of 2016, the international community promised around $2 billion in aid and investment for Jordan. The European Union also revised its preferential rules of origin, facilitating the export of products manufactured in Jordan, especially in the garment industry (Lenner and Turner 2018). Jordan committed to issue 200,000 work permits for Syrians, and to ease international investment in five SEZs. While the actual impact of these measures remains questionable (ILO 2017; Lenner and Turner 2018), international organizations and NGOs were quick to switch their agenda from emergency relief to development, as many officers confirmed during interviews in Amman.

By 2017, in Jordan, the "Californian ideology" of Silicon Valley had entered into an unlikely marriage with a humanitarian ethos reframed around the imperatives of refugee self-reliance and entrepreneurship, a marriage which Tom Scott-Smith (2015) defined as "humanitarian neophilia" (see also Barbrook and Cameron 1996). From the UNICEF's Innovation Fund to the "Ideas Box," the mobile library designed by Librarians without Borders in use in the community centers managed by the Danish Refugee Council, solutions to the Syrian refugee crisis were sought—or claimed to be sought—primarily through technology and the promotion of refugee entrepreneurship, with a particular focus on women and youth. The shiny high-tech veneer, however, did not erase the more concrete and long-lasting geopolitical preoccupations underpinning international donors' efforts directed toward Syrians in Jordan. The Jordan Compact's support to Syrian refugees' livelihood and the attempts at integrating them into the Jordanian economy had among their primary aims the promotion of stability, security, and the prevention of irregular migration toward Europe (Council of Europe 2016). In this context, places like KHBP opened their doors to refugees and humanitarian organizations. Hopes were rising high about the tech sector offering opportunities for young Syrians to express their talent and, in the process, develop Jordan.

The international community's concern with the labor and economic lives of refugees is hardly new (Easton-Calaabria 2015). The UNHCR Livelihoods Unit, established in 2008, identifies as its main tools and objectives "vocational and skills training, promoting entrepreneurship, supporting agriculture, livestock and fisheries, and strengthening access to financial services or microfinance" (UNHCR 2014: 14, as cited in Easton-Calabria 2015: 431). The "Whole of Syria" promoted by the United Nations through the Strategic Response Plan (SRP) pursues similar policies (Ilcan and Rygiel 2015). The plan's objective of strengthening "livelihoods and early recovery" is based on resilience-promotion, community self-reliance, and a decentered governance in which implementation is carried out through an extensive network of partners. The aim is to recast refugees from "passive recipients of aid" to "responsible, resilient subjects who survive through crisis" (Ilcan and Rygiel 2015: 337). While actual refugee participation in policy formulation and planning remains elusive (Easton-Calabria 2015), the responsibility for surviving and recovering from crises, especially from an economic point of view, is individualized. Coupled with the technological entrepreneurship narratives promoted through, among others, the UNHCR Innovation initiative, the neoliberal humanitarian governance characterizing the Syria SRP is but the latest development in a long history of governing displacement by making refugees economically viable.

"Coding," Borders, and Family Precarities

Founded in Jordan in December 2014, ReBootKamp (RBK)—the only coding boot camp in the Arab world according to its website—offers a sixteen-week program in computer programming. While the program is open also to Jordanians, many of its students are refugees. Besides private donors, the organization developed in collaboration with the UNHCR and the United Nations Development Program (UNDP), and has enjoyed a successful partnership with the latter that has allowed many young Syrians, Iraqis, and Yemenis to receive scholarships and loans covering the 5,700 JD (US$8,040) fee. The Danish Refugee Council also featured among the RBK partners. Its case highlights the convergence of national economic and humanitarian rationalities that frame the work of education start-ups, NGOs, and social enterprises in Jordan.

Despite the focus on innovation and technology, this convergence reproduces power relations imbued with colonial and racial tropes (Turner 2020). This emerged clearly from the analysis of the selection process at RBK, and from the interviews with its managers and, to a lesser extent, trainers. The main entry requirements to the program were motivational: commitment to the training and willingness to work in the Jordanian IT sector upon completion. While most of the refugee students had completed at least secondary school, and many had a university degree, formal education was not regarded as essential. RBK managers depicted secondary schools and universities in Syria and Jordan as excessively hierarchical and based on pedagogies that do not foster free, critical thinking and individual creativity (on "lack of critical thinking" as orientalist stereotyping in educational settings, see Moosavi 2020). Such perceptions of formal, public education resonated with the generalizing negative assessment of Jordanian and Syrian graduates by humanitarian and development professionals in Jordan. These viewed local graduates as having few, if any, marketable skills, and burdened by a sense of entitlement that led them to expect to find a stable job without much effort, possibly in state bureaucracies—a start-up era version of Syed Hussein Alatas's (1977) "myth of the lazy native."

The solution to this alleged impasse offered by the RBK coding boot camp is individual, and consists of making young refugees (and unemployed Jordanians) desirable employees in an aspirational emerging new economy. This transformation is achieved by combining a culturally specific version of the Silicon Valley work culture with humanitarian practices and values. As far as the technical training is concerned, the camp open-source pedagogy utilizes "agile principles: sprint learning, peer-based learning, problem-based learning, fail-based learning, heavily facilitated learning, psycho-social support" (interview with RBK manager, Amman 2017).

Syrian youths thus carefully deployed their strategic agency to navigate the variegated training and study opportunities offered by education start-ups, UN, international NGOs, and Jordanian charities close to the Hashemite government. However, at the RBK "Meet & Greet" event, an open day held in Amman's KHBP in April 2017 to allow perspective students to meet staff and alumni of the coding boot camp, unemployment was an experience shared by all the participants. None of the young Syrians met had joined to improve their "career perspectives." Rather, they were there "to find a job," as they put it. The difference in language denotes an important difference in attitudes and expectations. Most of them felt they had no chances of actual professional success, no matter what kind of degrees they held. The best they could hope for, if they were lucky, was finding decent work to support themselves and their families.

Such feelings were not without reason. As already mentioned, having no international legal obligations to refugees' social and economic rights, Jordan has very restrictive rules as to their access to the job market. Although these were partially mitigated by the Jordan Compact's commitment to issue work permits to Syrians, in 2017 access to qualified sectors of the job markets remained almost exclusively reserved to Jordanian citizens (Lenner and Turner 2018). Among other things, this meant that Syrian RBK graduates could only find employment through consultancy schemes, and not through regular work contracts. Coupled with Jordan's structurally high unemployment rates, RBK perspective students' grim outlook on the future appeared thus rather realistic.

Two months after completing the training, Mariam—"one of the technically most gifted coders we have ever trained," as one of the members of staff described her—had had job interviews at two different IT companies, but she was still waiting to hear back from them. At twenty-seven, she was looking for a job that would allow her to support her family of origin. Like Mariam, RBK students praised for their technical talent seemed to embrace the values of self-development and entrepreneurship. However, they did not look at professional and economic success as a merely individual endeavor. Commitments and responsibilities toward parents, siblings, spouses, future children, friends, and neighbors were often the main reasons to train as a coder and improve one's chances to find a good job. While the training proposed empathy, active listening, and collaboration as tools for personal growth and success, most of the young people I spoke to considered individual success as a way to build materially grounded and intimately connected relations of familiality and communal care.

Hanan was a refugee in her thirties with a civil engineering degree from a public university. By the time we met at the RBK event, her degree was already over five years old, and it had never been put to use, first because of war, then because of internal displacement. After her father's death, Hanan's family had finally relocated to Jordan, hoping to find some stability and perhaps a chance for resettlement to a third country through the UNHCR program, for which they had applied. Meanwhile, Hanan was trying other ways, both to improve her employment perspectives in Jordan, and to get a visa to travel abroad. Rather than engaging in a mere "timepass" in the absence of more meaningful ways to spend her time in Jordan (Wagner 2017), Hanan, like most of the refugee youths at RBK, was looking for another piece in the puzzle of her family's precarious livelihood.

As Hanan's experience shows, mobility is often the most challenging aspect of this puzzle. Like her, several other RBK graduates and students had applied for resettlement through the UNHCR, together with their families. The central and eastern Mediterranean routes featured often in the familial histories of the young Syrian software engineers. In 2014, Magid and his family had arrived in Egypt from Lebanon, where they had at first sought safety from the violence in Syria. In Cairo, Magid had worked for a shopping assistant for about eight months. Disappointed and increasingly frustrated with the little future perspectives that life in Egypt seemed to offer, and being lucky enough to be able to count on some financial support from his family, Magid had followed his aspirations and moved to Amman to enroll first for a scientific degree at the University of Jordan, and then for the RBK training. A few months after his arrival to Jordan, his two brothers who had remained in Egypt had decided to seek refuge in Europe, travelling to Italy via sea.

> They just took a boat to Europe. It took them twelve days to reach their destination. [...] No sleep, no eating until I heard back from them again. [...] My parents? No, my parents didn't travel that way. You can't send older people, your parents, on a dangerous trip like that.

While Magid's decision to move to Jordan was also determined by his own individual aspirations, both his and his brothers' trajectories of mobility were part of a transnational configuration of care and intersubjective responsibility. Once Magid's brothers had made it to their final destination, Germany, and received asylum there, they had applied for family reunification, getting their parents to travel to Europe safely. Like many of the young people enrolling for the training offered by RBK, they were thus hoping to find "good work" that would allow them to support members of their extended family and communities in Syria and in neighboring countries. Their economic selves were deeply embedded in relations aimed at countering the precarity produced by displacement and migration and refugee governance.

Conclusions

This study has highlighted the gap between the tech camp's narratives of success and the lived experience of young refugees in Jordan. It has shown how little young refugees actually engaged with the subject position of the brilliant, successful coder—the start-up economy winner. Instead, it was the needs of more vulnerable members of their families and communities—aging parents, unemployed siblings, and the like—that shaped the decisions they made in their economic lives. Actual, "decent" work remained scarce, legal access to it extremely limited, and young middle-class Syrians in Jordan were thoroughly aware of it. As Linda Herrera has eloquently put it, before growing evidence of the limits of start-up and entrepreneurship models, when not accompanied by initiatives aimed at more structural change, "it is unfair and disingenuous to propagate the myth that anyone with an idea, grit and determination" can be economically successful (2017: 42). To promise success in the IT sector to young women and men who find themselves "stuck," with very few options for international travel besides deadly dangerous, irregular migration via sea, seems incongruous at the very least.

That these youths would rather stick with their families as sources of economic, social, and moral support should come as no surprise. The point here is not to idealize refugee families as sites of resistance to neoliberal development. Rather, it is to show the inadequacies and contradictions of a model of economic integration targeting young refugees with promises of individual success, while actually offering little or no security, in a global context of shrinking budgets for international aid and increasingly restrictive migration policies. Livelihood policies that fail to take into account how the economic agency of refugees in precarious socio-legal conditions is embedded in familial relations of care, reciprocity, and responsibility are deemed to have limited effects. Such relations are moral, affective, and transnational, but also binding in their material implications. The professional and economic choices that made sense for my Syrian interlocutors, be they women or men, were those that were functional within their family and community relational space, and not simply those that maximized their individual success in the IT sector. Finally, some of the questions addressed in this chapter point to phenomena that are global in scale, and increasingly relevant for the sociology of displacement and humanitarianism in the Middle East. These include solutions to complex socio-political crises sought through technological innovation and the involvement of corporate actors and corporate governance tools in humanitarian delivery. The uneven results of these processes, in which humanitarianism and technology often merely reinforce old colonial and racist tropes (Turner 2020), call for further critical engagements with the question of refugee economies.

References

Ahmari, S. (2015), Welcome to Startup Egypt, *The Wall Street Journal*. https://www.wsj.com/articles/sohrab-ahmari-welcome-to-startup-egypt-1427315557

Alatas, S. H. (1977), *The Myth of the Lazy Native*, London: Routledge.

Baghaeen, S. G. (2006), "Redeveloping Former Military Sites: Competitiveness, Urban Sustainability and Public Participation," *Cities*, 23 (5): 339–52.

Barbrook, R. and A. Cameron (1996), "The Californian Ideology," *Science as Culture*, 6 (1): 44–72.
Council of Europe (2016), EU and Jordan adopted partnership priorities and compact, https://www.consilium.europa.eu/en/press/press-releases/2016/12/20/eu-jordan-partnership-priorities-and-compact/#:~:text=The%20EU%2DJordan%20compact%20foresees,Parliament%20on%2014%20December%202016.
Easton-Calabria, E. E. (2015), "From Bottom-up to Top-down: The 'Pre-history' of Refugee Livelihoods Assistance from 1919 to 1979," *Journal of Refugee Studies*, 28 (3): 412–36.
Ehrkamp, P. (2017), "Geographies of Migration I: Refugees," *Progress in Human Geography*, 41 (3): 816–22.
Ilcan, S. and K. Rygiel. (2015), "'Resiliency Humanitarianism': Responsibilizing Refugees through Humanitarian Emergency Governance in the Camp," *International Political Sociology*, 9 (4): 333–51.
ILO (2017), Work Permits and Employment of Syrian Refugees in Jordan: Towards Formalising the Work of Syrian Refugees, ILO Regional Office for Arab States. http://www.ilo.org/wcmsp5/groups/public/—arabstates/—ro-beirut/documents/publication/wcms_559151.pdf
INTAJ (2016), ICT and ITES Industry Statistics and Yearbook, Amman: INTAJ. Available at: http://intaj.net/wp-content/uploads/2017/12/ICT-ITES-INDUSTRY-STATISTICS-AND-YEARBOOK-2016.pdf
Kallio, K. P. (2018), "Leading Refugee Lives Together: Familial Agency as a Political Capacity," *Emotion, Space and Society*, https://doi.org/10.1016/j.emospa.2018.08.002
Lenner, K. and L. Turner (2018), "Making Refugees Work? The Politics of Integrating Syrian Refugees into the Labor Market in Jordan," *Middle East Critique*, 28 (1): 65–95.
Moosavi, L. (2020), "'Can East Asian Students Think?': Orientalism, Critical Thinking, and the Decolonial Project," *Education Sciences*, 10 (10): 286. https://doi.org/10.3390/educsci10100286
Mountz, A. and J. Hyndman (2006), "Feminist Approaches to the Global Intimate," *Women's Studies Quarterly*, 34 (1/2): 446–63.
Pascucci, E. (2018), "The Local Labour Building the International Community: Precarious Work within Humanitarian Spaces," *Environment and Planning A: Economy and Space*, 51 (3): 743–60.
Scott-Smith, T. (2015), "Humanitarian Neophilia: The Innovation Turn and Its Implications," *Third World Quarterly*, 37 (12): 2229–51.
Turner, L. (2020), "'#Refugees can be Entrepreneurs Too!' Humanitarianism, Race, and the Marketing of Syrian Refugees," *Review of International Studies*, 46 (1): 137–55.
UNHCR (2014), Global Strategy for Livelihoods. Available at: https://www.unhcr.org/protection/livelihoods/530f107b6/global-strategy-livelihoods.html (accessed February 23, 2022).
UNHCR (2017), Syria Emergency. http://www.unhcr.org/syria-emergency.html
Wagner, A. (2017), "Frantic Waiting: MGO Anti-Politics and 'Timepass' in Jordan," *Middle East – Topics & Arguments*, 9: 107–21.

II DIASPORA IN EUROPE

Muslims' Civic Participation and Voting in France, Québec, and English-Canada: Do National "Models" Play a Role?

by Emily Laxer, Jeffrey G. Reitz, and Patrick Simon

Introduction

In Europe and elsewhere, portrayals of a Muslim "other" increasingly pervade movements aimed at preserving distinct national identities. In several countries, the resulting debates have spawned campaigns to legally restrict the wearing of Islamic signs in public spaces and institutions. Full or partial bans of facial coverings are now in place in Austria, Belgium, Denmark, France, Germany, and the Netherlands. Headscarves are also prohibited in the French public school system, in some Belgian universities, and in Germany's court system.

European debates over Muslim religious signs find a remarkable parallel in the majority-French-speaking and historically Catholic Canadian province of Québec. In 2019, a two-decade-long debate over accommodations of minority religious practices culminated in a ban of religious signs among the province's public sector employees in positions of authority, including judges, police officers, crown prosecutors, and—most controversially—teachers. In justifying this ban to the public, the provincial government cited its commitment to *laïcité*, the French republican term for separation of church and state.

The banning of Muslim religious signs in and beyond Europe has renewed scholars' interest in the role of national discourses and policies of integration—what some call national "models"—in shaping the social, economic, and political incorporation of diasporic minorities, especially Muslims. This chapter examines whether the civic and political behaviors of the Muslim diaspora differ in three national settings whose integration "models" differently portray the limits and preferred mechanisms of political incorporation: France, Canada, and Québec. Using data from the 2008 Trajectories

---

Abridged from Laxer, E., J. G. Reitz and P. Simon (2020), "Muslims' political and civic incorporation in France and Canada: testing models of participation," *Journal of Ethnic and Migration Studies* 46 (17): 3677–702.

and Origins Survey in France and the 2002 Ethnic Diversity Survey in Canada, we find national "models" have limited effect on the civic and political engagements of Muslims. Association membership and voting are driven primarily by individual-level factors, and any cross-national differences seem to capture broader differences in national political culture that affect mainstream groups as much as minorities.

National "Models" and Political and Civic Incorporation

Research suggests countries' national integration "models" shape immigrants' political and civic engagement by demarcating membership in the nation. Anchored in law, institutions, and culture, these "models" assign the material and symbolic criteria of political and civic engagement, telling citizens how to participate in public life. In studying the effect this has on immigrants' political participation, scholars have invoked the concept of "political opportunity structures" (Bird 2005). By defining the normative frameworks of inter-group relations (Bloemraad 2006) and determining which types of claims are considered legitimate (Koopmans et al. 2005), they argue, countries' national integration discourses shape immigrants' access to political inclusion.

The French, Canadian, and Québécois "models" of integration differently define immigrants' national membership. France's republican discourse situates integration in the project of constructing a civic ideal of nationhood based on shared commitment to participation in a common public sphere. Immigrants are considered well-integrated when they shed their cultural and religious particularities to embrace *liberté*, *égalité*, *fraternité*, and *laïcité*. Despite an openness to immigration and naturalization (Hollifield 2014), newcomers must conform to the national ideal of citizen engagement in a culturally and religiously neutral public sphere (Laborde 2008).

In contrast, Canada's multicultural discourse of integration recognizes the group-based underpinnings of political incorporation. The original policy adopted by the Trudeau government in 1971 offered support for minority cultural organizations as part of an effort to incorporate them. Over time, multiculturalism has evolved into what many regard as a cornerstone of Canadian identity (Reitz 2011), which valorizes citizens' private cultural commitments and portrays these as legitimate bases of political belonging.

Within Canada, Québec has adopted a distinct approach to immigrant incorporation. With the 1960s Quiet Revolution, the provincial government replaced the Catholic Church to promote a secular and francophone national identity. To preserve that identity in the context of a growing immigrant population, Québec has adopted its own criteria—including French language proficiency—to select newcomers since 1991. The province has also distinguished itself by not embracing the federal multiculturalism policy, which many nationalists believe diminishes Québec's claims to sub-national identity by placing all minority groups on a level playing field. Québec's "interculturalism" (Bouchard

2011) approach valorizes diversity, but "within the limits imposed by the respect for fundamental democratic values, and the necessity of inter-community exchange" (Gagnon and Iacovino 2004: 375). While not official policy, interculturalism drives decision-making in government commissions, policy documents, and parliamentary debates in Québec.

French republicanism, Canadian multiculturalism, and Québécois interculturalism convey distinct messages about the parameters—and preferred mechanisms—of participation in the national polity. Both the republican and intercultural approaches explicitly identify the "limits" of tolerance for diverse viewpoints, including respect for democratic values, sexual equality, and nonviolence. By contrast, multiculturalism makes no reference to an official culture. Moreover, whereas multiculturalism portrays ethnicity as a legitimate component of citizenship, the emphasis on a common public culture in the republican and intercultural discourses implicitly relegates ethnicity to the private domain, rendering it an illegitimate basis for political mobilization.

Scholars disagree about the precise effects of "national models" on political incorporation. Some suggest multiculturalism facilitates engagement, both because it accepts group membership as a dimension of citizenship *and* because it welcomes engagement along ethnic lines (Bloemraad 2006). European studies corroborate this finding; immigrants residing in countries featuring inclusive integration policies exhibit higher levels of political trust (Wright and Bloemraad 2012) and engagement in domestic politics (Koopmans and Statham 2000). However, others warn multiculturalism discourages participation in mainstream politics by fostering social and residential ghettoization (Vertovec and Wessendorf 2009). In what is termed "reactive ethnicity," minorities adopt a conflictual stance vis-à-vis the host society due to perceptions of threat, persecution, and discrimination (Rumbaut 2008).

While providing no clear hypothesis, prior research leads us to expect differing patterns of engagement in France, Canada, and Québec. The greater preoccupation with forging *public* attachments in the republican and intercultural models may produce relatively high voting rates among Muslims and other minorities in France and Québec. Moreover, if we accept the argument that multiculturalism fosters community-based attachments by treating *private* ethnic commitments as bases of mobilization, Canada's multicultural discourse should foster relatively high rates of membership in local civic associations, particularly among minorities.

Data and Methods

To test these hypotheses, we compare the civic and political participation of Muslims in France, English-Canada, and Québec. In the absence of data permitting direct measurement of the impact of a "model," we treat the country (or province, in the case of Québec) as a proxy indicator. We use data from the 2008 Trajectories and Origins

Survey by Institut National d'Etudes Démographiques (INED) and the 2002 Ethnic Diversity Survey by Statistics Canada. With 21,000 and 44,000 respondents respectively, the surveys capture the social, economic, and political experiences of immigrants and ethnic minorities. Our analysis focuses on native- and foreign-born residents aged eighteen to sixty (for native-born children of immigrants, the sample is further limited to those between eighteen and fifty).

Regarding voting, we compare turnout in the most recent municipal elections, and in France's 2007 presidential and Canada's 2000 federal parliamentary elections. We measure civic engagement using a variable asking whether respondents report being members, or participating in the activities, of an association in the twelve months preceding the survey. To gauge ethnic-group engagements, we further distinguish membership in associations in which half or more members share an ethnic ancestry.

The two main independent variables are "religion/origins" and "generation status." Categories of the former are "non-Muslim, European," "non-Muslim, non-European," and "Muslim." The latter distinguishes the "mainstream" (born in France/Canada to two native-born parents), "immigrants" (foreign-born), and "second generation" (born in France/Canada to at least one foreign-born parent).

Muslims represent a much larger share of immigrants and second-generation minorities in France (39.4 and 26.8 percent respectively) than in Québec (19.7 and 2.2 percent) or in the rest of Canada (10.8 and 1.8 percent). In addition, more than one-third of Muslims in France are native-born, compared to 10.5 percent or less in Canada. The origins of the Muslim population also differ substantially. In France, those origins reflect the country's colonial history: three quarters report being born, or having parents who were born, in the Maghreb (Algeria, Morocco, Tunisia), with the rest from sub-Saharan Africa and Turkey. A significant proportion of Québec's Muslim population also hails from the Maghreb, while in English-Canada, Muslim minorities hail primarily from South Asia, Turkey, the Middle East, West and Central Asia, and sub-Saharan Africa.

Muslim minorities differ in individual characteristics known to influence political and civic incorporation. Canadian Muslims, as well as other minorities (not shown), possess higher than average levels of education, a factor that should increase their relative rate of participation. In France, Muslim minorities are distinguished by their lower-than-average educational attainment. In all three settings, minorities (including Muslims) are more often married with children, live in urban areas, and have a lower labor force participation and household income.

Results

We compare civic engagement across settings by examining the rate of participation in associations—in general, as well as in co-ethnic associations—for Muslims, other European and non-European minorities, and the mainstream. As Table 31.1 indicates,

Table 31.1 Participation in voluntary associations (non-sports), total and co-ethnic, mainstream and minorities by Religion/Origin, and Generation Status: France and Canada (including Québec)

		Member of association			Member of co-ethnic association		
		France	Canada outside Québec	Québec	France	Canada outside Québec	Québec
Mainstream		36.5	49.8	38.3	n/a	n/a	n/a
Non-Muslim, European	Recent immigrant (last 10 years)	29.3	35.8	39.7	4.5	11.7	n/a
	Long-term immigrant (earlier)	27.8	43.1	37.1	3.8	13.4	n/a
	Second generation	30.6	50.7	45.7	3.4	7.4	n/a
Non-Muslim, non-European	Recent immigrant (last 10 years)	27.4	33.0	34.7	5.8	14.4	n/a
	Long-term immigrant (earlier)	29.2	39.6	34.3	6.5	16.0	n/a
	Second generation	31.4	51.7	44.0	3.8	9.8	n/a
Muslim	Recent immigrant (last 10 years)	13.9	28.2		3.9	11.8	
	Long-term immigrant (earlier)	17.1	31.8	29.0	5.6	10.7	9.4
	Second generation	23.7	40.9		3.9	15.9	

Source: Trajectories and Origins Survey, 2009 (France), Ethnic Diversity Survey, 2002 (Canada)
Sample: All persons aged 18–60, 18–50 for second generation.

Canadian data excludes aboriginal Canadians, foreign-born who are not permanent residents and those born abroad with Canadian citizenship at birth.

mainstream rates of participation generally are higher in Canada than France, as shown in previous studies (Schofer and Fourcade-Gourinchas 2001). Rates for Québec are between what is observed for France and the rest of Canada. In each of the three settings, participation is less frequent for Muslims than for other minorities and for the mainstream.

Participation in co-ethnic associations is relatively less frequent in all three settings, but of interest because it reflects a multicultural basis for social organization. Table 31.3 (right-side) shows rates are substantially higher in Canada than France, for minorities of European and non-European origins, as well as Muslims. About 10 percent of Muslims in Canada (including Québec) participate in such associations, compared to less than 5 percent in France.

Turning to voting, we analyze turnout at the national and municipal levels in each setting using a sample of eligible voters (focusing in the case of national voting on the

2007 presidential election in France and the 2000 parliamentary election in Canada). Table 31.2 shows that in France, the voting rates of Muslim minorities in national elections are about 90 percent, only slightly below the mainstream (94.8 percent). In municipal elections, the Muslim voting rate is about 80 percent, only about 6 percent below the mainstream rate. Thus, in France, there is no discernible "Muslim voting gap" at national or municipal levels. In Canada outside Québec, the Muslim voting rate at the federal level is 65 percent, somewhat below the 70.9 percent turnout reported by non-Muslims non-Europeans, and well short of the 77.5 percent rate among the mainstream population. A similar pattern exists at the municipal level: the 50.4 percent Muslim voting rate is below the 55.3 percent rate for non-Muslim non-Europeans, and well below the 63.6 percent rate for the mainstream. Thus, not only is voter turnout generally lower in Canada than France, there is a more discernible gap between European and non-European minorities, and an even larger Muslim voting gap. Québec also shows a non-European minority gap, but the Muslim voting gap is impossible to determine, given the smaller sample size.

We use logistic regression to separate compositional from contextual effects, by controlling for the fact that voting is higher among older respondents, those who are married, better educated, currently employed, and have higher household incomes. Regression models also consider whether and to what degree association membership impacts voting. To probe these questions, we use a sample of eligible voters. Given the important effect of age on voting, and because Muslims in all three settings tend to be younger than average, we further limit the regression samples to respondents aged twenty-one and over. For the sake of parsimony, we focus on federal/presidential voting.

The results in Table 31.3 show that, in France, the moderately negative Muslim effect on voting (Model 1) is marginally impacted by group differences in civic association membership (Model 2). The addition of socio-demographic controls (Model 3) alters the picture, causing the "Muslim" coefficient to become more positive and insignificant. In

Table 31.2 Percent voting in last federal and municipal elections, mainstream and minorities eligible to vote, by religion/origin: France and Canada (including Québec)

	National federal/presidential election			Municipal election		
	France	Canada outside Québec	Québec	France	Canada outside Québec	Québec
Mainstream	94.8	77.5	83.1	85.9	63.6	67.9
European, non-Muslim	91.8	79.5	87	82.7	64.1	68
Non-Muslim, non-European	90.8	70.9	78.4	80.0	55.3	63.3
Muslim	89.4	65.3	80.9	79.6	50.4	60.2

Source: See Table 31.1.
Sample: See Table 31.1; citizens only (except including EU citizens for municipal voting in France).

Table 31.3 Logistic regression on national voting (expressed as relative odds), mainstream and minorities eligible to vote: France and Canada (including Québec)

	National (federal/presidential)												
	France						Canada (including Québec)						
	Model 1		Model 2		Model 3		Model 1		Model 2		Model 3		
	Coeff	P	Coeff	P	Coeff	P	Coeff	P	Coeff	P	Coeff	P	
Generation (Recent Immig rg)													
Longterm immig	2.991	***	2.959	***	4.222	***	3.473	***	3.405	***	2.763	***	
Second gen	3.408	***	3.395	***	2.633	***	2.119	***	2.025	***	3.030	***	
Origins and Religion (European non-Muslim rg)													
Non-European, non-Muslim	0.817	ns	0.818	ns	1.021	ns	0.576	***	0.573	***	0.765	***	
Muslim, non-European	0.707	***	0.731	**	1.125	ns	0.489	***	0.497	***	0.711	*	
Québec							1.742	***	1.754	***	2.118	***	
Québec*Non-European, non-Muslim							0.882	ns	0.889	ns	0.854	ns	
Québec*Muslim							2.055	ns	2.102	ns	2.235	ns	
Member of civic organization (Non-member rg)			1.541	***	1.516	***			1.390	***	1.317	***	
Member of co-ethnic organization			1.239	ns	1.331	ns			1.599	***	1.533	***	
Constant	3.221	***	2.890	***	0.744	ns	1.472	***	1.306	*	0.212	***	
(N, unweighted)	8,570		8,570		8,570		13,740		13,740		13,740		

Source: See Table 31.1.
Sample: See Table 31.2. Models 1 and 2 include variables shown. Model 3 includes controls for sex, age, marital/parental status, highest degree, household income, employment status, and urban/rural residence. Note: Canadian regressions are performed using bootstrap weights.

Canada, the more negative non-European and Muslim effects are partly explained by the controls added in Model 3, but the negative effects remain significant. Consistent with the descriptive findings, the results indicate that, including controls, rates of electoral participation are higher for minorities in Québec than in the rest of Canada. Once again, however, the Muslim difference is not significant.

The results of Table 31.3 also indicate that being a member of a co-ethnic association significantly increases the odds of voting in Canada (1.599 in Model 2) but not in France. This result partially supports the view that, in a multicultural society, the ethnic group is considered an important vehicle for engagement. Additional models (not shown) including an interaction term for region and association membership revealed no significant difference in the effect of membership (either overall or co-ethnic) on voting in Québec compared to the rest of Canada.

Discussion

Our objective was to determine, using comparable survey data, whether and how distinctive national "models" of integration impact the political and civic participation outcomes of Muslim diasporic communities. Based on descriptive and regression analyses of membership in associations and voting, the results only partly support the hypothesis that French republicanism, Canadian multiculturalism, and Québécois interculturalism significantly shape patterns of engagement.

For voting, rates of participation among minorities *relative* to the mainstream were highest in Québec and lowest in English-Canada. In both France and Canada, voter turnout is a function of age, education, and generation, with older, more educated native-born children of immigrants the most likely to vote in presidential (France) and federal parliamentary (Canada) elections. Cross-national differences become more discernible when we turn our attention to the prevalence and effects of co-ethnic association membership. Rates of co-ethnic membership are noticeably higher in English-Canada and Québec than France, a fact that may result from the differing legitimacy conferred on ethnic attachments by the integration "model" in each setting. Moreover, membership in a co-ethnic association has a stronger positive effect on voting in Canada and Québec than in France, corroborating theoretical expectations of the mobilizing role of ethnicity in multicultural societies.

Taken together, our results provide only mixed evidence that states' "grand narratives" (Alba and Foner 2014), or discourses of integration, bear a significant relationship to minorities' political and civic incorporation. While these discourses appear to influence co-ethnic forms of engagement, differences in activities like voting and mainstream association membership seem to derive mainly from variations in the structure of political institutions and in nation-specific cultures of participation. Further research to consider the effects of recent laws that prohibit certain religious signs on political participation is imperative. Indeed, preliminary studies indicate that laws like France's 2010 face veil ban and 2004 headscarf ban in schools have real material consequences, causing those targeted to face harassment and, in some cases, to consider taking refuge in their homes (Bouteldja 2013; Simon 2021). Yet, there are also signs that protest against such laws is taking shape at the organizational level, with the potential to mobilize targeted groups. For instance, Québec's 2019 law prohibiting religious signs in public sector positions of authority drew significant backlash from Civil Rights and Muslim organizations, and continues to be fought in the courts. It remains to be seen whether this kind of activism will translate into increased levels of political and/or civic engagement on the part of Muslims in Québec compared to France—where restrictive laws are well established—and English-Canada—where they have only recently, and largely symbolically, entered the political discourse.

References

Alba, R. and N. Foner (2014), "Comparing Immigrant Integration in North America and Western Europe: How Much do the Grand Narratives Tell Us?," *International Migration Review*, 48 (S1): S263–91.

Bird, K. (2005), "The Political Representation of Visible Minorities in Electoral Democracies: A Comparison of France, Denmark, and Canada," *Nationalism and Ethnic Politics*, 11 (4): 425–65.

Bloemraad, I. (2006), *Becoming a Citizen: Incorporating Immigrants and Refugees in the United States and Canada*, Berkeley: University of California Press.

Bouchard, G. (2011), "What is interculturalism?," *McGill Law Journal*, 56 (2): 435–68.

Bouteldja, N. (2013), *After the Ban: the Experiences of 35 Women of the Full- Face Veil in France*. York: Open Society Foundation.

Gagnon, A.-G. and R. Iacovino (2004), "Interculturalism: Expanding the Boundaries of Citizenship," in A.-G. Gagnon (ed.), *Quebec: State and Society*, 369–90. Peterborough: Broadview Press.

Henley, J. (March 16, 2017), "Europe's Governments Signal Relief after Dutch Election Defeats Far Right," *The Guardian*. https://www.theguardian.com/world/2017/mar/16/europes-governments-signal-relief-as-dutch-election-defeats-far-right

Hollifield, J. (2014). "France," in J. Hollifield, P. Martin, and P. Orrenius (eds.), *Controlling Immigration: A Global Perspective* 3rd edn., 157–87, Stanford CA: Stanford University Press.

Koopmans, R. and P. Statham (2000), "Challenging the Liberal Nation-state? Postnationalism, Multiculturalism, and the Collective Claims-making of Migrants and Ethnic Minorities in Britain and Germany," in R. Koopmans and P. Statham (eds.), *Challenging Immigration and Ethnic Relations Politics*, 652–96, New York: Oxford University Press.

Koopmans, R., P. Statham, M. Giugni, and F. Passy (2005), *Contested Citizenship: Immigration and Cultural Diversity in Europe*, Minneapolis: University of Minnesota Press.

Laborde, C. (2008), *Critical Republicanism: The Hijab Controversy and Political Philosophy*, Oxford: Oxford University Press.

Oltermann, P. (December 6, 2016), "Angela Merkel Endorses Party's Call for Partial Ban on Burqa and Niqab," *The Guardian*. https://www.theguardian.com/world/2016/dec/06/angela-merkel-cdu-partial-ban-burqa-niqab-german.

Reitz, J. G. (2011). "Pro-immigration Canada: Social and Economic Roots of Popular Views." IRPP Study, no. 20. Montreal: Institute for Research on Public Policy.

Rumbaut, R. G. (2008), "Reaping What You Sow: Immigration, Youth, and Reactive Ethnicity," *Applied Developmental Science*, 12 (2): 108–11.

Schofer, E. and M. Fourcade-Gourinchas (2001), "The Structural Contexts of Civic Engagement: Voluntary Association Membership in Comparative Perspective," *American Sociological Review*, 66 (6): 806–28.

Simon P. (2021), « Le genre de l'islamophobie : les musulman.es face aux discriminations en France », in Lepinard E., Sarrasin O. et Gianettoni L. *Genre et islamophobie : discriminations, préjugés et représentations en Europe*, 143–56, Lyon: ENS Editions.

Sioui, M.-M. (December 2, 2017), "L'article controversé de la loi sur la neutralité religieuse est suspend," *Le Devoir*. https://www.ledevoir.com/politique/quebec/514479/la-cour-superieure-suspend-l-article-10-de-la-loi-sur-la-neutralite-religieuse

Vertovec, S. and S. Wessendorf, eds. (2009), *The Multiculturalism Backlash: European Discourses, Policies and Practices*, London: Routledge.

Wright, M. and I. Bloemraad (2012), "Is there a Trade-off between Multiculturalism and Socio-political Integration? Policy Regimes and Immigrant Incorporation in Comparative Perspective," *Perspectives on Politics*, 10 (1): 77–95.

Rethinking Diasporas of the Middle East: Kurdish Diaspora as the Global South in the Global North

by Ipek Demir

Much of the critical literature on the Middle East, and of the diasporas from the Middle East has situated their discussions and examinations on the East/West axis. The Global South lens and the North/South axis itself have rarely been used as a way to examine the Middle East, or their diasporas. This is perhaps unsurprising, given the central role of Orientalism, Said, and postcolonial literature in the field of Middle East studies. My aim here is not to disown this important legacy or literature—as I indeed see them as central and insightful. My aim is to venture into new routes and ways of conceptualizing and examining diasporas. I argue that the Global South lens can help expand understandings and examinations of diasporas of the Middle East in general, and of Kurdish diaspora in Europe in particular.

The Global South scholarship has discussed globalization, modernity, development, and justice through challenging established understandings of these notions and their assumptions. Its primary intellectual contribution, in my view, has been its questioning of Northern epistemologies, especially how the North conceptualizes, and problematically reproduces, North-centric discourses on globalization, migration, inequalities, modernity, epistemology, gender, race, and so on. It has unpacked the ways in which dominant ways of understanding European history and modernity have created narrow and also inadequate understandings of history and thus of our today (e.g., Bhambra 2007; Chakrabarty 2000). It has examined how epistemic violence on others is created through Eurocentrism (e.g., Mignolo 2009; Santos 2014; Sayyid 1997).

Much can be gained by examining the diasporas of the Middle East by bringing in the insights of the Global South perspective and its mission to dislodge coloniality. Even though the geopolitics of the concept cannot be denied, the Global South is of course not a geography but a case of demanding decoloniality (Levander and Mignolo 2011). The Global South scholarship has its roots in postcolonialism, decoloniality, and earlier Third World perspectives on liberation. The fields of postcolonialism and decoloniality are fed from different historical origins and intellectual genealogies.

Postcolonialism has its origins in British and French colonialism, and decoloniality in the Latin American context, especially the Spanish and Portuguese colonies. Yet they have overlapping trajectories and make similar interventions in terms of attempting to dislodge both epistemic and material coloniality. Diasporas, and their mobilizations bring what I call foreignizations to the Global North (Demir 2017). Diasporas are both insiders and outsiders to Northern spaces. They expose the very entanglements of the North and South. Global South scholarship is thus uniquely placed to shed a light on how we can examine the ways in which diasporas intervene and dislodge coloniality in the new home and in the home left behind.

The foreignizations diasporas can bring to the Global North can be examined through an engagement with the work of Global South scholars who unpack the new possibilities the South offers as well as the invitations to foreignize. For example, Sousa Santos's "epistemologies of the south" (2014), Mignolo's call for "epistemic disobedience" (2009), Arturo Escobar's "relational ontologies" (2010), and Bhambra's "connected sociologies" (2014) provide plenty of examples of epistemological and ontological challenges to modernity and coloniality. The work of Sousa Santos seeks to denounce Northern models of production of knowledge due to its refusal to enter into a horizontal dialogue with other knowledges. Presenting the South as an alternative form of knowledge production, he underlines the "epistemicide" which these cultures face as well as the "learned ignorance" which the North perpetuates. He instead defends an "ecology of knowledge" whereby Northern and Southern modes of understanding enter into a non-hierarchical dialogue. Mignolo (2009) and Raewyn Connell (2007), on the other hand, focus on exposing the exclusions of the academic metropole and Northern theorizing. While Connell's work examines the erasures of the sociological canon which, she argues, rarely takes as its starting point the thought or experiences "generated in the majority of the world" (2007: 64), Mignolo's work makes interventions that question Northern epistemologies, calling for "decolonial thinking" and "epistemic disobedience" (2009). Escobar discusses the social movements from South America in the last two decades, especially the struggles in Chiapas, Oaxaca, Columbia, Ecuador, Guatemala, Peru, and others. He examines in detail the way in which they seek to establish relational ontologies that question the central divisions in liberal modernity—such as between the individual and community, nature and culture, developed and underdeveloped, civilized and uncivilized—demanding also a representation of nonhuman entities in their ontological visions. Bhambra (2007, 2014), on the other hand, has shown that a central tenet of bounded understandings of modernity has been the construction of modernity as endogenous to Europe (including its White settler colonies), and one where the rise of Europe/the West is seen as a miracle. In such understandings modernity is conceived as specifically a creation by Europe/the West, and Europeans/Westerners emerge as the originators (of modernity, ideas, creativity, industry, values, humanism). The South is not seen as having contributed to these. Even yet, encounters with the South are ignored or conceived as irrelevant to the miracle that is European/Western modernity. Such a perspective thus fails to recognize that the modern world is largely shaped by colonialism and empires and thus by and through the contributions of the South. As such this bounded yet still dominant view of modernity not only erases history but also reproduces ideas about the superiority of the North. It provides a one-sided and partial view of not just the South but also the North.

I argue that such bounded understandings of modernity, history, and today contribute to North's inability to deal with and accommodate racial and ethnic diversity. The North and its academia have for too long told a story of "a White past, and a multicultural present" (Naidoo and Littler 2004) when in fact diversity and plurality have been woven into the fabric of European/Western history and society for centuries. Such a miracle view also acts as a justification for hard and violent Northern borders and continues to shape and simmer underneath the migration policies—be it in the Mediterranean, the English Channel, or the southern US borders. Troubles over racial and ethnic diversity and migration cannot be resolved as long as postcolonial diasporas are conceived of as "others" rather than as constitutive of Europe/West. Previously excluded histories, of women and their contributions to our today have come to be recognized over the years, through feminist scholarly work and years of campaigning. Similarly, through the working-class struggle, resistance, and unionization, the expansion in higher education and the inclusion of those from the working class into universities, the contributions of the working class in terms of equality, liberty, and rights—be they Levellers or Chartists—are now better known. Just like women and the working class, diasporas have also significantly contributed to ideas about freedom and equality in Europe. Their struggle against discrimination, poor conditions, unequal treatment, their resistance, and uprisings, as well as their epistemic interventions should also be seen as part of expanding rights and freedoms in Europe and beyond.

An examination of diasporas from the Middle East and elsewhere provides plenty of examples of epistemological and ontological challenges to coloniality. A re-conceptualization of such diasporas of the Middle East as the "Global South in the Global North" enables us not just to expand our understandings of diaspora and do justice to their stories, but also refine our understandings of the Middle East and of Europe, their entanglements, of coloniality, of resistance, and of globalization. It would also help yield insight on gendered, racialized, economic, and epistemological inequalities related to the diasporas of the Middle East, through a more rigorous engagement with fields such as transnational feminism and critical race theory. We can focus on interconnections and intersections between different inequalities affecting the diasporas of the Middle East, rather than reproduce the methodologically nationalist discourses on diaspora of this region which have dominated the field (Demir 2022). It is time, I argue, for the scholarship on the Middle East to "give into" the Global South.

Secondly, by focusing on the Global South we can move from existing emphasis on the representations (of the Middle East and their diasporas) to that of what the diasporas are saying and how they are mobilizing. In the field of Middle East Studies, Orientalism has, rightly, had a firm hold. It has had successes in terms of deconstructing representations of the Orient, and has thus shone a light on the Western gaze. The strength of Orientalism is also its very failing—it examines representation, yet the voices and resistances of the subjects discussed are not often heard. By expanding further into the Global South scholarship, we can shift the attention from the Orient/Orientalized as a victim to one which has a voice. The Global South scholarship with its focus on social movements can shift that; it can help interrupt the way in which the Middle Eastern subjects are typically conceived, namely as a victim and instead focus us to think about them as actors, as part of movements, making claims, and so on. One way of doing this is through an examination of the ways in which diasporas, as the Global South in the Global North, dislodge coloniality. I seek to discuss this in relation to Kurdish diaspora in Europe.

The Global South in the North: The Case of Kurds in Europe

Kurds from Turkey are now a substantial part of European metropoles such as Berlin, London, Paris, and Stockholm, not only in terms of their numbers but also through their critical voice and activism. They have created a vibrant political space in Europe and continue ethno-political battles with Turkey at a distance. Kurds in Europe, like any other group, are not homogeneous. There are considerable differences in educational levels, language, class positions, and sectarian allegiances. More importantly, not all are politically engaged. The research and arguments underpinning this article focus on Kurdish diaspora, that is the highly political and mobilized Kurds who originate from Turkey. As I have discussed in previous work (Demir 2015), mobilized Kurds translate their suffering and rebellion to audiences in Europe as a means to challenge the way in which the Kurdish issue is typically narrated within Turkey and also presented by Turkey to Europe and beyond. Furthermore, they foreignize European publics by challenging their host countries' role in their own predicament. I argue that there are various ways in which mobilized Kurds attempt to foreignize Europe in their translations of their uprising and hardships. Below, I focus on three central and contemporarily important ones.

(i) Epistemological Interventions

Kurds of Europe are challenging the way in which knowledges created about them in Turkey are taken up and reproduced in Europe. This is especially visible in their struggle against the reproduction of Orientalist and backward depictions of Kurds and the presentation of the Kurdish issue in Turkey as a problem of terrorism. Founded upon the demise of the Ottoman Empire, Turkey's nation-building project saw the multi-ethnicity and multi-religiosity of the Ottoman order as major threats to Turkish modernization and nationalism. The nationalist elites who led these efforts mainly came from the military and bureaucratic cadres of the Ottoman Empire. They were deeply inspired by European Romantic nationalist thought and longed for a homogeneous, centralized, and secular nation-state. These in their eyes would ensure purity and strength, making Turkey "civilized," akin to the modernity of the European states. Such efforts to westernize and "reach the European level of modernity" required certain parts of the society to "do away with their backwardness," expressed in their so-called "primitive, feudal, and tribal" practices and thoughts, and to assimilate into the modern Turkish Republic. The sizable Kurdish population, alongside those who held a strong Muslim identity, were regarded as obstructions to these aspirations and to the state's homogenization efforts (Bozarslan 2007; Smith 2005; White 2007). The Kurds' refusal to assimilate into Turkishness came to be told as a story of refusal to adjust to modernity and to "civilize" in official Turkish discourse. This Orientalist narrative—reproduced in the media, in school textbooks, and via state institutions—coupled with the presentation of Kurdish demands for more autonomy and rights as a problem of terrorism, came to shape the way in which Turkey understood and presented the perennial Kurdish issue not only in Turkey but also to Europe. It is such discourses which the Kurds of Europe seek to challenge. They demand an epistemic change in how the Kurdish issue is understood in Europe. They foreignize European publics by retelling a counter-history of the homogenization efforts and the ensuing violence. Refusing to stay silent, Kurds interrupt the order of things in Europe by holding public demonstrations, rallies, and gatherings and questioning the silence of Europe on the ensuing violence and oppression Kurds face.

Kurds also force the European public to engage in the demanding job of listening and learning by correcting what they see as Turkish biases in their European interlocutors' discourses, including, for example, the use of "east of Turkey" instead of Kurdistan or the use of "Turkish" when referring to Kurdish people. They call for European media to refrain from doing reporting which solely relies on Turkish state discourse and mainstream media from Turkey. Through such online and offline translations of the Kurdish struggle and suffering, mobilized Kurds foreignize the European public sphere—albeit at times via uncomfortable renderings—and challenge the way in which knowledges created about them in Turkey are taken up and reproduced in Europe. In summary, epistemic violence and ignorance are combatted—albeit not always with success.

(ii) Exposing Links between the Kurdish Predicament and Europe: Current and Historical

Mobilized Kurds of Europe also attempt to heighten and sharpen European sensibilities, both current and historical. They highlight what they see as their host countries' action (or inaction) for the Kurdish predicament, as well as the opportunism of Europe in its dealings with Turkey. Nowhere has this been more pronounced than in the recent European migration crisis. Turkey hosts about 3.7 million Syrian refugees. In order to appease the anti-immigration sentiment and the popular politics of resentment in their countries, European leaders have aimed to stem the flow of refugees arriving in Greece through Turkey. In their desperation to seal the European borders, they signed a Refugee Readmission agreement with Turkey. According to the agreement, from March 20, 2016, all irregular "migrant" crossings from Turkey to Greece are returned to Turkey, and for each who is returned, a Syrian will instead be settled in an EU country. The Syrian refugee crisis has given Turkey immense political leverage and freedom to pursue what are regarded as authoritarian and anti-democratic policies and practices in Turkey and in its dealings with the Kurdish movement in Turkey and Syria. The criticism of this deal is one of the ways in which the Kurdish diaspora underline their host countries' involvement in the Kurds' predicament, troubling consensus and foreignizing Europe.

The Kurdish diaspora also foreignizes Europe historically, highlighting European involvement in the carving up of Kurdish lands in the first half of the twentieth century and supporting oppressive regimes politically and militarily in the region throughout the twentieth century. The Sykes-Picot (secret) agreement signed in 1916 carved up the Middle East into zones of influence and control. It put Syria and Lebanon under French rule, and Iraq, Transjordan and Palestine under British control. It also divided Kurds across four countries, creating artificial borders and paying little attention to religious, ethnic, or sectarian traits in the region. The Sykes-Picot agreement is regarded as central to the construction of the borders in the Middle East. Many of today's borders in the Middle East are an outcome of such colonial histories and various interventions. In this sense diasporic Kurds echo the "we are here because you were there" sentiment, which postcolonial diasporas in the UK—recalling colonial ties and imperialism—utilized in their responses to rising anti-immigrant discourses in the 1960s. This historical dimension has always been present in the minds of politicized Kurds in Europe. It has now captured the attention of other less politicized Kurds in Europe, allowing them to underline their current predicament by linking it to past injustices and imperialism in the Middle East, akin to the way in which other social movements of the Global South make connections between their contemporary marginalization and historical erasure and colonization.

(iii) Transnational (Kurdish) Indigeneity

The ongoing social and political transformations in Syrian Kurdistan (Rojava) have allowed Kurds across different borders in the Middle East and the diaspora to further connect emotionally as part of a transnational indigenous movement. While knowledges of spatial and temporal links with other Kurds have always existed for those closely involved in the Kurdish movement, developments in Rojava have strengthened the emotional and transnational ties of Kurds, as well as their relationship with the European left. Those living in Syria's Rojava cantons have established a communally organized entity that is based on what they call democratic autonomy. It claims to reject capitalism as well as reactionary ethnic or nationalist ideology and is radically feminist. It draws inspiration from radical-democratic thinking expressed in post-national and feminist discourses—though critical analysis of the divergences between the ideological underpinnings of democratic autonomy and its practical implementation do exist (e.g., Human Rights Watch Report 2014; Leezenberg 2016). Their platform has resonated with diasporic Kurds in Europe and with leftist groups and circles in Europe, such as the Confederal Group of the European United Left & Nordic Green Left (of the European Parliament), the General Federation of Trade Unions of the UK, and even European artists and cartoonists (e.g., the Italian Zerocalcare who wrote *Kobane Calling* [2015]). The Women's Protection Unit (YPJ)—that is the female Kurdish guerrillas—have been introduced to the world by *Marie Claire* (2014), a fashionable women's magazine, under the title "These Remarkable Women Are Fighting ISIS. It's Time You Know Who They Are." Even though such introductions might be seen as superficial, ignoring the history and struggle of women in the Kurdish movement, they have helped challenge received knowledges on gender and oppression in the Middle East, which have traditionally been constitutive of the North's framing of the region. The "Rojava Revolution" has energized Kurdish awareness in the Middle East and in Europe, further transnationalizing the Kurdish movement, sharpening Kurds' awareness and discourses of indigeneity and autonomy as well as connecting them to the European left. As such, new entanglements of the North and the South have taken hold.

Another interesting aspect of these developments is the overlap between the cultural and political mobilizations in Latin America and the democratic autonomy ideals of the Kurdish movement. The demands in Latin America are articulated in and through the Juntas de Buen Gobierno (boards of good governance) in Chiapas, the movements in Oaxaca, the uprisings in Ecuador and Bolivia, movements in Guatemala, Peru, Chile, Argentina, and Colombia, and the pueblos originarios. According to Escobar, their key arguments center around "the defence of territory as the site of production and the place of culture ... the right over a measure of autonomy and self-determination around the control of natural resources and 'development'; and ... the relation to the state and nation, most cogently articulated in the notion of pluri-nationality" (2010: 10). Such values and demands overlap with those of the Kurdish movement, which seeks not only liberation for Kurds along similar lines but also claiming democratic confederalism for the peoples of the Middle East. Most importantly, however, as part of the Global South, such movements in disparate parts of the world aim to challenge Northern epistemologies' assumptions about "native" populations and seek to enter into the international order as equals without reproducing atavism or portraying a determinative essence of indigeneity.

More than a decade ago, Gambetti (2009) examined and compared the spatial dynamics of the Kurdish and Zapatista movements. In the last few years, the Rojava movement has sown new relationships and bonds across disparate social movements and indigenous groups of the Global South. Kurdish foreignizations have begun to sow the seeds of conviviality between different Global Souths, which had not traditionally engaged with one another. The burgeoning conviviality created between, for example, the Zapatista and the Kurdish movements is worth watching out for as they may promote cosmopolitan justice-based solidarities across the Global South. They may constitute the next turn in "subaltern cosmopolitanisms" enabled by online and offline solidarities, which these two movements of the Global South are beginning to establish and promote (Sousa Santos and Rodríguez-Garavito 2005).

Conclusion

I argued that, as both insiders and outsiders to Northern spaces, diasporic groups living in Northern metropoles in Europe are uniquely placed both in terms of the foreignizations they bring to the North and the entanglements of the North and South which they expose. By taking the Kurdish diaspora living in European cities as my case study, I examined three central and contemporary ways in which mobilized diasporic Kurds foreignize, yet connect with, Europe: first, through their epistemic interventions; second, by exposing links between their predicament and Europe; and third, by advancing transnational indigeneity which also makes connections with the European left. Such foreignizations seek an epistemological change not only in how the Kurdish issue is understood and represented in Europe, but also in European self-understanding, modernity, and narratives concerning history. Moreover, by focusing on the questions Kurdish diaspora poses in Europe, I attempted to complicate our understandings of the Global South, moving diasporas of the Middle East from their typically conceived place, namely that of the Orientalized victim, and by instead tilting the North/South axis of Global South literature toward the East/West axis, and toward the Middle East and Kurds.

References

Bhambra, Gurminder K. (2007), *Rethinking Modernity: Postcolonialism and Sociological Imagination*, Basingstoke: Palgrave Macmillan.
Bhambra, Gurminder K. (2014), *Connected Sociologies*, London: Bloomsbury.
Bozarslan, H. (2007), "Kurdish Nationalism Under Kemalist Republic: Some Hypotheses," in Mohammed M. A. Ahmed and Michael M. Gunter (eds.), *The Evolution of Kurdish Nationalism*, 36–51, Santa Ana, California: Mazda Publishers.

Chakrabarty, D. (2000), *Provincializing Europe: Postcolonial Thought and Historical Difference*, Princeton: Princeton University Press.

Connell, Raewyn W. (2007), *Southern Theory: The Global Dynamics of Knowledge in Social Science*, Cambridge: Polity Press.

Demir, I. (2015), "Battlespace Diaspora: How the Kurds of Turkey Revive, Construct and Translate the Kurdish Struggle in London," in Anastasia Christou and Elizabeth Mavroudi (eds.), *Dismantling Diasporas: Rethinking the Geographies of Diasporic Identity, Connection and Development*, 71–84, London: Routledge.

Demir, I. (2017), "The Global South as Foreignization: The Case of the Kurdish Diaspora in Europe," *The Global South*, 11 (2): 54–70.

Demir, I. (2022), *Diaspora as Translation and Decolonisation*, Manchester: Manchester University Press.

Escobar, A. (2010), "Latin America at Crossroads: Alternative Modernizations, Post-liberalism, or Post-Development?," *Cultural Studies*, 24 (1): 1–65.

Gambetti, Z. (2009), "Politics of Place/Space: The Spatial Dynamics of the Kurdish and Zapatista Movements," *New Perspectives on Turkey*, 41 (Fall): 43–87.

Griffin, E. (2014), "These Remarkable Women Are Fighting ISIS. It's Time You Know Who They Are," *Marie Claire*, September 30, 2014. http://www.marieclaire.com/culture/news/a6643/these-are-the-women-battling-isis/ (accessed August 1, 2021).

Human Rights Watch Report. (2014), "Under Kurdish Rule: Abuses in PYD-run Enclaves of Syria," *Human Rights Watch*. https://www.hrw.org/report/2014/06/19/under-kurdish-rule/abuses-pyd-run-enclaves-syria (accessed October 26, 2020).

Leezenberg, M. (2016), "The Ambiguities of Democratic Autonomy: The Kurdish Movement in Turkey and Rojava," *Southeast European and Black Sea Studies*, 16 (4): 671–90.

Levander, C. and Mignolo, Walter. (2011), "Introduction: The Global South and World Dis/Order," *The Global South*, 5 (1): 1–11.

Mignolo, Walter. (2009), "Epistemic Disobedience, Independent Thought and Decolonial Freedom," *Theory, Culture & Society*, 26 (7–8): 159–81.

Naidoo, R. and Littler, J. (2004), "White Past, Multicultural Present: Heritage and National Stories," in H. Brocklehurst and R. Phillips (eds.), *History, Identity and the Question of Britain*, 330–41, Basingstoke: Palgrave Macmillan.

Sayyid, S. (1997), *A Fundamental Fear: Eurocentrism and the Emergence of Islamism*, London: Zed Books.

Smith, Thomas W. (2005), "Civic Nationalism and Ethnocultural Justice in Turkey," *Human Rights Quarterly*, 27 (2): 436–70.

Sousa Santos, Boaventura de (2014), *Epistemologies of the South*, Boulder: Paradigm Publishers.

Sousa Santos, Boaventura de and Rodríguez-Garavito, César A. (2005), "Law, Politics, and the Subaltern in Counter-Hegemonic Globalization," in Boaventura de Sousa Santos and César A. Rodríguez-Garavito (eds.), *Law and Globalization from Below: Towards a Cosmopolitan Legality*, 1–26, Cambridge: Cambridge University Press.

White, Paul J. (2007), "Citizenship Under Ottomans and Kemalists: How the Kurds Were Excluded," *Citizenship Studies*, 3 (1): 71–102.

Jews and Turks in Germany: Immigrant Integration, Political Representation, and Minority Rights

by Gökçe Yurdakul

Background

I wrote this work as a part of my post-doctoral studies at the Freie-Universität zu Berlin in 2008. Although it was published partially in edited books and peer-reviewed academic journals, it has never been published as a whole in English. There are significant studies on Jews and Turks (see Kastoryano 2002; Laurence 2001 for sociological studies, Marc Baer for historical ones, especially 2013, 2018), Jews and Muslims (Atshan and Galor 2020; Keskinkılıç and Langer 2018), and the role of Jewish memory for Muslims in Germany (Rothberg 2019; Özyürek 2018). There are more explorative ones that our students in the Humboldt-Universität zu Berlin have submitted as their MA thesis (Männlein 2019). I consider this paper as a part of this ongoing discussion on the cultural, interreligious, and political connection between minorities and immigrants in Germany. The newer, exciting and sophisticated research on the relations between Muslims and Jews in Germany is currently being conducted by researchers, such as Armin Langer and Elisabeth Becker Topkara. The following chapter has been previously published in the following books and journals: (2006) "'We Don't Want to Be the Jews of Tomorrow': Jews and Turks in Germany after 9/11," *German Politics and Society* 24 (2), 44-67 (with Michal Bodemann) and (2013) "Jews and Turks in Germany: Immigrant Integration, Political Representation and Minority Rights," *Rethinking the*

The study resulting in this publication was assisted by a post-doctoral research grant from the Berlin Program for Advanced German and European Studies with generous funds provided by the Freie Universität Berlin (2008–9). However, the conclusions, opinions, and other statements in this publication are mine and not necessarily those of the sponsoring institution. All translations between Turkish, German, and English are mine, unless otherwise stated. Earlier versions of this paper were presented at the Van Leer Institute Jerusalem (2009), Association for the Studies in Nationalities New York (2009), and Wissenschaftskolleg Berlin EUME Program (2009). I thank organizers and participants for their feedback. I am also grateful to Karin Goihl, Nadine Blumer, and Ian Leveson for their comments on earlier versions.

Public Sphere Through Transnationalizing Process: Europe and Beyond, Armando Salvatore, Oliver Schmidtke and Hans-Jörg Trenz (eds.). Palgrave Macmillan. Pp. 251-268. It has also been translated into German, and published partially or in full in German books and journals.

This chapter is on how Turkish immigrants have attempted to establish connections with the Jewish minority until 2008. The curious question is whether the findings of my research from 2008 are still relevant in 2020. In previous my research, I found that 1) Turkish immigrant leaders make analogies between *racism* and *anti-Semitism*, and recently have linked anti-Semitism and *Islamophobia*; 2) they refer to the Jewish community as a *structural model* to organize a political lobby; and 3) they take German Jewish trope as a model in order to *claim religious rights* in Germany. In their employment of the German Jewish trope, German Turkish leaders use different but overlapping **political strategies:** in their speeches, they seek ways to *solidarize* with the Jewish community; they search for ways to *cooperate* in campaigns and events; and they use *discursive models* to draw direct comparisons between anti-Semitism, racism, and Islamophobia. As a result, I could show that the Turkish immigrant leaders (please note I do not mean the complete Turkish immigrant groups in Germany here, I am referring to certain immigrant leadership who are politically engaged, and make claims to the state) engaged with the Jewish communities in Germany.

In fact, history proved me right. I had the chance to confirm my findings from 2008 during my research in 2012–14 on the ritual male circumcision debate, which affected Jewish and Muslim communities alike: On May 7, 2012, the Cologne regional court ruled that circumcising young boys was a form of previous bodily harm (*körperverletzung*). Although both Muslims and Jews circumcise infant boys as a religious practice, the Cologne court found that the child's "fundamental right to bodily integrity" was more important than the parents' rights, leaving Muslim and Jewish parents under suspicion of causing bodily harm to their children (Yurdakul 2016). After a lot of media debate and political controversy, Bundestag passed a new law in record time. I had the chance to follow in the debates in the backstage by interviewing Jewish and Turkish leaders who took part in the legal fight of this debate as well as the members of the German ethics council, who are for or against circumcision. With the introduction of a new circumcision law, *Bürgerliches Gesetzbuch (BGB) § 1631d Beschneidung des männlichen Kindes* (German Civil Code, Circumcision of Male Children), the debate on legal recognition and regulation of male circumcision in Germany seemed to be over. However, male circumcision debate is continuing as medical and legal discourses in order to criminalize and pathologize Jewish and Muslim religious practices.

Since 2012, there has been a spike in the discussions of anti-Semitism in Germany, and the role of Muslims in relation to anti-Semitism. Increase in anti-Semitic instances is statistically evident (statista.de 2020 Anti-Semitism in Europe) and monitoring and combatting against anti-Semitism is vital in Germany. Against this background, anti-Semitism commissioners are appointed by the local states after an official decision by the Bundestag in 2018 in order to monitor and combat against Anti-Semitism in German institutions. This has been a quite controversial process for two major reasons: First, it is (still) not completely clear what can be defined as Anti-Semitism in Germany, for example there was specific discussion that whether criticizing Prime Minister Netanyahu's politics in Israel can be a part of anti-Semitism or not (for a similar observation, please see the Independent Experts' Report on Anti-Semitism 2017, Federal Ministry of Internal Affairs). Second, it is (still) unclear what the anti-Semitism commissioners' role is in combatting anti-Semitism in Germany. Anti-Semitism commissioners had discretion on evaluating anti-Semitic statements. During this evaluation, heated media discussion turned into media sanctioning of particular scholars (please see Özyürek and Dekel's essay in *Die Zeit* 2020 on a specific case). Through this development, specifically Muslim communities became targets of policies with an assumption that anti-Semitism is inherent in Muslim communities (Özyürek 2018).

First Vignette

In July 2008, a public debate erupted about whether German Turks[1] could associate themselves with the German Jewish trope as a political model. The public controversy was sparked by a statement by Professor Faruk Sen, Head of the Zentrum für Türkeistudien (hereafter ZfT) in Essen.[2] Sen said in a newspaper interview that the Turks are the new Jews of Europe[3]:

> After the great extermination which aimed to clear Europe from Jews, 5 million 200 thousand Turks become the new Jews of Europe. Our people who have been residing in central and western Europe for 47 years; despite of the fact that they contribute to the economy with 45 billion revenue and 125 thousand entrepreneurs, they have been facing the discrimination and exclusion that Jews were facing, albeit in different scope and forms (translated from Turkish to English; *Referans Gazetesi, May 19, 2008*)

After making this comment, Professor Sen was severely criticized by public figures, including politicians, writers, and scholars.[4] The fiercest of these criticisms came from Nordrhein Westphalia-Integrationsminister Armin Laschet (Christian Democratic Union):

> [... [der Vergleich ist und bleibt inakzeptabel, er ist auch eine Verkennung deutscher Integrationspolitik. Die Aussage trifft insbesondere die deutsche Gesellschaft. [...] darf man so die Deutschen und die deutsche

> Gesellschaft nicht mit der Zeit vor 1945 vergleichen. Dieser Vergleich ist auch wissenschaftlich nicht haltbar und Sen spricht in seiner Funktion als ZfT-Direktor (Dirk Graalman interview with Armin Laschet, *Süddeutsche Zeitung, July 1, 2008*)

> [...] the comparison is and remains unacceptable, and it fails to consider the German integration policy. The statement hits the German society particularly hard. [...] one must not compare the Germans and German society with pre-1945 times in that way. Such a comparison is scientifically unfounded, and Sen speaks in his function as director of the ZfT (Dirk Graalman interview with Armin Laschet, *Süddeutsche Zeitung, July 1, 2008*)

Following this event, Sen officially apologized in the *Zentralrat der Juden*, and in an interview with the *Jüdische Allgemeine*, he accepted that his statement was "Ausrutscher"[5] (Tobias Kühn interview with Faruk Sen, 3 Juli 2008, front page).[6] As a result of the controversy,[7] and despite his public apology, Sen was first locked out of his office, then let go from his position at the Zentrum.

Second Vignette

In 2005, Aslı Bayram, born to a Turkish[8] guest worker family in Germany in 1981, won a beauty pageant and became Miss Germany. Following this, she was chosen to be the lead actress in a play about Jewish heroine Anne Frank. She was interviewed in *Die Zeit*, arguably the most popular intellectual weekly in Germany, concerning her success as a young woman in Germany. *Die Zeit* editors pointed out the paradoxical exchange of roles between Aslı and Anne Frank: "Aslı, die Muslimin, wird Anne sein, die Jüdin (Aslı, the Muslim, will be Anne, the Jew)" (*Zeit Magazin Leben*, 20 March 2008, p. 35). They also noted the similarities between Aslı's life and Anne Frank's life: both were victims of Nazi violence. Aslı says her family was often subject to Neo-Nazi verbal attacks in their hometown, Darmstadt. On February 18, 1994, the Bayram family's door buzzer sounded. Aslı opened the door to discover a neighbor who often swore at her and her sister. She called her father, and the neighbor shot both of them. Her father died, and Aslı was wounded. The neighbor was sentenced to nine years in prison but was released before completing his sentence. In a visit to Anne Frank's house, Aslı wrote the following in the guestbook; it has a double meaning, referring both to her life and to the victims of National Socialism in Germany: "Niemals vergessen" (*Zeit Magazin Leben*, 20 March 2008, p. 35).

Third Vignette

In its issue of September 23, 2004, the weekly Der Stern published a caricature, which went largely unnoticed by the German audience, but caused substantial indignation in the Turkish community. It showed a stereotypical elderly Turkish man with a dark moustache as he tried to crawl through the cat flap of a giant gate. The gate was labeled "European Union" and the cat flap was adorned with a two-liner in imitated Arabic script—even though famously, the Arabic script is not used in the Turkish language. In this caricature, not only an orientalist but also a common anti-Semitic structure became apparent: the image of the Jewish sub-human who infiltrates German society. Vural Öger, a prominent German-Turkish entrepreneur and deputy in the European Parliament, wrote a letter to the Stern magazine and accused the caricature of being defamatory, obscene, and wind in the sails of neo-Nazi propaganda. Öger concluded his letter as follows:

> Ein junger Türke mit deutschem Pass, nicht allein hierzulande schon auf die Welt gebracht, nein, auch erzogen, hat im Geschichtsunterricht von Hitlers Anfängen gehört und dann gemeint, das sei eine Zeichnung, wie sie damals auch im 'Stürmer' stand. Nur hätten die Juden andere Nasen bekommen. Hier im 'stern' sei die Nase durch den Schnurrbart ersetzt worden, sonst aber sei das alles derselbe rassistische Mist.
>
> *(Hürriyet, 2. Oktober 2004)*

> A young Turk with a German passport, not only born in this country, no, but also educated, heard about the beginnings of Hitler in history class and stated that this is the sort of illustration that was featured in the "Stürmer" back in the days. Jews had only been given new noses. Here in the "stern" magazine, the noses have been replaced by a moustache, but apart from that, it is the same racist crap.

Öger's comment and others like it represent a fundamental usage of the Jewish narrative by the Turkish leadership. They know that accusing Germans of anti-Turkish racism per se is only partly effective. Rhetorically far more effective is to associate Turkish concerns with those of Jews. This strategy compels Germans to listen to Turkish intellectuals, because on this point, the German environment is still vulnerable.

Introduction

From academia to the art scene to political debates, Turks and Jews are depicted as partners—both are victims of "racial" discrimination[9] in Germany. In this article, I attempt to show how political relations between immigrants and minorities play themselves out between Turks and Jews in Germany, specifically in terms of dealing with "racial," "ethnic," and religious discrimination. I examine how the political leaders of the numerically largest and most recent immigrant group, the Turks, take the German Jewish minority, pivotal because of its long history in Germany as well as its more recent past, as a model for their own future insertion in German society. And I explore how leading members of the Jewish community in Germany respond to Turkish immigrant leaders' attempts to make Jews their partners in fighting discrimination and seeking political solidarity in Germany.

The common theme in all three opening vignettes is how Turkish leaders in Germany refer to the German Jewish trope as a model for the "racial" discrimination that they encounter. In the first vignette, Sen argues that Turkish immigrants face discrimination even though they are financially successful, just like the Jews before the Second World War. The second vignette shows how a young German Turkish actress' life cuts across Jewish history in Europe. A victim of violent racist attacks, she takes on the role of Anne Frank and associates her experiences with hers. In the final vignette, Vural Öger scathingly notes that the anti-Turkish depiction in the German media resembles anti-Semitic propaganda before and during the Second World War. All three vignettes draw parallels between anti-Turkish racism and anti-Semitism.

Drawing parallels between racism and anti-Semitism is a one of several strategies used by German Turkish leaders in their bid to achieve political visibility. In fact, they **use the German Jewish trope as a political model** in three main areas: 1) they make analogies between *racism* and *anti-Semitism*, and recently have linked anti-Semitism and *Islamophobia*; 2) they refer to the Jewish community as a *structural model* to organize a political lobby; and 3) they take German Jewish trope as a model in order to *claim religious rights* in Germany. In their employment of the German Jewish trope, German Turkish leaders use different but overlapping **political strategies:** in their speeches, they seek ways to *solidarize* with the Jewish community; they search for ways to *cooperate* in campaigns and events; and they use *discursive models* to draw direct comparisons between anti-Semitism, racism, and Islamophobia.

In the first part of the chapter I focus on the theoretical background before turning, in the second part, to a discussion of the history of German Jews as a minority and German Turks as a major immigrant group. In the third part, I explore how German Turkish leaders refer to the similarities between anti-Semitism, racism against Turks, and Islamophobia. I discuss how Turkish immigrant leaders refer to Jewish associations as a structural model and a political lobby to organize as a minority in Germany.

Then, I explore how Turkish religious associations use the Jewish trope as a model in their bid to gain religious group rights. In the fourth part of the article, I explore the responses of the Jewish community members to the use of German Jewish trope as a model. Here, I delve into two contradictory views within the Jewish community: some are uncomfortable with the Turkish approach to Jews in Germany (I call these people *skeptics*), while others embrace their Muslim counterparts (*allies*). Finally, I propose a change in theoretical perspective to facilitate an in-depth exploration of immigrant integration in Western European societies.

Before moving on to a theoretical discussion, I would like to make three clarifications with respect to my terminology and analytical model. First, this article discusses how the German Turkish leadership builds upon the German Jewish trope, using it as a political model to gain political visibility and to strategize integration into the German society. The analytical model is not simply a comparison of Turkish and Jewish communities in Germany but a multifaceted analysis of how immigrants build upon the historical minorities of a country in order to create strategies of integration.

Second, the primary actor of this analytical model is the German Turkish leadership—not all Turkish immigrants in Germany. By German Turkish leadership, I refer to politically active members of the German Turkish community, those who are engaged with German politics and parliament. This is a small elite group with significant political visibility in the German politics and media. Their ideas may not reflect those of Turkish immigrants in Germany—a very heterogeneous group.

Third, I use the German Jewish model to refer to a specific identity construction, that of the German Jewish minority who were victims of the Holocaust and their descendants who live in Germany today and who solidarize around the *Zentralrat der Juden*. I am not referring to all Jews in Germany, neither those who have immigrated from the former Soviet Union as *kontingentflüchtlinge*, nor Israelis who have chosen to live in Germany.

Finally, I argue that the German Turkish leaders are actively creating strategies for integration, neither passively following the integration strategies of the German state authorities nor taking over Jewish strategies without modifying them to suit their own purposes.

Theoretical Challenge: Reconsidering Immigrant Integration

As a theoretical and political concept, immigrant integration concerns the extent to which immigrants become part of the majority society. In theoretical debates, immigrant integration is often measured by economic and social participation in the majority society. In studies that focus on immigrants in Western Europe and North America, the success or lack of success of immigrant integration is set on a continuum. In the most successful integration, immigrant communities resemble upper and middle classes of the majority society; members become blended almost seamlessly, leaving behind their cultural differences. In unsuccessful integration, at the other end of the continuum, immigrant communities associate themselves with the lower classes, creating their own residential areas and their own institutions, working against the "common good" of the society, and strongly maintaining their own traditions and religious practices.[10]

Earlier theories of immigrant integration in North American social sciences literature were based on the work of such writers as Robert Park of the Chicago School and Milton Gordon (*Assimilation in American Life* 1965). In these theories, immigrants are considered to be assimilating into a homogeneous American cultural model, and Gordon, for one, neglects to consider the modifications that immigrants may make to this cultural model. In addition, assimilation and upward mobility are seen as related to the social mobility of individuals, not to immigrant groups; early theories do not include the concept of changing ethnic boundaries over time. Subsequent understanding of immigrant integration, such as Edna Bonacich's split labor market (1980) or Alejandro Portes' ethnic-enclave theory (1992) are restricted as economic models; nor do they explain the social, cultural, and political integration of immigrants (Alba and Nee 1997; Schmitter-Heissler 1992), the dominating topic of contemporary discussions.

Hitherto, a neglected subject has been immigrant agency—the ability of immigrants to strategize their own integration into the majority society. A theoretical rethinking is apparent in models emerging in the context of globalization discussions of the 1990s and early 2000s. Such models include: *transnationalism, post-nationalism*, and an intensive discussion on *group rights* and *multiculturalism*[11] (see Bloemraad, Korteweg and Yurdakul 2008; Schmitter-Heissler 1992). And more recently, scholars are considering the problematic use of ethnicity (Brubaker 2004; Wimmer 2007). A new and more flexible model of immigrant integration uses "boundary drawing" as an analytical toolkit by which to take immigrant agency into account (Alba 2005; Korteweg and Yurdakul 2009; Lamont and Molnar 2002; Wimmer 2008; Zolberg and Woon 1999).[12] But as sophisticated as they are, boundary drawing analyses are inspired by a model based on the axis of "us" and "them." This analytical toolkit neglects in-depth cultural and historical meanings of the overall social context.

My work hinges on immigrant integration theories found in recent discussions. I note the need to consider immigrant agency within an historical context and in a cultural repertoire (Geertz 1976; Swidler 1986; also see Sayad 2004). I propose a multifaceted understanding of immigrant agency by taking the cultural and historical meanings of the social environment that shapes immigrant actions. Drawing on Clifford Geertz's "thick description,"[13] I argue that immigrant integration revolves around a culture repertoire which is continuously regenerated, learned, and adopted by the members of the group, sometimes anonymously and sometimes deliberately with well-known actors (Even-Zohar 2003; Lamont and Fleming 2005). I challenge the sociology of migration which reduces immigrant integration to models of "us" and "them." I propose a cultural repertoire with immigrant agency at its core. In other words, I suggest that we look at a "thick description" of immigrant integration (Geertz 1976).

This study of the inter-ethnic relations between Jews and Turks in Germany explores the integration of Turkish immigrant communities within their own cultural repertoire. How do German Turkish leaders draw upon German post-war history and its current effects on German society while they are negotiating their membership and belonging in German society? What strategies of integration are negotiated by immigrant elites with leading members of German society, including politicians, activists, and journalists? In what ways do German Turkish leaders refer to the Jewish model and how beneficial or detrimental is this in terms of defining their own integration strategies? Finally, how do the members of the Jewish community in Germany respond to the Turkish appropriation of the German Jewish trope as a model to negotiate membership and belonging?

Case Studies: Jews and Turks in Germany

Jews

Germany, the argument goes, is the last country in which Jews would want to live (Fleischmann 1980), but over the past decades, Germany has been turned into a land of memorials both large and small referring to the Holocaust. The Memorial for the Murdered Jews of Europe in Berlin occupies a site the size of two football fields across from Brandenburg Gate and is surely one of the most valuable pieces, symbolically and materially, of real estate in Germany. Another site of memory, the Jewish Museum in Berlin, opened to the public in 2001. The building, designed by Jewish architect Daniel Libeskind, is attached to what was to become the Berlin Museum, with almost organic passages, thereby symbolically implying that Jewish history is embedded in the history of Berlin (Young 2004). Still, the Jewish past exists primarily as museums and monuments, often under police protection and sometimes surrounded by barbed wire (Bodemann 1996; Legge Jr. 2003).

Today, however, German Jews are no longer "sitting on packed suitcases," and especially for Russian Jews, Germany is an attractive country in which to live. Obviously, the welfare system with its generous healthcare privileges is a major reason why Russian Jews (along with other immigrants) are attracted to Germany.

Further, with the arrival of Russian Jews, Jewish life in Germany became livelier. National Jewish organizations are thriving: the *Zentralrat der Juden* and *Zentralwohlfahrtsstelle* (Jewish social services), local Jewish congregations (*Jüdische Gemeinden*), community organizations and cultural centers in Berlin and elsewhere (e.g., the *Jüdische Kulturverein*), newspapers (e.g., *Jüdische Allgemeine*), bookstores, synagogues, restaurants, cemeteries, and museums. A church tax is collected by the state from Jewish community members in order to finance the communities. The *Zentralrat der Juden,* including rabbis and community leaders, enjoys national political recognition, and the *Jüdische Kulturverein* in Berlin and other Jewish groups organize numerous Jewish cultural events. Moreover, Jews are entitled to practice *shechita*, the religious slaughtering of animals, and they have their own religious schools. As they maintain a certain level of institutional separateness, however, it is questionable how or whether they feel at home in Germany, and some discussions in Berlin's *Jüdischer Kulturverein* debate whether a Jew should also call him/herself a German (Bodemann 2002; Brumlik 2004; Fleischmann 1980).[14]

A significant number of Israelis of German Jewish origin arrive in Germany to claim their grandparents' renounced German citizenships. On the one hand, these young people are drawn to Germany because of controversial Israeli politics, coupled with the long-lasting Israeli-Palestine conflict, the dilemma of joining the army at an early age, and the lack of safety in public life. On the other hand, they seek better employment opportunities, a vibrant cultural environment, and perhaps a discovery of their German roots (Oz-Salzberger 2001).

German law facilitates the acquisition of citizenship for former German citizens (and their descendants)—Jews mostly, who were persecuted during the Nazi period—irrespective of which other citizenships they may hold.[15] Because of the Holocaust, special conditions have been set up to encourage Jewish immigration to Germany. These new Jewish immigrants are eligible to apply for expedited citizenship. It is estimated that there are 5,000 Jews of German origin in Germany.[16] The total number of Jews in Germany is estimated to be 107,000 (Religionwissenschaftlicher Medien und Informationsdienst e.V. 2007).

German Turks

Seventeen years after Jews were exterminated in concentration camps, Turks started to migrate to Germany.[17] After the Second World War, when the Federal Republic needed a labor force to rebuild the country, the government decided to import labor from nearby countries like Turkey. Called guest workers, these Turkish migrant workers were usually unskilled or semi-skilled peasants running away from the lack of choice, scarcity of land, unemployment, and limited social services at home (Caglar 1994; Yurdakul 2009).[18] Some managed to reunite with their families after the Family Reunification Law of 1972, while others decided to stay permanently in Germany, leaving their families behind in Turkey.[19]

With the collapse of the Berlin Wall, a chaotic social environment and cheap labor from East Germany led to mass unemployment in the western part of Berlin (Joppke 2003; Yurdakul 2009). As the federal subsidy for industry in West Berlin was phased out and plants dismantled, Turks who worked in these factories lost their jobs. After 1989, those who came to Germany as workers in the 1960s and 1970s became increasingly dependent on welfare. The mass job dismissals have had long-term effects. Currently, German Turks lag behind majority society economically. In 2006, the unemployment rate for Turkish immigrants in Germany was 31.4 percent, compared to 10 percent for Germans (*Bundesagentur für Arbeit* 2007).

The first-generation immigrants often live transnational lives between Germany and Turkey, many spending six months in Turkey and six months in Germany. There are several reasons for this, including the availability of health-care facilities in Germany for former guest workers who are suffering from long-term disabilities due to the harsh working conditions in the German factories during and after the economic "miracle" years (Yurdakul 2009). Another factor is the presence of their children who are located in Germany and would prefer to stay there.

It is a fact that German Turks are low achievers in the *Bildungssystem*. Nevertheless, a significant number are successful in tertiary education (Kirsten, Reimer, and Kogan 2008). There are well-known German Turks in the political (Cem Özdemir), media (Nazan Eckes), literary (Emine Sevgi Özdamar), and art scenes (Fatih Akın), even though these are relatively few in number compared to the total population of German Turks. It is estimated that about 2.5 million Turkish immigrants live in Germany, constituting 3.8 to 4.2 percent of the German population, depending on the source.

One strategy to "integrate" German Turks into German society is to grant them German citizenship. In fact, statistics show that German citizens with Turkish background are higher achievers in the *Bildungssystem* than Turks without citizenship (Alber 2008). Since the introduction of a new citizenship law (*Staatsangehörigkeitsgesetz*), the German state has partially discarded the idea of *ius sanguinis* (law based on ancestral origin), and has started naturalizing the migrant population (Joppke 1998, 2003). According to the citizenship law, immigrant children born in Germany after the year 2000 will be granted German citizenship and their parents' native citizenship. To be granted permanent German citizenship, however, a child born in Germany has to give up the citizenship of his/her parents' native country between the ages of sixteen and twenty-three (*Beauftragte der Bundesregierung für Migration, Flüchtlinge und Integration* 2000). Although the exact number is unknown,[20] almost one fourth of the Turkish population in Germany hold German citizenship, approximately 500,000 people. Even so, the overall immediate effects of citizenship on immigrant integration remain unknown (Bloemraad, Korteweg and Yurdakul 2008).

Relations between Jews and Turks in Germany

A common (albeit rough) social pattern can be applied to Jews in Germany in the nineteenth century and Turkish immigrants in contemporary German society. In the early nineteenth century, a radical change took place in the German Jewish community; originally a poor, demographically dispersed population, it became economically and politically strong (Frankel and Zipperstein 2004). However, the assimilation of German Jews into middle-class German society was controversial in terms of maintaining differences and being "German" simultaneously. Historian Robin Judd, for example, has explored Jewish self-determination in legitimizing circumcision and kosher slaughtering during the Weimar Republic, specifically from the 1840s to 1933. The latter custom is evocative of the Turkish desire to have ritual slaughtering of animals according to Islamic traditions (*halal*), but is only one of many similarities.

The late nineteenth century also marked a migration of Eastern European Jews to Germany. These immigrants, who usually came from rural areas, were equally disliked by Germans and German Jews. Labeled *Ostjude*, they were pious, uneducated, had strange clothing and traditions, and tended to cluster in ghettos, having little to do with German society (Ascheim 1983). German Jews regretted being associated with these newcomers, who were an antithesis to the arguably well-assimilated German Jews.[21]

The nineteenth-century *Ostjude* and contemporary German Turks have a number of similarities. In both cases, religion is an important distinguishing feature: consider the piety of the *Ostjude* and the strong Muslim traditions of the Turks. Both groups look different: the strange clothing of the *Ostjude* and the German Turkish *kopftuch*. Also consider the ghetto self-exclusion of the *Ostjude* and the *parallelgesellschaften* of the German Turks, the uneducated *Ostjude*, and the low educational achievement of German Turks. Arguably, the most important problem of *Ostjude* was assimilation into German middle class—a situation evocative of German Turks today. A nineteenth-century remedy was to "integrate" the *Ostjude* into the German *Bildungssystem*; not surprisingly, this is the current strategy of integration for German Turks.[22] Eastern Jews and German Turks are similar on one more level: just as German Jews disliked *Ostjude*, so too middle-class secular Turks dislike *gastarbeiter*. For secular Turks, *gastarbeiter* and their children are "*Almancı*" a derogatory term, associated with the lower class, a lack of education, cultural incompetency, and a lack of social skills. German Jews, then *Ostjude*, and now German Turks have all been subjects of exclusion and "integration" debates in Germany. However, such debates have many facets; they are not based simply on similarities of exclusion and discrimination found in immigrant and minority populations.

Turkish immigrant leaders noted the commonalities between anti-Semitism and racism against Turks as early as the 1990s. A common strategy is to draw parallels between the Holocaust and the fire bombings of Turkish houses in Mölln and Solingen, and to argue that racism against Turks is an extension of anti-Semitism in Germany. Obviously, these two events are not comparable in scale, impact, or historical significance. However, Turkish immigrant leaders draw on Germany's anti-Semitic history to note the racism that continues to affect outsiders today.

However, the relationship between anti-Semitism and racism against Turks changed after 9/11 when the Turkish community began to be perceived as Muslims of Germany, not just an ethno-national community. Accordingly, some leaders of the Turkish immigrant community now point to the relationship between anti-Semitism and Islamophobia[23] rather than just to the relationship between anti-Semitism and racism against Turks. In essence, a political discourse of religious discrimination has replaced ethno-national discrimination.

Although Jews and Turks have both been subjects of discrimination in Germany, both hold stereotypes about the other's lifestyles, beliefs, and traditions, and as a result, arguably, they have minimal contact. In a conference I attended on Anti-Semitism and Islamophobia at the Friedrich Ebert Stiftung[24] (September 17, 2008), one of the leaders of *Jüdischer Gemeinde* in Berlin asked the following unfortunate question during the public discussion: "Why do Muslims not send their daughters to school?" Although her question shows how uninformed she is about one billion Muslims from Mali to Bangladesh, from Azerbaijan to Pakistan, the Turkish layperson on Berlin streets is not more informed about Jews in general,[25] often accusing "the Jews" of being the real perpetrators of 9/11 and being behind the financial market crash of 2008.[26]

Turkish governments have been historically pro-Israel. Turkey was one of the first to recognize the state of Israel. Moreover, a large number of Sephardic Jews were invited to the Ottoman Empire in 1492 when they were fleeing persecution in Spain and Portugal. Turkish government authorities commonly remind their Jewish counterparts of this in international meetings. Not surprisingly, they avoid mentioning the pogroms in 1955, the introduction of a "wealth tax" (*varlık vergisi*) on minorities in 1942 (Bali 1999, 2001), and the recent bombings of Istanbul synagogues in 2003. Contrary to its official statements, Turkey cannot be considered as minority-friendly, specifically because of its construction of Turkishness and the Turkish nation-state.[27] Anti-Semitism is no exception. Many people hold stereotypes about Jews and Judaism, as is obvious in the numerous bombings of and arson attacks on Istanbul synagogues, not to mention the ongoing controversy about "hidden Jews" who are supposedly committing crimes against the Turkish state (Bali 2008).[28]

Turks and Jews have stereotypical views of each other in Germany, perhaps as a result of lack of social contact, possibly because of journalistic hype about the Israeli-Palestinian conflict, but most likely because of a lack of proper education about each other's history and society. Given the lack of contact as well as the lack of knowledge about Jewish culture and customs, why do Turkish leaders in Germany approach the Jewish community in their efforts to achieve political visibility and to fight racism?

What Is a Jewish Model for German Turks?

Racism against Turks, Anti-Semitism, Islamophobia

Turkish immigrant leaders draw analogies between anti-Semitism, and the racism expressed against Turks and Islamophobia, one historically preceding the other, but both persistent over time.

Analogies between racism against Turks and anti-Semitism are pursued by secular Turkish associations. As I see it, this approach was stronger before 9/11 and has been gradually replaced by links between anti-Semitism and Islamophobia. As I have demonstrated elsewhere, *Türkischer Bund Berlin-Brandenburg* (*Turkish Federation of Berlin-Brandenburg*, hereafter TBB), a secular and social-democratically oriented immigrant association, applies the German Jewish trope to political discourse to show that racism in Germany today is an extension of anti-Semitic history (Yurdakul and Bodemann 2006). In a recent meeting, the spokesperson of the TBB, Safter Çınar emphasized that TBB will continue to cooperate with the *Jüdische Gemeinde zu Berlin* in various events, including a cultural exchange between Istanbul and Berlin.[29]

Arguably, TBB's decision to connect racism against Turks with anti-Semitism has not dramatically changed after 9/11, because it is a secular and social-democratic organization. However, the complex relationship between racism and anti-Semitism has gradually gained a different dimension after 9/11: Muslim immigrant associations, left-wing politicians,[30] and scholars have noted a legitimate connection between anti-Semitism and Islamophobia. In 2004, *Islamische Gemeinschaft Milli Görüs*' magazine, *Perspektive* published an issue on the relationship between anti-Semitism and Islamophobia and pointed out the similarities.[31]

A visible connection between anti-Semitism and Islamophobia is the comparison of local mosques (*hinterhofmoscheen*; literally meaning "in the backyard") to synagogues (Brenner 2007). In Berlin, a number of synagogues were historically built in the *hinterhof*; examples include the Rykestrasse, Joachimstalerstrasse, and Pestallozzistrasse synagogues.[32] Mosques are also located in the *hinterhof*, as well as in cellars. Today, a right-wing group, Pro-Köln is protesting the plan for a representative mosque in Cologne, using street marches and distributing leaflets to make their point. While criticizing the Pro-Köln movement, Bekir Alboga, previous spokesperson of *Koordinationsrat der Muslime in Deutschland* emphasized solidarity with the Jewish community against Islamophobia:

> Die rechtspopulistische Bewegung „Pro Köln' hat versucht, die Meinung der Menschen zu diesem Thema zu manipulieren und zu schüren. Da wurden zum Beispiel Schreiben mit dem Bild der Blauen Moschee, einem mächtigen Bauwerk mit sechs Minaretten, kopiert und in die Briefkästen verteilt. Nach dem Motto: So ein gigantisches Bauwerk wollen die Muslime auch in Ehrenfeld errichten. Unbelehrbare gibt es in jedem Land: nationalistisch oder rassistisch gesinnte Menschen. Andererseits dürfen wir das Problem nicht bagatellisieren. In Deutschland nehmen Antisemitismus, Islam- und

> Fremdenfeindlichkeit zu. Wir solidarisieren uns dagegen bundesweit auch mit den jüdischen Gemeinden.[33]

> The right-wing populist movement "Pro Köln" tried to manipulate and instigate the public opinion around this topic. Pamphlets showing the Blue Mosque, a mighty building with six minarets, were reproduced and distributed in letter boxes. Hinting at: The Muslims want to construct such a gigantic building here, in Ehrenfeld. There are unteachable people everywhere: people with racist or nationalistic attitudes. On the other hand, we must not trivialize the problem. In Germany, antisemitism, islamophobia, and xenophobia are on the rise. We, however, show solidarity with Jewish communities all across Germany.

However, *Zentralrat der Juden* is ambivalent about having an association with Turks or with Muslims in general. Charlotte Knobloch, current President of *Zentralrat* distanced herself from the mosque controversy and argued that Muslims should not compare themselves to Jews in Germany:

> Wir hatten über Jahrhunderte einen festen Platz in Deutschland, haben maßgeblich zur Kulturgeschichte Deutschlands beigetragen. Hitler hat uns das abgesprochen. Muslime müssen die Argumente für den Bau einer Moschee aus ihrer eigenen Geschichte schöpfen.[34]

> We have had a solid place in Germany for centuries and have made a significant contribution to Germany's cultural history. Hitler took that away from us. Muslims must create their arguments for building a mosque from their own history.

For centuries, we have had a steady place in Germany, we contributed decisively to the cultural history of Germany. Hitler denied us that. Muslims have to draw arguments for the construction of a mosque from their own history.

By distancing *Zentralrat* from the establishment of representative mosques, Knobloch refrains from showing solidarity with Muslims as Alboga claims to have done. Some members of *Zentralrat* do not share Knobloch's views: Stephan Kramer, Secretary General of *Zentralrat* announced that they will establish a center to conduct research on anti-Semitism and Islamophobia. *Zentralrat*'s ambivalence toward Muslim politics shows that the Jewish community is an unreliable ally for the Muslim associations who would like to use the Jewish minority as a model to establish themselves in Germany.[35]

Cumali Naz, *Vorsitzender des Münchner Ausländerbeirats*, places the mosque controversy within a freedom of religion discourse:

> 'Ich argumentiere ganz anders.' Die drei Weltreligionen hätten alle den gleichen Ursprung. Dieser Grundsatz müsse unabhängig von der Geschichte der einzelnen Religionen gelten. Schließlich sei das Recht auf freie Religionsausübung für alle im deutschen Grundgesetz verankert. 'Dazu gehört auch der Bau einer Moschee.'[36]

> "My argumentation is completely different." The three world religions share the same origin. This fundamental principle must hold true regardless of the individual history of each religion. After all, the right to freedom of worship is enshrined for everyone in the German Constitution. "This includes the construction of a mosque."

In this speaker's view, mosques and synagogues should be established according to the German constitution's principle of freedom of religion. According to Cumali Naz, these decisions should be made regardless of the historical background of the religious community.

Jewish Institutional Structures as Organizational Models

Turkish immigrant leaders build upon the German Jewish trope as an organizational model, for two reasons:

First, both Turks and Jews can benefit from *cooperation* against discrimination in Germany. The former has a large population, and the latter has experience in political lobbying. It is natural for them to work together. Kemal Önel is a young member of *Ülkümen-Sarfati Gemeinschaft*, an organization established by Jewish and Turkish youth in Germany.[37] He grew up in a German environment that had mixed ethnicities and religions. Kemal says that the context of discrimination for Turks and Jews is similar. Replicating the significance of Israel for Jews by mentioning Turkey, he associates himself with the Jewish discourse on a personal level: "Türkei ist eine Lebensversicherung [für die Türken in Deutschland]." Some organizations, such as *Kreuzberger Initiative gegen Anti-Semitismus*[38] and *Amira Anti-Semitismus im Kontext Migration und Rassismus*[39] work with Jewish communities to fight anti-Semitism in migrant neighborhoods and schools.

Second, Jewish institutional structures are used as models for religious associations to achieve the type of *community solidarity, collective unity*, and *political lobby* they believe is present in the Jewish community. Although Jewish organizations have different interests and are often in conflict, these conflicts are not readily apparent to the media or to outsiders. Unaware of possible contention within Jewish associations, an executive member of the *Türkische Gemeinde zu Berlin,* Ahmet Yılmaz glorifies the strong fellowship: "Ich wünsche mir von Allah, dass kein anderes Volk die Schwierigkeiten haben wird, die das jüdische Volk erfahren hat, aber ich wünsche mir von Allah, dass er alle mit einer Solidarität wie die der Juden untereinander versorgen würde." I ask Allah to make sure that no other people will encounter the same difficulties as those the Jewish people have encountered, but I ask Allah to bestow everyone with a solidarity like the one among the Jews.[40] Similarly, the Foreigner's Commissioner of *Tempelhof-Schöneberg* borough in Berlin, Emine Demirbüken, points to the economic power and intelligent political lobbying among Jews: "Die jüdische Gemeinschaft verbindet die wirtschaftliche Kraft mit ihrer intellektuellen Kraft. Doch die Türken hätten hier auch wirtschaftliche Kraft und viele Leute, die zweisprachig seien. Warum zeigten sie ihre Stärke den Deutschen nicht, und warum drängen sie sie nicht, Türken ernst zu nehmen?"[41]

But Turkish immigrant organizations are far from unified, and they do not have a strong political lobby in Germany. As a result of this Turkish fragmentation, German state authorities play down the role of immigrant organizations as their interlocutors, saying that the political disunity in the Turkish communities prevents them from establishing themselves as a strong political agency *vis à vis* German authorities (Yurdakul 2009).

In sum, Turkish immigrant leaders build upon Jewish institutional structures, using them as organizational models in two ways: first, cooperation—claiming that Jews have political experience in Germany; and second, collective unity—claiming that the strong Jewish political unity is a model for German Turks in their bid to fight discrimination and claim rights.

Claiming Group Rights

Turks also use the German Jewish trope when claiming group rights. One important difference between Jewish and Muslim associations is fiscal status. While churches and synagogues as statutory corporations (*Körperschaften*) in public law receive state-collected taxes (*Kirchensteuer*), the mosques do not have this right. This issue causes much resentment among Muslims in Germany, especially because their number far exceeds the number of Jews. They are, however, not sufficiently unified to establish political lobbies to demand corporation status in public law.[42]

The most striking examples of religious claims-making and the use of the Jewish narrative involve disputes over the religious education of Turkish Muslim children, wearing the headscarf in public places (Yurdakul 2006), and the right to eat religiously processed meat (*halal*). I will only focus on the case of ritual slaughtering in this chapter (also see Lavi 2009).

Granting *halal*, the ritual slaughtering of animals, has been an important cultural struggle for Turkish immigrants in Germany, especially as Jews are allowed to practice a similar slaughtering practice, known as *kashrut*. *Halal* requires that the animal's throat be cut with a sharp knife and the blood be drained. This contradicts the German regulation that animals should be stunned by electric shock before slaughtering. The situation for Turks periodically becomes controversial, especially before the Ramadan Feast that requires mass sacrifice and ritual slaughtering of certain animals, such as sheep and cattle. In 2004, Turkish butcher, Rüstem Altınküpe, struggled to provide *halal* meat to his clients during Ramadan (Evrensel 2002).[43] He was supported by various Turkish and Muslim associations and organizations that claimed the right to practice their religion in Germany. After days of public campaign in the media, and bureaucratic struggles with the German state, the Muslim community (i.e., the butcher) was given the right to slaughter animals with cutting objects, albeit under very strict conditions.

M.Y., head of the law office of Milli Görüş, a conservative religious immigrant organization associated with political Islam,[44] finds it natural to work with the German Jewish community on this and similar subjects. He participated in a panel discussion with politicians to defend the Muslim right to slaughter animals according to Islamic ritual. He says that the politicians in the panel discussion would not want to accept M.Y.'s arguments for allowing ritual slaughter for Muslims in Germany; however, he was questioning the fact the Jewish minority in Germany has exactly the same rights of ritual slaughter (Judd 2007; Yurdakul and Bodemann 2006). For him and for many Muslims in Germany, this is obviously not simply about slaughtering animals and eating meat—it is about practicing the laws of one's religion, as do Christians and Jews.

While Jews and Muslims are often in opposition, Turkish Muslim leaders, such as those of Milli Görüş, point to the parallel with German Jews in their efforts to claim religious rights from the German state. On the Jewish leaders' side, Sergey Lagodinsky from the *Jüdische Gemeinde zu Berlin* say that as long as there are justifiable links religious rights should be extended, not just to Jews, but to all minorities in Germany.[45] I will elaborate more on this below.

Responses of the Jewish Leaders to German Turkish Claims

Jewish leaders have two contradictory positions about German Turkish appropriation of the Jewish trope. Members of the first group, whom I will call *skeptics*, argue that German Turkish leaders are instrumentalizing Jewish identity in Germany, seeking solidarity with them to make their political claims visible. A more moderate group argues that solidarity between Jews and Turks is not possible, but certain cooperative events against racism are possible (e.g., Anetta Kahane, the leader of an anti-racist organization in Berlin). A more extreme faction argues that there can neither be solidarity nor cooperation. Jews must be cautious about establishing relations with Turks and other Muslim groups because of potential anti-Israel perspectives (e.g., journalist Henryk Broder and Chair of *Zentralrat der Juden*, Charlotte Knobloch).

The second group argues that Jews and Turks (and possibly Muslims) should show solidarity. I call this group *allies*. One topic that comes into discussion is the Israeli-Palestinian conflict as a part of Jewish-Turkish relations in Germany. Some argue that Israeli-Palestinian conflict should be avoided as a topic of discussion in order to solve immediate problems in Germany (e.g., Irene Runge of *Jüdischer Kulturverein*). Others argue that Israeli politics in Gaza and West Bank are unacceptable, and we should solidarize with Palestinians against Israeli politics (e.g., Rabbi Jeremy Milgrom).

Sceptics

Jewish leaders take exception with the German Turkish approach for two reasons. First, they argue that anti-Semitism is a unique phenomenon and cannot be compared to racism against another community. Second, they argue that solidarity between Turks and Jews is not possible. Such *skeptics* place the history of Palestine and the Israeli-Palestinian conflict at the heart of Turkish (i.e., Muslim) and Jewish relations. The following section looks more closely at these two issues.

1. "Opferkonkurrenz" ("victim competition"): The simplest definition of anti-Semitism is hatred against Jews. However, in practice, anti-Semitism can be extended to different political discussions. In my interviews with Jewish community members in Germany, it was obvious that the relationship between anti-Semitism and anti-Zionism is blurred and cannot easily be sorted out. Given the history of the Holocaust, German politicians and scholars refrain from making comments about Israeli politics.

Anti-Semitism takes a different twist for Henryk Broder, one of the most problematic Jewish thinkers in Germany and not necessarily a friend of Muslim immigrants. In July 2008, in a talk at the Domestic Affairs Committee of the German Bundestag, Broder said anti-Semites are not "a handful of weekend Nazis holding a demonstration in Cottbus," thereby covertly pointing to German politicians and writers.[46] Claiming that criticizing Israeli politics, for example in Gaza, is anti-Semitic, he says:

> Antisemitismus und Antizionismus sind zwei Seiten derselben Münze. War der Antisemit davon überzeugt, dass nicht er, der Antisemit, sondern der Jude am Antisemitismus schuld ist, so ist der Antizionist heute davon überzeugt, dass Israel nicht nur für die Leiden der Palästinenser, sondern auch dafür verantwortlich ist, was es selbst erleiden muss. [...]Wenn ich Ihnen in

> aller Demut und Bescheidenheit eine Empfehlung geben darf: Überlassen sie die Beschäftigung mit dem guten alten Antisemitismus à la Horst Mahler den Archäologen, den Antiquaren und den Historikern. Kümmern Sie sich um den modernen Antisemitismus im Kostüm des Antizionismus und um dessen Repräsentanten, die es auch in Ihren Reihen gibt.[47]

> Antisemitism and antizionism are two sides of the same coin. Where the antisemite was convinced that not he, the antisemite, but the Jew himself is responsible for antisemitism, the antizionist today is convinced, that Israel is not only responsible for the suffering of the Palestinians but also for what it has to endure itself. [...] If I may give you a recommendation in all modesty and humility: leave the discussion of the good old antisemitism à la Horst Mahler to the archaeologists, the antiquaries and the historians. Deal with the modern antisemitism disguised as antizionism and with its representatives, who are also present amongst you.

Such accusations[48] are almost taken for granted in Germany and are met with silence from a German audience. In Germany, defining anti-Semitism is a difficult, controversial, and ongoing debate both within Jewish communities and in majority society.

In a loose definition of the term, as we have seen, anti-Semitism is appropriated by Turkish immigrant leaders who seek to build upon the German Jewish trope. According to the leaders of the Jewish community in Germany, however, there are serious problems with how Turkish immigrant leaders point to parallels with German Jews. First, many Jews are offended and provoked by the fact that Turkish immigrant leaders draw comparisons between anti-Semitism, racism against Turks, and Islamophobia. During conferences on both sides of the Atlantic,[49] I found that Jewish audience members voiced their discomfort with this comparison. According to them, anti-Semitism is a unique phenomenon of hatred of Jews. It should not be categorized as a form of racism, as it downplays the significance of anti-Semitism.

Moreover, it is accepted that the Holocaust was a systematic killing of six million European Jews—an event unlike any other in world history.[50] When I proposed to take the Holocaust as a paradigm to fight against all kinds of genocides in the world, I was told that this would downplay the importance of the Holocaust. Anetta Kahane, leader of *Amadeu Antonio Stiftung*, an anti-racist organization, says:

> Das ist in verschiedenen Facetten antisemitisch konnotiert. Also zu sagen, wir sind die Juden von heute ... das ... impliziert eine Menge Abwertungen, 'ne Menge antisemitische Stereotype, 'ne Menge sozusagen

> Opferkonkurrenz ... all diese Sachen. Ich finde, das ist vor allem ein Missbrauch, das ist auch eine Relativierung vom Holocaust und all diesen Sachen.[51]

> This is connotated with antisemitism in various aspects. To say that we are today's Jews ... that ... implies a whole range of derogatory and antisemitic stereotypes, a lot of *Opferkonkurrenz* (victim competition) ... all of these things. Above all I think that this is an abuse, it is also a relativization of the Holocaust and all of these things.

For Kahane, it is normal to cooperate with some selected Turkish immigrant organizations[52] to fight against racism in Germany.[53] But it is not possible for Turks and Jews to be in solidarity in Germany, because they are from different *Verfolgungsgeschichte*. The natural counterpart for solidarity with Turks would be Sinti and Roma in Germany. Drawing parallels between anti-ziganism und anti-Semitism, Kahane said that Sinti-Roma and Jewish communities in Germany share the same history and a common cultural decoding that helps them understand each other and to solidarize in Germany. With respect to the Turkish leaders' choice of a Jewish model, she suggested we explore the "*frage der instrumentalisierung.*" In other words, she questions whether Turkish immigrant leaders are using the German Jewish trope merely to reach their political goals.

In sum, some *sceptics* have serious questions about how the German Turkish leadership builds upon the German Jewish model. The most significant question is whether anti-Semitism can be compared to racism against another ethnic group, or with Islamophobia for that matter. Similarly, some *sceptics* question *Opferkonkurrenz* (victim competition) and using the Holocaust memory as a political tool to gain political recognition.

2. Does Palestine Not Exist?: *Sceptics* also point to the Israeli-Palestinian conflict to highlight the problematic relations between Jews and Muslims, or in other words, Turkish Muslims in Germany. Many secular Turks in Turkey carefully differentiate themselves from Arabs[54] and disassociate themselves from Arabs who feel strongly about the Israeli-Palestinian conflict. But in Germany, Israeli-Palestinian conflict has a completely different connotation for Turkish immigrants. In neighborhoods such as Neukölln, shared by Turks, Palestinian refugees, and Lebanese immigrants, all residents tell similar stories—all have been affected by the anti-Muslim perspective.

In my interviews with members of German-Turkish and Jewish communities, talks often touched on the conflictual relationship between Muslims and Jews in Germany, placing Israeli-Palestinian conflict at the heart of the problem. Furthermore, in Germany (unlike Turkey), Turks are associated with Arabs in this dialogue because of their common problems with inner-city poverty, lack of access to proper employment, and discrimination in educational institutions, as well as immigrant background and discrimination history in Germany (Saad 2008).

A common perspective, especially in Jewish circles in Germany is that the history of Israeli-Palestinian conflict is a fundamental part of Muslim identity, regardless of territorial context. For example, in a workshop on Muslim-Jewish Dialogue in *Limmud*, a conference for Jews on Jewish themes,[55] some participants emphasized the importance of the Israeli-Palestinian conflict for Muslim-Jewish dialogue. The heterogeneity of Muslim practices and Islamic cultures around the world is often disregarded in such discussions; pro-Palestinian and anti-Israel perspectives appear to be fundamental to Islam. Therefore, many *sceptics* argue that it is problematic to establish relations between Muslims (including Turks) and Jews, because of the potential for anti-Israel politics.[56]

As counterpoint, I refer to a contextual understanding of the question of Israeli-Palestinian conflict for Jewish-Turkish dialogue which comes from two young social activists: Serhat Karakayali, a German Turkish project leader of *Amira*,[57] an organization against racism and anti-Semitism in Germany[58] and Sergey Lagodinsky, a legal scholar and prominent member of the Jewish community in Germany.[59] According to both, an *Opferperspektive* (victim perspective) unites Turks and other Muslims in their neighborhoods in Germany. They see themselves as victims of exclusion and discrimination, and they associate with other discriminated-against groups, such as Palestinians. Solidarity with Palestinians is partly due to this *Opferperspektive*, and partly, as Sergey Lagodinsky points out, a provocation of the majority society who is sensitive to Jewish issues in Germany. According to Karakayali, we cannot establish a dialogue among Muslim communities in Germany without addressing the Israeli-Palestinian conflict:

> [I]f we are not able to address the issue of the Palestinian question, as a legitimate question, we'll also not be able to, in the context of our project at least, we will not be able to talk to the people from the Arab communities about anti-Semitism. If we deny their right to speak about occupation, it's impossible [to establish a dialogue with them].[60]

In this case as well, pro-Palestinian perspective is a fact of Muslim identity in Germany. In fact, as Karakayali notes, ignoring Israeli-Palestinian conflict or preventing people from talking about it would cut off dialogue with Muslim youth.[61]

In sum, Israeli-Palestinian conflict is a significant problem affecting dialogue between Turks and Jews. *Skeptics* argue that Jewish leaders must be cautious about establishing relations with Turks, whom they equate with Muslims, because of possible anti-Israeli tendencies among their members. As indicated above, for many *skeptics*, anti-Israeli perspectives cannot be separated from anti-Semitism.

Allies

Some argue that Israeli-Palestinian conflict is not relevant for Muslim and Jewish relations in Germany because dialogue is taking place in a different cultural and social context. Irene Runge, head of the *Jüdischer Kulturverein*, says that her association seeks to cooperate with Muslim organizations.[62] In fact, *Jüdischer Kulturverein* has been in close contact with *Islamische Föderation in Berlin,* an organization known to have organic relations with *Milli Görüs Islamische Gemeinschaft.* This relationship has been criticized by many Jews who question the position of this latter Muslim organization toward Israel. Taking a critical perspective, Runge emphasizes that Jewish-Muslim dialogue in Germany should exclude the Israeli-Palestinian conflict, and should seek immediate solutions to current problems in Germany.[63]

Rabbi Jeremy Milgrom, who lived most of his life in Israel and now located in Berlin, has a different view.[64] He sees it as a part of his role as a Rabbi to facilitate Muslim-Jewish dialogue and also to protest against the human rights violations against Palestinians in Israel:

> My Jewish role as a Rabbi and in general working for justice and the relationship with the other populations in Israel, in the West Bank, in Gaza ... It became my life. It is a combination of inter-religious dialog, but also working for human rights.

Contrary to Runge's opinion, Rabbi Milgrom is a strong ally of Muslims in Germany, and he is one of the executive members of the *Jüdisch-islamischen Gesellschaft* Deutschland (Runge 2008), which is established by Muslims (mostly Turkish Muslims) and a few Jews. Although this organization has not been welcomed by many Jews, he argues for bringing Israeli-Palestinian conflict within the discourse in Germany while establishing formal organizations to create dialogue between Muslims and Jews.

In sum, Jewish leaders are divided into two camps in terms of German Turkish leaders' claim to build upon a German Jewish trope as a political model. Some leaders, such as Knobloch, Kahane, Broder are skeptical about establishing relations with generally with Muslims (which they also include Turkish Muslims) in Germany due to possible anti-Semitic tendencies. Some others, such as Runge are sympathetic to having formal alliances, or even establish common organizations to defend human rights in the Israeli-Palestinian conflict, such as Rabbi Milgrom.

Although Jewish leaders have different opinions about German Turkish leaders' claim, it is interesting that they refer to the Muslim identity as the defining characteristic of Turks. This is quite different in the Turkish leaders' side: They see an inclusive minority identity vis-a-vis a "German identity" as the basis of their relationship between Turks and Jews. In other words, the Jewish leaders see religion as a separating ground between Turks and Jews, whereas Turkish leaders see religious identity as a common ground for two minorities to connect.

Conclusion

In this article, my aim has been to explore the historical, cultural, and social dimensions of immigrant integration processes by focusing on inter-ethnic relations between Jews and Turks in Germany. Drawing on Clifford Geertz's "thick description," I argue for the significance of understanding immigrant integration within a social and cultural context, rather than focusing on the axis of "us" and "them." I use the term "cultural repertoire" to refer to the cultural meanings of the actions of deliberate or unknown social actors which give meaning to significant social actions, such as integration, that are attributed to a group.

By including the cultural repertoire while studying "immigrant integration," we can better understand integration processes, not only from the German state's perspective, but from that of the immigrant group, in this case, Turkish immigrants. This will help us to understand the social and cultural meanings of immigrant acts, helping to make "integration" a two-way process, rather than a state-imposed mandate. We can also see the social dynamics between ethnic groups, here German Jews and German Turks, and how they relate to each other in majority society. Until now, immigrant integration studies have focused on the relations between the majority society and immigrants. In this case, I show how immigrants build upon the experiences of other minorities.[65] I have also pointed out the problematic areas that hinder intensive political cooperation or even solidarity between Jews and Turks in Germany, such as *Opferkonkurrenz* (victim competition) and the Israeli-Palestinian conflict. The latter point shows the impact of Israel on diasporic Jewish communities and on the Turkish immigrant identity in Germany.

In sum, by focusing on Jews and Turks in Germany, I attempted to bring a different theoretical approach to immigrant integration studies, placing immigrant agency at the center and situating immigrants within their historical, social, and cultural contexts.

Notes

1 I use the term German Turks to refer to Turkish immigrants and their German-born children.
2 This Centre is arguably the most established center for research on Turkish immigrants in Germany. Further information can be found at: www.zft.de.
3 Sen's statement as it appears in the Turkish newspaper is as follows: "Büyük kıyım sonrasında Yahudilerden arındırılmaya çalışılan Avrupa'da 5 milyon 200 bin Türk, yeni Yahudiler haline gelmiş bulunuyor. 47 yıldır yaşlı kıtanın orta ve batısını da kendisine yurt edinen insanlarımız; aralarından 45 milyar euro ciro yapan 125 bin girişimci çıkardıkları halde, farklı ölçek ve görünümlerde de olsa, Yahudilerin karşılaştıkları ayrımcılık ve dışlamalara maruz kalıyorlar" (*Referans*, May 19, 2008).
4 His comments appeared in German newspapers and the European edition of the Turkish daily newspaper, *Hürriyet* in different ways. German newspapers focused on the appropriateness of the statement (TAZ, 5–6 Juli 2008: 11), questioning whether it offends Jews (TAZ, 3 Juli 2008: 12) and if there is a political motivation behind this controversy (FAZ, 3 Juli 2008: 2). The Turkish daily *Hürriyet*, however, discussed it as a political trap

of the FDP (Freie Demokratische Partei). They saw it as the FDP's attempt to replace Sen, who is a member of the SPD, with their own candidate (8 Juli 2008: 14), and they rarely discussed the appropriateness of the statement. The Turkish community in Berlin thought that Sen might be made Professor in the Turkish-German university (personal conversation with Safter Çınar, October 8, 2008, Berlin). However, this is yet to be confirmed.

5   This can be translated as "slip" or "gaffe."
6   In the same interview, however, Sen reiterated the anti-Semitic stereotype that Jews have a strong political lobby, and Turks should solidarize themselves with Jews (*Jüdische Allgemeine*, 3 Juli 2008: front page)
7   This controversy has been quite idiosyncratic. First, the original article by Sen was published in Turkish on May 19, 2008. But the controversy started in Germany in July 2008, and the time lapse is problematic. Second, some Turkish Jews backed up Sen's statement, and this has received little press coverage. Third, the Zentralrat der Juden had a press release stating that they had no apparent problem with the statement. Yet some German public figures were uncomfortable with it. These events can be traced in the first two weeks of July 2008 in German newspapers.
8   Unless otherwise indicated, "Turkish" will mean persons originating from Turkey, regardless of ethnicity.
9   Although I use the words, "race," "racism," "ethnicity," I am aware of their cultural limitations. For one, "race" is a term used to describe the differences between Whites and Blacks in the North American context. The history of the term "race" has developed differently in Germany, however, and its use is carefully avoided in public, including academia and media. Instead, *ausländerfeindlichkeit* is used to refer to racism against Turks (Mandel 2008). For another, as I will show in this article, "race" is a socially constructed concept (Goldberg 2002; Mills 1997); neither Turks nor Jews are "race," so they cannot be subjected to racism. However, the official definition of *United Nations Convention on the Elimination of All Forms of Racial Discrimination* is the following: "the term 'racial discrimination' shall mean any distinction, exclusion, restriction or preference based on race, colour, descent, or national or ethnic origin which has the purpose or effect of nullifying or impairing the recognition, enjoyment or exercise, on an equal footing, of human rights and fundamental freedoms in the political, economic, social, cultural or any other field of public life." Based on this definition, I use "race" and racism with caution, but with a broader understanding that racism includes all forms of "racial" discrimination.
10 Immigrant integration has two analytical components: class and race/ethnicity.
11 Multiculturalism appears as early as Milton Gordon's work (1965), but recent discussions on multiculturalism are fundamentally different from his modeling.
12 "Boundary drawing" analyses focus on imagined homogeneous immigrant groups.
13 Thick description is a term in cultural anthropology referring to the cultural meanings of human action within social contexts. A well-known example is the difference between wink, a socially meaningful action, and a twitch, an involuntary action. The emblematic study of thick description is Clifford Geertz' essay "Deep Play: Notes on the Balinese Cockfight" (1972).
14 The boldest statement is by Micha Brumlik, who has spoken firmly of German Jewish patriotism, in an article entitled "Dies ist mein Land" (this is my country). The title alludes to Lea Fleischmann's book, *Dies ist nicht mein Land* (1980). Also see Y. Michal Bodemann,

In den Wogen der Erinnerung. Jüdische Existenz in Deutschland (2002), 185; Micha Brumlik, "Dies ist mein Land," *Jüdische Allgemeine*, December 23, 2004.
15 Article 116 par. 2 of the German Constitution says: "Former German citizens, who between January 30, 1933 and May 8, 1945 were deprived of their citizenship on political, "racial," or religious grounds, and their descendants, shall on application have their citizenship restored. They shall be deemed never to have been deprived of their citizenship if they have established their domicile in Germany after May 8, 1945 and have not expressed a contrary intention ... The above mentioned group of people mainly includes German Jews and members of the Communist or Social Democratic Parties." Further information is available at "Information on obtaining/reobtaining German citizenship for former German citizens and their descendants who were persecuted on political, 'racial' or religious grounds between January 30, 1933 and May 8, 1945" at www.germany-info.org/relaunch/info/consular_services/citizenship/persecuted.html.
16 On the nature of "problematic counting of Jews," see Calvin Goldscheider, *Studying the Jewish Future* (2004).
17 Immigration from Turkey to Germany includes not only Turks, but Kurds and other ethnic and religious minorities, such as Alevites and Yezidis.
18 John Berger, *A Seventh Man: Migrant Workers in Europe* (1975).
19 Lenie Brouwer and Marijke Prister, "Living in Between: Turkish Women in Their Homeland and in the Netherlands," in *One-Way Ticket: Migration and Female Labour*, ed. Anne Phizacklea (1983). The family reunification law was a part of development policy toward foreigners in Germany that would facilitate their integration. These development policies included the introduction of the Action Program for Foreign Labor in June 1973 and changes in child allowances in January 1975. For detailed information, see Ulrich Herbert, *A History of Foreign Labor in Germany, 1880–1980: Seasonal Workers, Forced Laborers, Guest Workers* (1990).
20 German authorities do not register the ethnic background of German citizens due to the predicaments of the registry practice during the Holocaust.
21 Ascheim points out that German Jews were also regarded as "unintegrated" in the early nineteenth century.
22 German Turks who perform worst on the German educational achievement scale are used as a paradigmatic example of unsuccessful integration not only in Germany, but throughout the Western social sciences literature on immigration. Although the statistics vary slightly from year to year, a German Turkish young person is almost four times more likely to drop out of high school (*ohne abschluss*) than a German.
23 There is controversy over the use of this term. It is debated whether we should use anti-Muslim, anti-Islam, Islamophobia, and what we mean by each term. I use Islamophobia because it is used by the *Islamische Gemeinschaft Milli Görüs*, to which I refer throughout the article. Also see Kramer (2006) and TAZ (2006). I thank Mounir Azzaoui (Zentralrat der Muslime) for his insights about this topic.
24 Friedrich Ebert Stiftung is the cultural foundation of the Social Democratic Party in Germany. The proceedings from this conference were later published by the Foundation as a Policy Report Nr. 27 (2008).
25 Turks, in general, are not only uninformed about Jews and Jewishness, but their limited information is incorrect. In the open market in front of the *Ka De We*, one of the largest

shopping centers in Berlin, I was doing my usual weekly shopping at a Turkish stand. I asked the Turkish stand seller to give me a particular brand of yoghurt. He refused to sell me that brand, which he placed at a far corner of his stand. He said that particular yoghurt contained pork fat, and he would not sell it to me as a fellow Muslim. I confronted him, saying that the yoghurt container had a picture of a mosque on it. How was it possible to have pork fat in the yoghurt and a mosque picture on the container? He said that I should not be fooled by the container, as the owner of the yoghurt company was Jewish. Unaware that both Jews and Muslims avoid pork in their diet, the Turkish man associated pork eating, which Turks associate with promiscuity and dirtiness, with Jews. For more on the symbolic meaning of pork eating for German Turks, see Mandel (2008: 265–6).

26 I thank Helena Stern for insightful comments on this subject (December 10, 2008).
27 Consider the controversy over Turkish penal code, Article 301, which criminalizes "insulting Turkishness" (introduced in 2005, amended in 2008). The questioning of Turkish identity is racialized within the ongoing controversy about whether there was an Armenian genocide in 1915.
28 Some Turkish Jewish people living in Western Europe and North America claim that anti-Semitism does not exist in Turkey, and they criticize those of us who mention it as betraying our nation abroad.
29 Interview with Safter Çınar, October 8, 2008.
30 Certain politicians from the Green Party can be examples of this; Christian Ströbele proposed having Muslim religious holidays as public holidays in Germany, a proposal refused by the Islamische Gemenischaft Milli Görüs, perhaps to avoid public controversy.
31 This issue of *Perspektive* is available online and also as hard copy. The issue title is "Anti-Semitizm, Islamophobia ve Terör," published in Germany in March 2004, issue number 111. The online copy can be found at www.igmg.de. Please note that in the title, anti-Semitism is written in Turkish, but Islamophobia is written in German (the Turkish version would be "Islamofobi"). This and other spelling and grammar mistakes in Turkish in the journals of Milli Görüs point to the fact that the editors of this journal were mainly educated in German schools.
32 The possible trajectoral similarity between synagogues and mosques is not my point here, although perhaps historical and architectural similarities between synagogues and mosques would make an interesting research project. My focus is on the discourse analysis of the dialogue between Jewish community members and the German Turkish politicians.
33 Interview with Alboga in NGZ-online, released in 2007 and updated on February 15, 2008.
34 Interview with Knobloch in Merkür-online.de, 2007. This article is no longer available; previously it was located at http://www.merkur-online.de/regionen/mstadt/%3Bart8828,846794.
35 I am grateful to Ian Leveson for pointing out the fact that the position of the Jewish community toward Jewish-Muslim dialogue was different than the current one during the leadership of Ignatz Bubis.
36 Newspaper interview with Cumali Naz, 2007. This interview as a response to Knobloch is removed from the website of the newspaper but is available on personal blogs. See http://gruene-pest.com/archive/index.php/t-247981.html
37 Interview with assistants and interns in American Jewish Council in Berlin, July 21, 2008.
38 Interview with Aycan Demirel from KiGA on July 15, 2008.

39 Interview with Serhat Karakayali from Amira on October 22, 2008.
40 Interview with Ahmet Yilmaz from Türkische Gemeinde zu Berlin on May 8, 2003.
41 Interview with Emine Demirbüken at the Tempelhof-Schöneberg Rathaus on March 4, 2003.
42 It is referred as *Körperschaft des öffentlichen Rechts.* See Yurdakul 2009.
43 Also see Gokturk, Gramling and Kaes (2007: 226–8).
44 The name *Milli Görüs* refers to the political ideology created by the *Milli Nizam Partisi* (National Order Party) in Turkey during the 1970s. Because of its religious activities that threaten public order, political parties associated with *Milli Görüs* ideology were banned by the Constitutional Court in Turkey. It reappeared as a diasporic network of Turkish Muslims in Europe, specifically in Germany. However, it has a big disadvantage: it is listed with the *Bundesverfassungsschutz* (intelligence agency) as a "threat" to German democracy. It is considered part of a political Islam which prevents immigrants from achieving full integration into German society (Schiffauer 2004). The report states that *Milli Görüs* pursues anti-integrative efforts, especially Islamic education of children. Moreover, the report provides many statements taken from *Milli Görüs* publications, specifically anti-German and anti-Semitic statements in the *Milli Gazete*. The label of "threat" to German democracy restricts *Milli Görüs* activities and campaigns, and puts members under suspicion. *Milli Görüs* responded to the accusations of the *Innenministerium Baden Wüttemberg* in an informative brochure "Den Verfassungsfeind konstruieren" (2007).
45 Sergey Lagodinsky, a prominent member of the Jewish community in Berlin and a legal scholar argues that claiming rights in Germany by referring to the Holocaust is outdated. Interview with Lagodinsky, December 12, 2008.
46 Some examples are Hans-Christian Ströbele and Ludwig Watzal.
47 Broder 2008, available on various blogs online. Please see the references section for details. This speech is also available in English translated by John Rosenthal: "Anti-Semitism without Anti-Semites."
48 A Jewish writer might say, "You will find some of the latter among your ranks" in the German Bundestag. Consider also the above example of the Rabbi confronting German politicians in a panel discussion in Nordrhein Westphalia.
49 I was invited to give a talk at the "Immigration and Cultural Exchange: German Jewish Presences in the US and Post Cold War Germany" March 25–27, 2007, NYU Center for European Studies and Leo Baeck Institute, New York. I assumed that this was a typical response from an American Jewish audience, but to my surprise, I found it in Germany as well.
50 For a comparative work on the Holocaust, see Rosenbaum 1996; "Is Holocaust Unique?"
51 Interview with Anetta Kahane, September 11, 2008.
52 However, she refused to work with *Milli Görüs* through a proposal made by Schiffauer. And she would not do projects about Islamophobia or tackle anything that might threaten Israel. Interview with Kahane on September 11, 2008.
53 Follow-up interview with Kahane, November 17, 2008.
54 In fact, there is a significant anti-Arabism in Turkey: looking down on Arabs, downplaying Arabic culture, associating Arabs with being dirty, even calling stray black dogs "Arab." The following statement by Öger is evidence that some Turks want to distance themselves

from Arabs: "The actors of political Islam are not Turks. Jihad is not Turks' business. Palestine is not the problem of Turks" (Hürriyet, October 4, 2005).
55 This workshop "Who is Afraid of Muslim-Jewish Dialogue/understanding/cooperation?" was organized by Rabbi Jeremy Milgrom on May 18, 2008, Werbellinsee bei Berlin.
56 In his interview, Rabbi Milgrom mentioned that some members of the Jewish community have refuted the establishment of the *Jüdische-Muslime Verein* in Nürnberg; Milgrom is a member of the executive committee. Interview with Rabbi Milgrom on July 7, 2008.
57 Until now, *Amira* workers have talked to social workers in Muslim immigrant communities to fight against anti-Semitism among the youth in these neighborhoods.
58 Interview with Serhat Karakayali on October 22, 2008.
59 Interview with Sergey Lagodinsky on December 12, 2008.
60 Interview with Karakayali, October 22, 2008. Original in English.
61 The proliferation of Palestine themes in Muslim youth music, especially hip hop, shows that Karakayali is correct. In mixed ethnic hip-hop groups, German youth with Turkish (Islamic Power), Palestinian (Massiv), Egyptian (Scarabeuz) backgrounds deal with Palestinian issues in their lyrics. A popular example is Massiv who identifies himself as: "Ich hab 'n deutschen Pass aber Herkunft Palästina." (Massiv's song "Ich bin kein Berliner").
62 Interview with Irene Runge on July 10, 2008.
63 Irene Runge's contribution in the Limmud, May 18, 2008, Werbellinsee bei Berlin.
64 Interview with Rabbi Milgrom on July 7, 2008. Original in English.
65 This is a significant break from the existing literature, although there are some studies, such as Nancy Foner (2003).

References

Alba, R. (2005), "Right vs. Blurred Boundaries: Second-Generation Assimilation and Exclusion in France, Germany, and the United States," *Ethnic and Racial Studies*, 28 (1): 20–49.

Alba, R. and V. Nee (1997), "Rethinking Assimilation. Theory for a New Era of Immigration," *International Migration Review*, 31 (4): 826–74.

Alber, J. (2008), Paper Presentation in the session Immigrant Political Participation at the Germany-Turkey Common Challenges and Prospects Conference. Humboldt University, December 1–2.

Ascheim, S. (1983), *Brothers and Strangers: The East European Jews in German and German Jewish Consciousness, 1800–1923*, Madison: University of Wisconsin Press.

Atshan, S. and K. Galor (2020), *The Moral Triangle: Germans, Israelis, Palestinians*, Durham: Duke University Press.

Baer, M. (2013), "Turk and Jew in Berlin: The First Turkish Migration to Germany and the Shoah," *Comparative Studies in Society and History*, 55 (2): 330–55.

Baer, M. (2018), "Mistaken for Jews: Turkish PhD Students in Nazi Germany," *German Studies Review*, 41 (1): 19–39.

Bali, R. (1999), *Cumhuriyet Yıllarında Türkiye Yahudileri Bir Türkleştirme Serüveni (1923–1945)*, Istanbul: Iletisim.

Bali, R. (2001), *Musa'nın Evlatları Cumhuriyet'in Yurttasları*, Istanbul: Iletisim.

Bali, R. (2008), *A Scapegoat for All Seasons: The Donmes or Crypto-Jews of Turkey*, Istanbul: Isis.
Beauftragte der Bundesregierung für Migration, Flüchtlinge und Integration (2000), *Einbürgerung: Fair, Gerecht, Tolerant*, http://www.einbuergerung.de/ (Reached at December 28, 2008).
Berger, J. (1975), A *Seventh Man: Migrant Workers in Europe*, New York: Viking.
Bloemraad, I., A. Korteweg, and G. Yurdakul (2008), "Citizenship and Immigration: Multiculturalism, Assimilation, and Challenges to the Nation-State," *Annual Review of Sociology*, 34 (1): 153–79.
Bodemann, Y. M. (1996), *Gedächtnistheater. Die jüdische Gemeinschaft und ihre deutsche Erfindung*, Hamburg: Rotbuch Verlag.
Bodemann, Y. M. (2002), *In den Wogen der Erinnerung. Jüdische Existenz in Deutschland*, München: DTV.
Bonacich, E. (1980), "Class Approaches to Ethnicity and Race," *Insurgent Sociologist*, 10 (2): 9–22.
Brenner, M. (2007), "No Place of Honor," in D. Gokturk, D. Gramling and A. Kaes (eds.), *Germany in Transit: Nation and Migration 1955–2005*, 216–19, Berkeley: University of California Press.
Broder, H. (2008), *Anti Semitismus ohne Anti semiten* (reached at January 1, 2009). http://www.lizaswelt.net/2008/06/antisemitismus-ohne-antisemiten_16.html
Brouwer, L. and M. Prister (1983), "Living in Between: Turkish Women in Their Homeland and in the Netherlands," in A. Phizacklea (ed.), *One Way Ticket. Migration and Female Labour*, 113–29, London/Boston: Routledge & Keagan.
Brubaker, R. (2004), *Ethnicity without Groups*, Cambridge: Harvard University Press.
Brumlik, M. (2004), "Dies ist mein Land," *Jüdische Allgemeine*, December 23.
Çağlar, A. S. (1994), *German-Turks in Berlin: A Quest for Social Mobility*, unpublished PhD Dissertation, McGill University.
Ehrhardt, C. (2008), "Alleingänge und Entgleisungen," *Frankfurter Allgemeine Zeitung*, 3 Juli, p. 2.
Even-Zohar, I. (2003), "Culture Repertoire and Transfer," in S. Petrilli (ed.), *Translation Translation*, 425–31, Amsterdam: Rodopi.
Evrensel Gazetesi (2002), "Yüksek mahkemeden kurbana vize çıktı," in *Evrensel Daily Newspaper*, European Edition, January 16.
Fleischmann, L. (1980), *Dies ist nicht mein Land: eine Jüdin verläßt die Bundesrepublik*, Hamburg: Hoffmann und Campe.
Foner, N. (2003), "Immigrants and African Americans: Comparative Perspectives on the New York Experience across Time and Space," in J. G. Reitz (ed.), *Host Societies and the Reception of Immigrants*, 45–71, La Jolla: Center for Comparative Immigration Studies.
Frankel, J. and S. J. Zipperstein (2004), *Assimilation and Community: The Jews in Nineteenth-Century Europe*, Cambridge: Harvard University Press.
Friedrich Ebert Stiftung (2008), *Islamischer Anti-Semitismus und Islamophobia*, Berlin: Policy Report. Nr. 27. https://library.fes.de/pdf-files/akademie/berlin/05925.pdf (accessed March 14, 2022).
Geertz, C. (1972), "Deep Play. Notes on the Balinese Cockfight," *Daedalus*, 101 (1): 1–38.
Geertz, C. (1976), *The Interpretation of Cultures: Selected Essays*, New York: Basic Books.

Gokturk, D., D. Gramling and A. Kaes (2007), *Germany in Transit*, Berkeley: University of California Press.

Goldberg, D. T. (2002), *Racist Culture: Philosophy and the Politics of Meaning*, Malden: Blackwell.

Goldscheider, C. (2004), *Studying the Jewish Future*, Seattle and London: University of Washington Press.

Gordon, M. M. (1965), *Assimilation in American Life: The Role of Race, Religion, and National Origins*, New York: Oxford University Press.

Graalmann, Dirk interview with Armin Laschet (2008) "Das ist inakzeptabel." *Süddeutsche Zeitung*, 1 July.

Herbert, U. (1990), *A History of Foreign Labor in Germany, 1880–1980: Seasonal Workers/Forced Laborers/Guest Workers*, Ann Arbor: University of Michigan Press.

Hürriyet (2008), Kasap Rüstem'e yine engel çıkardılar (They block the Butcher Rustem Again), 4 August.

Hürriyet (2008), Sen'e Kulp Aranıyor (A Cover Needed for Sen's Case) 8 July, p. 14.

Islamische Gemeinde Milli Görüs (2004), "Brandanschlag auf muslimischen Schlachtbetrieb," November 26, http://www.igmg.de

Islamische Gemeinschaft Milli Görüs' magazine, *Perspektive* published an issue on the relationship between anti-Semitism and Islamophobia (2004).

Joppke, C. (1998), *Challenge to the Nation State: Immigration in Western Europe and the United States*, Oxford: Oxford University Press.

Joppke, C. (2003), "Multicultural Citizenship in Germany," in J. Stone and R. Denis (eds.), *"Race" and Ethnicity: Comparative and Theoretical Approaches*, 359–67, Oxford: Blackwell.

Judd, R. (2007), *Contested Rituals: Circumcision, Kosher Butchering and Jewish Political Life in Germany, 1848–1933*, Ithaca: Cornell University Press.

Kastoryano, R. (2002), *Negotiating Identities*, Princeton: Princeton University Press.

Keskinkılıç, O. Z. and Á. Langer (2018), *Fremdgemacht & Reorientiert—jüdisch-muslimische Verflechtungen*, Berlin: Verlag Yılmaz-Günay.

Kirschstein, Frank interview with Bekir Alboga (2008), "Ohne Gerechtigkeit geht es nicht," http://www.ngz-online.de/public/article/ngz-gespraeche/533602/Ohne-Gerechtigkeit-geht-es-nicht.html (December 19, 2008).

Kirsten, C., D. Reimer and I. Kogan (2008), "Higher Education Entry of Turkish Immigrant Youth in Germany," *International Journal of Comparative Sociology*, 49 (2–3): 127–51.

Korteweg, A. and G. Yurdakul (2009), "Gender Islam and Immigrant Integration: Boundary Drawing on Honour Killing in the Netherlands and Germany," *Ethnic and Racial Studies*, 32 (2): 218–38.

Kramer, G. (2006), "Anti-Semitism in the Modern World: A Critical Review," *Die Welt des Islams*, 46 (3): 243–76.

Kühn, Tobias interview with Faruk Sen (2008) "Wir wollen solidarisch sein," *Jüdische Allgemeine*, 3 July, p. 1.

Lamont, M. and C. Fleming (2005), "Everyday Anti-Racism: Competence and Religion in the Cultural Repertoire of the African American Elite," *Du Bois Review*, 2 (1): 29–43.

Lamont, M. and V. Molnár (2002), "The Study of Boundaries across the Social Sciences," *Annual Review of Sociology*, 28: 167–95.

Laurence, J. (2001), "(Re)constructing Community in Berlin: Turks, Jews, and German Responsibility," *German Politics & Society*, 19 (2): 22–61.

Lavi, S. (2009), "Unequal Rites: Jews, Muslims and the History of Ritual Slaughter in Germany," in J. Brunner and S. Lavi (eds.), *Juden und Muslime in Deutschland*, 164–84, Göttingen: Wallstein Verlag.

Legge Jr., J. S. (2003), *Jews, Turks, and Other Strangers: The Roots of Prejudice in Modern Germany*, Madison: University of Wisconsin Press.

Mandel, R. (2008), *Cosmopolitan Anxieties: Turkish Challenges to Citizenship and Belonging in Germany*, Durham: Duke University Press.

Männlein, D. (2019), *Boundary (Un-)Making in der postmigrantischen Gesellschaft— Perspektiven jüdischer und muslimischer politischer Repräsentant_innen in Deutschland*, Unpublished MA Thesis at the Department of Diversity and Social Conflict, Institute of Social Sciences, Humboldt-Universität zu Berlin.

Mills, C. W. (1997), *The Racial Contract*, Ithaca: Cornell University Press.

Öger, V. (2004), "Open Letter to the Stern," *Hürriyet Avrupa*, October 2.

Öger, V. (2005), "Interview," *Hürriyet Avrupa*, 4 October.

Özyürek, E. (2018), "Rethinking Empathy: Emotions Triggered by the Holocaust among the Muslim-minority in Germany," *Anthropological Theory*, 18 (4): 456–77.

Özyürek, E. and I. Dekel (2020), "Perfides Ablenkungsmanöver," *Die Zeit*, 10 July. https://www.zeit.de/kultur/2020-07/antisemitismus-debatte-holocaust-deutschland-rassismus-kolonialismus-diskriminierung-10nach8

Oz-Salzberger, F. (2001), *Israelis in Berlin*, Berlin: Jüdischer Verlag.

Park, R. E. (2005), "The Marginal Man," in K. Thompson (ed.), *Race and Culture. The Early Sociology of Race and Ethnicity*, 345–92, London: Routledge.

Portes, A. and M. Zhou (1992), "Gaining the Upper Hand: Economic Mobility among Immigrant and Domestic Minorities," *Ethnic and Racial Studies*, 15 (4): 491–522.

Religionswissenschaftlicher Medien und Informationsdienst e.V. (2007), *Religion in Deutschland: Mitgliederzahlen*. http://www.remid.de/remid_info_zahlen.htm (reached at January 1, 2009)

Rosenbaum, A. S. (1996), *Is the Holocaust Unique?: Perspectives on Comparative Genocide*, Boulder: Westview Press.

Rothberg, M. (2019), *The Implicated Subject: Beyond Victims and Perpetrators*, Palo Alto: Stanford University Press.

Runge, I. (2008), "Wer hat Angst vor dem Dialog?," *Jüdische Zeitung*, Haus Werner Media Berlin, June, p. 1.

Saad, F. (2008), *Der große Bruder von Neukölln*, Freiburg: Herder.

Sayad, A. (2004), *The Suffering of the Immigrant*, Cambridge: Polity Press.

Schiffauer, W. (2004) "Das Recht, anders zu sein," *Die Zeit*, November 18.

Schmitter-Heissler, B. (1992), "The Future of Immigrant Incorporation; Which Models? Which Concepts?," *International Migration Review*, 26 (2): 623–45.

Sen, F. (2008), "Avrupa'nın Yeni Yahudileri," (Europe's New Jews) *Referans Gazetesi*, May 19.

Simon, J. (2008), "Eine Jugend in Deutschland," *Zeitmagazin Leben*, 13, March 20, p. 35.

Swidler, A. (1986), "Culture in Action: Symbols and Strategies," *American Sociological Review*, 51: 273–86.

TAZ (2006), Deutsche Juden und Muslime Beginnen Dialog, May 26.

Unabhängiger Expertenkreis Antisemitismus (2017), *Antisemitismus in Deutschland—aktuelle Entwicklungen*, Berlin: Bundesministerium des Inneren.

United Nations Convention on the Elimination of All Forms of Racial Discrimination (2008), 26 December, http://www.unhchr.ch/html/menu3/b/d_icerd.htm.

Wimmer, A. (2007), *How (Not) to Think About Ethnicity in Immigrant Societies*, Working Paper No. 07–44, Oxford: Centre on Migration, Policy and Society.

Wimmer, A. (2008), "Elementary Strategies of Ethnic Boundary Making," *Ethnic and Racial Studies*, 31 (6): 1025–55.

Young, J. E. (2004), "Variations of Memory: Berlin to New York after 1989," unpublished conference presentation at the (Re)Visualising National History: Museology and National Identities in Europe in the New Millennium, University of Toronto, March.

Yücel, Deniz interview with Rıfat Bali (2008) "Faruk Sens Vergleich war populistisch," *Die Tageszeitung*, 5–6 July, p. 11.

Yurdakul, G. (2006), "Secular Versus Islamist: The Headscarf Debate in Germany," in G. Jonker and V. Amiraux (eds.), *Strategies of Visibility: Young Muslims in European Public Spaces*, 151–68, Bielefeld: Transcript Verlag.

Yurdakul, G. (2009), *From Guest Workers into Muslims: Turkish Immigrant Associations in Germany*, Newcastle: Cambridge Scholars Press.

Yurdakul, G. (2016), "Jews, Muslims and the Ritual Male Circumcision Debate: Religious Diversity and Social Inclusion in Germany," *Social Inclusion*, 4 (2): 77–86.

Yurdakul, G. and M. Bodemann (2006), "'We Don't Want to Be the Jews of Tomorrow': Jews and Turks in Germany after 9/11," *German Politics and Society*, 24 (2): 44–67.

Zaptcioglu, D. (2008), "Geschichten der Ausgrenzung," *Die Tageszeitung*, 3 Juli, p. 12.

Zolberg, A. R. and L. L. Woon (1999), "Why Islam Is Like Spanish: Cultural Incorporation in Europe and the United States," *Politics and Society*, 27 (1): 5–38.

III DIASPORA IN UNITED STATES

The Social Construction of Difference and the Arab American Experience, Revisited

by Louise Cainkar

Introduction

Sociological theories of race are a tough fit when it comes to Arab Americans. This is because these theories have been built on understandings of historic subordinations that served the domestic interests of white supremacy, such as territorial expansion and exploitation of cheap and free labor for profit. Although US race theory recognizes race as a social construction, it does not appear ready to acknowledge that new groups can be racialized. So, for example, dominant race theory does not help explain the status of groups whose racial position is tied to the rise of the United States as a superpower and its global—not domestic—interests, nor how these interests can cause shifts over time. It therefore does not account for why the racialization of Arab Americans produced some consequences that differ from those of historically racialized groups. For example, the outcomes of Arab American racialization are not tied to domestic socio-economic subordination, due in part to the racial project's different timing, objectives, and trajectory.

From a sociological perspective, Arabs who migrated to the United States in the first decades of the twentieth century held structural positions and faced barriers of prejudice and discrimination largely similar to other liminal-white groups (especially Italians). They were barred from a broad range of institutions run by mainstream whites, yet they largely lived among "white ethnics" in cities and small towns and led social lives that were intertwined with them, often resulting in second-generation intermarriages. Arab immigrants were allowed to own property, vote, run retail businesses, and travel across the country as goods peddlers. They worked in—and sometimes owned—factories, held government offices in a number of places, flourished artistically, and achieved a good degree of economic success. In many areas, they were your quintessential "middleman minority" shopkeepers, buying from dominant whites, selling to subordinated, racialized groups (Bonacich 1973). Yet there are important exceptions to this simplification of history; in certain cities and regions, for example, the right of Arabs to naturalize as US citizens was challenged by court clerks who asserted that

---

Originally, *Journal of American Ethnic History*.

they were not white. Gualtieri's (2009) scholarship shows us that Arab Americans staked claims to Christianity, to western civilization, and to difference from Chinese and African Americans in order to assert their Whiteness.

Overall, the Arab experience in the United States in the early part of the twentieth century displayed more social, political, and economic incorporation into whiteness than that of racially excluded African Americans, Asians, Native Americans, and Latinos. It was also vastly better than Arab American experiences over the past fifty years, which evidence a distinct pattern of racialization as non-white, a structural position created and reproduced by institutions of power that is measurable. This racialization is manifested in government policies of policing and surveillance, hate crimes, widespread discriminatory behaviors, physical insecurity, social and political exclusion, mainstream cultural representations, public perceptions and attitudes, and at times, immigration policies. There are some continuities between Arab communities past and present. In both periods and throughout the intervening years, Arabs have been highly entrepreneurial, heavily engaged in retail trade, and until the recent waves of Yemenis and Iraqi and Syrian refugees, have posted above average median incomes, in part a product of historic access to whiteness. At the same time that this trend toward self-employment may signal success, it also suggests blocked access to dominant forms of socio-economic mobility.

Religious factors may explain a small part of the differences in experience between past and present Arab American generations as the earliest Arab immigrants were more often Christian than Muslim, and thus allied with the dominant religion in the United States, while the reverse is now the case. But reducing historical changes in the Arab American experience to a Muslim-Christian dichotomy is not as analytically useful as it may appear. All major American Arab organizations, local and national, are staffed by members of both religious groups and share the same objectives: eliminating hyper-policing, discrimination, stereotyping, political exclusion, and vilification. Persons with Arabic-sounding names, whether Christian or Muslim, experience job discrimination and anti-Arab comments, and persons with the "Arab/Middle Eastern" phenotype are physically attacked regardless of religion. It is not clear that the American public has a differentiated view of the Christian versus the Muslim Arab; the utter simplicity of monolithic, anti-Arab messages has succeeded in precluding thoughtful distinctions. The negative experiences around which Arab American organizations have mobilized preceded by decades the September 11, 2001, attacks and laid the groundwork for the collective backlash that followed them.

Rather, it is global events and the relationship of the US government to them that explain the racialization of Arab Americans and the downturn in their American experience. Since the 1967 Israeli-Arab War, American news, film, and television narratives and images have persisted in using racialized tropes about Arabs, depicting them as inherently savage persons (terrorists) who need to be monitored and controlled. At the same time, Arab American voices of dissent (whether Christian or Muslim) have faced silencing and institutional exclusion. Due to global events and the political agendas of powerful institutional actors, the assimilation process, as Richard Alba and Victor Nee (2003) define it, went into *reversal* as social distance and group distinctiveness became more relevant, not less, for Arab American communities.

The theoretical construction that best captures the Arab American experience over time is racial formation, as initially developed by Michael Omi and Howard Winant (1994). The structural exclusion of Arab Americans from a wide range of social institutions has evolved from a plethora of "racial projects"—in the media, arts, news, pedagogy, academia, civil society, political organizations, public policy, and popular culture—in which social constructions of the essential differences of Arabs (and later Muslims) have been put forth so extensively as to become widely accepted as common sense, as evidenced in public opinion polls. Winant (2001) argued that public policies no longer can be legitimately sold to the public using racial typologies and stereotypes. Alba and Nee (2003) argued that the legitimacy of "overtly racist beliefs and practice have never been lower in the eyes of most Americans." I argue that discourses with socio-political objectives that stress essential cultural and civilizational differences are nearly identical replacements for racist ideas and are alive and well in the United States. My argument aligns with Naber's (2000) by locating US foreign policy interests as the key to Arab American racialization; these interests also explain Arab American invisibility and the racialization of Islam (Cainkar and Selod 2018).

Just as one can document and measure the process of becoming white,[1] a downgrading of the social status of Arabs in America through processes identified as racial formation is measurable: in public policies; policing; mainstream representations; social patterns of discrimination, separation, and exclusion; and in self-identification (see Shaheen 1984, 2001; Suleiman 1999).[2] In the late 1970s, pollsters Seymour Lipset and Martin Schneider found US attitudes toward Arabs "close to racist," and in the early 1980s Shelly Slade (1981) concluded that "Arabs remain one of the few ethnic groups that can still be slandered with impunity in America."[3]

Arab Americans have been racialized using dominant discourses about their inherent violence, which are propped up with confirming images (such as angry mobs) in a process tied to the rise of the United States as a superpower and its *foreign* (not domestic) policy interests. This stigmatization threw Arab American communities off their previous course in American society as it re-created them as "others," as people who stand in opposition to Americanness because of their inherent values and dispositions. Arab opposition to Israeli military occupation and dispossession was constructed as illegitimate through constructing Arabs as not only violent but also racist and anti-Semitic (Abu-Laban and Suleiman 1989: 18, 21). These social constructions effectively blocked Arab Americans from broader civic and political engagement; Arab American candidates for office and Arab American political donations were treated as poison and few political coalitions wanted Arab Americans in their ranks.

The domestic transformation of Arabs from a marginal white to structurally subordinate status was facilitated by the flexibility of whiteness and the historic and "observable" racial liminality of Arabs (a concept that can be extended to South Asians and Latinos). But, at its core, the social and political exclusion of Arabs in the United States has been a racial formation process because Arab inferiority has been constructed and sold to the American public using essentialist constructions of human difference, resulting in specific forms of structural isolation. In the 1990s, when Islamist challenges to American global hegemony became more powerful than Arab nationalism, these constructions were extended more broadly to Muslims and became grander—they became civilizational. The same representations were deployed, but instead of being about Arab culture they were about Islam and its "flawed civilization," as expressed in the clash of civilizations discourse popularized by Harvard scholar Samuel Huntington (1996). Seen as recently as 1943 by the Immigration and Naturalization Service as persons who shared "in the development of our civilization," affirming their whiteness and justifying their eligibility for naturalization, Arabs and Muslims were, by the 1990s, positioned by the "clash of civilizations" viewpoint as the cultural other—a categorization that had become an accepted scholarly perspective. The seemingly race-neutral lens of essentialized cultural and religious differences became useful after blatant racism had lost its power as an effective hegemonic tool (an outcome of the civil rights movement, according to race scholars). Nonetheless, the components of racialization were there: the assertion of *innate characteristics* held by all members of a *group* and the use of power to reward, control, and punish based on these determinations. In concordance with this global change, essentialized constructions of violent and backward Arabs were extended nearly seamlessly to Muslims.

Since race remains a fundamental tool for claiming rewards and organizing discipline in American society—and is something Americans know and understand—these notions of essential human difference have been corporealized, as if they were about color. Thus, race became the operant reference category for a woman voicing opposition to the construction of a mosque in her suburb, when she testified in 2004 at a hearing I observed: "I have no ill remorse for the Muslim race at all. I wish we could all live in peace, but … " (Cainkar 2009) The corporealization is also evident in the actionable but sloppy phenotypic category "Arabs, Muslims, and persons assumed to be Arabs and Muslims," terms without which no analyst can accurately describe the victims of hate crimes and verbal assault in the United States after the 9/11 attacks. The phenotype has become lethal; the first person killed in a post 9/11 hate crime was a Sikh, who was presumed to be "Middle Eastern."

Because the racialization of Arabs is tied to larger American global policies, the domestic aspect of this project is in the manufacture of public consent needed to support, finance, and defend these policies. For this reason, the most noted features of Arab exclusion in the United States are tactical: persistent, negative media representations, denial of political voice, surveillance, policies and strategies targeting their activism, and distortions of Arab and Muslim values, ways of life, and homelands (civilizational distortions). All of these actions are tied to the delegitimation of Arab claims around Palestine and silencing of dissenting voices in order to assert an informational hegemony.

Since the darkening of Arabs began in earnest after the beneficiaries of the US civil rights movement had been determined and the categories of "non-white" and "minority" had been set, Arabs have experienced the double burden of being excluded from the full scope of whiteness *and* from mainstream recognition as people of color. They are therefore still officially white and ineligible for affirmative action (Samhan 1999). As Saliba (1999) notes, while Arab Americans have been victims of racist policies, their experiences have been rendered invisible by dominant discourses about race. Their exclusion has been evident in multicultural pedagogy. Arabs have long been excluded from race and ethnic studies texts and, when mentioned, are often treated differently from other groups (Cainkar 2002). Consider the following quote from a race and ethnic studies textbook (Marger 2003: 165), which implies that, unlike other groups, Arabs are responsible for their own stereotyping:

> Perhaps more serious [than discrimination faced by Muslim women] is the persistence of negative stereotyping that has plagued Middle Easterners in the United States. The activities of *Arab terrorists* in the Middle East and elsewhere *have created* a sinister image of Arab and other Middle Eastern groups—an image that was greatly exacerbated by the attack on the World Trade Center in 2001. [emphasis added]

The exclusion of Arab Americans and their organizations from mainstream vehicles of dissent also left them with few powerful allies from the 1960s onward (although they have had some measurable local successes), allowing their challenges to hostile media representations, text-book biases, and selective policy enforcement to be ignored without repercussions (Zogby 1984). As they stood virtually alone, discrimination and the production of negative images flourished, pointing to the victory of strategies that ensured Arab exclusion from these groups.

Because the formation of Arabs as a unique "racial" group was a process with timing and purpose different from historic American racism, its objective manifestation also differs from that of traditionally subordinated groups: African Americans, Latinos, Asians, and Native Americans. Its impact is not well measured by indices of income, occupation, education, and segregation, because their racialization intervened in the ongoing trajectories of historically successful Arab American communities, and because a large percentage of post-Second World War Arab immigrants came to the United States with significant amounts of human capital. These facts have allowed Arabs to overcome some of the economic outcomes that usually correlate with subordinate status; at the same time, they mask the deep impact such subordinate status has on Arab communities with low levels of human capital.

The ways in which Arabs, Muslims, and persons assumed to be Arabs and Muslims were held collectively responsible for the 9/11 attacks (Cainkar 2009) should alone provide convincing evidence that their racial denouement had been sufficiently sealed before the attacks occurred. The public attribution of collective responsibility for the attacks required an *a priori* understanding that Arabs and Muslims should be seen as monolithic and culturally depraved, as groups racialized earlier were portrayed as obstacles to the progress of manifest destiny and as the white man's burden. In contrast, a primary correlate of whiteness is the attribution of modernity, rationality, and individuality, including individual culpability. When someone who is white commits an act interpreted as wrong or reprehensible, it is depicted by the organs of power as an individual act, one that has no reflection on the values and beliefs of other members of the white population. At the same time, paradoxically, the positive virtues of whiteness are represented as shared characteristics. But the violent act of any Arab or Muslim is rendered to represent entire societies and cultures, portrayed as a mechanical, civilizational act. As with Japanese internment in the United States during the Second World War, these racialized ways of thinking require *a priori* stigmatization and cultural constructions.

Widespread use of the "clash of civilizations" thesis by scholars, filmmakers, publishers, the media, the Christian right, and certain members of the US government—actions similar to what Omi and Winant call racial projects—cemented the social isolation of Arabs and Muslims before 9/11 and established the preconditions for collective backlash after the attacks. Since the backlash has been perpetrated largely by whites, it can be seen as a project further defining the boundaries of whiteness (Cainkar 2009). Research conducted in metropolitan Chicago showed that those who perpetrated these acts were often simultaneously displaying American flags, suggesting symbolic attempts to define the boundaries of the American nation and who lies outside of them.

Studies of the post 9/11 period amply demonstrate the imposition of collective responsibility for the attacks on Arab and Muslim American communities, irrespective of the fact that members of them did not plan or perpetrate them. Without much public discussion or debate, the US government implemented a range of domestic policies in the name of national security and the war on terrorism after the attacks of September 11. Twenty-five of the thirty-seven known government security initiatives implemented between the September 12, 2001, and mid-2003 either explicitly or implicitly targeted US Arabs and Muslims. They started with the round-up and detention of some 1,200 citizens and non-citizens, most of Arab and South Asian descent, who were referred to by the attorney general as "suspected terrorists." Profiling based on looks, names, and being in the wrong place at the wrong time characterize the contexts in which these persons were arrested and detained. None of them was ever convicted on a terrorism charge. Other measures included secret and indefinite detentions, prolonged detention of "material witnesses," closed hearings, secret evidence, government eavesdropping on attorney/client conversations, FBI interviews, wire-tapping, seizures of property, removals of aliens with technical visa violations, and mandatory special registration. Furthermore, public opinion polls showed broad support for these measures. Overall, there was little popular protest against any of these measures outside of Arab and Muslim American organizations and their limited allies. The popular support and lack of broad protest at the time show the degree to which the essentialized representations of Arabs and Muslims—propagated by the media and film industry, uncontested in pedagogy, and reflected in government policies and actions—were effective in constructing Arabs and Muslims as a distinct group (often reified in the artificial concept of "Middle Easterners") who merited a lesser set of rights.

At the very minimum, at least 100,000 Arabs and Muslims living in the United States personally experienced one of these repressive measures. Millions in Iraq and Afghanistan also paid the price in the US-led wars that followed, again pointing to "civilizational" responsibility. Understanding that race is a historically located social construct that has no fixed meaning and that it differentiates between human beings using discourses of human essences, we must ask: can policies that target persons on two continents, in three geographic regions, and through their messiness incorporate persons from three major religions, be considered part of a racial project? The answer is yes, because they use essentialized categories and understandings to create structural outcomes, which in turn become tied in the public's mind to a phenotype. Thus, a global project that included multiple subordinate populations has been amalgamated into a civilizational racial project.

Since the formation of Arabs as a unique racial group (distinct from white) was a socio-political process with timing and purpose different from historic American racism, Arabs have been left in the position of having no racial category (box) that makes sense. Arabs were in the midst of the process that rendered them non-white after the categories of race—White, Black, Hispanic, Asian and Pacific Islander, and Native American—had been set by the US government's Office of Management and Budget (OMB Directive 15). Arab American organizations have been advocating with the US Census Bureau since the 1980s for a category separate from white. Yet, the majority of Arab Muslims interviewed in a post-9/11 study conducted in the metropolitan Chicago viewed their social position in American society as subordinate and translate that status to a non-white racial position in a race-based social hierarchy. The data from this study also showed that when Arabs select the white box it does not necessarily mean that they identify with whiteness.

Conclusion

The racial formation processes experienced by Arab Americans differ in both historical timing and pretext from that of other groups in the United States. Unlike the historical argument of racial superiority and inferiority used to buttress the development of the United States as a country of white privilege, the fall of Arabs from the grace of marginal whiteness is traceable to the later emergence of the United States as a global superpower. The seemingly race-neutral lens of essentialized cultural differences and innate violence was promoted in the media and left to percolate by the educational system, thereby building support for government policies that targeted Arab Americans, justifying their political exclusion. This approach was effective and powerful because, while it buttressed US global policies, it did not appear blatantly racist.

Racial projects that moved Arabs into subordinate status began to clearly mark the Arab American experience in the late 1960s and provided momentum for the foundation of pan-Arab American activist organizations. In the 1990s, when Islamist challenges to American global hegemony became more powerful than Arab nationalism, these essentialized constructions were extended to Muslims and became grander; they became civilizational: Both Arabs and Muslims were represented as persons of inherently different values and dispositions than "Americans." These constructions were understood as race since race is a key category for organizing difference in the United States and is something Americans know and understand.

For decades, the protests of Arab Americans over surveillance and negative representations were silenced. The corporealization of the essentialized Arab/Muslim, embodied in images of dark haired, olive-skinned, and hook-nosed persons, came to life as "Arabs, Muslims, and persons assumed to be Arabs and Muslims" faced widespread attack after 9/11. Notions of collective, civilizational responsibility justified imputing to Arabs and Muslims a collective guilt for the attacks. As persons purportedly of a different civilization, Arabs/Muslims were counterposed to Americans and to whites—they were suspected, unsafe, and virtually circled.

Since the darkening of Arabs began in earnest after the beneficiaries of the US civil rights movement had been determined and the categories of "non-white" and "minority" had been set, Arabs have experienced the double burden of being excluded from whiteness *and* from mainstream recognition as people of color. Their isolation from mainstream vehicles of dissent left them with few powerful allies to contest their treatment in American society, leaving them open targets for collective punishment after the 9/11 attacks on the United States. While many Arab American activists recognized long ago that the road to their political inclusion and an end to the discrimination were in alliances with BIPOC communities, concerted efforts were made to exclude them because of their position on the Israeli military occupation of Palestinian lands. Longtime Arab American activist James Zogby (2107) refers to these measures as "campaigns of pressure" designed to make us "radioactive." Their domestic economic role as urban shopkeepers also placed strains on these relationships. Thankfully, this social and political isolation has changed. As the political right increased its use of Islamophobia for political gain during Barack Obama's first presidential campaign, efforts that continued through the election and presidency of Donald Trump, BIPOC, LGBTQ groups, and progressive white and Jewish organizations increasingly embraced Arab and Muslim Americans in joint solidarity (Ali et al. 2011; Cainkar 2019). By the time President Trump implemented the Muslim ban in 2017, Arabs and Muslims had a wide range of allies, leading in turn to increased solidarity over Palestine (e.g., see the *Journal of Palestine Studies* special issue on Black-Palestinian transnational solidarity).

Viewed over its one-hundred-year history, the Arab American experience is not well explained by prominent theories of race. The reason for this lies in a number of assumptions: that the creation of racially defined subordinate groups is a legacy of the American past (although the consequences of this history endure), and that no new racial groups will be constructed. It follows from these assumptions that no new group will experience downward movement on the color line, because in post-civil rights American society racial projects asserting the essential human difference of certain groups are no longer acceptable. I have shown that racializing processes are not just legacies of the American past, that racist ideas composed of social constructions of essential human differences can be effectively hidden behind new discourses, and that government policies promote these ideas. The fact that such policies are rooted in global matters instead of the domestic distribution of power and resources does not alter the fact that they instigate policing, domestic inequality, civic and political exclusion, stereotyping, and that they incite hate crimes, prejudice, and discrimination.

Notes

1. For the process of becoming white see Roedigger (1991) and Ignatiev (1995).
2. See, for example, Suleiman (1999), McCarus (1994), Abraham and Abraham (1983), Abu-Laban and Suleiman (1989), Bassiouni (1974), Cainkar (1988).
3. Stockton (1994), Lipset and Schneider (1977), and Zogby (1984: 21).

References

Abraham, S. Y. and N. Abraham, eds. (1983), *Arabs in the New World: Studies on Arab-American Communities*, Detroit: Wayne State University.

Abu-Laban, B. and M. Suleiman, eds. (1989), *Arab Americans: Continuity and Change*, Belmont: Association of Arab-American University Graduates.

Alba, R. and V. Nee (2003), *Remaking the American Mainstream: Assimilation and Contemporary Immigration*, Cambridge: Harvard University Press.

Ali, W., E. Clifton, M. Duss, L. Fang, S. Keyes, and F. Shakir (2011), *Fear, Inc.: The Roots of the Islamophobia Network in America*, Washington, DC: Center for American Progress.

Bassiouni, M. C., ed. (1974), *The Civil Rights of Arab-Americans: The Special Measures*, North Dartmouth: Association of Arab-American University Graduates.

Bonacich, E. (1973), "A Theory of Middleman Minorities," *American Sociological Review*, 38 (5): 583–94.

Cainkar, L. (1988), "Palestinian Women in the United States: Coping with Tradition, Change, and Alienation," PhD dissertation, Northwestern University.

Cainkar, L. (2002), "The Treatment of Arabs and Muslims in Race and Ethnic Studies Textbooks," Unpublished paper presented at the Annual Meeting of the American Sociological Association, Atlanta, Georgia, 2002.

Cainkar, L. (2009), *Homeland Insecurity: The Arab American and Muslim American Experience After 9/11*, New York: Russell Sage Foundation Press.

Cainkar, L. (2019), "Islamophobia and the US Ideological Infrastructure of White Supremacy," in I. Zempi and I. Awan (eds.), *Routledge International Handbook of Islamophobia*, 239–51, London: Routledge.

Cainkar, L. and S. Selod (2018), "Race Scholarship and the War on Terror," *Journal of the Sociology of Race and Ethnicity*, 4 (2): 165–77.

Fay, M. A. (1984), "Old Roots-New Soil," in J. Zogby (ed.), *Taking Root Bearing Fruit: The Arab American Experience*, 19–25, Washington, DC: ADC.

Gualtieri, S. (2009), *Between Arab and White*, Palo Alto: Stanford University Press.

Huntington, S. (1996), *The Clash of Civilizations and the Remaking of World Order*, New York: Simon and Schuster.

Ignatiev, N. (1995), *How the Irish Became White*, New York: Routledge.

Immigration and Naturalization Service (1943), U.S. Department of Justice, Immigration and Naturalization Service, "The Eligibility of Arabs to Naturalization," *INS Monthly Review*, 1: 15.

Lipset, S. M. and W. Schneider (1977), "Carter vs. Israel: What the Polls Reveal," *Commentary*, 64 (5): 22.

Marger, M. (2003), *Race and Ethnic Relations: American and Global Perspectives*, Belmont: Wadsworth/Thomson Learning.

McCarus, E., ed. (1994), *The Development of Arab American Identity*, Ann Arbor: University of Michigan Press.

Naber, N. (2000), "Ambiguous Insiders: An Investigation of Arab-American Invisibility," *Ethnic and Racial Studies*, 23 (2): 37–61.

Omi, M. and H. Winant (1994), *Racial Formation in the United States: From the 1960s to the 1990s*, New York: Routledge.

Roediger, D. (1991), *The Wages of Whiteness: Race and the Making of the American Working Class*, New York: Verso.

Saliba, T. (1999), "Resisting Invisibility," in M. W. Suleiman (ed.), *Arabs in America: Building a New Future*, 304–19, Philadelphia: Temple University Press.

Samhan, H. H. (1999), "Not Quite White: Race Classification and the Arab-American experience," in M. W. Suleiman (ed.), *Arabs in America: Building a New Future*, 209–26, Philadelphia: Temple University Press.

Shaheen, J. (1984), *The TV Arab*, Bowling Green: Popular Press.

Shaheen, J. (2001), *Reel Bad Arabs: How Hollywood Vilifies a People*, New York: Olive Branch Press.

Slade, S. (1981), "Image of the Arab in America: Analysis of a Poll on American Attitudes," *Middle East Journal*, 35 (2): 143–62.

Stockton, R. (1994), "Ethnic Archetypes and the Arab Image," in E. McCarus (ed.), *The Development of Arab American Identity*, 119–53, Ann Arbor: University of Michigan Press.

Suleiman, M. (1999), *Arabs in America: Building a New Future*, Philadelphia: Temple University Press.

Winant, H. (2001), *The World Is a Ghetto*, New York: Basic Books.

Zogby, J. (2017), "The History of Anti-Arab Sentiment Is Too Deep, the Pain Too Real," LobeLog, 16 July, https://lobelog.com/the-history-of-anti-arab-sentiment-is-too-deep-the-pain-too-real/.

Middle Eastern Muslims and the Ethical Inclusion of America as a New Homeland

by Mücahit Bilici

When in 1949 Sayyid Qutb, later to become one of the chief ideologues of the Muslim Brotherhood in Egypt, travelled to the United States for graduate studies, his observations of America as a country—and more importantly, as a culture—had a lasting impact on him. His time in small-town America (Greeley, Colorado) literally radicalized this young Egyptian man, creating in him a lifelong revulsion toward the Western societies where he had seen that, despite the accumulation of power and wealth, human lives were wasted on trivial concerns. Upon his return, he wrote *The America I Have Seen* (Qutb 2000 [1951]), a work in which he condemned American society. America, for Qutb, represented everything that Islam was not: one section bears the title, "America: The Peak of Advancement and the Depth of Primitiveness." A decade and a half later, as the number of students coming to the United States to pursue degrees greatly increased thanks to the Immigration and Naturalization Act of 1965, a significant portion of those Muslim immigrants, though much more moderate in their views of America than Sayyid Qutb, nevertheless continued to see America as a culturally impure and non-Islamic way station, if not an outright anti-Islamic land.

Today, however, Muslims in America occupy positions—congressman, journalist, entrepreneur; representative of the nation in science, in sport—that bespeak a deep engagement with their country's welfare, an unselfconscious commitment to its values. There are many American Muslim soldiers, among the most famous being the late Captain Humayun Khan (1976–2004), the son of Khizr and Ghazala Khan whose appearance at the 2016 Democratic National Convention precipitated an early airing of the Muslim-baiting tactics then-Presidential Candidate Trump would use in his ascent to power.[1] Another is Mansoor Shams, a Muslim marine who takes to the street to show Muslim patriotism to non-Muslim Americans by carrying a sign that says: "I'm a Muslim Marine, Ask Me Anything."[2] Many American Muslims are now eager to counter Islamophobia with their visibly Muslim patriotism. The transition from Qutb to Muslim marine is emblematic of the way America has gradually come to be included in the Muslim ethos, first as a legitimate surface and then as a new homeland. This chapter[3] provides a phenomenologically informed account of Muslim constructions of America as homeland. It begins by articulating the concept of home and what it means to feel at home. This

455

conceptual clarification is necessary for a proper understanding of cultural settlement. It continues with a brief inventory of the cultural idioms or topoi with which early Muslim immigrants—and some newly arrived Muslims today—made sense of their presence in America. This diasporic moment and vocabulary change over time as exposure and interaction lead to a more nuanced understanding. In addition to these cultural idioms, this chapter surveys the juridical tools by which Muslims religiously interpret America and engage gradually in ethical inclusion of America as a possible "homeland."

Theorizing the Concept of Homeland

How do we feel at home in a particular place? To put it another way, how do we convert a foreign land into a homeland? Home is where we are free from the judging gaze of strangers. The privacy of home is a needed deprivation (hence privacy) from the gaze of the public. Any land where "dwelling" (Heidegger 1971: 143) takes place becomes home. In the act of dwelling, we appropriate a given space by projecting onto it our subjective being (Levinas 1969: 153). This process continues until our subjective world achieves harmony with the intersubjective world (Berger and Luckmann 1966: 20). The relationship between privacy and publicness—or the subjective world and the objective world—is a two-way street. We come to feel at home when we begin to enjoy an "ontological complicity" between our habitus and the world in which we find ourselves (Bourdieu 2000: 135). As Bourdieu has noted, it is the correspondence between habitus and habitat that makes it possible to feel native (i.e., at home).

For immigrants and other displaced populations, the correspondence or balance that produces nativity is lost and needs to be restored. The immigrant undoes that alienation when she feels at home not only in the privacy of her home but also in the public culture of her society. Continuity between home and homeland thus requires the projection of what is private and subjective (i.e., the household, what is Muslim, communal) onto the public and intersubjective (i.e., the city, what is American, national). This native state of security—which tradition typically establishes via kinship—now in the modern world has to be achieved through multiple layers of citizenship.

Sociologists from Marx to Simmel early on warned modern societies against the damage done by disequilibrium between subjective and intersubjective cultures (Frisby and Featherstone 1997: 55–75; Simmel 1971). Simmel's "crisis in culture" is in many ways a pioneering study of homelessness in the general sense of the "homeless mind" of modernity (Berger, Berger and Kellner 1974). The process of alienation from the environment—or in Simmel's own terms, the loss of equilibrium between subjective culture and objective culture—was for him a tragic consequence of modernity, the result of industrialization and urbanization. In the present case, a similar alienation arises from the displacements of globalization. Any given society is an arena of reality construction (Berger and Luckmann 1966) where individual members share in the production of objective reality or common sense (*sensus communis*). The transformation of the Middle Eastern Muslim discourses on America needs to be construed in relation to the shifting sentiments Muslims experience as they overcome their initial sense of anomie—their loss of *nomos*.

Muslim immigrants who find themselves either at the frontiers or outside of the juridical limits of the traditional Muslim homeland (*dar al Islam*) experience a sense of alienation. Although we know from the recent literature on the idea of the "Muslim world" (Aydin 2017) that current conceptions of a unitary Muslim political geography are a relatively recent invention produced by colonial-era Muslim politics, the experience of not living in a Muslim-majority environment does give rise to new questions. For a long time, the Muslim imagination of "homeland" clearly did not include Europe or America, as Qutb's discourse showed. But the Middle East is no longer in the Middle East. The presence of significant diasporic communities in Europe and America has altered the Muslim sense of *dar al Islam*. That is precisely why Muslim communities can harbor such seemingly contradictory views about America, running the gamut from Anti-Americanism to American patriotism. What I am interested in here is the process through which those Muslims who once saw America as a place of "chaos" or "war" eventually came to embrace America as Islamic. As a "discursive tradition" (Asad 2009), Islam lends itself to historically specific reinterpretations across time and space.

Outside the Muslim Domicile

Medieval Muslim jurists developed a binary opposition to distinguish the legal status of Muslim-controlled lands from the rest of the world. They designated as *dar al Islam* (abode of Islam, abode of peace) the lands where Islam was dominant or had been naturalized as mainstream culture. By that classification, all other places fell under the category of *dar al harb* (abode of war, abode of chaos) or *dar al kufr* (abode of disbelief).[4] In this conception, *dar al Islam* becomes a spatial or geographic projection of the Islamic sacred canopy. Scholars have different opinions as to whether the canopy is held up by an Islamic political rule or by an Islamic mainstream culture even when the ruler is not necessarily Islamic (Al-Alwani 2003: 28; Ramadan 2002: 166). What is decisive in either case is whether a certain land has been subject to Islamic *nomos* and thus becomes conducive to an unrestricted, free practice of Islam. In short, *dar al Islam* describes a legal order (and not necessarily a political one) where geography is codified through the imaginary inscription of Islamic law. The remainder of that geography is mentally "nihilated" in order to create the sharp contrast that preserves "mental hygiene" (Berger and Luckmann 1966: 156; Zerubavel 1991: 37). This spiritual appropriation of land finds still another abstract expression in the juridical order of things. Identification of *qibla*, the direction of Mecca, is yet another form of religious appropriation of land, that is, introduction of *nomos*.[5]

As a juridical sphere, *dar al Islam* refers to the pacified, codified space enclosed within the canopy. Muslims living within *dar al Islam* are inhabitants of a familiar abode and members of a bounded community. This sphere that is under public law and familiar for jurisprudential purposes is surrounded by its constitutive other, *dar al harb*. What remains outside, therefore, becomes an extrajuridical, agonistic sphere. In that sense, *dar al harb* is similar to the Greek conception of "barbarian lands." Muslims venture into this unfamiliar abode only at their spiritual peril.

Concerned with the protection of Islamic identity, the classical Muslim jurists saw no reason why Muslims should move to *dar al harb* permanently. They strongly discouraged people from leaving the abode of Islam unless their departure was due to *darura* (necessity).[6] This extrajuridical sphere was thus incorporated into the legal canopy through the state of emergency; stay in that sphere fell under the paradigm of *exception*.

Darura or necessity occupies a special place in all legal traditions because it is the foundation of exception (Agamben 2005: 24). As a limit concept, it is the borderline between juridical order and bare life, between facticity and norms (Habermas 1996). Where public law (in this case, Islam) ends, political fact (the agonistic sphere) begins. Therefore, law melts under the conditions of necessity, as implied by the ancient maxim *necessitas legem non habet* [necessity has no law] (Agamben 2005: 1). Necessity has the power to render the illicit (*haram*) licit (*halal*). But this is not generalizable: necessity justifies only specific, individual cases of transgression through exception.[7]

The movement of Muslims from *dar al Islam* to *dar al harb* is a movement from inside legal order to outside of it, from law to exception. Law has two fundamental elements: norm and decision (Schmitt 1976: 10). In the state of exception, that is in *dar al harb*, the decision remains while the norm recedes. The new environment does not lend itself to the applicability of the norm developed inside the canopy and demands (a new) decision, an act of construction. At that very moment, the agency attributed to the law through reification falls back into the hands of the lawmaker.

The movement from rule (norm) to exception (decision) shifts our attention from the law itself to the lawmaker(s). What had been given, now becomes an explicit object of human construction. It is a shift from an already naturalized, habitualized reality to a reality that is witnessed at the moment of its construction by human subjects.

Therefore, as will become evident later in this chapter, the analogies made by Muslims themselves to the time of the Prophet Muhammad are not in vain: there are very real similarities between the contemporary frontiers (margins) of Islam and its center, its beginning. The similarities are both temporal (*hijra*, the early migration of Muslims and the first establishment of Islam)[8] and spatial (choosing *qibla* and operating on a land that is not yet *dar al Islam*). Stepping outside the canopy is therefore tantamount to a return to the pre-history of the canopy. At the frontiers, where *nomos* is absent, there is an originary indistinction (chaos, anomie). Here, exception reveals the historicity and contingency of the law. At the spatial margins of Islam, Muslims have to reenact what those who codified Islam in Muslim lands did many centuries ago. As Michel de Certeau has observed, "other lands restore to us what our own culture has seen fit to exclude from its own discourse" (De Certeau 1984: 50).

There are two possibilities for those who find themselves outside the canopy: they can either extend the canopy to cover them or engage in the construction of a new one. Extending the canopy under the paradigm of exception (*darura*) may be done for individual necessities, but if a large number of people take up residence not temporarily but permanently in what early jurists designated as *dar al harb*, can they still rely on *darura* as a paradigm?

The paradigm of *darura* enabled Muslims to make brief forays into *dar al harb*. Now that Muslims have permanently settled in what used to be seen as *dar al harb*, they have to transform necessity into law—bare life into canopy—and cultivate *nomos* on an anomic space. As the examples I give later will clarify, the movement from canopy to anomie is always temporary: it inevitably ends with arrival at a new canopy. Canopy construction, which is the construction of new reality, is similar to dwelling in that it has a temporal character. To put it bluntly, a guest who stays for too long is no longer a guest but a lodger. Whether temporal or spatial, the anomic liminality of *darura* expires either with a return to the canopy or the emergence of a new one.

So far, in my discussion of *darura*, the zone of exception, I have touched upon the relationship between *darura* and law and its manifestations in time and space. Before concluding this section, I shall briefly explain the reason why it came to prominence and the type of ethos *darura* engenders.

As a space of unenforceability of law or dispensation from the application of law, *darura* implies the impossibility of experiencing a given place as a fully justified homeland. Thus, it works as a temporary protective juridical shield (like a raincoat) for limited exposure to *dar al harb*. *Darura* gained jurisprudential prominence in modern times as a result of the processes that caused (dis)placement of Muslims into non-Muslim lands. These processes include colonialism in the past and globalization and Muslim immigration in the present day.

A juridical term designating the condition of "crisis times" and "unhomely places," *darura* has a particular ethos. This ethos is a "deficient mode of care" in the Heideggerian sense (Heidegger 1962: 83). The ethics of *darura* is negative. It demands avoidance, minimal involvement, and unsettlement. In a stricter sense, this ethos is a diasporic ethos, where home/land is elsewhere and the heart is there. In the next section, I give a quick overview of some prominent topoi of Muslim diasporic culture. Each topos reveals a certain aspect of the experience of Muslim immigrants.

Muslim Diasporic Imagination and the Justification of Mobility

Under the conditions of immigration, Muslims are displaced and disembedded from their original national environments. Diasporic conditions trigger the release of some Muslim idioms from their otherwise marginal status and pull them to the surface of the

Muslim imagination. There are several prominent root-paradigms (Turner 1974: 67) that immigrant Muslims in America employ in making sense of their experience. These include *hijra* (the Prophet Muhammad's migration from Mecca to Medina), *ummah* (the universal Muslim community), *dawah* (mission or propagation of Islam), and *jihad* (struggle, just war).

When the Prophet Muhammad and his followers were persecuted in Mecca, he migrated to the nearby city of Medina in the year 622 CE. This event occupies such a central place in the Muslim imagination that it marks the starting point of the Muslim calendar (called the *Hijri* calendar). *Hijra,* the movement from Mecca to Medina, is understood as a flight from chaos and oppression to a place of freedom that represents "the city" and "civilization" all at once. The Prophet's *hijra* thus constitutes the primary referent for the Muslim topos of *hijra,* migration. There is also a second event from the early days of Islam that contributes to the term's symbolic meaning: the migration of Muslim refugees to Abyssinia (present-day Ethiopia) in 615 CE.

Hijra is the primary idiom for Muslim immigrants who seek to frame their displacement—voluntary or not—in religious terms. It is not only the movement from one place to another or departure from one's native land that makes these historical events relevant to contemporary migrants, but also the fact that the destinations were in both cases non-Muslim. Thus, *hijra* gained prominence among Muslims in the United States as a way of providing a framework for their contemporary experience as immigrants (Haddad and Lummis 1987: 156). African-American Muslims even interpret their experience of slavery with reference to *hijra* and call *hijra* "The Greatest Migration" (Dannin 2002). At the other end of the spectrum, a fringe radical group of Muslim immigrants based in Britain employs the self-identification *Al-Muhajiroun* (the emigrants) (Wiktorowicz 2005).

The concept of *ummah* designates the global community of Muslims (Mandaville 2003; Roy 2006). It also refers to the community of followers of any prophet. Some Muslim scholars link *ummah* to the concept to *shahada* (witnessing). "The greatness of the Islamic *ummah* is to be understood in the fact that it is a community of the middle path which must bear witness to the faith before all mankind" (Ramadan 2002: 158–9). A non-territorial concept, it allows Muslims to transcend their ethnic, linguistic, and racial differences. In this imagined community, whose members are tied to one another through exposure to the scripture and belief in one God, Muslims relate to each other across time and space. In the words of Benedict Anderson,

> The strange physical juxtaposition of Malays, Persians, Indians, Berbers and Turks in Mecca is something incomprehensible without an idea of their community in some form. The Berber encountering the Malay before the *Kaaba* must, as it were, ask himself: "Why is this man doing what I am doing, uttering the same words that I am uttering, even though we cannot talk to one another?"

> There is only one answer, once one has learnt it: "Because *we* ... are Muslims".
>
> *(Anderson 1991: 54)*

Muslim experience of America is often compared to the Muslim experience in Mecca because Muslims discover and feel the extreme diversity within the Muslim community both during their pilgrimage in Mecca and upon their arrival in America. It is at that moment that the concept of *ummah* gains prominence as a way of acknowledging and overcoming differences. The appeal of the concept of *ummah* comes from both the diversity of Muslim communities and their minority status vis-à-vis non-Muslim majority society and the consequent need for solidarity.

Another key topos is *dawah*, which means religious propagation, fulfillment of the religious obligation of representing the faith to outsiders. *Dawah* is the primary mode of relating to the outside of the Muslim community. *Dawah* is not limited to proselytizing, but can include charity work and participation in community service. As much as it targets outsiders, the more immediate motivation for its deployment in a foreign setting is to protect the identity of insiders. As such it becomes a means of preserving religious identity and authenticity. It is an internally articulated means of engaging with the social environment. This sense of *dawah* is particularly relevant, for instance, for members of Muslim Student Association chapters on university campuses. As a female undergraduate Muslim student at the University of Michigan, Dearborn, once told me: "I am Muslim. I wear my Muslim identity wherever I go. Every action I make publicly is an act of *dawah*. It is especially important to me because I know that everything I do, every stance that I take, reflects the entire Muslim *ummah* whether I want it or not."

Of all the terms discussed here, *jihad* looms largest in the American psyche. It is a contested concept for both Muslims and non-Muslims. Jihad refers to the constant structuration of the self and the world along the lines of Islam. It literally means struggle; it is the equivalent of self-discipline in Protestant cultures. The concept covers a variety of struggles, ranging from spiritual self-restraint to the collective execution of a just war. Recent uses of the term in ethnic nationalism and global terrorism have, however, undermined its legitimacy in the eyes of non-Muslims.[9] Muslims themselves, in turn, employ the term increasingly reluctantly and uncomfortably. Yet they cannot do away with it, since it is part of Islam.

These key idioms have almost nothing to do with America *per se* as a destination for Muslim immigrants. They are root-paradigms that help Muslims make sense of their mobility/movement. It should be stressed that the prominence the terms enjoy here is absent in Muslim majority lands. The exception would be places where colonialism has had a disproportionate impact and thus induced the feeling of being a minority. Although American Muslims use these topoi from early on, they are like a certificate that authorizes their departure but does not deal with their destination. These topoi are extensions of old homelands; they hardly touch America.

Evolution of Muslim Perceptions of America

Immigrant Muslims' encounter with America starts well before their arrival in America, because America has already entered their minds as a phenomenon. The portrait that Muslims have of America is usually not based on direct experience, but on powerful images. America is a non-Muslim, arguably a Christian country. Is America *dar al harb*? And if so is it religiously permissible to stay in America for an extended period of time or even permanently? Some Muslims ask these questions, others do not. Not all Muslims are interested in religious justification of their presence in America. Some might not even be aware of the juridical terms discussed below. Moreover, some of them might be aware yet choose to ignore them in the face of some incongruity between the terms' implications and the reality of their own lives. People can choose to place themselves outside this particular juridical question by rejecting its relevance or avoid it altogether as a theoretical nuisance. Whether they embrace the relevance of the question or not, however, all Muslims engage in interpretation and produce a certain perspective on America (Haddad 2004: 32; Leonard 2003: 154). The fact that this question might not be an issue at all for some Muslims, of course shows the limits of religious discourse in the lives of individuals. For some people, even self-professed believers, Islam as a religion or Islamic law as a source of normativity carry little weight in determining the ways in which individual lives are lived in their worldly settings. However, given my focus on the legitimation or justification *within* religious discourse of Muslim presence in America, I limit my discussion to those who at least recognize the existence of the juridical terms analyzed here.

These questions have come to occupy a central place in American Muslim discourse. Especially after 9/11, according to an American Muslim pundit, such questions create a moral dilemma that needs to be resolved:

> Many Muslims who see Islam and the U.S. in a state of conflict have enormous problems in beginning to think of themselves as American Muslims. They want the prosperity and the freedom of America, but not its foreign policy or its liberal culture ... There are no simple solutions to this moral dilemma. The theological discussion will have to take American Muslims beyond the *dar-al-Islam* (house of peace) and *dar-al-harb* (house of war) dichotomy.
>
> *(Khan 2002: 10)*

Early Muslims considered living in American society a dangerous venture. It meant the risk of assimilation and moral decay. The students who constituted the kernel of American Muslim identity in the 1960s and 1970s wanted only to avoid the negative influence of American society (Schumann 2007: 11). This perception, however, changed over time (Mattson 2003: 03).

The terms or rather juridical tools available to Muslims for making sense of American space have outflanked the binary of *dar al Islam* versus *dar al harb*. The dichotomy, which existed so long as it was not challenged by direct experience, becomes problematic and insufficient when Muslims are actually in America. Reality interferes. The alternative or complementary concepts that were historically marginalized in the production of this binary are remembered, re-appropriated, and even invented by Muslims. Therefore, in addition to *dar al harb* and *dar al Islam,* Muslims in minority settings have brought back several notions, the most important of which are *dar al dawah* (abode of call, propagation) and *dar al ahd* (abode of treaty, contract). In place of the *dar al harb* versus *dar al Islam* dichotomy, we now have a continuum of *dar*s (abodes): (1) *Dar al Harb* (abode of war), (2) *Dar al Dawah* (abode of mission), (3) *Dar al Ahd* (abode of accord), and (4) *Dar al Islam* (abode of Islam).

This continuum, of course, implies no teleology. It is rather a spectrum of juridical terms providing religious meaning or justification for different discourses Muslims develop with respect to America. There are two broad paradigms under which we can classify the major juridical tools. They are either mobilized under the paradigm of *darura* or they are construed as part of an existing legal order or products of a newly articulated code that caters to the needs of Muslims in minority contexts. The first two categories of abode (*dar al harb* and *dar al dawah*), which fall under the paradigm of *darura*, are diasporic with respect to the American setting. The last two (*dar al ahd* and *dar al Islam*) come under the paradigm of law and are employed by Muslims in their post-diasporic moment, those who see or want to see America as home.

Let us now turn to the specifics of each of these categories. What are the consequences of perceiving America as an abode of war (*dar al harb*)? Who sees it as such and when? Such questions will be answered for each of the four categories used by Muslims as juridical "toolkit" (Swidler 1986). These juridical terms can be interpreted as symbolic stages in the Muslim internalization of America as a habitat.

Dar al Harb: An Impossible Homeland

For the perspective that sees America as abode of war *(dar al harb)*, America is *external* to Islam, and, as such, it is a source of anxiety and cultural threat. This perception is based on a lack of knowledge about what goes on inside America. America, in this view, is a monolith—completely profane and without legitimately perceptible nomos. America is a black box that can be treated only in its totality since it can be grasped in this understanding only from without. The ideal type for this conception is a visitor; it can be said to represent the common understanding of Muslim immigrants in the 1970s.

Changing immigration policies in the 1960s and Cold War politics opened the door for Muslim immigrants and students. Interestingly enough, the students from Muslim countries who came to America to study not only created the nucleus of a Muslim community, but also laid the ground for the formation of a number of major organizations, including the Muslim Students Association (MSA) and later the Islamic Society of North America (ISNA). Those Muslims who happened to be in America in this period believed that they were there under *darura*. They saw themselves as an outpost of Islam inside American space. They were geographic and cultural orphans, people out of place. Their plans to go back home kept them always in a precarious position, unsettled. *Dar al harb* (abode of war) characterized the perception of those Muslims, mostly students from Muslim countries, who were either religious to start with or became religious due to diasporic pressures during their studies at American institutions of higher education in the 1960s and 1970s. They set out to acquire America's science and technology without getting contaminated by its culture. Their plan to return home after the completion of their studies and their desire to avoid the influence of American culture defined their attitude toward American space. These students relied on funding from their home countries and were oriented toward their homelands.[10]

America was simply a meeting ground for Muslims from various countries. To the extent that care and involvement produce space (the world) for the situated subject, their American space was very small; their primary *concern* was political and cultural solidarity with the Muslim world and its rehabilitation through the acquisition of American scientific knowledge. The institutions built in this era catered to students and were concerned almost exclusively with the preservation of Islamic identity against the corrosive influence of American society. Publications of the time, such as *MSA News* and later *Islamic Horizons,* depicted the American environment as an undifferentiated culture having nothing to do with Islam (Schumann 2007: 16). America was technologically superior but morally bankrupt, a perception that echoed Sayyid Qutb's image of America. In the eyes of these identity-centric, diasporic Muslims, America was at worst an impure place, at best a neutral space for the encounter and education of Muslim activists from Islamic countries.

Their American location gave them room for maneuver and allowed them to mobilize technical and ideological resources for what Benedict Anderson calls "long-distance nationalism" (Anderson 1998: 58), which in this case meant long-distance Islamism. Even the notion of *dawah* which was activated in response to displacement— its temporariness notwithstanding—was an *introvert dawah* directed at students themselves. The purpose was to have "an impact on homelands by educating Islamic activists and preparing them for their future return" (Schumann 2007: 18). Inspired by the Islamic revivalist movements in Muslim countries, they interpreted their own experiences in terms of mobility, movement, or mobilization. The idea of returning home turned their stay into a prolonged transit. America was not a place to dwell; it was not home.

Today, most Muslims would reject the idea of America as *abode of war* and might even contest the applicability of the term altogether. As the community gains literacy in American culture and politics, such questionable concepts are removed from public display, an interesting phenomenon that Andrew Shryock observes among Dearborn Arab and Muslim communities and analyses under the rubric of "cultural intimacy" (Shryock 2004: 10–11). The culture of "America as *dar al harb*," survives, therefore, mostly in old community literature and biographical narratives about "Muslims then." One would expect the culture of *dar al harb* to have disappeared entirely over the last couple of decades, since today almost every Muslim sees Muslim presence in America as permanent. But it has not. I discovered this persistence when I talked to the imam of a mosque[11] in Detroit in 2007. This mosque, which has an Arabic name, self-identifies as *salafi*.[12] In terms of congregation, it appears to be predominantly Yemeni. Imam Talib, also from Yemen, is on a long-term visa and has been here for the last few years. One of the striking things about this mosque is that the imam does not speak any English at all and delivers his sermons only in Arabic. He does, however, use a translator. I interviewed him through one of the people who help translate his sermons and weekend classes. The following exchanges are selections from the interview.

I started by asking his opinion about the English language, since we were not able to communicate in it.

>Question: When one immigrates to America, a lot of things change. For example, here all the Muslims speak English. What do you think about the English language?

>Answer: English is good for giving *dawah*. When I came here there were some brothers who could speak both languages [English and Arabic]. That made it easy for me to do my own Islamic studies. If I go to English language classes, it will take a lot of driving. Also you know classes are mixed, men and women ... Muslims should learn this language, of course. If you do not know the language, it is going to be hard. We should give *dawah*.

>Kids in this country get very little Islam. Here in this masjid we try to focus more on Islam so that kids don't get *shirkiyat* and *khurafat* [violations of monotheism and deviation]. We want them to stay away from *shirk* [worshipping things other than the one God]. This is our focus.

>Q: What do you think about the *dar al harb* and *dar al Islam* distinction? What is America in your view?

A: America is a *kuffar* country [the land of disbelief, *dar al kufr* is synonymous with *dar al harb*]. It is a matter of who is dominant. The dominant identity in this country is *kuffar*. If we can have *dawah*, that is the most important thing. We need to show the people what Islam is. We should teach them.

Q: But Muslims have more freedoms here than in Muslim countries. Think of *hijab*, for example.

A: It is true we have more freedoms but it does not mean this country is better than the Muslim countries.

Q: Since you have plans to return to Yemen and won't stay in this country, what do you say to Muslims here, those who are going to stay.

A: I say, if they can go back, it is better for them. The future seems very hard here. It is hard to live as a family. It is hard. If something happens that will be good: if the government *puts all the Muslims in one place*, that will be good. Then we can live without mixing.

I left the mosque somewhat bewildered. I thought I had observed the whole spectrum of Muslims in the American context, but this was a truly extraordinary case: although many American Muslims believe that they live in "electronic internment" since 9/11, I had never met one who considered internment—be it electronic surveillance or physical imprisonment like what happened to Japanese-Americans during the Second World War—to be desirable. Here was a Muslim who was "in" America and believed that the best thing that could happen to Muslims living in this country was to be placed in a ghetto or camp. Interestingly enough, the Detroit-Dearborn area is currently the only place in America that could approximate a ghetto (Abraham and Shryock 2000). Yet the concentration of Arab Muslims in the area still seemed insufficient to this imam, as far as the protection of Islamic identity was concerned. The only justification for Muslims to stay in this country was *dawah*; otherwise, America was a *kuffar* (infidel) country, *dar al harb* (an abode of war), and to protect their religion, Muslims should leave as soon as possible. America was an insecure place and could never qualify as a homeland. This insecurity was not so much about civil rights and liberties—concerns shared by many Muslims—but about preservation of the faith and spiritual purity.

Most of the previous decades' Muslim immigrants—and some in the early stage of their immigration today—held a slightly tamer view of the American environment and the role of Muslims, perceiving themselves as an outpost of Muslim geography in an alien land. As long as their presence is temporary, they comfortably continue to hold the view that America can be *abode of war*. This ideal typical perception of America as *abode of war/chaos* changes only under the influence of direct experience and interaction. The concept of *dawah* (mission, call to Islam), which together with *darura* (necessity) is one of the two justifications for being in America, eventually outgrows the juridical category of *abode of war* and becomes the point of reference in itself. Limited engagement in the form of *dawah* ultimately leads to a perception of America as an open field for unlimited *dawah*. Dawah is no longer directed at other Muslims but the non-Muslim other. This change of orientation also marks the transition to the next stage, where America is perceived as a land of mission.

Dar al Dawah: An Outpost in "the Land of Possibilities"

As *abode of war,* America represented the absolute outside, the anti-homeland. As *abode of mission*, while still external to Islam, America is recognized as an adjacent space. It becomes a *frontier*. It is a target of concernful interest or a destination of risky spiritual venture. In this conception, America is a field of exploration that is at once dangerous and potentially beneficial. The most significant change this new perception entails is that America is no longer a monolith. The first, weak signs of differentiation emerge as the newcomer either reserves judgment about America or approaches it with caution. His presence is most likely temporary or in its early stages.

In the stage of *abode of mission*, the notion of *dawah* (mission) undergoes a shift in terms of orientation: now it explicitly targets non-Muslims. The introvert conception is replaced by an extrovert one as some involvement with America becomes possible. The primary concern is still the preservation of identity through a narrowly defined engagement with American society. Even though America is still in moral decay, Muslims are now seen as capable of contributing to its positive transformation: their reluctant involvement comes to designate a desirable partial participation. A shift also occurs from activism which targets Muslim students to activism aimed at contributing to an otherwise threatening environment. In this transformation, the Qur'anic idea of "promoting good and preventing evil" becomes a touchstone.

If previously the Muslim world and America were polar opposites, this time around, even though they are still largely monoliths, they each acquire negative and positive aspects the problems of the Muslim world and some virtues of America are acknowledged. The Muslim world or past homelands now lose their sharpness and complexity in the mind's eye of the immigrant, and this distancing from the past homeland is compensated by the development of a comparably limited "nearness" to the American environment. In terms of community development, this approach characterizes the 1980s. Early signs of recognizing America as a "nation of immigrants" emerge and the possibility of somehow fitting in becomes imaginable for the Muslim immigrant.

Yet even though the beginnings of settlement are observed, America's Muslims are still diasporic: their settlement has not yet fully disengaged itself from a movement that began elsewhere. Muslims who were in transit are now settled into "mobility" and outreach. In the process, *darura* (exception) becomes a conditional "stay." One can stay, but only to perform *dawah*! That is, a shift occurs from conditional visit to conditional stay. A necessity-based risk has become an opportunity-based one.

As a consequence of the shift, calling America *abode of war* becomes increasingly difficult and the term itself is seldom employed. As Mustapha, a young Muslim I interviewed, stated, "If America is *dar al harb* [abode of war], what does that add to you? What matters more is whether you as a Muslim change yourself and your environment." The formerly monolithic and impure surface of America is now seen as receptive to the inscription of Islam. Along the same lines, an essay published in 1985 in *Islamic Horizons* claims that,

> We cannot continue to throw out the baby of *dawah* with the bathwater of our disaffection towards this government and society. For clearly we have been placed here with a purpose ... If we plan to leave tomorrow, we still have today to work, to do our share ... .
> *(Omar 1985: 10, quoted in Schumann 2007: 21)*

At this juncture, Muslim institutions either change their orientation or institutions with a new orientation emerge in their stead: institutions oriented toward "non-American" Muslims in America and the Muslim world are replaced by a "global Muslim" discourse with some localization. The *Islamic Society of North America* (ISNA), established in 1982 in response to the fact that more and more of the students who had planned to return to their countries of origin ended up staying and forming families in the United States, is a perfect example of this new transformation. As the Muslim community ceased to be identified solely with university students, ISNA would cater to a population still diasporic in outlook but now inclined toward settlement. Its institutions begin to engage the American environment, but only on the grounds of ideology and a self-interest aimed solely at the dissemination of Islam. Still this reluctant settlement and narrow involvement transform the nature of the Muslim community from being a thin "outpost" of Muslims in an alien land to a "thicker" extension of the global Muslim community at large. To sum up, the ideological transition from 1970s to 1980s is one from students to families, from MSA to ISNA, from avoidance to protectionism through partial involvement.

Though this mindset had its heyday in the 1980s, it survives among American Muslims to this day. I saw it reflected in some of my conversations with community leaders. One such example was Imam[13] Haroon of Masjidun-Nur [Mosque of Light] in Detroit. Established in 1978, this inner-city mosque is at present predominantly African American. Although he was very conservative and introverted, his views about the American setting were more nuanced than those of the imam in the previous section. When asked about the distinction between *abode of war* and *abode of Islam,* he preferred to avoid the binary and emphasized instead the perception of America as "a land of possibilities" in the following manner:

> I have been able to pray at the airport, at the mall or at the bus station. Since I've been here it has been very easy to live Islam. I don't know what category America fits but we are free to live Islam and do *dawah*. Sometimes people are more welcoming.
>
> [America] is Allah's country. We're here to invite people to Islam. We are here for guidance. Some scholars say it is not permissible to stay in a non-Muslim land. *But what about those who are from here*? Where will they go? The earth is vast and for making a living anywhere is OK. Some *sahaba*s [companions of the prophet] did both living and *dawah*.

One can see in Imam Haroon's rather plaintive question, "But what about those who are from here?" the beginning of a possibility of Muslims being "from" America rather than merely "in" America. This nucleus of localization will soon blossom into other conceptions of America, but at this stage it remains an early sign of Americanness finding a foothold inside Islam. Despite the relative openness to and appreciation of the American environment, his response to my question on interfaith activism, which I use as an index of involvement with the social environment, revealed the striking ambivalence produced by the perception of America as *abode of mission*: "No, we don't do interfaith activities. My personal opinion, I don't feel the need for it. We respect but don't talk ... The main thing is *dawah*, it is an imperative for us."

Dar al dawah basically takes Muslim immigrants just up to the threshold of settlement; it marks the limit of the diasporic orientation. The negative connection with the environment (through the juridical device of *darura* (necessity)) is now replaced by a narrowed yet positive connection (based on a redefinition of *dawah* (mission)). At this point, the neat division "anything Muslim is good, anything American is evil" starts to erode. Yet the Muslim subject is still mentally located in another homeland and has only a limited justification for his presence in America.

Dar al Ahd: From Mission to Dialogue

As *dar al ahd* (abode of accord) America is *neighbor* to Islam and a party to an accord; it is a source of mutual benefit. America is religiously justified and protected by religious laws such as the injunction that Muslims must obey the law of the land wherever they live. America thus becomes even more differentiated and emerges as a peaceful opportunity space for Muslims, but one that has not yet been fully internalized or naturalized. The benefits and opportunities now supersede the risks. This conception's ideal type is a resident: his presence is permanent with the reservation that it might one day be possible that he will have to leave. *Abode of accord* represents a cautious embrace and the early stage of settlement. Many Muslims interpret *abode of accord* with relative comfort due to its resonance with the social contract theories of American society. *Abode of accord*, therefore, symbolizes the first cultural encounter of the immigrant Muslim with American citizenship. While for *abode of war* and *abode of mission*, the Muslim just happens to be in America, in the conception of *abode of accord* he begins to see himself as part of a larger society in which he, too, has a stake. It thus allows Muslims to imagine a place of their own inside American society, creating the possibility of an American Muslim cultural "ghetto"—in the positive sense of the term within a liberal society. More specifically, *abode of accord* represents a communitarian understanding of membership in American society, where private autonomy is slightly expanded and buttressed as an adequate domain for the survival of Islamic identity. The sense of belonging that *abode of accord* generates is located in the spectrum between protected subject and full citizen.

Muslims who see their new environment in this way no longer hold themselves apart from majority society, but still preserve their distinct identity. They share with the rest of the society a culture in which Islam seeks a place. The idea of *abode of accord* therefore lends itself to a spectrum of existence from reluctant participation to hopeful and safe engagement with the American environment.

In 1999, the Mauritanian sheikh Abdallah Bin Bayyah was invited by the Zaytuna Institute, a neo-traditional center of Islamic learning in California, to speak to American Muslims in the Bay Area. He delivered his lecture in Arabic, translated by American convert Shaykh Hamza Yusuf. Interestingly enough, the sheikh begins his lecture, a series of juridical recommendations for Muslims living as a minority in non-Muslim lands, with the recognition of this fact:

> In contrast to Muslims living in the dominant Muslim world at large, you are, in many ways, strangers in a strange land. The Messenger of Allah said that the conditions of the stranger are blessed conditions. It also means "they have paradise" for bearing the burden of alienation. An Arab proverb is, "oh stranger in a strange land, be a man of courtesy and cultivation." The meaning of estrangement [is not that] you should not work with others or that you should avoid the dominant society and distance yourselves completely from it.[14]

After examining the needs and conditions of Muslims in diaspora, the sheikh discusses the problem of the status of lands where Muslims are minorities. He criticizes the dichotomy of *abode of war* and *abode of Islam*.

> Most people think that the world is divided into two abodes, the abode of peace and the abode of war. The abode of peace is the land of the Muslims, *dar al-Islam*, and the abode of war is everywhere else ... This idea is wrong. There are three abodes: there is the abode of peace, the abode of war, and then there is the *abode of treaty* where there is a contractual agreement between two abodes.

The sheikh then explains the relationship between immigrant Muslims in America and their country of immigration by referring to his entry into the country. His personal border crossing becomes an illustration of entry into *abode of accord/ contract*.

> For instance, when I came into this country, they issued me a visa, and I signed something. In the issuance of the visa and my signing of it, a legally binding contract occurred. It was an agreement that when I came into this country, I would obey the laws and would follow the restrictions that this visa demanded that I follow. This was a contractual agreement that is legally binding according even to the divine laws. In looking at this, we have to understand that the relationship between the Muslims living in this land and the dominant authorities in this land is a relationship of peace and contractual agreement—of a treaty. This is a relationship of dialogue and a relationship of giving and taking.

As far as Muslim community leadership is concerned, the idea of *abode of accord* appears to have been the dominant conception in the 1990s. Since 9/11, however, it has been criticized by Muslim public intellectuals who urge a complete transition to the conception of America as an *abode of Islam*. Muqtedar Khan, a Muslim professor of political science who became prominent after 9/11, finds the idea of *abode of accord* an inadequate and morally problematic position for Muslims in the United States (Khan 2002: 8). From another perspective, Tariq Ramadan, a European Muslim intellectual, finds the same term untenable due to its dependence on the old dichotomy of *abode of war/abode of Islam*. Instead he proposes *dar al dawah* (abode of call)—using a sense different from my own discussion above—and he even calls for a total abandonment of the idea of *abodes*: "At a time when we are witnessing a strong current of globalization, it is difficult to refer to the notion of *dar* (abode) unless we consider the whole world as an abode. Our world has become a small village and, as such, it is henceforth *an open world*" (Ramadan 2002: 147).

Dar al Islam: "Thinking without Accent"

Encouraging Muslim political participation, Muslim political activist and president of the American Muslim Alliance, Agha Saeed, wrote that Muslims need generations who "not only speak without accent but also think without accent" (Saeed 2002: 55). To him, "thinking without accent" means changing the orientation of Muslims in America from preoccupation with the Muslim world to taking an interest in American domestic issues. Criticizing immigrant generations for being too much invested in goings-on in their countries of origin, Saeed finds hope in new generations of Muslims who would instead regard America as both home and homeland.

In the conception of *abode of Islam* or *abode of peace*, the ideal type is a citizen, a person who feels at home in America, thereby achieving equilibrium or symmetry between the subjective culture (Muslim identity) and the objective culture (American culture). America no longer remains a mismatched habitat for a Muslim habitus developed elsewhere. Rather it becomes an American Muslim habitus in an American habitat. As such, even immigrant parents who might not consider America their homeland would not hesitate to call it the homeland of their children.

When I asked a Bangladeshi community leader in Hamtramck, Michigan, what he thought of America as a new home for Muslims, he replied, "There is no return, we have settled here." When I said, "But you know there are Muslims who have reluctance because of the distinction of two abodes ... " his response came very quickly.

> Oh no, no. I take one poet, he said: [quotes first in Bengali, then translates freely] "China is mine. Arabian Peninsula is mine. Japan is mine. America is mine. I'm a Muslim. All the world is my country." That is my understanding. I decided to live over here, I'm a citizen of this country, this is my country. It is my children's country.

In the three previous perceptions of America, Muslims remained outside the fray where American politics was concerned. It is only with the conception of America as *abode of Islam/peace* that membership in American society begins to translate into active citizenship and political participation. If *abode of accord* (*dar al ahd*) designated an American environment not incompatible with Islam, *abode of peace* (*dar al Islam*) designates an American environment that is actually perceived as Islamic. Muslims who regard America as *dar al Islam* actually consider American values to be lost or alienated Islamic values. As Ingrid Mattson, one of the past presidents of ISNA, notes, "among the most interesting efforts to permit Muslims a full embrace of American identity is the attempt to show that the constitutional democratic structure of America is almost equivalent to the political structure of an ideal Islamic state" (Mattson 2003: 207).

The legal structures of democratic society become an extension of Islamic political order, if not an unnoticed embodiment of it. "Implementing the Sharia [Islamic law], for a Muslim citizen or resident in Europe [or America], is explicitly to respect the constitutional and legal framework of the country in which he is a citizen" (Ramadan 2002: 172).

The perspective identifying Islam with American values tends to emerge among American-born children of immigrants (i.e., second and third generations) and convert Americans seeking harmony in their double identity. For example, Robert Dickson Crane, a former advisor to President Nixon and convert to Islam, argues that "the basic principles of Islamic law are identical to the basic premises of America's founding fathers, but both Muslims and Americans have lost this common heritage" (Crane 1997). This was the implicit theme of the keynote speech that Hamza Yusuf of Zaytuna Institute delivered in 2007 in Chicago at the annual convention of ISNA. He argued that not only are Muslim and American values aligned, but American Muslims are the true inheritors and present-day bearers of "old-fashioned American values" which otherwise have been lost in the modern world.

A land of freedom (especially religious freedom) and democracy, America in this view becomes a heterogeneous arena of good and bad, right and wrong. Just like historically Muslim lands, America also has its share of bad things. But it is up to Muslims to live Islam. They can contribute to its culture and society not only by their faith but also through their hard work and service. America is no longer an opportunity space or a land of possibilities; it is a privilege for Muslims. As such it places them in a special status with regard to both America and the global Muslim community. American Muslims see themselves as having a special location and a historical responsibility—indeed, a number of contemporary Muslim intellectuals have called it a "manifest destiny" (Khan 2002: 1).

Muslim writers publish articles with such titles as: "Life, Liberty and Pursuit of Happiness are Islamic Values."[15] The pursuit of happiness—which had been regarded by Sayyid Qutb, under the paradigm of *abode of war*, as antithetical to Islam—is now seen as part of Islam. Islam becomes an *American religion*, part of the landscape of American civil religion in the minds of Muslims themselves, as interfaith consciousness matures and interfaith activism intensifies.

Now America is home and the wider Muslim world is the target of outreach. At the stage of America as *abode of Islam*, the shift of perspectives is complete. Muslims see things from the "point of view" (i.e., location) of their new home/land, America. They are now set to make strategic incursions into the Muslim world, seeking to derive benefits from it (in the form of cultural resources) while avoiding its problems (corruption, authoritarianism). Whereas previously only converts had behaved in this way, it now becomes a common practice among the children of American immigrants. New generations of Muslims often criticize the "cultural Islam" of their parents, which they see as immigrant confusion of culture with religion. What had once been approached with suspicion (i.e., America, the *abode of war*) is now naturalized and what was natural for their parents (i.e., overseas culture) has now become an object of suspicion.

As American Muslims gain relative autonomy vis-à-vis other Muslims, America becomes in their eyes an increasingly complex entity. America presents manifold eidetic appearances, while the Muslim world shrinks to a few ideal types. The rise and fall of "minority fiqh" (*al fiqh al aqalliyat*) among American Muslims in the early 2000s, authoritatively presented by late jurist Taha Jabir Al-Alwani (2003), was a symptom of the passing of the diasporic moment. What rose to replace it was a citizenship ethics in which American Muslims no longer see themselves as merely an outpost of overseas Islam. This transition finds its expression in the proliferation of Gen-Z Muslims who meld unabashed Islamic self-expression with American-style activism in various domains of public life: as media personalities and social media influencers, environmental activists, new generation philanthropists and crowdfunders, racial justice educators, and gender justice advocates.

Conclusion

The emergence of an American Muslim ethos and the development of a sense of being at home in America reverse the relationship between *dar al Islam* and *dar al harb*. America becomes the land of order and pure reality, while the homeland of immigrant parents retreats into chaos and anomie.

With the passage of several decades—and spurred on by the urgency of responding to the realities of a post-9/11 world—Middle Eastern and South Asian immigrant Muslims have succeeded in the discursive task of ethically including America in their imagination as a new Muslim homeland. As Muslims settle in America, either the American *nomos* becomes legible to them or they introduce a new Islamic *nomos* onto the American surface. Often the two possibilities converge.

This chapter has traced the transition from the paradigm of exception (*darura*) to the construction of legal order on a previously anomic space. As we have seen, the *abode of chaos/abode of peace* binary faces an irruption of experience and is shattered into a plurality of new categories—and, as a consequence, the Muslim lifeworld in America becomes religiously legitimate and meaningful. Examining the stages of this process reaffirms that there is no such thing as a monolithic Muslim perception of America, a salient reminder at a time when Muslim loyalty to the American nation is still viewed with skepticism.

Taking a phenomenological approach to the immigrant experience sensitizes us to the fact that the human being and the world he or she inhabits are much less dissociable then our liberal conceptions of citizenship would tend to suggest. In an important sense, the immigrant does not move from one part of the world to another. He moves from one world to another. Truly "being" in that new world demands an unmaking and remaking of self, a shift from the deficient mode of care which is a disposition of non-attunement toward the new environment to an attitude of involvement, openness, and attunement. A proper phenomenology of the immigration experience—that is, of the processes of dissociation from the past and *there* and re-sociation with the now, the *here*—reveals a transformation from chaos and confusion, from life as a constant state of exception, to attention, receptivity, and nomos. This is creative work, both on the part of the immigrant and on the part of the society that receives her. Immigration, with its discordance between habitus and habitat, ceases to define a person only when concordance is established between habitus and new habitat in a gradual process of mutual appropriation.

Notes

1. Edward E.Curtis IV, "Blood Sacrifice and the Myth of the Fallen Muslim Soldier in the US Presidential Elections after 9/11," in M. Khalil (ed.), *Muslims and US Politics: A Defining Moment*, Cambridge: Harvard University Press, 2019, 50.
2. Aymann Ismail and Jeffrey Bloomer, "How a Muslim Marine Is Changing Minds," *Slate*, August 24, 2018, https://slate.com/news-and-politics/2018/08/muslim-marine-mansoor-shams-confronts-islamophobes-to-change-their-minds.html, accessed July 2020.
3. This chapter draws on the research and findings of my earlier study, Mucahit Bilici, 2011, "Homeland Insecurity: How Immigrant Muslims Naturalize America in Islam," Comparative Studies in Society and History 53 (3): 595–622.
4. Such distinctions were common in the medieval world and not limited to Muslims: "There has always been some kind of *nomos* of the earth. In all ages of mankind, the earth has been appropriated, divided and cultivated. But before the age of the great discoveries, before the sixteenth century of our system of dating, men had no global concept of the planet on which they lived ... Every powerful people considered themselves to be the center of the earth and their dominion to be the domicile of freedom, beyond which war, barbarism, and chaos ruled" (Schmitt 2003: 351).
5. The Jewish religious idea of the *eruv* is in many ways comparable to the Muslim idea of *qibla* and the notion of *dar al Islam*. An *eruv* is a symbolically appropriated place where space is codified and made –literally navigable during the Sabbath. The single most important social function of the *eruv* is the creation of a communal domain through a religious marking of the public sphere. The *eruv* sets aside a portion of the public sphere and turns it into a communal sphere (Cooper 1998; Rosen-Zvi 2004).
6. American Muslim scholar Nuh Ha Mim Keller describes *darura* as vital interest: "How is it possible that the ruling of Allah could vary from place to place? One scholarly answer is found in the Islamic legal concept of *darura* or "vital interest" that sometimes affects the *shari'a* rulings otherwise normally in force. Although the fundamental basis of Islamic law is that it is valid for all times and places, Allah Most High, in His divine wisdom, stipulates in Surat al-Hajj that "*He has not placed any hardship upon you in religion*" (Qur'an 22:78)" (Keller, Nuh Ha Mim. 1995. "Fiqh for Muslims Living as Minorities." Available at http://www.masud.co.uk/ISLAM/nuh/fiqh.htm, accessed May 10, 2008).

7   A Shia handbook that I obtained from the Islamic Center of America in Dearborn, where it is used as a textbook for English-speaking youth and converts, addresses the issues of Muslim minorities in the West. It states that "A believer is allowed to reside in non-Muslim countries provided that his residing there does not become a hurdle in the fulfillment of his or her religious obligations" (Al-Hakim 1999: 42).
8   "During the early days of Islam, a number of Muslims took refuge in the non-Muslim land of Abyssinia in order to preserve their faith. This episode bears particular significance [for the situation of Muslim minorities today] because it occurred at a time when the foundations of Islamic law and *fiqh* [jurisprudence] were still being established" (Al-Alwani 2003: 30–1).
9   The author of *Jihad vs. McWorld*, for example, notes that "while for many Muslims it may signify only ardor in the name of a religion that can properly be regarded as universalizing, I borrow its meaning from those militants who make the slaughter of the 'other' a higher duty" (Barber 1996: 17).
10 Oil-producing countries like Saudi Arabia had disproportionate ideological influence during the early decades of Muslim immigration to the United States.
11 I have chosen to suppress the name of the mosque and refer to its imam by a pseudonym in deference to his concerns about publicity. He also expressed reluctance at the idea of recording the interview. The dialogue is based on my notes taken during our conversation.
12 A movement in Sunni Islam, Salafism seeks to restore the golden age of Islam by purging what it perceives to be later cultural influences and innovations. It is a modern form of Puritanism in Islam.
13 I spoke mostly to imams on the question of "*dar*"s because imams occupy a privileged position in the hermeneutic community of Muslims as interpreters of Islamic law and as individuals who feel the need for reconciliation of such juridical notions with their new settings. While at first blush they might seem likely to articulate opinions on juridical issues that their congregations are not even aware of, I have found that imams in America are actually quite representative of the communities they lead. Unlike in many Muslim countries, where imams are appointed by the state and are expected to hew to a centrally approved religious line, American mosque leadership is at least quasi-democratic and quite responsive to the concerns of congregants. The imams' opinions can therefore be treated as representative of the normative orientation of their respective communities. Secondly, the problem of legitimation of America as a homeland via Islamic juridical tools is a collective problem that demands expert opinions: the communities of believers themselves expect such matters to be handled by those who lead them legally and spiritually. One obviously needs to note that this general tendency is even stronger among Shia Muslims than Sunni ones.
14 Bayyah, Abdallah bin. 1999. "Muslims Living in Non-Muslim Lands." Speech delivered in Santa Clara, CA. July 31. Available at www.zaytuna.org, accessed April 2006.
15 The annual ISNA Convention held in Washington, DC in 2009 bore the same title: "Life, Liberty and the Pursuit of Happiness."

References

Abraham, N. and A. Shryock, eds. (2000), *Arab Detroit: From Margin to Mainstream*, Detroit: Wayne State University Press.

Agamben, G. (2005), *State of Exception*, trans K. Attell, Chicago: University of Chicago Press.

Al-Alwani, T. J. (2003), *Towards a Fiqh for Minorities: Some Basic Reflections*, London: The International Institute of Islamic Thought.

Al-Hakim, A. H. (1999), *A Code of Practice for Muslims in the West*, London: Imam Ali Foundation.

Anderson, B. (1991), *Imagined Communities*, revised edn., London: Verso.

Anderson, B. (1998), *The Spectre of Comparisons: Nationalism, Southeast Asia and the World*, London: Verso Press.

Asad, T. (2009), "The Idea of an Anthropology of Islam," *Qui Parle*, 17 (2): 1–30.

Aydin, C. (2017), *The Idea of the Muslim World: A Global Intellectual History*, Cambridge: Harvard University Press.

Barber, B. R. (1996), *Jihad vs. McWorld*, New York: Ballantine Books.

Berger, P. L. and T. Luckmann (1966), *The Social Construction of Reality: A Treatise in the Sociology of Knowledge*, New York: Anchor Books.

Berger, P. L., B. Berger, and H. Kellner (1974), *The Homeless Mind: Modernization and Consciousness*, New York: Vintage Press.

Bourdieu, P. (2000), *Pascalian Meditations*, Stanford: Stanford University Press.

Cooper, D. (1998), *Governing Out of Order: Space, Law and the Politics of Belonging*, London: Rivers Oram.

Crane, R. D. (1997), *Shaping the Future: Challenge and Response*, Littleton: Tapestry.

Dannin, R. (2002), *Black Pilgrimage to Islam*, Oxford: Oxford University Press.

De Certeau, M. (1984), *The Practice of Everyday Life*, trans Steven Rendall, Berkeley: University of California Press.

Frisby, D. and M. Featherstone, eds. (1997), *Simmel on Culture: Selected Writings*, London: Sage Publications.

Habermas, J. (1996), *Between Facts and Norms: Contributions to a Discourse Theory of Law and Democracy*, Cambridge: MIT Press.

Haddad, Y. Y. (2004), *Not Quite American? The Shaping of Arab and Muslim Identity in the United States*, Waco: Baylor University Press.

Haddad, Y. Y. and A. T. Lummis (1987), *Islamic Values in the United States: A Comparative Study*, Oxford: Oxford University Press.

Heidegger, M. (1962), *Being and Time*, trans J. Macquirre and E. Robinson, New York: HarperCollins.

Heidegger, M. (1971), *Poetry, Language, Thought*, trans A. Hofstadter, New York: Perennial Classics.

Khan, M. A. M. (2002), *American Muslims: Bridging Faith and Freedom*, Beltsville: Amana Publications.

Leonard, K. (2003), "American Muslim Politics: Discourse and Practices," *Ethnicities*, 3 (2): 147–81.

Levinas, E. (1969), *Totality and Infinity: An Essay on Exteriority*, Pittsburgh: Duquesne University Press.
Mandaville, Peter G. (2003), *Transnational Muslim Politics: Reimagining the Umma*, London: Routledge.
Mattson, I. (2003), "How Muslims Use Islamic Paradigms to Define America," in Haddad, Smith and Esposito (eds.), *Religion and Immigration: Christian, Jewish and Muslim Experiences in the United States*, 199–216, Walnut Creek: Altamira Press.
Qutb, S. (2000), "The America I Have Seen: In the Scale of Human Values," in K. Abdel-Malek (ed.), *America in an Arab Mirror: Images of America in Arabic Travel* Literature – *An Anthology*, 9–28. New York: Palgrave Macmillan.
Ramadan, T. (2002), *To Be a European Muslim*, Leicester: The Islamic Foundation.
Rosen-Zvi, I. (2004), *Taking Space Seriously: Law, Space and Society in Contemporary Israel*, London: Ashgate.
Roy, O. (2006), *Globalized Islam: The Search for a New Ummah*, New York: Columbia University Press.
Saeed, A. (2002), "The American Muslim Paradox," in Y. Y. Haddad and J. I. Smith (eds.), *Muslim Minorities in the West: Visible and Invisible*, 9–28, Walnut Creek: Altamira Press.
Schmitt, C. (1976), *The Concept of the Political*, New Brunswick: Rutgers University Press.
Schmitt, C. (2003), *The Nomos of the Earth*, trans. G. L. Ulmen, 1950, reprint, New York: Telos Press.
Schumann, C. (2007), "A Muslim 'Diaspora' in the United States?," *The Muslim World*, 97 (1): 11–32.
Shryock, A. (2004), *Off Stage, On Display: Intimacy and Ethnography in the Age of Public Culture*, Redwood City: Stanford University Press.
Simmel, G. (1971), *On Individuality and Social Forms*, Chicago: The University of Chicago Press.
Swidler, A. (1986), "Culture in Action: Symbols and Strategies," *American Sociological Review*, 51 (2): 273–86.
Turner, V. (1974), *Dramas, Fields, and Metaphors: Symbolic Action in Human Society*, Ithaca: Cornell University Press.
Wiktorowicz, Q. (2005), *Radical Islam Rising: Muslim Extremism in the West*, Lanham: Rowman & Littlefield.
Zerubavel, E. (1991), *The Fine Line: Making Distinctions in Everyday Life*, New York: The Free Press.

Between Sacred Codes and Secular Consumer Society: The Practice of Headscarf Adoption among American College Girls

by Mustafa Gürbüz and Gülsüm Gürbüz-Küçüksarı

The Islamic headscarf continues to be a contentious issue in many Western countries, and it is not going away anytime soon. Although headscarf can be used as a symbol of political resistance, reducing it to a political symbol only hinders multiple meanings that Muslim women themselves attach to it and denies agency to them. This research specifically focuses on how hijabi women reproduce their Muslim selves through stigma management in the United States.

The American social context has two main dynamics that are relevant to our research: First, contrary to France where there is an official ban against the veil, the practice here represents private choices of individuals, and does not convey a political meaning against a restrictive state rule. Yet, secular lifestyle and preconceptions about Muslims make headscarf adoption stigmatized in American culture. Inspired by Goffman's work (1963) on stigma, we found that Muslim women consciously present their headscarf adoption practice as "liberating," using American repertoire in their self-identity reproduction.

Second, unlike some Muslim majority countries where the practice becomes a social norm, headscarf adoption provides a powerful source for identity (re)construction from a marginalized minority group. Our analysis shows how headscarf adoption suggests a wide-ranging repertoire for multiple identity constructions of American Muslim college students, including primarily religious, feminine, moral, and communal identities.

The full citation to the original work as follows: Gurbuz, M. E. and G. Gurbuz-Kucuksari (2009), "Between Sacred Codes and Secular Consumer Society: The Practice of Headscarf Adoption among American College Girls," *Journal of Muslim Minority Affairs* 29 (3): 387–99, DOI: 10.1080/13602000903166648

Consumer Society and Stigma

Zukin and Maguire argue that the rise of consumer culture has been a part of a larger social secularization process, in which the modern creation of a "choosing self" has been realized (Zukin and Maguire 2004: 180).[1] Capitalist consumer culture has enabled two contradicting demands: (1) eliminating the traditional forms of culture by stigmatizing them as "backward" and (2) calling for a rich array of diverse self-identity expressions including traditional ones. In terms of the headscarf practice, capitalist secularization process and the consumer culture of the modern society has both (1) stigmatized the headscarf adoption as backward and (2) enabled the headscarf to become a vehicle of identity re-construction with new meanings.

Goffman points out that "an attribute that stigmatizes one type of possessor can confirm the usualness of another, and therefore is neither creditable nor discreditable as a thing in itself" because "the normal and the stigmatized are not persons but rather perspectives" (Goffman 1963: 137–8). In the capitalist consumer society, it is not hard to understand why the practice of headscarf is seen as a sign of oppression. Specifically, religious dress codes have been condemned as being an instrument for the social control of the body. This mode of understanding leads people to see headscarf adopters as un-modernized, backward, not open-minded, radically religious, and non-free. In short, the socio-contextual factors of American society enable stigma process working for headscarf adopter by reducing her in one's mind, in Goffman's words, "from a whole and usual person to a tainted, discounted one" (Goffman 1963: 3).

Malika's story articulates how the stigma ruins young Muslims' self-esteem:

> I felt like people discriminated against me, because I made them feel uncomfortable by wearing the hijab. I was strong for two years and then I just decided to unveil. I was very young, and I wasn't strong enough to deal with self-esteem issues, adults and my own classmates attacking me verbally among other things. Then, I decided to wear hijab again.[2]

On the other hand, the stigma on Muslim women can also work to empower an identity reconstruction. The attachment of positive meaning to the headscarf seems very interrelated with the negative attitudes and stigma in American society that labels the practice as a symbol of oppression: It is no coincidence that almost all of the respondents reported that they see headscarf as "a symbol of liberation."

What follows are the multilayered self-identity constructions we identified through our interviews with American college students.

Hijab as Vehicle to Redefine Religious Identity

Under the pressures of implicit secular norms and due to the stigma attached to scarves, the performer of religious identity usually starts to explain the reasoning of the hijab to others. This "educational accounting" helps Muslim women to explain their beliefs in a deliberate pedagogical form in which the account giver combats stigma by correcting stereotypes (Marvasti 2005). Giving informational substance to audience, the Muslim women dwell into what Goffman calls "normalization" after the stigmatization process (Goffman 1963: 3).

Almost all interviewees, in one way or another, stated that they wear hijab because of their desire to actively appreciate their religious identities. This is how they normalize their donning of hijab as a performance of religious identity. As Fatimah, a nineteen-year-old Bengali-American, asserted: "I am covering myself for protection and as a duty to God. I am not, however, hiding myself from the world ... Through hijab, I find I have grown for the better as a Muslim and as I am a full-time Muslim."

Another student expressed strength in her belief: "Hijab doesn't just mean a head covering for women, it is a modest dress code for all Muslims."

The educational accounting further reinforces one's own religious identity. As Aisha, a Pakistani-American student, expressed: "I think wearing hijab has definitely worked for the better for me. I became more assured of myself. Through having to defend my reasons for wearing it, I have acquired more knowledge of Islam."

Thus, by defending their beliefs, the Muslim women transform their ascribed Islamic identity into an achieved status. The feeling to acquire an Islamic identity as a personal choice seems very attractive to young Muslims since it reflects their "American" side. In most cases, however, they feel that their American identity enforces them as being free individuals having independent choices. Therefore, their choice to wear headscarf makes them better Americans as well as better Muslims.

Hijab as an Expression of Gender Identity

Hijabi women deal with stigmatization by explaining it to be a protection of their femininity. They see headscarf as a "shield" and "protection" from the American secular lifestyle. The metaphor of shield leads a new definition of feminine identity as Abida, a twenty-one-year-old Arab American, put it:

> Wearing hijab has made me a stronger woman; I feel that I have a stronger sense of self, since people listen to me rather than look at my body ... Many people critique hijab as a force to oppress women and curtail a woman's freedom. My life is more focused on matters that are

> important to me, rather than finding the nicest hairstyle that will attract attention, or even dress in order to deter unwanted gazes and comments.

What we see in Abida's account is not an emphasis on religious obligation but, instead, her dissent against definitions of liberation in terms of external beauty. Abida, rather, gives her own definition of being empowered:

> It is easy to forget the "oppression" that women are confronted with daily via mass media who display images of the "ideal woman." The unrealistic goal of obtaining the ideal body to flaunt steals our time that we could dedicate to helping others, learning, educating, or any number of things. When we are free from the constraints of the society we are truly liberated, and I feel anything but oppressed.

Thus, the concepts of freedom, self-respect, important values, and liberation are redefined through American repertoire. The practice of hijab is intertwined with true liberation. Being a slave of God is emphasized in a liberating manner: obey God in order to be free from social pressures. Yet, we should realize these accounts' gender emphasized characteristics. The adopters' emphasis on liberation comes with a new characterization of femininity. Nadeema, a third-year college student, asserted that her attractiveness of personality should be more important than her sexual attractiveness: "I don't need to worry about men checking me out, or talking to me for sexual reasons … I find it more impressive to have a male attracted to my personality, sense of modesty, values, internal beauty, and obviously so much more than only he can see and enjoy."

Nadeema added that she avoids going to certain places such as entertainment clubs because her adoption of the headscarf becomes a constant reminder of her identity. For her, the headscarf symbolizes not oppression but rather "a shield against the danger of getting dirty looks from perverted guys, verbal and sexual harassment, provocative fashions and, most of all, being viewed as a piece of meat."

Thus, contrary to the Western idea that the practice of hijab is a controlling mechanism over women's bodies, some Muslim women rather believe that their hijab provides a greater physical mobility in public space since they feel free from the male gaze.[3] The view of the headscarf as a shield is shared by another college student, who asserted that her wearing of headscarf is not only a "reminder" for her but also helps others: "they understand the limits to approach me."

However, this attempt of shaping the desired response from others does not always bring success for the adopters of the headscarf who are stigmatized. The headscarf adopters as stigmatized individuals usually are getting either much positive reactions or much negative one. As another interviewee described it: "From strangers, the reaction is usually mixed. Some are outright rude or presumptuous, glaring at me in the subway, making comments, or teasing. Others have sincere curiosity and are extremely friendly. At times they are too friendly."

Having extreme reactions in either way, the headscarf adopter becomes more assured of her connection with other headscarf adopters. In fact, this point is particularly related to the collective identity reproduction, which we elucidate in the following sections.

Hijab as a Reconstruction of Cultural Identity

As some scholars pointed out, modesty is also seen as a feature of being Arab, or Indonesian, or Nigerian among the Muslim immigrant communities as being the minority group in United States, and therefore Islamic identity is simply considered as an ingredient in that particular national identity (Haddad et al. 2006: 17). Thus, the donning of the headscarf reinforces the cultural identities as well.

Moreover, as discussed in previous sections, American cultural and social environment generally remains as "foreign" in the eyes of immigrants due to the threat of assimilation in the melting pot of the United States. Tabassum Ruby's study among immigrant Muslim families in Canada, for instance, indicated that adopters of veiling practice in the host land are stricter in the use of their hijab than are those "back home" (Ruby 2006: 59). We might argue that people become more loyal to their traditions and identity symbols if their group identities are threatened by the larger society.[4]

Unlike the other respondents, Husna does not only refer to religious concerns but also mentions how she finds the practice as a symbol of modesty. Husna's story also reveals some Muslim immigrant girls' search for conformity with their indigenous culture. Confirming Ruby's findings in Canadian context, a number of informants emphasized their enthusiasm to keep their own cultural identities in a racist environment.

Hijab as a Venue to Establish a Collective Identity

Given that one's individual identity is hardly distinct from her communal identity, we should study the collective experiences of Muslim women as development of a peculiar consciousness that they are representing Islam. This dimension of the identity reproduction is not only related with stigmatization of Muslim women in negative ways; but also, the high-level expectations of the larger Muslim community from the headscarf adopters.

Hence, the social expectation has twofold dynamics that set the context. The first dynamic is explained in previous sections of the work, that is outsiders' (i.e., non-Muslims) negative expectations because of their oversimplification, which produces stigma for all headscarf adopters as being one group who are oppressed by their consent, non-free, radically religious, and unmodernized.

Second dynamic is related with common expectation from Muslim community that the headscarf adopter represents their religion. Most Muslims' deep respect to the headscarf practice sometimes leads them to expect seeing headscarf adopters in certain ways. Thus, the headscarf adopters are often likely to be encountering a much positive encouragement or a negative frustration from their social environment because they are seen as representatives of a group rather than simple individuals. Twenty-year-old Amina's account succinctly describes the situation:

> Many people assume that a woman who wears a veil is better than other Muslim women and that she is much more religious than a woman who doesn't wear one. That's she is very strict in her beliefs and is not flexible. I think that this is all wrong. When Muslims say these things they are making Muslims the "other" and the ostracized just as much as a non-Muslim who puts barriers between "us" and "them".

Although Amina does not like to be seen as a claimer of piety, she is positive with sharing a communal identity of Muslimness:

> Wearing hijab has definitely increased by spirituality because people see me in it and they see me foremost as Muslim. Often times the way people identify you is the way you identify yourself, so it definitely strengthens my identity of being a Muslim woman.

What is interesting in Amina's account is that the communal identity reproduction usually comes with an idea of individual strengthening and self-development. We can catch the similar feelings of being more independent in other girls' accounts as well. One interviewee, Faheema, an eighteen-year-old Pakistani-American, stated her appreciation of the communal identity as the following:

> I feel that wearing the veil has enabled me to express my identity as a Muslim woman more openly. Additionally, it has made me conscious that since it identifies me as a Muslim woman, I have to make sure that my actions and behaviour are in accordance with Islam. Wearing the hijab makes me a representative of Islam, and therefore, I am required to project it in a positive light so that others will not see Islam with negativity.

Thus, even the communal identity of Muslimness is perceived by these college students as a "great freedom" and a liberating practice in nature.

Conclusions

The headscarf adoption in a secular consumer society has diverse meanings, supporting multiple source of identity reproduction for Muslim college students. The students' special emphasis on liberating face of the headscarf is not a coincidence. Stigmatization of headscarf as a symbol of oppression is challenged by the adopters with an image of "a liberated woman" agency. Despite that the lines between these religious, gender, cultural, and communal identities are blurry, an active claim of the practice has empowered the students. Through stigma management, marginalized Muslim women interpret the practice with a wide-ranging repertoire for multilayered identity formations—an enriching experience that may not be observed in social contexts of the Muslim world where the practice is part of the everyday life.

Notes

1 The concept of "choosing self" was developed by Don Slater, see Slater (1999).
2 All names of the respondents have been changed to protect their identities.
3 A number of studies pointed out that the hijab enables Muslim women's greater mobility in social interactions in public. See, for example, Odeh (1993), Ruby (2006).
4 As Shaffir (1978: 41) notes, "A feature common to groups that perceive the outside world as a threat is the belief that they must resist the assimilative influence of the larger society ... (This helps the) group members to feel more committed and increases their awareness of their separate identity."

References

Goffman, E. (1963), *Stigma: Notes on the Management of Spoiled Identity*, Englewood Cliffs: Prentice Hall.
Haddad, Y., J. Smith, and K. Moore (2006), *Muslim Women in America: The Challenge of Islamic Identity Today*, New York: Oxford University Press.
Marvasti, A. (2005), "Being Middle Eastern American: Identity Negotiation in the Context of the War on Terror," *Symbolic Interaction*, 28 (4): 525–47.
Odeh, L. A. (1993), "Post-Colonial Feminism and the Veil: Thinking the Difference," *Feminist Review*, 43: 26–37.
Ruby, T. (2006), "Listening to the Voices of Hijab," *Women's Studies International Forum*, 29 (1): 54–66.
Shaffir, W. (1978), "Canada: Witnessing as Identity Consolidation: The Case of the Lubavitcher Chassidim]," in H. Moll (ed.), *Identity and Religion: International, Cross-Cultural Approaches*, 39–57, Beverly Hills: Sage.
Slater, D. (1999), *Consumer Culture and Modernity*, Cambridge: Polity Press.
Zukin, S. and J. S. Maguire (2004), "Consumers and Consumption," *Annual Review of Sociology*, 30: 173–97.

Index

1001 Nights 155

Abd al-Raziq, Ali 151
Abu-Lughod, Janet 156, 257
Abu-Lughod, Lila 328, 335, 358, 378
Achille Mbembe 25, 372
Afghanistan 6, 174, 187, 188, 220, 359, 360, 451
African National Congress 24–5
Agamben, Giorgio 364, 458
Ahmadinejad, Mahmoud 61, 62, 191, 338
Al-Alwani, Taha Jabir 457, 474, 476
Alatas, Syed Hussein 387
Al-Azhar 153
Al-Bassusi, N. 270, 277, 279, 285
Alevis 178, 212, 224
Algeria 68, 74, 163, 164, 377, 396
Al Khalifa monarchy 88, 91, 97, 98
Al-Minya 272–4, 276–8, 280, 282, 284–5, 288–9 n.16
AlSayyad and Castells 357
Aly, Anne 357
Al-Zawahiri, Ayman 167, 175
Amin, Sajeda 270, 277, 279
anger 38–9, 201, 201–2
An-Na'im, Abdullahi 151
apartheid 3, 11, 23–30
appliances 136, 266–8, 282, 288 n.6
Arab Spring 13, 68, 71, 88–94, 96, 100, 102, 128–9, 163, 164, 165, 166, 167, 170, 174, 245, 249
Arab uprisings 2, 3, 11, 12, 13, 67–73, 96–7, 99–103, 129, 196, 200, 202, 203
Asabiyya 223–4
Asad, Talal 177, 178, 183, 457
Ayatollah Khamenei 60
ayma 275–6, 284, 286–7
authoritarianism 81, 96, 100, 157, 233, 260

Bahrain 3, 13, 68, 70, 88–94, 96, 98, 99, 100, 101, 102, 103, 164, 174, 188
  women 96–9, 100–3
Bakhtin, Mikhail 157

Bayat, Asef 50, 71, 89, 249, 333, 334
Beirut
  gay friendly 319, 320, 323
  inequalities 322, 323
  LGBTQ life 320, 321, 322, 323
  narratives of exceptionalism 320, 321, 322
Ben Ali 70, 73, 88, 90, 188
bereaved 35, 38–40
Bhambra, Gurminder K. 403, 404
Bhatt, Chetan 354
Bigo, Didier 220, 354, 355, 356
border
  border protection 353, 354, 355, 358, 360
  entry 353
  externalization of borders 358, 360
  fortress Europe 358
  surrogate borders 356
  transnational border 354
  virtual border 355
borders 105, 155, 349, 376, 385, 387–90, 408
Bosnia 167, 208, 220
Bourdieu, Pierre 270–81, 287, 312–15, 329, 330, 377, 456
Bowen, John R. 357, 358
Bulliet, Richard 156
bullying 14, 119, 122
Buyid (state) 151

Cairo 73, 80, 81, 82, 83, 129, 197, 199, 200, 246, 248–59, 272–3, 275–82, 284, 288–9 n.16, 389
Caliph 150, 156
capital accumulation 140
capitalism 140, 142, 145, 183, 217, 218, 325, 409
  relationship between religion and 133, 138
CEDAW (the Convention on Elimination of All Forms of Discrimination Against Women) 97
celebrations 266, 268, 270, 274, 279, 286, 287 n.5, 289 nn.16–17
Cherlin, Andrew J. 270

China 67, 143
Christian 196–203, 273, 288, 446
   in Israel 239–40
   in Lebanon 323, 325
Christianity 207, 217, 446
   early 151, 155
Christian-Muslim relations 196
citizenship
   citizen-spectator 355, 356
   citizenship tests 357
   global 151, 152
   at margins of 357
civic participation
   association membership 394–5
   co-ethnic associations 395, 398
   impact on voting 396–8
   of Muslims 395
civil society 68, 71, 151–3, 155, 260
civil war 158, 164, 174
   in Lebanon 187, 189, 223
civility 74, 160
class 321, 322, 323, 324, 423
   middle- 15, 17, 19, 67, 68, 69–72, 191, 192, 268, 275, 278, 279, 280, 285–6, 294
clothing 221, 299, 300, 302, 306, 310, 311, 312, 314, 315, 423
coding 384
   coding boot camp 387–8
collective identity 34–41, 483
colonialism 82, 150, 210, 328, 377, 394, 405
Combatants for Peace (CFP) 35–7, 40–1
commerce 136
   global 149, 151, 155–6
commodification 140
confirmatory actions 37–8, 39–40, 41
Connell, Raewyn 404
constellations
   digital constellations 343–4
   in A Queer New 343
consumption 29, 268, 270–1, 277, 279, 281, 285, 311
   of Islamic fashion 292
control, partial 150–5
Copts or Coptic Christian *See* Christian
cosmopolitanism 298, 319, 320, 321
credit 156, 266–7, 274–5
cultural capital 156, 197, 234, 311–15, 323, 326
cultural invasion 60
cultural turn 312

culture 328–35
   global 150, 160
curriculum 14, 116, 117, 120

Da'esh (ISIS) 75
Danish Refugee Council 387
Dar al Ahd 463, 469, 472
Dar al Dawah 463, 467, 469, 471
Dar al harb 457, 458, 459, 462–8
Dar al Islam 457–8, 462–3, 472, 474
Darura 458–9, 463, 464, 467, 468, 469, 474, 475
dating 338–43
Dawah 460–1, 463, 464, 466–8
Debord, Guy 353
decoloniality 403–4
democracy 62, 67, 75, 84, 96, 103, 127, 128, 142, 147, 163, 168, 170, 378, 439, 473
development 20, 50, 97, 105, 106, 108, 112, 140–2, 144, 145, 350, 354, 359, 378, 384, 385–7, 390, 437
dialogue 37
diaspora 213, 219, 220, 405
   Kurdish 190, 403, 406, 408, 410
   Muslim 357, 359, 393
   Turkish 211, 212, 214, 215, 216, 225
diaspora politics 205, 211, 212, 224
dismissal 201
DITIB (Turkish-Islamic Union for Religious Affairs) 181, 184, 215
Diyanet 177–84, 212, 214–16, 225
demonstrations 37–8, 40, 41, 46, 51, 81, 89, 213, 251, 252, 256, 341, 370, 371, 372, 407
dowry 269, 288 n.7
dress, or clothing
   Islamic dress 292, 294, 295, 300, 303
Duffield and Waddell 359

Early Republican Period (Turkey) 178, 180
economic self-sufficiency 266–7, 285
Edin, Kathryn 270
education
   in Jordan 387
Education and Training Organization of Tehran 61
Egypt 68–9, 71–4, 78–86, 137, 163, 164, 165, 170, 173, 196, 198, 199, 200, 201, 202, 203, 265–6
   labor market 269

Index

marriage expenditures 272, 279, 281
   middle-class 270
Egypt Labor Market Panel Survey 288 n.8
Egyptian pounds (EGP) 274
elections 18, 20, 61, 68, 70, 74, 75, 90, 98, 99, 101, 103, 163–73, 191, 213, 396, 398, 400
electoral platforms 163, 168, 174, 175
El-Kholy, Heba 284
embodiment 310–16, 341
emotions 196, 197, 199–203, 310, 312, 315–16
engagement 265, 267–8, 272–81, 283, 285–6, 287 n.1, 288 nn.11–12, 16
Ennahda (Tunisia) 164, 167, 170, 171, 173
entrepreneurship 384–8, 390
epistemological interventions 405–7, 409
equality, women 168
Escobar, Arturo 404, 409
Ethnic Diversity Survey (Statistics Canada) 394, 396
ethnographic 81, 196, 197, 202, 320, 326, 329, 349, 362, 384
Europe 109, 110, 112, 113, 146, 151, 181, 182, 184, 190, 205, 206, 208, 215–16, 220–2, 242, 357–60, 389, 393, 407–10
European Union 105, 141, 207, 386
exception 177, 178
The exceptionalism thesis (of Turkish secularism) 178
exercise spaces for women 59, 62
   framed as a problem 59, 62
   framed as a solution to problems 59, 62

family 384–5
   family precarities 387–90
Family Guidance Bureaus (AIRB) 182
fashion
   cosmopolitan 298, 306
   modern 303
Fatah 36, 37, 368
Fatimid (state) 151
fear 36, 38, 118, 199, 200, 201
   wall of 68, 74
Feldman, Allen 355
femininity 283, 296, 316, 329–33, 481, 482
focus groups 301, 302, 303, 306, 307
Foucault, Michel 58, 63, 154, 242, 355
Freedom and Justice Party (Morocco) 164, 170

furniture 266–8, 274, 276, 279, 281–3, 285, 287 n.5

Galilee 16, 238
Gambetti, Zeynep 410
gay tourism 319
Gaza
   2008–2009 War in Gaza 40
   2014 War in Gaza 34, 40
Gaza Strip 23, 25–6, 28–9, 366, 368, 378
gender 323–5
   matrimonial transactions 270–2, 282–7
gender politics 57–9, 63, 338
gender segregation 59, 63
   and the establishment of women-only parks 63
General Federation of Bahrain Trade Unions (GFBTU) 88, 91–3
general strike 81, 88, 89, 90, 91–3, 94
geography, in Islam 155
gihaz 268, 276, 280–2, 285, 288 n.11
Global South 105, 106, 320, 350, 365, 403–10
Goffman, Erving 270–81, 479–81
Goitein, Shelomo Dov 155
governance
   blaming 354
   hypergovernance 354, 358, 359, 360
   outsourcing sovereignty 354
"Grand narratives" 400
Gülenist 144, 145, 146
Gulf 67, 71, 75, 92–3, 131, 143, 218, 274, 321–2
   model 132–3, 135, 137–8

Habibi, Shahla 60
habitat 456, 463, 472, 475
habitus 191, 312–14, 456
   Muslim 472
Hashemite Kingdom of Jordan 385–6, 388
headscarf 142, 221, 222, 291–2, 293–4, 296, 302, 304, 314–15, 332, 351, 428
   adoption 479–85
headscarf bans
   France 401
   Turkey 145, 391, 399
Heidegger, Martin 456
heteroglossia, 157–8
   and inquisition, 158–9
Hezbollah (Lebanon) 164, 192

488

homeland 456
homo Islameconomicus 145
housing 266–8
humanitarian innovation 384, 390
   and colonialism 384, 387, 390
   UNHCR Innovation initiative 387
   UNICEF Innovation Fund 386
   and racialization/racialized tropes 384
humanitarian technology 385–6, 387, 390
Huysmans, Jef 351

Ibn Abd al-Aziz, Umar 152
Ibn Hanbal, Ahmad 154
Ibn Tashfin, Yusuf 152
Ijaza 156
Indonesia 164
Information & communication technologies (ICT) 384–7
inquisition, versus heteroglossia 158–9
interculturalism (Québec) 394, 395
   impact on minorities' civic participation and voting 395
international law 23–4, 26–7
   asylum policy 358, 359, 360
   avoiding state responsibility 359
international migration
   Australia 356, 357, 358, 359
   containment 354, 358, 359, 360
   EU 355, 358, 359, 360
   Fortress Europe 358
internet in Iran
   internet censorship 341
   internet usage 341, 344
intersectionality 222, 328–30
Iranian postrevolutionary state 57–9
   conflict and negotiation 57, 63
   flexibility and adaptability 57
   modernity of 57, 63
Iran 57–64, 134, 153, 189, 191–4, 235, 338–44
Iraq 68, 164, 189–90, 192–4, 220, 359
Islam See *Muslims*
Islam in the West
   Australia 356, 357
   domestication of 357, 358
   Euro-Islam 357
   France 356, 357
   Islamophobia 357, 358
   moderate Islam 357
   Muslim stigmatization 356, 357
   radicalization of 357
   revival of 358
   securitization of 358
Islamic banking 131, 132, 134, 135–7, 168
Islamic doctrine 57–8, 63
Islamic ethic 140, 141, 143
Islamic Horizons 464, 468
Islamic movements 167, 168, 170
Islamic political parties 163, 169–71
Islamic revolution 57
Islamic State 167
Islamism 205, 206–7
Islamization 173, 216, 225
Islam's marriage with neoliberalism 140, 141
Israel
   discrimination of Palestinian citizens 18–20
   education of Palestinians in 15
   mixed towns 16–18
   Palestinian citizens 15–22
   Palestinian middle-class 15
   Palestinian representation in municipal councils 20
   settler colonialism 15–16, 20–1, 25, 28, 237
Israelis 34–5, 36–41
Israeli Defense Force 36, 37
Israeli military occupation 35, 36–40, 41
I'tilaf al-Karama (Tunisia) 173

Jamaat-e-Islami (Pakistan) 170
Jerusalem 23, 26–7
jewelry 266, 268
Jihad 163, 168, 461
Jordan 105–13, 163, 164, 321–2, 366, 384–90
   Refugee Compact 105–6, 384
   special economic zones 105–6, 110, 385–6
Jüdischer Kulturverein 421, 430, 433
Justice and Development Party (Morocco) 164, 166, 170, 171, 173
Justice and Development Party (Turkey)
   See AKP

Karbaschi, Gholamhossein 59
Kemalism 140, 142, 180, 182
Kenya 167
Khalidi, Tarif 153–4
Khatami presidency 61
Khomeini 45–9, 51–4, 153
King Hussein Business Park 385
kiswa 268, 282

kontingentflüchtlinge 418
Körperschaften 355, 361, 428
Kurds 121, 187, 189–94, 212, 224, 350, 406–10
Kurdish indigeneity 408–10

labor movement 88, 90, 92, 94
land relations 140, 147
laïcité 178, 211, 393, 394
Latin America 409–10
Lebanon 68, 164, 188, 189, 220, 234, 319, 321–6, 366
Leitkultur 209–10, 222
LGBTQI+ dating 339, 343
liberalism 168, 207, 210
Libya 67, 71, 74, 133, 163, 174, 188, 360

Mahfouz, Asmaa 328, 335
Malaysia 133, 134, 170, 172
Mali 174
management of religion 177
marketing
　Islamic 294, 306
marriage
　age at 265–6, 273–4, 287 n.2
　costs of 267–8, 274–5
　courtship and 272, 277, 279
　delayed 273–7
　financing 274–5, 277–8, 280, 285, 289 n.12
　material barriers to 267, 271, 285
　normative barriers to 285
marriage expenditures 270, 275
　class position 279–81
　functional importance of 275–9
　gendered 282–5
　groom and bride 267–9, 274–86, 287 n.5, 288 nn.11–12, 16
　negotiations over 275–6, 282, 284, 286, 288 nn.12, 16
　parental assistance with 266, 269, 285
　social meanings of 269–71
　strategies for covering 271, 273–5
masculinity 283, 344
Maspero massacre 200, 203, 250, 254
Massell, Gregory J. 358
Mattson, Ingrid 472
MAXQDA program 272
McNay, Lois 330
Mediterranean 155, 389, 405
Middle East and North Africa (MENA) 196, 266–7, 269, 273, 285

Mignolo, Walter 403–4
migration 105, 106, 107, 112, 118, 206–9, 211, 220, 274, 353–60, 386, 389, 390, 403, 405, 419
minority 194, 196, 198
　fiqh 474
　rights 168, 171, 172
modernity 57, 140, 141, 143, 145, 234–5, 319–20, 324, 326, 403–5, 407, 456
modernity and progress 320, 321, 322
modernization 63, 131, 141, 143, 152, 203, 217, 218, 257, 310–11, 331, 350, 406
modesty 59, 234, 299, 300, 306, 483
Modood and Ahmad 357
monocultural school 118, 119
moral shock 37
Morocco 163, 166, 171
Morsi, Mohamed 74, 167, 196–7, 246, 251–2, 256, 259, 260
motherhood, construction of 59, 62
movement, free 155–6
muakhar 275, 287, 288 n.14
Mubarak 70, 73, 82, 84, 88, 90, 129, 188, 196, 199, 203, 251–2, 260
Muhammad (prophet) 157, 458, 460
Muhtasib 150
Mukhabarat (security forces) 68
multiculturalism (Canada) 394, 395
　impact on minorities' civic participation and voting 395
Muslim Brotherhood (Egypt) 164, 166, 167, 170, 173, 196, 201, 251, 253, 254, 256, 455
Muslim women
　emancipation 357, 358
　female circumcision 358
　veil 59–60, 221, 302, 305, 328, 351, 358
　　compulsory 59
　veiling 302, 311, 483
Muslimizing 205, 208, 211
Muslims
　association memberships of 397
　legislative restrictions affecting (*see also* "headscarf bans") 393, 401
　origins of
　　in English-Canada 396
　　in France 396
　　in Québec 396
　voting by 397–8

490

Nakba 37, 366, 378
Naqshbandi 144–6
narrative identity 330
Nasser, Jamal Abd al- 80, 153, 260, 288
National Congress Party (Sudan) 164
National integration "models" (see also "Grand narratives")
    impact on minorities' civic participation and voting 394–5, 400–11
    and political opportunity structures 394
National Socialism 415
nation-building 350, 359, 406
Neda Agha-Soltan 328
neoliberal history making 140, 141
neoliberalism 27–8, 67, 69, 75, 140, 141, 219, 224, 248, 249
neostatist perspective 140, 142
New York 343
Nigeria 167, 174
non-governmental organizations 28, 71, 106, 365
nostalgia 222, 257
Nour Party (Egypt) 167, 175

Occupy Wall Street 67
orientalism 358, 403–6
Oslo Accords 26–7, 240
Özyeğin, Gül 333

Pahlavi dynasty 3, 57
Pakistan 133, 134, 137, 170, 174
Palestine 23–30, 34, 37, 71, 108, 164, 239, 430, 432, 448, 452
Palestine Liberation Organization 26
Palestinian Authority 26, 28, 240, 349, 363, 370, 378
Palestinian citizens of Israel 15–16, 23, 25
Palestinian workers 28–9
Palestinians 23–30, 34–5, 36–41, 107–8, 238–43, 362–, 366–7, 372–7
Pan-Malaysian Islamic Party 170
Parents Circle/Families Forum (PCFF) 35, 38–41
Parliamentary elections 74, 98, 101, 163, 164, 165, 213
Party of God (Lebanon) 164
Party of Light (Egypt) 166–7
peace organizations 34, 35, 36–40
People's Republican Party 178
Persian language 338, 339, 341, 343

pilgrimage 128, 149, 156, 214, 461
policy shifts 57, 59, 62
political liberalization 61, 96, 97, 99
politics of resentment 140, 147, 408
populism 129, 205, 206, 207, 211, 220, 222
postcolonialism 403–4
precarity 14, 343–4, 350, 389
    and family 387–90
Presidential Center for Women's Affairs and Participation 60, 62
prestige 234, 269–71, 279, 281, 286–7
public schools 116, 117, 121, 122, 177

Qalibaf, Mohammad Baqir 62
queer in Iran
    queer online dating 339–42
    queer resistance 342
    queerness 338
queer life and exclusions 324, 325
Qur'an 155, 173, 182, 293, 307
Qutb, Sayyid 455, 457, 464, 473

racial capitalism 23–5, 27, 30
radicalism 217–19, 224
radicalization 205–6, 208, 209, 211, 217–18, 220–1, 224
Rafsanjani presidency 59–60
Ramadan, Tariq 469
Rashidun 152
"Reactive ethnicity" 395
realignment of Turkish capital 142
Reed, Joanna M. 270
reform era (1996–2004) 61
refugees 23, 25
    detention of 354, 356, 359, 360
    displacement by war 359
    employment 109–11
    EU Policy 358, 359, 360
    harmonization of policy 358
    history in Jordan 107–9
    humanitarian crisis 359
    labor precarity 109–12
    NGOs 110–11
    people smuggling 359, 360
    Syrian 105–6, 108–12, 113, 115–16, 146, 320, 325, 384–7, 408, 446
regulation of religion 178
relational sociology 67
Renaissance Party (Tunisia) 164, 167, 170, 171
rent 71

representation (political) 69
Republicanism (France) 393, 394, 395
    impact on minorities' civic participation and voting 395
    secularism (see also *laïcité*) 393, 394
respectability 330–3
revolution 88, 89, 94
Rihla 156
ritual male circumcision 413
Rojava 193, 408–9
role reversal 118
Roma 170, 432

Safavid (state) 151
Saladin 156
Salafist 166–7
Saleh, Ali Abdallah 70, 74
Salvatore, Armando 160, 413
Saudi Arabia 88, 90, 92, 93, 94, 134, 137, 146, 153, 215, 218, 281
Schools of Imams and Preachers 177, 179
sectarian boundaries 196, 197
sectarianism 196
secularism 168
    European 210
    Turkish 177–9, 180, 184
security
    human security 354
    insecurity 354, 355, 359
securitization
    fear 353, 354, 355
        of Islam 358
        of migrants 353, 354, 356
    risk management 355
    as saving lives 359, 360
self-sufficiency, economic 266–7, 285
sexuality in Iran
    sexual education 340
    sexuality assemblages 344
    sexuality discourses and orientation 338–40, 343, 344
Şeyhülislam 179, 180
shabka 268, 274, 276, 279–81, 285, 287, 288 n.13
Shari'a 163, 168, 170
    as an anarchist system 152
    and autonomy 154
    and waqf 153
Shojaee, Zahra 62
Shura 168, 170, 171, 173

Silicon Valley 143, 386, 388–90
Singerman, Diane 270
Sisi (al-) 68, 197, 203
Siyasa 152–4
snowball sampling techniques 272
social class *See also* class 270–2, 281, 310–16, 328–30, 335
    matrimonial transactions 267–8, 270–2, 278–82, 285–7
social contract 68, 69, 73, 75, 355, 470
social meanings 269–71
social movements 30, 34, 74, 79, 159, 217, 404, 406, 408, 410
    literature 205
    theory 334
solidarity 30, 38, 48, 50, 82, 94, 129, 216, 218, 220, 223, 351, 370, 373, 375, 417, 425, 428, 429, 430, 432, 435, 452, 461, 464
Sousa Santos, Boaventura de 404, 410
South Africa 24–5, 365
Spivak, Gayatri 328
start-up 387–9
state
    complexity 58
    disabling of undesired effects 57, 64
    enabling of desired effects 57, 64
    maturation of 59, 63–4
    negative, prohibitive, and repressive power 57–8, 64
    patriarchal 57
    productive capacity of 58, 63
    repressive power of 58, 63
    situatedness in a regional and global system of governance 58
state feminism 96, 102
state institutions 57–9
    reflexivity of 59
storytelling 36–7, 38–9, 41
subdued behaviors 199
sub-Saharan Africa 67, 269, 396
Sudan 68, 74, 108, 113, 164
Sungur, Ceyda 328, 335
surveillance
    ban-opticon 355, 356
    panopticon 355
    policing 353, 354, 355
Sykes-Picot agreement 408
symbolic capital 271, 279–81, 286–5
    face and 271

492

Syria 67, 75, 187–94, 359, 384–6
  children 4, 14, 116, 117, 118, 121
  parents 14, 117, 121, 122
  Syrian refugee crisis 384–90
  "Whole of Syria" 386

Taleghani Park 60
Tehran Parks and Green Space Organization 61–2
Telegram
  dating on Telegram 341
  Telegram application 339
Temporary Education Centers 14, 116, 118, 121, 122
terrorism 205, 206, 217, 218, 221, 224
  counter-terrorism 356
  homegrown terrorism 359
  London 7/7 2005 356
  moral panic and 357
  September 11, 2001 353, 356
  war on terror 356, 359
Tesettür 292–5, 297, 301–11, 302–4, 305–6
thick description 419
Trajectories and Origins Survey (Institut national d'études démographiques) 393–4, 395–6
Trump 242, 351, 452, 455
Tunisia 70, 73, 74, 88, 90, 163, 164, 167, 171, 173
Turkey (Türkiye) 109, 113, 115–7, 140–6, 164, 170, 173, 174, 177–9, 181–4, 189–94, 211–16, 310–11, 315–16, 328–35, 406–8, 421–2
  AKP (Justice and Development Party Turkey) 128, 140–7, 164, 170, 172, 173, 175, 177, 181–4, 190, 211–6, 225, 307
  Istanbul 141–3, 218, 293, 295, 296, 301, 302
  Konya 293, 295, 296, 301, 302, 304
  Welfare Party 170, 307
Türkischer Bund Berlin-Brandenburg (Turkish Federation of Berlin-Brandenburg) 425
trust
  building trust 36–41

Ulama 135, 151, 153, 155
Ummah 137, 460, 461
unemployment 385–7
UNHCR 385–7
United Arab Emirates 71, 88, 92, 94, 385
UNPD 387

Upper Nazareth (Nof Haglil) 18–20
urban planning 26, 60, 373, 379
urbanization 59, 60, 63, 129, 223, 456
urban space 60, 249, 321, 341, 344, 364
'urf 154

Veblen, Thorstein 270
victim competition 430, 432, 435
visual methodology 295

Wahhabism 153
waithood 266–8, 271, 285
Waqf 153
West, Candace 271
Weber, Max 72, 131, 147, 188, 329
Werbner, Pnina 358
West Bank 21, 23, 25–6, 28–9, 35, 107, 237, 238, 240–2, 362, 366–9, 375, 376, 377–9
women
  mental and physical health 60–3
  -only parks 60–1, 63
Women's Paradise 63
women's rights 47, 97, 100–3, 168, 170, 171, 172
work
  culture 388
  permit 387
  precarious 386
World Bank 60, 105–9, 113, 144
  -inspired structural adjustment policies 60
World Health Organization 62

Yemen 67, 68, 70, 73–5, 174, 188, 189, 203, 359, 465
  Yemenis 387, 446
young women 253, 282, 294, 302, 304, 328–35, 390
youth
  high-caste 269
  in MENA 266
  qualitative interview 272
  waithood 267–8
Yusuf, Hamza 473

Zan-e Rooz magazine 59
Zapatistas and Kurds 409–10
Zentralrat der Juden 415, 418, 420, 426, 430, 436
Zimmerman, Don H. 271
Zionism 25

493